DOCUMENTS OF AMERICAN
THEATER HISTORY

DOCUMENTS OF AMERICAN THEATER HISTORY

Volume 1

Famous American Playhouses

1716-1899

William C. Young

American Library Association, Chicago 1973

Library of Congress Cataloging in Publication Data

Young, William C   1928–
  Famous American playhouses, 1716–1899.

  (His Documents of American theater history, v. 1)
  Bibliography: p.
  1. Theaters—United States—History. 2. Theater—
United States—History. I. Title.
NA6830.Y67   792′.0973   72–9837
ISBN 0–8389–0136–0

International Standard Book Number 0–8389–0136–0 (1973)

Library of Congress Catalog Card Number 72–9837

  Printed in the United States of America

To
THELMA REINHARD MORREALE
Whose love of the American theater
has inspired her students
and all who knew her

Contents

Illustrations

facing page

Preface to Documents of American Theater History

DOCUMENTS OF AMERICAN THEATER HISTORY, a multivolume anthology of primary and secondary source reading, is intended as a basic reference tool for librarians, scholars, students, and others interested in the American theater. Although not a narrative history, the present work is the first systematic documentary history of the theater in American society and culture. Thorough documentation of sources is in this discipline, as in all fields of study, the necessary precondition for definitive narrative history.

The need for such an anthology of primary and secondary documents about the American theater is obvious. Most of the books from which I have excerpted quotations have been out-of-print for many years and are extremely difficult to obtain. Moreover, most of the pertinent letters, diaries, and regional histories, being in manuscript form, are available only to specialists who have access to the libraries in which they are housed. Also, although a number of old newspapers and journals from the eighteenth and nineteenth centuries have been microfilmed, these sources are without indexes and hence the locating of specific references is difficult, tedious, and time-consuming. As even the average university library possesses only a few of these sources on micro-film, one must seek to obtain copies through interlibrary loan, a process that can take a number of weeks.

The organization of these volumes follows a logical analysis of the American theater in its several structural and functional components:

Famous American Playhouses contains documents describing the development of the playhouse in America, not only in New York but in other major cities and on the frontier as well. University and summer theaters are also included.

Famous Actors and Actresses on the American Stage contains accounts of performers, their performances as seen by their contemporaries, and their ideas on creating roles.

Designers for the American Stage, which includes set, costume, and lighting designers, documents their theories of design in words and illustrations.

Directors and Producers on the American Stage deals specifically with the theatrical managers of the early companies and with the rise of the modern producers and directors.

Playwrights of the American Stage includes materials about the most important of the American playwrights, from Thomas Godfrey to the writers of the 1960s. A number of minor playwrights are also included.

Major Events of American Theater History presents documents dealing with specific events and also traces some important movements in the American theater.

As each topic of theater history has presented its own peculiar difficulties, I have outlined the criteria for selection in the introduction to each subseries.

Even more basic, however, than the differentiation of component topics of theater history in America, has been the selection of documents. The types of documents used include diaries, letters, journals, autobiographies, newspaper reviews and clippings, magazine articles, playbills, publicity materials, and architectural descriptions. The authenticity of each document had to be evaluated according to its source, and therein lay the difficulty. Theater reviews, for example, are in varying degrees colored by the prejudices of reviewers. I have tried, whenever possible, to present contrasting views so that the reader may arrive at a just appraisal. Many times "autobiographies" purportedly written by actors have, in fact, been written by their publicity agents or ghost writers. I have tried, therefore, to avoid autobiographical writings unless they deal with an actor's philosophy of acting, his impressions of his fellow actors, theater managers, directors, and producers, or his description of a particular theater which he visited or in which he worked. I have left the story of the actors' lives and anecdotes about them to their biographers.

As far as possible, I have relied on contemporary sources. Frequently, however, I have preferred a modern document whenever it seemed to contain a more accurate account than an older contemporary source. There are, of course, oftentimes real difficulties with con-

temporary sources. William Dunlap, for example, wrote his *History of the American Stage* in 1832, yet he relates many events (and incorrectly many times) from the eighteenth century, citing dates and performances (often grossly inaccurate) and coloring his remembrances with his strong prejudices, but all the time treating his work as history. William Wood's *Personal Recollections of the Stage* many times records incidents fifty years after they happened. The same is true of Noah M. Ludlow's *Dramatic Life As I Found It*, which was published in 1880 but records events from the early years of the actor's life. These are primary sources, then, but they are not always the best sources for a particular incident. Time and prejudice often distort the memory of the reminiscer. Newspaper accounts often correct the dates of performances or details about certain playhouses given in such autobiographical works as these, and hence their importance for these volumes. Notwithstanding their limitations, autobiographical works are important because they are the remembrances of men and women who lived through the times under discussion.

Removal in time and noninvolvement give perspective not available to participants or well-meaning friends whose works represent a small piece of the puzzle of events in history. An overall view is needed however, one which will be able to place an actor, a theatrical manager, a playhouse, or an event into a larger picture. Consequently certain secondary sources become very important in a documentary study of history. The sound scholarship of someone like Joseph N. Ireland, as he writes about the earliest theaters in New York City, certainly throws greater light on many of the first playhouses than do the newspaper accounts or journals of the day.

In the same way, an architect's assessment of a certain theater has greater value to the student of playhouses than do all the rhapsodizings of some journals about the elegance and magnificence of the same theater. The first relates the facts from an expert's point of view, while the other gives us commentary and local color which make for interesting social history.

I have, therefore, tried to select my accounts judiciously, seeking to achieve a balance between primary and secondary sources that I feel will best aid the student who is interested in American theater history. Then, through the use of a selected bibliography, I have attempted to inform the reader where other materials can be found that may be profitable to him in his studies.

A word should be said about the illustrations used in these volumes. Many of them are quite rare, particularly those of the eighteenth- and early nineteenth-century actors and actresses, playhouses, designers, directors, and events. For the most part these pictures have been taken from contemporary sources that are identified in the legends. The illustrations form an integral part of this work, for they show the development of the American playhouse, the use of costume, the hair styles, and the production techniques over more than two centuries.

Inconsistencies in spelling, punctuation, and typographical errors have not been pointed out by the use of *sic*. It should be understood that the selections in this collection of documents have been copied verbatim, including punctuation and misspellings from the original. The only change has been in using modern type for the archaic letter *s* and superior letters in the eighteenth-century writings. All other spelling, punctuation, and typographical errors remain untouched.

When a work in another language is included, the translation is mine unless otherwise noted.

As I read thousands of documents concerning the establishment and growth of the American theater in the course of this work, my excitement for the theater was matched by the discovery of the hidden richness of our theater history recorded within the materials in scattered library collections of all kinds. I sincerely hope that the readers of these volumes will be able to develop a deeper love and appreciation for the theater in this country after reading these documents, and that libraries will be encouraged to collect and preserve theatrical materials.

Preface to Volumes 1 and 2

The focus of the first two volumes in this series is the American playhouse as a physical structure. Various aspects of performance will be treated in other volumes, as will some of the dramatic historical events that occurred in these theaters. For example, accounts of the assassination of President Abraham Lincoln in Ford's Theater and the burning of the Iroquois Theatre in Chicago will be found in the final volume of this series, *Major Events of American Theater History*.

An explanation should be given of the criteria for the selection of theaters included in these volumes, which are basically three: historical, architectural, and social and cultural importance. First of all, historical importance of a playhouse has been a major consideration, not only as the house related to the development of the American theater, but also as it might have been the focal point for some historical event. The event itself will be described in the final volume of the series, but the playhouse is described here. The term "historical importance" needs to be defined for the reader of these volumes. By it I refer to the importance that a certain playhouse may have had in the development of the American theater. Very little is actually known about the three Williamsburg, Virginia, theaters, and yet they are of great historical importance because the Williamsburg Theatre of 1716 was probably the first playhouse erected in the American colonies. The Astor Place Opera House in New York City was not only a very comfortably built theater, but it was also the site of the Astor Place Riots in the nineteenth century. Likewise the Eagle Theatre in Sacramento was certainly not notable for its beauty; in fact it was little more than a tent. It was important, however, because this little mining-town playhouse was the first theater in California. The Dallas Theater Center achieves historical importance for the reason that it was the only theater to be designed and built by the famous American architect, Frank Lloyd Wright. It also contains a number of interesting features that are described in the second volume of this series. The Loeb Drama Center of Harvard University is historically important as the first fully automated theater, so flexible that the auditorium can be changed from a proscenium theater to an arena stage, to a thrust stage.

Some theaters have been included, not for their own historical importance as theaters, but for their importance as an institution in theater history. Good examples are the Bowery Theaters. I have included all five Bowery Theaters to show the continuity involved in this important institution. As one building burned, another would rise in its place, often within a ninety-day period. The Bowery as an institution continued for decades. The same kind of progression is used in the treatment of Thomas Maguire's various Jenny Lind Theatres in San Francisco, the first two of which were destroyed by fire and the third of which became the city hall of San Francisco in a rather questionable and quick deal which netted Maguire a sizable profit.

Another group of theaters has been included for historical importance as theater prototypes. There was little uniqueness in various theater structures during the eighteenth and nineteenth centuries, although many of the new playhouses contained some minor innovations. The theaters of the early twentieth century had a great sameness about them, finding their only uniqueness in the style of decoration adopted, whether Moorish, Georgian, or Oriental. There has been no need, then, to include a great number of these theaters, no matter how interesting their stories might be in local history. I have chosen only a few to serve as theatrical prototypes.

Architectural importance has been another of the prime criteria, particularly as the American playhouse, which in the beginning was based on the English playhouses, began to assume new forms. Architectural significance is especially characteristic of those twentieth-century theaters that have become centers of structural experimentation. Harvard University's Loeb Center, already mentioned, is an example, as are the Dallas Theater Center and the Mummers Theatre in Oklahoma City.

Again architectural prototypes have played an important role in my selection of playhouses. Since World War II constant experimentation has been taking place, particularly in academic and regional theaters. I have selected some experimental theater designs, not because these theaters were necessarily the first of their kind, but because they represented some significant variation of an architectural prototype. For example, the Loretto–Hilton Center of Webster College is included because

it is a most interesting variation of the Loeb theater's completely flexible staging area, but without the latter's sophisticated and expensive automation.

The growth of the cultural center, with its multitheaters, has been documented because it represents a movement in many metropolitan areas, a movement, however, which has brought with it many financial problems, as will be seen in the documents pertaining to these centers.

Finally, some playhouses have been included for their social and cultural importance. Again the idea of the prototype has been used. Piper's Opera House in Virginia City, Nevada, was chosen not only for its bizarre history, but also because it was typical of a kind of frontier theater that had to adapt itself to its inauspicious surroundings. Elitch's Gardens Theatre in Denver not only is the first of the modern summer theaters still in use, but its development forms an important part in the theater history of the West. The Salt Lake Theatre is remarkable, not for its architecture, but for the fact that it was built by a religious group to furnish entertainment for the city. Since it was rather isolated from the usual train route, which dictated a "playing city" for the star or road company, the importance of its stock company is readily seen. Brigham Young even had his daughters act in the company on occasion to give respectability to acting in his community.

The omission of certain playhouses will be of special concern to various readers who are particularly interested in regional theaters, college and university playhouses, and summer theaters. Those people who have made a study of the theater in the South may regret that I have not included any of the Kentucky playhouses, or the theaters in Richmond and Petersburg, Virginia, in Annapolis, Maryland, in Memphis and Nashville, Tennessee, and in numerous other places. Those interested in playhouses in the North will find that numerous New England playhouses have been omitted, as well as theaters some might find important in New York, New Jersey, Ohio, and Pennsylvania. Summer theater buffs may not find their favorite place of amusement listed.

I gathered sets of documents on more than 400 theaters; of these only 199 withstood the critical test of analysis. Two hundred and one theaters were eliminated either because they failed to meet my three basic criteria or because information concerning them was fragmentary and incomplete, a result of the failure of the reportorial process. A few theaters presented in detail in later volumes are not included here to avoid repetition.

In the chapter introductions I have explained the reasons why the theater flourished in certain areas of the country, while in others it could not gain a foothold until rather late in our history. Clearly, density of population made possible the opening of numerous playhouses in New York and Philadelphia in the eighteenth century. Even in the larger cities of colonial America there was difficulty in filling the playhouses for long seasons. Sometimes the same company would play seasons each year in two or three cities. The South, being basically agrarian and sparsely populated, did not have the population of a sufficient size to support many theaters, and so Charleston and New Orleans became the major theater centers in this part of the country. Even well into the nineteenth century there were so few southern cities with large populations that theatrical companies such as those of Samuel Drake, Noah Ludlow, and Sol Smith went from one town to the next, playing only a few weeks at a time in a single area up and down the Ohio and Mississippi river valleys.

In New England the Puritan aversion to "frivolous" entertainment plus small population centers retarded the growth of theater until the latter part of the eighteenth century, and even then the number of playhouses did not increase rapidly.

Most of all, it must be remembered that these volumes cannot achieve comprehensiveness. Consequently the prototype theater is used as a technique of selective representation. Local theaters in various areas are important, many such theaters having had their moments

of glory which should be recorded and remembered, but their remembrance lies with local history. The present work must confine itself to the theater on a national level.

Little theater groups have made their contribution to American theater history, and many of the more important of these production groups will be considered in the final volume of the series. Here we are concerned with theaters and not theater groups. An exception has been made in the favor of the Provincetown Playhouse, which has been included as an example of the decline of the large, elaborate playhouse and of the production of dramas of quality in spite of the most unsatisfactory conditions imaginable.

Although the focus of these volumes is the playhouse, social history does emerge as a by-product. In many instances, particularly during the eighteenth century, there were few detailed descriptions of the playhouses; consequently whatever information we have must be gleaned from letters, diaries, and critiques of performances. In some cases the information available seemed, at first reading, to have little to do with the subject at hand. Although Washington Irving's "Jonathan Oldstyle" letter is a social commentary on theater audiences at the beginning of the nineteenth century, we also learn much about the Park Theatre: seating accommodations, lighting, ventilation, etc. Alice Lewisohn Crowley's description of the beginning of the Neighborhood Playhouse, Helen Morosco's biography of her husband, in which she tells of his struggles in opening the Morosco Theatre, and various other excerpts used are much more social history than description of a certain playhouse. They are used because they provide us with the best description we have.

Oddly enough, descriptive materials concerning the physical aspects of many of the playhouses built between 1910 and 1929 are difficult to obtain, as the primary emphasis of available material is on the performance of the play given at the opening and not on the theater itself. In New York City for several years during the time mentioned, there was a new playhouse opening practically every week throughout the season, with the only differentiating aspects being minor differences in decor, a fact which reporters understandably scorned to mention in their stories.

This lack of descriptive materials about the playhouse has also been true of the summer theaters, many of which had very simple beginnings. Few of the local papers ever described the playhouse itself, confining their reviews and comments to the performances; even pictures of the interiors of these playhouses are very difficult to obtain.

In the selection of documents, preference has been given to eye-witness accounts and contemporary reports; however, the reader will note a number of exceptions to this statement when secondary sources or even quite modern documents have been used. For example, the first entry on the Williamsburg Theatre of 1716 is from a book published in 1958. The primary source materials concerning this earliest playhouse are quite fragmented and mostly legal in nature; therefore, I have found it more practical and helpful for the reader to use Marcus Whiffen's summary of the archaeological and archival findings, which are included in his *The Public Buildings of Williamsburg*.

Also, I have used works by various early theater historians if I felt that they perhaps had access to materials not now available, or if their work has been particularly illuminating about a certain theater or its background.

Certainly one of the most valuable aspects of these volumes is found in the many illustrations of the playhouses. The eighteenth-century theaters are of particular interest, but I would also direct the reader's attention to the pictures of Niblo's Gardens, as an example of the early American summer theater, of Chapman's Temple of the Muses, probably the first showboat ever to visit New York City, and of the frontier theaters. The pictures in volume 2 show the architectural evolution of the regional and university theaters to their present level of architectural and technical excellence.

The main divisions of volumes 1 and 2 are New York theaters, regional theaters, university playhouses, and summer theaters, and the arrangement is chronological within these categories. Notice should be taken that the date used is not the date that a certain playhouse was founded, but the date of the building described. The founding dates, however, are included in the introductory notes. Volume 1 begins with 1716 and ends with 1899; volume 2 begins with 1900 and ends with the opening of the John F. Kennedy Center for the Performing Arts in 1971.

Each volume has three indexes: an index to the playhouses, arranged alphabetically; an index by geographical location; and, finally, an index to the names and theatrical specialties of architects, artists, builders, decorators, designers, directors, managers, producers, and owners of the playhouses treated. The final index is not intended to be comprehensive, that is, to contain the names of actors and actresses or the names of the plays presented in the various playhouses; it deals solely with those involved in the building and managing of the theaters.

Acknowledgments

A project of this scope would not be possible without the assistance of many wonderful people who have helped in many ways to bring this reference work into being, and it is the very pleasant task of the author to acknowledge some of these people at this time. Any omissions are purely unintentional.

A special note of appreciation must be given to the staff of the Watson Library of the University of Kansas for their invaluable assistance: Judith Castle, Microfilms; Marilyn Clark, Interlibrary Loan; Marianne Griffin, Interlibrary Loan; Marjorie Karlson, Reference; Eugenea Wilson, Photocopy; and Linda Crosby, Geraldine Dangerfield, and Alberta Wright. They have made my task a pleasant one and have gone far beyond the call of duty to be of help to me.

Also, the staff of the Lawrence Public Library have given unsparingly of their time and resources in aiding me, and so my thanks to Mary Murphy, Bonita Dillard, Sue Hess, and Elizabeth Barlow for their friendly helpfulness.

The following people have been most cooperative in assisting me with this work: ALABAMA: Birmingham Southern College, Dr. Arnold S. Powell. CALIFORNIA: University of California at Berkeley, Irene Moran; University of California at Los Angeles, Chandler Harris; California Historical Society, Lee L. Burtis; California State Library, Carma R. Leigh; Los Angeles Public Library, Lois M. Jones; Music Center Operating Company, Joel M. Pritkin; Pasadena Playhouse, Mrs. James N. Ebright and Ross Eastty; San Diego Old Globe Theatre, Linda Truesdale; San Diego Public Library, Mrs. Marion L. Buckner. COLORADO: Denver Public Library, Hazel Lundberg; Elitch's Gardens, John Gurtler. CONNECTICUT: American Shakespeare Festival, Morton Langbord; Yale University Crawford Theatre Collection, Dorothy Crawford; Yale University School of Drama, Judith Drucker. DISTRICT OF COLUMBIA: Arena Stage, Alton Miller; United States Department of the Interior, Gordon Chappell. GEORGIA: Atlanta Historical Society, Richard T. Eltzroth; Atlanta Pubic Library, Judy W. Nichols; Emory University, Ruth Walling; University of Georgia, Mrs. William Tate. ILLINOIS: Chicago Historical Society, Larry A. Viskochil; Chicago Public Library, Janet R. Bean; University of Illinois, T. E. Ratcliffe, Gilbert G. Wright.

IOWA: Grinnell College, William Deminoff; University of Iowa, Amy Pratter. LOUISIANA: William R. Culison, Connie G. Grif-

Acknowledgments

fiths; Le Petit Théâtre du Vieux Carré, Emma D. Genre. MARYLAND: Maryland Historical Society, Nancy G. Boles, Mrs. Robert H. McCauley, Jr. MAINE: Ogunquit Playhouse, Robert A. Schanke. MASSACHUSETTS: Boston Public Library, J. A. Monahan; Cape Playhouse, Dr. Edward Tracy; Harvard University Theatre Collection, Helen D. Willard; Harvard University Loeb Drama Center, George Hamlin. MINNESOTA: Guthrie Theater, Nancy B. Miller; Walker Art Center, Mrs. Martin Friedman; Macalester College, Mary M. Hill. MISSOURI: Missouri Historical Society, St. Louis, Mrs. Fred C. Harrington, Jr., Ruth K. Field; St. Louis Public Library, Elizabeth Tindall; Webster College–Loretto–Hilton Center, Nita S. Browning, Walter Perner, Jr. NEVADA: Nevada Historical Society, L. James Higgins, Jr. NEW YORK: Cooper–Hewitt Museum of Decorative Arts and Design, Xenia Cage; Lincoln Center for the Performing Arts, Susanne Faulkner, Bill Schelbe; Museum of the City of New York, Charlotte La Rue; New York Historical Society, James Gregory, James J. Heslin. NORTH CAROLINA: University of North Carolina, Chapel Hill, Nan N. Friend. OHIO: Cincinnati *Enquirer*, Brady Black; Cincinnati Historical Society, Mrs. John K. Major; Cincinnati's Playhouse in the Park, Patricia Gerhardt; Cleveland Play House, Fanny Arms.

OKLAHOMA: Mummers Theatre, Mack Scism. OREGON: Oregon Shakespearean Festival Association, Pam Creedon. PENNSYLVANIA: Free Library of Philadelphia, Rosalie J. Coyle, Diane Welch; Carnegie–Mellon University, Helen A. Lingelbach, Elizabeth Kimberly; University of Pennsylvania, Nancy Huntington, David Kagan; Bucks County Playhouse, Marcia A. Frazier. SOUTH CAROLINA: Charleston Library Society, Virginia Rugheimer; South Carolina Historical Society, Mrs. Granville T. Prior. TEXAS: Alley Theatre, Claudia Autrey; Dallas Theater Center, Paul Baker; Trinity University, Sara M. Golding, Caroline Robertson; University of Texas, W. H. Crain, Frederick J. Hunter, Jane A. Combs. UTAH: Utah State Historical Society, Margaret D. Lester. VIRGINIA: Barter Theatre, Owen Phillips; Colonial Williamsburg, Marylee G. McGregor, Edward M. Riley; Virginia Historical Society, Virginius C. Hall, Jr. WASHINGTON: University of Washingon, Ellen Smock.

Dr. Fredric M. Litto of the University of São Paulo, Brazil, has made helpful suggestions and encouraged me in this project.

I also wish to acknowledge my appreciation to my typist, Betty Allen, who is a real expert in her field and has made my task much easier because of her expertise.

To the Publishing Services staff of the American Library Association, my special note of thanks. Richard A. Gray, Senior Editor, Miss Marion Dittman, former Managing Editor, and Miss Pauline Cianciolo, Executive Editor, have had faith in this project from the beginning, before a single word was written, and they and Miss Helen Cline, Production Editor, have helped in innumerable ways. Expert editors are the most priceless assistance that any writer can have, and I deeply appreciate the untiring efforts of my editors in my behalf.

Finally, I wish to express my heartfelt thanks to Thelma Morreale, Chairman of the Department of Speech and Drama of Baker University, and to Colby H. Kullman of the University of Kansas, for their assistance, advice, and encouragement throughout the long period of gathering materials and writing. Without them and their help, these volumes would not have been possible.

Famous American Playhouses
1716-1899

Chapter 1

American Playhouses in the Eighteenth Century

The history of the development of the American playhouse is still rather obscure. It was thought for a long while that the first playhouse in the American colonies was that used by the Lewis Hallam company in Williamsburg, Virginia, in 1752, and, in fact, a centennial celebration was held in 1852 in honor of this event. As our knowledge of the American theater grew, however, earlier playhouses were discovered in New York, Philadelphia, and Williamsburg. At the present time it is fairly well accepted that the first actual playhouse in the American colonies was built in Williamsburg, Virginia, by William Levingston and opened on October 12, 1716. Of the playhouse itself we know very little, since there was no newspaper in Virginia at that time, and the few documents discovered have been of a legal nature.

It is doubtful that any earlier playhouse will be discovered, since conditions in the American colonies prior to that date were most unfavorable to the establishment of any type of permanent theater. There is a record of a court case in Virginia in 1665, in which William Darby of Accomac County, Virginia, was under indictment for presenting a play, *Ye Bare and Ye Cubb*, on August 27, 1665. His two accomplices were Cornelius Watkinson, another landowner, and Philip Howard, a servant. There is no record, however, as to where the play was presented, and no text of the play itself any longer exists.

One might well ask why it took the theater so long to gain acceptance in the colonies when it was such a popular form of entertainment in England, both before and after the Restoration. The first playhouse in Williamsburg did not open its doors until one hundred and ten years after the first settlement at Jamestown, Virginia, which is just a few miles from Williamsburg. The answer is basically simple: the colonists were too busy carving a home for themselves out of the wilderness to have time for such an unnecessary frill as a theater. Homes, churches, schools, and places of business were to be built, land had to be cleared, and the necessities of life had to be provided before thoughts could turn to entertainment on the large scale of a playhouse.

Then, too, in order to support a playhouse, a fairly large center of population is needed. Prior to the American Revolution, there were in 1774 only five major urban centers in the colonies: Boston, Charleston, Newport, New York, and Philadelphia. None of these cities was really large. Philadelphia had a population of under 40,000: New York,

1

25,000; Boston, 20,000; Charleston, 15,000; and Newport, 12,000. By the time these population figures were reached, New York, Charleston, and Philadelphia each had a playhouse, and they could not have supported more than one.

Of course, religious proscriptions against drama were in effect in the Puritan-dominated New England colonies, where theatrical performances were strictly forbidden by law and where an itinerant actor would have been *persona non grata*. There was also a hostile religious element in Philadelphia and even in New York. This meant that the lower middle and southern colonies, which had the smallest populations, were the only ones in which drama could very readily find a home. Williamsburg was the perfect place for the first theater in the colonies, since it was the largest town in Virginia and the capital city of that colony; but even here there was difficulty and the first playhouse was not long in use as a theater.

Another basic question that cannot easily be answered is: What form did the early playhouse take? The answer is not simple, for there are no pictures of the earliest playhouses, no plans extant, no sketches, no newspaper descriptions. All is speculation. Some writers have proposed that the early Williamsburg theater was probably based on plans for a playhouse in England, but there is absolutely no historical evidence or artifacts that would support any such proposals. On the contrary, facts point to the probable crudity of the early playhouses, with makeshift stages and seating arrangements, a minimum of scenery, and poor lighting. Although early newspapers refer to a "box, pit and gallery" arrangement such as would be found in the English theaters, some accounts and newspaper announcements indicate that these playhouses were merely long rooms with a raised platform at one end and roped-off areas at the sides for "boxes" and at the back for a "gallery."

It is only normal to suppose that the early American playhouses were shaped by the frontier conditions found in the colonies. Certainly as the theater moved west the crudest of conditions existed.

The American playhouse during the eighteenth century evolved from improvised playing areas, often in warehouses and deserted stores, to quite beautiful theaters, such as those in Boston, Philadelphia, New York, and Charleston at the end of the century. The playhouses in these cities could well be compared to the English theaters of the same period.

There can be no doubt that the American playhouses of the latter part of the eighteenth century were modeled after those in England and often built according to the same plans used for certain English theaters. The stage area was of the proscenium type, the proscenium being an opening in the stage wall behind which the scenery and the front curtain were hung. The auditorium was semicircular and surrounded by several tiers of boxes, which opened into corridors behind them. The equivalent of present-day orchestra seats was referred to as the pit, while the cheapest seats were in the gallery in the highest of the tiers.

Unlike the twentieth century proscenium-type theater, there was a large forestage extending into the audience, and it was here that the acting took place. The box-set, which recreates the illusion of an actual room and has workable doors and windows, was not yet in use. Instead, painted drops set the scene. Actors made their entrances through pairs of stage doors, which were located in front of the proscenium—two doors on each side of the stage. Boxes over these doors were called stage boxes and were much in demand by spectators who wished to be seen at the theater.

Lighting during the eighteenth century was by candle and oil lamps. A huge chandelier was suspended over the audience, and the candles remained lighted during the performance. Washington Irving complained of the candles dripping wax onto the spectators seated in the pit. There were other candles in the boxes and in front of the boxes. It is little wonder that the hazard of fire was so great in these early playhouses.

Documentation for these theaters is often sparse and, particularly in the early days, relies on memoirs, letters, journals, and, later on, newspaper accounts of the openings of the playhouses. The photographs included of theaters described in this chapter will be of particular aid to the reader in his reconstruction of the playhouses of colonial and post-Revolutionary America.

1. FIRST WILLIAMSBURG THEATRE
Williamsburg, Virginia
Opened 1716(?)

Although there are records of plays performed in English in the American colonies as early as 1665, the first known playhouse was built in Williamsburg, Virginia, in 1716. The promoter of this enterprise was William Levingston, who, assisted by his indentured servants, Charles and Mary Stagg (who were dancing masters), built a playhouse on the Palace Green.

The absence of a newspaper in Williamsburg at this date makes it extremely difficult to ascertain the exact date of the opening of the theater. The Department of Research of Colonial Williamsburg has carried on extensive investigations concerning the theater, and its findings are related by Marcus Whiffen:

1:1 . . . In November that year, 1716, Levingston purchased three lots on the east side of Palace Street. Since the holding of the lots was subject to the usual condition that houses should be built upon them within two years of purchase, the theatre had to be up by November 1718. A letter from [Governor] Spotswood to the Board of Trade, complaining that when he gave an entertainment in celebration of the King's birthday in May 1718 "eight Counsellors would neither come to my House nor go to the Play w'ch was Acted on that occasion," shows that it had been opened before then— that it had in fact been built "with all convenient Speed," as the indenture stipulated.*

1:1. Marcus Wiffen, *The Public Buildings of Williamsburg* (Williamsburg, Va.: Colonial Williamsburg, 1958), pp. 112–17.

*Refers to the indenture agreement between Levingston and the Staggs recorded on July 11, 1716, at the York County Courthouse.

THE FIRST PLAYHOUSE

The remains of the foundations of this theatre, identifiable beyond all reasonable doubt by their location and their character, were excavated in 1947. They show that it was about 30 ft. wide by 86 ft. 6 in. long and stood end-on to the street. The slightness of the foundation walls suggests a frame building, and a reference to weatherboards in a *Virginia Gazette* advertisement of 1745 confirms the structural evidence. It had no basement.

In the absence of more positive information about the form and character of the building, one may fairly ask if it was a proper theatre, with the internal arrangements of a typical English theatre of the period, or something nearer to a barn. However, there is nothing at all to suggest that it was not a proper theatre, or playhouse (as it is called in most of the contemporary references). And the determination of those who lived in Williamsburg or frequented the town during the public times to have everything after the London mode surely makes it unlikely that they would have put up with anything less.

Granted that it was a proper playhouse, it is possible to picture it, if not with accuracy, at least with some assurance of not being wildly wrong. Externally it is plain to the point of bareness, with a gable roof, shingled, rising to a height of between thirty-five and forty feet; the weatherboards of the walls are painted red. Doors of domestic size, placed laterally, admit to the auditorium and (at the end farther from the street) to the stage; in deference to the climate of Virginia there are several small windows. Passing inside by the southwest entrance we find ourselves in a lobby; opposite the door is the pay-box, while to the right is one of the two "pit passages," which flank that part of the house and provide the only means of access to it. (The gallery pay-box and stairs are reached separately by the north-west entrance.) Traversing the pit passage, which is about twenty feet long, only three feet wide, quite unlit, and not altogether savory, we emerge into the pit itself. Our first impression, accustomed as we are to a later tradition of theatre architecture, is of extreme smallness; if a play was being given, an impression of extreme overcrowding would be added to this. On either side of the house, in two tiers, are the boxes; at the back is the gallery; the seats in both pit and gallery are plain wooden forms, without backs. The interior is painted generally blue-green, but fine splashes of colour are supplied by drapes of red moreen in the boxes, hung there as much for acoustical as decorative reasons. Turning towards the stage, we find the orchestra where we would expect it. But the proscenium doors, giving on to the forestage in front of the curtain on either side, with balconies above them, are "legacies from Elizabeth's day" that were abandoned in the nineteenth century; it is through these doors, not through the scenery, that the actors make their exits and their entrances. The curtain is of green baize, though not precisely what is meant by baize today, and the scenery behind it slides in horizontal grooves; this method of scene changing, "almost unknown outside the British stage," is one of the factors that has enabled Mr. Levingston to build his theatre without a deep basement such as the Continental European system demands. The character of the scenery, and the workings of such intriguing accessories as the cloud machine and the thunder run, are matters of theatrical rather than architectural history; the reader who has a curiosity about them must be referred to the luminous pages of Sothern.*

PLAYHOUSE INTO COURTHOUSE

Levingston is described in the indenture of 1716 as a merchant, elsewhere as a gentleman and sometimes as a sur-

*Richard Sothern, a theater historian.

geon. His varied talents did not save him from financial difficulties, and about 1723, having mortgaged and lost possession of the Playhouse and his own dwelling (which stood next to it), and having acquired much experience in litigation, he moved to Spotsylvania County; he died at Fredericksburg in 1729. . . .

. . . In 1735, before Stagg's death, John Blair, as executor of Archibald Blair to whom the property had been mortgaged in 1721, sold the three lots by Palace Street to George Gilmer, surgeon and apothecary. Gilmer moved into the house that Levingston had built for himself, but conveyed the Theatre to a group of thirty-one subscribers, which included Governor Gooch and many other prominent people. A period of amateur productions, with plays acted by "the young Gentlemen of the College" or "Gentlemen and Ladies of this Country," followed. But it did not last long; by December 1745 the Playhouse had "not been put to any Use for several Years," and was "now going to decay." The words are those of a petition to the subscribers from the City Corporation, representing "that they have no Publick Building within the City, wherein to hold their Common Halls and Courts of Hustings," and no money to build one with—

"Wherefore they shall esteem, and always acknowledge it as a singular Mark of your Good Will and favour, if you will be pleased to bestow Your present Useless House in this Corporation, for the use of aforesaid They intending to repair and alter it by their own Subscription. If this request be granted."

The request was granted, and the *Virginia Gazette* for December 19 contained the following advertisement:

"The Play-House in Williamsburg, being by Order of the Common-Hall of the said City, to be fitted up for a Court-House, with the necessary Alterations and Repairs; that is to say, to be new shingled, weatherboarded, painted, five large Sash Windows, Door, flooring, plaistering and proper Workmanship within; Notice is hereby given to all such as are willing to undertake the doing thereof, That they offer their Proposals to the Mayor who will inform them more particularly what is to be done."

. . . The Playhouse-turned-Courthouse was demolished in 1769 or 1770. . . .

2. DOCK STREET THEATRE
Charleston, South Carolina
Opened February 12, 1736

The first performances that are recorded in Charleston, South Carolina, took place on January 24, 1735, when Otway's tragedy, *The Orphan*, was given in the "Court Room." Apparently the play was well received, since a playhouse was built to open the following year.

The South Carolina *Gazette* exactly one year later announced the opening of the Dock Street Theatre:

2:1 On Thursday, February 12 will be opened the New Theatre in Dock Street in which will be perform'd 'The Recruiting Officer.' Tickets for the pitt and boxes will be delivered at Mr. Charles Shepheard's on Thursday the 5th February. Boxes 30s., pitt 20s., and tickets for the gallery 15s., which will be delivered at the theatre the day of playing.
N.B. the doors will be opened all the afternoon. The Subscribers are desired to send to the stage door in the forenoon to bespeak places, otherwise it will be too late.

The theatrical season was a very short one, for it closed with a production of *The Orphan* on March 23, 1736. Apparently the venture was not a financial success, for the sale of the theater was carried in the South Carolina *Gazette*, in the form of a poem:

2:1. South Carolina *Gazette*, Jan. 24, 1736.

2:2   ON THE SALE OF THE THEATRE
How cruel Fortune, and how fickle, too,
To crop the Method made for making you!
Changes tho' common, yet when great they prove,
Make men distrust the care of Mighty Jove.
Half made in thought (though not in fact) we find
You bought and sold, but left poor H. behind.
P.S.—Since so it is ne'er mind the silly trick.
The pair will please, when Pierrot makes you sick.

The Dock Street Theatre continued in use until July 1749, when it was sold, and nothing is heard of the building after that date until February 1935, when the Federal Works Administration program of the United States decided to sponsor a "restoration" of the theater. This "restoration" was completed and the theater opened on December 1, 1937, with a performance of Farquhar's *The Recruiting Officer*, the same play that opened the theater in 1736.

The 1736 Dock Street Theatre remains a mystery, for nothing is known about it except its location, the fact that there was a "box, pit and gallery" arrangement, and those few other facts that can be gleaned from the advertisements in the South Carolina *Gazette*. A special brochure published at the time of the opening of the new Dock Street Theatre in 1937 says that the reconstruction "has recaptured the original spirit by all means which architectural taste and research could suggest."

3. PLUMSTED'S PLAYHOUSE
Philadelphia, Pennsylvania
Opened January 1749(?)

In January 1749 a company of players under the direction of Thomas Kean and Walter Murray offered a short season of plays in a temporary playhouse on the outskirts of the

2:2. South Carolina *Gazette*, May 23, 1736.

city of Philadelphia. The theater was set up in the warehouse of a prominent Philadelphian, William Plumsted, whose reputation was certainly not injured because of his connection with the players, for he was elected Mayor of Philadelphia the following year.

Whether the Murray-Kean company was a professional one is open to conjecture by theater historians, since nothing is known of either of the men before their appearance in Philadelphia in 1749 or after their appearance in Williamsburg in 1751. Some historians have conjectured that the company continued to perform for a number of years, but historical evidence is woefully lacking. If the company was a professional one, amateurs were added during their time in America, since a young Philadelphia woman, Nancy George, joined the company, much to the displeasure of many Philadelphians.

Because of the antipathy of many people to the theater, little documentation is available concerning it. William Dunlap describes the playhouse as it appeared during the 1754 season:

3:1 The first regular company of comedians* opened their theatre, the store-house of Mr. William Plumsted, at the corner of the first alley above Pine Street, and commenced playing in April, 1754, with the tragedy of *The Fair Penitent*. The place has since been occupied as a sail-loft, and the remains or traces of scenic decoration were to be seen within forty years. This was called the new theatre. The word "new" seems to have applied to all the places or buildings used by this company, although there had been no previous establishment of the kind. The prices of admittance were, box 6s; pit 4s; gallery 2s 6d. . . .

The house was, as might be expected, full to overflowing. In the course of the

evening a great tumult was occasioned by the discovery of one of the unfriendly petitioners in the pit. He was considered as a spy, and peace was not restored until he was hustled out. . . .

Plumsted's warehouse, which was a large building made of unglazed brick, continued to stand until the middle of the nineteenth century.

4. FIRST NASSAU STREET THEATRE
New York City
Opened March 5, 1750

The company of players under the direction of Murray and Kean left Philadelphia in February 1750 and went to New York, petitioning the governor on their arrival for permission to perform in New York City. No playhouse was erected, but a temporary theater was arranged for the presentation of their plays beginning on March 5, 1750, as is evidenced by the following announcement from the New York *Gazette and Weekly Postboy*:

4:1 Last week arrived here a company of comedians from Philadelphia, who we hear have taken a convenient Room for their Purpose in one of the buildings lately belonging to the Hon. Rip Van Dam Esq., deceased, in Nassau Street, where they intend to perform as long as the season lasts, provided they meet with suitable encouragement.

Further background concerning the First Nassau Street Theatre is given by Joseph N. Ireland:

4:2 This building, belonging to the Hon. Rip Van Dam, deceased, once Governor of the Province of New York, was situated on the east side of Nassau street and Maiden lane, on lots now known by the numbers 64 and 66. [1866] It was con-

3:1. William Dunlap, *A History of the American Theatre*. 2 vols. in 1. (New York: J. & J. Harper, 1832), 1:31–32.

*This was the company of Lewis Hallam, which arrived in America in 1752.

4:1. New York *Gazette and Weekly Postboy*, Feb. 26, 1750.

4:2. Joseph N. Ireland, *Records of the New York Stage*, 2 vols. (New York: T. H. Morrell, 1866–67), 1:2–3.

3. Plumsted's Warehouse, Philadelphia. Etching by G. Vandergrucht, published in George Heap and Nicholas Scull, *An East Prospect of the City of Philadelphia* (London, 1754). Courtesy of the Harvard Theatre Collection.

10. Southwark Theatre, Philadelphia, 1766. Engraving, after a drawing by Edwin F. Durang based on the research of Charles Durang, 1868. Courtesy of the Free Library of Philadelphia.

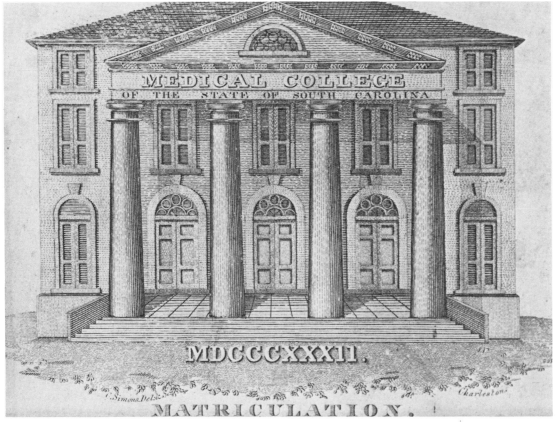

15. Charleston Theatre, Charleston, S.C. Engraving and drawing by C. Simons. The portico was added in 1830. The engraving shows the building in its later use, as a medical college. Courtesy of the South Carolina Historical Society.

verted into a church in 1758, by a congregation of German Calvinists, who in 1765, erected in its stead a more substantial building, which remained standing as lately as 1810. Dunlap's statement that the Old *Dutch* Church was built on the site of the old Theatre, has confused many readers with regard to its location, who suppose that he referred to the building now used for the United States Post Office. That church was erected in 1729, long before Van Dam's building was used for theatrical purposes. . . .

The New York *Gazette and Weekly Postboy* contained an advertisement of the opening bill:

4:3   By his Excellency's Permission
         at the Theatre in Nassau Street.
On Monday the 5th day of March next
will be presented the Historical Tragedy
         of "King Richard III."
Wrote originally by Shakspeare
and altered by Colly Cibber, Esq.

In this play is contained The Death of Henry 6th, the artful acquisition of the Crown by King Richard, the Murder of the Princes in the Tower. The Landing of the Earl of Richmond and the Battle of Bosworth Field.

Tickets will be ready to be delivered by Thursday next, and to be had of the Printer thereof.
         Pitt 5/.   Gallery 3/.
To begin precisely at half an hour after 6 o'clock and no Person to be admitted behind the scenes.

A theater historian, T. Allston Brown, described the theater in some detail.

4:4   The first Nassau Street Theatre was located on the east side of Kip (now

Nassau) Street between John Street and Maiden Lane. Kean and Murray appeared here March 5, 1750. The room in which the performances were given was in a wooden building, which belonged to the estate of the Hon. Rip Van Dam.

It was a two-storied house, with high gables. The stage was raised five feet from the floor. The scenes, curtains, and wings were all carried by the managers in their "property" trunks. A green curtain was suspended from the ceiling. A pair of paper screens were erected upon the right and left hand sides, for wings. Six wax lights were in front of the stage. Suspended from the ceiling was the chandelier, made of a barrel hoop, through which were driven half a dozen nails, into which were stuck so many candles. Two drop scenes, representing a castle and a wood, bits of landscape, river, and mountain, comprised the scenery. The opening bill was "Richard III." The company consisted of Messrs. Jago, Scott, Marks, Woodham, Taylor, Tremain, Master R. Murray, Nancy George, Mrs. Taylor, Mrs. Davis, and Mrs. and Miss Osborne. They acted twice each week, and the season lasted five months. . . . That my readers may know what a crowded house was, I will state that there were 161 pit tickets at five shillings each, ten box tickets at eight shillings each, and 121 gallery tickets at three shillings each. This was the capacity of the house.

5. SECOND WILLIAMSBURG THEATRE
Williamsburg, Virginia
Opened October(?) 1751

The Murray and Kean Company closed their New York season on June 17, 1751, and went south to Annapolis, Maryland, and Williamsburg. Since the original playhouse in Williamsburg had been turned into a courthouse in 1745, there was no structure adequate to the needs of the players; therefore, there was an appeal for funds to raise a new playhouse as soon as the players arrived. An offer

4:3. New York *Gazette and Weekly Postboy,* Feb. 26, 1750.
4:4. T. Allston Brown, *A History of the New York Stage from the First Performance 1732 to 1901.* 3 vols. (New York: Dodd, 1903), 1:2–3.

was made in the *Virginia Gazette,* August 1751:

> 5:1 By permission of his Honour the President. Whereas the Company of Comedians that are in New York intend performing in this City, but there being no Room suitable for a Play-house, 'tis propos'd that a Theatre shall be built by way of Subscription, each Subscriber advancing a Pistole* to be entitled to a Box Ticket for the first Night's diversion.

The site of the new theater is located by Lyon G. Tyler in his book on Williamsburg as being on "two lots of the Eastern side of Eastern Street (Waller Street) just back of the Capitol. On this the new playhouse was erected, the deed being dated September 2, 1751."† Nothing more is known of the playhouse or its opening except a brief announcement in the *Virginia Gazette:*

> 5:2 On Monday a Company of Comedians opened at the New Theatre near the Capitol in Williamsburg with "King Richard III" and a tragic dance composed by Monsieur Denoier called "The Royal Captive."

The season proved a short one, for by the middle of November the company had traveled on to Petersburg. They did return to Williamsburg the following April, however, for another short season at the theater, and this was their last appearance there.

6. THIRD WILLIAMSBURG THEATRE
Williamsburg, Virginia
Opened September 15, 1752

The arrival of Lewis Hallam and his professional troupe of actors from England signaled the true beginning of professional theater in

America. The group, which made the journey from England aboard a ship called the *Charming Sally,* arrived in Williamsburg early in June 1752. William Dunlap, who knew Lewis Hallam, Jr., writes of the company and their dramatic presentations in Williamsburg. The account, though interesting, is not always accurate.

> 6:1 . . . As the first settlers of Virginia were of the established English Church and that form of religion was supported by law to the exclusion of all others, it is probable that William Hallam was induced to send his company thither in preference to the other colonies, from the knowledge that Episcopalians were then more liberal in regard to the Drama than most other sects, although not less intolerant in respect to religious creeds or worship than their Presbyterian brethren, and more so than most other denominations of Christians.

The foresight exercised by the Hallams in preparing their company for immediate action on their arrival in America merits applause. The pieces had been selected, cast, and put in study, before embarkation; and during passage they were regularly rehearsed. The quarterdeck of the Charming Sally was the stage, and, whenever the winds and weather permitted, the heroes and heroines of the sock and buskin performed their allotted parts, rehearsing all the plays that had been selected, particularly those fixed upon to form the first theatrical exhibition which was to enliven the wilds of America.

It is easy to imagine the fun which these rehearsals, with the drilling of the corps, must have created among the tars. We know the salutary effect of the admirable plan of that skilful navigator Parry, who, by introducing the amusements of the theatre, when his ship was locked up amid

---

5:1. *Virginia Gazette,* Aug 29, 1751.

*A pistole was a gold Spanish coin then in use and worth approximately $4.

† Lyon Gardiner Tyler, *Williamsburg, the Old Virginia Capital* (Richmond, Va.: Whittet & Shepperson, 1907), p. 226.

5:2. *Virginia Gazette,* Oct 21, 1751.

6:1. William Dunlap, *A History of the American Theatre.* 2 vols. in 1. (New York: J. & J. Harper, 1832), 1:12–15.

the gloom of a half-year's polar night, preserved the health of his crew by preserving their cheerfulness. Sailors are peculiarly alive to dramatic representations —in that, as in some other points, they resemble children; and the novelty of having such a set of passengers, with the humour of many of the pieces rehearsed, must have delighted Jack; while the nautical drollery of the audience must have been occasionally a source of quaint amusement to the players.

The circumstance of a complete company of comedians crossing the Atlantic together and regularly drilling during the voyage, each one in his respective line, must have given a degree of precision to the first dramatic performances in the New World, which is found wanting in many theatres, even metropolitan, at this time.

Williamsburg was then the capital of Virginia; and thither the players proceeded from Yorktown, the place of their landing. Upon application made to Governor Dinwiddie, permission was granted to erect or fit up a building for a theatre. Hallam found a building which he judged to be sufficient for his purpose, and proceeded to metamorphose it into box, pit, gallery and stage. It was a long house in the suburbs of the town, probably erected as a store-house by the early emigrants; it was unoccupied, and the manager purchased it. This was the first theatre opened in America by a company of regular comedians, and although within the boundaries of the metropolis of the Ancient Dominion, the seat of William and Mary College, and the residence of all the officers of his majesty's government, was so near the woods that the manager could stand within the door and shoot pigeons for his dinner, which he more than once actually did. This theatre was situated on the spot occupied now by the house of the late Judge Tucker. After its destruction by fire, another was erected below the Old Capitol. The reader will observe

that the proprietors of this enterprise had not included an orchestra in the plan of their establishment; but fortunately a professor of music had been before them as a pioneer of the fine arts, and Mr. Pelham, who taught the harpsichord in the town, was engaged with his instrument to represent that splendid assemblage of wind and stringed instruments which we now look for in an orchestra.

On the fifth of September, 1752, at Williamsburg, the capital of Virginia, the first play performed in America by a regular company of comedians was represented to a delighted audience. The piece was *The Merchant of Venice*, and it was followed by the farce of *Lethe*. Thus Shakespeare had the first place in time as in merit as the dramatist of the western world, and Garrick the honour of attending upon his master. *Lethe* was at that time new even in London, and a popular afterpiece. . . .

That the playhouse used by Hallam was the same one built for Murray and Kean is a certainty, as indicated in this announcement in the *Virginia Gazette:*

6:2 The Company lately from London have altered the Playhouse to a regular theatre fit for the reception of Ladies and Gentlemen and the execution of their own performance, and will open on the first Friday in September with a play called "The Merchant of Venice," written by Shakespeare. Ladies engaging seats in the boxes are advised to send their servants early on the day of the performance to hold them and prevent trouble and disappointment.

The opening of the playhouse was heralded in quite a large advertisement in the *Virginia Gazette:*

6:3   By permission of the
        Hon. Robert Dinwiddie, Esq.,
    His Majesty's Lieutenant Governor

6:2. *Virginia Gazette,* Aug. 21, 1752.
6:3. *Virginia Gazette,* Aug. 28, 1752.

and Commander in Chief of the Colony
and Dominion of Virginia
By a Company of Comedians from London
At the Theatre in Williamsburg
On Friday next,
being the 15th of September, will be
presented a Play Call'd
"The Merchant of Venice"
(Written by Shakespear)
The part of *Antonio* (the Merchant)
to be perform'd by Mr. Clarkson
Gratiano, by Mr. Singleton.
Lorenzo (with songs in character)
by Mr. Adcock.
The part of *Basanio* to be performed
by Mr. Rigby.
Duke, by Mr. Wynell.
Salanio, by Mr. Herbert.
The Part of *Launcelot* by Mr. Hallam.
And the Part of *Shylock* (the Jew)
to be perform'd by Mr. Malone.
The Part of *Nerissa* by Mrs. Adcock,
Jessica, by Mrs. Rigby
And the Part of *Portia*
to be perform'd by Mrs. Hallam.
With a new occasional Prologue.
To which will be added a Farce, call'd
"The Anatomist,"
or
"Sham Doctor."
The Part of *Monsieur le Medecin*
by Mr. Rigby.
And the Part of *Beatrice*
by Mrs. Adcock.

No Persons whatsoever to be admitted behind the Scenes. Boxes 7s 6d. Pit and Balconies 5s 9d. Gallery 3s 9d. To begin at Six o'Clock.

Vivat Rex!

The discrepancy in dates of the opening of the theater between Dunlap and the announcement in the *Virginia Gazette* can perhaps be explained by the adoption of the Georgian calendar in the American colonies in 1752. In this change, eleven days were actually "lost," since the calendar skipped eleven days from September 2nd to the 14th.

Again, little is known of the physical characteristics of this playhouse, since there are no extant pictures, and the descriptions are mostly of the plays and players rather than the playhouse itself. A number of authors have recreated the playhouse from the account in a novel, *The Virginia Comedians*, by John Esten Cooke, published in 1854. The novel is set in 1763 and Lewis Hallam is still the manager of the playhouse (even though Hallam left the colonies in 1754 and died in 1756). The description, however, is an interesting one.

6:4   CHAPTER III

The "old Theatre near the Capitol," discoursed of in the manifesto issued by Mr. Manager Hallam, was so far old, that the walls were well-browned by time, and the shutters to the windows of a pleasant neutral tint between a rust and dust color. The building had no doubt been used for the present purpose in bygone times, before the days of the "Virginia Gazette," which is our authority for many of the facts here stated, and in relation to the "Virginia Company of Comedians"—but of the former companies of "players," as my lord Hamlet calls them, and their successes or misfortunes, printed words tell us nothing, as far as the researches of the present Chronicle extend. That there had been such companies before, however, we repeat, there is some reason to believe; else why that addition of "old" applied to the "Theatre near the Capitol." The question is submitted to the future social historians of the Old Dominion.

Within, the playhouse presented a somewhat more attractive appearance. There was "box," "pit," and "gallery," as in our own day; and the relative prices were arranged in much the same manner. The common mortals—gentlemen and ladies—were forced to occupy the boxes, raised slightly above the level of the stage, and

6:4. John Esten Cooke, *The Virginia Comedians*. 2 vols. (New York: D. Appleton & Co., 1854), 1:44–47.

hemmed in by velvet-cushioned railings, —in front, a flower-decorated panel, extending all around the house,—and for this position were moreover compelled to pay an admission fee of seven shillings and sixpence. The demigods—so to speak— occupied a more eligible position in the "pit," from which they could procure a highly excellent view of the actors' feet and ankles, just on a level with their noses: to conciliate the demigods, this superior advantage had been offered, and the price for them was, further still, reduced to five shillings. But "the gods" in truth were the real favorites of the manager. To attract them, he arranged the higher upper "gallery"—and left it untouched, unincumbered by railing or velvet cushions, or any other device: all was free space, and liberal as the air: there were no troublesome seats for "the gods," and three shillings and nine pence was all that the managers would demand. The honor of their presence was enough.

From the boxes, a stairway led down to the stage, and some rude scenes, visible at the edges of the green curtain, completed the outline.

When Mr. Lee and his daughters entered the box which had been reserved for them, next to the stage, the house was nearly full, and the neatness of the edifice was lost sight of in the sea of brilliant ladies' faces, and strong forms of cavaliers, which extended—like a line of glistening foam—around the semicircle of the boxes. The pit was occupied by well-dressed men of the lower class, as the times had it, and from the gallery proceeded hoarse murmurs and the unforgotten slang of London.

Many smiles and bows were interchanged between the parties in the different boxes; and the young gallants, following the fashion of the day, gathered at each end of the stage, and often walked across, to exchange some polite speech with the smiling dames in the boxes nearest.

Mr. Champ Effingham was, upon the whole, much the most notable fop present; and his elegant, languid, *petit maitre* air, as he strolled across the stage, attracted many remarks, not invariably favorable. It was observed, however, that when the Virginia-bred youths, with honest plainness called him "ridiculous," the young ladies, their companions, took Mr. Effingham's part, and defended him with great enthusiasm. Only when they returned home, Mr. Effingham was more unmercifully criticised than he would otherwise have been.

A little bell rang, and the orchestra, represented by three or four foreign-looking gentlemen, bearded and moustached, entered with trumpet and violin. The trumpets made the roof shake, indifferently, in honor of the *Prince of Morocco*, or *King Richard*, or any other worthy whose entrance was marked in the play-book "with a flourish." But before the orchestra ravished the ear of every one, the manager came forward, in the costume of *Bassanio*, and made a low bow. Mr. Hallam was a fat little man, of fifty or fifty-five, with a rubicund and somewhat sensual face, and he expressed extraordinary delight at meeting so many of the "noble aristocracy of the great and noble colony of Virginia," assembled to witness his very humble representation. It would be the chief end and sole ambition of his life, he said, to please the gentry, who so kindly patronized their servants— himself and his associates—and then the smiling worthy concluded by bowing lower than before. Much applause from the pit and gallery, and murmurs of approbation from the well-bred boxes, greeted this address, and the orchestra, having struck up, the curtain slowly rolled aloft. The young gallants scattered to the corners of the stage—seating themselves on stools or chairs, or standing, and the "Merchant of Venice" commenced. *Bassanio* having assumed a dignified and lofty port, criticised *Gratiano* with courteous and lordly wit:

his friend *Antonio* offered him his fortune with grand magnanimity, in a loud singing voice, worthy the utmost commendation, and the first act proceeded on its way in triumph.

7. SECOND NASSAU STREET THEATRE
New York City
Opened September 17, 1753

Hallam's company of players arrived in New York in June 1753, carrying a letter from Governor Dinwiddie of Virginia testifying to their ability as actors and to their good character. For some reason, however, the social climate of the city had changed from the previous year, when Kean and Murray's troupe of players had acted there, and Hallam was not given a license for his troupe, who thus were without work until September. After entreaty by Hallam, permission was finally given by the Governor of New York and the company opened on September 17, 1753, with Steele's comedy *The Conscious Lovers*. The playhouse used by Kean and Murray was found too small for the purpose, so it was pulled down and a new theater erected in its place. The plight of the players is explained by Hallam in *Gaine's Mercury*.

7:1   The case of the London Company of Comedians, lately arrived from Virginia, humbly submitted to the Consideration of the Publick; whose servants we are, and whose protection they intreat.

As our Expedition to New York seems likely to be attended with a very fatal Consequence, and ourselves haply censured for undertaking it without assurance of success—We beg leave humbly to lay a true state of our case before the worthy inhabitants of this city; if possible endeavor to remove those great obstacles which at present lie before us, and give very sufficient reasons for our appearance in this part of the world where we all had the most sanguine hopes of meeting a very different reception; little imagining

7:1. *Gaine's Mercury*, July 2, 1753.

that in a City—to all appearance so polite as this, the Muses would be banished, the works of the immortal Shakespeare and others, the greatest geniuses England ever produced, deny'd admittance among them, and the instructive and elegant entertainment of the Stage utterly protested against: when without boasting we may venture to affirm that we are capable of supporting its dignity with proper decorum and regularity.

In the infancy of this scheme it was proposed to Mr. William Hallam, now of London, to collect a Company of Comedians and send them to New York and other colonies of America. Accordingly he assented and was at vast expence to procure Scenes, Cloaths, People, &c., &c., and in October, 1750, sent out to this place Mr. Robert Upton in order to obtain permission to perform, erect a building and settle everything against our arrival; for which service Mr. Hallam advanced no inconsiderable sum. But Mr. Upton on his arrival found here that sett of pretenders with whom he joined, and unhappily for us quite neglected the business he was sent about from England; for we never heard from him after.

Being thus deceived by him, the company was at a stand till April, 1752, when by the persuasion of several gentlemen in London, and Virginia Captains, we set sail on board of Mr. William Lee (Master of the ship 'Charming Sally') and arrived after a very expensive and tedious voyage at York River, on the 28th of June following, where we obtained leave of his Excellency the Governor, and performed with universal applause and met with the greatest encouragement; for which we are bound by the strongest obligations to acknowledge the many and repeated instances of their spirit and generosity.

We were there Eleven Months before we thought of removing, and then asking advice we were again persuaded to come to New York, by several gentlemen whose names we can mention, but do not think proper to publish. They told us we should not fail of a genteel and favourable reception—that the Inhabitants were generous and polite—naturally fond of Diversions rational, particularly those of the Theatre: nay they even told us that there was a very fine Play House building and that we were really expected.

This was encouragement sufficient for us as we thought, and we came firmly asssured of success: but how far our expectations are answered, we shall leave to the Candid to determine, and only beg leave to add, That as we are People of no Estates, it cannot be supposed we have a Fund sufficient to bear up against such unexpected Repulses. A Journey by Sea and Land, Five Hundred Miles is not undertaken without money. Therefore if the worthy Magistrates would consider this in our Favour, that it would rather turn out a Publick Advantage and Pleasure, than a Private Injury, They would, we make no doubt grant us permission and give us an opportunity to convince them that we were not cast in the same mould with our Theatrical Predecessors; or that in Private Life or Publick Occupation we have the least affinity to them.

The archives of the New-York Historical Society contain the following letter by a Mathew Clarkson concerning the building of the new playhouse in New York City, which shows the prevailing attitude toward the theater. The letter is dated July 17, 1753.

7:2 . . . We are to have the diversions of the Stage the Season. There are Severall actors from some part of Europe who after much Solissitation have at last obtained leive of his Excellency to perform. They talk of building a house for that purpose and have offered themselves to Subscribe £100 for the Encouragement of it. This is a Malencholy Story among considerate

persons that so Smale aplace as this Should Encourage the toleration of such publick diversions. People are dayly murmuring at the badness of the times as tho' they were actually concerned for their Interest but their conduct proves acontradiction to it. For men in every Profession are ever fond of some party of pleasure or other and as if they had not room enough to Spend their money that way they must for all put themselves under greater temptations in going to the play house. This I speak with regard to those who are Scarcely above want. These sort of people are the most fond of it which makes the Toleration of Publick Diversions the greater Nusance to a Place Especially as it Contains So few Inhabitants.

The second performance by the company was again *The Conscious Lovers* and was attended by Philip Schuyler, who told of the experience in a letter to a relative in Albany dated September 21, 1753.

7:3 . . . The schooner arrived at Ten Eyck's wharf on Wednesday, at one o'clock, and the same evening I went to the play with Phil. You know I told you before I left home that if the players should be here I should see them, for a player is a new thing under the sun in our good province. Phil's sweetheart went with us. She is a handsome brunette from Barbadoes, has an eye like that of a Mohawk beauty, appears to possess a good understanding. Phil and I went to see the grand battery in the afternoon, and to pay my respects to the governor, whose lady spent a week with us last spring, and we bought our play tickets for eight shillings apiece, at Parker and Weyman's printing-office, in Beaver Street, on our return. We had tea at five o'clock, and before sundown we were in the Theatre, for the players commenced at six. The room was quite full

7:2. Mathew Clarkson to "Dear John" July 17, 1753, The New-York Historical Society, New York City.

7:3. Benson J. Lossing, *Life and Times of Philip Schuyler*. 2 vols. (New York: Mason Bros., 1860, 1873), 1:68–69.

already. Among the company were your cousin Tom and Kitty Livingston, and also Jack Watts, Sir Peter Warren's brother-in-law. I would like to tell you about the play, but I can't now, for Billy must take this to the wharf for Captain Wynkoop in half an hour. He sails this afternoon.

A large green curtain hung before the players until they were ready to begin, when, on the blast of a whistle, it was raised, and some of them appeared and commenced acting. The play was called The Conscious Lovers, written you know, by Sir Richard Steele, Addison's help in writing the *Spectator*. Hallam, and his wife and sisters all performed, and a sprightly young man named Hulett played the violin and danced merrily. But I said I could not tell you about the play, so I wil forbear, only adding that I was no better pleased than I should have been at the club, where, last year, I went with cousin Stephen, and heard many wise sayings which I hope profited me something. . . .

8. CRUGER'S WHARF THEATRE
New York City
Opened December 28, 1758

Following an eleven-month season in Williamsburg, the Hallam troupe had played in Philadelphia in the Plumsted warehouse and in New York in Murray and Kean's Nassau Street Theatre. They then made their way south to Charleston, South Carolina, where they supervised the building of a new theater and, following a season there, embarked for Kingston, Jamaica. It was here that Lewis Hallam died in 1756 and the company disbanded.

In 1758, however, Mrs. Hallam remarried and with her husband formed a new company to tour the American colonies. Her new husband, David Douglass, was not particularly notable as an actor, but as a manager of a theatrical company he made an important contribution to the development of professional theater in America.

Douglass and his company arrived in New York and, since the Nassau Street Theatre was no longer available, built a new theater on Cruger's Wharf. Douglass, however, did not know the ways of the Americans and had neglected to obtain the permission of the governor of the colony for the company to perform in New York. Such permission, when it was asked, was promptly denied by the city magistrates, who had been offended by his neglect in obtaining their permission. Douglass resorted to an old English trick for players to circumvent the law and announced that the playhouse would be opened as a "Histrionic Academy."

8:1 Mr. Douglass, who came here with a Company of Comedians, having applied to the Gentlemen in Power for permission to play, has (to his great mortification) met with a positive and absolute denial. He has represented that such are his circumstances and those of the other members of his company that it is impossible for them to move to another place; and tho', in the humblest manner, he begged the Magistrates would indulge him in acting as many Plays as would barely defray the expenses he and the Company have been at in coming to this city, and enable them to proceed to another, he has been unfortunate enough to be peremptorily refused it. As he has given over all thoughts of acting, he begs leave to inform the Publick that in a few days he will open a Histrionic Academy, of which proper notice will be given in this paper.

The announcement further infuriated the magistrates, and the "Histrionic Academy" never opened. Instead, Douglass was forced to publish an apology in *Gaine's Mercury:*

8:2 Whereas, I am informed that an advertisement of mine, which appeared some time ago in this paper, giving notice that I would open an Histrionic Academy, has been understood by many as a declaration

8:1. *Gaine's Mercury*, Nov. 6, 1758
8:2. *Gaine's Mercury*, Dec. 11, 1758.

that I had proposed under that colour to act plays without the consent of the Magistracy;

This is, therefore, to inform the publick that such a construction was quite foreign to my intent and meaning—that so vain, so insolent a project never once entered my head; it is an imputation on my understanding to imagine that I would dare, in a publick manner, to air an affront on gentlemen on whom I am dependent for the only means that can save us from utter ruin.

All that I proposed to do was to deliver Dissertations on Subjects, MORAL, INSTRUCTIVE, and ENTERTAINING, and to endeavor to qualify such as would favour me with their attendance—TO SPEAK IN PUBLICK WITH PROPRIETY. But as such an undertaking might have occasioned an Enquiry into my Capacity, I thought the Publick would treat me with greater Favour—when they were informed I was deprived of any other means of getting my Bread, nor would that have done more than barely supplied our present Necessities.

The expenses of our coming here—Our Living since our arrival, with the charge of Building, &c. (which, let me observe, we had engaged for before we had any Reason to apprehend a Denial), amounted to a sum that would swallow up the profits of a great many nights acting, had we permission.

I shall conclude with humbly hoping that those Gentlemen who have entertained an ill opinion of me from my supposed Presumption, will do me the favour to believe that I have truly explained the advertisement, and that I am to them and the Publick

A very humble and very
Devoted Servant,

David Douglass

Dec. 8th, 1758

Whether this letter or some other means won the permission of the magistrates to per-

form is not known, but permission was given and the theater opened on December 28, 1758, with the play *Jane Shore*.

Concerning Cruger's Wharf Theatre, as with so many of the colonial American playhouses, little is known of the physical characteristics of the playhouse other than can be discerned from the advertisements for the performances that appeared in the newspapers of the period.

8:3   At the THEATRE
On Mr. Cruger's Wharf
This present Monday, will be presented
a Comedy written by
Captain Farquhar, called
THE INCONSTANT,
or the WAY TO WIN HIM
and the farce of the MOCK DOCTOR
On Wednesday, 3d Inst., a Tragedy,
called THE ORPHAN,
or the UNHAPPY MARRIAGE.
On Friday, the 5th, the Comic Scenes of
THE SPANISH FRYAR

With entertainments as will be expressed in the bills. Tickets to be had at the Printing Office in Hanover Square, at the Coffee House, and at the Fountain Tavern, and nowhere else.

The Doors for the Gallery will be opened at Four O'clock, but the Pit and the Boxes, that Ladies may be well accommodated with seats—not till Five—and the Play begins precisely at Six.

Box, 8 shillings. Pit, 5 shillings.
Gallery, 2 shillings.

N.B.—No more tickets will be given out than the House will hold. And positively no money taken at the door.

9. SOCIETY HILL THEATRE
Philadelphia, Pennsylvania
Opened June 25, 1759

Douglass and his company ended their brief season in New York City on February 7th and moved to Philadelphia. Because of

8:3. *Gaine's Mercury*, Jan. 1, 1759.

religious opposition, Douglass decided to erect a new theater outside the city limits. He received the permission of Governor Denny to perform, in spite of strong Quaker opposition, and the company opened a successful six-month season on June 25 with a performance of *Tamerlane*.

Dunlap tells us all that we actually know about the playhouse:

9:1   In the year 1759, David Douglass opened the second theatre in Philadelphia. It was situated at the southwest corner of Vernon and South Street, at a place formerly called "Society Hill."

Strictly speaking, this was the first theatre opened in Philadelphia or its suburbs, unless we call every place a theatre which is fitted up for the temporary exhibition of plays. This was, however, the first building erected as a theatre. The manager had cautiously taken his stand without the precincts of the city authorities, in what is called the Southern Liberties, but this did not prevent the revival of the civil strife of 1754. The Quakers and others arrayed themselves in opposition, and applied to Judge Allen (probably because the place was within the peculiar limits assigned to his rule), with denunciations of the players, and petitions that his power might be exerted for the putting down of these intruders, these disturbers of the sleepy quiet of the formal city. The judge gave them an answer which must have been very unpalatable. Watson says he rejected the petition, and among other matter told the petitioners that "he had learned more moral virtue from plays than from sermons." What was the consequence? The playhouse was opened, and the wife of the judge fell sick and died. Such is the warning which tradition has handed down to us that wives may hereafter prevent their husbands giving countenance to theatres.

9:1. William Dunlap, *A History of the American Theatre*. 2 vols. in 1. (New York: J. & J. Harper, 1832), 1:38–39.

It is probable that Douglass, profiting by experience, had applied to Allen, and obtained his permission before he ventured to erect a theatre, thus avoiding the prohibition which had troubled him at New-York.

This temple of the dramatic Muse was, as may be supposed, an ordinary wooden building, and was afterward converted into three dwelling-houses, which are still standing at the corner of Vernon and South Street. The inhabitants of Philadelphia remember Mr. and Mrs. Douglass, Miss Cheer, and Miss Morris, as the most prominent performers of that day.

Arthur Hornblow in his admirable book on the American theater adds a little more information to Dunlap's account.

9:2   It was late in the spring of 1759 when Douglass and his players reached Philadelphia. The new theatre was situated at the southwest corner of Vernon and South Streets, on what was known as "Society Hill." It is believed that the manager preferred to put-up a building in this locality instead of using the old theatre in Plumsted's warehouse, where Hallam had played, because Society Hill, being beyond the city limits, was out of the jurisdiction of the town authorities. This time he had taken a precaution to secure Governor Denny's sanction to perform. Permission was granted on condition that the company gave one performance for the benefit of the Pennsylvania Hospital. But in spite of this official support the hostility continued, the Quakers going so far as to apply to Judge Allen for an injunction against the players. The story goes that the judge not only dismissed the application, but retorted with a quiet chuckle that he had always got more moral virtue from plays than from sermons. Shortly after this, the judge's wife died and the

9:2. Arthur Hornblow, *A History of the Theatre in America*. 2 vols. (Philadelphia: Lippincott, 1919), 1:104–5.

"antis" were prompt to pronounce this domestic misfortune Heaven's judgment for having given encouragement to profane stage plays.

Balked in one direction, the Quakers tried to stop the performers in another. On May 22, 1759, they presented an address to the House setting forth that "they have with real concern, heard that a company of stage players are preparing to erect a theatre and exhibit plays to the inhabitants of this city which they conceive, if permitted, will be subversive of the good order and morals which they desire may be preserved in this government." The elders of the Lutheran German Congregation of Philadelphia and the Presbyterian Synod of New York and Philadelphia presented similar petitions. The House could not ignore these representations and a bill against play-acting was presented May 28 and passed May 31. This put Governor Denny in a dilemma. He had given Douglass his permission and he wanted to keep faith with him. So he witheld the bill until June 15 when he returned it with some amendments. The measure was finally passed but was set aside in the King's Council September 2, 1760.

Meanwhile, Douglass had not been slow to take advantage of the respite thus afforded. He began his season at the new theatre on Society Hill on June 25 and remained open until December 27.

10. SOUTHWARK THEATRE
Philadelphia, Pennsylvania
Opened November 12, 1766

Douglass's company toured American towns from Newport, Rhode Island, to Annapolis, Maryland, building theaters wherever they went. These playhouses, however, were of a very temporary nature, and one, in Newport, Rhode Island, was blown down in a storm scarcely a year after it was built.

The Southwark Theatre in Philadelphia was a building of a more permanent nature,

and one that was to be used for many years. Dunlap, although he makes a major error in the date, describes the Southwark Theatre thus:

10:1   The Thespians did not visit New-York from 1759 to 1761, but, in the year 1760, Douglass built a larger theatre in Philadelphia, and, after giving a benefit at Society Hill for the college of the city, "for improving youth in the fine art of psalmody and church music," he opened the theatre in Southwark, which remained the only theatre of the metropolis of Pennsylvania, until the building of the beautiful house in Chestnut Street, erected for Wignell and Reinagle in 1791, of which hereafter.

The house erected in 1760 was of sufficient size for the population at that time and long afterwards, and well adapted for theatrical representations. It was principally of wood, and painted red, without external decoration, and in its appearance no ornament to the city. It was partly burnt some years ago, and is now used as a distillery. Once pouring out a mingled strain of good and evil, it now dispenses purely evil. Yet distilleries are not stigmatized in society. This place was used for the exhibition of players, though not the performance of plays, as late as August, 1800, when Messrs. Hodgkinson and Barrett opened it with portions of plays, recitations, and music, for two nights.

John Durang in his memoirs mentions the Southwark Theatre several times, and his comments are informative. In the following excerpt he refers to the theater as it stood in 1786, twenty years after its opening.

10:2   In the fall, Messrs. Hallam and Henry returned from New York, collected their

10:1. William Dunlap, *A History of the American Theatre.* 2 vols. in 1. (New York: J. & J. Harper, 1832), 1:40–41.

10:2. John Durang, *The Memoir of John Durang, American Actor, 1787–1816.* Ed. by Alan S. Downer (Pittsburgh: Univ. of Pittsburgh Pr., 1966), p. 26.

17

company and opened the Philadelphia old theatre in South Street. In rainey weather it was most impossible to get to the theatre within a square for mud [and] water; yet the people would flock to it. They where oblight to make a footway in every direction on a wed day. One evening a rain came during the performance and the audiance, unprepared for the mud, men and women where obliged to wade through the mud and water up to the calf for a square.

Again Hornblow is able to add some details to our knowledge of the new playhouse.

10:3   While the drama in America still had its narrow minded defamers, the more liberal and intelligent part of the community enjoyed seeing good plays well acted, and did not hesitate to patronize the playhouse. The drama, he [Douglass] considered, was worthy of a more substantial home than the flimsy wooden buildings which until now had given shelter. He determined, therefore, to erect in Philadelphia a theatre of a more permanent character. As a result of this decision, he built the old Southwark Theatre in South Street, above Fourth, the original walls of which are still standing, and which continue to be used for dramatic performances until the beginning of the Nineteenth Century. This was the first permanent theatre erected in America.

The upper part of the building was of wood, only the walls of the first story being of brick. It was partly destroyed by fire in 1821. Soon afterwards the walls were raised, and it was known for many years as Young's Distillery, which fact prompted Dunlap, in 1832, to remark facetiously: "Once pouring out a mingled strain of good and evil, it now dispenses purely evil." It was an ugly, ill-contrived affair both outside and inside. "The brickwork," says Seilhamer,* was rude but strong, and the wooden part of the building rough and primitive. The whole was painted glaring red. The stage was lighted by plain oil lamps, without glasses, and the view from the boxes was intercepted by large wooden pillars supporting the upper tier and the roof."

The erection of the new theatre naturally aroused a storm of protest. The Quakers looked upon it as an unlawful encroachment on their religious views and habits and presented the Assembly a remonstrance demanding that the proposed "stage-playing" be forbidden on the ground that plays "divert the minds of unwary youths and prevent their becoming useful members of society." Governor Penn, less bigoted than the subscribers, refused to entertain the complaint and the antitheatrical party found themselves powerless.

The season at Southwark theatre began November 21, 1766, the players being now known as the American Company. The organization was, in fact, American in more than name. The early actors were all English, but now that could no longer be said of the company.

One of the most important events of this season in Philadelphia was the presentation of the first play by an American author to receive a professional production—*The Prince of Parthia* by Thomas Godfrey, which had its debut on April 24, 1767.

11. JOHN STREET THEATRE
New York City
Opened December 7, 1767

The John Street Theatre was built by David Douglass in 1767 and remained the leading theater in New York for the next thirty

---

10:3. Arthur Hornblow, *A History of the Theatre in America.* 2 vols. (Philadelphia: Lippincott, 1919), 1:120–21.

*George Seilhamer, a theater historian of the 19th century, who wrote *History of the American Theatre* in 1891.

years. The building of this playhouse elicited a number of comments in the local newspapers, and one of these articles is reprinted here.

11:1 The Mirror. (Numb. IV.)

To Mr. David De Speculo.

Sir,

Reading *Parker's Gazette* a few days ago, I was much pleased with a paper called the *Mirror,* on the subject of beauty; the author I think discovers a knowledge of human-nature, at the same time that his concern to correct it does honour to his benevolence. You seem, Sir, to write as much with a view of pleasing and entertaining your readers, as of employing your leisure hours; and therefore I take the liberty of sending you a few thoughts upon a subject, which equally respects the entertainment and improvement of the town—I mean the Play-house—. Few are ignorant, that whoever attempts to recommend any thing, that pious and well-disposed people erroneously think disadvantageous to morality, must expect opposition from every sophism, that can give the least appearance of reason to prejudice, or tend to justify the virulence of mistaken zeal. It is difficult to convince men of errors imbibed in infancy and confirmed by education, and therefore those who attempt to establish opposite opinions, for the most part undertake a task too arduous for their abilities. These, however, are disadvantages to which every unpopular doctrine is subject, and would deter me from saying any thing in vindication of the stage, did I not flatter myself, that Mr. De Speculo's acquaintance with the world has divested him of every prejudice, and that his liberal way of thinking, will secure to me all the candour necessary to determine, on which side of the question truth preponderates.

The advantages of the theatre, come under two heads; Instruction and Amusement—. The objections raised against it, are drawn, first, from the expence attending it, and secondly, from an ill-grounded supposition, that it tends to the corruption of morals. Of these in their order—

That it is calculated for Instruction, appears, from its being the best school in which a knowledge of mankind can be acquired, and from its tendency to refine and polish the manners of the audience: That the knowledge of human nature is necessary to all who are conversant with mankind, and whose success in every enterprize depends upon prudence and discretion, need not be insisted upon; it is a proposition to which few will refuse their assent.—The only question then is, whether the stage advances this kind of knowledge? That it does will appear from the following considerations.—The success of every play depends upon its similarity to nature; human nature is the subject of every play;—therefore, every play, which in its exhibition meets with applause, proves that its author understands human nature.—Now from whom can we expect better lessons in any science, than from those whom the united voice of the whole people declare proficient in it. It is agreed on all hands, that an acquaintance with mankind is necessary, and therefore, no one can pretend to act consistent with reason and his own principles, and yet refuse to frequent the Play-house.—This argument, Sir, in my opinion is conclusive, and proves demonstrably, that, considering the Theatre in the light as a school, it ought by all means to be encouraged.

Whether it has a tendency to refine and polish the manners of a people, let experience determine; with those who are conversant with history, the point is clear in its favour; but the misfortune is that people in general are ignorant of the transactions of former ages, and for the sake of such, I must beg leave to mention that there never was a nation in which a

11:1. New York *Gazette*, Dec. 3, 1767.

Theatre has been erected, that was not more polite, more refined, and more civilized after, than before they had a taste for theatrical representations: Whence it follows, that dramatic writers have done more towards expelling barbarism and introducing good manners, than any other, or all other causes put together.—The Athenians were more civilized after the time of Eschylus, than before.—The Spartans never had a stage, and from the beginning to the end of their government, their court resembled a rendezvous of ruffians and assassins, than a polite assembly of well-bred gentlemen. Rome never cultivated the arts of peace, or knew the value of science, till their accidental acquaintance with the Greeks introduced a taste for dramatic performances. And to come to later times, what did Great-Britain know about good manners or the belles lettres before Shakespear gave the stage a general influence, or by publickly exposing the foibles, opened a way to the improvement of the times. Thus, a number of facts conspire in establishing the importance of the stage, and remove every objection that can be made to its utility.

Whoever denies that the stage is capable of affording the most rational entertainment, betrays a secret, which I should think it his interest to conceal; namely, an unpardonable want of taste: Does it not abound with every thing necessary to inform the judgment, and enrich the imagination? There we are led thro' all the mazes in which the characters of men are inveloped, their motives of action laid open, and the means made use of to accomplish their ends, explained. There, wit and politeness shew themselves in the dress of elegance, in all the splendor of delicate refinement. There the fancy is entertained with the finest imagery; all nature, every art and science their flowers to embellish the stage.—What place can be better fitted for rational entertainment,

what person of taste can bear to hear it decried? Rather let it become the object of public care, and let us consider the patrons of the Theatre, as the friends and guardians of polite erudition. If there be any weight in the objections urged against the expediency of a Play-house, it consists in the one raised from the expence attending it; tho' I am far from thinking this sufficient to counterbalance the advantages resulting from it.—There are many parents, who willingly spare two or three hundred pounds, to give a son what is called a college education; and no one looks upon this as extravagant, because all conceive it to be useful: They conceive it to be useful, because it qualifies a youth for a learned profession, or at least enables him to pass thro' life with greater advantage and more reputation.—This case applies exactly to the Theatre, it is as reasonable to purchase knowledge in one way as another, and when we compare the knowledge gained at college, with what may be acquired at the Play-house in point of utility, the latter certainly merits the preference; the one being merely speculative, the other practical; And yet, so inconsistently do the generality of mankind act, that many make it their business to calumniate what they ought to recommend; and lectures against the Play-house, are as common, as admonitions against the world, the flesh, and the devil.

Whoever attempts to maintain that the Theatre is a friend to immorality, in my opinion, discovers little knowledge of human nature.—They tell us that many plays abound with obscenities, some of them treat religion with disrespect; true, they do so, but this is so far from being an argument against them, that in my opinion it evinces their use: Don't imagine I am going to say any thing in favour of obscenity or irreligion; this is by no means my intention. Nature has wisely implanted in the breast of every man, an internal sense of beauty and deformity;

the one is followed by an agreeable, the other by a disagreeable sensation!—A distorted feature, a withered limb, an ill-natured countenance, and a thousand other objects of this kind, occasion pain and uneasiness in the spectator, and strongly urge him to avoid them. In like manner, when we are informed of a horrid parricide, a cool deliberate murder, base ingratitude to a benefactor, a malicious calumny; this bare recital shocks us, and we are immediately fired with resentment against the perpetrators. In short, as deformity need only be exposed to become disagreeable, so sin and immorality need only be mentioned, to be rendered odious. The plays, therefore, which publish the vices that infest society, increase the number of their enemies, they teach us how to guard against them, and instead of promoting the cause of immorality, give strength to the interest of virtue.

Besides, if I am rightly informed, the Play-house in this city was erected under the licence and approbation of those, whom it is our duty to imitate, and who are too well affected to the country, to encourage any thing that might injure its welfare. I assure you, it gave me great pleasure to hear, that some of the first rank and figure among us, refused to countenance a measure, which two or three busy people had concerted to discourage it. Their example, I think, should silence popular clamour, and induce us to neglect the common place censures of testy individuals.

Thus, Sir, you have my sentiments respecting the expediency of a Theatre, as fully as the limits of a letter will permit, and if you honour them with a place in the Mirror, I shall think it such a mark of your approbation, as will induce me to continue the correspondence.

I am, Sir, your humble servant,

Dramaticus

A rather brief description of the John Street Theatre was written by William Dunlap. Although Dunlap was only one year old when the playhouse was built, he later became one of the managers of the theater and had his comedy, *The Father, or, American Shandyism*, produced there by the American Company in 1789.

11:2 In the summer of 1767, the theatre in John Street, New-York, was built very much upon the plan of that in the Southern liberties at Philadelphia, already mentioned.* It was principally of wood; an unsightly object, painted red. The situation of this house was on the north side of the street, nearly opposite to the present Arcade (1832). It was about 60 feet back from the street, having a covered way of rough wooden material from the pavement to the doors. There is reason to believe that at this time the dressing-rooms and green-room were under the stage, for, after the revolution, Hallam and Henry added on the west side of the building a range of rooms for dressing, and a commodious room for assembling previous to being called to go on. Two rows of boxes, with a pit and gallery, could accommodate all the play-going people at that time, and yield to the sharers eight hundred dollars when full, at the usual prices. The stage was of good dimensions, as far as memory serves, equal to that of Colman's theatre, originally Foote's, in the Haymarket, London.

Royall Tyler was the first American playwright of comedy to have his work produced by a professional company. *The Contrast* was written in a very brief time, perhaps less than two weeks, and was undoubtedly inspired by a performance of *The School for Scandal* that he viewed at the John Street Theatre. One scene, in particular, describes the interior of

11:2. William Dunlap, *A History of the American Theatre*. 2 vols. in 1. (New York: J. & J. Harper, 1832), 1:51–52.
*The Southwark Theatre in Philadelphia.

21

a playhouse, presumably the John Street Theatre. The character Jonathan is famous as a precursor of the famous shrewd Yankee character that now took its place on the American stage.

11:3 *Jenny*: So, Mr. Jonathan, I hear you were at the play last night.

>*Jonathan*: At the play! why, did you think I went to the devil's drawing-room!

>*Jenny*: The devil's drawing-room!

>*Jonathan*: Yes; why an't cards and dice the devil's device; and the play house the shop where the devil hangs out the vanities of the world, upon the tenterhooks of temptation. I believe you have not heard how they were acting the old boy one night, and the wicked one came among them sure enough; and went right off in a storm, and carried one-quarter of the play-house with him. Oh! no, no, no! you won't catch me at a play-house, I warrant you.

>*Jenny*: Well, Mr. Jonathan, though I don't scruple your veracity, I have some reasons for believing you were there; pray, where were you about six o'clock?

>*Jonathan*: Why, I went to see one Mr. Morrison, the hocus-pocus man; they said as how he could eat a case knife.

>*Jenny*: Well, and how did you find the place?

>*Jonathan*: As I was going about here and there, to and again, to find it, I saw a great crowd of folks going into a long entry, that had lantherns iver the door; so I asked a man whether that was not the place where they played hocus-pocus? He was a very civil kind man, though he did speak like the Hessians; he lifted up his eyes and said—"they play hocus pocus tricks enough there, Got knows, mine friend."

>*Jenny*: Well—

11:3. Royall Tyler, *The Contrast*, Act III, sc. 1.

>*Jonathan*: So I went right in, and they shewed me away clean up to the garret, just like a meetinghouse gallery. And so I saw a power of topping folks, all sitting around in little cabbins, just like father's corn-cribs; and then there was such a squeaking with the fiddles, and such a tarnal blaze with the lights, my head was near turned. At last the people that sat near me set up such a hissing—hiss—like so many mad cats; and then they went thump, thump, thump, just like our Peleg threshing wheat, and stampt away, just like the nation; and called out for one Mr. Langolee,—I suppose he helps act the tricks.

>*Jenny*: Well, and what did you do all this time?

>*Jonathan*: Gor, I—I like the fun, and so I thumpt away, and hiss'd as lustily as the best of 'em. One sailor-looking man that sat by me, seeing me stamp, and knowing I was a cute fellow, because I could make a roaring noise, clapt me on the shoulder and said, you are a d----d hearty cock, smite my timbers! I told him so I was, but I thought he need not swear so, and make use of such naughty words.

>*Jessamy*: The savage!—Well, and did you see the man with his tricks?

>*Jonathan*: Why I vow, as I was looking out for him, they lifted up a great green cloth, and let us look right into the next neighbor's house. Have you a good many houses in New York made so in that 'ere way?

>*Jenny*: Not many; but did you see the family?

>*Jonathan*: Yes, swamp it; I see'd the family.

>*Jenny*: Well, how did you like them?

>*Jonathan*: Why, I vow they was pretty much like other families;—there was a poor, good natured, curse of a husband, and a sad rantipole of a wife.

Jenny: But did you see no other folks?

Jonathan: Yes. There was one youngster, they called him Mr. Joseph; he talked as sober and pious as a minister; but like some ministers that I know, he was a sly tike in his heart for all that: He was going to ask a young woman to spark it with him, and—the Lord have mercy on my soul!—she was another man's wife.

Jessamy: The Wabash!

Jenny: And did you see any more folks?

Jonathan: Why they came on as thick as mustard. For my part, I thought the house was haunted. There was a soldier fellow, who talked about his row de dow dow, and courted a young woman; but of all the cute folk I saw, I liked one little fellow—

Jenny: Aye! Who was he?

Jonathan: Why, he had red hair, and a little round plump face like mine, only not altogether so handsome. His name was Darby:—that was his baptizing name, his other name I forgot. Oh! it was Wig—Wag—Wag-all, Darby Wag-all;*—pray, de you know him?—I should like to take a sling with him or a drap of cyder with a pepper-pod in it, to make it warm and comfortable.

Jenny: I can't say I have that pleasure.

Jonathan: I wish you did, he is a cute fellow. But there was one thing I didn't like in that Mr. Darby; and that was he was afraid of some of them 'ere shooting irons, such as your troopers wear on training days. Now I'm a true born Yankee American son of liberty, and I never was afraid of a gun yet in all my life.

Jenny: Well, Mr. Jonathan, you were certainly at the play-house.

Jonathan: I at the play-house!—Why didn't I see the play then?

Jenny: Why the people you saw were players.

George C. D. Odell in his *Annals of the New York Stage* discusses the John Street Theatre in some detail, using the information from Dunlap's work as a basis for his comments on the exterior, while the description of the interior is based on a single picture allegedly from the period 1777–83, which has since proved to be spurious. Some of Odell's comments concerning the setting of the play-house as well as its history are of great interest.

11:4   In 1767 cattle pastures extended above Grand Street, and the town reckoned distances by docks rather than by blocks. At least I seem to feel a preponderance of wharves and slips in ploughing through old newspapers of the period, papers in which little beyond the latest shipping intelligence finds harbourage. But enough remains in advertisements at least, to revivify the little city laved by the waters of traffic, to awaken a tender curiosity as to the Fly Market, east of Maiden Lane, as to Pie-Alley, Cart and Horse Alley, and other quaintly-named localities long since nominated in prose. The Broadway, with, if Dunlap may be believed, its two or three dwellings gable-end towards the street; the Bouwerie—the Boston Road—stretching out into almost a wilderness, but lined on each side for a little way, at least, with farms whose fruit-trees overhung the orchard walls; this was the milieu in which our famous theatre lived and thrived or failed, according to the exigencies of the season. Of course, the Battery, with the Bowling Green near, and Fort George, with its barracks and governor's mansion and its orthodox

---

*The part of Jonathan was played originally by Thomas Wignell, leading comedian of the John Street company. Darby Wag-all is a character in John O'Keefe's *The Poor Soldier,* a popular comic opera that had been performed quite often by the John Street company. It is obvious, however, that Jonathan's description of Darby Wag-all is actually a description of Tyler's friend Thomas Wignell.

11:4. George C. D. Odell, *Annals of the New York Stage.* 15 vols. (New York: Columbia University Pr., 1927–49), 1:110–11.

church, constituted the acme of social distinction for a self-satisfied community. Even if we could revive the theatre in its pristine state, how could we ever hope to recapture the setting of that town on the tip of the tongue of Manhattan? a town of fewer than 20,000 inhabitants, unschooled, mostly, in the commonplaces of culture known to their descendants, though living, in some cases in great luxury? The fame of the Walton house, home of a family of merchant princes, extended, we are told, to the mother country; and its lavish hospitality and gorgeous entertainments led to a belief in London that the colonies could be taxed to any limit. The Walton house is said to have been the finest in pre-Revolutionary America. . . .

The story of the John Street establishment—a matter of thirty years—breaks into four clearly differentiated periods, and each of those periods it will now be my pleasing task to consider in detail. The first extends from the opening of the house by Douglass on the 7th of December, 1767, to the closing of all theatrical activities throughout the Colonies by resolution of Congress in 1774. The second is that of the military actors, who entertained the more or less willing population of New York during the occupation of the city by the English army; amateurs who displayed their talents from 1777 to to 1783. The third era extends from Lewis Hallam's tentative, not to say timid offerings in the summer of 1785 to the departure of Wignell and Mrs. Morris in 1789, with a subsequent season (1791–92) without the cooperation of those artists. The fourth and most brilliant episode—1793 to 1798—is dominated by the compelling personality of the talented and versatile John Hodgkinson. I shall prosper just so far as I succeed in revivifying these four epochs in the life of the old theatre. . . .

J. N. Ireland was able to add a little more

to our knowledge of this important early playhouse.

11:5 In the summer of 1767, a new Theatre was built on the northerly side of John Street, near Broadway. It stood much longer than any of its predecessors, and was used for the purpose for which it was erected for more than thirty years. Long after, its site, and perhaps the original building, was occupied by a carriage factory, and is now covered with storehouses adjoining Thorburn's seed and agricultural establishment, and in the rear of lots Nos. 17, 19, and 21. By a renumbering of the street, the entrance lot, which is but a wide alley-way leading to the rear, is now known as No. 17, but a half century ago it was No. 15. The building was an unsightly object, principally of wood painted red, and stood about sixty feet back from the street, having a covered way of rough wooden material from the pavement to the doors. The stage was of good dimensions, and the dressing room and green room were originally under it, but after the Revolution, they were removed to a wing added for the purpose, on the west side. The auditorium was fitted up with a pit, two rows of boxes, and a gallery, and when full at usual prices would contain $800. The John Street Theatre was first opened by Mr. Douglass, on the 7th of December, 1767. We transcribe the opening bill:

By Permission of his Excellency,
the Governor,
by the American Company
at the THEATRE in John Street,
this present evening
a comedy called
THE STRATAGEM

Archer . . . . Mr. Hallam
Aimwell . . . . Mr. Henry

11:5. Joseph N. Ireland, *Records of the New York Stage*. 2 vols. (New York: T. H. Morrell, 1866–67), 1:42–43.

Sir C. Freeman .... Mr. Malone
Sullen .... Mr. Tomlinson
Foigard .... Mr. Allyn
Gibbet .... Mr. Woolls
Boniface .... Mr. Douglass
Lady Boniface .... Mrs. Harman
Mrs. Sullen .... Mlle. Cheer
Dorinda .... Mlle. Hallam
Cherry .... Mrs. Wainwright
Gipsy .... Mrs. Wall

AN OCCASIONAL EPILOGUE,
by Mrs. Douglass.
To conclude with the dramatic
Satire, entitled
LETHE

Aesop .... Mr. Douglass
Mercury .... Mr. Woolls
Tattoo .... Mr. Malone
Frenchman .... Mr. Allyn
Fine Gentleman .... Mr. Wall
Drunken Man .... Mr. Hallam
Mrs. Tattoo .... Mlle. Hallam
Mrs. Riot .... Mrs. Wainwright

To begin exactly at Six o'clock
Vivant Rex et Regina.

No person under any pretext whatever can be admitted behind the scenes. Tickets, without which no person can be admitted, to be had at the Bible and Crown in Hanover Square, and of Mr. Hayes at the Area of the Theatre. Places in the boxes may be taken of Mr. Broadbelt at the Stage door. Ladies will please send their servants to keep their places at four o'clock.
Boxes, 8 s.   Pit, 5 s.   Gallery, 3 s.

12. CHURCH-STREET THEATRE
Charleston, South Carolina
Opened December 22, 1773

Charleston was a very prosperous and thriving city with a population that enjoyed cultural events. Theatrical performances had been given in the community from the early part of the eighteenth century, and several theaters had been built but had not been able to survive over a long period of time. By 1774, however, the city was basking in its prosperity and was ready for playhouses of a more permanent nature.

The South Carolina *Gazette* tells of the building of a new playhouse and other important buildings.

12:1   Besides the stupendous work now nearly completed by Christopher Gadsden, Esq., at the North end of this Town which is reckoned the most extensive of the kind ever undertaken by any one man in America, it is amazing to observe the other improvements that have within a very few years past been made here and are daily carrying on. More than six new and commodious wharves have been added to our water-front. In the same period a great Assembly Room has been built, and within six months past an elegant Theatre established by which a Company of Comedians are handsomely supported.

White Point is almost covered with houses, many of them very elegant. Several excellent academies have been established for the education of the Youth of this Province; great attention is also paid to the Fine Arts, the St. Cecilia Society warmly patronized music, while many Gentlemen of Taste and Fortune are giving the utmost Encouragement to Architecture, Portraiting and the ingenuous performances of the first capital Landscape Painter that visited America, whose works will do him Honour.

And shall it be said that such a People will suffer themselves to sink into Slavery?

Documentation for the Church-Street Theatre is difficult, since the issues of the South Carolina *Gazette* from December 20th to the 27th, 1773, are missing; however, Seilhamer was able to reconstruct the details from some

12:1. South Carolina *Gazette,* Jan. 9, 1774.

documents and sources that were available to him:

12:2   In Rivington's *Gazette*, under date of July 27th, 1773, it was announced that a large subscription had been solicited and was raising for building an elegant theatre in Charleston, S.C., in which Mr. Douglass' American Company would perform during the winter. Mr. Douglass evidently had gone to Charleston on this business before the close of the New York season, leaving Mr. Henry in charge, as it was announced he would sail thence for Philadelphia on the 30th of August with Captain Blewer, "having secured the patronage of the gentlemen of that city, which will enable him to build and open an elegant theatre before Christmas." This indicates that the Charleston Theatre was built upon a plan similar to that which enabled Mr. Douglass to build the theatre at Annapolis, in 1771. The house was not large, but it was more commodious than either the Southwark Theatre at Philadelphia or the John Street Theatre in New York. It was said of it that it was elegantly finished and well supplied with new scenery. How long this theatre stood is uncertain, but it does not seem to have been used as a play-house after the Revolutionary war. Previous to the erection of this building entertainments such as the concerts of the St. Cecilia Society were given in a large, inelegant structure, situated, Josiah Quincy, Jr., says in his "Journal," down a yard.

The New Charleston Theatre was opened on the 22nd of December, 1773, with "A Word to the Wise" and "High Life Below Stairs." This was the beginning of a season of fifty-nine nights, during which as many as forty-eight distinct plays and twenty-nine farces were given. The season lasted until the 19th of May,

1774, a period of five months. When it closed a complete list of the performances, from the beginning, was printed in the South Carolina *Gazette*. As already mentioned, this is the only complete list of any season before the Revolution, except for the Annapolis engagement of 1760. It is, however, in every way more interesting than the Annapolis repertoire. The good people of Charleston had not only an opportunity of witnessing the American Company's last performance before the Revolution and of seeing the performers at their best, but the list of performances presented for their approbation is almost bewildering in extent and variety. Nearly everything that then held the stage was produced at least once during the season. . . .

Seilhamer also quotes an account of the opening of the Church-Street Theatre that appeared in Rivington's *Gazette* but probably was copied from the South Carolina *Gazette*.

12:3 OPENING OF THE CHARLESTON THEATRE —On Wednesday last the new theatre in this town was opened with Mr. Kelly's "Word to the Wise" and "High Life Below Stairs," with an occasional prologue spoken by Mr. Hallam and Mrs. Douglass. The performance gave universal satisfaction. Mr. Hallam in particular in *Captain Dormer* displayed his extraordinary theatrical talents in a most splendid manner. Indeed, all the performers did great justice to their characters; but that gentleman's superior abilities were so remarkably striking that we could not pass them over unnoticed. The house is elegantly furnished and supposed for the size to be the most commodious on the continent. The scenes, which are new and well designed, the dresses, the music and what had a very pleasing effect, the dis-

12:2. George O. Seilhamer, *History of the American Theatre*. 3 vols. (Philadelphia: Globe Printing House, 1889–91), 1:329–30.

12:3. George O. Seilhamer, *History of the American Theatre*. 3 vols. (Philadelphia: Globe Printing House, 1889–91), 1:331.

position of the lights, all contributed to the satisfaction of the audience, who expressed the highest approbation of their entertainment.

The season was a long and successful one, and Douglass made plans to return to Charleston for another season, as is indicated in this announcement in the South Carolina *Gazette*:

12:4   CLOSE OF THE CHARLESTON SEASON

On Friday last the theatre which opened here the 22d of December was closed. Warmly countenanced and supported by the public the manager and his company were excited to the most strenuous efforts to render their entertainment worthy of so respectable a patronage. It was considered how late it was in the season before the house could be opened, the variety of scenery and decorations necessary to a regular theatre, the number of plays represented and that almost every piece required particular preparations, it must be confessed that the exertions of the American Company have been uncommon and justly entitles them to those marks of public favor that have for so many years stampt a merit in their performances. The choice of plays hath been allowed to be very judicious, the director having selected from the most approved English poets such pieces as possess in the highest degree the *utile dulce*, and they entertain and improve the mind by conveying the most useful lessons of industry and virtue. The company have separated until the winter, when the New York Theatre will be opened. Mr. Hallam being embarked to England to engage some recruits for that service. The year after they will perform at Philadelphia, and in the winter following we may expect them here with a theatrical force hitherto unknown in America.

Scratch me, countryman!—and I'll scratch thee.

12:4. South Carolina *Gazette*, May 30, 1774.

13. HARMONY HALL
Charleston, South Carolina
Opened July 11, 1786

The Church-Street Theatre, built in Charleston in 1773 and mentioned as being so "elegant," by 1786 had been demolished or used for other purposes, for no further mention is made of it. In its place a new theater was raised by an actor named Godwin. The first mention of this theater is in the New York *Independent*.

13:1   We hear from Charleston, S.C., that a principal merchant of that city and a Mr. Goodwin, comedian, have leased a lot of land for five years and have erected a building called Harmony Hall, for the purpose of music meetings, dancing, and theatrical amusements. It is situated in a spacious garden in the suburbs of the city. The boxes are 22 in number, with a key to each box. The pit is very large and the theatrum and orchestra elegant and commodious. It was opened with a grand concert of music *gratis* for the satisfaction of the principal inhabitants, who wished to see it previous to the first night's exhibition. The above building has cost £500 sterling. Salaries from two to five guineas per week, and a benefit night every nine months is offered to good performers.

Godwin, seeking to publicize his new enterprise, inserted an advertisement in the Charleston *Morning Post* and *Daily Advertiser*.

13:2   TO THE PUBLIC

Mr. Godwin has leased a Lot of Land next to the Louisburg Hotel, without the city, for a term of years, and having erected a building thereon to be known by the name Harmony Hill, he proposed

13:1. New York *Independent*, Aug. 5, 1786.
13:2. Charleston *Morning Post* and *Daily Advertiser*, June 9, 1786.

to establish the same as an Academy for Oratory, Music, Dancing and Fencing.

In the course of the year will be given some two or three benefits for public uses and charitable purposes. Every possible exertion will be used to render the amusements of Harmony Hill rational and innocent and in every way worthy the approbation of the sensible and polite inhabitants of South Carolina.

Mr. Godwin most respectfully assured those Ladies and Gentlemen who may patronize him, that gratitude shall write their names in his heart and lead him to acknowledge the obligation that will so much honour him.

A reporter visited the new theater and assessed it:

13:3   A correspondent, feeling a curious propensity to view Harmony Hall, obtained permission from the Manager, and was astonished to find such a beautiful little theatre could be completed in so short a time. If a similar genius and industry are exerted in promoting the entertainments proposed to be exhibited, Harmony Hall will undoubtedly be a place of resort for the fashionable and the polite.

The formal opening of the theater was announced in a full-page advertisement in the Columbia *Herald*.

13:4   OPENING OF HARMONY HALL
Tuesday Evening July 11th
at Seven O'Clock
By Desire will be performed
A Grand Concert of Music. In Three Acts
Selected from the most
Celebrated Composers, etc.
Between the Acts to be exhibited a
Variety of Paintings of
Ancient and Modern Heads,
With a Lecture by Mr. Godwin
Prologue—Tragic and Comic Muse,

13:3. Charleston *Morning Post* and *Daily Advertiser*, June 30, 1786.
13:4. Columbia *Herald*, July 11, 1786.

The Celebrated Dr. B. Franklin with the motto affixed to his bust at Paris, etc.
After the Second Act Transparencies
and an Ode by Mr. Godwin, then
"Bucks Have At Ye All"
After the Third Act of the Concert
a Hornpipe
Then a Foreign Gentleman will perform
a few choice pieces with a
Pantomimical Dance called
"L'Amour du Vin"
Italian Shepherd by Mr. Godwin.
Peasant by Mons. Carré.

. . . .

A person will attend at the office of Harmony Hall every Day to let Boxes. Front Boxes are for parties of Ten and Side Boxes for Parties of Six. Each box has a key to be given to the Person who takes it. The Gate fronting Boundary Street will be open at Half Past Five O'Clock and the Concert commence at Seven.

Tickets for the Pit at Five Shillings each, to be had at Mr. Waller's store on Beal's Wharf, at Bowen and Markland's No. 11 Elliott Street and at the office above mentioned.

No admittance to the Boxes but by Parties. No more tickets for the Pit are issued than to the number of persons it will accommodate; therefore Ladies and Gentlemen are desired to apply for tickets early as the Doorkeeper is under a binding engagement to reject money at the Door. N.B. New Heads, with Singing and Dancing each night of the Concert.

The opening received good news coverage, the following commentary appearing in the *Morning Post* on July 14:

13:5   The Theatre at Louisburg is constructed upon as good a concerted plan, and has as cheerful an appearance as any erection for public exhibitions we ever remember to have seen on a similar scale. Certainly it is not fit to be put in a line

13:5. Charleston *Morning Post*, July 14, 1786.

of comparison with the Capital theatres of Europe as to glare and magnificent appearance, for many of these buildings originally cost immense sums, and are every year altered and ornamented; but then this great display of magnificence utterly destroys any ideas that a critical spectator may entertain of propriety, and consequently deadens the effect which dramatic compositions are calculated to have upon the passions. In a theatre where the ornaments before the curtain are glittering and grand, behind it everything must be magnificent, so that to preserve uniformity, chamber-maids are dressed in gowns of rich silk and common tradesmen's wives in robes of tissue or brochade. An alderman is represented on the stage in a dress that would be highly ornamental for a king and a tragedy queen is so loaded with ornaments that it is with difficulty she can move under them.

The opening doors to each box give a thorough circulation to the air exceedingly grateful to the auditors.

It will not be remiss if the painter retouches Thalia's features, for as it was, she appeared to be a Birmingham composition, whilst her pensive sister was set-off as Fanny's darling child. . . .

Apparently the Harmony Hall venture was doomed to failure from the outset. Seilhamer remarks:

13:6 . . . Beginning in September the season lasted until the close of March, but it does not appear to have been a very prosperous one. The list of performers that I have been able to cull from the Charleston papers is, of course, far from complete, but it is sufficiently full to show the ambitious character of Godwin's management and to indicate the failure of his plans. Indeed, success must have been im-

possible from the outset. In a city where the "principal inhabitants" rush to see the house for nothing, they are not likely to pay afterwards to witness the performances that take place in it.* In thus throwing away the receipts of his first night Mr. Godwin made a fatal mistake, for it is evident that the new theatre was his chief attraction. He was without a company of competant players to begin with, and when he at last secured a few people who had had some experience on the stage, it was too late to recover from the mistakes made in the beginning. . . .

14. NEW EXHIBITION ROOM
Boston, Massachusetts
Opened August 16, 1792

Although Boston, with the first college in America, was an intellectual center in the American colonies, it was also the stronghold of puritanism. Consequently, the theater had never taken root in the "Athens of the North." William Dunlap's observations concerning the prohibition of the theater in the Commonwealth of Massachusetts are interesting, if not completely accurate.

14:1 Massachusetts, both as a colony of Great Britain and as an independent state, had been forbidden ground to all Thespians. As early as the year 1750, before any of that dangerous class of people had ventured over the Atlantic, the General Court of Massachusetts, that is, in the language of other parts of our country, the House of Assembly or Representatives, passed an act to prevent stage-plays and other theatrical entertainments. The historian of Massachusetts says, that the cause of "this moral regulation" was that two young Englishmen, assisted by

*Godwin offered a free performance on opening night in order to acquaint the public with his new theater.

13:6. George O. Seilhamer, *History of the American Theatre*. 3 vols. (Philadelphia: Globe Printing House, 1889–91), 2:205–7.

14:1. William Dunlap, *A History of the American Theatre*. 2 vols. in 1. (New York: J. & J. Harper, 1832), 1:242–44.

some townsmen, tried to represent Otway's tragedy of *The Orphan*, and the inhabitants were so eager to see the entertainment, that some disturbances took place at the door of the coffeehouse where they were amusing themselves. This so alarmed the lieutenant-governor, council, and house of representatives, that, "for preventing and avoiding the many and great mischiefs which arise from public stage-plays, &c. which not only occasion great and unnecessary expenses, and discourage industry and frugality, but likewise tend generally to increase immorality, impiety, and a contempt of religion," they enacted as follows: "that from and after the publication of this act, no person or persons whatsoever may, for his or their gain, or for any price or valuable consideration, let, or suffer to be used or improved, any house, room, or place whatsoever, for acting or carrying on any stage-plays, interludes, or other theatrical entertainments, on pain of forfeiting and paying for each and every day, or time, such house, room, or place, shall be let, used, or improved, contrary to this act, twenty pounds. And if, at any time or times whatsoever, from and after the publication of this act, any person or persons shall be present as an actor in or spectator of any stage-play, &c. in any house, &c. where a greater number of persons than twenty shall be assembled together, every such person shall forfeit for each time five pounds. One-half to his majesty and one-half to the informer."

Such were the feelings and opinions of the representatives of the people of Massachusetts in 1750; "but," says the author of Dramatic Reminiscences in the New England Magazine, "as the Puritanic sentiments of the older inhabitants gave place to more liberal and extended views in religion, and morals, much of the prejudice against theatrical amusements subsided."

By 1791 there was widespread feeling among the people of Boston that a playhouse would be very desirable, and action was initiated in the state legislature to attempt a repeal of the law of 1750, but to no avail. Even such a liberal as Samuel Adams was listed as an opponent to the theater! Dunlap continues his story:

14:2   The secession of Wignell from the old American Company, and his crossing the Atlantic in search of performers, caused the immediate voyage of John Henry, also for the same purpose. It has been stated that Mr. and Mrs. Morris and Stephen Wools were sharers in the *scheme* of the old company. Harper was not. Mr. and Mrs. Morris took their part with Wignell, and were, during his absence, to seek employment. Harper was not engaged with either party. Wools adhered to the property in which he was a sharer, but was left for the present unemployed.

Under these circumstances, the above-named four individuals united for the purpose of trying their fortunes in Boston, invited by the efforts for the establishment of a theatre which a portion of the inhabitants were making. Notwithstanding the refusal of the legislature to repeal the law of 1750, a number of gentlemen formed an association for the purpose of introducing the drama. A committee was formed to carry their purpose into effect, and ground purchased on which to erect a building in Broad-alley, near Hawley-street. The committee were, according to Mr. Buckingham, "Joseph Russell, Esq., who also acted as treasurer to the association, Dr. Jarvis, General Henry Jackson, Joseph Barrell, and Joseph Russell, Jun." "A theatre in every thing but the name" was erected. A pit, one row of boxes, and a gallery, could contain about five hundred persons, and it was called the "New Exhibition Room." "The boxes formed three sides of a regular square, the stage making the fourth. The scenery

14:2. William Dunlap, *A History of the American Theatre*. 2 vols. in 1. (New York: J. & J. Harper, 1832), 1:246–47.

was tolerably well executed." But before its completion, Charles Powell arrived from England, and advertised an entertainment, which he called "The Evening Brush for rubbing off the Ruse of Care," to consist of songs and farcical recitations. This was on Monday, August 13, 1792, and on the 16th, the New Exhibition Room was opened by Harper as manager, with feats on the tightrope by Mons. Placide, songs by Mr. Wools, feats on the slack rope and tumbling by Mons. Martine, hornpipes and minuets by Mons. and Madame Placide, and the gallery of portraits by Mr. Harper, the manager. "These entertainments," says the New England Magazine, "continued with slight variations, for several weeks.

15. CHARLESTON THEATRE
Charleston, South Carolina
Opened February 11, 1793

The Charleston Theater of Thomas Wade West and John Bignall is a classic illustration of the danger of reconstructing a theater on partial evidence. For many years, because a historian of the Charleston stage had misread existing documents, it was thought that the Charleston Theatre of 1793 was the most magnificent playhouse erected in the United States up to that time. Recent evidence, however, proves that the theater when it opened hardly lived up to the claims of the builders. The structure cost twice as much as Wade and Bignall had originally estimated, and even then the outside was not completed until 1830, when a portico was added. The interior was relatively simple, at least for the first season.

The plans for the theater were on a grand scale, as is seen from this correspondence from Charleston, which appeared in the *New York Magazine.*

15:1 On Tuesday last the ground was laid off for the new theatre on Savage's Green.

15:1. *New York Magazine*, Sept. 1792.

The cornerstone of the foundation is to be laid the 20th inst. The dimensions, we are informed, are as follows:—125 feet in length, the width 56 feet, the height 37 feet; with an handsome pediment, stone ornaments, a large flight of stone steps and a court yard palisaded. The front will be in Broad-street and the pit entrance in Middleton-street. The different offices will be calculated so as not to interfere with each other; the stage is to be 56 feet in length, the front circular, with three rows of patent lamps; the boxes will be constructed so that small parties may be accommodated to a single box; to every box there will be a window and a venetian blind; three tiers of boxes decorated with 32 columns; to each column a glass chandelier with five lights; the lower tier balustraded; the middle and upper boxes paneled; fancy painting, the ground French white, the mouldings and projections silvered; in the ceiling there will be three ventilators. The frontispiece, balconies and stage doors will be similar to those of the opera-house, London. The theatre is to be built under the immediate direction of Mr. West. When it is considered that this gentleman has had nearly thirty years experience in many of the first theatres in England; that he is to be assisted by artists of the first class, Captain Toomer and Mr. Hobam, we may expect a theatre in a style of elegance and novelty. Every attention will be paid to blend beauty with conveniency, and to render it the first theatre on the continent. The contractors have engaged to complete the building by the tenth of January next.

Originally £2500 had been raised by West and Bignall, but it was soon evident that this would represent only about one-half the sum needed to open the theater in a form simplified from the original plans. Further subscribers were obtained and the theater finally opened on February 11, 1793. The following review is from the Charleston *City Gazette and Daily Advertiser:*

15:2 Monday evening the New Theatre was opened with "The Highland Reel" and "Appearance Is Against Them." Whilst we express our approbation of the zeal and activity exerted by the managers, in the rapid erection and fitting up this theatre—we must at the same time pay a just tribute of applause to the liberality and taste evinced by them in the scenery, decorations and embellishments; which, however, they may be exceeded by gaudy glitter, can nowhere be surpassed in neatness and simple elegance. The curtain rose at the appointed hour, to a very numerous and genteel audience, when Mr. Bignall delivered an occasional prologue with the nicest discrimination and appropriate feelings.

The opera was well cast and the principal parts performed with a spirit and truth of colouring, which affords a pleasing presage of the elegant and refined enjoyment our citizens are likely to experience on this most rational amusement. . . .

The emphasis in the review on the "neatness and simple elegance" of the playhouse hardly seems in accord with the earlier announcement of the lavishness of the appointments. The following year the playhouse was redecorated and it may be that much of the planned decorations were added at that time, but the extent of these decorations is not known.

Perhaps one of the more interesting innovations in the Charleston Theatre was an "air conditioning" system, which was installed in 1794 especially for the benefit performance of Mrs. Edgar by her husband, who claimed credit for the invention of the system. Eola Willis records the announcement that appeared concerning this improvement in the playhouse.

15:3 Mr. Edgar being informed that on the night of his benefit the audience were

15:2. Charleston *City Gazette and Daily Advertiser*, Feb. 13, 1793.
15:3. Eola Willis, *The Charleston Stage in the Eighteenth Century* (Columbia, S.C.: The State Co., 1924), p. 224.

considerably inconvenienced with the heat, he has since that time been studying how to remedy the evil and is now most happy that he can announce to the public, whose liberality he has so particularly experienced, that he has completed an air-pump of such construction as to render the theatre pleasant and comfortable, even in cases of crowded audiences.

Mr. Edgar is indebted for his idea to the inventor of those air pumps that are often used on board ships of war. . . . In public places in England, too, he has witnessed the utility of it, where its approved effect has been generally acknowledged. . . . It is so contrived as not to intercept the view of the audience; it indeed takes up a little room in the gallery, which then cannot hold as many as before, but the advantage which might arise from that, Mrs. Edgar cheerfully gives up for the general accommodation. . . .

In 1830 some architectural changes were made to the exterior of the building, the main alteration being the addition of a large portico with four columns. The exterior face-lifting made the building one of the handsomest in Charleston.

The Charleston Theatre was sold to the new Medical College of South Carolina in 1833.

16. BRICK MARKET THEATRE
Newport, Rhode Island
Opened July 3, 1793

Companies of comedians had made forays into Rhode Island as early as 1761, when David Douglass took his troupe to Newport to perform. At that time Douglass, fearing the reaction of New Englanders to the frivolities of the theater, cautiously announced a "series of brief Moral Dialogues," which were so well received that he built a temporary theater there. This playhouse later was demolished in a storm.

It was not until February 1793 that the General Assembly of Rhode Island gave the town council of Newport the power to grant licenses for theatrical entertainment. The only stipulation was that "the State House in that town not be used for that purpose."

In May 1793 Alexander Placide, who was to be the founder of the French Theatre in New Orleans, was given permission to repair and renovate the old Brick Market for use as a playhouse. The following quotation is from the *Bulletin* of the Society for the Preservation of New England Antiquities.

16:1 In 1762 the brick market was built on a lot given to the town by the proprietors of the Long Wharf. It was erected by the town by the proceeds of lotteries granted for that purpose by the General Assembly. It measures in Thames Street 33 feet and on the passage to the Long Wharf 65 feet—built after the Ionic order, three stories high, under the direction of Peter Harrison, architect. It was intended for a public granary, but was never used for that purpose. The lower storey was made a market and the second and third stories let out for the retailing of goods and also for offices. An entry ran through the two upper stories, on each side of which were separate rooms, hired for and used as before stated. The watch house was and is in the rear part of the building, on the lower floor. Immediately after the revolutionary war the upper part was used only as a printing office, but in 1793 Alexander Placide rented the upper stories and fitted them for a playhouse, since which it has undergone little or no alterations.

The Brick Market Theatre, which was later named the Newport Theatre, remained in use as a playhouse until 1842.

17. FEDERAL STREET THEATRE
Boston, Massachusetts
Opened February 3, 1794

16:1. N. M. Isham, "Report on the Old Brick Market," *Bulletin*, Society for the Preservation of New England Antiquities, 6, no. 2:21 (1915). The quotation is from the Appendix, compiled by Edith Tilly.

The struggle to establish a legitimate playhouse in Boston, the bastion of puritanism, had been a long one, but it culminated with the opening of the Federal Street Theatre in February, 1794. The theater, unlike so many of the other eighteenth century playhouses, was a handsome one, in both exterior and interior. Seilhamer in his *History of the American Theatre* tells something about the playhouse and its opening.

17:1 After Joseph Harper's unsuccessful attempt to establish a theatre in Boston, in the Summer and Autumn of 1792, the friends of the drama were more persistent than ever in their efforts to have the obnoxious prohibitory act of 1750 repealed. They finally succeeded early in 1793, and, on the 9th of April a meeting was held to open subscriptions for building a house for theatrical exhibitions. The number of shares was limited to 120 at $50 per share, no one person being allowed more than two shares. The site selected was the corner of Federal and Franklin Streets, where a commodious brick building 140 feet long, 61 feet wide and 40 feet in height was speedily erected. The new theatre was plain and substantial, without architectural pretensions, with the exception of a colonnade in Federal Street. One of the first acts of the trustees was to appoint Charles Stuart Powell, who had played with Harper the previous year, sole manager, and early in June, 1793, it was announced that he would sail for England in a few days to engage a company for the new theatre. Unlike Mr. Henry, Powell found no Hodgkinson at Bath eager to engage with him, nor, like Mr. Wignell, was he able to secure a force that would have been creditable even in London. His predecessors had exhausted the immediate supply of talent eligible for the American market. The company secured for the first season

17:1. George O. Seilhamer, *History of the American Theatre.* 3 vols. (Philadelphia: Globe Printing House, 1889–91), 3:227–30.

at the Boston Theatre comprised Mr. and Mrs. Powell, Mr. and Mrs. Baker, Miss Baker, Mr. and Mrs. Collins, Mr. and Mrs. Jones, Messrs. Bartlett, Kenny, Nelson, and Snelling Powell, a brother of the manager, Mrs. Abbott and Miss Harrison, afterward Mrs. S. Powell. These were all without reputation in the country from which they came, and such fame as they afterward acquired was confined to America.

When Mr. Powell arrived with his company he found the theatre ready for occupation, and so he proceeded to begin his campaign. The opening night was the 3d of February, 1794, with "Gustavus Vasa" and "Modern Antiques" as the initial productions. The season lasted until the 4th of July following. Probably no theatre in the United States was ever opened with such formality and decorum. The rules and regulations adopted by the trustees were very elaborate and very strict. No infraction of them was allowed. Mr. John Hastings, the box-keeper, inadvertently let a few places in the boxes before the official announcement of the opening night was made. For this he was hauled over the coals in the *Mercury*, and Mr. Powell apologized in a card, as did Hastings also. For the preservation of order both within and without the theatre a Master of Ceremonies was appointed. That this office was considered one of great dignity is apparent from the fact that Col. John S. Tyler was appointed to fill it, and so highly were Colonel Tyler's ·services appreciated that he was accorded the first regular benefit of the season. Not only was a master of ceremonies appointed to see that those who had taken seats should be accommodated according to contract, to direct the manner of setting down and taking up those who came to the playhouse in carriages, and to suppress "all kinds of disorder and indecorum," but the trustees reserved to themselves the power of dismissing any performer either on the stage or in the

orchestra—a power to be exercised in the form of a request to the manager. Singularly enough, the first complaint was made against the manager himself. . . .

William Clapp, Jr., one of the earliest chroniclers of the Boston stage, described the playhouse in some detail.

17:2   The theatre in those days was considered a fine specimen of architecture and creditable to the architect, Mr. Bulfinch. It was a lofty and specious edifice substantially built of brick, with some stone facias, imposts, etc. It was one hundred and forty feet long, sixty-one feet wide, and forty feet high. The entrances to the different parts of the house were distinct, and at the time the opponents of the theatre made strong use of this fact, alleging that by affording a special door to that portion of the house usually the resort of the vile of both sexes, a premium on vice was offered. In the front there was a projecting arcade, which enabled carriages to land company under cover. The interior of the building was tastefully decorated. The stage opening was thirty-one feet wide, ornamented on each side by two columns, and between them a stage door and projecting iron balcony. Over the columns a cornice and a balustrade were carried across the opening; above was painted a flow of crimson drapery and the arms of the Union and of the State of Massachusetts blended with emblems tragic and comic. A ribbon depending from the arms bore the motto, "All the world's a stage." At the end of the building a noble and elegant dancing room was constructed, fifty-eight feet long, thirty-six feet wide and twenty-six high, richly ornamented with Corinthian columns and pilasters.

More details concerning the interior are

17:2. William W. Clapp, Jr., *A Record of the Boston Stage* (Boston & Cambridge: James Munroe & Co., 1853), pp. 19–20.

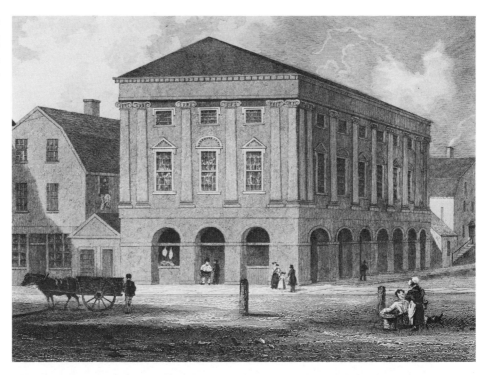

16. Newport Theatre, Newport, R.I. Engraving, 1831, after a drawing by W. Goodacre, Jr. Courtesy of the Harvard Theatre Collection.

OLD FEDERAL STREET THEATRE, BOSTON.

17. Old Federal Street Theatre, Boston, as it appeared after the remodeling that followed the fire of 1798. Engraving. Courtesy of the University of Pennsylvania.

18. Chestnut Street Theatre, Philadelphia, 1804. Aquatint by W. Ralph, after an engraving by William Birch, 1804. Benjamin Latrobe designed the portico, completed in 1804. Courtesy of the Free Library of Philadelphia.

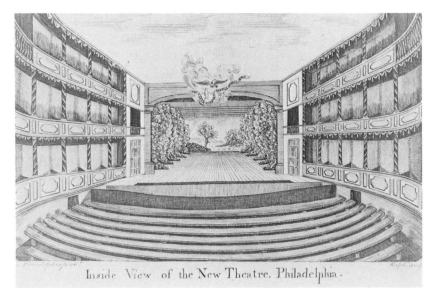

Inside View of the New Theatre. Philadelphia.

18. Interior, Chestnut Street Theatre, Philadelphia. Engraving by W. Ralph, after a drawing by S. Lewis, published in *New York Magazine* (1794). Courtesy of the Cooper-Hewitt Museum of Decorative Arts and Design, Smithsonian Institution.

furnished by Mary Caroline Crawford in her study on the American theater:

17:3   The new theatre was located at the corner of Federal and Franklin Streets, and with its opening on February 3, 1794, the dramatic history of Boston may be said properly to have begun. It was called the Boston Theatre (later the Federal Street Theatre) and was under the management of Charles Stuart Powell and Baker. It had been erected from plans furnished by Charles Bulfinch, then a young man, and a contemporary thus describes it:

"It was one hundred and forty feet long, sixty-two feet wide, forty feet high; a lofty and spacious edifice built of brick, with stone facings, iron posts and pillars. The entrances to the different parts of the house were distinct. In front there was a projecting arcade which enabled carriages to land company under cover. After alighting at the main entrance, they passed through an elegant saloon to the staircases leading to the back of the boxes. The pit and gallery had separate entrances on the sides.

"The interior was circular in form, the ceiling composed of elliptical arches resting on Corinthian pillars. There were two rows of boxes, the second suspended by invisible means. The stage opening was thirty-one feet wide, ornamented on either side by two columns, between which was a stage door opening on a projecting iron balcony. Above the columns a cornice and a balustrade were carried over the stage openings; and above these was painted a flow of crimson drapery and the arms of the United States and the commonwealth blended with emblems tragic and comic. A ribbon depending from the arms bore the motto, 'All the world's a stage.'

17:3. Mary Caroline Crawford, *The Romance of the American Theatre* (Boston: Little, 1913), pp. 114–15.

"The boxes were hung with crimson silk, and their balustrade gilded; the boxes were tinted azure and the columns and fronts of the boxes straw and lilac. At the end of the building was a noble and elegant dancing pavilion, richly ornamented with Corinthian columns and pilasters. There were also spacious card and tea rooms and kitchens with the proper conveniences."

Great state was observed in performances here. The "guests" were met by a bewigged and bepowdered master of ceremonies and escorted to their boxes. Thence, the feeble light of candles or by means of the more objectionable, because smoky, illumination of whale-oil lamps. Moreover, they might freeze in winter, for all the effective heating apparatus provided. Very likely it was to keep warm that the gallery gods threw things. At any rate, the orchestra was obliged to insert a card in the newspaper requesting the audience to be more restrained in the matter of pelting the musicians with apple cores and oranges. The music, by the way, was of high standard, Reinagle of Philadelphia being director. In short, though Boston had come on slowly, it was now conceded to possess the finest theatre in the country.

18. CHESTNUT STREET THEATRE
Philadelphia, Pennsylvania
Opened February 17, 1794

The Chestnut Theatre, although conceived as early as 1791 and completed by January 1793, could not open for thirteen months after its completion because of the plague that was ravaging the Philadelphia area. Thomas Wignell had assembled a brilliant company of players in England and had brought them to America, but they were unable to begin performances at the new playhouse until February 17, 1794. The theater is described by Charles Durang, actor and stage manager, whose father was a performer and dancer with the Old American Company of Lewis Hallam, Jr.

18:1   We come now to a more particular recital of the circumstances connected with
the history of the new theatre, in Chestnut street. This theatrical edifice was
commenced in the year 1791. The corner
stone was laid by Mr. Reinagle, a Master
Mason, in Masonic form, and an address
delivered by Jared Ingersoll. It was
erected by a company upon a tontine
principal.

Mr. Richards, a celebrated artist at
London, and a brother-in-law to Mr.
Wignell, furnished a plan for the building, which was a perfect model of the
Bath Theatre, England. I often saw the
model lying in a property-room over
the dome. The house was very comfortable in every particular for the actors.
The dressing-rooms were numerous in the
wings. Three or four persons only dressed
together. There were two green-rooms,
but not with a view of making the sal-
aried distinction, that then existed at
London. One green-room was used for
musical rehearsals, dancing practices, &c.,
and it was a place where the juvenile
members of the corps might indulge their
freaks unrestrainedly. The principal green-
room was adjacent to the prompt side, in
the west wing. In this apartment the perfect etiquette of the polished drawing-
room was always preserved. Things of
that kind now-a-days bear an inverse
ratio to the antiquated notions of good-
breeding. We are now bound to "*catch
the manners living as they rise.*" We will
here give an architectural description of
the old house, from *Dr. Mease's* picture
of Philadelphia, published in 1811.

"The theatre in Chestnut, near Sixth
street, was founded in the year 1791, and
enlarged and improved, as it now stands
(1811), in 1805. It presents a handsome
front on Chestnut street of ninety feet,
including two wings of fifteen feet each.
The centre building is ornamented with
two spirited and well-executed figures of
Tragedy and Comedy, (by Rush,) on
each side of the great Venetian window,
over which, in two circular tablets, are
emblematical insignia. (These figures are
now in the niches of the present house.)
The top of the centre building is crowned
by a pediment. The wings, opened by
large windows, recede a little from the
front above, but project below twelve feet,
to the line of the street, and are faced
with marble. These pavilions are decorated by emblematical figures, in tablets,
and are connected together by a colonnade of ten fancy Corinthian columns.
The extreme depth of the theatre is one
hundred and thirty-four feet; the interior
is judiciously and handsomely arranged.
In the wings are the green-rooms and
dressing rooms, &c. Through the projecting wings or pavilions you pass to the
stairs of the galleries, under the colonnade. The left-hand door leads to the pit,
but to the boxes you ascend in front, by
a flight of marble steps, enter the lobby
and pass to the corridors, which communicate with all the boxes. Those in
front of the stage are disposed in form
of an amphitheatre. The seats of the
whole, with those of the pit and gallery,
are arranged so as to give the spectator
the greatest advantages.

"The stage occupies a front between
the boxes of thirty-six feet, and runs back
upwards of seventy-one feet. Over the
stage, occupying a part of the entablature
and plafond of the front scene, is an emblematic representation of *America* encouraging the drama, under which are
the words, 'For useful mirth or salutory
woe.'

"The fronts of the lodges or boxes,
together with the ceiling are handsomely
gilt and decorated, hung with corresponding drapery between the columns. The
scenery of the stage is well arranged, and
calculated both for convenience, comfort

18:1. Charles Durang, "The Philadelphia Stage.
From the Year 1749 to the Year 1855," University
of Pennsylvania Library, Philadelphia. Excerpt from
chap. 30.

and elegance of arrangement. The theatre is computed to hold about two thousand persons, of which number nine hundred may be accommodated in the boxes."

The description ends with the following just tribute by the worthy doctor to the old management:

"It is but justice to say that, whenever required, the proprietors of this theatre have cheerfully lent their assistance in promoting any undertaking for the public good, and that occasionally the interest of religion has been promoted by their benefactions; but the poor, the public charitable institutions for medical relief, and those for gratuitous education, nay, the afflicted, whether from fire or pestilence, in other cities of the Union, have on numerous occasions received the benefit of their voluntary labors."

Admissions like the above, so freely and disinterestedly expressed, speak "trumpet-tongued" in the stage's behalf against the fanatical calumniators, who treat its *salutary uses* in modifying public amusements with the intolerance which should not be directed against its abuses. "It is not *fair* to argue *against* the *use* from the *abuse* of anything."

The theatre was in a condition for performance before Mr. Wignell was able to engage a proper company. Mr. Reinagle, who was in this city, determined to try the qualities of the house in a musical entertainment. In accordance with this determination, the new theatre was opened to the public on Saturday evening, April 2d, 1793, with "a grand concert of vocal and instrumental music." In this entertainment there were engaged Mr. Reinagle, Mr. Boulay, Mrs. Morris, Mr. Petit, Mr. Mallet, Mr. Harper, Mr. Kozeluch, Mr. Guenin, Mr. Rand, Mr. Solomans, and Master Duport, who danced between the parts. . . .

The opening of the Chestnut Street Theatre in Philadelphia received only a brief comment from William Dunlap, who, after all, had vested interests in the New York theater and did not show a particularly avid interest in other dramatic centers in the country.

18:2   After the long delay occasioned by the yellow fever, Wignell opened the splendid theatre, which had been prepared for him in 1792, on the 17th of February, 1794. He had brought from England Mr. Milbourne, an excellent scene-painter, who decorated the house and furnished the necessary scenery, as far surpassing any stage decorations heretofore seen in the country as the building surpassed former American theatres.

The plan of the building was furnished by Mr. Richards, who was Wignell's brother-in-law, and secretary to the Royal Academy. The model was burnt when house was consumed. Mr. Richards likewise presented to the managers several very fine scenes, and the beautiful drop-curtain, which was destroyed likewise by the fire of 1820.

The part of the theatre before the curtain formed a semi-circle, having two complete rows of boxes, and, higher up, on a line with the gallery, side-boxes. The boxes were supported by pillars formed of bunches of reeds, tied together with red fillets and gilt. Festoons of curtains and numerous chandeliers gave a brilliant effect to the whole. The first dramatic pieces presented to the public of Philadelphia by the new company were *The Castle of Andalusia* and *Who's the Dupe*.

The orchestra, under the direction of Reinagle, who sat at the harpsichord, was as much superior in power and talent as the other departments of the Drama.

Shortly after the opening of the Chestnut Street Theatre, a French refugee, Moreau de Saint-Méry, visited the theater and recorded his impressions:

18:2. William Dunlap, *A History of the American Theatre*. 2 vols. in 1. (New York: J. & J. Harper, 1832), 1:223–24.

37

18:3   Philadelphia has two theatres. The older of the two, which is closed, is located at the corner of Cedar and Fourth Streets at the edge of the city.

The new theatre, which stands on the northwest corner of Chestnut and Fourth Streets, has an unimposing brick facade and certainly does not look like an important public building. The entrance is rather small and seems no different from that of an ordinary house. The interior, however, is quite handsome.

The auditorium shaped by the tiers of boxes is an agreeable semi-eliptical shape. There are three tiers of boxes with fifteen boxes in each tier. Of these fifteen, the five boxes which face the stage have seven rows of benches each seating five people, so that each of these five boxes can hold thirty-five people. The ten boxes on the sides have two rows of benches, each seating four people. Each tier of boxes, then, can hold two hundred and fifty-three people for a total of seven hundred and fifty-five. The pit, which descends from the first tier of boxes to the orchestra pit, has thirteen rows of benches, each bench seating thirty people, so that the pit has a capacity of about four hundred spectators.

The auditorium is painted gray with gold ornamentation. The third tier of boxes even has some small gilded railings which add a note of elegance. The boxes, between which a small column partially obstructs the view, are papered in red, the very color of which is a proof of bad taste.

The performance is lit by the dim light of four-pronged chandeliers placed in alternate boxes beginning with the middle of the second box on either side. The chandeliers are S-shaped and are made of gilded iron.

The orchestra pit is large enough for thirty musicians sitting in two rows facing each other.

The forestage is quite large. The sides of the proscenium wall represent the facades of beautiful houses, but they face too sharply towards the stage. Also the rows of columns in the boxes tend to obscure the view.

The stage, which is large, is lit by oil lamps, as in France, which are capable of being dimmed for darker or night scenes.

The auditorium is acoustically satisfactory. One can see well from all points in the auditorium except from the back of the second tier of boxes where the slope of the floor of the third tier cuts off the view of the top of the rear stage. Moreover, from some points in the theatre one cannot clearly distinguish people seated in the back of the boxes with the seven rows of benches.

The price of tickets for seats in the first and second tiers of boxes and of the boxes in the third tier which seat eight people is one gourde per person.* Seats in the pit are three-quarters of a gourde and only half a gourde for gallery seats located in the third tier above that section of the second tier with the five boxes containing seven rows of benches.

The corridors are large and commodious. In each box there is a louvered window located in the upper part of the partition leading to the corridor. This provides ventilation without opening the doors of the boxes.

Some women sit in the pit as well as men, but these are not the ladies of fashion. Women also sit in the gallery, as do the colored people, who have nowhere else to sit.

The scenery is newly painted and well-executed. The play itself was well-acted.

18:3. Moreau de Saint-Méry, *Voyage aux États-Unis de l'Amerique.* Ed. by Stewart L. Mims (New Haven: Yale Univ. Pr., 1913), pp. 372–74.

*A gourde is the monetary unit used in some of the Caribbean Islands, where Saint-Méry was born and practiced law. There are one hundred centimes to a gourde, and a gourde was worth approximately $.20 in American money.

The theatre, called the New Theatre, was built by stockholders who rent it to the directors. The company of actors not only performs at this theatre, but also travels to Baltimore for a season there. Their efforts produce about six percent interest on the stockholders' investment.

The actors are quite good; the plays are mainly English, very coarse and not very appealing to the French taste.

Spectators eat and drink in the pit. The refreshments, which are sold from an attractive little stand in the main corridor, are about fifty percent more expensive than in town. This naturally occurs when a franchise is given for the refreshments.

Most of the musicians are Frenchmen who earn their living by playing in the theatre.

19. FRENCH THEATRE
Charleston, South Carolina
Opened April 12, 1794

This study is concerned with American playhouses and not those built by other national groups, *i.e.*, French, German, or Yiddish. The French Theatre in Charleston is mentioned, however, for two reasons: (1) to use as an example illustrating the contribution of the foreign language theater to the cultural life of the early American theater; and (2) because the leader of the enterprise was Alexandre Placide, founder of a family of actors who were important in the American theater in the late eighteenth and early nineteenth centuries.

The first permanent French theater in the United States was the Théâtre St. Pierre in New Orleans, which opened in 1791. The French Theatre in Charleston was the second permanent playhouse. French actors had toured the country for some time, but, in the case of Charleston, had played in the Charleston Theatre of West and Bignall. They were so well received that a playhouse was erected for the purpose of presenting plays in French. The Charleston *Gazette and Daily Advertiser* carried the following announcement:

19:1   The French actors propose to open their Theatre in the course of next week, and being desirous that their first performance may be an act of public utility, they mean to give it for the benefit of their unfortunate brethren, the American prisoners in Algiers.

The musicians which will compose the orchestra of their theatre, animated with the same sentiments with which the actors are penetrated, offer their services without any wish of payment for the representation, being always ready to assist their brothers whenever occasion shall unfortunately make it necessary. They will announce in a few days the day fixed for their début as well as the piece that will be performed; after which they will play regularly three times a week. Their performances will consist of dancing, pantomime—ballets and fancy dances; Harloquin-pantomimes, rope-dancing with many feats and little amusing French pieces; and to satisfy many who wish it, the grand pieces of the French theatre. Being willing to offer to those who are learning the French language a sure way of perfecting themselves, the theatre being a place where the French language is spoke in its purity, they propose to the admirers of the French language a fourth representation weekly by subscription, to be composed of tragedies, dramas and the first comic pieces.

Two editions later, the *Gazette and City Advertiser* published notification of the first performance:

19:2   SATURDAY EVENING,
                APRIL 12, 1794:
     The Theatre will be opened for the benefit of the American Prisoners in Algiers.

19:1. Charleston *Gazette and Daily Advertiser,* Mar. 26, 1794.
19:2. Charleston *Gazette and Daily Advertiser,* Mar. 28, 1794.

1ST—PYGMALION

Scene lyric of the celebrated John James Rousseau with the Interludes in music by the same author. Mr. Dainville will perform the part of *Pygmalion* and Mrs. Val, that of *Galatea*.

2ND—DANCING ON THE
TIGHT ROPE

by Signor Spinacuta and Mr. Placide.

To conclude with a Grand Ballet-Pantomime intermixed with dances and allemandes, called "The Three Philosophers, or The Dutch Coffee House," in which Mr. Dainville will perform the part of *Mr. Vandervek*, Mrs. Val that of *Mrs. Vandervek*, and Mr. Francisquy that of the *Lover*. Doors to be opened at six o'clock and the performance to commence at seven o'clock.

Eola Willis is able to identify the site of the playhouse:

19:3 On the 12th day of April, 1794, the French Theatre, which was later called the City Theatre or Church-Street Theatre, was opened in a brick building on the west side of Church Street between St. Michael's Alley and Tradd Street. The Mesne-Conveyance files give the site as: No. 40 Church—50 x 6 x 245 ft. On south, Thos. Smith, Esqr, west, Sam'l Prioleau and north, Rev. Mr. Robt. Smith. This building was known as Sollee's Hall, and here an excellent company of comedians, pantomimists, and ropedancers inaugurated the French Theatre.

20. HOLLIDAY STREET THEATRE
Baltimore, Maryland
Opened September 25, 1794

The arrival in America of the Thomas Wignell company of actors occurred at a most inopportune moment, for in September 1793 an epidemic of yellow fever was at its height

in Philadelphia and it was impossible to contemplate opening the new Chestnut Street Theatre at this time. Since Wignell was under heavy financial obligations for bringing his players to America, he began to search for temporary engagements for his troupe until the yellow fever epidemic abated in Philadelphia. It was during this period that he purchased land in Baltimore and solicited funds to raise a playhouse, the Holliday Street Theatre.

Alonzo B. May (1856–1912) was a Baltimore musician and author who wrote a history of the city's theaters based on newspaper accounts and hearsay evidence. The account of the Holliday Street Theatre, therefore, is interesting, but perhaps not always reliable.

20:1   HOLLIDAY STREET THEATRE

The lot forming the site of this venerable historical Thespianic monument was purchased on November 30, 1793, through the agency of Thoroughgood Smith and Robert Gilman, by Thomas Wignell, an actor and manager, and Alexander Reinagle, a professional musician, from Robert Holliday esq. who also owned other property in the vicinity. The Deed verifying the transaction is recorded in the Land Records of Baltimore City in Liber. N. G. No. M. M. Folio 408, etc. The enterprise of these pioneers was rendered very difficult and hazardous from a financial standpoint, by reason of the existing conditions. These will be duly set forth in this volume in chronological order, and the many transitions of the affairs of Baltimore's Old Drury recorded as accurately as our information permits.

It is a notable fact that the Holliday Street Theatre is the sole remaining establishment, in the country, hallowed by the

19:3. Eola Willis, *The Charleston Stage in the Eighteenth Century* (Columbia, S.C.: The State Co., 1924), p. 237.

20:1. Alonzo B. May, "May's Dramatic Encyclopedia of Baltimore" Ms. 995. Maryland Historical Society, Baltimore. I would like to express my appreciation to the Maryland Historical Society and to Nancy G. Boles, Curator of Manuscripts, for permission to use this holograph manuscript.

genius of Kean, Cook, Cooper, Duff, Jefferson and others, whose names have shed an imperishable lustre on the Stage. One by one, the Theatres in which these brilliant Stars so shone, have yielded either to the ravages of fire, or the energy of improvement, (if every change from the old to the new; may be properly designated.) until of them all "Holliday Street," remains a glorious lone memorial of the past; the Drama's classic home in America.

WIGNELL AND REINAGLE

When Thomas Wignell landed with his Theatrical company, in September 1793, in America, the Yellow Fever was raging. That he was the proprietor of a large organization is evidenced by the fact that "before the Philadelphia house could be opened," he had incurred an indebtedness of nearly twenty thousand dollars. The fever raged so violently that he was obliged to find accommodation for the members of his troupe in different villages in New Jersey. The delay in performing "accumulated in salaries alone, a monstrous debt, nearly every performer having claims, by the terms of the contract made in England, for his pay, from the moment of his arrival.["] For ten preceding years, the organization and plans of each season had been changed or defeated by this destructive epidemic. In 1880 Wignell opened a Theatre in Washington. His company is frequently numbered between seventy and eighty persons. The management was on the sharing plan; graduated by the winter salaries; and was continued by his successors for a long series of years with great advantage, indeed, until the "Star" System was introduced, to the speedy ruin of those safe, comfortable companies, and finally to the irretrievable financial embarrassment of the larger establishments. In 1802 Wignell died, Mrs. Wignell and Reinagle succeeded in the management, Reinagle having been a joint proprietor

with Wignell. Reinagle had been made a partner because of his musical abilities; the audiences in Philadelphia insisting that Wignell should furnish good musical features, which he always did, with a large orchestra, at great expense. At his demise the stage management devolved professedly on Warren, but Wood did the actual work of the position.

On August 19th 1794 the following advertisement appeared.

NEW THEATRE

["]Persons desirous of becoming Subscribers to the New Theatre of Messrs. Wignell and Reinagle, are respectfully informed that there are 5 shares unappropriated, of One Hundred Dollars each. Subscribers to draw interest at six per cent till the money is repaid; and to be entitled to a Free Ticket for the first season for each share. Application to be speedily made to Thorowgood Smith, and Robert Gilmore, esqs."

A HEARTY WELCOME

The Maryland Journal announced the advent of the new play house in this eloquim, "The inhabitants of Baltimore and its vicinity, will soon have the opportunity of being gratified with the most refined and rational Amusement which a liberal mind is capable of enjoying. The animated sentiments of immortal Authors, when clothed in the smooth robe of pathetic eloquence, cannot fail to awaken the most dormant of human faculties, and, by exciting a laudable emulation, rouse the noblest principles of the soul in imitation of the virtues and achievements of the heroes of the Drama. In all ages, since the first innovation of dramatic achievements, the stage has been justly celebrated for its tendency to reform manners, and give an elegant polish to society; its felicity in exposing the baser part of mankind cannot be too warmly admired, and the beautiful representations of the rewards of virtue, which every well-written play exhibits, must cause the honest, generous breast to glow with the strongest consciousness of rectitude, and additional self-satisfaction. The public may anticipate the full enjoyment of all the ravishing sensations which the superior talents of able theatrical performers, assisted by the attractive charms of melodious music, are capable of conveying to the soul. The ingenious conduct of Messrs. Wignell and Reinagle, the peculiar taste displayed in their selection, and the singing abilities of their company, have already merited and received the loudest applauses of a distinguished part of our country; and from the convenient situation and accommodation of our New Theatre, but particularly from the address of the Managers, the public have everything that is pleasing to expect."

THE OPENING SEASON

The announcement of the first performance at this Theatre, was couched in the following words. This, however, did not take place as proposed.

NEW THEATRE

The Public is especially acquainted that the entertainment for the Season commences on Wednesday the 24th inst (August) with the Comic Opera of
Love in a Village
And a Comedy in two Acts, called
Who is the Dupe?
Places for the Boxes to be taken on Tuesday, at the office in front of the Theatre from the hour of 10 till 2, and on the Day of Performance.
Boxes, 7s. 6d.　　Pit, 5 s. 7½ d.
Floreat Republica

From the Maryland Journal of Wednesday, September 24th, 1794, we also get the following:

"The Public are respectfully acquainted that the opening of the
New Theatre
Is Unavoidably Postponed until Thursday, the 25th instant, when a

favorite Comedy will be performed (for the first time here) called
Every One has his Fault
With an occasional Overture, composed by Mr. Reinagle.
End of the Comedy
A Scotch Pastoral Dance
In which will be introduced a New Highland Reel composed by
Mr. Francis
called
The Caledonian Frolic.
To which will be added a
Comic Opera
In two Acts called
The Flitch of Bacon:
or, Dunmore Priory.
Love In a Village is obliged to be postponed on account of the indisposition of Mrs. Warnell, etc. Subscribers to the New Theatre are requested to send for their Tickets of Admission, to the Store of Mr. Clarke, bookseller in Market Street, on Thursday. Places for the Boxes to be taken on Tuesday, at the Office, in front of the Theatre.
No money changed.
The manager requests gentlemen and ladies who procure Tickets at the office of the Theatre to
Always Bring Exact Change,
as No Change will be given, owing to the confusion it occassions in the hurry of business. The gentlemen and ladies are requested to send their
Servants to Keep Places,
by a quarter to five o'clock. (No numbered chairs, or Coupons then, accommodation must be secured by scrambling for the best seats on hard benches) and to direct them to Withdraw, as soon as the company (i.e. audience) is seated, as they Cannot on Any Account be permitted to Remain."

The second performance was Love in a Village, and a two act Farce called the Lovers Quarrel, or Like Master, Like Man.

Only a small number of the members of the corps appeared on this occasion, the cast including Moreton, Green, Harwood, Wignell, Mrs. Francis and Mrs. Rowson. The scenery used was the production of Milburn. The rates of admission established on this interesting initial evening prevailed for a long time. The entree to the Boxes cost the sum of One Dollar, while a ticket entitling its holder to a seat in the Pit, was sold for seventy-five cents.

The Doors were opened at a quarter after five o'clock, the curtain being raised at fifteen minutes past six.

The opening performance was attended by a numerous and brilliant audience, who deservedly bestowed their reiterated plaudits, on the very skillful performances of the company. Thus encouraged, Fennell, Chalmers, Cleveland, Whitlock, Blisset, Darley Jr, J. Warrell, Mrs. Marshall, Mrs. Shaw, Mrs. Cleaveland, Miss Rowason, Mrs. Bates, Miss Warrell and Miss Broadhurst appeared in the production of the Comedy, The West Indian, and the Comic Opera, Rosina.

Of this effort a local critic wrote, "The refined entertainment the lovers of the Drama received, from the correct and spirited performance of the first three nights entertainments, so judiciously selected by the Managers, led us to most sincerely regret the unavoidable suspension of such pleasing and rational amusements, And it was with infiite satisfaction, we last night attended their recommencement. The Comedy of the West Indian was well received with that applause the exertions of the Performers so justly merited, particularly by Mrs. Marshall, Mrs. Shaw, Whitlock and Chalmers, who so effectually caught the spirit of the Author, and wore their assumed characters with such natural ease, that for a time we forgot the scenes repeated were but fiction. Before the curtain drew up, we were informed by Mr. Moreton that Mr. Morris has at short notice under-

taken the character of Stockwell, on account of Mr. Fennell having been unavoidably detained at Annapolis. We sincerely hope that it is not indisposition that detained him. At the same time, we cannot but add, that if he has, from any other cause, neglected to attend, his non-appearance must be considered not only as an inattention to the interest of the Managers, but an evident proof of disrespect to the Public, and we are pained to be under the necessity of reminding him that any public performer, however eminent, still owes something to those friends by whom the consequence is created, and by whom they are caressed and supported. Mrs. Warrell as Rosina, looked and spoke with fascinating simplicity. Miss Broadhurst was all innocent vivacity in Phoebe. They both sang with great taste, but Mrs. Warrell does not seem recovered from her indisposition, and we hope to see her at a future period in full possession of those vocal powers, by which it is so well known she can charm her delighted hearers.

["]Mr. Francis was correct and pleasing as William, nor is there any fault to be found with the whole performance, except we just hint to Mr. Green to lop off a little of that superabundant Low wit, in the Irishman with which he last night Endeavoured to embellish the part...."

The Holliday Street Theatre remained an institution in Baltimore for 123 years before it was demolished in 1917. That year the Baltimore *Sun* carried the story of the theater, some of which merely repeats the previous documents and is, therefore, omitted.

20:2   PASSING OF OLD HOLLIDAY STREET
BRINGS WEALTH OF REMINISCENCES
The Holliday Street Theatre is to be torn down. In a few short months this historic structure will have disappeared to make room for the Civic Centre, plans

20:2. Baltimore *Sun*, Mar. 17, 1917.

for which have finally been completed. After rising nightly with but few interruptions for 123 years the curtain of Old Drury, as the playhouse was called in its early days, will fall for the last time this spring.

Built for Messrs. Wignell and Reinagle, the former an actor and the latter a professor of music, and called by them the New Theatre, the opening was announced for August 24, 1794, with the comic opera "Love in a Village" and a comedy in two acts called "Who Is the Dupe?" Boxes, 7s6d; pit, 5s7 1/2d.

The theatre not being ready, the opening was postponed until September 25. . . .

The New Theatre was opened at the time appointed, the performance commencing at a quarter past six in the evening, when a large and brilliant audience assembled and "deservedly bestowed their reiterated plaudits on the very skillful performance of the company."

A curious feature of the times were the requests in the play-bills that persons bring the exact change with them and that ladies and gentlemen send their servants by a quarter past five o'clock to keep their places for them.

John P. Kennedy, the author, who lived in the hey-day of the old house, wrote of it thus: "What a superb thing it was! It had something of the splendor of a great barn, weather-boarded, milk-white, with many windows, and to my conception looked with a hospitable, patronizing, tragi-comic greeting down upon the street.

"It never occurred to me to think of it as a piece of architecture. It was something above that—a huge, mystical Aladdin lamp that had a magic to repel criticism, and filled with wonderful histories. There was a universal gladness in this old Baltimore when the word was passed around, 'The players are come.'

"It instantly became everybody's business to give them a good reception. We ran after them in the streets as something very notable to be looked at. 'There goes Old Francis!' was our phrase; not that he was old, for he was far from it, but because we loved him. It was a term of endearment. And as for Jefferson! Is there anyone now who remembers that imp of ancient fame?

"This must have been the older Jefferson, the father of our own 'Rip.' I cannot even now think definitely of him as a man, except in one particular, that he had a rather prominent and arching nose. In regard to everything else he was a proteus, the nose always being the same. He played everything that was comic, and always made people laugh till tears came to their eyes."

WOMAN GUIDES DESTINIES

Thomas Wignell died in 1803 and the management of his theatrical enterprises devolved upon his widow, Mrs. Merry, and Alexander Reinagle, his partner. The new management opened under the stage nominal direction of William Warren, though the labors of the office fell to the share of William B. Wood. In 1809 Reinagle died and Warren and Wood formed a copartnership. October, 1809, found John Howard Payne, author of "Home Sweet Home," then known as Master Payne, "the Young Roscius," in the full tide of popular favor in Baltimore. He appeared at the Holliday Street Theatre as Young Norval, Hamlet, Romeo, Tanered, Octavian, Frederic, Rolla, Achmet and Zaphna. His benefit proved a crowing [crowning] triumph and the receipts reached the (for that time) extraordinary amount of $1,160.

In 1810 Mr. Wood purchased Mr. Warren's interest and the autumn season opened with the illustrious Fennell at the head of an exceptional company which included Mr. and Mrs. Jefferson.

The storm of war was now threatening the country and its effects were soon felt in the theatres. The season of 1811 was a discouraging one, although the Baltimore company was strengthened by the engagement of Fennell and Payne and "The Lady of the Lake." The latter averaged $419 a night, the largest receipts for any one night being $711, "an increase which was due to the happy introduction of an elephant."

WAR COMPELS OMISSION OF SEASON

Owing to the excited war feeling prevailing in Baltimore, the season of 1812 was omitted. In the meantime the liberality of the Baltimore public had induced the management to remove the old wooden structure with its quaint scenery and cheap properties and in May, 1813, the new structure, which was built of brick for a joint stock company by Col. James Mosher and was called the Baltimore Theatre. The program for the opening performance included a comedy, "The West Indian" and Mr. Jefferson in "The Sleep Walker; or Which Is the Lady?" with "an occasional Patriotic address, commemorative of the late brilliant naval victories."

"STAR-SPANGLED BANNER" IS SUNG

Soon after the opening of the new Holliday Street Theatre is was distinguished by the singing of "The Star-Spangled Banner." The anthem was first sung by Charles Durang at a restaurant which adjoined the theatre and was then sung nightly at the theatre. An old bill of 1818 announced the first illumination of the theatre with gas and during a performance of "Aladdin" in that year the gas lamps unexpectedly went out, in consequence of an omission to open one of the gasometers.

This put an abrupt end to the performance. The theatre was supplied with gas by the Baltimore Gas Company. During this season James Wallack made his first appearance in Baltimore at the theatre in the roles of Macbeth, Pizarro, Hamlet, Coriolanus, Octavian and Richard III.

EDMUND KEAN APPEARS

The season of 1821 was begun by the first appearance in this city of Edmund Kean in the character of Richard III followed by "Othello," "Merchant of Venice," "King Lear," "Macbeth," "Julius Caesar" (the first time played in this country) and "Hamlet." The autumn season of 1821 presented the first appearance here of the elder Booth in all his best Shakespearean roles. From this time until 1854, though remarkable companies presented the finest of plays, the theatre was run at a loss, and in 1856 it was sold at auction to John Grason, and in the autumn of the same year Messrs. John T. Ford, Kunkle and Moxley leased the house.

COMES UNDER THE MANAGEMENT OF JOHN T. FORD

Under Mr. Ford's management the establishment attained a degree of popularity and prestige never before known in the theatrical annals of Baltimore. In 1859 James J. Gifford remodeled the theatre for Mr. Ford, and in August it was opened by Stuart Robson as Tony Lumpkin in "She Stoops to Conquer." In 1870 Mr. Ford purchased the theatre. The season of 1873, which was doomed to so sudden and disastrous a termination in August, opened with a spectacular drama, "The Ice Witch," and in September Boucicault's play "After Dark" was placed on the boards and played twice. After the performance a fire burst out in the theatre and in a short time consumed it.

IS DESTROYED BY FIRE

Soon after the burning of the theatre, Mr. Ford associated himself with his eldest son, Mr. Charles E. Ford, who is now one of the managers of Ford's Grand Opera House, which was built shortly after this time. In November they began the rebuilding of the Holliday Street Theatre, and August, 1874, it was reopened with the same play, "After Dark," with an immense audience crowding all parts of the playhouse.

During Mr. Ford's management the works of two dramatists were produced for the first time. "Boy Martyrs" and "East Lynne," the former written and the latter dramatized by C. W. Tayleure, and "De Soto" and "Senior Valliento" by George W. Miles.

HISTRIONIC GENIUSES GRACED THE BOARDS

The stock company which played at the Holliday Street Theatre at this time included such actors as Robert Mantell, Henry Miller, Stuart Robson, A. W. Albaugh, Mrs. Whitlock, sister of the matchless Mrs. Siddons, and aunt of Fannie Kemble; Laura Keene, Lucie Western, and upon this stage appeared three generations of Jeffersons, Junius Brutus, Edwin and John Wilkes Booth, the elder Hackett, Mrs. Arnold, who married David Joe and was mother of Edgar Allan Poe; John Darley, father of F. O. Darley, the designer; Fannie Kemble, the Florences, Charles Kean, Mme. Celeste, E. L. Davenport, Ristori, Matilde Heron, Patti, Mario, Sontage, Piccolommo, Mme. Bishop, and many others equally illustrious. Mr. Ford was identified with the careers of many of the great theatrical lights of the period, all of whom played at the "Old Drury," among them John S. Clark, John E. Owens, Charlotte Cushman, E. A. Sothern, Edwin Forrest, John Adams, Joseph Jefferson, Lotta, Maggie Mitchel, Julia Dean and James Sibley Wallace.

Edwin Booth courted and married Mary Devlin, a member of Mr. Ford's stock company. Several years after her death he was playing the "Apostate" at the Holliday Street Theatre and was wounded in the arm by George Vandenhoff. . . .

21. PROVIDENCE THEATRE
Providence, Rhode Island
Opened September 2, 1795

The theater situation in Providence was much the same as that in its sister town of Newport. The first touring company of players was that of David Douglass, who visited Providence in the summer of 1762 following his successful season in Newport. The group played only a short season here before they moved south for the autumn season.

The next group of note to play in Providence was the company assembled by Joseph Harper, one of the prominent members of the Hallam and Henry group. It was this company of comedians that had been playing in the New Exhibition Hall in Boston when it was closed by the authorities as an infringement of the laws of the Commonwealth of Massachusetts. Harper made his way across the state line to Providence and there, after assessing the disposition of the people of Providence toward stage presentations, began a season that opened on December 10, 1792. These entertainments were given in the courthouse. The season was a short one, since Harper had commitments in Philadelphia in January, but so cordial had been his reception in Providence that he returned there in 1794.

During this engagement the Harper company found that the friends of the drama in Providence had provided a semblance of a theater in rooms adjoining the old Coffee House. Here Harper began his season on December 30, 1794, and continued until April 13th. The theatrical presentations met with such approbation that on April 14th a group of men met at McLane's Coffee House to discuss the building of a permanent theater in Providence. Charles Blake, who in 1868 wrote about the Providence stage, chronicles the meeting and its aftermath:

21:1 . . . The next day, April 14, a meeting of gentlemen interested in the permanent establishment of the stage in the town was held at McLane's Coffee House, and subscriptions for a new theatre were so liberally promised that a building com-

21:1. Charles Blake, *An Historical Account of the Providence Stage* (Providence, R.I.: George H. Whitney, 1868), pp. 51–52.

HOLLIDAY STREET THEATRE (BALTIMORE) IN 1859.

20. Holliday Street Theatre, Baltimore, 1859. The theater pictured opened in 1813, replacing the original theater built in 1794. Courtesy of The Hoblitzelle Theatre Arts Library, The Humanities Research Center, The University of Texas at Austin.

22. Haymarket Theatre, Boston. Watercolor by Robertson, 1798. Courtesy of the Harvard Theatre Collection.

23. Park Theatre and St. Paul's Chapel, New York. Watercolor by C. Milbourne, 1798. Courtesy of The New-York Historical Society, New York City.

mittee was immediately appointed to make the necessary contracts, with the understanding that the work was to be completed at Commencement time. John Brown gave the lot, and subscribed for seven shares of stock. Messrs. T. L. Halsey, Sr., John Corliss, Cyprian Sterry, and George and Jeremiah Olney were also liberal in their subscriptions. As soon as a sum sufficient for the completion of the building had been guaranteed workmen began to prepare the frame, and on Thursday, August 6th, 1795, commenced raising the edifice. The work was pushed forward with energy, and when it seemed doubtful whether it would be possible to have it ready for use at the time proposed, the prospect was at once brightened by a demonstration of good will from a quarter where it was scarcely looked for. All the carpenters, clubbing together, formed a "bee," and, abandoning all other employments, laboured without fee or reward upon the edifice until opening night. As the work progressed the town was on tiptoe with expectation, and such was the general good feeling prevailing that it was manifest that the drama was to become a permanent institution.

This theatre was situated at the corner of Westminster and Mathewson streets, on the site now occupied by Grace Church. It was eighty-one feet long by fifty feet wide, fronting on Westminster street. Access to the interior was gained by three doors in front; the entrance to the boxes being in the middle, that to the pit on the East, and that to the gallery on the West side. Over the middle door was suspended a light wooden canopy, which served both for ornament and for protection from rains. The theatre contained two tiers of boxes, a gallery, and a pit. The proscenium was sixteen feet high by twenty-four wide; and over the arch was a scroll bearing the motto: "Pleasure the means; the end virtue," a pithy sentiment worthy of adoption by every theatrical manager. The few scenes that were prepared were tolerably good; but as no act drop was painted, the traditional green curtain was obliged to serve a double purpose.

22. HAYMARKET THEATRE
Boston, Massachusetts
Opened December 26, 1796

Charles Stuart Powell, who had served as manager of the Federal Street Theatre when it opened, had been dismissed by the trustees after two seasons. The ostensible reason was that Powell had not been able to recruit a really distinguished company, such as that of the Chestnut Street Theatre in Philadelphia or the John Street Theatre in New York City. Powell, in retaliation, set about planning a new theatre that would be a competitor to the Federal Street playhouse. Seilhamer gives some of the background of the financial arrangements for the new house.

22:1   On the 11th of April, 1796, Charles S. Powell advertised proposals for building a new theatre in Boston. The capital was placed at £3,400—two hundred shares of stock at $60 per share—making $12,000 in American money. Such was the eagerness with which the shares were taken that on the 18th of May an advertisement was printed for bids for the contract for furnishing stone for the new building. Each share of stock carried with it free admission to the theatre during the season, and the desire to become stockholders was so great that some Boston mechanics even undertook to give their labor in payment for their shares. So rapidly was the work pushed forward that before the close of the year the house was ready for occupancy. The new theatre was situated near the corner of Tremont and Boylston Streets, and was an immense wooden pile, over-

22:1. George O. Seilhamer, *History of the American Theatre*. 3 vols. (Philadelphia: Globe Printing House, 1889–91), 3:354.

topping every building in the vicinity. It had three tiers of boxes, together with a pit and gallery. . . .

Further details of the playhouse are added by Dunlap.

22:2   In the course of the spring of 1796, the project of building a new play-house in Boston was started, a subscription opened, and almost immediately filled up. Such was the prevailing taste for theatrical performances, that men of capital were willing to invest their property to almost any amount in the erection of theatres; and mechanics did not hesitate to take shares in payment for labour. Contracts were made, the building went on rapidly, and, before the first of January, 1797, the Haymarket theatre, an immense wooden pile, proudly overtopping every other building in the metropolis, was completed. It is believed that the idea of raising a rival playhouse was first suggested by C. Powell, or some of his friends, who thought him injured by the proprietors of the Federal Street Theatre; but there was another and more potent principle exerted in producing the establishment than mere theatrical rivalry, and that was political feeling. Political excitement between the parties then denominated Federal and Jacobin was high and furious. Every man joined himself to one or the other of those parties, and each was jealous of the ascendancy of the other. It was suspected, and not without some reason, that party politics, which pervaded almost every private as well as public concern, had some influence in the management of the Federal Street house; and that the trustees, who were all of the Federal school of politics, had upheld and justified the manager in the introduction of pieces tending to provoke resentments and animosities of their political opponents. . . .

22:2. William Dunlap, *A History of the American Theatre*. 2 vols. in 1. (New York: J. & J. Harper, 1832), 1:271–74.

In the month of December, the Haymarket theatre was completed. It was an immense building, constructed entirely of wood. It had three tiers of boxes and a gallery. The lobbies and staircases were spacious and convenient. On each side of the stage was a suite of dressing rooms, constructed in the wings, projecting from the second story to the main edifice, and nearly on a level with the stage. The entrance to the pit was up a flight of steps. The theatre was opened on Monday, the 26th day of December. . . .

23. PARK THEATRE
New York City
Opened January 29, 1798

The eighteenth century was a time of experimentation in the American theater, for, from the beginnings in 1716, the traveling companies of actors were seeking to discover whether the cities of the American colonies could support a permanent playhouse. The early theaters were temporary affairs, since in many instances a playhouse was erected and the company would remain there for only a month or sometimes even less. The Southwark and John Street theaters were of a more permanent nature, although still rather crude, and it was not until after the American Revolution that permanent theaters of distinctive architecture began to appear. The 1790s in particular were extremely important in the growth of the American playhouse, and certainly the opening of the Park Theatre in New York City heralded the ascendancy of that city as the theater capital of the United States.

Dunlap, who was one of the lessees of the new theater, tells of the impetus to build a splendid new playhouse in New York City.

23:1   It was not to be expected that the inhabitants of New-York would be content with a paltry wooden theatre in John Street, when their neighbors and rivals,

23:1. William Dunlap, *A History of the American Theatre*. 2 vols. in 1. (New York: J. & J. Harper, 1832), 1:265–66.

who outdid them at all times in fish and butter, had a new brick splendid building in Chestnut Street, the centre of Philadelphia fashion. Accordingly, a scheme for a new theatre, to surpass all new theatres, had now been some time in agitation. Eighty subscribers at 375 dollars each were obtained, making the sum of 30,000 dollars. This was to be sufficient. The number of subscribers was increased to 100; and more it was soon found were wanted. It was reported that Hodgkinson* was to go to England and leave his partner to manage in America; but the partners were by this time, to use the common phrase, "at swords' points"; neither was the one fitted for the mission abroad, nor the other to manage at home. . . .

There was financial difficulty from the beginning of the project, and until the time of the opening there was much dissension even concerning whether the stockholders would be admitted free to the first performance. Dunlap chronicles these difficulties at length:

23:2   At length, on the 29th of January, 1798, the new theatre was opened in an unfinished state, and with a scanty supply of scenes. The scenery, machinery, and stage, were under the direction of Mr. Charles Ciceri, heretofore mentioned. The landscapes were painted by Mr. Audin, his assistant. The play of the night was *As You Like It,* the farce was *The Purse.* The house was opened with an address written by Dr. E. H. Smith and spoken by Mr. Hodgkinson. A prelude was performed, written by Mr. Milne, and called *All in a Bustle.* The house was overflowing, but such was the confusion, from the press of the crowd, and the want of such precautions as experience would have suggested, that great

numbers entered without paying at the doors or delivering tickets. Mr. Cooper, seeing the confusion and the want of energy in one of the door-keepers, took his place, and restored order at one of the entrances. The amount received on this first evening of performance was 1,232 dollars. The next night, January 31st sunk to 513, and the third, with Mr. Chalmers' first appearance in the new theatre, to 265 dollars. The succeeding week only averaged 333 each evening. The theatre in John Street was soon after pulled down, and on the site three houses were built. . . .

Ireland locates the new theater and describes it in greater detail.

23:3   The New Theatre, as it was styled for many years—the Theatre, Park as it was afterward designated by its managers—or the Park Theatre, as more commonly called by the public, stood in Park Row, about two hundred feet east of Ann Street, and nearly opposite the present fountain, on lots now numbered 21, 23 and 25.

It occupied a space of eighty feet by one hundred and sixty-five feet deep, running through to Theatre Alley in the rear, where a wing was attached.

It was one of the most substantial buildings ever erected in New York, and though externally devoid of architectural pretension, was in its interior harmoniously proportioned and admirably well adapted for the purposes of sight and sound.

The plans for its construction were originally furnished by Marc Isambard Brunel, the celebrated French engineer and builder of the Thames Tunnel, who, during the stormy days of the French Revolution, was in exile in America.

It is doubtful if they were ever carried out—that for the exterior, which in-

*John Hodgkinson, who was joint lessee of the new theater with Dunlap.

23:2. William Dunlap, *A History of the American Theatre.* 2 vols. in 1. (New York: J. & J. Harper, 1832), 2:12–13.

23:3. Joseph N. Ireland, *Records of the New York Stage.* 2 vols. (New York: T. H. Morrell, 1866–67), 1:172–73.

cluded a range of fluted pilasters by way of ornament, certainly was not, and for many years the front wall remained perfectly plain and barn-like in appearance.

An engraving of the original design may be seen in the New York Directory for 1796.

The Park Theatre was first projected in the year 1795, and was intended to be ready for occupation in October, 1797. Its estimated cost was raised by subscription of one hundred and thirteen shares of $375 each, making the sum of $42,375. Its actual cost, owing to the inexperience and mismanagement of its builders, amounted to more than $130,-000. After several years profitless ownership, the original proprietors parted with it to Messrs. Beekman and Astor, who held it until its destruction, in 1848. Its first lessees were John Hodgkinson and William Dunlap, who opened it to the public, in an unfinished state, on the 29th of January, 1798. . . .

The opening of the theater was reviewed in the *Daily Advertiser.*

23:4 On Monday evening last, the New Theatre was opened to the most overflowing house that was ever witnessed in this city. Though the Commissioners have been constrained to open it in an unfinished state, it still gave high satisfaction.

The essential requisites of hearing and seeing have been happily attained. We do not remember to have been in any Theatre where the view of the stage is so complete from all parts of the house, or where the actors are heard with such distinctness. The house is made to contain about 2,000 persons. The audience part, though wanting in those brilliant decorations which the artists have designed for it, yet exhibited a neatness and simplicity which were highly agreeable. The stage was everything that could be wished. The scenery was executed in a most masterly style. The extensiveness of the scale upon which the scenes are executed, the correctness of the designs, and the elegance of the painting, presented the most beautiful views which the imagination can conceive. The scenery was of itself worth a visit to the theatre.

The company are known to the public, and they played with great spirit. We indeed think it the best company of comedians which has yet appeared on the boards of any Theatre in this place, and we presume they will this season receive an uncommon share of public patronage.

Great credit is due to the Messrs. Mangins, who were the architects of the house, for their skilful and commodious arrangements, and too much cannot be said for the science of Mr. Ciceri as the machinist, and for his taste as scene painter. They are artists who would do honour to any country, and a great acquisition.

The interior of the theater is described in detail by T. Allston Brown:

23:5 The theatre was three stories high, of stone, with about six steps up to the box entrance, and three green baize doors from the outside lobby. There was a box office on the right hand as you entered. In a niche in the centre of the building was, some time after the house was erected, a statue of Shakespeare on a pedestal. The extension lobby was wide and carpeted, and in cold weather two blazing fires were kept at either end of the lobbies. There was a box door at each box of the first tier, and a box keeper ever ready to open to the audience. The interior was tastefully ornamented in light pink and gold. There were three tiers of

23:4. New York *Daily Advertiser*, Jan. 31, 1798.

23:5. T. Allston Brown, *A History of the New York Stage from the First Performance in 1732 to 1901.* 3 vols. (New York: Dodd, 1903), 1:12.

boxes, a gallery and a pit. There were no chairs in either boxes or pit, but cushioned seats. The proscenium had stage doors and about four or five private boxes. The stage was at all times well arranged and provided with most excellent scenery. The prices of admission were: boxes, $1; pit, 50 cents; gallery, 25 cents. No lady was admitted to the first or second tier unless accompanied by a gentleman. The theatre held $1,700. Although the house was opened before it was completed, it was finished and elegantly furnished during the summer of 1789, by Mr. Dunlap, the manager. Notwithstanding its popularity, this theatre was subject to all the ups and downs of financial experience, as may be inferred from the fact that during its opening season one of the original managers, Mr. Hallam, withdrew, and at the close of the first season the other one, John Hodgkinson, also gave up his managerial control. . . .

Washington Irving was a great theater buff and aften visited the Park Theatre. Many of his impressions are recorded in the "Jonathan Oldstyle" letters, which were published in the *Morning Chronicle* in 1802. Some of his impressions of the audience that frequented the Park Theatre are found in his letter of December 3, 1802.

23:6 MR. EDITOR:

My last communication mentioned my visit to the theatre: the remarks it contained were chiefly confined to the play and the actors; I shall now extend them to the audience, who, I assure you, furnish no inconsiderable part of the entertainment.

. . . As I entered the house some time before the curtain rose, I had sufficient leisure to make some observations. I was much amused with the waggery and humour of the gallery, which, by the

23:6. New York *Morning Chronicle*, Dec. 3, 1802.

way, is kept in *excellent* order by the constables, who are stationed there. The noise in this part of the house is somewhat similar to that which prevailed in Noah's ark; for we have an imitation of the whistles and yells of very kind of animal. This, in some measure, compensates for the want of music, as the gentlemen of our orchestra are very economic of their favours. Somehow or another, the anger of the gods seemed to be aroused all of a sudden, and they commenced a discharge of apples, nuts, and gingerbread, on the heads of the honest folk in the pit, who had no possibility of retreating from this new kind of thunderbolts. I can't say but I was a little irritated at being saluted aside of my head with a rotten pippin; and was going to shake my cane at them, but was prevented by a decent looking man behind me, who informed me that it was useless to threaten or expostulate. They are only *amusing themselves* a little at our expense, said he; sit down quietly and bend your back to it. My kind neighbor was interrupted by a hard green apple that hit him between the shoulders—he made a wry face, but knowing it all to be a joke, bore the blow like a philosopher. I soon saw the wisdom of this determination; a stray thunderbolt happened to light on the head of a little sharp faced Frenchman, dressed in a white coat and small cocked hat, who sat two or three benches ahead of me, and seemed to be an irritable little animal. Monsieur was terribly exasperated; he jumped upon his seat, shook his fist at the gallery, and swore violently in bad English. This was all nuts to his merry persecutors; their attention was wholly turned on him, and he formed their *target* for the rest of the evening.

I found the ladies in the boxes, as usual, studious to please; their charms were set off to the greatest advantage; each box was a little battery in itself, and they all seemed eager to outdo each other in the havoc they spread around. An arch glance in one box was rivalled by a smile in another, that smile by a simper in a third, and in a fourth a most bewitching languish carried all before it.

I was surprised to see some persons reconnoitering the company through spy-glasses; and was in doubt whether these machines were used to remedy deficiencies of vision, or whether this was another of the eccentricities of fashion. Jack Stylish has since informed me, that glasses were lately all *the go;* though hang it, says Jack, it is quite *out* at present; we used to mount our glasses in *great snuff,* but since so many *tough jockies* have followed the lead, the bucks have all *cut* the custom. I give you, Mr. Editor, the account in my dashing cousin's own language. It is from a vocabulary I do not well understand.

I was considerably amused by the queries of the countrymen mentioned in my last, who was now making his first visit to the theatre. He kept constantly applying to me for information, and I readily communicated, as far as my ignorance would permit.

As this honest man was casting his eye round the house, his attention was suddenly arrested. And pray, who are these? said he, pointing to a cluster of young fellows. These, I suppose, are the critics, of whom I have heard so much. They have, no doubt, got together to communicate their remarks, and compare notes: these are the persons through whom the audience exercise their judgments, and by whom they are told when they are to applaud and when they are to hiss. Critics! ha! ha! my dear sir, they trouble themselves as little about the elements of criticism, as they do about other departments of science and belles-lettres. These the beaux of the present day, who meet here to lounge away an idle hour, and play off their little impertinences for the entertainment of the public. They no more regard the merits of the play, nor of the actors, than my cane. They even strive to appear inattentive; and I have seen one of them perched on the front of the box, sucking the head of his stick, and staring vacantly at the audience, insensible to the most interesting specimens of science representation, though the tear of sensibility was trembling in every eye around him. I have heard that some have even gone so far in search of amusement, as to propose a game of cards in the theatre, during the performance. The eyes of my neighbor sparkled at this information—his cane shook in his hand—the word *puppies* burst from his lips. Nay, says I, I don't give this for absolute fact: my cousin Jack was, I believe, *quizzing* me (as he terms it) when he gave me the information. But you seem quite indignant, said I, to the decent looking man in my rear. It was from him the exclamation came: the honest *countryman* was gazing in gaping wonder on some new attraction. Believe me, said I, if you had them daily before your eyes, you would get quite used to them. Used to them, replied he; how it is possible for people of sense to relish such conduct? Bless you, my friend, people of sense have nothing to do with it; they merely endure it in silence. These young gentlemen live in an indulgent age. When I was a young man, such tricks and follies were held in proper contempt. Here I went a little too far; for, upon better recollection, I must own that a lapse of years has produced but little alteration in this department of folly and impertinence. But do the ladies admire these manners! Truly, I am not conversant in female circles as formerly; but I should think it a poor compliment to my fair countrywomen, to suppose them pleased with the stupid stare and cant phrases with which these votaries of fashion add affected to real ignorance.

Our conversation was here interrupted by the ringing of a bell. Now for the play, said my companion. No, said I, it is only for the musicians. These worthy gentlemen then came crawling out of their holes, and began, with very solemn and

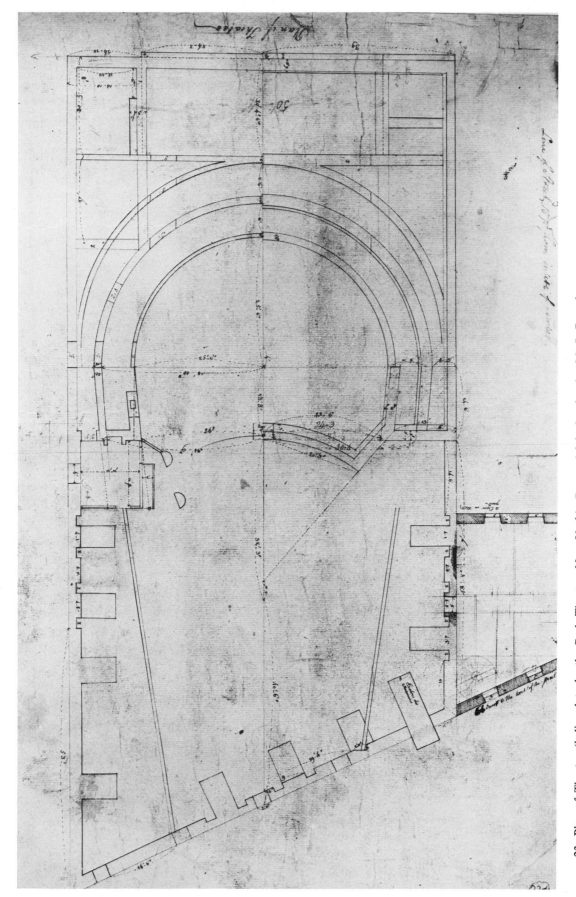

23. Plan of Theater (believed to be the Park Theatre, New York). Pen and ink drawing by M. I. Brunel. Courtesy of the New-York Historical Society, New York City.

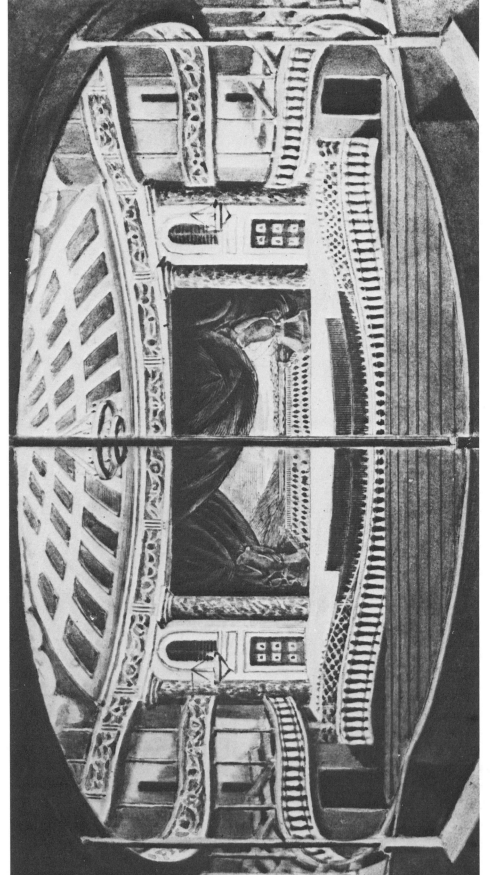

23. Interior, Park Theatre, New York, ca. 1805. Watercolor, based on a woodcut used as the frontispiece to the "Address of the Opening." Courtesy of the J. Clarence Davies Collection, Museum of the City of New York.

important phizzes, strumming and tuning their instruments in the usual style of discordance, to the great *entertainment* of the audience. What tune is that? asked my neighbor, covering his ears. This, said I, is no tune; it is only a pleasing symphony with which we are regaled, as a preparative. For my part, though I admire the effect of contrast, I think they might as well play it in their cavern under the stage. The bell rung a second time—and then began the tune in reality; but I could not help observing, that the countryman was more diverted with the queer grimaces and contortions of countenance exhibited by the musicians, than their melody. What I heard of the music, I liked very well; (though I was told by one of my neighbors, that the same pieces have been played every night for these three years;) but it was often overpowered by the gentry in the gallery, who vociferated loudly for *Moll in the Wad, Talley ho the Grinders,* and several other *airs* more suited to their tastes.

I observed that every part of the house has its different department. The good folks of the gallery have all the trouble of ordering the music; (their directions, however, are not more frequently followed than they deserve). The mode by which they issue their mandates is stamping, hissing, roaring, whistling; and, when the musicians are refractory, groaning in cadence. They also have the privilege of demanding a *bow* from *John* (by which name they designate every servant at the theatre, who enters to move a table or snuff a candle); and of detecting those cunning dogs who peep from behind the curtain.

By the by, my honest friend was much puzzled about the curtain itself. He wanted to know why that carpet was hung up in the theatre? I assured him it was no carpet, but a very fine curtain. And what, pray, may be the meaning of that gold head, with the nose cut off, that I see in front of it? The meaning—why, really, I can't tell exactly—though my cousin,

Jack Stylish, says there is a great deal of meaning of it. But surely you like the *design* of the curtain? The design,— why really I can see no design about it, unless it is to be brought down about our ears by the weight of those gold heads, and that heavy *cornice* with which it is garnished. I began now to be uneasy for the credit of our curtain, and was afraid he would perceive the mistake of the painter, in putting a *harp* in the middle of the curtain, and calling it a *mirror;* but his attention was *happily* called away by the *candle-grease* from the chandelier, over the centre of the pit, dropping on his clothes. This he loudly complained of, and declared his coat was *bran-new.* Now, my friend? said I; we must put up with a few trifling inconveniences, when in the pursuit of pleasure. True, said he; but I think I pay pretty dear for it;—first to give six shillings at the door, and then to have my head battered with rotten apples, and my coat spoiled by candle-grease; by and by I shall have my other clothes dirtied by sitting down, as I perceive every body mounted on the benches. I wonder if they could not see as well if they were all to stand upon the floor.

Here I could no longer defend our customs, for I could scarcely breathe while thus surrounded by a host of strapping fellows, standing with their dirty boots on the seats of the benches. The little Frenchman, who thus found a temporary shelter from the missive compliments of his gallery friend, was the only person benefited. At last the bell rung again, and the cry of *down, down, down —hats off,* was the signal for the commencement of the play.

If, Mr. Editor, the garrulity of an old fellow is not tiresome and you chuse to give this view of the New-York theatre, a place in your paper, you may, perhaps, hear further from your friend.

JONATHAN OLDSTYLE

Chapter 2

Nineteenth-Century Playhouses to the End of the Civil War

After an important period of playhouse building in the 1790s, theater construction came to a standstill at the turn of the century. Certainly this was not caused by a decrease in population, for in 1800 New York had grown to 60,489, Philadelphia to 69,403, and Boston to 33,250. The growth in Charleston was less rapid, its population rising only to 20,473.

Other problems, however, controlled the destiny of the theater in the United States at this period. Chief among the difficulties was the growing unrest between England and the United States that was to result in the War of 1812. The animosity between the two nations was felt to some extent in the theater, where the majority of players still were British.

The economic situation during the early years of the nineteenth century were very unsettled. Because of the Napoleonic Wars, American commercial interests ebbed, and the coming of the War of 1812 brought even worse economic conditions to the new nation.

By the 1820s, however, the situation had improved economically and politically, and the United States began to gain economic and social stability. Thousands of immigrants poured into the East coast cities, many of which doubled their populations within a twenty-year period. The population of New York City soared to 202,589 by 1830, while Boston's population rose to 61,392 in the same census, and New Orleans to 46,310.

With the increase of population due to immigration came a new and greater interest in theatrical entertainment. Many of these immigrants came from European backgrounds where there had not been the same proscription against the theater as was found among some earlier British settlers. Although other playhouses had opened earlier in the century in Washington, Philadelphia, and New York, certainly the opening of the Bowery Theatre in 1826 signaled the beginning of theatrical entertainment for the masses.

As the floods of immigrants deluged New York City, the number of theaters increased accordingly. By 1850 New York City could boast of a half million people, and there seemed to be a theater to suit all tastes: opera, serious drama, variety entertainment, and circus. Huge playhouses were built, some of them seating more than three thousand spectators. These "temples of the muses," as the reporters loved to call them, were lavish in their decorations. In 1845 there was even a showboat in the city, complete with limelight so that the ship could be seen at a distance as the light pierced the sky in lower Manhattan.

Perhaps the major change in theatrical management occurred with the shift from the stock company—a group of actors and actresses employed by a theater and acting exclusively in that theater—to the star system, by which an eminent actor from England (or later from the continent or the United States) would tour the playgoing cities, acting in favorite roles. The star was supported in his role by members of the stock company of the theater in which he was playing. As competition between the numerous theaters became more intense, each theatrical manager felt that he must hire more name stars in order to attract theatergoers. The star, realizing his importance, began to demand and receive increasingly higher salaries, often far out of proportion to his ability, while the members of the stock companies, many of whom were far superior in acting ability to the star, received a pittance by contrast.

Theatergoing became respectable and the local newspapers hired drama critics, who regularly reported on the openings of the various playhouses and their attractions. News of any new theaters that were being built was sometimes reported for months before the theaters actually opened. Not only was the theater now respectable, but Americans, and particularly New Yorkers, had become avid lovers of the performing arts.

As "theater for the masses" became popular, there was a change from classical repertoire in various theaters, such as the Bowery, and variety entertainment attracted a huge following. Two men in particular were important in the development of this field of entertainment in the United States: Phineas Taylor Barnum and Tony Pastor.

Barnum was an extraordinary showman who knew what his audiences liked and gave them what they wanted. He sought to appeal to people of various tastes when in 1842 he opened his American Museum, a combination of sideshow and theater. Here he exhibited many of his "curiosities" and at the same time presented dramas in his "Moral Lecture Room."

Both Barnum's contributions and those of Tony Pastor are discussed more fully in

Chapter 4, which treats the New York theaters from 1865 to 1900. They were both the products, however, of this turbulent era of change in America, sensing the entertainment needs of the masses of people who crowded into America's urban areas.

The documents included in the present chapter reflect the transition that was taking place in the American playhouse from 1800 to 1865, a period that saw the adoption of gas as a means of lighting, the beginning of the use of the box set, the disappearance of the stage doors, and the use of the area behind the proscenium as the major acting area. These documents also reflect the general fear of theater fires and record the claims that the new playhouses were safer than ever.

24. UNITED STATES THEATRE
Washington, D.C.
Opened June 1800

Soon after the beginning of the new century, Thomas Wignell and his Chestnut Street Theatre company journeyed to the new city of Washington, D.C., to establish a theater season in the nation's capital. One of the actors in the company, who later became the manager of the Chestnut Street Theatre in Philadelphia, was William B. Wood, who is one of the chief chroniclers of the early American stage. It is from him that we gain what little information we have about the first theater in Washington, although it must be remembered that he wrote his *Personal Recollections of the Stage* late in his life and published the work in 1855, and as a result, his memory is not always as accurate as one would wish.

24:1   In the spring of the year 1800, Mr. Wignell received a pressing request to establish a theatre at the new city of Washington; and to facilitate this purpose, fortunately, a building was offered every way suitable, situated nearly in the centre of the new metropolis. A company of gentlemen had erected, but not com-

24:1. William B. Wood, *Personal Recollections of the Stage* (Philadelphia: H. C. Baird, 1855), pp. 55–57.

pleted, (for the purpose of a large hotel originally,) the extensive building, subsequently known for many years as the post-office and patent office, unfortunately afterwards destroyed by fire. It consisted of a large, spacious centre building, with two extensive wings. The former was offered by the proprietors as an eligible structure for our purpose; and its capacious size afforded ample space for such accommodation as would be required in furnishing dramatic entertainments to the citizens of Washington, Georgetown and Alexandria, as well as of the extended neighborhood around. In the size and loftiness of this central edifice Mr. Lenthall found full scope for the completion of his purpose, while the manager prepared, at Philadelphia, scenery, an artificial dome, and the embellishments of the audience part, so as to have them in readiness to be put up without delay upon their arrival at Washington.

But poor Wignell's ill-fortune, constant to him on all occasions, did not fail to check his plan, so well contrived and at a large cost. On the way to Washington a furious storm of rain invaded the wagons, and drenched the tasteful labors of the painters so seriously as to make it necessary to repaint nearly the whole, besides occasioning a considerable delay in opening the house. Not a jot discouraged, however, this excellent man persevered in his exertions; and after innumerable difficulties incident to the unprovided state of the place, and at great expense, he at length opened.

THE FIRST THEATRE IN WASHINGTON

With an appropriate address, written by the late Thomas Law, Esq., who continued to aid the enterprise, not only with his pen and his influence, but with his purse; he was ably seconded by several other gentlemen of liberality and taste. The opening play of "Venice Preserved" was well acted by Messrs. Wignell, Cooper and Mrs. Merry, as Jaffier, Prince and Belvidera, and warmly received and

applauded by the audience, more numerous, as well as splendid, than can be conceived from a population so slender and so scattered. The encouragement continued to exceed his expectations, yet fell very far below his expenditure, as his company consisted of every one of the persons who composed the Philadelphia establishment. Mr. Wignell's main object was to obtain a footing in Washington, where he might keep together his company during the summer, in the event of a recurrence of the pestilence, which was regarded as but too probable. It may be justice to add, that he ever expressed a degree of pride at having established a theatre at the metropolis of our country, and acted on the first night of any performance at the foundation of what was properly entitled *The National Theatre*. From the citizens of Washington the principal performers received the most gratifying attention and hospitality. Many of us commenced at this period acquaintances and friendships which have continued with unabated kindness through a long course of succeeding years. Of the large company presented by Mr. Wignell, there remained forty-three years afterwards only Mrs. Darley, (then Miss E. Westray,) Cooper and Blissett.

. . . The partial success of Mr. Wignell's experiment encouraged some friends of the drama, a few years afterwards, to erect a more durable dramatic temple on the Pennsylvania Avenue. . . .

On 1901 A. J. Mudd, an eminent historian who was interested in the theater, read a paper for the Columbia Historical Society entitled "Early Theatres in Washington City." In this account he was able to clarify a number of facts concerning this first playhouse.

24:2 . . . The history of the Washington stage dates from the removal of the seat of the National Government to this city. The

24:2. A. J. Mudd, "Early Theatre in Washington City," *Columbia Historical Society Records* 5:65–66 (1902).

removal began in May, 1800, and by July all of the then existing six Executive Departments were in full working order in Washington. At that time there were two theatres in Philadelphia, one known as "The Old Theatre" and the other as "The New Theatre."

The "New Theatre" was under the management of Messrs. Wignell and Reinagle. The season in Philadelphia closed May 19 and the company came to this city to open "an elegant little theatre" called the "United States Theatre," fitted up in the "Lottery" or "Great Hotel." This hotel was erected by Samuel Blodgett and was situated on the south front of the Square, where the old Post Office Department now stands. So far as I have been able to learn there is no record of the exact time that the opening took place, but it was probably in June. A storm which raged a short time before the opening of the theatre overflowed the creeks, many horses were drownded, and the scenery of the theatre was almost entirely destroyed. Among the members of the Philadelphia company were the celebrated comedian, Mr. Warren, father of William Warren, the famous comedian of later years; Mr. Francis, Mr. Wood, Mr. Bernard, another noted comedian; Mr. Cain, Mr. Blissett, Mr. Darley, Mr. Warrell, Mrs. Merry, Mrs. Snowden, Mrs. Morriss, Mrs. Warrell, Miss Broadhurst, Mrs. Oldnixon and Miss Arnold. The managers were also actors. The company played in Washington "with great reputation but no proportionate profit,"* and closed the season about September 15, 1800

25. WASHINGTON THEATRE
Washington, D.C.
Opened November 16, 1804

Four years after the Chestnut Street company under the management of Wignell

and Reinagle played in the first theater in the new capital city, a regular playhouse was opened. The difficulties in building this theater are related by Professor Mudd.

25:1 . . . Early in 1803 a number of prominent citizens of Washington met and opened subscriptions for the purpose of building a theatre.

At a meeting of the subscribers held in Tunnicliff's Hotel on the night of Wednesday, April 20, 1803, a number of offers of donation of ground was considered, a site was selected and arrangements made for erecting the building. The site selected was the northeast corner of Eleventh and C Street, Northwest, fronting 135 feet 4 inches on Eleventh Street and 64 feet on C Street. That site is now occupied by Kernan's Lyceum.

At that meeting, in addition to the subscriptions of money, a number of persons subscribed labor—digging, carpentering, plastering, etc. The shares were placed at $50 each, and on May 4, the subscribers were called on to pay into the hands of Mayor John P. Van Ness, Chairman of the Building Committee, on the tenth of that month, the first instalment of their subscription, being one-fifth or ten dollars on each share.

Ground was broken early in June, and the second instalment was called for, to be paid June 10. The third and fourth instalments were soon requested to be paid, and those persons who had failed to respond to the first and second calls were urged to do so at once.

Reports were circulated which were calculated to injure the project and shake the confidence of the subscribers in their building committee. A meeting of the stockholders called by the building committee was held at Lovell's Hotel Wednesday, July 20, 1803, to which the committee made a report of the progress of

Claypole's Advertiser, Philadelphia, September 11, 1800.

25:1. A. J. Mudd, "Early Theatre in Washington City," *Columbia Historical Society Records* 5:68–71 (1902).

the work and also as to their management of the affairs entrusted to them. A resolution was adopted reciting that the stockholders were highly satisfied with the progress which had been made with the erecting the Theatre; that the committee deserved the thanks of the meeting; that the building had progressed as expeditiously as could have been expected; and that the reports were unjust and highly disapproved.

On August 1, the subscribers were requested to hand in their fifth and last instalment, and those who were delinquent in both money and labor subscriptions were urged to come forward at once and make payment so that the building might be finished with the dispatch which was particularly desirable.

In June, 1804, the Theatre Committee called a meeting of the subscribers and other gentlemen desirous of promoting the building of the Theatre. This meeting was held at Rhode's Tavern and was organized by calling Hon. Robert Brent, Mayor of Washington City, to the chair, and Stanley Byus was appointed Secretary.

After the committee had made report of the progress of the work a resolution was adopted providing for the appointment of a board of Directors to continue in office for one year. The resolution also provided that the Board should immediately proceed to raise by such means as they should deem eligible and necessary funds, and thenceforth apply the same to the completion of the building, and to procure a dramatic company when the prospects respecting the completion of the theatre should in their opinions warrant the same. . . .

The subscribers were slow in responding to the requests of the committee for payment of their subscriptions and on August 4, 1804, an urgent appeal was made by the Directors to all persons who had subscribed money to make immediate payment, to those who had subscribed materials to furnish them, and

to those who had subscribed labor to apply to the superintendent of the work and work out their shares.

In order to provide additional funds to expedite the work the Directors at a meeting held October 2, resolved to dispose of twelve free tickets at two hundred dollars each, one-half to be paid in shares previously subscribed or thereafter to be subscribed, and the other half in cash subject to redemption by the stockholders of the Theatre, or their assigns, at or after the expiration of seven years, on the repayment of two hundred dollars.

Work was pushed as much as possible and the Theatre was competed early in November, 1804. It was opened Friday, November 16, under the name "Washington Theatre," the opening being postponed from Wednesday, 14, on account of the inclemency of the weather. The initial performance consisted of a "Grand Medley Entertainment by the celebrated Mr. Maginnis from London who had performed in most of the Capital Cities of Europe and America." Mr. Maginnis announced that the exhibition had been brought to perfection after twenty years' study together with an expense of $5,000, and that no person could form a full idea of its merits without being a spectator. The entertainment was composed of songs, magic, dancing, pictures, and spectacular effects. Mr. Maginnis varied the features of his exhibition nightly and gave his last performance December 17. . . .

26. VAUXHALL GARDEN THEATRE
New York City
Opened May 10, 1806

The institution known as "summer theater" started early in American theater history. Mount Vernon Garden opened in 1800 and was very popular from the time of its inauguration. Vauxhall Garden, however, was more important as a summer attraction, since some of the actors from the excellent Park Theatre company were hired to perform and the offerings were of high caliber. Information concerning these summer theaters is difficult to find, for although the local newspapers carried their advertisements, little is mentioned about them. T. Allston Brown, in his history of the New York stage, related some facts about the playhouse.

26:1   The place of amusement known as the Vauxhall Garden and Theatre was situated on the west side of Fourth Avenue, opposite Cooper Institute Park. It ran through to Broadway, as far up as Astor Place, including what is now called the Astor Library and Lafayette Place. It was opened by Mr. Delacroix May 10, 1806. They engaged a portion of the Park Theatre company (as they were idle during the summer), and gave an entertainment called "Animal Magnetism" and a concert. Among the members of the company was Mr. Poe, father of Edgar Allan Poe, who made his first appearance in New York July 18, 1806, with his wife. It is said that neither Mr. Poe nor his wife possessed a very large amount of dramatic talent, although Mrs. Poe (formerly Miss Arnold), who had performed at the John Street Theatre, became a favorite with the audiences. Vauxhall was an extensive plot of land, created apparently in imitation of the Vauxhall of London. As a garden, it presented a handsome area of open ground in its centre, surrounded with the remnant of once luxuriant forest trees. There were long avenues of dimly obscured paintings, set in green frames, illuminated after nightfall with lamps. An aeronaut used to make daily ascensions. It was first destroyed by fire Aug. 10, 1807. The premises were soon rebuilt and again resumed their position as a popular resort. In the summer of 1838, Gates, the comedian, appeared as manager. He was a great favorite on the Bowery, and, with the idea that he would succeed in a summer theatre, he gathered an excellent company and opened the

theatre June 13, 1838. At the close of this season, 1837–38, not less than ten different places of amusement were open for the benefit of the citizens of New York. . . .

27. WALNUT STREET THEATRE
Philadelphia, Pennsylvania
Opened February 2, 1809

The Walnut Street Theatre is the oldest theater in America still in use. It was opened originally as a circus in 1809, was remodeled two years later into a playhouse, the Olympic Theatre, and was used by the Chestnut Street company when the old Chestnut Street Theatre burned down. The Walnut Street Theatre has had a varied and interesting history, and the accounts used here are from various periods of that history.

The first document is written by Charles Durang, who acted in the Chestnut Street Theatre company when it played at the Walnut Theatre from 1820 to 1822.

27:1   We have hitherto noticed incidentally the opposition which the Chestnut street theatre began to encounter in 1809 from the circus of Pepin & Breschard, at the northeast corner of Ninth and Walnut streets—an opposition which in 1811 increased to a regular theatrical rivalry, with a good dramatic company and fine equestrian talent. We have purposely refrained from saying much on this topic, because we desired to devote a separate chapter to the history of this circus, and of the first season of its existence as the Olympic theatre.

Pepin & Breschard's "new circus" opened February 2d, 1809. Pepin was a native of Philadelphia, and was said to have sprung from the little French colony, located on the lot of ground at the northeast corner of Pine and Sixth streets. Those French emigrants and refugees,

26:1. T. Allston Brown. *A History of the New York Stage from the First Performance in 1732 to 1901.* 3 vols. (New York: Dodd, 1903), 1:172–73.

27:1. Charles Durang, "The Philadelphia Stage. From the Year 1749 to the Year 1855." University of Pennsylvania Library, Philadelphia. Excerpt from chap. 48.

some of whom came from Acadia, Nova Scotia, and some from France and St. Domingo, had erected temporary abodes on that lot, and there for some time they maintained themselves independently, by industry in the arts and trades. This little settlement was known by the name of "the neutral houses," and some of our most respected citizens are descendants from the pioneers of that emigration. Breschard was a Frenchman of excellent address and fine personal appearance. Both the managers were very graceful and talented equestrians. Their company was numerous and well appointed. Their stud of horses was thoroughly broken, and composed of splendid animals. Their wardrobe was new, costly, and, indeed, the best thing of the kind that had been seen in the country. Horses, riders, and all appertenances, were brought with them from Spain. They were invited hither by Don Leonis, the Spanish consul for this port. He then resided in the row of houses opposite to the ground on which the circus was built. He negotiated for the vacant lot, procured it for Pepin and Breschard, and, having completed every necessary arrangement for the erection of the building, invited those gentlemen with their corps to the country. The building, we believe, was commenced in March, 1808. It covered the same ground which the Walnut street theatre does now, with the exception of the stage, which was added to it about two years after the circus was opened. The house was very spacious. The dome over the ring was an immense affair, it had from the pit the appearance of being some eighty feet in height, and looked very oriental, and magnificently imposing. In the wings were offices and apartments to reside in. The exterior presented no architectural beauty or ornament. It was simply a plain brick building. The same walls are now standing, with the exception of the front on Walnut street, which was entirely rebuilt, from designs by Mr. Haviland, in 1828. In the latter year Mr. Cowell became the lessee of it. He completely gutted the interior, leaving nothing but the walls standing, and built an entire new theatre, stage and andience department, the whole resting on a new foundation and interior walls, as it now stands. The outward walls, being deemed insecure, this course was considered necessary. Mr. Haviland, in the alterations, evinced great skill and taste. After the house was reconstructed by Mr. Cowell, he did not retain it, and never opened it. It remained thus until the failure of Mr. W. B. Wood, in the new Arch street theatre, when it was opened, for the first time, by Messrs. William Rufus Blake and Inslee, on the 1st of January, 1829, with a very talented company, to immense audiences. Notwithstanding the flattering prospects attending this enterprize, the management became bankrupt in the spring. We should have stated that after the destruction of the old Chestnut street theatre by fire, in 1820, Warren & Wood took the "Olympic," removed the huge dome referred to, and placed a flat ceiling in its stead, with other necessary alterations to aid the voice in speaking. The actors could not be satisfactorily heard in the house as it then stood. . . .

Warren and Wood moved their Chestnut Street Theatre company to the Walnut Street Theatre after the fire in 1820 and played there for two years, until the opening of the New Chestnut Street Theatre. Wood reminisces about the theater in his memoirs.

27:2   We began again in Philadelphia, on the 11th November, 1820, at the building still known as the Walnut street theatre, at the corner of Ninth and Walnut. The house having been originally constructed only with a view to circus purposes, and subsequently imperfectly changed to dramatic uses, required expensive improve-

27:2. William B. Wood, *Personal Recollections of the Stage* (Philadelphia: H. C. Baird, 1855), pp. 249–50.

ment in every part. The performers' dressing-rooms, the green-room, and indeed nearly every portion of the building needed alteration. With great labor and cost the house was prepared for opening on the day I have stated. Every possible provision for safety, comfort and attraction in the choice of pieces had been liberally made, but unfortunately our company was not strong. Commencing with little spirit after our late calamity, we felt slight hopes of the future, and opened appropriately enough with the "Poor Gentleman" and the following announcement:

TO THE FRIENDS OF THE DRAMA

"The managers respectfully inform the friends of the drama and the public in general, that the building formerly known as the Olympic theatre, has lately undergone a complete alteration, and been converted into a splendid and convenient theatre. The ponderous dome has been wholly removed, and replaced by a light and elegant ceiling. The stage has been brought forward several feet, and finished in the best manner, for the purposes of the drama. A pit has been erected, which for space and elegance has never been equalled in any theatre on the continent, while the lobbies and boxes have received the most essential improvement. A large and convenient new door has been opened on Ninth street, by which the audience of the pit may leave the theatre without meeting the other part of the audience, and avoid the delay formerly experienced. The pit lobby now occupies all the space of the former pit of the Olympic theatre, and offers much promise of room and convenience to visitors.

"A survey of the theatre has been taken, the result of which will be seen in the following certificate:

"The subscribers having viewed and examined the improvements made in the Olympic theatre, by Messrs. Warren and Wood, are decidedly of the opinion, that it is firmly and substantially secured in a workmanlike manner, and calculated to sustain amply the weight and pressure of an overflowing house.

William Strickland, Architect
Philip Tustin
Joseph Randall
Alexander Hampton

Philadelphia, November 7th, 1820."

As has been stated, the Chesnut Street Theatre company was not successful in the new house and was overjoyed when the New Chestnut Street Theatre was ready for occupancy in 1822.

In 1828 the management of the Walnut Street Theatre was assumed by Joe Cowell, who proceeded to renovate the structure completely. His comments follow:

27:3   In consequence of the extraordinary success which had attended the temporary alteration of the Walnut-street Circus, the proprietors were easily persuaded to convert it into a permanent theatre. A lease on my own terms was granted for ten years. To my experience was left the general detail of the improvements, and the celebrated John Haviland was chosen as the architect, and the present Walnut-street Theatre was erected withinside the walls of the old building. Scarcely had the note of preparation been sounded, when an *entirely-new theatre* was proposed to be built in Arch-street by some property-holders in that neighbourhood. Building theatres was supposed to be an excellent investment of capital at that time, and a good excuse for the elderly, sedate, Quaker-bred gentlemen to take a peep at a play, or a look at what was going on behind the scenes in the character of a stockholder.

It had already been proved past a doubt to my mind and poor Warren's pocket, that Philadelphia would not or could not

27:3. Joe Cowell, *Thirty Years Passed among the Players in England and America*. 2 vols. (New York: Harper & Bros., 1844), 2:83.

support more than one establishment of the sort; and *the one* the public would most probably select, in despite of my popularity, would most likely be the *new one,* and I began to tremble for the consequences. While I was wavering as to the course I should pursue, through the instrumentality of my friend Hamblin I received an offer from the proprietors of the Tremont Theatre at Boston to undertake its direction for forty weeks, for the sum of four thousand five hundred dollars, which, after duly weighing all the consequences, prudence, and the persuasion of my friends, induced me to accept. And that I did *I have most heartily regretted ever since.* . . .

One other writing of interest concerning the Walnut Street Theatre is that of Francis Courtney Wemyss, who details his career in his book *Twenty-six Years in the Life of an Actor and Manager.* Wemyss took over the management of the theater in 1834.

27:4   My first business after my arrival at Pittsburgh, was to dispatch my artist, W. Russel Smith, (a name since well known in the annals of fame,) to Philadelphia, to decorate the interior of the theatre. And well did he execute that work. The design was formed thus: each tier of boxes was decorated with paintings representing some celebrated battle in the history of the United States; around the dress circle were placed medallions of the heads of the Presidents; around the second tier, the heads of the celebrated generals, and around the third tier, the heads of the naval heroes; between each medallion and its corresponding painting, was a large burnished gold star, the whole forming on a pink ground, the most pleasing interior I ever saw. I have seen them more gaudy, but never one so chaste and beautiful. . . .

27:4. Francis Courtney Wemyss, *Twenty-six Years in the Life of an Actor and Manager* (New York: Burgess, Stringer & Co., 1847), pp. 234–35.

28. NEW WASHINGTON THEATRE
Washington, D.C.
Opened August 8, 1821

The third theater to be opened in Washington in a twenty-one year period had its debut on August 8, 1821. The other Washington Theatre had been rebuilt and reopened as the Washington City Assembly Rooms.

The new house was quite small, seating only seven hundred people, and was hardly the splendid playhouse one would expect to find in the capital city of a great nation. Certainly New York, Philadelphia, and Boston could all boast of better theaters, but it must be remembered that the population of Washington was still quite small at this time and could not support even one playhouse for a long season of plays.

Professor Mudd writes a brief description of the theater:

28:1   A new Theatre was erected on Louisiana Avenue, between Four-and-one-half and Sixth Streets, and was completed about August 1, 1821. It was not large, but was more commodious than the former Theatre and was fitted up in better style. The building was arranged to hold about 700 persons and the acoustic properties were good. Liquor was excluded from the box lobbies and smoking absolutely prohibited in all parts of the building. Separate boxes were provided for colored people. The new Theatre was also called "Washington Theatre," and opened Wednesday, August 8, 1821, under the management of Messrs. Warren and Wood, with the Philadelphia and Baltimore Company, after an absence of two years. They received a very cordial welcome. . . .

Joe Cowell, who was an actor and manager in America for a number of years, mentioned playing at this theater in 1828.

28:1. A. J. Mudd, "Early Theatre in Washington City," *Columbia Historical Society Records* 5:77–78 (1902).

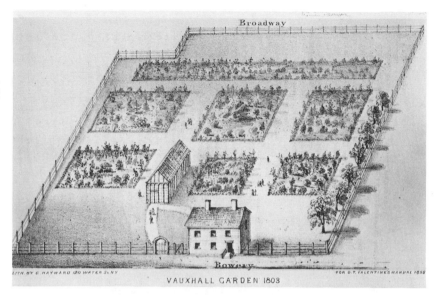

26. Vauxhall Garden, New York, 1803. Lithograph, for D. T. Valentine, *Manual of the Corporation of the City of New York* (1856). Courtesy of the Museum of the City of New York.

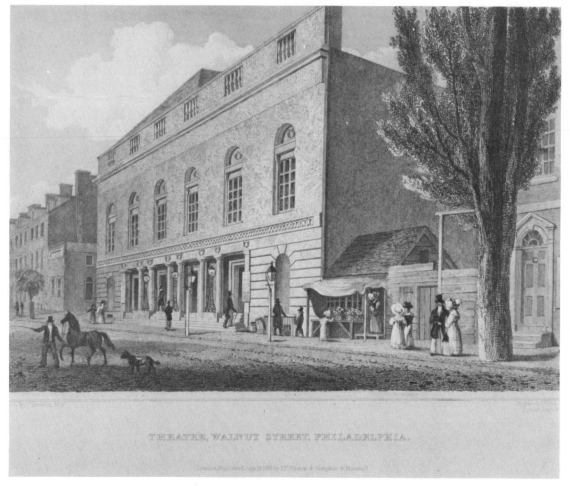

27. Walnut Street Theatre, Philadelphia. Engraving, after a drawing by C. Burton; published by I. T. Hinton & Simpkin & Marshall (London, 1831). Courtesy of the Cooper-Hewitt Museum of Decorative Arts and Design, Smithsonian Institution.

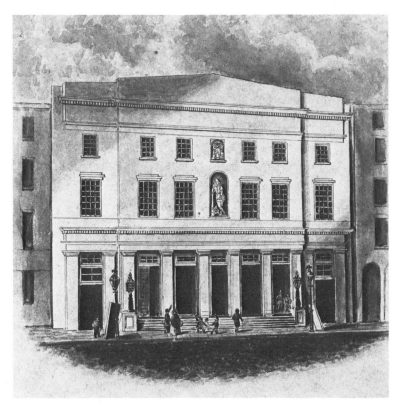

29. New Park Theatre, New York. Watercolor by A. J. Davis. Courtesy of the J. Clarence Davies Collection, Museum of the City of New York.

Interior of the Park Theatre, One of the Early Playhouses Downtown.

29. Interior, New Park Theatre, New York. Watercolor by John Searles, 1822, in the collection of The New-York Historical Society, New York City. Courtesy of The Hoblitzelle Theatre Arts Library, The Humanities Research Center, The University of Texas at Austin.

28:2   Washington City could then only boast of a very small theatre, in a very out-of-the-way situation, and used by Warren and Wood as a sort of summer retreat for their company; where the disciples of Isaac Walton, with old Jefferson at their head, might indulge their fishing propensities, without having them interfered with by either rehearsal or study.

Now Miss [Clara] Fisher had so turned the heads of the public in Baltimore, that I thought it a safe experiment to try if she couldn't turn the heads of the government, then in session, and I hired the theatre for an optional number of nights. "There is nothing like getting up an excitement," Pelby used to say. I immediately set a swarm of carpenters at work to bang out the backs of the boxes and extend the seats into the lobbies, which, in all the theatres built since the awful loss of life by the Richmond fire, were ridiculously large in proportion to the space allotted to the audience. As the house had seldom or ever been full, small as it was, my preparing it to hold twice the number which had ever been tried to get in appeared somewhat extraordinary. Mashing down thin partitions, in an open space, plastered into a ceiling, is a most conspicuously dusty and noisy operation, and attracted, as I wished, numerous inquiries —the doors being all thrown open—and my people were instructed to say, that "the house wasn't half large enough to accommodate the crowds which would throng to see Clara Fisher." The plan succeeded to a nicety. Never had there been such a scramble for places before in the capital—I mean in the theatre. At the end of two days every seat was secured for the whole of her engagement.

On the afternoon of the first performance I got a note from John Quincy Adams, then the President, requiring a certain box for that evening, directed to

"Mr. Manager of the Theatre"; and I sent a reply, regretting that he couldn't have it. . . .

29. NEW PARK THEATRE
New York City
Opened September 1, 1821

The old Park Theatre remained the favorite theater with New York audiences for well over two decades, until it was destroyed by fire on May 24, 1820. The company was kept intact by moving operations temporarily to the Anthony Street Theatre until a new Park could be built on the same site as the former playhouse.

The setting was not very impressive to young Joe Cowell, who arrived in New York City from England on October 23, 1821, to act in the playhouse beginning on October 31. In his memoirs he writes of his impressions of the theater on his first day in the city.

29:1   I salied up Wall-street and through Broadway. The pavement was horrible, and the sidewalks, partly brick and partly flagstones, of all shapes, put together as nearly as their untrimmed forms would permit. The Park, which Scovill had spoken of with enthusiasm, I found to be about the size of Portman Square, but of a shape defying any geometrical term to convey the form of it. It had been surrounded by a wooden, unpainted, rough fence, but a storm on the first of September, the power of which we had felt the full force of, twenty days after, on the Atlantic, had prostrated the larger portion, together with some fine old buttonwood-trees, which either nature or the good taste of the first settlers had planted there, and the little grass the cows and pigs allowed to remain was checkered o'er by the *short cuts* to the different streets in the neighborhood. The exterior of the theatre was the most prisonlike-looking place I had ever seen appropriated

28:2. Joe Cowell, *Thirty Years Passed among the Players in England and America.* 2 vols. (New York: Harper & Bros., 1844), 2:82.

29:1. Joe Cowell, *Thirty Years among the Players in England and America.* 2 vols. (New York: Harper & Bros., 1844), 2:56–57.

to such a purpose. It is not much better now; but then it was merely rough stone, but now it's rough cast, and can boast of a cornice. Observing the front doors open, I ventured in, and, opening one of the boxes, endeavoured to take a peep at the interior of the shrine at which I was either to be accepted or sacrificed; but, coming immediately out of the daylight, all was dark as Erebus. A large door at the back of the stage gave me a glimmer of that department, and groping my way through the lobby, I felt, at the extremity, a small opening, and proceeding, as I intended, very cautiously, tumbled down three or four steps, and was picked up at the bottom by some one in the dark, who led me on the stage.

"Have you hurt yourself?" said this immensely tall, rawboned fellow, with his shirt sleeves rolled up over an arm the same size from wrist to the shoulder.

"No," I replied, "but I wonder I didn't."

"Have you any business here?" said he.

"No, nothing particular," said I.

"Then you can go out," said he, and he pointed to the opening at the back.

I took the hint and direction, and found myself in an alley knee deep with filth the whole width of the theatre. I continued my walk up Broadway, and as I went the houses diminished both in size and number, and in less than a mile I was out in the country. On my return, the theatre doors were open, and the audience already assembling. Phillips, the singer, was the "star," and the performance, "Lionel and Clarrissa." The opera had not commenced, but I took a seat, with about twenty others, in the second tier. The house was excessively dark; oil, of course, then was used, in common Liverpool lamps, ten or twelve of which were placed in a large sheet-iron hoop, painted green, hanging from the ceiling in the centre, and one, half the size, on each side of the stage. The fronts of the boxes were decorated, if it could be so called, with one continuous American ensign, a

splendid subject, and very difficult to handle properly, but this was designed in the taste of the upholsterer, and executed without any taste at all; the seats were covered with green baize, and the back of the boxes with whitewash, and the iron columns which supported them covered with burnished gold! and looking as if they had no business there, but had made their escape from the Coburg. The audience came evidently to see the play, and be pleased, if they possibly could, with everything; the men, generally, wore their hats; at all events, they consulted only their own opinion and comfort in the matter; and the ladies, I observed, very sensibly all came in bonnets, but usually dispossessed themselves of them, and tied them, in large bunches, high up to the gold columns; and as there is nothing a woman can touch that she does not instinctively adorn, the varied colours of the ribands and materials of which they were made, were in my opinion a vast improvement to the unfurnished appearance of the house. . . .

The opening of the New Park Theatre was covered by a reporter for the New York *Evening Post*. In his review he gives a brief "history" of the New York theaters. It is interesting that in less than eighty years so much fiction had crept into the historical remembrances of the past, and much of what the reporter drew from is completely inaccurate.

29:2   In submitting the above view of the theatre to our friends, we cannot avoid offering our congratulations on the rebuilding and entire completion of this costly edifice, which opens THIS EVENING for the first time. While every latitude of opinion and freedom of thought may be allowed to those who are prejudiced against the Drama, it is the duty of the press to afford every countenance and support to an institution which forms an important feature in the arts and sci-

29:2. New York *Evening Post*, Sept. 2, 1821.

ences of the country, and which is considered, by many, the channel of a salutary amusement, and the indispensable appendage of a rich and refined city.

The Park Theatre was destroyed by fire on the morning of the 25th May, 1820, and for several months nothing was done towards rebuilding it. Messsrs. Astor and Beekman, the enterprising proprietors, though suffering a severe loss from the calamity, did not hesitate to embark once more in the costly experiment, confiding in the liberality and good taste of our citizens, for that protection and support which is anticipated from an enlightened community.

In rebuilding the Theatre no expense has been spared; every thing which could unite comfort, taste, and splendour has been liberally afforded; and the Theatre, for the first time, is completely finished in every department.

The history of the New-York Theatres is a brief one. The first which our oldest inhabitant remembers, was fitted up in a store of Cruger's wharf, near Old-slip, in which a company of Thespians performed very badly, if history tells truth. The company was composed of roystering young men, full of tricks and mischief; who used to gambol in the fields where St. Paul's church now stands, and who spent their nights at the boat house, in Broad near Wall-street, and amused themselves with snap dragons and hot cockles, during the winter evenings. The store was soon pulled down, and with it their stage and decorations. The first regular Theatre built in New-York, was about the year 1750, and was a stone-building in the rear of the Dutch Church in Nassau-street, near Maiden Lane. Old Hallam, the father of old Hallam, "if we may be allowed the expression," was the Manager. He had a tolerable good company, which he picked up in several towns in England, and who had courage to prepare themselves for a six month's voyage, and cross the Atlantic to amuse the promising city of New-York.

In this Theatre, the sterling English tragedies and comedies were performed. Hallam took his company to Jamaica and the Theatre was pulled down. About the year 1769, Phil Miller, well known to the town for a plodding, active, managing man, obtained permission of Governor Coldes, to build a Theatre and act plays, which he did in Beekman-street, a few doors below Nassau-street. This was a wooden building, in poor condition, with paper scenery, and a wretched wardrobe. The whole was destroyed by a mob created by the stamp act. Phil Miller lost his house and his company. He was a jocose fellow, and played Justice Guttle with great humour.

Hallam's company returned from Jamaica, reinforced by several performers of merit, among them was Henry. They built the Theatre in John-street, which was spacious and well arranged, and had an excellent company. This Theatre was destroyed by fire, and a company of gentlemen united in the purchase of a lot, and commenced the Park Theatre, upon which a considerable sum of money was expended; and, from embarrassments and mortgages, it was finally sold to Beekman and Astor, the present proprietors, and continues to this day in their possession.

It will be thus perceived, that in ratio with the increase of the city and population, the Theatres have likewise improved, and the present may be considered the most splendid, and, taken altogether, the first in the union.

The Theatre fronting the Park is *eighty* feet; *fifty-five* in height to the top of the cornice, and *one hundred and sixty-five* feet deep. Adjoining the side of the building in Theatre alley, is a substantial wing, containing the green room, dressing rooms, and other indispensable apartments, connected with the house; the whole neatly finished and fire proof. A very important improvement will be discerned in the lobbies and entrance. In the former Theatre, a small vestibule led to a flight of narrow and dangerous steps, opening in the lobby, and particularly inconvenient on a crowded night.—The entrance from the doors to the boxes is perfectly level; the doors, of which there are *five* to the boxes, *two* to the pit, and *one* to the gallery, all open *outward*. The vestibule, or ticket lobby, is nine feet wide, and *forty seven and a half* feet long. Here the company are perfectly sheltered from the weather, while tickets are procured from the office at each end. From this the audience enter the check doors to the corridor or box office, through a double colonnade of *fourteen* Ionic columns.—The stairs to the 2d, 3d, and 4th tier of boxes, lead from each end of this colonnade, and are *seven* feet wide, with mahogany rail and bannisters throughout. The lobby at the narrowest part is 147 feet wide. It will, therefore, at once be perceived, that the lobby is sufficiently spacious to contain the whole audience, which can, with great ease, leave the house through the vomitorias on the least alarm.

The saloon or coffee room is on the second floor, and fronts the street; it is 60 feet in length, 16 wide, and 17 in height, with large arched windows. The punch room is of similar dimensions, on the third story. The form of the interior is that of the *Lyre*, measuring at the stage boxes 52½ feet. The stage, at the drop curtain, is 38 feet wide and 70 deep from the front, and forty feet to the ceiling.

In each of the circles there are *fourteen* boxes, which are supported by *fifteen* small columns, 6 feet 6 inches in height. In the first tier they are of burnished gold; the upper pillars are bronzed with gold, caps and bases; these columns are conveniently situated, and recede 16 inches from the front, which gives a fair view of the audience, and prevents the sight being obstructed.

The decorations on the box fronts continue without division, and are in the Grecian style. The first circle is a balustrade, relieved on a crimson ground, similar to the cushions of the box seats. The pannels of the second tier or circle are painted in imitation of *Basso relieve* on a fawn colored ground; the figures of light stone color represent boys with wreaths of flowers, supporting medallions of dramatic poets. The centre group are Tragedy and Comedy. The third circle is the Greek doric cornice, with enrichments, which continues around the proscenium. The fourth tier, which is the front of the slips and galleries, is enriched with a double scroll ornament, interspersed with eagles, encircled with wreaths.

The ceiling is a flat surface, painted in imitation of a cone, open to the sky, and divided into eight pannels, enriched with emblems of the four elements, and eagles supporting trophies of war; a Greek fret and open balustrade crown the top of the sky.

The proscenium is composed of four doric columns without bases, 21½ feet high, painted in imitation of yellow marble, with white marble caps. They support the full entablature, with enrichments between the triglyphs, and which constitute the fronts of the third circle of boxes. From the cornice, over the columns, springs an eliptic vault of 53 feet, receding from the auditory 15 feet, terminating in front of an eliptic arch 15½ feet high. The vault or dome is divided into pannels of a fawn color, with light stone stiles. The stage doors which stand between two of the above mentioned columns, on each side, are enriched with eagles and dramatic devices. A crimson drapery over the arch of the cone, completes the decorations of the auditory; the uniform color of the house is fawn, with light stone color. Leading from the orchestra are two private boxes, with adjoining rooms appropriated for the proprietors.

The whole of the audience part of the house is lit with patent lamps. There are three chandeliers in the auditory, containing thirty-five lamps, which with those in front of the stage and the side lights to the wings make 203 lights, exclusive of the orchestra, lobbies, &c.

We have been thus particular in our description of the Theatre, that our readers abroad and at home, may have a perfect idea of the convenience and elegance of the building, and may do justice to the spirit of the proprietors, and the talent of those employed on the building. It is with pride we announce, that the persons engaged in the superintending the re-building of the Theatre, the Architect, Painters, Masons, and Carpenters, are *Americans* who never have been abroad or have seen a foreign Theatre. This is an additional evidence of the ability of our native artists.

The stage and machinery, which is admirably finished and much admired, was executed under the immediate direction of Mr. George Concklin, who had the entire charge and responsibility of that department. Mr. Hugh Reinagle, was the architect who finished the designs, and under whose inspection the house was erected and finished, commencing in January, and completed this day; and we venture to say with confidence that the reputation of Mr. Reinagle, will sustain no diminuition by this building; on the contrary, it will receive additional weight from public opinion and approbation. There is an entire new set of scenery, adapted to the various requirements of the Drama; the whole executed by *Mr. Reinagle* and *Mr. John Evers*, an artist of promise, and the assistants. The drop scene represents a rich damask crimson curtain drawn up by gold cords and tassels into festoons of drapery, a porch of mosaic workmanship, with a balustrade in the centre, and beyond the ballustrade is an equestrian statue of Washington; the back ground seen under the folds of the Curtain is a distant prospect of the characteristic scenery of the Hudson River. On each side of the scene, is an enriched vase on a pedestal partially obscured by the drapery thrown over them.

The mason work was under the direction of *Mr. Berwick*, whose activity and ability is justly commended. The construction of the audience part of the house, was under the direction of *Mr. Heath*, who selected all the materials, the beauty and sound finish of the workmanship, are proofs of his industry and ability, and of the attention and ability of his foreman, Mr. Cox.

The roof is shingled and covered with tin; the whole completely fire proof.

The front of the building is covered with the newly invented Reinagle & Berwick oil cement, in imitation of our brown free stone, and gives it a handsome and smooth finish.

The lamps, hangings, and glasses, are all American manufacture; and, after the iron railing is completed round the Park, the building will be an ornament to that street. The house will hold 2,600 persons, and is under the management of Messrs. Price and Simpson.

Thus, commences a new era in the dramatic annals of our city.

30. CHESTNUT STREET THEATRE
Philadelphia, Pennsylvania
Opened December 2, 1822

Philadelphia's "Old Drury" burned on April 2, 1820, about six weeks before the old Park Theatre was to be gutted by flames. The manager, William B. Wood, tells of his distress at being notified of the loss.

30:1   ... At this moment we were overtaken by a calamity, which once more threw all our plans into confusion and distress. Our Philadelphia season closing on the 29th of March, the company repaired to Baltimore for the usual Spring

30:1. William B. Wood, *Personal Recollections of the Stage* (Philadelphia: H. C. Baird, 1855), pp. 236–39.

term. We commenced cheerfully, on the 3d of April, with "Wild Oats" and "Ruffian Boy," notwithstanding a severe snow storm. On the succeeding morning I was awakened at an unusually early hour by a visit from our old property-man, Charley Ward, who will be remembered by all persons that visited the theatre any time within twenty years of the date I am speaking of. He presented, silently, a number of letters, which rather perplexed me, as I had so recently left home, where Mrs. Wood's illness now detained my family. The first I glanced at bore an extra superscription. It ran thus:

Philadelphia, April 3d, 1820

"Dear Wood:

This letter bears sad news for you. Early last evening, your beautiful theatre was wholly consumed by fire. Yours,

Richard Bache, Post Master."

Warren was apprised of our misfortune by letters from home, and hastened to meet me, that we might decide what course it was necessary to pursue. Altering the order of plays for a few nights, we hastened to Philadelphia, in time to witness the last wall topple to the ground, and the smoking ruins of our favorite house. The destruction was so complete that the green room mirror, a beautiful model of a ship, and the prompter's clock, were alone preserved. The expensive gas works shared the common fate. It is not generally known that the *stockholder's* property consisted of the walls alone. The scenery, lights, wardrobe, and other appointments having been purchased from them by the managers some years before. The loss was very great, as the property had been liberally augmented and improved through a long series of years. The most irretrievable part, was the splendid English scenery, presented to Wignell in 1793 by Richards, Hodges and Rooker, artists of the first reputation in their day. The wardrobe was of great extent, includ-

ing the whole of the dresses from Lord Barrymore's theatre, as well as those from a French establishment recently purchased. The library and music were of an extent and value unknown to any other American theatre. Two grand pianos, costing 100 guineas each, a noble organ, used in the "Castle Spectre," and other chapel scenes, and models of scenery and machinery, imported at a large cost, swelled the sum of our misfortune. The appointments of every kind were most ample and complete.

It has been a question whether we were prudent in accumulating so much property, and of so perilous a character. It is necessary to state, that until within a few months of the disaster we had been guarded by insurance to a considerable amount, but the frequency of fires, as well as alarms, rendered the offices reluctant to venture on the risk of theatres and certain dangerous manufactories; and while we were actively engaged in applications to different offices here and elsewhere, our policy expired. The stockholders were more fortunate, for their insurance fully covered their loss. I must add that notice had been given to them that the risk would be declined at the termination of the policy, which would have occurred a month after the date of the conflagration.

The destruction was by many imputed to the malice of an incendiary. This charge, however, is liable to much doubt, as being wholly unsupported by any probable evidence. Every possible inquiry and investigation failed to give to the greatest sufferers, the managers, the slightest reason to believe it any other than the result of accident. The corner of the building on Carpenter street, nearest to which the fire first appeared, had long been appropriated to the use of a fire company, and the latticed window of this apartment looked full upon the staircase of our theatre, which part of the building was first on fire. It is therefore more reasonable to believe that, during the frequent alarms of fire which occurred about this time, a spark might have fallen from the lanterns or torches usually hung upon this latticed window, and smouldered for some time. The house was so easily accessible on every other side of the building, that an incendiary would scarcely have hazarded discovery by using for his purpose a place visited almost hourly by some one of the fire companies. It is remarkable that the occupants of the refectory, immediately adjoining the engine house, were annoyed the whole day by a strong smell of fire, without any one thinking to look in upon the theatre. The season had closed on the previous Thursday, and no person had entered it after Friday.

No immediate plans were made to rebuild the theater, so the managers, Warren and Wood, made arrangements to lease the Walnut Street Theatre. After redecorating that playhouse they played there for two seasons; however, these seasons were not successful financially. In the meanwhile, plans were made to rebuild "Old Drury." Wood, in his memoirs, does little to describe the new house.

30:2 Much attention had been bestowed on the safety as well as the comforts of the audience, by large doors of exit and entrance to the boxes. A convenient and handsome entrance had been provided to the pit from Sixth street, thus preventing the confusion of too many auditors meeting at the Chestnut street doors; the gallery entrance was from the rear of the house, on Carpenter street. This excellent arrangement, however, proved unsatisfactory to a portion of the public. On the second week we were surprised to learn that serious objections had been made to the pit entrance, but we were unable to learn on what the objection was founded. . . .

30:2. William B. Wood, *Personal Recollections of the Stage* (Philadelphia: H. C. Baird, 1855), p. 290.

The best description of the New Chestnut Street Theatre is probably the one furnished by Charles Durang, who was intimately acquainted with the theater.

30:3 The first Chestnut street theatre, destroyed by fire in April, 1820, was rebuilt in 1822. The stock was divided in shares of six hundred dollars. Messrs. Warren and Wood were the lessees, and the house was erected after the plans of William Strickland, Esq., architect. The opening bill was as follows:

NEW THEATRE
(A vignette wood cut of the front elevation of the building)
"The theatre will open for the season on MONDAY EVENING, December 2d, 1822, with
AN OCCASIONAL ADDRESS
Written by Charles Sprague, Esq., of Boston, and to be spoken by Mr. Wood.
After which Mr. Sheridan's celebrated comedy of the
SCHOOL FOR SCANDAL

Sir Peter Teazle . . . . Mr. Warren.
Sir Oliver Surface . . . . Mr. Francis.
Charles Surface . . . . Mr. Wood.
Joseph Surface . . . . Mr. H. Wallack.
Sir Ben Backbite . . . . Mr. Johnson.
Crabtree . . . . Mr. Jefferson.
Rowley . . . . Mr. Hathwell.
Moses . . . . Mr. Burke.
Careless (With a song) . . . . Mr. Darley.
Trip . . . . Mr. J. Jefferson.
Snake . . . . Mr. Greene.
Servant to Joseph . . . . . . Mr. Scrivener.
Servants to Sir Peter . . . . . .
                    Messrs. Parker and Murray.
Lady Teazle . . . . Mrs. Wood
Lady Sneerwell . . . . Mrs. Lefolle.

30:3. Charles Durang, "The Philadelphia Stage. From the Year 1749 to the Year 1855." University of Pennsylvania Library, Philadelphia. Excerpt from chap. 75.

Mrs. Candour .... Mrs. Francis.
Maria .... Mrs. H. Wallack.
Maid .... Mrs. Greene.

The whole of the Scenery and Drop Curtain entirely new designed by Mr. H. Warren and executed by him, Messrs. R. Anders, J. Jefferson, and J. Darley. To which will be added the popular and interesting

drama of the

WANDERING BOYS or,

THE CASTLE OF OLIVAL

Conat de Croissy ..... Mr. H. Wallack.
Paul   The Wandering .... Mrs. Darley.
Justin   Boys   ... Mrs. H. Wallack.
Hubert .... Mr. Burke.
Roland .... Mr. Darley.
Gregoire .... Mr. Hathwell.
Labin .... Mr. Jefferson.
Gaspard .... Mr. Scrivener.
Sentinel .... Mr. J. Jefferson.
The Baroness .... Mrs. Jefferson.
Mercelline .... Mrs. Francis.
Louise .... Miss Hathwell.

"On Wednesday the tragedy of "Damon and Pythias, or, The Test of Friendship," with other entertainments.

"The managers respectfully announce that Mr. Cooper is engaged for a number of nights during the season.

"Mrs. Entwhistle and Mr. Wilson (from the Charleston Theatre) are also engaged for the season.

"Lord Byron's historical play of the "Two Foscari"; Colman's new musical drama of the "Law of Java"; "The Two Pages of Frederick the Great"; M. G. Lewis' melo-drama of "The Wood Daemons"; Shakespere's tragedy of "Julius Caesar"; will undoubtedly be revived, and various other new pieces will be immediately produced. N.B. The box sheet will be opened on Saturday. Places in the boxes may be taken of Mr. Johnson, at the box office, from 10 until 1; and on days of performance from 10 until 4 o'clock.

"Checks not transferable. Proper officers are appointed who will rigidly enforce decorum.

"The doors will be opened at a quarter past 5, and the curtain will rise at a quarter past six precisely. Box, one dollar; Pit, 75 cents; Gallery, 50 cents. Children under 12 years, half price. Thirty-five seats in the orchestra, for sale nightly, at box price."

On the back of the first night's bill was printed the following description from the pen of the architect:

"The managers of the new theatre have the pleasure to inform the public that the house will open for the season on Monday evening, December 2d. They feel much satisfaction in being able to state that the arrangement and distribution of their new building is such as will afford strength, safety and convenience to the audience upon which so much depends in the establishment of a new era in the drama of this enlightened city.

"That the public may feel satisfied of the fixed determination of the managers to pay every attention to the decorum of the house, they avail themselves of this early opportunity of giving the following description of the building together with their rules of order:

"The approach to the boxes is from Chestnut street, through a close arcade of five entrances, opening into a vestibule fifty-eight feet long, by eighty feet in width, communicating at each end with the box office and a withdrawing ladies' room. From the vestibule are screen doors, immediately opposite, and corresponding with the openings of the arcade, leading into spacious lobbies, warmed with fireproof furnaces, and calculated to contain upwards of one thousand persons. Double flight of stairways communicate with a spacious saloon and coffee rooms, together with the lobbies of the second and third floors. The audience part of the house is described upon a semi-circle of forty-six feet in diameter, containing three rows of boxes, resting upon cast-iron columns, and secured with iron sockets from the foundation to the dome. The whole being combined, internally, with a strong wall bounding the lobbies and supporting the roof. The dress circle of the boxes is formed by a seat in advance of the columns, covered with a splendid canopy projecting in front of the second row of boxes, in the style of Covent Garden Theatre, London.

"The peculiar form given to this part of the house places the mass of the audience within thirty-five feet of the stage, securing to them the important objects of distinct sound and perfect scenic view —an advantage which the best theatres of Europe do not possess, although they may exceed it in magnitude.

"The dome is forty-six feet in diameter, rising six feet to the crown, which is perforated, and formed into a ventilator, from which is suspended an elegant chandelier, nine feet in diameter, containing sixty patent lamps enriched with appropriate ornaments.

"The effect produced by this concentration of light will be great, inasmuch as the whole of the audience part of the house can be brilliantly illuminating without resorting to the detached lamps which have been in common use, and which is destructive to finish decoration.

"The proscenium is forty-six feet by twenty-five feet—an opening well calculated to exhibit the best exhibitions of the drama. The tympanum, over the center of the stage, is chastely decorated with an appropriate design, exhibiting the claims of Thalia and Melpomene to the genius of Shakespere, over which is seen the motto, "To raise the genius and to mend the heart."

"There are two doors of entrance to the pit from Sixth street, through a passage fourteen feet in width, which passage enters a lobby paved with brick, communicating with a bar-room, and private stairway leading into the box office on the west side of the building. The pit floor is laid on a solid inclined plane of brick and mortar and will accommodate four hundred persons. The orchestra will contain from forty to fifty persons, independent of the musicians, and is to be approached from the box office by a private stairway. The gallery has its entrance from Carpenter street through a passage situated on the outside of the building, leading to a lobby and a bar-room, and will contain two or three hundred persons. It may be here proper to observe that the whole building will contain upwards of two thousand persons, and that the doorways are numerous and wide, opening outwards into the surrounding streets. The principal front is on Chestnut street, being ninety-two feet by one hundred fifty, built of marble, in the Italian style; the leading features of which are an arcade, supporting a screen of composite columns, and a plain entablature, flanked by two wings, and decorated with niches and basso relievos, representing the tragic and comic masks, with the attributes of Apollo.

"The greatest attention will be paid to the decorum of the theatre, and special officers of police appointed, especially engaged for the preservation of order, and every violation of propriety will be referred immediately to the magistracy, without the least respect to persons.

"In obedience to the suggestion of several friends of the drama, children under twelve years of age will be admitted to the boxes, pit and gallery at half price. A part of the orchestra is appropriated to the use of the audience, for which tickets may be had in the morning at the box office. No smoking can be permitted except in the coffee-room of the third row.

Warren and Wood"

The New Chestnut Street Theatre was in use until May 1, 1855, when the last performance was given and the theater demolished.

31. CHATHAM GARDEN THEATRE
New York City
Opened May 17, 1824

Chatham Garden was originally opened in 1822 by Henry Barriere and quickly became the favorite summer theater in New York City. So popular was the Garden that Barriere decided to erect a permanent playhouse, which was opened on May 17, 1824.

The New York *Evening Post* carried the following advertisement:

31:1 NEW THEATRE————CHATHAM GARDEN

The public is respectfully informed, that the elegant THEATRE, in Chatham Garden, will be open on THIS Evening, May the 17th. The Proprietor begs leave to inform his friends and the public, that he has used his best endeavors to procure such a company of Performers as, he hopes, will meet the wishes, and secure the approbation of the generous and enlightened citizens of New York. During the season, every novelty within the reach of his power, will be brought forward, and neither labour nor expense will be spared to render the entertainments worthy of public patronage.

THE PRIZE ADDRESS

To be spoken by Mrs. Entwhistle.
On Monday evening, May 17th,
will be presented,
Cherry's admired Comedy of
SOLDIER'S DAUGHTER

Governor Heartall,	Mr. Kilner
(his first appearance here these three years)	
Frank Heartall,	Barrett
(his first appearance here these two years)	
Malfort Senior,	Allen

31:1. New York *Evening Post*, May 17, 1824.

Malfort Junior,	Moreland
(his first appearance here these two years)	
Ferret,	Stone
Simon,	Sommerville
Timothy Quaint,	Simpson
William,	Byers
George, (his first appearance here)	Collins
Widow Cheerly	Mrs. Entwhistle
(her first appearance here these two years)	
Mrs. Malfort	Durang
Julia,	Miss Oliff
Mrs. Fidget,	Mrs. Kilner
Susan,	Allen

End of the play, the

ORIGINAL EPILOGUE
To be spoken by Mrs. Entwhistle.
To conclude with the laughable
farce of
RAISING THE WIND.

"Doors open at half past 6; performance to commence at half past 7 o'clock.

"Admittance to the Boxes, 50 cents; to the Pit, 25 cents. Children under twelve years of age, with their parents or guardians, to the boxes, half price.

"Seats may be secured on application at the Box Office, during the day."

A description of the building is found in the New York *Mirror* of May 15, 1824.

31:2 This new and tastefully-embellished edifice was not opened on Monday evening, as we prematurely announced in the last MIRROR, several of the party not having arrived. It will, however, positively be opened on Monday evening next, with the favorite comedy of the "*Soldier's Daughter*"; previous to which the Prize-Medal Address will be spoken by Mrs. Entwhistle. In the meantime we present our readers with the following brief description of the house:

Chatham Garden Theatre is an oblong, square building, extending westward over

31:2. New York *Mirror*, May 15, 1824.

30. New Chestnut Street Theatre, Philadelphia. Engraving, after a drawing by R. Goodacre, 1831. Courtesy of the Cooper-Hewitt Museum of Decorative Arts and Design, Smithsonian Institution.

THEATRES AND HALLS OF AMERICA.

No. 11.—Interior of the Reconstructed Chestnut-street Theatre, Philadelphia, Pa.

30. Interior, New Chestnut Street Theatre, Philadelphia. Engraving. Courtesy of the Free Library of Philadelphia.

INTERIOR OF THE CHATHAM THEATRE, NEW YORK 1825.

FROM AN ORIGINAL DRAWING BY A.J.DAVIS.

31. Interior, Chatham Garden Theatre, New York, 1825. Lithograph, from a drawing by A. J. Davis. Courtesy of the Museum of the City of New York.

several adjacent lots, and presenting to the Garden an eastern front of sixty-five feet.

The *entrance* to the Theatre is through the Hall of the dwelling-house, in Chatham-street, the same as last year. On entering the Garden, which has been much improved, you proceed onward to the fountain, which throws up a refreshing column of pure water, directly in front of the folding-doors of the Theatre. Passing through these doors, you ascend, by a double flight of stairs, (to the right and left,) to the lobby of the first circle of boxes.

On gaining the interior of the house, you find it comprising two circles of boxes, and a pit, capable of containing thirteen hundred persons; four hundred of whom may be comfortably seated in the pit. The area of the auditory is a semi-circle of forty-five feet span, from one side of the stage to the other, and thirty-one feet deep, from the centre box to the stage.

The opening of the stage, at the drop-scene, is thirty-two feet in width, and twenty feet nine inches in height; the scenery is twenty-three feet wide, by sixteen and a half feet high, being very little less than that of the Park Theatre. The depth of the stage is not quite forty feet.

There are twelve boxes in each circle, which will contain nine hundred persons. These boxes are supported by columns, painted in imitation of a pale green-and-white marble; caps and bases of gold.— The fronts of the boxes, and the *proscenium*, are of one uniform character, (as is the ceiling), and painted with a delicate fawn colour, of two shades, slightly varying from each other, with pannels of a pale sky-blue. The *proscenium*, and front boxes, are highly enriched with fine *basso relievo* ornaments, of figures and trophies, of pure classical designs, done in France, of the finest models from the antique.

On each side of the stage, in front of the *proscenium*, is a superb alabaster vase, from Italy, of the most exquisite workmanship, and the largest we have ever seen, being over five feet in height; they stand on pedestals of green marble, with brown marble plinths. Just above these vases, and over the stage-doors, are four fine *alto relievo* busts, (by a French artist in this city,) of Washington, Jefferson, Franklin, and Jackson, encircled with wreaths of relief gold, with golden figures of Fame on each side.

Above the cornice, which divides the *proscenium* into two stories, corresponding with the height of the two circles of boxes, are painted niches, with statues of Shakspeare and Garrick. In the sides of the *proscenium*, parallel with the boxes, are the private boxes, (directly over the stage doors,) decorated with crimson curtains. On each side of the stage is a splendid chandelier; and over the centre of the pit three large chandeliers are suspended from a *triangle*, which is decorated with a light gauze drapery.

The boxes project about six inches, and are raised on a frieze, decorated with projecting ornaments in relief gold; beneath which, around each circle, is a neat crimson drapery, high enough to be no obstruction to the sight from the back seats. The whole of the interior of the boxes is lined with crimson cloth, the seats covered with green. The cushions on the front of the boxes are crimson, with brass nails and fringe.

The ceiling over the pit is arched, with a ventilator of nine feet diameter in the centre, leading to the cupola, from which descends the triangle which supports the three superb chandeliers before-mentioned.

Every attention has been paid to render the house as cool and pleasant as possible, during the summer season. For this purpose, openings are left all around the ceilings of the lower and upper boxes, and the partitions at the back of the boxes are likewise left open, so that a person can witness the performances without taking a seat within. A moveable green blind is placed in each box-door, and at the back of the centre boxes in the circle, which can be closed or left open at pleasure. The ceilings of the upper boxes are very lofty, which gives an air of elegance to this part of the house, which we have never seen in any other theatre. It is lighted with a number of glass lanterns, suspended from the ceiling, and the view of the stage is equally as good as from the first circle.

One of the most agreeable arrangements for the comfort of the audience, is a spacious balcony, extending the whole front of the theatre, (projecting near to the temple of the *Naiades*,) and overlooking the whole garden. This delightful retreat is entered through doors from the lobby of the first circle; and here the fresh air can be enjoyed, freighted with the perfume of the garden, and cooled by the playing of the fountain. Here, also, every refreshment can be procured from the bars, which are in both the lobbies; and here the sentiments of friendship may be interchanged, or any topic discussed, without molestations or interruption.

The pit has a greater elevation than usual, so that there is no part in which the auditors can be situated where they will intercept the view of each other. For the greater facility of discharging the audience from the boxes, there are flights of stairs at each extremity of the first lobby. The pit has two large passages, and in the spaces on each side are elegant bars, richly stocked with every species of refreshment.

The garden has been extended to Augustus-street, with a gate-way, to be opened at the close of the performance. As the building stands insulated from all others, there is a free circulation of air on all sides.

The interior of the Theatre, as well as the scenery, has been designed by Mr. Hugh Reinagle; mortar-builder and mechanist, Mr. George Conklin, whose ingenuity in the mechanism of this stage, is as conspicuous as it is in that of the Park Theatre, the stage and machinery of which were under the sole direction of

Mr. C. when Mr. Reinagle re-built that house for Messrs. Beekman and Astor.

32. LAFAYETTE THEATRE
New York City
Opened July 4, 1825

The Lafayette Theatre opened on July 4, 1825, as the Lafayette Amphitheatre, presenting circuses, equestrian dramas, and ballets. The theater was located on the west side of Laurens Street. After two years of operating as a circus it was completely renovated and opened as a theater on September 19, 1827, with a company of actors headed by Henry Wallack.

An account of the redecoration and renovation is given by Ireland in his *Records of the New York Stage.*

32:1   THE LAFAYETTE THEATRE was entirely rebuilt this season, by Mr. (C.W.) Sanford, from the plans of Mr. Grain, and on its completion was acknowledged to be the largest and most splendid theatre in the Union. The front was of Eastern white granite, presenting a novel and beautiful appearance, and the interior was decorated in a style equally chaste and elegant. The boxes were supported by bronze columns, with Ionic capitals carved and gilded, and a superb dome— the latter attracting universal admiration for the beauty and harmony of the proportions. The stage was one hundred and twenty feet deep, and, in part, one hundred feet wide, being larger than any then existing in England or America. It was considered a vast improvement that it was lighted from above, and that the stage machinery was also managed from the same elevated position. . . .

The New-York *Mirror and Ladies' Literary Gazette* described the new theater in detail. The picture of the playhouse alluded

32:1. Joseph N. Ireland, *Records of the New York Stage.* 2 vols. (New York: T. J. Morrell, 1866–67), 1:578–79.

to in the first paragraph is the one reproduced in the present volume.

32:2 We present to our readers a front view of the LaFayette Theatre, engraved expressly for this paper by Mr. Eddy, from a drawing by Mr. Davis.

This building, the largest and most splendid ever erected for theatrical purposes in the United States, is located in a section of the city which has sprung into existence, and arrived at maturity, in so short a period as to astonish even those who were daily witnessing its progress, but which, to the occasional visitor, could scarcely be realized.

It is located in Laurens-street, about 100 feet north of Canal-street, and extends in depth, from Laurens to Thompson-street, about 200 feet. The front, of which the plate is a correct representation, is built of Eastern white granite, and presents one of the most beautiful exteriors in the city. The lobbies are spacious, and thoroughly ventilated by twelve windows in each tier, seven on the south and five on the north side of the building, which, in addition to the advantage they will give this house in the summer season, are peculiarly neat in their appearance. The interior is the most elegant in the country, and is decorated in a style equally chaste and splendid. The boxes are supported by bronze columns, surmounted by Ionic capitals beautifully carved and gilt, and the elevation of each tier is sufficient to give auditors upon the rear seats as full a view of the stage and proscenium as those upon the front benches. A ventilator is placed over the door of each box, which answers the purpose better than if inserted in the box doors, which we find by experience to be a great annoyance to those who sit near them. The saloons, which are very elegant, and admirably arranged, upon the level of the lobbies, are kept in a very

32:2. New-York *Mirror and Ladies' Literary Gazette,* Oct. 6, 1827.

superior style by Mr. Stevenson, late of Chatham Garden, whose activity and gentlemanly manners are well calculated for this department.

The elegance and beauty of the dome attract the immediate attention of the spactator. A superb gas chandelier is suspended from the centre, directly under the ventilator, shedding a light over the whole audience, like the splendour of the midday sun. The proprietor has judiciously dispensed with the gallery. The proportion of the house and the dome are therefore preserved, and the gallery audience, which is proverbially the most unruly and noisy, is excluded. The proscenium is in admirable proportion, and finished by an arch thrown from the entablature, to the front of the dome, so as to form a sounding board; and notwithstanding the great size of the house, we observe that the performers are distinctly heard throughout it.

The fronts of the boxes are embellished in a style wholly new, designed by Mr. P. Grain. The figures in each pannel are cut in relief, shaded and gilt, and project about four inches from the ground work, which is green. The pannel is surrounded by a richly carved and gilded moulding, and the whole is classically beautiful, and surpasses any thing of the kind that we have ever seen.

The stage, with its scenery and machinery, exceed all former attempts in this country. It is one hundred and twenty feet deep, and in some places one hundred feet wide, being greater than any known in the United States or Great Britain. The machinery is managed above the scenes, and the stage lights are also placed above. This is the greatest improvement of the whole. The light is more natural, and imparts an unequalled brilliancy to the productions of the artist. It also strips the stage from the lamp ladders which prevented the wings from being opened beyond a certain width, so that now the width of the stage presented to the audience may be increased at pleasure. The effect of this arrangement is strikingly exemplified in the splendid procession scene of the Bride of Abydos, which presents a spectacle far more imposing than we have ever witnessed. . . .

33. FIRST BOWERY THEATRE
New York City
Opened October 23, 1826

The opening of the Bowery Theatre signified a new era in New York theatrical history, for the Bowery was to have a very long history (although several different buildings were to house the theater). It was a theater that would furnish entertainment for the masses, unlike the Park Theatre, which catered to the tastes of a higher class of clientele with its presentation of the finest works in drama.

Certainly there was a need for another theater, since New York had grown to a population of nearly 125,000. The new playhouse was planned as early as 1823. Soon after it was opened, Joe Cowell, the theatrical manager, wrote:

33:1   . . . The yellow fever gave so broad a hint as to the necessity of buildings better prepared in the upper sections of the city, that New-York increased in that direction with a rapidity that was truly astonishing. A very superior theatre was erected on the site of the old Bull's Head Tavern in the Bowery; a short time before considered out of town, and used as the cattle mart. The control was placed in the hands of Charles Gilfert, a highly-accomplished German, whose chief ambition was to manage a theatre on an extensive scale, and be considered *more knave than fool*," in both of which desires he was fully gratified; for the establishment given to him to conduct infinitely exceeded in its extent and appointments any-

thing then on the continent, and everybody agreed he was a consummate rogue. Thoughtless, extravagant, and unprincipaled as to the means used to obtain on the instant his real or imaginary wants in his private station, he carried with him the same reckless spirit to control the fortunes of others. Large inducements were held out to the various members of the profession to join the concern, and an excellent, but very costly, company was engaged; and though the overflowing houses attracted by the newness, and, perhaps, superiority of the entertainments, were ruinous to the Park, the expenditure quite equalled the receipts. Barrett was the stage-manager; and though at that time not distinguished by the title "Gentleman George," he was as deserving then of the appellation as now. But if one had been selected which would have more clearly conveyed the idea of an inconsiderately liberal, kind-hearted man, it would better have described his intrinsic character. As an actor in smart, impudent servants, eccentric parts, bordering on caricature, and light comedy, where the claims to the gentleman do not exceed those required for Corinthian Tom, he is excellent. He has attempted to perform some old men lately; in consequence, I suppose of his whiskers getting gray; but, if he'll take my advice, he'd better dye them, and stick to his old line of business; six feet four is too tall to fit the common run of elderly gentlemen nowadays. . . .

Joseph N. Ireland told of the Bowery Theatre and its background.

33:2   The vast improvements made in the eastern section of the city, and its great increase of population, including many wealthy and fashionable citizens who located their residences in the Seventh, Tenth and Fourteenth Wards, (since, in their turn, deserted for more westerly

33:1. Joe Cowell, *Thirty Years Passed among the Players in England and America*. 2 vols. (New York: Harper & Bros., 1844), 2:72-73.

33:2. Joseph N. Ireland, *Records of the New York Stage*. 2 vols. (New York: T. J. Morrell, 1866–67), 1:521–22.

situations) induced the formation of a company for the purpose of erecting a theatre in the Bowery, on the site of the old Tavern and Cattle Market, known as the Bull's Head, then belonging to George Astor. Messrs. Gouverneur, Graham, James A. Hamilton, George W. Brown, P. M. Wetmore, T. L. Smith and Gilfert, were the projectors of this enterprise, and in process of time a very elegant structure was completed, having externally the similitude of white marble, with a spacious portico and lofty columns supporting an entablature and pediment. The size, both of the stage and auditorium, was greater than any theatre in the country, the latter being able to seat about three thousand persons, and in point of decoration it was unsurpassed. It was fondly hoped by its proprietors that it would prove to be the favored dramatic temple of New York, and that all other city theatres would sink subordinate in comparison, and consequently, though popularly known as the Bull's Head Theatre, it was determined to give it the more comprehensive title of THE NEW YORK THEATRE, Bowery; a name which it retained until it came into the hands of Hackett and Hamblin, who designated it simply THE BOWERY THEATRE; though the latter, in a fit of naturalized patriotism on the occasion of the Anderson riot at the Park, in 1831, proclaimed a change, and announced it as the AMERICAN THEATRE, by which its bills were headed for a year or two, after which its present title was resumed.

The management of the NEW YORK THEATRE, which hereafter, for convenience, we shall simply call "The Bowery," was intrusted to Mr. Charles Gilfert, and his experience as a manager and skill as a musician, aided by the undoubted taste of his accomplished wife, were deemed sufficient guarantees of his fitness for the post.

Mr. George Barrett was engaged as stage-manager, Mr. Taylor from the Park,

as leader of the orchestra, and Messrs. Coyle and Serra, very meritorious artists, as scene-painters. The prices of admission were at first fixed at fifty cents for the boxes and pit, and twenty-five cents for the gallery, but a few nights' experience proved that to keep a portion of the house free from admixture with the vulgar and unrefined, it would be necessary to discriminate between the box and the pit, and the admission was raised to seventy-five cents for the former, and reduced to thirty-seven and a half for the latter, which soon produced the desired effect. . . .

The Theatre was first opened to the public on Monday evening, October 23rd, 1826, and the brilliant experiment of lighting the stage with gas, then first attempted, was hailed with the greatest satisfaction by an audience which crowded the building in every part. . . .

The critic of the New York *Mirror* had a rather short review for such an auspicious event.

33:3 A most crowded audience attended the opening of the New-York Theatre on Monday evening. The house is difficult to describe, but we shall attempt it in our next. To say the building, inside and outside, right side and left side, is splendid is saying no more than what everybody acknowledges, and no more than what all the editors have already told their readers. Every term has been exhausted in its praise, and every tongue has spoken of its magnificence. A Frenchman would declare, "it was *grand*—it was *magnific*—it was *very well*," and these words would sum up *his* descriptions as they would do ours for the present. . . .

The *Mirror* had promised a description in the next edition, but such was not forthcoming because of the indisposition of the drama critic.

On May 26, 1828, the Bowery Theatre was completely destroyed in a fire, the great

33:3. New York *Mirror*, Oct. 28, 1826.

nemesis of so many theaters in the eighteenth and nineteenth centuries in America. The New York *Mirror* commented on the disaster:

33:4   The particulars of the destructive conflagration which destroyed, on Monday evening last, this elegant and costly fabric, must already have been made known to our readers. We understand that arrangements are in a state of great forwardness for erecting another and still more beautiful edifice, on the site now occupied by smouldering and blackened ruins, and that it is intended to construct it with an Aladdin-like rapidity, greater even than that which excited the astonishment and admiration of the public, when the other sprung, as the poets of antiquity say that Minerva did, at once into a full grown and beautiful existence. It has been ascertained that the loss incurred by the owners and lessees is not great, as the edifice, and the greater part of the *properties*, were insured to the amount of their value; and, as this insurance was divided among a number of offices, the evil will be much less severely felt than might have been expected.

Had there been a copious supply of water at hand, the extent of this lamentable devastation might easily have been restricted to much narrower limits, and the noble fabric of which we are speaking would not now lie a mass of black and smoking ruins. This is a subject on which we have often expressed our sentiments and wishes; and we cannot avoid embracing the present occasion of again adverting to it, and calling upon the corporation to do what they may in emulation of Philadelphia, which, in this respect, bears away the palm from every city in the United States, while she is surpassed by none in the old world.

It is very much to be desired, also, that the proprietors of the lots in that vicinity, may erect uniform and handsome houses of durable materials, to supply the place

33.4. New York *Mirror*, May 31, 1828.

of the miserable rookeries which this conflagration has transmuted to ashes.

34. NIBLO'S GARDEN THEATRE
New York City
Opened July 4, 1827

Niblo's Garden Theatre was to have a long and much respected history, for it served the public with entertainment of high quality for nearly seventy years. Like many other theaters of the day, it had its beginning as a summer theater in a lovely garden setting. So popular did it become with the people of New York City, however, that the playhouse became a year-round theater and continued until 1895 as a theatrical institution.

34:1   In early years, say 1800, a circus and training ground for race horses, called the Stadium, was established on the northeast corner of Broadway and Prince Street. The site was a portion of the old Bayard farm, and was purchased by S. Van Rensaelaer for $15,000. Shortly after the war of 1812 the inclosure was used as a drill ground for militia officers. Early in 1823 the Columbian Gardens, devoted to summer night entertainments, occupied the site, and many singers, dancers, and specialists of that day appeared there. William Niblo took a lease of it, and resolved to convert it into an ornamental garden for the public. Large trees were transplanted from distant woods; choice flowers and plants mingled with rarest exotics; fountains gushed and threw their spray into the sunbeams. In the centre of this garden a neat temple was erected and dedicated to music. The entertainments given consisted of instrumental music and a display of fireworks each evening. On July 4, 1827, the Sans Souci Theatre came into existence on this spot, the manager and proprietor being Mr. Gilfert, and the opening performance

34:1. T. Allston Brown, *A History of the New York Stage from the First Performance in 1732 to 1901.* 3 vols. (New York: Dodd, 1903), 1:175–77.

LAFAYETTE THEATRE,

LAURENS ST. NEAR CANAL ST. N.YORK.

ENGRAVED BY JAMES EDDY, FROM THE PLAN AND DESIGN OF PETER GRAIN.

FOR THE NEW-YORK MIRROR,

AND LADIES' LITERARY GAZETTE.

1827.

32. Lafayette Theatre, New York, 1827. Engraving by James Eddy, from the plan and design of Peter Grain; for the *New-York Mirror and Ladies' Literary Gazette* (1827). Courtesy of the Cooper-Hewitt Museum of Decorative Arts and Design, Smithsonian Institution.

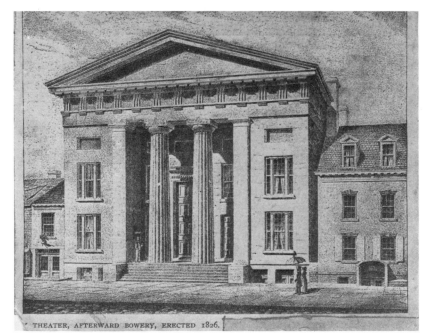

THEATER, AFTERWARD BOWERY, ERECTED 1826.

33. American Theatre, Bowery (First Bowery Theatre), New York. Courtesy of The Hoblitzelle Theatre Arts Library, The Humanities Research Center, The University of Texas at Austin.

34. Niblo's Garden Theatre, New York. Etching by S. Hollyer, 1827. Courtesy of the Museum of the City of New York.

consisting of "The Hundred Pound Note."
The Bowery Theatre burning down, Mr.
Niblo commenced the erection of a theatre, and in fifteen days from the time the
foundation was laid a commanding and
handsome theatre was actually completed
—comprising a spacious stage, a parquet,
and two circles of boxes, capable of holding 1,200 persons. In the dramatic company were W. B. Chapman, Anderson,
Stone, Geo. Barrett, and Mrs. Jone; Herr
Cline the tight-rope dancer also appeared.
Mr. and Mrs. Blake acted in the opera
"Rosina" on Aug. 6. The season terminated on August 19, 1827. George Holland appeared in "Whims of a Comedy."

The following is a copy of one of the
programmes of the day:

THEATRE SANS SOUCI

LAST NIGHT   GREAT ATTRACTION

"Mr. Walton, Howard, Chapman, Mrs.
Lacombe, Mrs. Blake, Mons. Mathis, Herr
Cline, and the Parisian dancers. Tuesday
evening, August 19, 1828, will be presented the opera of "Rosina." This is
probably the only opportunity which will
ever occur of presenting this popular and
admired opera, with decidedly the strongest cast ever offered in America:

Captain Belville . . . . Jas. Howard
Mr. Belvil . . . . Thomas Walton
William . . . . W. B. Chapman
Irishman . . . . Allen
Rosina . . . . Mrs. Lacombe
Phoebe . . . . Mrs. W. R. Blake

"Song by Mr. Walters, after which
Mons. Mathis will, for the first time, as-
tonish the audience by the surprising and
peculiar feats of strength and agility, and
now, for the first time in New York, give
his imitations of the celebrated Sans
Sama. He will also appear as the French
Hercules and perform his wonderful feats.
Celebrated Indian War Dance by Mr.
Schinotti; song, Mr. Howard; Herr Cline
on the elastic cord; duet by Howard and
Walton; the Parisian Dancers, Mons. Bar-

biere, Mme. Labasse, and Mlle. Rosalie,
who will appear in Trojan Pas de Trois;
the whole to conclude with Mons. Mathis
in the comic scene "The Cobbler upon
Stilts Five Feet High." Prices of admission: Boxes, 50 cts.; pit, 25 cts. The entrance to the theatre is by the north gate
on Broadway."

On May 18, 1829, the "Sans Souci"
was converted into a free concert saloon,
and opened with a music festival. Mr.
Niblo soon erected a larger and more
perfect theatre which he called Niblo's
Garden. The stage was 75 ft. wide, 67 ft.
deep, and 44 ft. high.

A programme of Niblo's in 1830 shows
that the price of admission had been
slightly increased. A ticket admitting a
gentleman and lady sold for $1, but single
tickets cost 75 cents. Mr. William Mitchell
opened here June 3, 1834, with a large
and talented company. Among the productions was "The Revolt of the Harem,"
with Mmes. Dejardin and Vallee, Miss
Partington, Korpony, Mons. Marten, and
Mr. Wells in the principal roles. Mitchell
was not successful. . . .

35. TREMONT STREET THEATRE
Boston, Massachusetts
Opened September 24, 1827

A quarrel within the ranks of the Federal
Street Theatre company in Boston led to the
formation of a new playhouse, the Tremont
Street Theatre. Supposedly, one of the actors,
William Pelby, demanded a much larger salary,
and Henry J. Finn, the actor-manager of the
old Federal Street Theatre, declared that he
was unable to meet his demands. This was
probably true, since the old playhouse was
failing financially at that time. Pelby used this
rebuke as an excuse to start a new theater
company, an act that proved disastrous to the
old playhouse. The Tremont Street Theatre
opened on September 24, 1827, triggering a
rivalry with the Federal Street Theatre that
ended two years later with the closing of the
old house.

The historian of the Boston stage, W. W. Clapp, writes of the beginnings of the new playhouse and its founding.

35:1   A site of land was the next step to be taken. It was proposed to buy the Washington Garden property, and erect there a first class theatrical temple, and some of the stockholders of the theatre in Federal street were disposed to sell the whole of their property, but the land in Tremont (then Common) street was finally agreed upon and purchased. It had been previously used for Gragg & Brigham's livery stables. The foundation walls were laid in May. There was some trouble in naming the theatre. It was proposed at first to call it the "Franklin," the "Columbia," etc. etc.; but in June, the trustees agreed that the edifice should be designated the TREMONT THEATER, and the application made to the legislature for an act of incorporation was made in the name of the "Stockholders of the Tremont Theatre."

As a matter of record, we give below the act of incorporation. Only two of the gentlemen, who petitioned for it, survive:—

Commonwealth of Massachusetts,
A. D. 1827.
AN ACT
TO INCORPORATE THE PROPRIETORS OF
THE TREMONT THEATRE.
"Sec. 1. *Be it enacted by the Senate and House of Representatives, in General Court assembled, and by the authority of the same,* That Thomas H. Perkins, Edward D. Clark, Charles F. Kupfer, Thomas Brewer, John Redman, and Oliver Mills, and all such persons as are or may be associated with them, for the purpose of erecting and keeping a theatre in Boston, and their successors, be, and they are hereby made a Corporation, by the name of the Proprietors of the Tre-

mont Theatre; and by that name they may sue and be sued, have a Common Seal, and have and enjoy all the powers and privileges, and be subject to all the duties incident to Corporations; and they shall have power to make, and at their pleasure to alter, such by-laws, for the management and regulation of their corporate property and concerns, as to them may appear expedient; *provided,* the same be not repugnant to the Constitution or Laws of this Commonwealth.

"Sec. 2. *Be it further enacted,* That said Corporation be authorized to purchase, take and hold, the land on which said Proprietors are now erecting a Theatre on Common street, in the city of Boston; and such other real and personal estate as may be the necessary and proper appendages of a Theatre, and manage and direct the operations of the same as a corporate body; *provided,* the whole real estate shall not exceed one hundred thousand dollars, and the personal estate shall not exceed fifty thousand dollars.

"Sec. 3. *Be it further enacted,* That the said corporate property shall be divided into shares of equal value, and no transfer of a share shall be valid, until such transfer be recorded by the Clerk of the Corporation; and such shares may be attached on mesne process, and taken and sold on execution according to law.

"Sec. 4. *Be it further enacted,* That any one or more persons named in the first section of this act, be authorized to call the first meeting of said Proprietors, for the purpose of organizing the Corporation, to be holden at such time and place as he or they shall appoint, by giving ten days notice thereof in an advertisement, to be published in one or more of the Boston newspapers.

"Sec. 5. *Be it further enacted,* That this act may be altered, amended, or repealed, at the discretion of the Legislature.

[Approved by the Governor,
June 16th, 1827.]"

35:1. William W. Clapp, Jr., *A Record of the Boston Stage* (Boston and Cambridge: James Munroe & Co., 1853), pp. 250–53.

On the fourth of July, the same year, (1827,) the corner-stone was laid. It is at the north corner, fronting on Tremont street. No ceremony of any note took place. A few remarks were made by the chairman of the building committee. A box containing copies of the newspapers of the day, English and American coins, and a copy of the act of incorporation, was securely soldered by Edward D. Clark, Esq., the well known auctioneer, and placed beneath. Inside of the box was the following record engraved on a silver plate:—

COMMONWEALTH OF MASSACHUSETTS.

"On the fourth day of July, in the year of our Lord one thousand eight hundred and twenty-seven, and the Independence of the United States of America, the fifty second, this inscription was deposited by the Proprietors of the Tremont Theatre, in token of laying the *Corner Stone*.

Treasurer—W. H. Gardiner.

Secretary—Washington P. Gragg.

Building Committee—Edward H. Robbins, Jr., Oliver Mills, John Redman, Solomon Towne, James Page, James McAllaster, Charles F. Kupfer, Edward D. Clark, Alpheus Cary.

Architect—Isaiah Rogers.

Lessee—William Pelby.

President of the United States—John Quincy Adams.

Governor of Massachusetts—Levi Lincoln.

Mayor of the City of Boston—Josiah Quincy."

There is a slight change between the list first given of the first building committee and the last, which was made during the process of erection.

The theatre was erected in a very short time. Its heavy granite front at that time was the admiration of the people, and the papers of the day recorded its progress with pride. Mr. Pelby offered, early as May, 1827, a premium of *one hundred dollars* in money or plate to the author of the best poem, of not less than fifty or more than seventy lines, to be recited at the opening of the theatre, and a committee was appointed to award the prize.

The proprietors and managers of the old theatre were determined, however, not to allow the rival house an easy conquest, and Mr. Finn was despatched to England for recruits, and the interior of the theatre was thoroughly renovated. The excitement produced by this state of things was very great, equalling almost that which now precedes a local election. Many—and especially the older portion of the community—adhered to the "Old Drury." It was there that they had first beheld Hodgkinson, Fennel, Cooke, Cooper, and others, and their associations with the house were of too pleasant a nature to be broken off for any trivial cause, and their affections too permanently located to be won by any new beauty. There were others who were equally partial to the new house—they had either been instrumental in its erection, or were attracted by the novelty of the project; and, consequently, as the time approached for the opening of both houses, there was some little boasting about the relative merits of the two companies engaged, Finn, having arrived from England with strong reinforcements *per Coral* and *Brookline*, and Pelby, having scoured the American market, offering large salaries for any available talent.

The Federal Street commenced the campaign on the 17th of September, 1827, with the "Rivals" and the "Young Widow." The company consisted of several recruits from England.

Mr. Thomas Flynn, from the respectable provincial theatres and the Haymarket, was engaged as principal tragedian. Poor Tom died a few years since, poor as poverty. His career was a remarkable one, and his tomb-stone should bear the inscription, "He was his own worst enemy." Tom Walton, from the Theatre Royal, York, England, came out as principal singer. Mr. Geo. Andrews, who married Miss Woodward from the Liverpool "boards," as low comedian, Mr. King from Drury Lane, and Miss Rivers as leading actors. Miss Rock came out as a star. Mr. and Mrs. Bernard, (formerly Miss Tilden,) and Mrs. C. Young, were important additions from other theatres in the country. . . .

The playhouse was much too small ever to have a great financial success, and in 1843 was sold to the Baptist Church, the last performance being on June 23, 1843.

The following account of the preview opening of the Tremont Theatre appeared in *The Traveller*:

35:2 *Tremont Theatre.*—This new and splendid Temple of the Muses was lighted up on Wednesday evening, for the first time. The effect was brilliant beyond description. Only three scenes were displayed, and the manner in which they were changed was so rapid and skilful as to appear more the effect of magic than of human agency. These were—a palace scene, occupying with its twelve wings the entire stage, and rendered splendid throughout by its oriental beauty and magnificence—a Gothic scene, representing at once all the architectural grandeur of an ancient cathedral—and the drop scene, which for classic design and elaborate execution, has certainly never been surpassed by any similar effort in this part of the country. It represents the ruins of the Colisseum, at Rome; and some idea of the imposing character of the painting may be formed, when it is recollected that this famous amphitheatre, commenced by Vespasian and finished by Domitian, gave constant employment during the reign of those princes, to more than twelve thousand Jews; and when completed, is said to have been capable of containing eighty-seven thousand spectators seated, or one hundred thousand

35:2. *The Traveller*, Sept. 21, 1827.

standing! The representation, like the architecture of this stupendous theatre, which was perfectly light, is so just in its proportions, as to appear much smaller than it really is. The effect of this scene, as well as the others, would be much heightened, we think, if they were displayed by a light less brilliant, than that which, as it were, completely illumined the house on Wednesday night. However, the reader will soon have an opportunity of judging of this matter for himself.

As present appearances indicate a general wish to witness the opening performances; and as probably no small portion of those desirous of obtaining seats for the first night will be unable to attend them; the manager has determined to repeat the Prize Poem, and all other performances, without variation, on Tuesday evening. We mention this now more particularly for the information of persons at a distance, as we have seen it stated in the Providence papers, and otherwise heard it mentioned, that many from Providence, Salem, and other towns, were contemplating a visit to our city at the opening of the new house.

Since writing the above we have been favoured with the following description of the decorations of the interior of the establishment; and gave it as we received it, though a part was contained in an article in our last.

The Boxes—The fronts are painted of a delicate blue color, ornamented with groupes of figures (in basso-relievo) in compartments painted by Mr. Hubard, and splendid, burnished gold mouldings. The seats are handsomely cushioned, and from the second and third tiers of boxes are suspended elegant cut glass Chandeliers, from gold brackets.

The Proscenium—In the centre near the ceiling is a bust of Shakspeare, with the emblems of the comic and tragic muse; and on either side two female figures with wreaths, cornucopias, &c. &c. The Cove of the proscenium is in pannel work. Immediately below is a representation of Apollo drawn in a Chariot, attended by the muses, &c. painted by Mr. Hubard; below is a splendid cornice of the Ionic order with gilt cubical plinths; crimson and gold drapery completes this part of the proscenium.

The Ceiling—Is painted in compartments of light straw color, representing a dome, with gold wreaths, mouldings and rosetts—by Mr. Hardy.

The Pit—Is cushioned and every other seat furnished with a back.

The Scenery—Which is entirely new and has been several months in active preparation, was designed by Mr. H. Isherwood, principal Artist of the establishment, and executed by him, Messrs. Hardy, Reinagle and Edgar. The whole is said to have cost more than ten thousand dollars.

The new Act Drop was painted by Mr. H. Isherwood and designed by Isherwood and Edgar.

36. SECOND BOWERY THEATRE
New York City
Opened August 28, 1828

The first Bowery Theatre was gutted by flames on May 26, 1828. The fire occurred about 6:30 in the evening, when it was discovered that the stables next door to the theater were on fire. No lives were lost, but the playhouse and its contents were a complete loss.

36:1 . . . The building was insured for $60,000, but the scenery, wardrobe, and properties were only partly covered. When the fire broke out the players were all in their rooms dressing for the drama of "The Gambler's Fate," for the benefit of Mrs. Gilfert, but happily no lives were lost. Charles Gilfert had the ground cleared in twenty-four hours after the fire

was extinguished, and in the remarkable short space of ninety days from the date of the destruction of the old house the doors of the new one were opened to the public. The new building was very beautiful and commodious. The front was made of stucco, made to resemble marble, and had six columns to support the roof, the entire front being of Doric architecture. The curtain, instead of rolling up, divided in the centre, and was drawn up into festoons. During the rebuilding Gilfert dispatched agents to Europe for artistes of every description, and to him belongs the credit of bringing to this country the first good theatrical orchestra. . . .

The drama critic for the New-York *Mirror and Ladies' Literary Gazette* described the building in great detail.

36:2 THE NEW BOWERY THEATRE
The rapid growth and improvement of New-York, the celerity with which immense structures are reared, and in many instances the architectural beauty of their formations and ornaments, are subjects of surprise and admiration to strangers, and reflect great credit on the enterprise and taste of our citizens. But in no single instance has any work been effected among us, which, in all respects, so justly authorises pride and self-gratulation, as the one of which a view is given in the plate which accompanies the present number of this paper. The ashes of the conflagration which destroyed, with numerous other buildings, one of the fairest and most stately edifices of our city, had scarce become cool, before another, surpassing the first in size and solidity, in the splendour of its internal decorations, and the architectural grandeur of the exterior, sprung from the smouldering ruins, astonishing all beholders by the rapidity of its growth, and charming them with the beauty of its proportions. In a shorter

36:1. Joseph N. Ireland, *Records of the New York Stage*. 2 vols. (New York: T. J. Morrell, 1866–67), 2:104.

36:2. New-York *Mirror and Ladies' Literary Gazette,* Aug. 23, 1828.

time than it takes the flower to unfold itself from the stem that winter has left bare and withered, did this magnificent fabric arise, under the plastic care of the architect and artist, preventing us only by its massive fixedness from looking upon it as the creation of enchantment. Yet, though every thing has been accomplished with unprecedented quickness, nothing seems to have been slighted; and notwithstanding the bustle and apparent disorder necessarily incident to the consummation of such a gigantic undertaking, the result clearly shows that it has been "regular confusion,"

"A mighty maze—
but not without a plan."

In a former number of the Mirror we gave our readers an account of the destruction of the New-York Theatre, Bowery; since which time, and in the incredibly short period of sixty-five working days, Mr. Gear, the contractor and builder, has completed the structure. To the skill, assiduity and enterprise of this gentleman, who singly undertook the erection of this edifice, an exalted degree of credit is due. To Mr. Sera, the architect, who designed the whole, and to whose tasteful pencil all the rich decorations of the interior are to be ascribed, too much praise cannot be accorded.

The architecture of the new theatre is at once simple and elegant. There is no confusion of ornaments, no blending of styles, no discordance of proportions; but, while the separate parts are beautiful in themselves, the *tout ensemble* delights the spectator with its Doric simplicity and grandeur. It is too often the case that the eye of taste is offended, in this city, with abortive attempts in the science of building, where the projectors display the absurdity of their notions, by a strange mixture of orders and a ludicrous assemblage of incongruous ornaments, till they deserve the comment of Apelles, when a picture of Venus, gorgeously attired, was ostentatiously exhibited before him, by an

unskilful painter: "Friends," said the favourite of Alexander, "if thou has not succeeded in making the goddess fair, at least thou has made her *very fine*." Of the Bowery Theatre, however, the very reverse is true, and a forcible exemplification is afforded of the fact, that the rudest materials, by having a harmonious disposition and combination, are susceptible of being wrought into forms of the most impressive beauty; as, in music, by an artful arrangement and succession of the simplest sounds, the soul may be moved with pleasure of the most thrilling nature.

The front of the building is covered with a newly invented stucco, (of extraordinary durability,) in excellent imitation of marble. It is of the Grecian Doric order, comprehended in one large portico, shown in a colonnade of six detached Doric columns supporting an entablature and pediment. The porch is sustained by a flight of seven marble steps, which are protected at either end by a large abutment. These abutments are each divided into two compartments, by the Pit and Gallery entrances, which pass through them, descending from the street by a flight of marble steps to the paved basement floor. The different compartments of the abutments, four in number, are surrounded by as many large Grecian candelabras, eight feet high, of an antique form, and elegantly executed in iron. Immediately behind the candelabras runs a light iron railing, enclosing the abutments, and extending thence across the extreme ends of the platform of the porch to the actual front. The width of the portico is fourteen feet. There are five large doors, with a corresponding window over each, opening into the saloon. Twelve of these doors communicate with the audience part of the house, and are so constructed that they open either inward or outward, thus adding greatly to convenience, besides diminishing the danger to be apprehended from a fire occurring within the edifice. Indeed, the means of escape in the event of such an unfortunate contingency, are so numerous and obvious, that no reasonable ground for fear arises on this score. The exterior of the building is entirely fireproof, not an inch of wood-work being exposed in any part. The three doors of entrance open from the front into a spacious vestibule, brilliantly lighted with gas, and terminating at the ends in two offices, which occupy the two remaining doors of the front. The one of the right is the ticket-office; the other the private office of the managers. The admission from the vestibule to the corridors is by three Venetian doors, corresponding in size and situation with the three front entrance doors, and each surmounted with a fan-light window. These doors allow a free circulation of air, and add greatly to comfort during the warm season of the year. In winter closed doors are to be substituted.

The corridor is traversed, from end to end, by a richly sculptured Grecian Doric cornice, supported by two detached columns and two pilasters of the same order. On the right and left hand a spacious and beautifully finished flight of stairs, inclosed by an open mahogany balustrade, ascends to the lobby of the second row of boxes, and thence to the third. Brilliant gas burners illuminate the landing-place of the staircase, and are interspersed at proper intervals, throughout the corridor. The lobbies are rendered cool and airy by windows opening into them, on either side of the edifice, which are protected, as are all the windows and doors of the house, by massive iron shuttery.

The entrance to the saloons is from the centre of the second lobby. It is a commodious and well arranged apartment, richly furnished and ornamented, the furniture being of blue, to correspond with the ground of the boxes, and the ornaments, also, in the same style as those of the interior, which we shall presently describe. Two rooms close the extremities, the one being a retiring-room, and the other the coffee-room. The whole suite is sumptuously lighted with glass lamps of an antique fashion.

On entering the box-circle, the spectator is dazzled with the blaze of light that suddenly bursts upon him; and it is some time before he can ascertain the particulars of the commingled splendour and beauty which the hand of liberality and taste has spread here with unsparing luxuriance. As soon, however, as his mind can trace the general effect to its several causes, his attention becomes fixed upon the dome as the most inviting object of beauty. This rises, with a graceful curve, from a circle corresponding with the sweep of the boxes, and in shape is a concave semi-spheroid, very triflingly oblate, the lower part, or edge, overhanging the gallery, as the gallery overhangs the row of boxes beneath it, and, extending on the opposite side, to the proscenium. The dome is divided into four pannels, in which appropriate emblematic figures are richly and beautifully executed in gold, and boldly relieved on a ground of light blue. On the dividing spaces between the pannels are painted four intertwined vines, terminating at the bottom with as many wreaths of flowers, supported on golden arrows. A broad, rich Grecian border surrounds the lower part of the dome, beneath the pannels; and garlands of flowers, on golden ribbands, are wreathed around the circles formed by the ventilators. The centre figure of the dome represents a female in the act of scattering flowers over the audience, and furnishes an apt illustration of the line, in the second prize-poem,

"The drama comes to strew her choicest flowers."

The ground of the triangular sections, between the circle of the dome and the proscenium, is a beautiful pink, on which are displayed tasteful ornaments in Arabesque, painted to imitate figures sculptured from marble.

The back wall of the boxes forms a segment of about two thirds of a circle; but the front, with a convenient deviation from the awkward regularity of such a figure, recedes from the stage in a curve, so as to form somewhat of an irregular conchoid, or, to compare it with a familiar object, so as to resemble a horseshoe, considerably flattened at the centre. By this means the spectators in the side-boxes have the advantage of sitting almost facing the stage; and scenic exhibitions will consequently be witnessed by them with more pleasure than they otherwise could experience. The ground of the boxes, like that of the dome, is a light blue, edged with a narrow border of white, and surmounted in elegant and imposing contrast, by the crimson cushions of the fronts. The ornaments, which are extremely rich and massive in their appearance, are of embossed gold. Those of the front row represent the griffin; of the second, two eagles, supporting a wreath; the third, a harp; and the fourth, a beautiful wreath—all in Arabesque. The boxes project one seat over the columns, the under part of which projection is so curved as to form a segment of about one fourth of a circle, supported by richly carved and gilded Corinthian leaves. The columns represent each an entire shaft of white marble surmounted by a golden capital.—From the base of the dress-circle to the pit, the front is painted in imitation of *Griole d'Italie*.

The proscenium is likewise a splendid effort of genius. It is painted in imitation of Parian marble. The sides are slightly curved and have been constructed with an especial view to the assistance of sound. The stage-doors are ornamented with two cornelian columns of the Ionic order, supporting a richly sculptured architrave. Gilded balconies are thrown across the stage-windows, which open into private boxes, small and tasteful in the extreme. The whole is surmounted by medallions, on one side—of Thalia; and on the other—of Melpomene, with appropriate emblematic devices. The under side of the arch of the proscenium is edged with a rich border of gold, in Ara-

besque; and in the centre is the head of Apollo, with golden rays diverging in every direction. On the front, in the centre, directly opposite the audience, is a finely executed bust of Shakspeare, and on the right and left are figures of Fame in an attitude of extending a wreath to crown him.

The drop-curtain is entirely done away with in this theatre, having been superseded by a splendid drapery-curtain, as rich as it is novel. The plan has very recently been introduced in one of the principal theatres of Paris, and the committee which superintended the erection of this establishment deserves great praise for the liberal and enterprising spirit that prompted the adoption of this expensive and tasteful alteration, before the change had been instituted not only in any other theatre in this country, but in England. Frequenters of dramatic entertainments must have noticed the disagreeable effect frequently produced by the falling of the drop-curtain, particularly when it descends to slow and solemn music, cutting off, in its downward progress, first the tops of the scenes, then the heads of the performers, and then gradually closing the view of the spectator in a most unnatural and ludicrous manner. . . .

Before the opening of the new theater the architect, Mr. Sera, published a letter that he had sent to the Committee of the New York Theatre Association and that, in turn, elicited a published reply.

36:3   NEW YORK, August 20, 1828

Gentlemen—The new Bowery Theatre being completed, I avail myself of this early occasion to express to you my sincere and grateful thanks for the confidence you have reposed in me, and the unmerited kindness with which you have supervised my labours, and advanced my views. Seldom has such a stupendous edifice been erected without any thing occur-

36:3. New York *Evening Post*, Aug. 21, 1826.

ring to mar the harmony of those concerned; but in the present instance, the most perfect harmony has prevailed between all the departments, thus greatly facilitating operations, as well as augmenting the satisfaction of all concerned. Of Mr. Greer, in particular, I feel myself urged to speak in terms of sincerest admiration; we met as strangers; yet, notwithstanding the hurry, perplexity and fatigue necessarily incident to carrying into execution the vast design of this fabric, which he has consummated in one incredibly short period of time, his conduct has been uniformly urbane and gentlemanly, never opposing useless objects to my wishes, but on the contrary, accelerating my program by every means in his power.—Of his talent and skill there can be no need for my feeble eulogy, while the proud monument of ability and enterprise which he has erected remains; and his sentiments and manners as a gentleman are likewise well known to you—but of these I could not forbear to speak.

With the warmest wishes for your prosperity, I have the honor to be, very respectfully, your obedient servant,

Joseph Sera.

To the Committee of the New York Theatre Association.

NEW-YORK, Aug. 20, 1828.

The Committee of the New York Association, appointed to superintend the erection of the Bowery Theatre, have received the communication addressed to them by Mr. Sera, and it affords them much pleasure to reciprocate his expressions of satisfaction at the successful and gratifying termination of their labours.

The Committee feel it their duty to state their entire satisfaction with the zealous attention and skillful ability evinced by Mr. Sera in the discharge of his arduous duties; and they are confident they but express the sentiments of all who have viewed the building, in awarding to them the highest degree of praise for the tasteful and beautiful exhibition of his designs.

The Committee cheerfully join with Mr. Sera in the expressions of their admiration of the talents, judgement, and energy displayed by Mr. Geer in the execution of the edifice in a style of workmanship, and with a celerity unexampled in this, and it is believed unsurpassed in any country.

It is by no means the smallest source of gratification enjoyed by the Committee, that the extensive arrangements connected with the building, have progressed with uninterrupted harmony and perfect good feeling.

To Mr. J. Sera, Architect and Artist, New York.

37. ARCH STREET THEATRE
Philadelphia, Pennsylvania
Opened October 1, 1828

The already overcrowded theatrical scene in Philadelphia saw another major addition in 1828 with the opening of the Arch Street Theatre under the management of William B. Wood, one of the former managers of the Chestnut Street Theatre. As he states in his memoirs, Mr. Wood entered the management of the new house with great reluctance and with the idea that the Walnut Street Theatre, which had been doing poor business, was to be demolished. This did not prove to be the case, and Wood soon found himself in a literal struggle for survival in the new theater.

37:1   The next principal feature of this amateur management (for there were many minor changes) were arrangements of a very extensive character for fashionable performers from England. The starring system was about, in effect, though not professedly, to be tried in contrast with

37:1. William B. Wood, *Personal Recollections of the Stage* (Philadelphia: H. C. Baird, 1855), pp. 346–51.

the former stock arrangements, of which "Tom and Jerry" had been a not inappropriate finale, as a prelude to this new scheme. A considerable number of our own performers were discharged—not from any suggestion of either incompetency or decline, nor from any want of good conduct anywhere, but from the enormous expense which it was said the promised succession of new English performers had involved. These strange proceedings I am sure were not suggested by Warren; who, on the contrary, hardly knew how to announce them to his old friends. My own salary—that is, the promise of it—was largely increased, and its amount fixed at the large sum formerly received by Mrs. Merry. I saw pretty clearly, however, I thought, that bankruptcy would be the end of these fantastic measures—for in a theatre any violent and sudden change may be called fantastic—and that although I might for a short time receive nominally more than I had expected, yet that in the end I should probably be paid in a way known in the insolvent court as payment by a ticket. Standing in no position of confidence to the management, I was therefore silently looking at the prospect about, around and before me, and expecting either that the theatre itself would sooner or later disappear from under me—or that I might find it necessary to be disengaged from it, if it continued in name to exist—when I learned that a number of gentlemen, dissatisfied by what had already been done, and thinking that they saw a benefit to property about them, had entered upon the scheme of another theatre in Arch street. At this time every one supposed that the Walnut street house, never a good one for theatrical representations, was about to be demolished, and give way to private houses. The other project, therefore, went on. The stock was rapidly subscribed, and the edifice erected almost before Mr. Warren knew that it was certainly in progress. While debating on some other prospects, I received an in-

vitation from the stockholders of the new building to become the lessee. I had great hesitation in accepting the offer. The whole new enterprise was in a measure irregular, although if, as every one supposed, the Walnut street house was about to be torn down, a new theatre would be requisite. It had, too, somewhat the aspect of a schism from the Chestnut street theatre, though it was so less, perhaps, than was believed. Under any circumstances, I well know what it was to get a company of new performers into *drill* at short notice. Even good performers require to be familiar with one another before they can play easily and with proper correspondence. The growth of our old theatre had been, as a natural growth commonly is, *gradual*. It had therefore been sure. I knew as yet very imperfectly what company the Arch street theatre was likely to have; and I knew no more of the principal persons by whom the theatre was owned, and would of course in all great matters be controlled. Independent of this, I had, to a great extent, built the Chestnut street theatre. It was a beautiful, convenient and excellent house. I had up to that time many pleasant associations with it, and I felt somewhat as if I was abandoning my own offspring. However, being quite unable to control the new course of operations there—certain that they would not only ultimately, but would very soon, end in failure—uncertain how long, even if I desired to remain, I could find it possible to do so—and not being doubtful that my retirement would be willingly received whenever offered, I accepted the offer so politely made me from Arch street. Mrs. Wood not long before had of necessity ended her connection with the Chestnut street managers, where her services, though always acceptable, were neither rendered by her nor received by the direction as she could desire. *I entered therefore upon my new management from necessity*, and with feelings of reluctance and great doubt as to the issue. Still, as we were credibly informed that arrangements were in progress for pulling down the Walnut street house—a matter really resolved upon, though afterwards defeated or abandoned—and as it was certain that the Chestnut street theatre, under its new direction, was not likely to prove a formidable rival to us, the prospect was not entirely dark. We had had very numerous applications for engagements, and the prominent situations were filled by persons of good natural capacities. The important line of business formerly done by Warren was entrusted to an actor named Reese, of much ability. S. Chapman, who had quitted Warren from some dissatisfaction about salary, was appointed stage manager, and director of the pantomime and melo-dramatic departments, an office for which he had real ability. An inexperienced judge, however sagacious, would have said that we had in all respects a good theatrical community. But all, and even more than all, the disadvantages I had anticipated from a new and sudden theatrical enterprise were now about to be encountered. In the very outset I was doomed to feel the immense advantage of an old, settled and regulated establishment, as compared with one that was new and suddenly brought together. The actors had each their own ways. They had come irregularly from different places, where many of them had been superior to the persons about them. They were jealous of one another. They had been trained, so far as trained at all, in different schools of acting. Their internal jars, and dissensions were not proper subjects of my management, and if they had been, could not have been controlled by it. There was no unanimity among them. They were all "pulling different ways." Each desired to be *the feature*; and the course of stage business, instead of working smoothly, in correspondence and with ease, was irregular, disturbed and uncomfortable. Many of the performers, as I have intimated, had come from minor establishments, where the absence of system and discipline had bred habits of neglect and insubordination, which were so fixed as to render vain even a hope of reformation. By one of those casualties which happen in the oldest and best communities, but which in them is always provided for, and is capable of being relieved against—one of the principal actors was suddenly taken ill, after all the plans of the season had been fixed. This compelled us to a frequent change of casts, which were greatly injurious to the attractions which we could otherwise have presented. I had no confidence in Mr. S. Chapman's stability, and I knew that the advance of salary, for the want of which he had left Warren, would take him back again. There was nothing left to keep us going at all, but a resort to the starring system; a miserable resort, and one certain to end in the destruction of the drama. Annoyance arose from the frequent and almost incessant offers of advice and suggestions from persons interested in the edifice and property, but wholly ignorant of its business necessities. . . .

The management of Wood at the New Arch Street Theatre ended in disaster for the theater and the company. The theater was not to become a strong one until a number of years later under the management of Mrs. John Drew.

The *United States Gazette* carried the following on the new playhouse:

37:2 The following description of the [Arch Street Theatre] has been received, and may prove interesting to the lovers of the drama, and friends to the improvements of our city. Mr. Strickland, the architect, has contracted to complete it by the first of October, but from the great advancement of the building, and the number of persons employed, it is highly probable that it will be completed some time sooner, and opened by Mr. Wood, the manager, with a powerful establishment.

37:2. *United States Gazette,* June 10, 1828.

The dimensions of the Theatre now building in Arch street are 70 feet by 155 feet—The front, which is to be made of marble, will consist of a Colonnade between two wings formed by coupled columns 16 feet in height and 2 feet in diameter, supporting an Entablature and Balustrade of the Roman Doric Order.

The entrances of the Vestibule and Lobbies of the Boxes are by a flight of marble steps 42 feet in length rising to the platform of the Colonnade. Those to the Pit will be through the wings. The Box Treasurer's offices will be in the wings; and the stair ways to the upper Lobbies will commence at each end of the vestibule.

The ground plan of the Boxes will be in the form of a horse shoe 40 feet across its shortest dimension at the stage Box; rising in three tiers or rows, and containing three ranges of seats in each tier on the sides, and five in the circular front. These boxes will be bounded by a strong brick wall separating them from the lobbies which will be carried up through each tier to support and strengthen the roof of the building:—

The supports of the boxes will consist of Cast Iron Columns fashioned in imitation of the Thyrsis of Bacchus—They will recede upwards of 4 feet from the front of the Boxes, and be founded on a strong stone wall forming the back of the Pit.—The first row or tier of Boxes will decline 2 feet from the circular front towards the stage;—and the Pit will extend under the first row of Boxes in the form of an alcove, and will command a fine view of the stage at all points. This part of the house will contain between 5 and 600 persons, and will be approached by two wide entrances paved with brick, leading directly from Arch street.—The coffee room will be over the vestibule in front, and on a level with the second lobby floor.

The stage will extend back to the depth of 155 feet from Arch Street, where it will be increased in width 30 feet upon a ten feet wide alley, communicating with Sixth st.; The entrances to the stage and gallery will be immediately from the above mentioned alley and sixth street. —The foundation walls will be of the most substantial stone work, and the superstructure of the best brick work 22 inches in thickness.—The side walls of the whole building will be carried up at this thickness to the square of the roof, where a parapet wall will be raised, and coped with stone 2 feet above the Eaves.

The building will contain, including the Pit, Boxes and Gallery, about 2000 persons.

38. NATIONAL THEATRE
Washington, D.C.
Opened December 7, 1835

By 1835 the nation's capital had outgrown its Washington Theatre, built in 1821, and a group of interested investors decided to build a larger playhouse on a much grander scale. The result of their plans was the National Theatre, which opened December 7, 1835. The old Washington Theatre did not close, as was anticipated, however, but continued under the management of Francis C. Wemyss.

Professor Mudd writes of this new theater:

38:1 In August, 1834, a movement for a new Theatre was inaugurated and a stock company was organized for that purpose. Sealed proposals were invited until September 8, for the erection of a new Theatre to be located on the open space included between E Street on the north, Pennsylvania Avenue on the south and Thirteenth Street on the east. The principal front was to be on Thirteenth Street and to be 76 feet six inches in width. The building was to run back 150 feet on Pennsylvania Avenue and 153 feet on E Street, and was to be of the Roman Doric

38:1. A. J. Mudd, "Early Theatre in Washington City," *Columbia Historical Society Records* 5:84–85 (1902).

style. The edifice was not erected on this triangle, but on the site of the present National Theatre. It was completed in the fall of 1835, and at a meeting of the stockholders held November 3, the name of "National Theatre" was unanimously agreed upon.

The National Theatre was opened December 7, 1835. A prize opening address, written by Mr. Vose of Baltimore, was spoken by Mrs. Hughes, and the comedy of "The Man of the World" was performed, Mr. Maywood being the *Sir Pertinax Macsycophant*, and the afterpiece was the musical farce "Turn Out."

The *National Intelligencer* printed the following account of the opening:

"The new and magnificent establishment was finely patronized on Monday evening, December 7, 1835, by a very full house. The parquet and boxes were filled with ladies and gentlemen, and the "tout ensemble" must have formed a highly gratifying "coup d'oeil" to the spirited manager, precursor, it is hoped, of what he may expect throughout the season, providing he realizes the assurance and promises which he made. The form of the first tier of boxes is embellished with slight sketches in imitation of bas-relief, and surrounded by correspondent ornaments representing brilliant events in maritime history, discovery and naval achievements. The second tier of boxes is ornamented in similar style, referring to victories, treaties, agriculture, etc. The proscenium shows the same colors and style of ornaments. In the arch thereof is a representation of the Declaration of Independence, supported on the wings of Time. The curtain displays an equestrian statue of Washington in front of rich drapery, which is partly drawn aside and displays the tomb of Washington, Mount Vernon, etc. It is intended as a substitute for the green curtain, and the change will doubtless be approved of. The machinery and stage arrangements, all excellent of their kind, are by Mr. Varden; and the whole was lighted by new and splendid lamps made expressly for this establishment."

With the opening of the National Theatre a new order of things was inaugurated. The "gallery gods" were sent aloft and the pit, which in the early days had been appropriated by the most boisterous portion of the audiences, became the parquet and was patronized by the best class of theatre-goers. . . .

In another article about the theater in Washington, Professor Mudd made further observations concerning the National Theatre.

38:2   As is well known Washington was an unpaved city and the streets were badly lighted. When it rained the streets were filled with mud puddles. In fact a communication signed by a member of Congress was printed in the *National Intelligencer* in 1835 complaining that the lamps were not lighted and that people could not walk in the streets at night without falling into mud holes. It was also stated that about that time it cost $10 for a hack to take a party to and from the theatre. As a consequence of these uncomfortable conditions the performance often did not take place on nights when the weather was very inclement.

As Washington grew in size and importance the population moved westward and a movement was inaugurated to build a more modern theatre, and nearer the center of the city. This movement resulted in the organization of a stock company of prominent citizens, and plans were drawn for a new theatre to be built on the triangular park in front of the present National Theatre. August 26, 1834, proposals were invited for the erection of the structure. Later, ground was purchased about where the theatre now stands, the plans were changed, and No-

38:2. A. J. Mudd, "The Theatre of Washington City from 1835 to 1850," *Columbia Historical Society Records* 6:223–25 (1903).

vember 26 proposals were again asked for. The building was begun early in 1835 and finished in November of that year. It was of Roman Doric, resting on a basement 13 feet 6 inches in height with a portico 41 feet 6 inches long by 12 feet 9 inches in breadth, consisting of four brick Roman Doric columns 29 feet 6 inches in height with antae, entablature, and balustrade. The front was 76 feet 6 inches wide, the building running back 150 feet and 50 feet in height. It was stuccoed in imitation of granite and had five large doors and a like number of windows in front.

The parquette was arranged so that the floor could be removed in order that the building might be used as an amphitheatre. The stage was 68 x 71 feet.

The dome was painted a pale cerulean blue and was divided into four allegorical designs. The first represented the Genius of the Institutions of the country, designated by Power and Wisdom repelling Tyranny and superstition. The second represented Truth at the altar from which the Spirits of War and Peace had taken the sword and torch. The third represented the Goddess of Wisdom presenting a medallion of Washington to the Goddess of Liberty, who returned a wreath to crown her favorite son—Fame proclaiming Victory and Peace. The last represented Justice protecting and guiding the commerce and manufactures of America. All the ornaments of the interior were of a national character representing, either by allegorical design or historical illustrations, important events in the history of the country. What had in the earlier theatres been known as the pit was done away with and in its place a parquette was substituted and connected with the lower boxes. Then there was the first gallery or first tier, the second tier and the gallery. A part of this gallery was set apart for persons of color.

The theatre was leased to Messrs. Maywood, Rowbotham and Platt of the Chestnut Street Theatre, Philadelphia. . . .

The prices of admission were: First tier of boxes and parquette $1, second and third tiers 50 cents, gallery 25 cents.

The doors were opened at a quarter-past 6 and the performance commenced at 7 o'clock, but later the hours were changed to 5:45 and 6:30, so that the entertainments might conclude at as near ten o'clock as possible. . . .

39. THIRD BOWERY THEATRE
New York City
Opened January 2, 1837

In 1830 Thomas S. Hamblin became joint lessee of the Bowery Theatre with James H. Hackett. There was no pretension to the presentation of the great dramas of the past and present, but rather a concentration of what the crowds wanted—melodramas with action; in fact, during their regime the Bowery became known as "the Bowery Slaughter House." The theater certainly gained the enmity of the critics and all who professed to be lovers of great drama. The New York *Herald* wrote:

39:1   We have now five theatres in full blast in New York. Here's the Park, the National, the Franklin, and Mrs. Hamblin's, and the Bowery. Can they all succeed? Can five theatres be supported here? Certainly not. One, if not two, must go down. Now who will go down first? The appearances indicate that the Bowery must go on the rocks. The other theatres have some pretensions to character and respectability—the Bowery is without exception the worst and wickedest that ever stood a month in any city under heaven.

This sentiment was certainly an overstatement, and one that the crowds obviously did not share, since the Bowery, as an institution, lasted some hundred and three years. Perhaps, however, the critic who wrote these words felt justified when, a few weeks after they were published, the Bowery burned to the ground.

39:1. New York *Herald,* Aug. 29, 1836.

35. Tremont Theatre, Boston, 1827. Lithograph. Courtesy of the Harvard Theatre Collection.

36. Bowery Theatre, New York, 1828. Engraving, from a drawing by A. J. Davis; for the *New-York Mirror and Ladies' Literary Gazette* (Aug. 23, 1828). Courtesy of the Cooper-Hewitt Museum of Decorative Arts and Design, Smithsonian Institution.

37. Arch Street Theatre, Philadelphia. Engraving and drawing by Yeager. Courtesy of the Free Library of Philadelphia.

39. Third Bowery Theatre, New York. Etching. Courtesy of The Hoblitzelle Theatre Arts Library, The Humanities Research Center, The University of Texas at Austin.

Again like the phoenix the Bowery rose from its own ashes, and by January 2 the theater was ready to open once again to its adoring public. The following description is from the New York *Herald* the evening of the opening:

39:2   AMERICAN THEATRE, BOWERY

In presenting to the public the prospectus of an old established Theatre, under a new management, the subscriber feels called upon to state fully his plans as to its future regulation, in order to convince his friends, and the public in general, that the character of the Theatre is not likely to deteriorate in his hands. It is scarcely necessary to say, that the erection of a building so superior completed in the short space of 54 working days, at a time when the money market was exceedingly tight, has been a matter of no small difficulty; but the same conviction which first induced the undertaking, has been sufficient to carry it out triumphantly—viz., that, in this city, enterprise and industry never failed of encouragement and support. This belief has been confirmed to the subscriber through many years of public service, and having acted upon it in the more circumscribed line to which he has been hitherto confined, he feels no doubt of a similar success in the bolder effort he now makes.

The Bowery Theatre has been built by Mr. James Phillips, the contractor, and reflects great credit upon that gentleman for the substantial and elegant manner in which he has accomplished it.—Calvin Pollard, Esq., has gained in public estimation, fresh laurels for the taste and discrimination he has displayed in his capacity of architect to the Theatre.

The building is about eight feet higher than before; it will be supplied with large tanks of water in case of fire; the pit extends under the boxes, and is capable of containing 800 persons more than that of Drury Lane, London; the dome and pro-

39:2. New York *Herald,* Jan. 2, 1837.

scenium, including the balcony boxes, are so constructed that, by a piece of ingenious machinery, they can in an instant be moved back so as to throw open the entire stage for processions, &c.

Signors *Guidicini, Chizzola* and *Alba,* the well known and celebrated Italian artists, have had the entire chore of the ornamental painting, and every facility has been afforded to their magnificent conceptions. The dome is ornamented with five superb chandeliers, in Grecian *basso relievo,* with a crown of *tableau* representing Apollo, surrounded by the Muses; this is intersected by hexagons of gold ornaments, embracing a drop, terminating in the centre with festoons of flowers. The Fourth Tier, painted in Raffelo style, intercepted with five pannels, blazoned in ornamented groups. Third Tier represents bases in gold frescos, with festoons of flowers, suspending a circle, each containing the head of Medusa, blazoned on gold ornaments. Second Tier represents rich wreaths of gold, suspending bronze candelabra superbly chased, intercepted by tableaux, with illusive groups and gold cornices.

First Tier represent Grecian border variegated *basso relievo* and *raffielo.* Gold shields supporting five ornamented pannels, each emblazoned with classic groups and rich ornaments.

The Proscenium is composed of pannels ornamented in bas relief—in the center a superb tabulum with a portrait of Shakspeare.

The Drop Curtain is superbly classical, representing a magnificent vestibule in Rome, with the celebrated conflict between Horatti and Curatti.

The construction of the Stage has been under the direction of Mr. William Daverna, the master carpenter to the Theatre. The Scenery, which of course is entirely new, and of the most beautiful description, has been executed by Messrs. Walker, Jones, Grain, and assistants. Above 300 new and magnificent dresses made under the direction of Mr. Lewis, master of the wardrobe, have already cost the enormous sum of $6000. In complete accordance with all these superb arrangements, is the company engaged, which shall be the fullest and most efficient in the Union; in proof of which, he needs only give amongst other distinguished names those of Miss Ann Waring, (whose great talent in every branch of her profession are too well appreciated to need comment here), Miss Cushman, Mrs. Herring, Messrs. G. Jones, the American tragedian, Wm. Sefton, Kilner, Gates, Blakely, Anderson, Edwin, &c., &c.

The subscriber also announces with pleasure having secured the services of Miss Louisa H. Medina, as Dramatist and literary Censor of the Theatre, being the first and only dramatic authoress in the Union, whose magnificent and successful pieces contributed so largely to the fame of the Bowery Theatre, previous to its destruction.

All these arrangements are calculated to ensure to the public a well conducted Theatre, and those outwardly connected with the good order and attendance of the establishment will be no less scupulously attended to, and it only remains for the subscriber to look to a munificent and discriminating public for that support which it never denies to well regulated efforts joined to a sincere desire to please.

W. Dinneford.

40. NEW CHARLESTON THEATRE
Charleston, South Carolina
Opened December 15, 1837

The old Charleston Theatre of 1793 was sold in 1832 to be used as the Medical School of South Carolina, and so for five years the city of Charleston was without a first-class theater. In 1835 a group of local businessmen bought a large lot on Meeting Street and organized "The Charleston New Theatre Company." The group included William A. Carson, Richard Cogdell, Harry Gourdin, Samuel Rose, and Robert Witherspoon, who was made chairman of the new company. An architect and builders were selected and the work begun.

The playhouse was completed late in 1837 and was officially opened on December 15 of that year. A complete description of the theater and the opening appeared in the Charleston *Courier*:

40:1   THE NEW THEATRE

After a long sleep, Rip Van Winkle like, the Drama has again lifted up her head among us under the most favorable auspices. She is again wide awake with renovated beauty and attraction.

"To teach the young idea how to shoot,
To pour fresh instruction o'er the mind"

not by the cant, the dullness of ignorance, but by, "holding as 'twere the Mirror up to Nature," to show virtue her own theatre—even her own image—vice her own deformity—the very age and body of the time, its form and pressure."

It is not our intention to enter into any vindication of dramatic exhibitions. Whatever some may think, we are sure that notwithstanding

"Sunt bona, sunt mediocris, sunt maia pluria," or as we should say in plain American, in these utilitarian days, *notwithstanding its abuses*, many of good taste, as well as of the patriotic, and the lovers of good order, will always be found to advocate the stage.

Cicero, we believe, will be admitted to be pretty good authority on this subject. In one of his Epistles, it may be remembered, he observes, that no human invention of genius and art is so well calculated as the Theatre to inspire virtuous energies in a people, and ennobles their actions. But we need not multiply instances from the citation, which we could easily do, to sustain our position, a thousand names might also, if it were necessary, be adduced from the ranks of the learned and pious in modern times as

40:1. Charleston *Courier*, Dec. 18, 1837.

professing sentiments favorable to the legitimate Drama. "What Cato did, and Addison approved," cannot be altogether wrong.

As the writer of this is among those who believes that we are taught many useful lessons from the stage, he cannot but cordially congratulate his fellow-citizens upon the completion of their new and elegant Theatre in Meeting-street.

This splendid edifice has been constructed from designs by, and under the immediate supervision of, Mr. REICHARDT—an architect of considerable celebrity, a pupil of the celebrated SCHINKEL in Prussia. To the assiduity of Mr. CURTIS, and to Messrs. FOGARTIE AND SUTTON, the builders—to Mr. SERA, and to Mr. CHIZZOLA, to whose tasteful pencils the scenery and decorations of the interior are to be ascribed, much credit is due. Too much praise, likewise, cannot be accorded to Mr. WITHERSPOON, the Chairman of the Directors, and to the other public spirited and liberal gentlemen associated with him in the good cause.

The architecture of the Theatre is at once simple and elegant. The front, when completed, will be stuccoed in imitation of free stone. It is a building in the Grecian style, comprehended in two stories on a high basement—the first story having an arcade form main entrance to the building—the upper story showing a portico of four Ionic columns, supporting an entablature and pediment. The porch is attained by a flight of steps, protected by a large abutment at either end. There are three large doors on the first entrance, with two windows on each side, with corresponding windows over each in the second story, opening into an elegantly furnished saloon. The three doors of entrance open from the front (as most other Theatres do) into a spacious vestibule, on one side of which is the ticket office, and on the other a withdrawing room for the ladies, handsomely carpeted and fitted up with mirrors and lamps.

From the vestibule you pass into a corridor by doors corresponding with those already mentioned. From the corridor, (or lobby as generally termed) the boxes are entered, which form a segment of about two thirds of a circle, receding as they approach the stage, something in the shape of a horseshoe. All the benches provided with sofa seats, covered with crimson moreen. The backs of the boxes are painted a peach blossom color—perhaps of all colors, the best adapted to display the beauty of the fairer part of the audience.

The Parquet or Pit is connected with the dress circle of Boxes, and is divided off into nicely cushioned seats, after the plan of the French Theatre—this is a decided improvement, and will add so much to the comfort and accommodation of the audience, as all the seats are numbered, and can be taken, that we should not be surprised to find this part of the Theatre, nightly the resort of the elite and fashion of the city.

We noticed also, a decided improvement in the diminution of the size of the pillars that support the second and third tiers of boxes—those of our Theatre being of wrought iron, and only 2½ inches in diameter.

The ornaments of the interior though, exceedingly rich, are yet simple and indicative of the nicest taste. The proscenium particularly attracted our attention —it is formed by four Ionic pilastres of the richest order with complete entablature and ornamented frieze—the caps are rendered still more effective by being gilt, and the shafts of the pilastres considerably enriched by gilt mouldings.

Of the comingled splendor, and beauty of the Dome, we cannot speak in too high terms of admiration. It is divided into twelve compartments, and sub-divided by gilt mouldings, and ornamented with arabesque and emblematic figures richly and beautifully executed in the brightest colors. The dividing spaces or medallions between the compartments, are to be filled up with appropriate dramatic designs, already executed by a distinguished historical painter of the North, and which unfortunately did not arrive for the opening but will be found in their places in the course of the next week; this we are informed is also the case in regard to the ornaments in relievo prepared for the 2d and 3d tier of boxes. At the summit of the Dome a circular opening of eight feet diameter is left for the suspension of an elegant chandelier of the same dimensions —containing forty-eight lamps with strong reflectors—the ornamental part of it executed in the richest style. It is from the factory of CORNELIUS & Co., in Philadelphia, and is on an entirely new principle, this being the first time it has been applied to the lighting of a Theatre in America. We must not neglect to mention, however, that the saloons and lobbies are all brilliantly illuminated by very rich bronze hanging lamps.

It would occupy too much of our time thoroughly to describe the magnificence of this splendid Temple of the Muses, and to enumerate all the beauties which struck us as worthy of being particularized. We will, therefore, conclude this hasty and consequently very imperfect sketch, by merely recording in addition to what we have already said that the scenery and drop curtain, the former Messrs. SERA, NIXON, and WILLIAMS, and the latter by Mr. CHIZZOLA, are of the most effective kind, and executed in the highest degree of art.

Our most pleasing task, however yet remains. It is to record that on Friday evening, Dec. 15, 1837, this beautiful building, so well adapted to its object, was opened to the public for the first time, under the management of Mr. ABBOTT. At the hour appointed for the rising of the curtain, it was literally crammed in every part; many had to go away from the doors, unable to get in. Mr. LATHAM, the stage manager, came forward under the most deafening applause. Having received, what I am sure

he must have felt as a warm and encouraging welcome to our *new boards* and to our *old city*, he delivered a poetical Address, written for the occasion, by our highly distinguished fellow citizen, W. GILMORE SIMMS, Esq.

From the length of our article, we are prevented at present from making any remarks upon the merits of the company. From the specimen afforded us on Friday evening, we auger most favorably of its genteel ability, but more of this anon.

The same edition of the Charleston *Courier* contained some further information about the new playhouse and its opening.

40:2 The Theatre.—It will be perceived that Miss ELLEN TREE is to make her first appearance this evening, in the character of JULIANA, in the play of *The Hunchback*. This will ensure to the enterprising managers a full attendance.

The Drop Curtain alone, first exhibited on Saturday evening last, is sufficient attraction to draw a good house—it is a most inimitable specimen of Scene Painting, and certainly reflects great credit on the Artist, Mr. CIZZOLA. . . .

41. NATIONAL THEATRE
New York City
Opened August 29, 1838

The Bowery Theatre became increasingly unpopular with the reporters of the New York *Herald*. They felt that the crowds who frequented the playhouse were coarse and lower-class, not at all the fashionable people who should attend the theater. They were joyful, then, when a new competitor appeared on the scene, and reported the following bit of news:

41:1 The United States Gazette (Chandler editor) has the following—"A New York manager has engaged a considerable number of performers in England, which are said to be very attractive. A Miss Sheriff

40:2. Charleston *Courier,* Dec. 18, 1837.
41:1. New York *Herald,* Aug. 27, 1838.

seems to arrest public attention, and to be highly spoken of by those who have strong attachments for the Theatre. She is an actress of great execution."

The "New York manager" is Mr. Flynn, the magnificent Lord Adolphus Fitzclarence (he was taken for him in England) of the Opera House in Chapel Street. To-night he has a rehearsal— Monday he opens.

The Bowery may as well put out its lights, or be rented for a loafers' alms house establishment; and as to Hamblin,* he can have the choice of either hanging or drowning himself—no matter which. We are happy that we have at last caught a gentleman to manage the National Theatre, so that Mr. Simpson (at the Park Theatre) may not monopolize all the respect and esteem of the public. Mr. Flynn is such a clever man to boot, and so is his lady also—heaven bless her pretty face.

The National Theatre was not a new playhouse, but was the renovated Italian Opera House, which had opened in 1833 and had not done well. The following article tells a little about the house:

41:2   The playhouse known as the National Theatre was situated at the southwest corner of Leonard and Church Streets. It was opened as the Italian Opera House by a stock company, who had purchased the site at a low price, November 18, 1883, with the opera of "La Gazza Ladra". . . .

. . . The admission was $2 for the sofa seats, $1.50 for the boxes, $1 for the pit, and 75 cents for the gallery. The arrangement of the house was a novelty to this country. What constituted the *parterre* in other houses was in this divided into three parts. The one (parquet) facing the orchestra was occupied by those who

study comfort, and not to be annoyed by the close proximity of the instruments. This retreat communicated with the first tier of boxes. The pit was spacious and accommodating. Projecting from the front boxes was a circle, or amphitheatre. On each side of the pit were the windows of the *bagnoires*, or private boxes, for the *dilletanti*. The stage was very large, and afforded every facility for grand spectacles; the dome was magnificent being beyond description. The building cost $110,000, the ground lots costing, besides, $65,000.

Being situated in an inconvenient and poor neighborhood, the National Theatre was never a popular resort, and its fortunes were uniformly disastrous, except with Italian opera. The first season continued, with several interruptions, until July 21, 1834, the performances being entirely of Italian opera. It held, at the prices charged, $1,400. . . . The season was advertised for forty nights, but the large audiences encouraged the management, and twenty-eight extra nights were added. A supplemental season followed, beginning November 10, 1834.

A cessation of the season occurred Dec. 23, and, after being resumed, continued until May 15, 1835. . . . At the conclusion of the season, the theatre was leased by Henry Willard and Thomas Flynn, who opened it as the National Theatre, August 29, 1836 (an address by Jonas B. Phillips being spoken by Mrs. Thomas Flynn), with "The Merchant of Venice": Shylock, Junius B. Booth; Bassanio, Andrew Pickering; Lorenzo, Plumer (who afterwards became a negro minstrel; Launcelot, Thomas Placide; Portia, Mrs. Flynn; Nerissa, Clara Woodhull; Jessica, Mrs. Conduit. The afterpiece was "The Man With the Carpet Bag," in which, as Grimes and Wrangle, William Mitchell and Charles S. Howard (who became the brother-in-law of Mrs. John Hoey) respectively made their first appearances in America. . . .

---

*Hamblin was manager of the Bowery Theatre.
41:2. T. Allston Brown, *A History of the New York Stage from the First Performance in 1732 to 1901.* 3 vols. (New York: Dodd, 1903), 1:240–41.

This theatre was sold at auction in November, 1846, for $75,000, and purchased by Mr. Mauran, a merchant of this city, and James H. Hackett, and they leased it to James W. Wallack. Mr. Hackett had a private box therein, to which he gave the Bonapartes a standing invitation, of which privilege they almost nightly availed themselves. . . .

42. DORRANCE STREET THEATRE
Providence, Rhode Island
Opened October 29, 1838

The fortunes of the theater had never been smooth in Rhode Island, as was seen in the beginnings of professional theater in Newport and Providence. Although many people were genuinely interested in seeing the cause of the theater advanced in the state, others still viewed it as an immoral influence in the community and fought any incursions it made into the life of the people. Blake's account of the building of the Dorrance Street Theatre in Providence shows the difficulties encountered by the proponents of this enterprise.

42:1   Another long time passed, and Providence had no theatre, although the need of one was seriously felt. Accordingly, a number of public-spirited gentlemen decided to erect on the east side of Dorrance street, between Weybosset and Pine streets, one that should be a credit to the city for its appearance and capacity. They appointed a building committee, consisting of Messrs. Jamess G. Anthony, John Gould, John A. Littlefield, John W. Richmond, and Ezra Dodge, who selected Mr. Buckling as the architect, under whose direction the work was begun on the 28th of May, 1838.

This enterprise from its inception was exposed to the slings and arrows of enemies. As soon as the ground was broken by the workmen, Mr. Samuel Wheeler, a very well meaning citizen, conceived the

plan of committing the city authorities to hostility towards the projected theatre; and, with this design, he zealously laboured in procuring signatures to a memorial, in which the Board of Aldermen were prayed "to take such immediate action in relation to the erection of a new theatre, as would indicate a determination to refuse all licenses for such purposes." The memorial was presented on the 18th of June and the consideration of the subject was then postponed one week. On the 25th of the same month, the board again assembled, and found that during the intervening time many additional signatures had been obtained to Mr. Wheeler's document, swelling the whole number to about six hundred. The Second Baptist Society, whose house was directly opposite the site chosen for the theatre, also presented a memorial, representing in substance, that they had erected a house of worship in a retired and peaceful situation, in which they had hoped to hold their meetings undisturbed, but that the theatre would prevent their doing so, and impair their rights as a Christian society; and also setting forth that theatrical amusements are opposed to the true interest of the community at large. After a discussion of the subject, the board passed a resolution "that, however much the members may regret that a building for theatrical purposes is now erecting, they consider it premature and inconsistent with former usages to give their opinion as to the propriety of granting licenses to theatres, or anything else, until a request for the same is made by persons interested."

The work upon the new theatre now advanced with rapidity, and competent managers were desirous of obtaining a lease as soon as it should be completed, providing a license could be procured. On the 22nd of October, a petition was presented to the Board of Aldermen, from Mr. James G. Maeder, the eminent musician, representing that he and others had become lessees of the new building called

42:1. Charles Blake, *An Historical Account of the Providence Stage* (Providence: G. H. Whitney, 1868), pp. 222–25.

"Shakspeare Hall," on Dorrance street, for the purpose of theatrical representations; that he had engaged a stock company respectable in talent and character, who were well aware that they could not hope to be sustained by the public, unless they should maintain a reputation for professional and private good character; and that he intended to enforce such regulations as would conduce to good order, especially forbidding the sale of wines and strong liquors upon the premises, and excluding all persons of notoriously bad character; and asking a license for one year. After a full hearing of the parties interested, the license was granted on the conditions named in the petition, subject to such regulations as the board might thereafter deem expedient. One hundred dollars for the use of the city, and ten dollars for the state, constituted the fee exacted. It was stipulated that performances should not be given either on Saturday or Sunday evenings, and they should always be terminated before twelve o'clock at night. The sheriff of the county and two police constables were appointed to attend at "Shakspeare Hall" to keep order, at the expense of the manager.

The theatre was a stone edifice, one hundred and ten feet in length, by sixty-five in width; and the stage was a little more than fifty feet deep. The exterior was plastered and pointed in imitation of granite, and had pilasters in front and a granite basement. The principal external decoration was a medallion bust of Shakspeare. The interior was beautifully decorated by accomplished artists; the ceiling representing a dome with a sun in the centre, surrounded by the signs of the zodiac in gold. This was the work of Mr. Heister, then eighteen years of age, and now the ablest scenic artist in America. The fronts of the boxes were exquisitely painted in panels. The auditorium contained, besides a pit, two tiers of boxes and a gallery of semi-circular form, and could seat about thirteen hundred spectators. The act-drop represented a moon-light view of the Capitol at Washington. The entire cost of the theatre was twenty thousand dollars.

The inauguratory performance took place October 29, 1838, and consisted of "The Soldier's Daughter," and "A Pleasant Neighbour." . . .

43. FOURTH BOWERY THEATRE
New York City
Opened May 6, 1839

The misfortunes of the Bowery Theatre continued when, on February 18, 1838, the playhouse was once again gutted by fire, barely thirteen months after the building had been opened to the public. In his chronicle of "The Theatre in America," T. Allston Brown told of the loss.

43:1 This theatre was again destroyed by fire Monday morning, February 18, 1838. About 2 o'clock flames were seen issuing from the rear of the theatre, in that portion of the building occupied by the carpenter. In two hours the building was in ashes. The performance was over at 12 o'clock, and although the last piece was a nautical melodrama, very little gunpowder was in requisition during its progress. The building belonged to a joint stock company. The ground was the property of Hamblin, who was in receipt of $8,000 per annum from the theatre as ground rent. Junius Brutus Booth was to have commenced an engagement the same night, as Richard, with a reduction in the prices to fifty and twenty-five cents. The building was insured by $35,000. The scenery, dresses and properties were totally uninsured, and were valued at $60,000. The fire was supposed to be the work of an incendiary.

For nearly a year after the Bowery was supposed to be a thing of the past, but it was rebuilt and opened May 6, 1839 by Thomas Hamblin, as manager and proprietor. The initial performance

43:1. T. Allston Brown, "The Theatre in America," *The Clipper* (1888).

was "Nick of the Woods," with Joseph Proctor (his first appearance in this city) as the star. . . .

Descriptions of the Bowery Theatre of 1839 are very scarce. An engraving in the *Illustrated London News* of May 24, 1845, shows the theater in flames, but certain external features are clear. There were four Corinthian columns, a flight of steps leading to the front entrance, and a promenade balcony.

The New York *Herald* had a rather meager description.

43:2   *BOWERY THEATRE.*—This new and splendid building opens to-night for the first time, under the management of its sole proprietor, Mr. Jackson. The elegance of the internal arrangements—the comfort to be found in all parts of the house—the magnificence of the new scenery, and the talent of the artists engaged for the season, leave nothing to desire to the most fastidious theatrical *amateur*. . . .

The *tout ensemble* is intended to excite the admiration of the visitor, and will answer fully the most sanguine expectations. This theatre, raised phoenix-like, from its smouldering ruins, with more brilliancy that it was ever known to possess, will certainly become the favorite resort of fashion, and will, no doubt, meet at its opening, with liberal patronage.

We invite the public to call at the New Bowery this evening, and we feel confident that they will not be disappointed in what they see.

The Spirit of the Times adds very little in its description.

43:3   The *Bowery Theatre* opened on Monday last with an overwhelming audience. The house has been reconstructed in an approving manner, obviating the many difficulties the audience experienced in the old theatre, and presenting a clean and tasty appearance. The paintings on the box fronts and on the ceiling are clever, and the chandelier adds much to the comfort and beauty of the interior. The pieces during the week have been "Money" and the spectacle of the "Sleeping Beauty."

44. NEW CHATHAM THEATRE
New York City
Opened September 11, 1839

The New Chatham Theatre, which opened in 1839, was one of the more popular theaters of its time, although it was not a great financial success and had a quick change of managers after its opening. Brown gives the background of the venture:

44:1   One of the most popular of New York's playhouses in its day was The Chatham Theatre, situated on the East side of Chatham Street, between Roosevelt and James streets. It was projected by Thomas Flynn and Henry Willard, who opened it Sept. 11, 1839, with Flynn as manager. The opening play was "A New Way to Pay Old Debts," with J. R. Scott as Sir Giles Overreach and Mrs. Thomas Flynn as Margaret Overreach. The farce was "Family Jars." In the company were Mrs. C. R. Thorne, Emily Mestayer, Mrs. Judah, Mrs. Blake, J. Hudson, Kirby, C. R. Thorne, Stevens, and C. Mestayer. Kirby was a tragedian whose strong point was his dying scenes. This gave rise to the saying of the gallery gods, who often slept through the tame portions of the play: "Wake me up when Kirby dies." On Nov. 21 "The Happy Man" was played for the first time in America. The first season was rather eventful, though by no means prosperous to its managers. Numerous comedies and standard plays were produced, and J. R. Scott, J. B. Booth, James Anderson, William Rufus

43:2. New York *Herald*, Aug. 4, 1839.
43:3. *Spirit of the Times*, May 18, 1839.

44:1. T. Allston Brown, *A History of the New York Stage from the First Performance in 1732 to 1901*. 3 vol. (New York: Dodd, 1903), 1:297–98.

Blake, Mlle. Celeste, and other popular actors played engagements here. In January, 1840, the theatre was closed, owing to differences between the two managers. Charles R. Thorne bought Mr. Willard's interest in the house, and, in conjunction with Mr. Flynn (February, 1840), managed it for two weeks to a losing business, when Mr. Flynn, fearing a continued loss, sold his interest to Mr. Thorne for $500. The latter gentleman kept the house open for four years with success. Such stars as the elder Booth, T. D. Rice, John Sefton, M. and Mme. Le Compte, Mme. Celeste, John R. Scott, Henry Wallack, Mary Duff, James S. Browne, Bill Williams, Henry Placide, Edwin Forrest, Josephine Clifton, and others appeared. At the expiration of his four years' lease Thorne sold out to his stage manager, Mr. Stevens, and A. W. Jackson.

Some additional information concerning this playhouse is furnished by Odell.

44:2 The sense of weariness attendant on a study of the minor theatres of New York during the years from 1824, when Barrière started his campaign at Chatham Garden Theatre, down to and beyond the period we are now treating, arises from the utter sameness of offering at all the houses, one and several. How New York could have endured the constant succession of the same stale farces, dramas, and melodramas is beyond my powers of conjecture, especially as most of the pieces were certainly not acted as well as at the Park, and later at the National. The uselessness of these enterprises impresses one with a sense of economic waste. In 1840, according to Hough, the population of New York City was 312,710; one sees the utter futility—especially in those desperately hard times—of the multiplying of theatres. Yet such multiplication continued with insane feverishness; the

44:2. George C. D. Odell, *Annals of the New York Stage.* 15 vols. (New York: Columbia Univ. Pr., 1927–49), 4:375–76.

burnt National was replaced, and a committee was organised to build Wallack a new theatre—to be called the Metropolitan—at the corner of Broadway and Chambers Street. This I learn from references in the paper, the Spirit of the Times, and from an advertisement in the Evening Post of November 6th, wherein we are informed that "the arrangements of the committee being now completed, stockholders and all persons disposed to subscribe to stock of the New Theatre . . . . . at Broadway and Chambers street, are invited to attend a meeting at the Astor House, on Monday . . . the 11th November, at 7 o'clock, for the purpose of choosing trustees and hearing the Report of the committee on arrangements."

Fortunately, this scheme fell through. But New York was, next season, to have a newly rebuilt National, on the site of the old, and, for the season of 1839–40, it could attend performances at the New Chatham Theatre, built for Thomas Flynn and Henry E. Willard from designs by Samuel Purdy. It stood on the south-east side of Chatham Street, between Roosevelt and James Streets, and would seat comfortably—according to the Spirit of the Times, for September 7, 1839—2200 spectators, 500 in the first tier, 400 in the second (exclusive of private boxes) 300 in the third, 800 in the pit, and 200 in the gallery. James Anderson (long of the Bowery) was stage-manager, and Marmaduke White, scene-painter.

The opening bill (September 11th) presented familiar actors in A New Way to Pay Old Debts and Family Jars; could any bill less justify the building of a new theatre, even though J. R. Scott played Sir Giles Overreach and the once so popular Barnes was on hand for his inimitable Delph, in the farce? The remaining actors might be guessed by my astute reader—Harrison, Russell, Goodenow, Crouta, Mr. and Mrs. W. Jones, Mrs. Bannister, George Stanley, Mrs. Flynn, and Mrs. Williams (late Miss Verity). There were still two groups of actors in New York—those who appeared at the Park and those who did not. From the large resident list of the latter any new theatrical enterprise selected its cohorts. Boston and Philadelphia, not to say Charleston, New Orleans and Baltimore, all had their own companies, far from Broadway, but, let us hope, happy. Among Flynn's new actors, here, was Henry E. Stevens, who played Lord Lovell in the Massinger play; he will remain with us for some years of our journey.

The Spirit of the Times: A Chronicle of the Turf, Literature and the Stage, a weekly magazine, had the following article about the New Chatham Theatre. The projected date of opening, however, is incorrect, for the playhouse opened September 11th, not the 9th.

44:3   In relation to this theatre, we make use of the words of the "Times," which is becoming, or has already become, the best daily theatrical paper in the city. The new theatre is now finished, and will open for the season on the 9th of September, with a very good company. It is inferior in its capacity but to two other theatres in the city, and in its accommodations, to none. By accurate measurement, it will hold twenty-two hundred persons, all seated. Of this number, the first tier will hold 500; the second, exclusive of private boxes, 400; the third, 300; the pit, 800, and the gallery, 200. Among other superior accommodations, is that of a ladies' saloon, attached to and only accessible from the first tier. The managers have in contemplation to give the legitimate drama, and well varied popular entertainments.

The celebrated London pantomimists, Messrs. Brown, King, and Gibson, have been engaged, and are hourly expected. Mr. Anderson, one of the best stage managers in the country, has quitted the Bow-

ery theatre, and is engaged in the same capacity at this house. Mrs. Bannister, a lady of superior talents, is also engaged for the first "business" in old women.

45. MITCHELL'S OLYMPIC THEATRE
New York City
Opened December 9, 1839

The destruction of the National Theatre by fire in 1839 threw a number of actors and stage technicians out of work. Among them was William Mitchell, the stage manager of the company and a first-rate actor. Mitchell took the opportunity to lease the Olympic Theatre, a relatively new playhouse built in 1837, and here presented comedies and other light entertainment at cut-rate prices. Since it was a time of serious financial difficulty in the country, the people responded very well to Mitchell's policy of low prices and humorous productions.

The *Spirit of the Times* carried the following announcement:

45:1   Mr. Mitchell, late Stage Manager of the National, has hired this house, which he will endeavor to conduct as nearly as possible upon the "Wyche street" plan. Mrs. Bailey and Mrs. Plumer; Brown, Williams, Horncastle, and others, will aid the Manager with their powers of attraction, and light comedy and burletta are likely to be extremely well played. The plan is to have nothing but stars throughout the season. May success wait upon the enterprise!

The same edition of the *Spirit of the Times* had an advertisement for the opening of the theater.

45:2   MITCHELL'S OLYMPIC THEATRE
MR. MITCHELL, of the late National Theatre, would respectfully inform his friends and the public in general, that he has taken a lease of the above establishment, which will be opened on MON-

44:3. *Spirit of the Times,* Sept. 7, 1839.

45:1. *Spirit of the Times,* Dec. 2, 1839.
45:2. *Spirit of the Times,* Dec. 2, 1839.

CHARLESTON THEATRE, CHARLESTON, S. C.

40. New Charleston Theatre, Charleston, S.C. Engraving by Burn. Courtesy of the South Carolina Historical Society.

OLD NATIONAL THEATRE, CORNER OF LEONARD AND CHURCH STREETS.

41. National Theatre, New York. Engraving by Richardson, after a drawing by Waud. Courtesy of The Hoblitzelle Theatre Arts Library, The Humanities Research Center, The University of Texas at Austin.

45. Mitchell's Olympic Theatre, New York. Drawing by Green, based on an 1840 woodcut; published in R. M. De Leeuw, *Both Sides of Broadway* (New York, 1910). Courtesy of the Museum of the City of New York.

46. Boston Museum, Boston. Lithograph. Courtesy of The Hoblitzelle Theatre Arts Library, The Humanities Research Center, The University of Texas at Austin.

DAY EVENING, Dec. 9, 1839, when will be produced, for the first time in this country, a drama called **HIS FIRST CHAMPAGNE**; Richard Watt, Mr. Browne; Horatio Craven, A. M. Horncastle; Glump, Mitchell; Miss Bygrove, Mrs. Plumer; Mary Grubb, Miss Randolph.

After which, the burletta of NO! Andrew, Mitchell; Maria, with songs, Mrs. Bailey; Frederick, with songs, Mr. Horncastle.

To conclude with **HIGH LIFE BELOW STAIRS**; Lord Duke, Mr. Browne; Sir Harry, Mr. Mitchell; Lovell, Mr. Horncastle; Mrs. Kitty, Miss Randolph; Lady Charlotte, Mrs. Jones.

Boxes, 50—Pit, 25 cents. Private Boxes, $5. Doors open at half past six o'clock, and the performances will commence at 7 o'clock precisely.

**A full and efficient police is engaged, and the strictest order and decorum will be preserved.

T. Allston Brown calls Mitchell's Olympic "the most popular place of amusement ever known in New York." This most certainly is an overstatement, but the playhouse was assuredly a very popular one. Brown tells us a little more concerning the theater.

45:3 Undoubtedly the most popular place of amusement ever known in New York was Mitchell's Olympic Theatre, situated at 442 Broadway, between Howard and Grand streets, which was originally built for Henry Willard and William Rufus Blake. The auditorium was small, the pit being wholly devoted to the male sex, and was entered by a subterranean passageway running beneath the boxes and furnished with distinct ticket-venders and doorkeepers. The first and second tiers of boxes, shut off from the lobby by a series of doors, were set aside for ladies and the

gentlemen who accompanied them. A bar-room on the second tier was liberally supplied with liquors and other refreshments. The property was owned by Mr. Spofford, of the firm of Spofford, Tileston & Co. It was opened Sept. 13, 1837, by Willard & Blake, as the Olympic with "Perfection," "The Lady and the Devil," and "Married Life." One of the leading dramatic critics of the day characterized it as "a parlor of elegance and beauty." The stage appointments were excellent, and the scenery was considered to be marvellous. When the house opened the prices of admission were 75 cents to the boxes, and 37½ cents to the pit. Oct. 20 they were reduced to 50 cents to the boxes, and 25 cents to the pit. . . .

46. BOSTON MUSEUM
Boston, Massachusetts
Opened June 14, 1841

This venerable institution had the distinction of being under the managership of the same family for more than forty years. It was built by Moses Kimball and opened in 1841. For the first two seasons musical entertainments took place; then, beginning September 4, 1843, regular dramatic performances were offered. The venture was so successsful that a new Museum was built on the east side of Tremont Street, between Court and School Streets, and was opened November 2, 1846.

Some background of the establishment is given by W. W. Clapp.

46:1 We have alluded incidentally in previous chapters to the Boston Museum. This popular place of amusement is now a feature of this city. From a very humble beginning, it has increased and strengthened, till it has attained a name which is as enviable as it is well-deserved.

On the 14th of June, 1841, the "Boston Museum and Gallery of Fine Arts," was

45:3. T. Allston Brown, *A History of the New York Stage from the First Performance in 1732 to 1901.* 3 vols. (New York: Dodd, 1903), 1:264.

46:1. William W. Clapp, Jr., *A Record of the Boston Stage* (Boston and Cambridge: James Munroe & Co., 1853), pp. 469–72.

opened by Mr. Moses Kimball and associates, in the building erected for the purpose at the corner of Tremont and Bromfield streets. The collection of natural curiosities was the same that formerly belonged to the New England Museum, but many additions were made, and several valuable curiosities were added. There had been several museums in Boston, but this new place differed from all others, from the fact that it had a spacious music saloon over the Museum, capable of holding 1200 persons. The walls of the saloon were hung with pictures, and the stage was sufficiently capacious for the performance of vaudevilles, etc. The drop scene was very neat and appropriate, and the place was quite comfortable and cosey. The hall was dedicated on the 14th by a grand concert, in which Mr. Sinclair, (father to Mrs. E. Forrest,) and Miss Melton, were the attractions. These entertainments proved very acceptable to the public, and in course of the first twenty months, Yankee Hill, Dr. Valentine, Mr. Walcott, Miss Rock, Dempster, Mr. Young, Mr. and Mrs. Maeder, S. C. Massett, Miss Moss, Mrs. Seymour, Edward Kendall, Miss Sarah, Knight, the Indian Warriors and Squaws, Mr. Love, the polyphonist, the Rainer Family, Signor Blitz, the Mysterious Gipsey Girl, Major Stevens' Diorama of the Battle of Bunker Hill, the Miss Shaws, were at different times exhibiting at the Museum.

In February, 1843, Mr. Kimball engaged John Sefton and Mrs. Maeder to bring out "Operattas," and on the 6th inst., the "Masque Ball" was brought out. This was the commencement of dramatic representations at the Museum, and in the fall of the same year an efficient *corps dramatique*, under W. H. Smith, was organized, and performances were given. On the 25th of September, 1843, Miss Adelaide Phillips ("only ten years old") made her first appearance as *Little Pickle*, and gave promise of that advancement which she has since made. Miss Phillips,

by the kindness of her friends and Jenny Lind, is now in Europe perfecting her vocal acquirements under competent masters, and a brilliant future is in store for her. The Museum attracted all classes, and it was the resort not only of the middling and lower classes, but of the more wealthy residents, for the pieces were well put on the stage, and the actors above mediocrity. The Museum was then and is now patronized by a large class who do not frequent theatres, but who have a nice perception of the difference between tweedle-*dum* and tweedle-*dee*. We have noticed, however, that many who make a first attempt at countenancing theatricals at the Museum, may shortly after be found at the regular theatres, and the Museum has thus done much towards increasing the lovers of the drama. The production of the moral play called "The Drunkard," written by W. H. Smith, decided the fate of the Museum, for it attracted to the house an unprecedented number of visitors, and established permanently the popularity of Boston Museum. In the year 1846 the present Museum was built by Mr. Kimball and his associates, and on the 2d of November of that year the first entertainment was given. The building, designed by H. & J. E. Billings, and erected under the superintendence of Anthony Hanson, is admirably adapted for the purposes for which it was built. It was during the season of 1846–7 that "Aladdin" was brought out, which had a run of eight weeks, and was performed ninety-one times to crowded houses. Mrs. George Barrett also appeared, and has attracted since then a very large amount of money to that house. To record in detail the various performances or the novelties that have been offered, would, at this time, be a repetition of what is still fresh in the memory of our readers. Mr. Kimball is one of the shrewdest managers in this country, and has at all times in reserve sufficient attractions to render him independent of stars, though of late years this place has been the scene of Mr. Booth's performances, when in Boston. Mr. W. H. Smith, as stage-director, has no equal in this city, and to his efforts may be attributed a large portion of the success of the Museum. Mr. Comer, as leader of the orchestra and musical director, rendered the most efficient services, while Mr. Warren is a host in himself, and Mrs. Thoman, Mrs. Vincent, Mr. J. A. Smith, G. H. Finn, and others, are highly esteemed. There is not a theatre in this country which is more agreeable for an actor than this. Behind the scenes all is harmony, and a degree of etiquette is observed, which should be introduced into every theatre. . . .

The famous actor Otis Skinner remembered his visits to the Museum as a boy, and recorded his impressions in his autobiography, *Footlights and Spotlights.*

46:2   My theatre-going probably began when I was about five. Charlie and I were frequently allowed, on a Saturday afternoon, to accompany our parents across the Charles River from Cambridge to the Boston Museum. This dignified place of amusement was exempt from Puritan prejudice; its very name gave it a propriety denied to other theatres. A visit there was most instructive. In orderly alcoves, shelves of minerals, cases of stuffed birds, fossil remains, and curiosities from various parts of the world formed a collection that was presided over by busts and portraits of gentlemen whose respectability no one could doubt. A large painting called THE ROMAN DAUGHTER hung over the entrance into the hall of curiosities, representing a beautiful matron who visited her starving father in prison and nurtured him by suckling his parched old lips at her breast. I was duly impressed by an ingenious piece of faking known as BARNUM'S JAPANESE MERMAID, a mummy, the size of a small cat, with

female head, hair and breast, arms and claws of an animal and the tail of a fish. I used to wonder why the Japanese were so clever in catching mermaids.

But the place of dread in this enchanted palace was the gallery of waxworks on the upper floor. Here I drank horrors by the bucketful. There were the Siamese Twins in ill-fitting black suits, the ligature of realistic wax binding their bodies in perpetual companionship. And Daniel Lambert, the celebrated fat man, seated in a huge chair, a diminutive wax boy struggling to hand him a mug of beer the size of a coal scuttle which he was receiving with great joy.

A particular terror was wrought upon me by a moral lesson called THREE SCENES IN A DRUNKARD'S LIFE and another entitled THE PIRATES' CABIN. The dominant feature of these silent and awful dramas was blood—lots of it. The DRUNKARD and his family had begun their pestilential career pleasantly and prosperously. Father, Mother, Son and Daughter were seated about the festal board, the expression of their faces fixed in a beatific trance, and the gorgeousness of their raiment only matched by that of the wall-paper and the tablecloth. They were drinking champagne, the cotton wool foam of which was greatly in need of dusting. This was the first step in their downward path. The second house, meaner—much meaner; furniture and tablecloth shabby and the drink RUM—labeled in bold letters on the family bottle. The fashionable garments of the first scene were things of the past. Son and Daughter were degenerate and obviously bilious; Mother's rum had not agreed with her; and Father was truly no fit company for any one. In the last group the family had moved up to the garret and again changed their clothes to their disadvantage, except Daughter who had found profitable employment in the streets and had blossomed into colors like the butterfly. The others were sad sights. Father, shrunken and haggard, a

46:2. Otis Skinner, *Footlights and Spotlights* (Indianapolis: Bobbs-Merrill, 1924), pp. 13–16.

sore in the corner of his mouth, had just dealt Mother a blow with the gin bottle, and the poor soul lay prone in her dingy calico dress, rivers of blood ebbing from a hole in her waxen head. Son had become a moron, and Father was being arrested by a policeman at the very moment of murder.

Horror mounted on horror in THE PIRATES' CABIN, where the immorality of piracy was set forth in lasting lesson to the youth of Boston who had formed the habit of sailing up the salt creeks of the Charles on heavily armed rafts in search of treasure galleons. Never was such scene of carnage as that cabin presented. Corpses oozing blood, and pirates, armed to the teeth, gloating over them. A particularly awful ruffian was standing in the foreground with ax uplifted to tap a fresh blood supply in the head of a gentleman with white whiskers. A beautiful maiden raised arms of supplication over him, and the pirate captain descended the companionway with an arresting gesture.

These were the gory objects that pursued my waking and sleeping hours. Especially did they busy themselves at night and hide under my bed and in the dark corners that pirates and drunkards know about. Sometimes, after dusk, I was sent to Kennedy's Bakery in the main street of Cambridge, on the servant's bread-baking evenings, for a cent's worth of yeast, and then there was an inevitable chase of these hobgoblins in my wake. Sometimes they would get ahead of me and hide behind trees and in black doorways, and little it mattered that I jangled the penny vigorously in my tin pail! That scared them not at all; my path was sore beset by demons. Nor in my dreams did they cease from troubling, but came flocking in new forms, committing dire deeds.

The recollection of this horror chamber lies far deeper than the plays I saw. These were given in what, for politic reasons, was first termed, "The Lecture Hall" of the Museum, and which gradually assumed the proportions of a stage and auditorium. Ministers of the gospel could freely patronize such a place of entertainment; their attendance was even sought on a complimentary basis. That, perhaps, is why my family became frequent patrons of the Museum at a time in my life when the play was a mixture of things too vast for my infantile mind. . . .

The Boston *Transcript* carried the following announcement on the day of the opening of the Boston Museum (June 14, 1841):

46:3 THE BOSTON MUSEUM AND GALLERY OF FINE ARTS, at the corner of Tremont and Bromfield streets, is opened today by Mr. Kimball, the proprietor; and the first Concert will be given there this evening by Mr. Sinclair and Miss Mellon, in the Saloon.

The hall is fitted up in most beautiful style, ornamented with a large number of paintings and sculpture by the most eminent artists; among others, is the splendid historical painting by Suly of the passage of the Delaware. The cabinets are filled with a great variety of birds from all parts of the world; also are to be found a numerous collection of quadrupeds, including a giraffe; Indian and Chinese curiosities without number. Taken together, this is by far the best collection of curiosities we have ever seen, and everything is arranged in the most perfect order. The Saloon is large enough to seat 900 persons, who can all be comfortably accommodated. The Drop Scene is a beautiful painting, from the pencil of R. Jones.

No expense has been spared in the fitting up, and we trust the enterprizing proprietor will reap a rich reward for his labors. The price of admission is only 25 cents to the whole, including the concert, which brings it within the means of all.

46:3. Boston *Transcript,* June 14, 1841.

47. CHAPMAN'S TEMPLE OF THE MUSES
New York City
Opened April 2, 1845

Undoubtedly one of the most unusual playhouses ever to be opened in New York was Chapman's Temple of the Muses, for it introduced New Yorkers to the showboat. Although this form of entertainment was new to the East coast, it was not new to the people living along the Ohio and Mississippi rivers, where the Chapman family had taken their showboats since the summer of 1831. Further description of the Chapmans and their floating theaters is contained in the next chapter.

In 1844 the Chapmans, who had been eminently successful with their river showboats, decided to take a showboat to New York City. There they anchored the playhouse at the foot of Canal Street and opened their season April 2, 1845. Little is known about the engagement, and there are no records to show that the Chapmans returned for another season.

Two announcements appeared in the New York *Herald*.

47:1   THIS SPLENDID ESTABLISH-MENT, about which so much has been published, commonly called the Floating Theatre, will open with a powerful cast, tomorrow, (Wednesday) evening, near the foot of Canal street. She will be brilliantly lighted with Gas, made on board, and surmounted with the largest Drummond Light* ever made. Particulars tomorrow.

47:2   TEMPLE OF THE MUSES

The Floating Theatre, lying between Charlton and Canal streets, opened here last evening, with some appropriate dramatic entertainments. The Saloon, which will hold more than Palmo's Opera House, is divided into commodious boxes and pit, with a large stage, well painted interior, and scenery and fixtures of the best style. It is lighted with gas, and a brilliant Drummond Light burning at the top, outside, indicates the whereabouts of this "Leviathan of the deep," to the visitor.

The most detailed description of this theatrical novelty was in the *Herald* of a later date.

47:3 . . . It was constructed out of one of the old southern steam packets called the "Virginia," has a 42 feet beam, perfectly flat bottomed, 22 feet wide, with a keel of about 26 inches; she is about 385 tons burthen, 90 feet in length, and near upon 50 feet high, and draws about seven feet of water. The entrance is ten feet wide, placed about midships, where there is also an engine of about ninety horse power. The stage, parquette, and boxes are aft, and have altogether a very neat and chaste appearance.

It has a roomy little stage, four private boxes in the proscenium, one tier of boxes, a pit, and is capable of seating 1,200 persons comfortably. The parquette is 42 feet wide by 36, the opening of the proscenium 27 feet; the stage is 42 feet wide and 45 feet deep; and the scenery is 16 feet high. The space between the wings is about four feet. At the back of the stage are two dressing rooms for the ladies; and beneath the stage are the dressing rooms for the male performers, together with dining room and bed rooms for the whole company, engineers, &c. In the bows is a large and elegantly furnished salon, in which all the good things of this life are disposed of, on terms the most reasonable. It is about 36 feet deep by about 40 wide; in which are two handsomely fitted up bars, well furnished with good eatables and drinkables. The handsome marble-topped tables, the splendid mirrors and some elegant paintings—the

47:1. New York *Herald*, Mar. 31, 1845.

*The lime, or calcium, light was developed by Drummond in 1816.

47:2. New York *Herald*, Apr. 3, 1845.

47:3. New York *Herald*, Apr. 7, 1845.

beautiful cut ground glass shades to the lamps give this part of the vessel a gay and elegant appearance. A brilliant "Drummond light" surmounts the establishment, illuminating the whole neighborhood, and directing visitors to this floating dramatic temple. The whole establishment is brilliantly illuminated with portable gas, manufactured on board by E. S. Driggs, who has patented the apparatus, which is perfectly safe. The whole is so constructed that the north wind will scarce affect it, and she has already budgeted more than one heavy blow. She was moored in the river during the gale of the 12th of Dec. last, and stood it nobly.

The orchestra has nine musicians. The scenery is from the pencil of Mr. Grain, one of the best artists in the country. Among the company are Mesdames Mossop and Sutherland, and Messrs. Saunders, Sutherland, and others, to which has been added Mr. T. G. Booth, a light comedian of considerable talent. The entertainments during the past week have consisted chiefly of a new national drama from the pen of C. H. Saunders, and some very clever farces and vaudevilles. Mrs. Timm did not appear, in consequence of severe illness, and Mrs. Mossop, formerly of the Olympic, sustained her character. We seldom, or never, saw the amusing farce of "Loan of a Lover" performed in better style than it was on Saturday evening, by the principal members of the company. This evening the vessel will be moored at the foot of Chambers street, and on other evenings of the week at various other slips towards the Battery, and on the East river; after which it will proceed up the North river to visit several towns on its banks—after which the establishment will visit the principal cities and towns on the navigable waters of this country, under a coasting license.

This floating theater was a converted steamboat, which, when remodeled, had a seating capacity for 1,200 persons and even a bar for the convenience of the customers. The Temple of the Muses was open for entertainments to the people of New York City for about a month and then was moved up the Hudson River, stopping at various points along the river where entertainments were given.

48. FIFTH BOWERY THEATRE
New York City
Opened August 4, 1845

The fourth catastrophic fire to destroy the Bowery Theatre occurred on April 25, 1845, and once again the popular playhouse was reduced to rubble. With the building of the fifth Bowery Theatre in August 1845, however, there was a period of eighty-four years before this playhouse was destroyed by fire in 1929, never to be rebuilt.

Once again, T. Allston Brown in his series on "The Theatre in America" tells of the fifth Bowery Theatre and the destruction of its predecessor.

48:1 . . . E. L. Davenport's benefit was announced for April 23, 1845, but the theatre took fire early in the evening before the doors were opened, and was, for the fourth time, entirely destroyed.

The fire originated in the carpenter shop, spread from there to the gas house attached to the theatre, and finally to the theatre, of which nothing but the blackened porticos of the columns remained. The flames spread with such rapidity that nothing was saved, the actors losing their wardrobe. The theatre was rebuilt from designs by Mr. Trimble, was leased to A. W. Jackson. The front of the theatre had a magnificent aspect, which rendered it as imposing as that of any other public building in the city. There were four massive, fluted columns, with rich friezes, above seven marble steps which led to the main entrance. The capitals were modelled from those of an Athenian temple. On the north and south sides of

48:1. T. Allston Brown, "The Theatre in America," *The Clipper* (1888).

the edifice were the entrances to the pit and gallery, wholly disconnected from the entrance to the boxes. Attached to the second tier saloon was a balcony of excellent construction, which proved an excellent withdrawing place in the Summer season, for those who wish to lounge between the acts. The lobbies were extensive, and the shape of the boxes of the most approved form. The depth from the boxes to the stage was fifty-two feet; the width, thirty-nine feet. The pit held eight hundred spectators very conveniently. The orchestra was so constructed as to give the leader a view of all the musicians, thus rendering his task less severe than it would be in an ordinarily shaped one. There were twelve private boxes and four tiers, the gallery forming a portion of the upper one, the whole so extensive as to seat three thousand persons, and yet so constructed as to allow the spectators farthest removed from the stage to hear with distinctness. The stage was eighty-five feet deep and seventy-one wide, the breadth of the curtain thirty-two feet, and so arranged that the whole could be thrown open to the production of spectacles.

The house was opened Aug. 4, 1845, with "The Sleeping Beauty" and "Charles II". . . .

The Spirit of the Times did not send a critic to the opening night of the theater, but did send one the following night.

48:2 THE BOWERY.—We visited this theatre the first night after it opened. It was not crowded, indeed not half full, although *of course* we heard daily how *bang up* were the houses. The house itself is very large and prettily ornamented. The depth of the pit, measuring from the orchestra to the boxes, is immense. From the first box on each side of the stage, the boxes run back to the number of five, before the curve commences. The result is that in these five boxes on each side,

48:2. *Spirit of the Times*, Aug. 9, 1845.

you must sit obliquely, or screw yourself round in your seat very much, to see the stage. We are told in this respect it is like Drury Lane. In the Park theatre the reader may recollect that the curve or semi-circle to which we allude springs from the stage, or the first boxes, at farthest.

There are sixteen boxes at the Bowery in place of fourteen as at the Park, and each seat in the boxes (save perhaps the stage box) will hold one more, we apprehend, than the corresponding seats at the Park. The boxes contain, usually, six seats each. We have said enough to indicate the great capacity of the house to hold numbers. At the same prices, we should think it would contain twice the money that the National can. In the second tier the back seats on each side, must, we think, be quite low. Though not short ourselves, we found it impossible to see the front of the stage while seated in one of them. The proscenium boxes are ten in number, if we recollect right. (We enter into these details because many of our readers may never visit the house.)

The coloring and ornamental work of the boxes and house are generally in good taste,—not gaudy at all, but not striking. They do not compare with the principal city theatres, either in richness or beauty. . . .

The Bowery Theatre of 1845 was thoroughly renovated and redecorated in 1862, reopening on July 14th of that year. It was renovated again in 1879 and reopened on September 11, when it was officially renamed the Thalia.

49. BROADWAY THEATRE
New York City
Opened September 27, 1847

The new theatrical season of 1847–48 saw the opening of an important new theater, which was to be of first rank importance for the next ten years. The Broadway opened on September 27, 1847, with an outstanding stock company that included Henry and Lester Wallack, soon to be distinguished theatrical managers in their own right. The architect for the building was J. M. Trimble, who had built the Olympic and was to be responsible in the future for a number of New York's finest theaters. Brown comments:

49:1   The original projector of the "Old Broadway Theatre" was Thomas S. Hamblin, but just as he was about beginning operations, the Bowery Theatre, then under his management, was destroyed by fire, involving him in a loss of $100,000. Col. Alvah Mann, then commenced the erection of it, and, after spending $14,000, was obliged to call in the aid of Mr. Raymond in order to complete the building. The lot upon which this theatre was built was on the east side of Broadway between Pearl and Anthony (now Worth) Streets, at what are now known as 326 and 328 Broadway. It would accommodate 4,500 persons, having seats for 4,000. There was an immense pit to which only men and boys were admitted. The price of admission was twenty-five cents and the seats were plain benches without backs, and on crowded nights the jam used to be terrific. The first and second galleries were called the dress and family circles. Three rows of benches were set apart in the latter for the accommodation of colored persons. It was one of the best arranged places of amusement in the city, and was modelled after the Haymarket Theatre, London, Eng. When he first opened here Ethelbert A. Marshall, the manager, was partial to English actors, but it was not long before many Americans were found among his *corps dramatique*. Here Edwin Forrest and W. C. Macready won their greatest laurels. Although Macready was regarded by the general public as the greatest actor of his day, his vanity and egotism, and his supercilious treatment of his subordinates, made him unpopular in his own profession. Sometimes he rendered himself ridiculous on the stage by assuming characters unsuited to his years. He would persist in playing Claude Melnott because he had been the original representative of that part. The opening of the "Old Broadway" took place Sept. 27, 1847. The company consisted of Fanny Wallack, Rose Telbin, Miss Winstanley, Miss Carman, Mrs. Hield, Helen Matthews, Henry Wallack, John Lester (Wallack), Thomas Lynne, J. M. Dawson, Thomas Vache, Henry Hunt, C. W. Hunt, Mesdames Watts, Bernard, Sargeant, and Chapman, the Misses Gordon, Fitzjames, George Vandenhoff, G. Chapman, H. Bernard, J. Everard, Dennison, William Fredericks, E. Shaw, J. Bernard, J. Kingsley, J. Walters, Thompson, Allen, and Miles, St. Clair and Celeste. Alvah Mann, proprietor; G. H. Barrett, acting and stage manager; W. E. Anderton, prompter; J. M. Trimble, architect; J. R. Smith and G. Heister, scenic artists, Andrew J. Allen, costumer; Samuel Wallis, properties; Mr. Galbraith, stage carpenter and machinist. The initial performance was "School for Scandal." . . .

50. ASTOR PLACE OPERA HOUSE
New York City
Opened November 22, 1847

A theater that would become notorious in American theater history opened on November 22, 1847. The Astor Place Opera House was to be the new home of Italian opera in New York City but, like its predecessors, it was doomed to be a financial failure and finally to open its doors to dramatic entertainments. The tragedy that led to the theater's notoriety and finally its demise occurred in 1849 with an appearance of the great English tragedian, William Macready. The circumstances surrounding his appearance led to the "Astor Place Riots," which are discussed in detail in the last volume of this series, *Major Events of American Theater History*.

49:1. T. Allston Brown, *A History of the New York Stage from the First Performance in 1732 to 1901*. 3 vols. (New York: Dodd, 1903), 1:367–68.

FLOATING THEATRE.—"TEMPLE OF THE MUSES," NEW YORK.

47. Chapman's Temple of the Muses, New York. Engraving, published in the *Illustrated London News* (May 7, 1845). Courtesy of The Hoblitzelle Theater Arts Library, The Humanities Research Center, The University of Texas at Austin.

THE OLD BOWERY THEATRE. 1860.

48. Fifth Bowery Theatre, New York, 1860. Lithograph, for D. T. Valentine's *Manual of the Corporation of the City of New York* (1863). Courtesy of The Hoblitzelle Theatre Arts Library, The Humanities Research Center, The University of Texas at Austin.

THE BOWERY THEATRE IN 1872.

48. Fifth Bowery Theatre, New York, 1872. Engraving, published in *New York Dramatic Mirror*. Courtesy of The Hoblitzelle Theatre Arts Library, The Humanities Research Center, The University of Texas at Austin.

49. Broadway Theatre, New York, 1850. Courtesy of The Hoblitzelle Theatre Arts Library, The Humanities Research Center, The University of Texas at Austin.

ASTOR PLACE OPERA HOUSE.

50. Astor Place Opera House, New York. Engraving, after a drawing by J. H. Souter; published in *Illustrated London News* (Feb. 12, 1853). Courtesy of The Hoblitzelle Theatre Arts Library, The Humanities Research Center, The University of Texas at Austin.

The New York *Herald* critic attended the opening and his comments appeared the next day.

50:1   ITALIAN OPERA—OPENING OF
THE ASTOR THEATRE

Last evening was a memorable era in the fashionable and meteorological annals of New York. The weather was unpropitious outside—it was dark, misty, grisly, disagreeable, deceptive. The first appearance in the interior of the Astor Theatre, of the new Italian *troupe* was equally doubtful, dark, when the chandelier was out, foggy, uncertain, vociferous, applauding, and all sorts of noises, and all sorts of feelings in private. Such a rush of well-dressed ladies, ill-dressed gentlemen, beautiful female faces, and Wall-street worn male countenances, was never seen in the history of Manhattan Island. As the carriages rolled one after the other up to the entrances, discharging loads of beauty, elegance, diamonds, lace, in all the varieties, of music and millinery, the mind was lost in the contemplation as to what would be the results of all these doings, at the final settlement of accounts next spring. The rent is already paid—but how will the poor artists come out! When all were seated, the *coup d'oeil* of the house was beautiful in the extreme; it was filled from top to bottom, from pit to gallery, from the foot of the mountains of humanity up to the upper edges of the clouds of heavenly sentiment. The only drawback was the half hour of deficient gas and light. But what can be said of the *troupe*? of the *prima donna*, the *tenoré*, the *basso*, of all of them, from the first manager down to the very lamplighter! The applause, from time to time, was vociferous: thump, thump, thump; bravo, bravo, bravo. Opinions, however, to the aggregate result were varying and contradictory, fat and lean, like pork steaks. The *troupe*, it was said by many first-rate critics, was the best we ever had

in this city, not even excepting the Garcia company. Oh! oh! But what would good judges say? what would the real critics determine?—We think that the best way is to consider them for the season as the best *troupe*—the finest artists—the most interesting divinities, that ever have been in New York, from the first era of Italian opera to the present day.

But notwithstanding such an indulgent opinion entertained by many, there were others who said that such vocalists could not pass muster in London or Paris, even as third-rate artists. Yet we have enthusiasm among us, growing as rank as prairie grass; and numbers there are extravagant in feeling, energetic in action, who maintain that Grisi and Jenny Lind have found their match at last in the Astor Theatre of New York; that we are a happy and lucky people in having imported from Italy, unknown to all the rest of Europe, artists of the first talents, whom none ever dreamt or thought we could obtain. We think we shall side with this party, and think we shall regard the *troupe* as equal to anything in Paris or London. We do so, because it is a delicious and pleasing fancy, and corresponds with the position we have been gradually assuming in the other departments of human life—in war, in trade, in cotton, in corn, in whiskey, in sausages. We mean to make New York the metropolis of the world, and to compel London to vacate her post. We mean to make Paris take off the fashions from Broadway as soon as stitched up; and all the rest of Europe to imitate what takes place here, both in war and commerce—in paying debts, and paying dividends—as well notes of hand as well as notes of music.

Upon the whole, however, last evening was a brilliant reception. The company was brilliant—the house brilliant—the diamonds brilliant—the eyes brilliant—all but the everlasting chandelier. Everything went off with the greatest *éclat*, and in the present movement, in the midst of doubt and difficulty among the critics,

50:1. New York *Herald,* Nov. 23, 1847.

we are determined to believe that Grisi and Jenny Lind are not such extraordinary singers after all; that Tamborini, Rubini, and even the great Lablache—great in fat and circumference, truly—are nothing at all beyond those whom we can produce at a dollar a ticket in New York. We have paid fifteen dollars—rental price —for one seat to hear Jenny Lind. To hear our *prima donna* is only 87½ cents, cash in advance, wholesale value. Of course you get more music for a shilling in New York than in London—and even still more of mush and milk. On the whole, the fair vocalists of the *troupe* are a fair average of Italy; but the males are only from fair to middling; and even a shade below that. But, wait for another night.

The fashionable world is now completely organized—the opera is successful —white kid gloves are all the go—and the *canaille* must keep themselves a respectful distance from Astor Place hereafter. Read and obey.

By April the house had closed for lack of support, but William Niblo, of Niblo's Garden, took over the management of the theater during the summer of 1848 and was very successful with a program of drama, music, and ballet. The Astor Place Opera House remained a successful theater presenting dramatic performances until the tragic riots of 1849, which killed twenty-one persons and wounded thirty-six more.

51. BURTON'S THEATRE
New York City
Opened July 10, 1848

William E. Burton not only was an actor of note, but also had had extensive experience as a theatrical manager in Philadelphia, Washington, Baltimore, and New York. In 1848 he leased a relatively new theater known as Palmo's Opera House and changed the name to Burton's Theatre. The theater became one of the most popular playhouses in New York City. Palmo's Opera House had been built in 1844 and was an exquisitely designed and decorated theater. Burton opened his playhouse on July 10, 1848, to the following review in the New York *Herald*:

51:1   Last night, this theatre (lately Palmo's), opened for the season, under the most flattering and favorable auspices. A numerous audience filled the boxes, parterre, and galleries, to witness various performances. Great expectations were raised by such names as Brougham, for stage manager; Loder, musical director; and Fredericks as ballet master. Nor were the high raised expectations of the public disappointed. This theatre, from the changes and decorations it has undergone, is now a beautiful resort, and a comfortable place of public amusement. The new company which has been selected, will bear comparison with that of any Theatre in the Union, Mrs. Chapman, of Philadelphia, in the burletta of "Maidens, Beware," delighted the audience. She was rapturously applauded, and loudly called for at conclusion of the piece. That laughable and lightly entertaining farce of "Raising the Wind" was admirably performed. Mr. Crisp, as Jeremy Diddler, surpassed every one we have ever seen in this difficult character. His performance was a master-piece, and the applause and delight of the audience were such as to prove that his talent was well appreciated. The "Irish Dragoon," a new farce, was perfectly successful, nor could it be otherwise with such real and genuine talent as that which Mr. Brougham displayed. In addition to all these pieces, the Viennoise troupe performed some of their best dances, and, upon the whole, the opening was crowned with great success, affording a highly flattering prospect for the future. The little theatre, from what we saw last night, bid fair to become a favorite and fashionable resort of the downtown gentry. The enterprising manager and talented company fully deserve

51:1. New York *Herald*, July 11, 1848.

the success which we doubt not they will meet with.

Some facts concerning the physical aspects of the house are found in Brown's *History of the New York Stage.*

51:2 The place of amusement known as "Palmo's Opera House" was erected upon the site of Stoppani's Arcade Baths, Nos. 39 and 41 Chambers Street, by Sig. Ferdinand Palmo, who had accumulated a little fortune as proprietor of the Café des Mille Colonnes, in Broadway, between Hospital and Duane Streets. It was the ambition of his life to establish a theatre in which the music of his own beloved Italy might find a permanent home, and he had sufficient confidence in the taste and liberality of the public to believe that his investment would be remunerative. His was the fourth attempt to introduce Italian opera in this city, and the second to give it individual habitation. The venture proved disastrous, and poor Palmo sacrificed all that he possessed, and became eventually dependent upon the charity of others, after serving as a cook in a hotel and in several restaurants. It was a small theatre compared to those of the present day, and would seat hardly eight hundred persons. The house was well constructed, ingeniously contrived for acoustic purposes; in fact, it was as convenient and comfortable as any theatre could be. . . .

. . . William E. Burton was the next lessee. The theatre had terribly run down, and Burton's speculation was regarded as a suicidal affair. He opened, however, July 10, 1848, and gave it his own name.

The whole establishment had a thorough renovation; a new proscenium was erected, and private boxes constructed; a new drop curtain was painted by Mr. Hiegle. John Brougham was stage man-

ager. "Maidens, Beware!," "Raising the Wind," "The Irish Dragoon," and three ballet divertisements by the Viennoise children formed the initial program. . . .

52. NEW NIBLO'S GARDEN THEATRE
New York City
Opened July 30, 1849

Niblo's Garden had continued its popularity; a fire, however, destroyed the house. Mr. Niblo then planned a new, much larger, and more permanent theater, which he opened to the public July 30, 1849. The New York *Herald* of July 31 carried a review of the opening and the new theater.

52:1   NIBLO'S OPENING NIGHT
In spite of Mr. Niblo's request for the indulgence of his friends for the unfinished state of some parts of his establishment, we were much astonished to witness the wonderful effects he had achieved in the opening of his fashionable place of amusement. The interior of this splendid theatre is finished, and it is a beautiful specimen of architectural art, which does great credit to its decorators and painters, MM. Allegri and Molini, two of the best scenic and decorative artists in this country. The proscenium is illustrated in the Moorish style, and copied from those admirable *circleurs* of the Alhambra of Granada. The two ranges of boxes are beautifully ornamented, and the curtains and scenaries are of very elegant style. One of the most remarkable improvements of Niblo's Garden are the seats of the boxes, which are well cushioned and give comfort to those who find room upon them. As a *tout ensemble*, the aspect of the house is very fine. The theatre is airy, and, of course, comfortable for the numerous public who will undoubtedly patronise the establishment for the Napoleon of theatrical managers. The audience last evening was very large and composed of the most respectable people

51:2. T. Allston Brown, *A History of the New York Stage from the First Performance in 1732 to 1901.* 3 vols. (New York: Dodd, 1903), 1:337–39.

52:1. New York *Herald,* July 31, 1849.

of our city. The Ravels made their new debut in their well known farces, panto-mimes, and acrobatic feats, which were, and will be, as before, the great attraction of Niblo's Garden. The tight-rope, the "Italian Brigands," and "Vol-au-Vent," completed the entertainment, and excited all the old enthusiastic approbation, laughter, and applause which we have witnessed and heard for the last ten years. The second performance of the Ravel family will take place this evening, and will consist in the exercises of the *danse de corde*; to be succeeded by the panto-mime of the "Milliners, or the Hungarian Rendezvous," and to conclude with the fairy play of the "Magic Trumpet." We are certain that Niblo's Garden will have another large audience; and this enter-prising manager deserves to see his place filled, for he has made every effort to build an elegant theatre, and has thus far entirely succeeded. The stage manage-ment is in the hands of Messrs. Chippen-dale and Sefton, two well-known public favorites. What with the excitement of all the arrangements, the beauty and spa-ciousness of the theatre and saloons, the loveliness of the fashionable ladies who fill the boxes, the admirable performances of the orchestra, led by Signor Lamana, and a hundred other attractions, Niblo's new theatre cannot fail to equal in at-tractiveness and prosperity, to the old "Garden." What more could Mr. Niblo wish?

53. BROUGHAM'S LYCEUM
New York City
Opened December 23, 1850

John Brougham was a talented and pop-ular young writer and stage manager who had spent two years as the chief writer at Burton's Theatre. In 1850 he decided to launch his career as a theatrical manager, obtained sup-port, and built a new theater, which opened on December 23, 1850. The playhouse filled the need for a quality house to take the place

of Mitchell's Olympic Theatre, which had closed.

The following excerpt places the new theater geographically:

53:1   The Theatre known as "Brougham's Lyceum" was situated on the west side of Broadway, two doors below Broome Street, and built on the lot formerly occu-pied by what was called the "Mourning Store." It was opened Dec. 23, 1850, with "Esmeralda," by John Brougham. During the time it was building, and on Aug. 5, 1850, the rear of the building fell to the ground, killing two of the la-borers. Mr. Brougham put all the money he could raise into the enterprise, and borrowed a great deal from Edwin P. Christy, the minstrel manager. During the first season it was a brilliant success, but subsequently, owing to architectural changes in the neighborhood, it became necessary for Mr. Brougham to assume new obligations. In making a loan he signed a paper which he supposed gave him the sole lease of the premises for a series of years. Instead of that, one of the parties took advantage of his legal rights, and, because on the instant Brougham did not furnish $15,000, the amount of his demand, the sheriff entered and took possession of the theatre. . . .

The opening of the theater was covered by the New York *Herald*:

53:2   BROUGHAM'S LYCEUM
                THE OPENING NIGHT

This new temple of Thespis was opened last evening, before a brilliant and crowded audience, with an *éclat* which prognosticates its future to be tri-umphant. In this city, where a vast vari-ety of places of dramatic resort are already established as universally ac-

53:1. T. Allston Brown, *A History of the New York Stage from the First Performance in 1732 to 1901*. 3 vols. (New York: Dodd, 1903), 1:472.
53:2. New York *Herald,* Dec. 24, 1850.

knowledged favorite theatres of the art, it requires no small efforts and no mean talents, to make an opening and secure a patronage, amongst our playgoers; yet if we may judge from the overwhelming audience, the unbounded applause, and the excellence of the whole corps, Brougham's Lyceum is destined to hold a prominent position as a home of the drama in New York. The entrance, which is spacious, is in Broadway, within a few doors of Broome street, and the building extends to Mercer street. The interior of the theatre presents a very pleasing *coup d'oeil*, and is capable of containing about 1,800 or 2,000 persons. The seats in the dress circle are elegantly covered and will accommodate about four hundred; the pit, or parquette, is finished in a similar style, and will contain comfortably about an equal number of visitors. The family circle is spacious and well arranged, and the panels are most tastefully formed of iron work, painted in white and gold, and from each panel is suspended a chastely exquisite chandelier; the proscenium is quite pleasing and not gaudy, and the whole presents a very pretty little theatre. All the artists connected with its erection deserve unqualified commendation; Mr. Trimble, the well known builder, has added another "story" to his architectural fame, and the masonry, by Mr. George J. Knight, is solid and enduring, and must afford full confidence as to safety and stability of structure. It reflects the highest credit upon both these gentlemen. The exquisite carving is by Mr. Allegri, and the ornamental iron works by Jackson and Co. The act drop, which is most artistically painted with a softness of style and a clearness of representation, is from the pencil of Mr. Heister, the able scene painter of the Broadway theatre. The opening entertainment commenced with a humorous and appropriate address entitled "Brougham & Co.," in which the whole company were introduced. It was very playful and entertaining, but can be appreciated only when

admirably acted, as it was last night. It would be injustice to attempt to describe it. Brougham made the first bow, and commenced his rigamarole, after the deafening plaudits which greeted him had ceased, and at the end of every verse introduced with a happy line each member of his company—first his stage manager, Mr. Henry Lynne; then Mrs. Vernon, Mrs. Blake and Mrs. Brougham, who were each most cheeringly received. Miss Kate Hern (our own Kate) was received with a warmth that she deserves, and which convinces us that she will be a great favourite as she has been elsewhere. She will doubtless prove one of the most attractive members of the corps. Miss Mary Taylor, too, who brought forward her sister as a new aspirant for that favor which she herself has never failed to receive at the hands of a New York audience, was greeted with great applause. Mrs. Loder's reception showed that she was not forgotten. Mrs. McDill, a lady of very prepossessing appearance, bids fair to be a favourite on these boards. Then came Miss Gould, from London, Mrs. Dunn, Mrs. Lyster, Mr. Owens, Mr. Phillips, and a host of others, whom in good time we will notice but at present we cannot do justice to. The orchestra, conducted by Mr. George Loder, is efficient and correct, and reflected the highest credit on the musical ability of that gentleman. The overture was performed with well studied and faultless accuracy. A young lady, from the Academie Royal, Paris, Mademoiselle Ducy-Barre, made her first appearance in this country as the *danceuse* of the Lyceum, and we are pleased to say that she is likely to be not the least of the attractions offered to the public; she is graceful and buoyant in her execution of the Terpsichorean art, and was received with a burst of applause, which must have convinced her that Americans can welcome a stranger, who, by ability, proves deserving of their hospitality. She was supported by Mr. Smith, the ballet master of the theatre.

54. WALLACK'S LYCEUM
New York City
Opened September 9, 1852

Undoubtedly the finest repertory company in nineteenth-century America was that of Wallack's, which for more than thirty years stood for the highest degree of excellence and taste in the drama. Wallack's Lyceum was built on the ruins of Brougham's Lyceum, which failed financially. The importance of this theater and its opening is explained by Odell.

54:1   Decidedly one of the most important events in the history of the New York stage was the establishment of Wallack's Theatre. One reads old playbills with more or less depression; immediately on getting into a file of Wallack programmes one realises that one has entered a realm where beauty and elegance almost invariably prevail. There was nothing haphazard about the productions of this house throughout its best years; care for minutest details distinguished the management, a finish of acting glorified every play, and the best the English dramatist had done was presented on that stage, night after night, for years. Nothing like Wallack's Theatre, I am convinced, had existed in New York previously to 1852; nothing quite like it existed after 1880. I say this in full recognition of the claims of the old Park, of Burton's, and of the later Daly's. The serene excellence of Wallack's for nearly thirty years surpassed them all. Will the skeptical, instead of condemning me, read, as I have done, patiently and lovingly through files of daily papers and nightly playbills, covering all the years involved, and see, candidly, if I am right? Such reading will show why refined playgoers, whether resident here or briefly sojourning, went to Wallack's, without inquiring as to the play to be acted. There was the perfect

performance by the best company in America; what mattered the play?

Wallack's Lyceum sprang from the failure of Brougham's Lyceum. The playbill for the opening night—September 8, 1852—promises new decorations, embellishments, etc. The spacious lobbies in front of the theatre had been painted in fresco by Harvest and Youngling, "who have just achieved so great a triumph of taste and skill in the decorations of the Metropolitan Hotel." The boarded partitions formerly separating the entrances to the boxes and parquet had been replaced by ornamental balustrade, and the sofas of the boxes and parquet had been entirely remade, with patent spring seats. "In the large space at the back of the Parquet, where, formerly a crowded house would compel visitors to stand, comfortable sofas, to accommodate Ninety Persons, have been placed." Two new private boxes had been added, and the interior had been entirely repainted and regilded; altogether, the management felt justified in announcing this as "One of the Most Beautiful and Commodious Theaters in the World." Besides, arrangements had been made for additional ventilation.

The playbill sets down Wallack as lessee, "John W. Lester" as stage manager, and Charles Wallack, another son, as treasurer. I am surprised to find fifteen players in the band, directed by Tyte. The price of admission to the parquet and dress circle was fifty cents; to the family circle twenty-five cents; to orchestra seats, seventy-five cents. Private boxes were, according to size, five or seven dollars. The performances began at seven-thirty. And thus started the great Wallack's Theatre.

The review of the opening appeared in the New York *Herald*:

54:2   The Lyceum, which has been closed for several months past, re-opened under

54:1. George D. C. Odell, *Annals of the New York Stage*. 15 vols. (New York: Columbia Univ. Pr., 1927–49), 6:213.

54:2. New York *Herald*, Sept. 9, 1852.

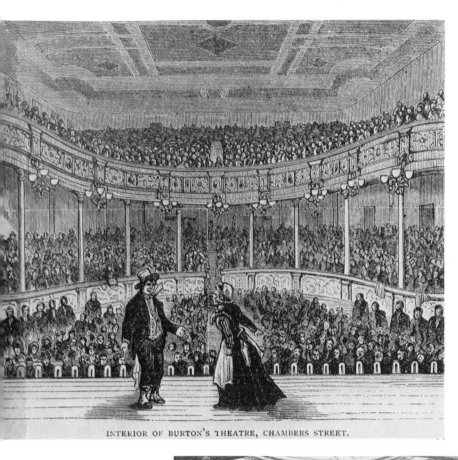

INTERIOR OF BURTON'S THEATRE, CHAMBERS STREET.

51. Interior, Burton's Theatre, New York. Engraving. Courtesy of The Hoblitzelle Theatre Arts Library, The Humanities Research Center, The University of Texas at Austin.

52. Interior, New Niblo's Garden Theatre, New York. Engraving, published in *Ballou's Pictorial Drawing-Room Companion* (Feb. 24, 1855). Courtesy of The Hoblitzelle Theatre Arts Library, The Humanities Research Center, The University of Texas at Austin.

INTERIOR VIEW OF NIBLO'S THEATRE, NEW YORK.

FEBRUARY 24, 1855.

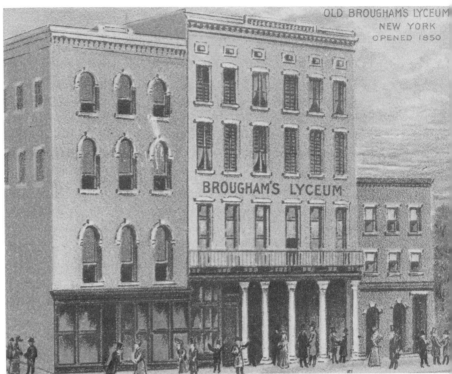

53. Brougham's Lyceum, New York. A cigar card, "Between the Acts." Courtesy of the Hoblitzelle Theatre Arts Library, The Humanities Research Center, The University of Texas at Austin.

ENTRANCE TO THE NEW BOSTON THEATRE, WASHINGTON STREET.

55. New Boston Theatre, Boston. Engraving by Peirce, after a drawing by Champney; published in *Ballou's Pictorial Drawing-Room Companion* (July 21, 1855). Courtesy of The Hoblitzelle Theatre Arts Library, The Humanities Research Center, The University of Texas at Austin.

new and better auspices last evening, under the management and proprietorship of Mr. Wallack. The theatre has undergone many improvements since it has passed into his hands. The sofas of the boxes and parquet have been renovated and heightened. Two new and handsome boxes have been added, the entrance and lobbies ornamented, and the whole interior of the house has put on a fashionable and elegant appearance. The performance of last evening commenced with the excellent comedy of "The way to get Married," with Blake, Walcott and Lester supporting the characters of Toby Allspice, Dashaila and Tangent; and Mr. H. B. Phillips, that of Caustic. These gentlemen are already well and favorably known to the play going public, and a criticism of their performances would be supererogatory; suffice it to say that each seemed to strive on this occasion to surpass anything he had done before in the same line. And in this we think they were successful. They certainly managed to keep the audience in a continual roar of laughter. Mrs. Backland played Clementina extremely well, and Julia Faulkner and Lady Sorrel, were also well sustained by Mmes. Hale and Cramer. With such names occurring in the stock company, the season cannot but be successful at the Lyceum—which, besides, possesses the attraction of a very fine orchestra. . . .

55. NEW BOSTON THEATRE
Boston, Massachusetts
Opened September 11, 1854

In 1854 there was a definite need for a new first-class theater in Boston, for the old Boston Theatre had burned in 1852 and the Tremont Street Theatre had been sold to a church group. The new Boston Theatre, which opened in 1854, was, perhaps, the most advanced playhouse built during this period, with excellent facilities for various types of stage entertainments. A history of this theater was written in 1908 by Eugene Tompkins, who

was manager from 1830 to 1906. Part of it is quoted here.

55:1   The Boston Theatre was opened in 1854, and was so far in advance of the times that even to-day no theatre in the world has been able to surpass it in all important particulars. In beauty of line, in acoustic properties, in ventilation, in ease and economy of heating, in generosity of entrances and lobbies, in comfort and celerity of exit, in size and capabilities of stage, it has been a model for all the large theatres in this country. No other theatre in the world has presented so many notabilities to the public, from tragedians and grand opera singers to negro minstrels and various performers, from orators and clergymen to ballet dancers and athletes. Scarcely any world-famous artist in the last fifty years has missed making his or her appearance at the Boston Theatre, and myriads of words have fallen from their lips for its beauty, its comfort, and its unparalleled acoustics.

The old Boston Theatre on Federal Street was destroyed in 1852, and the Tremont Theatre having gone into the possession of a religious society, it was felt that an adequate place of amusement was needed in the city. Consequently, on April 28, 1852, a meeting which had been called by Joseph Leonard, the auctioneer, was held at the Revere House to consider the building of a new theatre. The meeting was called to order by Joseph N. Howe. E. C. Bates was chosen chairman, and B. F. Stevens secretary. Addresses were made by Mayor Benjamin Seavern, Gardner Brewer, and other prominent citizens, and a committee, consisting of John E. Bates, Gardner Brewer, Otis Rich, and John E. Thayer, was appointed to select a site and solicit subscriptions. Among those who signed the petition for a charter were David Sears,

55:1. Eugene Tompkins and Quincy Kilby, *The History of the Boston Theatre, 1854–1901* (Boston and New York: Houghton, 1908), pp. 1–12.

Oliver Ditson, and General John S. Tyler.

On May 15, 1852, the Boston Theatre Company was incorporated with a capital stock of $200,000, which was afterwards increased to $250,000, the price of the shares being placed at $1000 each. The Melodeon estate on Washington Street was bought, together with the rear land, which had been owned by the Boston Gaslight Company, the total cost reaching $163,348.80.

A prize of $500 was offered for the best design of a theatre, and was won by H. Noury, the building being constructed from his design by the Boston architects, E. C. and J. E. Cabot and Jonathan Preston, the latter being appointed supervisor. The building covers 26,149 feet of land and has a present seating capacity of 3140. Comparatively few structural changes have been made in the theatre since it was built, the greatest being in 1888, when ten feet were cut from the front of the stage, thus bringing the audience so much nearer the players. In 1890 the great cut-glass chandelier was taken down and its place was filled by eight smaller electric clusters, thus removing the danger of accident from the fall of the whole or a part of the massive structure, a danger far more apparent than real, yet within the bounds of possibility. This chandelier was of immense size and weight, and was composed of thousands of cut-glass prisms. When lighted, it had the appearance of a great glowing jewel, and was the admiration and delight of generations of theatre-goers. A strange comment on the uncertainty of fashion is furnished by the fact that when this chandelier was taken down, nobody could be found to purchase it, or even to remove it for the value of the material of which it was composed. It was dismantled and stored above the dome of the theatre, where it now lies, neglected and forgotten, within a few feet of the scene of its long-time glory.

The construction of the dome was a work of genius in engineering, as it was a serious problem to carry so large an expanse of ceiling without help from below. It was here that wire lathing was used for the first time on record, as it was not practicable to sustain so great an area of plastering with ordinary wooden laths.

The paneled clock over the proscenium was unique in its novelty, and is still the only one of the kind in this country, though its counterpart may be seen at the Hoftheater in Dresden, Saxony.

The staircase which leads from the Washington Street lobby to the upper gallery is ingeniously contrived to be self-supporting and in no way dependent upon the walls beside it, but springing free and clear from the basement below. Its integrity is shown in the fact that in all its more than fifty years of service it has borne its burden of millions of hurrying human beings without a crack or strain of any kind. It is spiral in form and measures nine feet in width, being constructed of oak, which even now shows but few signs of wear from the countless feet that have trodden its broad surfaces. The grand staircase leading from the main lobby to the first balcony also shows the excellence of its material, there being practically no appearance of wear after its half-century of faithful service.

The ladies' room on the first floor, the smoking-room on the second floor, and the spacious lobbies of the family circle and gallery occupy in themselves an area greater than the entire auditorium of many a smaller theatre. Although the seating capacity of the house is so much larger than that of any other in the city, it is a pleasing fact that the sign "Standing Room Only" has been shown oftener in the Boston Theatre than in any other local playhouse.

The auditorium is ninety feet in diameter and is almost circular in shape, flattening slightly towards the stage. The distance from the curtain to the back of the auditorium is eighty-four feet. The height of the dome is fifty-four feet.

The four private boxes on either side of the auditorium should be considered principally as an architectural feature, as they were intentionally kept in the background, that they might not interfere with the view from the orchestra circle and balconies.

The stage backs on Mason Street, where are the stage-door for the use of actors and working staff, and the great scene-doors, which have height enough to admit the largest pieces of scenery and sufficient width to permit the passage of tally-ho coaches, fire engines, or the bulkiest properties that may be needed. The proscenium opening is forty-eight feet in width by forty-one in height. There is a sub-cellar beneath the stage with a depth of about thirty feet, which allows the sinking of the highest flats and wings. The stage itself is irregular in shape, being much deeper on the side toward the south. Its capabilities are known the world over, and it has been since its first construction a standard for commodiousness and mechanical perfection. . . .

56. NEW YORK THEATRE
New York City
Opened September 20, 1854

The New York Theatre was built on the site of the old Metropolitan (Tripler Hall) Theatre, which burned. The new theater, although it had an excellent architect and was basically a good playhouse, never attained much popularity as a quality theater and received bad notices from the beginning, as with the following criticism from the New York *Times:*

56:1   NEW YORK THEATRE

Last evening the play of "The Wife" was given here—the leading characters by Miss JULIA DEAN and Mr. E. EDDY. It is the policy of "stars" of course to produce those pieces in which they most excel, but if they were all of

56:1. New York *Times,* Sept. 21, 1854.

"The Wife" stamp it is scarcely possible that that policy would tally with the interest of the management. A more cold and cheerless performance than that of last evening we have seldom listened to. The patient look of endurance with which the audience sat out the five acts was more threatening than satisfactory, and must be observed by the keen eye of the manager with a feeling different to hopefulness.

Of the performances last evening we have little to say. Miss JULIA DEAN in the character of *Mariana* is too well known in that character to draw forth any useful remark. Her conception is pure, womanly, and modest, and her reading good, but intoned too much. In Mr. EDDY we recognize the valuable addition to the few good actors we have in New York. As *St. Pierre* he was admirable, and we are glad to say appreciated. Some portions of his performance were better than we have ever heard before; such for instance as the description of the Swiss home, and in the fourth act where he obtains the confession. In person, in voice, and in that great secret of stage success, repose, Mr. EDDY possesses great advantages. He is judicious, quiet, and eminently picturesque; in a word, he is good, and we are glad to welcome him to a sphere where his talents will be welcomed and appreciated.

It would be an ungrateful task to speak particularly of any other characters in the play. Excepting the gentleman who played the Friar they were uniformly bad. Judging from our experience of last evening we should say the stock company of the New York Theatre requires strengthening, in nearly every department.

The scenery is wretched; the dresses tawdry and common; the stage furniture inappropriate and flashy. Perhaps some amount of allowance should be made for these short-comings, in consideration of the hasty manner in which the theatre has been constructed and opened. We should feel disposed to make this allowance were it not for the uniform badness of the company, scenery, dresses and properties. In view of that uniformity, we are constrained to believe there is something radically wrong, which unvarnished and stern truth alone can remedy.

A word or two about the theatre may not be out of place. In an architectural point of view it reflects great credit on the builder, J. M. Trimble; the design is at once elegant and convenient. Compared with NIBLO'S new theatre, it is, perhaps, the best of the two, although in minute particulars of ornamental work, NIBLO'S has the advantage, and unquestionably so in regard to gas fixtures, &c. The strong point of the NEW YORK is the dome. This is elaborate in conception, carefully studied, and exquisitely executed. The proscenium is also very fine, although the heads of the Caryatids appear to be disproportionately large.

The general seating of the house is arranged as follows: the parquette has sofa, covered with crimson cloth, surrounded by a tier of open boxes, on a level with the stage, furnished with a sofa and six chairs each, and a succession of sofas extending back to the entrances from the vestibule. There are two galleries with circular seats extending around to the proscenium, so arranged as to enable the spectator to see every part of the stage with the greatest facility. The house will comfortably seat 3,000 to 3,500 persons, and is so substantially constructed that the most perfect safety is assured, however great the crowd.

The acoustic properties of the house are decidedly good for operatic purposes. Every sound can be heard, *that is a continuous sound.* It comes to us pure and unbroken. As there does not appear to be any double, or echo, the qualities of the building will be admirable for musical purposes. This fact was sufficiently illustrated by the orchestra, whose performance of the overture to "Zampa" afforded us a good opportunity of catching all the contrasts in the best possible man-

ner. The orchestra, by the way, is a good one, and worth listening to, except in the divertisement music.

For dramatic purposes, the acoustical peculiarities are rather objectionable. Unless the artist is distinct and deliberate in his enunciation, the mere tone of his words, and not the syllables, predominates. We have before referred to Miss JULIA DEAN'S customary intonation. Ordinarily this produces a rather pleasant effect, and compensates in a most satisfactory manner for larger physical effort. This intonation, however, is totally unsuited for the NEW YORK THEATRE. Several times last evening, Miss JULIA DEAN appeared to be singing to the audience; her words were indistinguishable, nothing but a melodious and continuous sound could be heard. Mr. EDDY was the only artist whose method seemed to be improved by this quick transmission of sound.

57. LAURA KEENE'S THEATRE
New York City
Opened November 18, 1856

In 1856 Laura Keene, who was a very popular actress, decided to become a theatrical manager. She remodeled an already existing theater, hired a competent stock company, and began her first season on November 18, 1856. The house was a large one, seating 1,800 persons. Remodeling of the theater cost more than $74,000.

The New York *Times* described the opening night:

57:1   LAURA KEENE'S THEATRE

An acceptable and very beautiful addition to the world of amusement was made last night by the opening of Miss Laura Keene's new theatre. This edifice erected by J. M. Trimble, Esq., is located on the east side of Broadway, a few doors above Houston street, and is entered through a facade of Corinthian columns lightly but

57:1. New York *Times,* Nov. 19, 1856.

120

strongly cast in iron. The hall is paved with black and white marble, and looks elegant, especially at the part where it is surmounted by the ornamental dome.

The interior of the house is extremely pleasing, and bears some general resemblance to Wallack's; but the coloring is different, and the proportions more simple. The proscenium is chaste, and depends more on form than color for its effect. Two large female torchbearers are placed on either side, and from their flambeaux much of the light that illumines this part of the stage is shed. The stage itself appears to be unusually well proportioned and is fifty-two feet in depth.

Most of the decorations of the house are in white and gold, with the exception of the ceiling, which is beautifully painted with allegorical figures, tablets, &c. The effect is very pleasing. The great crowd of the first night is not favorable to a just perception of the acoustical excellences of a new building, but in spite of all the surging and struggling we heard distinctly every word of MISS KEENE'S opening speech; from this fact we anticipate much. The theatre is just about the size for hearing and seeing with comfort. It will seat about 1,800 persons.

There was a large amount of enthusiasm last night, and when the curtain rose peals of applause greeted the fair manageress. The National Anthem sung, MISS KEENE stepped forward and addressed her audience in a forcible, business-like speech, after which the opening performance commenced—Shakespeare's "As you like it."

58. NEW BOWERY THEATRE
New York City
Opened September 5, 1859

The Old Bowery Theatre, which had been in operation since 1837, suddenly found that it had a new rival bearing the same name. The New Bowery opened to great acclaim on September 5, 1859. The dramatic critic of the

New York *Herald* wrote the review of the theater:

58:1 THE NEW BOWERY THEATRE— OPENING NIGHT

People who never visit what is called the east side of the town don't know what they miss. The district bounded by Chatham square, Division street, the Bowery, Eighth street and the East River, is a city entirely distinct in almost everything but language from the remainder of the metropolis. The Bowery itself is always full of bustle and gayety at night. Not so cosmopolitan nor so well dressed, perhaps, as the Broadway promenaders, yet the *habitués* of the Bowery are quite as independent, and certainly have an equally good opinion of themselves. They have, too, excitements and necessities. Among other things the theatre. Beyond other things, we might say, the theatre, for the theatre is almost the only amusement of the working man. To the working boy it is Elysium. For a shilling he gets four hours of the drama, in a crude stage to be sure, but still the drama knights, heroes, distressed maidens, funny servants, a terrible plot and a striking denouement.

So the commencement of any new theatrical enterprise in the Bowery is an event of the highest importance, not only to the manager, but to each individual of the audience. Every man and boy of them seems to have an individual interest in the matter. It is no wonder, then, that the opening of the new Bowery theatre, which took place last evening, should have created an immense sensation. The affair took the form of an ovation from the outset.

The new theatre has already been described at some length in the HERALD. It is situated between new Canal and Hester streets, two blocks north of the old Bowery and on the same side of the way. The dimensions are the most ample

58:1. New York *Herald,* Sept. 6, 1859.

of any theatre in this country. In the auditorium there are seats for over four thousand persons, and the stage is no less than fifty feet wide at the proscenium arch and nearly one hundred feet deep. The immense building was crowded last night long before the performances commenced, and many people—almost as many, we should think, as there were inside the house—were unable to gain admission. The crowd without the doors obstructed the sidewalk for two or three blocks north and south of the theatre, and the crush about the doors was terrific. The pit entrance was the scene of an immense jam, and the conversation of the juvenile portion of the audience was more graphic than elegant.

Within the theatre the general view was exceedingly spirited. The spacious pit, the orchestra stalls, private boxes, and three tiers of amphitheatrical seats, presented an array of earnest, eager, and enthusiastic faces which would stir up the most *blasé* man to a degree of sympathetic announcement. The house itself was freely but not unfavorably criticized. It is spacious and comfortable, the lobbies, corridors and doorways being ample enough for all practical purposes. In the ocular and auricular view of the affair, the house is, *on dit*, quite perfect. A full view of the stage is to be had from almost every seat in the auditorium, and the stage is admirably constructed. The decorations are in white and gold, and in the plainest and best possible taste. The theatre is well lighted, and it seemed to us, properly ventilated. The audience embraced all conditions of humanity. In the orchestra we noticed more than one *habitué* of the Broadway theatres. The pit was jammed with the *democracy*, unwashed and unterrified, to the number of a couple of thousand, and we have rarely seen the boys come out more strongly. Before the curtain rose they interchanged opinons upon nearly all mundane subjects. They talked about politics, the weather, newspapers, plays, &c., in the

most audible and refreshing way. Peanuts, of course, were plenty—(what would the Bowery do without peanuts?) In the boxes above numerous forlorn people prowled about; getting a glance at the stage over or through a vista made by two or three rows of hats. Others stood patiently through the whole performance, and among these amiable persons were several of the (so called) softer sex. The ladies can always stand a good deal of fatigue in the theatrical way.

Altogether, it is rarely that we have seen so gay a scene as presented by the new Bowery Theatre last night. When the curtain rose and displayed the members of the company, with the managers, Messrs. Fox and Lingard, in the centre of the group, with Miss Cappell, the leading actress of the theatre, the managers pronounced a suitable opening address in prose. The managers were received with the most enthusiastic demonstrations of applause. The same honor was given to the salient points of the address, which was followed by the singing of the "Star Spangled Banner," all of which were received with true Bowery unction.

Mr. Hillyard's fine act drop, representing the arms of the State upheld by the Muses, had an appreciative yell, and the audience amused itself while the actors were preparing for the second piece by paying its *devoirs* to the distinguished persons in the house. John Brougham, in the retirement of a private box, was espied by the serried ranks of petites, vehemently cheered, and appealed to in the most lovable way for a "speech," which not being down in the bills was not given. Really, it was asking too much.

Still, through all the bustle and confusion, the most perfect order was preserved. The time-honored sergeant-at-arms, with his rattan, was on hand, but not being members of Congress, the boys attended closely to business and paid particular heed to the more important scenes of the play, which was a curiously, wonderfully and fearfully constructed drama—"The Orange Girl of Venice." How the boys cheered when the patriotic youth triumphed over the aristocratic scoundrel, revenged a parent's murder and freed his country at the same time. The heroine came in for her full share of applause, and the grave and severe portion of the plot was duly enlivened by the low comedian, who, as usual, is victimized by the soubrette. Then there was a comic pantomime and other pleasant things, which were duly relished.

The plays afforded but little opportunities for the actors, but, nevertheless, the company seem to be a fair one. The public is well acquainted with Mr. Fox, who is, deservedly, a favorite with the audience. The leading *tragedienne*, Miss Cappell, promises well, and Mr. Edwards is excellent in the stern fathers, who always, happily, relent before the curtain falls.

Altogether, Messrs. Fox & Lingard, who have purchased the theatre from Hon. James R. Whiting, who commenced building it in May last, have made a good beginning. They have the public voice in their favor, and their success is indubitable.

59. WINTER GARDEN THEATRE
New York City
Opened September 14, 1859

The new Winter Garden Theatre was located in the remodeled Tripler Hall. This theater was to see one of the famous performances of the nineteenth-century American stage when the Booth brothers made their appearance in *Julius Caesar* on November 25, 1864. Junius Brutus Booth, Jr., played Cassius; Edwin, Brutus; and John Wilkes Booth, Marc Anthony. It was the first and only joint appearance by the three brothers, although Edwin and John Wilkes Booth acted together on other occasions.

In the original stock company of the theater, which was to be under the direction of Dion Boucicault, one of the most famous playwrights of the nineteenth century, was Joseph

Jefferson III. He recalls the Winter Garden Theatre in his *Autobiography*.

59:1 My starring venture was attended with what is termed qualified success; not with what could be called positive failure; still I felt that the time had not yet arrived for the continuation of such a rash experiment.* Just at this juncture William Stuart made me an offer of an engagement at his new theater, the Winter Garden, which place was to be under the direction of Dion Boucicault. I accepted the offer, at a much larger salary than I had ever received, and was enrolled as a member of the company. The title of "Winter Garden" had been adopted from a place of amusement in Paris, where plays were acted in a kind of conservatory filled with tropical plants. If I remember rightly, the treasury of the management was not in what could be called an overflowing condition; and although the actors whom they engaged were quite strong, the horticultural display was comparatively weak. Some sharp-pointed tropical plants of an inhospitable and sticky character exuded their "medicinal gums" in the vestibule, and the dress circle was festooned with artificial flowers so rare that they must have been unknown to the science of botany. To give these delicate exotics a sweet and natural odor they were plentifully sprinkled with some perfume resembling closely the sweet scent of hair oil, so that the audience as they were entering could "nose" them in the lobby. Take it altogether, the theater was a failure; for, added to the meager decorations, the acoustics were inferior, and the views of the stage from the auditorium unpardonably bad. To make amends, however, for these shortcomings, Mr. Boucicault had secured a strong company; not so

59:1. Joseph Jefferson, *The Autobiography of Joseph Jefferson* (New York: Century Co., 1889), pp. 207–8.
*Jefferson had been acting with Laura Keene at her theater and had had a bitter experience working with the actress.

far as great names were concerned, but they had been carefully selected with regard to the plays that were to be produced. . . .

The drama critic of the New York *Times* was more gentle than Mr. Jefferson in his criticisms of the theater:

59:2   OPENING OF THE WINTER GARDEN

The upward march of the City population is fast making itself felt on our places of amusement, and the power of the tide was never more strickingly illustrated than at the opening of the so-called "Winter Garden" of MR. STUART last night.

The said Winter Garden is no garden at all, but a neat, charming, brilliant and fairy-like theatre, which, in the course of a few weeks, has replaced, as by a sort of Aladdin's enchantment, the doomed and disconsolate old Metropolitan Theatre. Lying just opposite Bond-street, it receives at high-water mark the two great streams which feed our theatres, and is the joint reservoir of our hotels and our homes. It is near enough to the Metropolitan and the St. Nicholaas, and not too far from Fifth-avenue and Fourteenth-street. This is an advantage, to be sure, which it shares with MISS KEENE'S delightful little theatre. But the Winter Garden (we suppose we must so call it) has other and altogether novel merits of its own, numerous and emphatic enough to account for the enthusiasm with which a new version of that exquisite story, the "Cricket on the Hearth," was received last night by one of the largest, most effective and solidly remunerative audiences we have ever seen assembled in a New York theatre. As we have no time now for extended criticism of the play and the players, the performance having closed at a very late hour—mainly, we presume, in consequence of what the engineers would call the heating of the new machinery—we can only say, in general

59:2. New York *Times,* Sept. 15, 1859.

terms, that the *début* of the new enterprise was thoroughly satisfactory and full of golden promise. The building fully bears out all our anticipations of its qualities. Vast as the crowd last night was, the atmosphere of the place was constantly and universally agreeable, and the system of ventilation deserves, therefore, special commendation as the first real success in this important direction, which has been achieved in a New York place of amusement. Another marked and noticeable feature of the new theatre is the orchestra, which of itself would constitute charm enough to secure a succession of brilliant audiences. Conducted by that most admirable of violinists, Mollenbauer, and made up of thoroughly-cultivated musicians, its performances were marked throughout the evening with a delicacy, grace, refinement and musical value equally new and encouraging. The decorations of the house we have already described. They bear the test of the blazing gas-light bravely. The elevated taste which reigns throughout the whole interior, from the mauve-volor and gold of the vestibule to the graceful floral ornaments of the grand circle, is nowhere more conspicuous than in the drop-curtain, which was painted by RUSSELL SMITH of Philadelphia, and is a genuine *chef-d'oeuvre* of the art. The "Cricket on the Hearth," the opening piece of last night's performances, was tumultuously received. It is a very clever dramatization, and is cast as it could be cast nowhere else than at this theatre. Mr. JEFFERSON, despite a faint suspicion of Americanism, makes a most pathetic and pitiful as well as quaint old Plummer. Miss AGNES ROBERTSON is an incarnate DOT in respect to *naiveté* and touching archness. She was a little dreary with her *patois* in the opening scenes, but this disappeared as the play went on, and in the more serious passages of the second and third acts the audience was visibly reached and moved. Mrs. JOHN WOOD as *Tilly*

Slowboy, looked a Venus in Calico, and made herself irresistibly comical by her positively delicious stupidity. She sang a song of course, and such a song as cannot be easily described and will doubtless receive the attention of all philosophers. Miss SARA STEVENS acts that part of blind *Bertha*, in which Mrs. Hoey won so many laurels, with singular skill and feeling. A little more care bestowed upon the singular management of the features in such a part will make Miss STEVENS' *Bertha* the most delicately truthful character which this promising actress has yet sustained. Mrs. Allen was young, lovely and unhappy, as it was set down that she should be. But what shall we say of Mrs. BLAKE! This thoroughbred actress was completely in her element as the widow of a victim of the Indigo crisis, and "looked-back" from beneath her miraculous head-dress with a dignity and naturalness worthy the best old days of the stage. Mr. HARRY PEARSON was a kind of *John Brodie* in his part of *Perrybingle*, and gave great reality to the best and most touching passages of the rôle. Mr. JOHNSTON'S *Tackleton*, too, was conceived in a higher vein than this artist has accustomed us to expect from him. His power of facial expression proves to be as varied as it is vigorous, and, save for a slight suspicion of extravagance in the demoniacal glee with which *Tackleton* disappears from the presence of *John Perrybingle* when his mission of evil is completely fulfilled, the character could not have been rendered with more *finesse* as well as force. Mr. DAVENPORT'S love-making is altogether appropriate to Mrs. ALLEN'S loveliness; and of the whole cast we have, therefore, really scarcely a word to say save in commendation, which is not our specialty.

The scenery, painted by Messrs. HAYES & HAWTHORNE, takes rank with the best work of its kind which New York has seen. The stage machinery was hardly in fair running order last night,

however, and did less than justice to some of the most novel effects. There were plenty of pretty fairies thrown through the piece; and as the characterization of the New Theatre may be summed up in three words—comfort, taste and female beauty—it needs no ghost of a critic come from Broadway at midnight to foretell for it a high, genuine and permanent success.

60. NEW WALLACK'S THEATRE
New York City
Opened September 26, 1861

The Wallack's Lyceum had been opened in 1852 in the same theater that had housed Brougham's Lyceum. The theater had thrived and was noted as having the best repertory company in New York City, but the time now came for the Wallacks to build their own theater, a playhouse that would incorporate all the ideas they had developed over the past twenty years as managers of the finest stock company in America.

The new theater was moved farther uptown, occupying the site on the northeast corner of Broadway at Thirteenth Street, and opened its doors to the public on September 26, 1861. The New York *Times* drama critic was in attendance and wrote the following review of the play and the theater:

60:1 Many years ago, when actors were a more shabby class than they are now, and the stage was regarded as the most convenient and best lighted path to perdition, there existed in this metropolis a theatre called the Park. Being the only place of amusement of any consequence, it speedily became popular. Artists who came to this country waited upon the manager with fear and trembling. They crooked the pregnant hinges of the knee to his awful garrulity. They listened to his little shibboleth of art and rejoiced. It was well for them that they did, for the Park, like an aesthetical boa-constrictor, crushed

60:1. New York *Times*, Sept. 28, 1861.

what it did not swallow. To make money, it was necessary to play at the Park, to know anything of acting it was necessary to have graduated from that Temple of the Muses. Critics of easy virtue wrote tremendous disquisitions on the affinity of all that was truly great with all that was done at the Park, breathing the salubrious atmosphere of Mount Parnassus, looked down like gods, upon the common people. About this time there arrived in this country a gentlemen whom we now call the "veteran manager." He was in the prime of life: gifted with rare talents as an artist, and still rarer faculties as a manager. For some reason he did not "see" the Park. Doubtless he was told, as we are even now told, that it was the best piece of amusement in the world. Some eminent tragedian, smelling strongly of tobacco, undoubtedly recommended him with exuberant generosity to try the provinces. But shutting his eyes alike to perfection and disinterestedness, this newcomer resolved to open a theatre of his own. You may imagine if you like the jokes of the low comedy man, the lofty scorn of the leading tragedian, the sarcastic considerateness of the manager, and the beery doubts of the critics, when the news became known in the purlieus of the Park Theatre. If, in our day, the Governor of Coney Island were to send a missive to the Mayor of New York, warning him to remove the women and children because it was his intention to bombard the City within twenty-four hours, the surprise could not be greater. But the public, which looks to facts, accepted the thing with favor. Mr. WALLACK opened his theatre, and from that day to this has been quietly accepted as the best manager we have ever had. The rosy fiction that nothing could ever surpass the glories of the Park, has vanished into that very thin air which old and superseded actors are apt to use when they "blow" about their former triumphs.

Just now, when the tendency of man-

agements is to drag down theatrical performances to the lowest level of sensuous glitter and senseless gabble, it is something to see Mr. WALLACK stepping forth on a new stage to enter upon a new career. It means at least that there will be one honest and authoritative voice raised in the cause of art. We do not fear that it will be unheeded. The public must weary of the trash that other establishments present; and turn to Mr. WALLACK for what is pleasant and profitable. He who takes care of the beautiful invariably finds that the useful (such, for instance, as money, newspaper puffs and glory) will take care of themselves. A German gentleman named GOETHE, who knew a thing or two, discovered this long ago.

The new comedy with which Mr. WALLACK inaugurated this season of healthful mimicry and wholesome illusion, is from the pen of the inexhaustible TOM TAYLOR. In London it was called "The Duke in Difficulties"—a title which was suggestive of the plot. Here it is called "The New President," which from the confusion of idea it is apt to produce, does not strike me as an improvement. There are many characters in the piece, and witty dialogue—a little too much perhaps. The story is slight enough. A Duke of a small German State having been deserted by his Court and ministers at a moment when he most needed their presence for the purpose of impressing a powerful visitor with a sense of his importance, hands over the portfolios of office to a company of actors and actresses, who immediately assume the responsibilities of their station, and mingle with distinguished visitors and profound diplomats with all the unrestrained freedom of the footlights. There is little more in the plot to be recorded; the dramatist's opportunity being in the distribution of the dialogue, and the next repartee when it occasions. The histrions are charmed with the nobles, and the nobles with the histrions. Neither has seen precisely the

DRAWN BY CHARLES COPELAND
LOOKING FROM THE STAGE INTO THE LARGEST THEATRE IN AMERICA
THE INTERIOR OF THE BOSTON THEATRE, WHICH SEATS 3172 PERSONS

55. Interior, New Boston Theatre, Boston. Drawing by Charles Copeland, published in *Gleason's Drawing Room Companion* (1854). Courtesy of The Hoblitzelle Theatre Arts Library, The Humanities Research Center, The University of Texas at Austin.

59. Destruction of the Winter Garden Theatre, New York, March 23, 1867. Wood engraving. Courtesy of The New-York Historical Society, New York City.

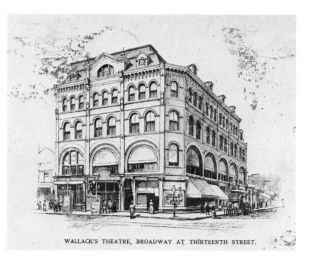

WALLACK'S THEATRE, BROADWAY AT THIRTEENTH STREET.

60. New Wallack's Theatre, New York. Published in *New York Dramatic Mirror*. Courtesy of The Hoblitzelle Theatre Arts Library, The Humanities Research Center, The University of Texas at Austin.

61. Interior, Ford's Theater (restored), Washington, D.C., 1968. Photo by W. H. Spradley, 1968. Courtesy of the National Park Service, U.S. Department of the Interior.

61. Ford's Theater (restored), Washington, D.C., 1969. Photo by W. H. Spradley, 1969. Courtesy of the National Park Service, U.S. Department of the Interior.

same sort of thing before. The ease and abandon of the ladies breaks like Spring sunshine through the frigid reserve of the dignitaries, and the magnate for whom the festive occasion has been prepared, expresses himself charmed with a Court so singularly unconventional. There is, of course, a strong undercurrent of intrigue, and floating on its surface a pleasant little episode about a young girl and her mother, who turn out in the end to be related to the Duke.

Mr. TAYLOR is seldom wordy, but he is frequently exhaustive. Knowing the value of a good theme, he is apt to make the most of it. Diplomacy has always been one of his hobbies. Like BULWER, he has a genius for the *pros* and *cons* of statesmanship. In this play he is exposed to peculiar temptation. On the one hand, he has a group of characters who act by precedent, and speak with the voice of VATTEL; on the other, a number of quick, lively people, who trust to a ready mother-wit to rescue them from the exposure which a knowledge of their imposition would bring about. An intellectual fencing-match could be conducted with smaller weapons than these. Mr. TAYLOR lunges and parries, but he is somewhat lengthy and proud of his dexterity. The first act, in particular, is too long, and must evidently be cut. On the first night the performance was not over until 12 o'clock, and this without any usual delay between acts. In a literary point of view the play is one of Mr. TAYLOR's best. It is written easily, and with great correctness and elegance to diction. Mr. WALLACK has placed it upon the stage with his usual care. The pic-nic scene in the second act is prettily devised, and effective.

The principal parts were played by Mr. LESTER WALLACK, (who had to make a little speech at the end of the entertainment,) Mrs. Hoéy, Miss Mary Gannon, Miss Henriques, Mrs. Vernon, Mr. Blake, Mr. Charles Fisher, Mr. Floyd and Mr.

Reynolds. They were so well played that we are unwilling to do more than record these well-known and thoroughly esteemed names. A company of such sterling excellence should not be spotted with superfluous flattery.

The incidental music was written by Mr. Robert Stoepel, who has resumed the *baton* as orchestral conductor. An effective overture on popular airs, was received with great tumult by the audience, and subsequently an admirable musical panorama of Broadway, (similar to the one played by DODWORTH some years ago,) descriptive of the sounds one may hear on that thorough-fare, brought down the house with genuine applause. Mr. Stoepel is one of the best informed musicians of this country and as a composer is remarkable for the graceful elegance of his style. It is a gratification to know that so competent a conductor has been found for Mr. WALLACK'S fine band. We venture to say that the musical department of the establishment will not be the least of its attractions.

61. FORD'S THEATER
Washington, D.C.
Opened August 27, 1863

It is most unfortunate that Ford's Theater, which was the scene of the assassination of President Abraham Lincoln, has been so damned by the public. Most histories of Washington, D.C., as well as guidebooks over the past hundred years, have merely referred to the building as the place where Lincoln was shot and mentioned nothing of the history of this playhouse.

Ford's Theater was originally the First Baptist Church of Washington, D.C., and services were held in the building from 1834, when it opened, until 1859, when the congregation joined with another one. The building had stood vacant for nearly two years when John T. Ford, a theatrical manager from Baltimore, bought the church and had it renovated into a theater. The venture proved successful; however, a fire destroyed the edifice on December 30, 1862. Ford immediately made plans to rebuild the playhouse and opened it on August 27, 1863. The architect was James J. Gifford, who designed the new brick playhouse to be an outstanding one, seating 1,700 people.

The Washington *Daily Chronicle* of August 26 announced the opening:

61:1   This evening the first performance at this beautiful temple of the Drama will take place. The enterprise of the manager is one involving the outlay of many thousands of dollars, and as Mr. Ford seems determined that nothing shall be omitted on his part to establish a first class theater in this city, we hope that the public will be as ready to support him as he has been to expend money. Those who visit his new theater will see that in every respect it is far superior to his old one, which was burned down last winter, and on the site of which the present establishment is built. The piece selected for the opening is the spectacular drama of the "Naiad Queen," which for beauty of scenery and elegance of appointments and dresses, is not surpassed by any we know of.

The opening of the theater had to be postponed an evening, but when the house opened on August 27 it met all expectations of the public, as revealed in the critic's comments in the Washington *Daily Chronicle*:

61:2   OPENING NIGHT OF FORD'S NEW THEATER.—Mr. Ford must have retired to rest last night, or this morning, as the case may have been, with the gratifying consciousness that he is a well-established favorite with the Washington public, and that his splendid new theater is a success beyond all doubt or possibility of reversal. Notwithstanding the disappointment on Wednesday evening—for though unavoidable on Mr. Ford's part, it was no less a disappointment to his friends and the public—the house last evening was crammed to its utmost capacity, in parquette, dress and family circles. Every foot of standing room was occupied, the auditory seeming as though they were piled up against the wall, so dense was the assemblage. The dress circle was a fine sight alone, while the view of the whole assemblage was positively exciting to look upon.

It gives us great pleasure to say, as the result of personal observation, that this new theater is in every sense a great success. The interior of the building, though the finishing touches are not yet completed, is truly elegant. It is not so gaudy and glittering as perhaps we expected to find it, but it is truly handsome, and in perfect taste. Nothing is overdone, and assuredly nothing is poor or merely pretentious. The *tout ensemble* is most pleasing. There is nothing so ornamentative as to attract your attention from what is going on on the stage; but the moment your eye has taken in all the features of the immense building, eye and taste are satisfied, and the mind is placidly occupied with the idea of completeness. The colors are in harmony; they are sufficiently light to give sense of coolness, and yet sufficiently quiet to bear the artificial light without disturbing the sense of repose so essential to places of public amusement. It is a pity that others do not realize this idea as well as Mr. Ford has done.

The next best thing about this beautiful house is that the ventilation is perfect. This was well tested last night. We confess to some apprehension on the subject as we saw the throngs pouring in, notwithstanding the assurances that had been given in relation to it. But although there could not have been less than three thousand persons present, and the performance was necessarily very prolonged—indeed, the house may be said to have been

61:1. Washington *Daily Chronicle*, Aug. 26, 1863.
61:2. Washington *Daily Chronicle*, Aug. 28, 1863.

"jammed" from half-past seven to half-past eleven, the atmosphere was almost as wholesome for breathing at the first, as at the last. This, considering the location of the building, is a great achievement on the architect's part. Both the parquet and dress circle—we believe the family circle, also—are furnished with cane-bottomed chairs, which are immeasurably superior to the old style of padded cushions. The private boxes are very elegant.

And what is at least of equal importance is that the building is constructed on sound acoustic principles. In this respect nothing is left to be desired. With experience in this matter, we should say there is not a building in the United States of equal size that is so perfect in this particular. There is not the slightest echo or obstruction, and the actors have no need to strain their organs of speech in order to make themselves heard.

It would be hardly proper to criticize or in any way to comment upon the production of the "Naiad Queen" under the circumstances of last evening. There was unavoidable delay between the acts, for the piece is one largely of scenic effect. These delays the audience took with perfect good temper, knowing what difficulties attended the performance, and how solicitous Mr. Ford had been to gratify all by an early opening of his theater. The scenes and spectacles were truly splendid when presented, and the performers bore themselves most admirably under their difficulties. They doubtless felt that they had the hearts of their audience, which is always a good actor's best stimulus. . . .

The story of Mr. Lincoln's assassination in the theater will be recounted in the final volume in this work, *Major Events in American Theater History*, but following this tragic act, on April 14, 1865, Ford's Theater was closed and guards posted at the doors. In June Ford determined to commence the presentation of plays at Ford's Theater once again, but public resentment prevented the reopening, and the War Department ordered the building closed. Later the government purchased it, making it into a storage and office building.

As early as 1946 bills were introduced in Congress to restore the theater as a historic landmark, but the authorization for such a restoration did not come until 1964, when Congress voted funds for the project. The project was completed and the rededication of Ford's Theater took place on April 14, 1967, 102 years after the assassination of President Lincoln. An announcement of the restoration appeared in the New York *Times*:

61:3 RESTORED FORD THEATER
      TO BE DEDICATED
       APRIL 14

The restored Ford's Theater in Washington is expected to be dedicated next April 14, the 102d anniversary of Lincoln's assassination there.

Sixteen plays, many that were performed at Ford's before it ceased to be a theater, will be presented in the 600-seat house. Among them will be "The Rivals," "She Stoops to Conquer," and "The Imaginary Invalid." In addition, existing or original plays dealing with the Lincoln era will be put on.

The program is being collated by Michael Dewell, coproducer with Frances Ann Dougherty of the National Repertory Theater, in conjunction with Lucille Lortel of the American National Theater and Academy. A resident company will be organized by N.R.T. Funds will be sought from foundations, United States Office of Education and the National Council on the Arts.

The restoration of the theater to its original state was authorized as an historic heritage by Congress at a cost of $2,730,000. It will contain a Lincolnia museum, where a documentary on the significance of the theater will be shown.

61:3. New York *Times*, Sept. 26, 1966.

From 1931 until 1964 the house was used as a museum. Reconstruction work started last Jan. 5.

SAW BOOTH IN PLAY

Between 1862 and 1865, Lincoln saw nine offerings at Ford's. One was "The Marble Heart," in which John Wilkes Booth, the assassin, was the leading actor. The records show that Lincoln attended two performances of "Henry IV" on consecutive nights.

The last play seen there by him was "Our American Cousin." He was assassinated during Act III, Scene 2. A reproduction of that scene is being designed by Sointu Syrjala. He is also designing the stage rigging. The contract calls for the installation of his work by March 1. Mr. Syrjala is a scenic designer for the stage and television as well as art director for industrial films.

Asked how he obtained the commission from the Interior Department, Mr. Syrjala said yesterday:

"I had gone to Washington in 1956 to do research for the scenery of Robert Montgomery's television program, 'Good Friday, 1865' (the day of Lincoln's assassination) and met Randle B. Truett, chief historian of the Interior Department's National Capital Region.

USED BRADY PHOTOGRAPHS

"He gave me photographs taken by the Civil War's celebrated photographer, Matthew Brady, showing the interior and exterior of Ford's. Those helped me in designing part of the scenery of 'Our American Cousin' and the Presidential box for 'Good Friday, 1865.'

"Two years ago I was assigned to draw what the stage of Ford's was like and the theater. Aiding me in my work was George J. Olszewski, an historian on the Interior Department's staff."

"Our American Cousin," witnessed by the Lincolns and a party of three, was written by Tom Taylor, a British dramatist, who wrote more than 70 plays. The performance was a benefit for Laura Keene, a popular actress, who appeared in it.

The story concerned the daughter of a baronet who, under duress, is about to marry the lawyer who drove her father into bankruptcy. She is saved from that fate by a clerk in the lawyer's office.

The suggestion to give live performances at Ford's was made by Actors Equity in 1964 and approved by Secretary of the Interior Stewart L. Udall. Architects participating in the reconversion are William M. Haussmann, Charles W. Lessig and the firm of Macomber & Peter.

Chapter 3

The Theater Moves West, 1800-1865

American history from its inception has always been influenced by its western frontier, and the early part of the nineteenth century was an age of great expansion to the West. During the early decades of the century settlements were developed along the Ohio and Mississippi rivers, but with the discovery of gold in California in 1849 there began one of the greatest population movements this country has ever known. Literally overnight new communities came into existence in California, Nevada, and Colorado, and some of these towns died as quickly as they were born as old mines petered out and new strikes were made.

New Orleans became an excellent city for theatricals; a French troupe presented plays shortly before the turn of the nineteenth century. The American Theatre was built in 1823 and was soon followed by the beautiful St. Charles Theatre. Visitors from Europe often commented on the loveliness of the well-appointed playhouses in this leading southern city.

The first playhouse to be built west of the Mississippi River was erected in St. Louis in 1837. Theatrical performances began in

Chicago about the same time, with the building of the Rialto Theatre in 1838.

In California, where there was plenty of gold and too little entertainment, it was not long before a type of crude playhouse was opened in Sacramento and named the Eagle Theatre. As the population of California continued to grow, particularly in San Francisco, the theater became the most popular form of entertainment and numerous playhouses opened their doors. These San Francisco theaters often rivaled their New York counterparts and sometimes even surpassed them in luxury. The hazard of fire in the San Francisco area, however, proved to be great, and few of these theaters lasted for a long period of time.

With the promise of huge salaries, the stage stars from the East coast and Europe made the arduous journey to the West coast to perform, and many of them made their fortunes there. These performers acted under the most severe handicaps in the mining towns, but they found that the miners could be very hospitable and a few months of deprivation could lead to handsome financial rewards. Lotta Crabtree, one of the favorites of the California circuit, made her stage debut in

1855 at the age of eight, and although she possessed very little dramatic talent, her banjo-playing, singing, dancing, and general gaiety had earned her a fortune by the time she retired in 1891.

The stories of the theater moving west are among the most fascinating sagas of American theater history, as performers acted in tents and saloons, on riverboats, in the dining rooms of frontier hotels, or in the open air. The documents in this chapter illustrate the ingenuity of the performers on the American frontier and the adaptability of the playhouse to frontier conditions.

62. AMERICAN THEATRE
New Orleans, Louisiana
Opened January 1, 1824

New Orleans was probably the most cosmopolitan city in the nation during the first thirty years of the nineteenth century. There were large French- and Spanish-speaking populations in addition to other national groups; in fact, at one time the English-speaking audience was much in the minority.

The first theater was a French-speaking one, and it was not until 1817 that English dramas were presented. Sol Smith, one of the most important actors and managers in the West in the nineteenth century, gives a brief sketch of the opening of New Orleans to English-speaking theater companies.

62:1   The English Drama was introduced into the city of New Orleans in December, 1817, by a commonwealth company.

The performances took place in the St. Philippe Theatre, afterward the Washington Ballroom. In 1818 Mr. Aaron Phillips took a company to New Orleans and performed in the French Theatre, Orleans Street. Mr. James H. Caldwell came the same year with a company from Virginia, and occupied the St. Philippe Theatre, afterward removing to the French Theatre, which he occupied three evenings of each week, alternating with the French company,—a compromise having been effected with Mr. Phillips, who, with the principal members of his company, enlisted under Mr. Caldwell's banner. The then great tragedian, Cooper, performed an engagement this season, receiving, as I have been informed, $333 per night!

The foundation of the American Theatre, Camp Street (now the Armory Hall), was laid in 1821, and it was opened in an unfinished condition. In 1824 it was finished and regularly opened, with a company competent to give proper effect to the regular drama. The season was a profitable one to the manager, and satisfactory to the public. . . .

Sol Smith's partner in many of his theatrical ventures, Noah M. Ludlow, was a part of the New Orleans theatrical scene in the early years as an actor. In his memoirs he mentions many details of the building of the American Theatre.

62:2 . . . Before taking a final leave of the New Orleans season of 1822–23, I wish to state that Mr. Caldwell, having commenced building a theatre in that city in May, 1822, had in May, 1823, got it to a condition—though not completed— that permitted him to perform in it *one night*, which was the 14th of May, 1823, the entertainments being the comedy of the "Dramatist," and the comic opera of the "Romp." This building was known as the "Camp Street Theatre," and stood on the west side of Camp, a few yards below Poydras Street. The interior of the building was destroyed by fire many years ago, but the walls were left standing, and it was reconstructed inside and occupied as a large auction mart, and such it had continued up to the date of this writing [1880].

62:1. Sol Smith, *Theatrical Management in the West and South for Thirty Years* (New York: Harper & Bros., 1868), p. 49.

62:2. Noah M. Ludlow, *Dramatic Life As I Found It* (St. Louis: G. I. Jones & Co., 1880), pp. 247–50.

When Mr. Caldwell commenced building the Camp Street Theatre, its location was considered by many of his friends to be a very injudicious one. They said "it was too much out of the way"; "surely ladies would never go there"; they thought "people would never go above Canal Street to visit a theatre." Canal Street was then considered the upper boundary of the city proper; beyond that was only known as the "Faubourg Saint Marie." But Mr. Caldwell had more acumen, and a better comprehension of his business than many of his would-be advisers. He knew—and he was right—that where there is a desire in a community for theatrical amusements, and wealth to minister to it, people will always find the ways and means to gratify that desire, even at the cost of some personal inconvenience. Mr. Caldwell knew that the history of theatres showed that they have always proved to be a nucleus for various other kinds of business; that they invariably draw a population around them, and the Camp Street Theatre would probably be no exception to such general results. During the first two seasons of this theatre, the streets leading to it above Canal Street were without pavement for carriages or footmen. Those who had not the means for riding had to walk on Camp Street from Canal, on pieces of timber laid together, forming a pathway about two and a half feet in width, made of boat gunwales purchased from Western traders who had brought their stock to New Orleans on "flat-boats," and having no further use for the boats, sold them on very cheap terms. . . .

An era of importance in the history of New Orleans was the opening of this theatre, *lighted with gas*. This was the first building lighted by such means in the city of New Orleans. It was an individual enterprise of Mr. James H. Caldwell, who had "gas-works," on a limited scale, erected on the same lot on which his theatre stood. His next act of importance was lighting one side of Camp, from Canal Street to the theatre. It was two years, I believe, before Mr. Caldwell could induce city authorities to allow him to light a portion of Canal Street; finally, with great exertions for a number of years, he succeeded in forming a "gas company," for the purpose of lighting New Orleans. Of this company, Mr. Caldwell was president for a long succession of years.

The noted Irish actor and comedian, Tyrone Power, visited the United States in 1833 and acted in the American Theatre in New Orleans. His impressions of the theater and the audience are of special interest.

62:3   On Monday the 5th I attended rehearsal at the American Theatre, and was pleased to find it a large, well-proportioned house, with three rows of boxes, a pit, or *parquette*, as it is termed, subdivided as in the French Theatre: each seat is numbered, and, being taken at the box-office, is secured to the purchaser for any part of the evening. The company was a very tolerable one; and in the person of a nephew of Mr. W. Farren's, I found an adjunct of much importance to me—an excellent old man.

My next anxiety was about my audience, not its numbers, as I was assured every seat in the house was disposed of, and this as far as could be allowed, for every night I might perform; but I felt solicitous with respect to its character and composition, of which I had received very discouraging reports. I kept however my apprehensions to myself, resolved to do my best after my own fashion, and abide the result as I best might.

On Tuesday I made my *début*; and never was man more agreeably surprised than myself when, after making my bow, I for the first time took a rapid survey

62:3. Tyrone Power, *Impressions of America in 1833–1835*. 2 vols. (London: Carey, Lea & Blanchard, 1836), 1:171–74.

of the aspect of the house: the *parquette* and dress-boxes were almost exclusively filled with ladies, *coiffées* with the taste which distinguishes French women in every country, and which becomes peculiarly striking here, where are to be seen the finest heads of dark hair in the world, many wore bonnets of the latest Parisian fashion, and all were more dressed than it is usual to be at theatres in America. This attention to costume on the part of the ladies, added to their occupying the pit, obliges the gentlemen to adopt a corresponding neatness; and hence it occurs that, when the New Orleans theatre is attended by the belles of the city, it presents decidedly the most elegant-looking auditory of this country.

For myself, I found them in manner equal to their appearance; a greater degree of repose and gentility of demeanor I never remember to have noticed in any mixed assembly of any place. So much for report, which informed me I should find the American house here filled by noisy planters from the up-country and boisterous Mississippi boatmen. Let me however add, that my personal friends assure me a class of families attend my performances that is but rarely seen within this theatre, which the creoles do not usually patronize; and that this extreme decorum and exclusive appearance are assured by the places being all secured by families.

This may in some sort be true; but at most can only apply to the *parquette*, dress, and private boxes; the mixed population is still here; and, after nightly observation, rendered acute by interest and anxiety, I must assert that, taken generally, I do not desire to meet an audience whose behaviour more decidedly justifies the terms respectable and intelligent.

The least prolonged tumult of approbation even is stilled by a word to order: and when it is considered that here are assembled the wildest and rudest specimens of the Western population, men owning no control except the laws, and not viewing these over submissively, and who admit of no *arbiter elegantiarum* or standard of fine breeding, it confers infinite credit on their innate good feeling, and that sense of propriety which here forms the sole check on their naturally somewhat uproarious jollity.

Let me add, that my first engagement was for twelve nights, four nights per week; that I, on my return from Natchez, acted a like number, with equal patronage; and that on no one night was I afforded an occasion of making an exception to the opinion I have above honestly recorded, certainly with greater pleasure, because in asserting the truth I feel I am at the same time performing an act of justice.

Gibson's Guide and Directory on the State on Louisiana (1838) has the following description of the American Theatre:

62:4   CAMP STREET THEATRE

The "Camp," as it is familiarly termed, was the first American Theatre built in the State of Louisiana: it stands on the west side of Camp street, between Gravier and Poydras, and for the earliest building of its kind, is a handsome and spacious structure. It is 60 feet wide, and 160 in depth. This theatre was built by James H. Caldwell, the founder of American Drama in the South and West, and who not being able to obtain the assistance of the grand Lodge, laid the foundation stone himself, with all the masonic ceremonies, on the 29th of May, 1822. On the 14th of the following May, it was opened with Reynolds's comedy of the 'Dramatist,' and the farce of "the Romp." The ground, the building and furnishing of the Theatre, cost $120,000. From the period of its opening until the year 1833, it re-

---

62:4. *Gibson's Guide and Directory on the State of Louisiana* (New Orleans: J. Gibson, 1838), pp. 317–18.

mained under the management of Mr. Caldwell; who in that year leased it to Messrs. Russell and Rowe, whose time expires in May 1838. At the time of laying the foundation of the "Camp theatre" there were no houses nearer to it than at the corner of Common street, and it was with great difficulty, it could be reached in wet weather. In this theatre has almost every distinguished dramatic artist appeared; and to this pioneer undertaking of Mr. Caldwell may be traced the immediate, and rapid rise of the second Municipality. Within its walls the national drama first found a fit abode: and from year to year, it has gone on improving until few, if any, establishments in the Union, could boast of producing plays in superior style. From want of width on the stage, the scenery is necessarily painted on drops: the "parquette" will accommodate about 150 persons: there are two rows of boxes, and a large gallery. The house altogether is competent to seat about eleven hundred persons, above and below, and few are there among our worthy populations but have some agreeable reminiscence connected with the "little Camp."

63. CHAPMAN'S FLOATING THEATRE
July 1831

One of the most colorful theaters to be found in nineteenth-century America had its birth with the advent of the showboat. It was a normal outgrowth of the American frontier, a frontier that stretched over hundreds of miles but was so sparsely settled that the population centers could not support a regular playhouse.

The first floating theater of which there is any record is that of the Chapman family, who sailed the Ohio and Mississippi rivers, stopping at settlements along the rivers and acting their plays for the audiences that would gather to see them. Philip Graham wrote a history of this showboat and others in 1951, and a small portion is reproduced here.

63:1   A little more than a decade after Noah Ludlow had left the River for the more pretentious land theatres, the first deliberately planned showboat was launched, in the summer of 1831, at Pittsburgh. The boat had been designed by William Chapman, Sr., formerly of London, since 1827 of New York and Philadelphia. In reality, the whole Chapman family planned it. The master craftsman, Cyrus Brown, had built it. With little ceremony, but with much pride both builder and family watched the small craft, no larger than a keel boat, slide off the ways and bob jerkily onto the Ohio. William Chapman, Sr.; his wife, Sarah; their two sons, William, Jr. and George; their two daughters, Caroline and Therese Sarah; William, Jr.'s wife, Phoebe, a gifted musician whom he had married three years before leaving England; Grandmother Chapman; the grandson, Harry, aged nine, son of Samuel who had died in Philadelphia the year before: they were all there, tense, tired, and happy, for this boat was to be not only their profession but also their home and their great adventure. "Mama Chapman" probably said least and felt most when the white flag took the breeze and proclaimed in her red piquéd letters the name FLOATING THEATRE.

These Chapmans, America's first showboat family, were labeled by early dramatic critics also America's most remarkable theatre family. Noah Ludlow wrote that he had never met elsewhere in the profession of the stage a group possessing such versatility and unusual ability. . . .

. . . According to legend, William Chapman with difficulty persuaded the keeper of the Old Red Lion Hotel, on the bank of the Allegheny River on the north side of town (Pittsburgh), to rent him lodgings for his family, and, each evening

63:1. Philip Graham, *Showboats* (Austin: Univ. of Texas Pr., 1951), pp. 9–14.

after supper, also the dining room for the presentation of plays. The good landlord feared that the presence of actors, especially since their number included women, might injure the reputation of his house, but he was reassured when Chapman promised that the chief fare would be Shakespeare.

No record exists of the plans and the arguments of the Chapmans between their first performance in the Old Red Lion dining room and the launching of their theatre boat three months later. Yet the imagination easily bridges the gap. The conditions were these: a clannish family, well trained in the drama with a strong professional ideal that looked not so much toward stardom as toward a warm and unified domestic arrangement; a past that included both traveling and lodging in vans; an immediate environment difficult in the matter of available lodgings and theatres, but very enthusiastic in the matter of river boats and the new uses to which they were being put; a desire to travel through a region where the rivers were almost the only means of transportation and where the inhabitants were said to be drama-hungry. The showboat was the inevitable result. Certainly it represented a characteristic development on the frontier, the adapting of an Eastern institution to the Western environment. Few families ever realize so completely their ideal as the Chapmans probably did when they climbed aboard their FLOATING THEATRE.

Eleven people embarked on the drama barge on that July evening in 1831. For in addition to the nine members of the family, there were two unidentified persons, one a riverman and the other an unnamed extra actor. The plan was to drift with the current down the Ohio and the Mississippi, stopping where an audience seemed likely, and in late winter to sell or junk the boat at New Orleans. If the experiment proved enjoyable and self-supporting, they planned to return to

Pittsburgh by steamer, build another boat and repeat the trip the next year.

A surviving woodcut shows that the boat was crudely constructed, resembling a large garage set down on a small barge. It was a little more than one hundred feet long and sixteen feet wide. A contemporary, the redoubtable Noah Ludlow himself, writes his impression of the boat into his sparkling *Dramatic Life as I Found It*:

"The enclosed portion of the boat, measuring one hundred feet long and fourteen feet wide, was divided into a narrow, shallow stage at the stern (the front of the theatre), a pit in the middle for the white audience, and a small gallery at the bow (the rear of the theatre) for the colored people. White muslin draw-curtains and tallow candle footlights equipped the staff. Hard board benches, securely fastened down, ran the entire width of the boat. Though these were without backs or cushions, audiences have testified that the only undesirable seats were exactly in the center, under the tallow-dropping chandelier, which was a hogshead hoop with candles attached."

Noah Ludlow's partner, Sol Smith, also wrote about the Chapman Floating Theatre. One amusing incident in particular depicts theater life on the river.

63:2 The "Chapman family," consisting of old Mr. Chapman, William Chapman, George Chapman, Caroline Chapman, and Harry and Therese Chapman (children), came to the West this summer, opened a theatre at Louisville, and afterward established and carried into operation that singular affair, the "Floating Theatre," concerning which so many anecdotes are told. The "family" were all extremely fond of fishing, and during

63:2. Sol Smith, *Theatrical Management in the West and South for Thirty Years* (New York: Harper & Bros., 1868), p. 89.

the "waits" the actors amused themselves by "dropping a line" over the stern of the ark. On one occasion, while playing the STRANGER (act iv, Scene 1), there was a long wait for Francis, the servant of the misanthropic Count Walborough.

"Francis! Francis!" called the Stranger. No reply.

"Francis! Francis!" (a pause). "Francis!" rather angrily called the Stranger again.

A very distant voice—"Coming, sir!" (a considerable pause, during which the Stranger walks up and down à la Macready, in a great rage.)

"Francis!"

Francis (entering). Here I am, Sir.

Stranger. Why, sir, did you not come when I called?

Francis. Why, sir, I was just hauling in one of the d——dest big catfish you ever saw!

It was some minutes before the laughter of the audience could be restrained sufficiently to allow the play to proceed.

It is said of this Floating Theatre that it was cast loose during a performance at one of the river towns in Indiana by some mischievous boys and could not be landed for half a dozen miles, the large audience being compelled to walk back to their village.

64. ST. CHARLES THEATRE
New Orleans, Louisiana
Opened November 30, 1835

James H. Caldwell, who in 1823 had erected the American Theatre on Camp Street in New Orleans, twelve years later began to build a new, more lavish theater, to be called the St. Charles. The playhouse was to be the finest erected in America until that date. *Gibson's Guide* (1838) describes the theater.

64:1　This magnificent temple of the Drama was, like its humble neighbor, built en-

64:1. *Gibson's Guide and Directory on the State of Louisiana* (New Orleans: J. Gibson, 1838), pp. 313–14.

tirely by James H. Caldwell, to whose enterprise and energy the upper section of our city owes so much. But the professors and admirers of the drama, owe him still more. What has required a long period of years, a large number of rich patrons, and a variety of favorable circumstances to effect elsewhere, the industry and professional enthusiasm of one man has accomplished here. Mr. Caldwell, and his company of actors arrived in this city from Virginia in December, 1819, per schooner Betsey, and on the 7th January, 1820, they made their first appearance in New Orleans, at the St. Philip street Theatre. Their opening performance of the "Honey Moon" and "Three and the Deuce," brought $700, the utmost capacity of the house. Shortly after the new (present) French Theatre in Orleans street was opened, and the company forthwith removed to it, and for three seasons continued to play in it four nights a week, and in St. Philip-street Theatre on the other three. On the 29th May, 1822, the foundation stone of the Camp-street Theatre was laid, and the house opened on the 14th May, 1823.

On the 9th May, 1835, the corner stone of the great St. Charles Theatre was laid; and though in its process of building, its enterprising owner had to contend with ninety days of continued rain, it was opened, as resolved on by Mr. Caldwell, on the 30th November, in the same year, with the "School for Scandal" and "Spoiled Child." This magnificent structure, erected by the unassisted energies of one man, has a frontage of one hundred and thirty-two feet, and a depth of a hundred and seventy-five. Its capacity, and accommodations within, correspond with the magnitude of its *exterior*. The grand saloon is 129 feet by 26; it has four tiers of boxes, surmounted with enormous galleries: at the back of 47 of its boxes, are convenient *boudoirs*, or retiring rooms. In the centre of the dome is suspended a magnificent chandelier—

twelve feet in height, thirty-six feet in circumference, weighing 4200 weight and illuminated with 176 gas lights. This brilliant article was manufactured by Brooks & Hughes, of London, and contains 23,300 cut glass drops, weighing 9 cwt. and 9 grs., has 23 cwt. of brass work and 9 cwt. of iron in its construction. From the curtain to the back of the boxes, is 78 feet; across the boxes, 71 feet. The proscenium is 50 feet, with an opening of 44 feet. From the pit floor to the ceiling, is 54 feet; and from the stage to the roof, 62. The scenery is 44 high, and 48 wide, with the wings; and from wall to wall, the stage is 96 feet wide, and 78 feet deep, from the Orchestra line.

From these proportions, contrasted with those of any other theatre in the Union, some idea may be formed of the beauty and extent of the St. Charles, and its splendor is quite proportionate to its dimensions. Its cost was $350,000, and it stands on the east side of St. Charles street, near Poydras, the prominent monument of zeal and industry, ever raised to the honor of an individual citizen in his life time.

Noah Ludlow, who had acted with Caldwell's company and now was a theatrical manager in his own right, wrote about Caldwell and the building of the new theater in New Orleans.

64:2   At the close of this New Orleans season, May 28, 1833, Mr. Caldwell took a formal leave of the stage, and made a speech, in which he declared his determination to abandon management and the cares of an actor forever. To that end he leased his theatres to his late stage-manager, Richard Russell, and his late treasurer, James S. Rowe. How long Mr. Caldwell kept to this resolution will be seen in the sequel.

64:2. Noah M. Ludlow, *Dramatic Life As I Found It* (St. Louis: G. I. Jones & Co., 1880), pp. 403–6.

Notwithstanding Mr. Caldwell took a formal leave of the stage, both as an actor and a manager, we find him, according to his own statement (see "Dramatic Authors" of James Rees, page 56), laying the corner-stone of a large theatre on the 9th of May, 1835, which he opened on the 30th of November of the same year,—seven months, lacking nine days, from the laying down of the corner-stone. This great building was the "St. Charles Theatre," the *first* of that name, and the one destroyed by fire on March 13, 1842, of which more will be said hereafter.

I have always had doubts of the sincerity of Mr. Caldwell when he declared, as before stated, his determination of abandoning the profession of the stage forever. I considered it then, and do now, nothing more than a *ruse*,—a stroke of policy, with an eye to the future. Mr. Caldwell was ambitious to become president of the "Gas Bank" at New Orleans, of which he was already a member of the board of directors; an ambition not censurable, and a position which he well deserved, inasmuch as he had been one of the most active and efficient persons in establishing the gas-works of that city, and in obtaining a charter for that bank, the offspring of the gas company. It was not long ere this ambition was gratified. His situation as president of that bank gave him influence with the directors, sufficient to enable him to procure large loans from the bank; and to those loans he had recourse when his own treasury became exhausted. He mortgaged the ground and the improvements, as far as the latter had advanced, and by these means, in the short period of time as before stated, he erected in New Orleans the largest theatre in the United States at that time.

Notwithstanding that Mr. Caldwell sought every opportunity during a period of about twenty years to "crush me," as he said in 1824 he would, yet I have always been, and shall still be, ready to accord to him that meed of praise which his enterprise and exertions for the Drama most justly merit; but I am unwilling that certain false statements put forth by interested parties to glorify him at the expense of others shall remain on record, without at least a protest against them, and a statement of facts as they actually transpired, void of all false coloring.

Mr. James H. Caldwell has been put forward by Mr. Rees, in his pamphlet entitled "Dramatic Authors of America" (1845), as *the* man, and the only one who had up to that time done any thing towards the founding or advancement of the Drama in the West and South-West. It was evidently an afterthought of Mr. Rees, and one entirely forcign to the character of his pamphlet. What his motive could have been for introducing a subject so entirely extraneous is best known to himself. Mr. Caldwell was no "dramatic author," or at least not known as such. He may have dramatized "Eugene Aram" from Bulwer's novel, as stated by Mr. Rees, but if it was ever acted, it could not have been more than once or twice; it certainly did not "please the million," or it is likely I should have heard of it. I was well aware of the theatrical management of Mr. Caldwell, and, in general, of any new play produced by him, during a period of forty years, yet never did I know of his having written and performed a play of his own. In speaking of Mr. Caldwell, Mr. Rees says: "As this gentleman's name is associated with the history of the theatres in the South, of nearly all of which he was the founder," etc. Now, these words are decidedly at variance with the facts of the case; there is no "history" yet published, I am confident, wherein Mr. Caldwell is noted as the *founder* of the Western and Southern theatres, unless Mr. Rees means his pamphlet as the "history." Neither was Mr. Caldwell "the *founder* of nearly all the theatres of the South," taking the word *founder* as set down by

Dr. Johnson, as used by Addison, viz.: "One from whom any thing has its origin or beginning." There is not a city or town south or west of the Alleghany Mountains, in which Mr. Caldwell performed, that was not visited and occupied by regular dramatic companies for years before Mr. Caldwell ever saw them. Mr. Caldwell and company performed for the first time in the South at New Orleans, on January 7, 1820, in the St. Philip Street Theatre,—the same building in which I first produced the English Drama, December 24, 1817.

The cities of Louisvile, Frankfort, and Lexington, Kentucky, were occupied first with a regular company of comedians under Samuel Drake, Sr., in the fall of 1815; Cincinnati, by William Turner's company, in 1810 and by Collins & Jones and company, 1820; Nashville, by N. M. Ludlow and company, in summer of 1817; Natchez by the same, in the fall of 1817, and New Orleans by same, 1817; Huntsville, Alabama, by same, 1818; St. Louis, Missouri, by same, 1819; Mobile, by same, 1824; Montgomery, by same, 1827, and at other towns by the same at later dates,—all being a presentation of the Drama for the *first* time by regularly constituted companies of comedians.

A person reading Mr. Caldwell's statement, as set down by Mr. Rees in his pamphlet, would suppose that he had built nearly all the theatres of consequence in the West and South up to 1845. Let us see how this will agree with the facts in the case. We will begin in the South, where Mr. Caldwell commenced his operations. For the first three years that the gentleman performed in New Orleans, he occupied the theatres standing on St. Philip and on Orleans Streets. The former, the one occupied by myself and company two years prior to his arrival in the city, the latter was the French theatre, where he performed alternate nights with the French company. The third theatre occupied by him stood on Camp Street, and was built by Mr. Caldwell from his own means and by borrowing $14,400 for a term of ten years, each subscriber of $300 to have a ticket of free admission for that time, or until he returned the money. The fourth theatre occupied by him was the first "St. Charles," on St. Charles Street, near Poydras. This was erected by Mr. Caldwell from his own means and his own credit; with the former he bought the ground, on which, from the latter, he obtained a loan from the "Gas Bank" of New Orleans, sufficient to enable him to erect the building. I will here cheerfully say this was the largest and most magnificent theatre that has been built in the South or West even to the time of this present writing. . . .

Later in his narrative Ludlow writes about the burning of this magnificent playhouse in 1842.

64:3   Early in the year 1842, Mr. James H. Caldwell rented his St. Charles Theatre for one month to Signor Marti, manager of the Tacon Theatre, Havana; the Signor promising to present to the New Orleans public a series of Italian operas by his grand troupe of singers from the Tacon Theatre. The troupe was a good one, and the operas produced were performed in a very superior style. They commenced about the 1st of March, proceeding in a very satisfactory manner to the public, when on Sunday evening, the 13th of that month, about six o'clock, the great St. Charles Theatre was said to be on fire. I was at my residence, on Carondelet Street, and when the alarm was given I stepped to the door and was told, "The theatre is on fire." Fearful that it was our own, I hurried out in that direction, but soon discovered the crowd gathered on St. Charles Street, opposite to the theatre. Being apprehensive that our own theatre

64:3. Noah M. Ludlow, *Dramatic Life As I Found It* (St. Louis: G. I. Jones & Co., 1880), pp. 549–50.

might become endangered by the conflagration of that large building, I summoned all the carpenters, scene-shifters, and others of our establishment, and had them prepare to remove our scenery and other property whenever I should give them the word to do so. While gazing on the magnificent building, I saw, with feelings of sorrow, the flames drawn into the back windows, which had been left open. In a few minutes they were seen bursting from the side windows, and I saw then the total destruction of the building was inevitable. It was a sad sight; and although a rival theatre, I felt sincere regret in beholding such a grand temple of the Muses swept away, and probably lost forever to the good city of New Orleans,—a city where the people had always supported the legitimate Drama with princely liberality.

The opera troupe met with no loss of property, excepting a few dresses which had been sent to the theatre for that night's use. The fire that destroyed this theatre commenced in the workshop of an undertaker, immediately adjoining the rear of it, where a quantity of shavings and other combustible materials had, in the process of coffin-making, accumulated. By some means, I believe never known, these became ignited; and the workshop being on that day (Sunday) not occupied, and also hidden from view of any one passing in the street, was fully on fire before discovered, and the flames creeping up the rear of the theatre. Before engines could be got to play upon the flames, the fire had found a way into the theatre, and the whole interior was filled with the raging element of destruction. . . .

65. ST. LOUIS THEATRE
St. Louis, Missouri
Opened July 3, 1837

The St. Louis Theatre of Ludlow and Smith represents a landmark in American the-

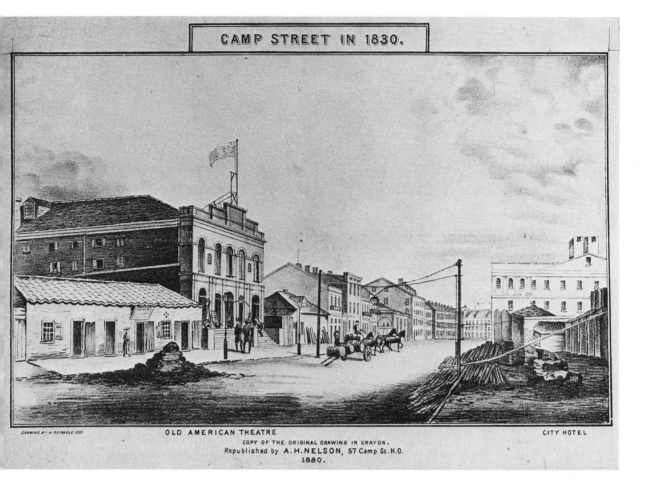

CAMP STREET IN 1830.

DRAWING BY H. REINAGLE 1830.
OLD AMERICAN THEATRE
CITY HOTEL
COPY OF THE ORIGINAL DRAWING IN CRAYON.
Republished by A. H. NELSON, 57 Camp St. N.O.
1880.

62. American "Camp Street" Theatre, New Orleans, 1830. Lithograph of a drawing by H. Reinagle, 1830; published by A. H. Nelson (New Orleans, 1880). Courtesy of the Louisiana Collection, Special Collections Division, Tulane University Library.

St. Charles Theatre.

64. St. Charles Theatre, New Orleans. Engraving, published in *Gibson's Guide and Directory on the State of Louisiana* (New Orleans, 1838). Courtesy of the Rare Book Room, Special Collections Division, Tulane University Library.

65. St. Louis Theatre, St. Louis. Lithograph and drawing by J. C. Wild, published in his *The Valley of the Mississippi* (St. Louis, 1841). The columns and portico were never added, although the columns were constructed and stored in the playhouse. Courtesy of the Missouri Historical Society.

ater history, since this was the first regular English-speaking theater to be opened west of the Mississippi. Plays had been given by traveling troupes of players who set up temporary stages, but this was a building erected for the purpose of the drama. Noah Ludlow tells in his book of the building of the playhouse and its opening.

65:1   As I have previously said, I reached St. Louis on the 10th of April. The prospect for the early opening of the new theatre looked very unpromising; every object out of doors was covered with snow. Making my way to the building, as the first object of interest to me, I entered through one of the basement openings, waded to the centre of the great area, looked up at the four walls, without any roof on them, and felt a sensation as though my heart was sliding down into my boots. All looked cold and discouraging, and I began to resolve in my mind at what time in the summer or fall we should be able to open the house to the public. While I stood thus in gloomy mood, my head-carpenter, Mr. Crowl, arrived at the building, and a few minutes' conversation with him changed the condition of my feelings greatly. He informed me that the heavy timbers for the roof were all ready to be put in their places; that the flooring joists for the lobbies and boxes and parquet were all in a condition to be put in; the stage and lobby flooring were ready to be laid; in short that the timbers for the inside heavy work were ready to be adjusted in their proper places.

I should have mentioned before this, that during the previous fall, about the time I was preparing to leave St. Louis for the South, Mr. Crowl informed me that he was afraid the front wall of the theatre would have to be taken down, and it was at that time as high almost

as intended to be ultimately. He said that the openings in the wall were so many and so large that he feared the spaces between would not be sufficiently strong to sustain the weight that would be upon them when the roof should be put on; and advised that there be some alteration of the front portion of the building. This alteration, after some consultation with the other members of the building committee and a competent architect, was decided should be made. Some of the openings of the inner wall of the vestibule were to be closed, and then the two walls, the outer and the inner, were to be put up anew, and as they were rebuilt, filled in with what bricklayers term *groating*, the best quality of lime; that is, lime reduced to a fluid condition, and poured in between the bricks forming the wall. This was found to be quite sufficient; for, after standing for more than ten years without a single crack appearing, these two walls were pulled down to make way for the present building, the custom-house and post-office, and the bricks of these walls came out in solid blocks, like large slabs of stone. On visiting the workshop or paint-room of our scenic artist, Mr. J. R. Smith, I found he had got ready eight pairs of "flats" (centre-scenes), and with their appropriate "wings" (side-scenes); the dome, also, of the auditory, painted in sections, ready to be put in its place at the proper time, and other work which it is not necessary to speak of here. Without delay we made a contract for the lathing and plastering required, and put workmen upon all the different departments not already under contracts. We also had to make arrangements for lighting the house, which had to be done by spirit-gas, coal-gas not having at that time been introduced into the city of St. Louis. This lighting was effected by means of branch-lamps suspended around the front of the boxes; the stage having for the "foot-lights" (front lights), square tin

65:1. Noah M. Ludlow, *Dramatic Life As I Found It* (St. Louis: G. I. Jones & Co., 1880), pp. 475–79.

141

boxes, with large burners for spirit gas, a similar kind of box, only of triangular shape, being used behind each wing, with reflectors attached, to throw the light to the centre of the stage.

After obtaining a general idea of the work to be done before the house could be opened, and weighing the difficulties, I came to the conclusion that we might be able to open the house to the public on the 4th of July, the anniversary of our national independence. And this was my reply to the numerous inquiries of "when I expected to commence the theatrical season," which was generally met with the response, "You cannot do it!" As the work progressed, my conjectures became strengthened; and being bantered with bets of hats, boots, etc., that I would not open on the 4th of July, I accepted some of them, and the sequel will show the result.

About this time I began to discover that we were proceeding on too extravagant a scale for our means, although they had been more than doubled on the amount that we had originally started upon. As I said before, Col. M. L. Clarke's ideas were always formed upon a large scale, and as they expanded, new ones would arise of still larger dimensions; and in this way it was generally found that his conclusions of today were considerably in advance of those of yesterday. He had insisted upon having a *grand front* to the building, such as should "make it an ornament to the city." To this end he had contracted at the East, upon his own responsibility, for caps and bases of four magnificent Corinthian columns, intended to support a *grand front portico*, and for which he generously said he would pay out of his own purse, should the stockholders object to the expense.

These columns were never put up, but remained stored away under the stage of the theatre until the building was sold to the United States government; and what become of them I have never heard.

As the work progressed, I became each day more impressed with the importance of our opening the theatre to the public on the 4th of July, if the interior of the building could be got into a proper condition; in fact, it became almost a matter of *necessity* that we should do so, for our season in Mobile had been prolonged much beyond the usual time; the weather had become quite warm in that Southern latitude, and the audiences diminishing rapidly in numbers. In addition to this, my partner was almost daily urging me by letter to hasten matters to a point that would enable us to occupy the house with our company, for our weekly receipts at Mobile were falling below the current expenses.

Under the pressure of these circumstances, every effort was made that promised to forward the work to a condition that would allow us to begin our season; and about the middle of June I wrote to my partner that I thought he might rely on our being in a position to commence our season on the 4th of July, and advising him to make his arrangements to be in St. Louis by the 1st.

On the 1st of July the company did arrive from Mobile, and the following Monday, the first play-day of the week, and my birthday, the 3rd of July, I decided on for the opening of the new theatre. The inside of the theatre was very conveniently arranged, consisting of three tiers or galleries of seats and a parquet. The first tier, or "dress circle," would seat about three hundred persons; the second tier, or "family circle," about three hundred and fifty; the third tier or "gallery," about four hundred and fifty, and the parquet about four hundred. The entrance to the first and second tiers and parquet was through a large vestibule twenty feet in depth by forty in width, thence through three large doors into the lobby of the first tier, which was uncommonly wide. Through the centre of the first tier was the passage to the parquet, and on each side of the lobby a flight of stairs leading to the second tier. The entrance to the gallery was from the outside of the building, to a flight of winding stairs, having no connection with the other entrances. The stage was about forty-five feet in depth, from the front of which to the front of the dress-circle was about fifty feet. The house being designed for a summer theatre, was constructed with a number of very large windows on each side, and the seats in the first and second tiers surrounded with handsome balustrades, turned of cherry wood, which being highly varnished, looked like mahogany. There was a ladies' retiring-room on a level with the first tier, furnished with refreshments and conveniences suited to such visitors. On a level with the second floor was a saloon for gentlemen, furnished with refreshments. Both of these saloons were closed before the conclusion of the season; the first, because a very small proportion of the lady auditors ever visited it, a notion having sprung up among some of the leading ones that their visits to the saloon might be misconstrued, apprehensions that the situation did not necessarily warrant. The gentlemen's saloon was closed because it was found to be an annoyance to the occupants, not only of the second, but of the first tier. There were three large doors opening from the saloon to the *auditorium*, and the loud talking that frequently took place there disturbed many persons who came to hear and enjoy the performance on the stage; so we shut that up before the season terminated.

On the opening of this house I made it a beginning of a reform which I adhered to and carried forward in after years in all the theatres under my management. This was to refuse admission to any female to the performance who did not come attended by a gentleman, or some one having the appearance of a man of respectability, not even in the third tier; and women notoriously of the *pave* never, under any conditions, admitted.

The result of these rigid measures was that the third tier in our theatres was as quiet and orderly as any portion of the house.

On one occasion our vigilance for a time was eluded by two females of questionable character; one of them, in male attire, came as a gallant of the other. This usurper of the "inexpressibles" was imposingly finished up with a fine curly black wig and a killing pair of whiskers to match, and should most likely have avoided detection had there not been present, unfortunately for the intruders, an old gallant of one of them, who, eyeing closely this rather *distingué* youth, winked at him in a peculiar way, which wink was answered by a half-smothered laugh. This was too good a joke for him to keep, and he mentioned it to the head officer of our police, Mr. D. Busby, who, calling aside the *soi-disant* gentleman, and questioning him, he "confessed the cape," and was then permitted quietly, but on the instant, to quit the theatre with his "Dulcinea." It must be remembered that there were no *matinees*, as at the present day, when ladies can attend without male gallants.

I had a hard struggle for this scheme of reformation. There were several attempts made by lewd women and their bullies to pass the door-keepers having obtained tickets by sending boys and servants for them under the names of respectable citizens. However, I foiled their stratagems through the vigilance of a private policeman, well acquainted with such kind of persons by sight, and who knew how to deal with them. From time to time, for some two or three years following my management in St. Louis and Mobile, and in subsequent years in New Orleans, I had sent to me through the post-office threatening missives, such as "cowhidings," "fisticuffings," and "shootings," and the like, for refusing admission to these *filles de joie*; but I persisted in my course, and finally gained my point.

The opening to our first performance was a matter of "touch and go" with us. The scaffolding that had been used to put up some decorations for the front of the boxes was being pitched out of side windows as the audience were coming in at the front doors, that had been opened promptly upon the time advertised. I did not perform on the stage the first night, nor until some week or so afterward, having as much as I could attend to in organizing the forces that were to be brought into action in the new house.

Elsewhere in his narrative Ludlow comments:

65:2   The *exterior* of the front of this building was never finished according to the plan, which embraced a portico of sixty feet on Third Street, supported by four large columns of the Corinthian order. But the building had cost so much when opened, that it was thought advisable by the stockholders—of which body Ludlow & Smith held the largest number of shares held by any one party—to defer the finishing of the front to a more favorable time; and thus it remained until it was sold to the government of the United States, on the site of which was erected the present custom-house, post-office, and other offices of the government. This theatre, the first large one in its capacity, was second only to the first St. Charles Theatre of New Orleans, in all the cities of the West and South. . . .

66. RIALTO THEATRE
Chicago, Illinois
Opened May 10, 1838

The first building in Chicago used for theatrical purposes was the historic old Sauganash Hotel, which was appropriated by two men, Isherwood and McKenzie. Here, beginning in October 1837, plays were presented in the dining room of the old hotel. The sea-

son lasted probably not more than six weeks.

The following year, however, the first building designed as a regular playhouse opened and was called the Rialto Theatre. Facts about this theater are related by A. T. Andreas in his *History of Chicago,* which he published in 1885.

66:1   The next authentic record carried this narrative onward to the spring of 1838, at which period the drama in Chicago assumed a more distinctive form. The experimental season proved a satisfactory one to the managers, and they concluded to return to this place, with the intention of establishing a permanent theater. In April Isherwood & McKenzie petitioned the Council as follows:

Chicago, April 28,1838

"Dear Sirs: Intending to resume our theatrical amusements in your city, we would respectfully solicit the action of your honorable body in reference to a license granting us the privilege to 'strut and fret our (year) upon the stage,' for one year and after the 12th day of May, A.D. 1838. Intending (subject to your decision on this point) to make ourselves the permanent residents of your city, we have, at much expense and trouble, commenced the adapting and fitting up of the upper portion of the 'Rialto' (a room thirty by eighty) as a theater; and intend to fit it up in such a manner as to reflect credit upon our infant city. We trust, under all the circumstances of the case, the license will be made as moderate as is consistent with justice. We should like, if possible, the exclusive privilege, but do not urge it. The early action of your body on this subject is respectfully requested.

We remain, gentlemen,
Your obedient servants,

Isherwood & McKenzie."

65:2. Noah M. Ludlow, *Dramatic Life As I Found It* (St. Louis: G. I. Jones & Co., 1880), p. 407.

66:1. A. T. Andreas, *History of Chicago.* 3 vols. (Chicago: A. T. Andreas Co., 1884–86), 1:475–77.

The building referred to was a wooden structure, erected in 1833 or 1834, by John Bates, for an auction-room. Prior to 1838 this place was used by various parties as an auction-room. According to J. M. Hannahs, "It was at the very center of business and resort; the only bridge on the main river being at that time at Dearborn Street, and one of the principal hotels, the Tremont House, being on the same block. The only eating-house, the City Refectory, as it was called, was on the east side of the street, nearly opposite the theater; and the auction-rooms, which, as before stated, were, previous to the establishment of this theater, the only place of amusement in the town, were in the immediate neighborhood. Above all, there was adjoining the theater the famous "Eagle," kept by Isaac Cook, which was the resort of politicians; and as every man was, in those days, a politician, it will be readily understood that the theater was at the center of gravity." Dr. Egan, the wit of the company, named the place the "Rialto," for obvious reasons. Thus, it will be seen, that although the Sauganash was the birthplace of dramatic art in Chicago, the Rialto was the nursery of the muse, and from within the walls of this historical pile issued the infant's feeble wails as it struggled for existence. The building stood on the west side of Dearborn, Nos. 8 and 10, between Lake and South Water streets, and was "a den of a place, looking more like a dismantled grist-mill than a temple of anybody. The gloomy entrance could have furnished the scenery for a nightmare, and the lights within were sepulchral enough to show up the coffin scene in 'Lucretia Borgia.' But for all this, those dingy old walls used to ring sometimes with renderings fine enough to grace grander Thespian temples; though there was a farce now and then somewhat *broader* than it was long." So wrote that genial critic, Benjamin F. Taylor, when subsequently commenting on those early days.

Manifestly the public quite agreed with Mr. Taylor on the subject of the Rialto as a theater site, for on sooner had the action of Messrs. Isherwood & McKenzie been known than the following remonstrance was sent to the Council:

"To the Honorable the Common Council of the City of Chicago: Your petitioners would represent to your honorable body that they have understood that a petition is pending before your honorable body for the license of a theater, to be held and maintained in the room of the Rialto, which is a wooden building, and surrounded by wooden and combustible buildings. Your petitioners would further represent that theaters are subject to take fire, and (are) believed to be dangerous on that account to property in their vicinity, and that insurance cannot be obtained on property in their vicinity, except at greatly advanced premiums. And your petitioners do solemnly protest against the granting of such license to keep a theater in such building, and thereby endangering the property and lives of your petitioners.
Chicago, May 1, 1838.

> J. Young Scammon, William Osborn, E. G. Ryan, Joseph L. Hanson, Henry Brown, O. H. Thompson, Thomas R. Hubbard, Curtis Haven, I. R. Gavin, William Jones, Erastus Brown, Mahlon Ayers, C. Beers, William H. Adams, H. B. Clarke, J. Ballard, Walter Kimball, William H. Taylor, Alanson Follansbe, E. K. Rogers, King, Walker & Co., Tuthill King, A. N. Fullerton, Nelson Tuttle, B. F. Knapp, G. W. Merrill, E. S. Kingsbury, J. H. Woodworth, S. Burton, J. A. Smith, Lewis N. Wood, B. W. Raymind, E. S. Brown, Giles Spring."

The matter was referred, by the Council, to a special committee, consisting of Messrs. H. L. Rucker, Eli B. Williams and Grant Goodrich, who were empowered to decide upon the propriety of issuing a license.

Grant Goodrich submitted a minority report, in which he forcibly expressed his antagonism to the new theater. The basis of this antagonism was, primarily, the unsuitableness of the Rialto as a public hall, located as it was "in one of the most compact blocks in the city, composed chiefly of wooden buildings. . . ."

Acting upon the judgment of the majority report, the Council granted the license prayed for, dating it from May 20, 1838; but the tax imposed on the managers was fixed at $100, instead of the sum recommended by the majority of the committee ($125 per year).

Fortified by this official indorsement, Messrs. Isherwood & McKenzie fitted up an auditorium in the Rialto, with boxes, gallery and pit, supplying seating for about four hundred persons. The stage furnishings were improvements on those of the Sauganash Theater, but they were scarcely worthy of commendation. Dropping the title Rialto, the place was renamed "The Chicago Theater," and a stock company of actors was employed, several of whom since attained distinction in the profession. . . .

Joseph Jefferson III, the famous actor and comedian, recalled the new theater in his *Autobiography*:

66:2   . . . And now for the new theater, newly painted canvas, tack-hammer at work on stuffed seats in the dress-circle, planing-boards in the pit, new drop-curtain let down for inspection, "beautiful!" —a medallion of Shakspere, suffering from a severe pain in his stomach, over the center, with "One touch of nature makes the whole world kin" written under him, and a large, painted, brick-red

66:2. Joseph Jefferson, *The Autobiography of Joseph Jefferson* (New York: Century Co., 1889), pp. 22–24.

drapery looped up by Justice, with sword and scales, showing an arena with a large number of gladiators hacking away at one another in the distance to a delighted Roman public; though what Justice had to do with keeping these gladiators on exhibition was never clearly explained by the artist. There were two private boxes with little white-and-gold balustrades and turkey-red curtains, over one box a portrait of Beethoven and over the other a portrait of Handel—upon unfriendly terms, glaring at each other. The dome was pale blue, with pink-and-white clouds, on which reposed four ungraceful ballet girls representing the seasons, and apparently dropping flowers, snow, and grapes into the pit. Over each season there floated four fat little cherubim "in various stages of spinal curvature."

My father, being a scenic artist himself, was naturally disposed to be critical, and when the painter asked his opinion of the dome, he replied:

"Well, since you ask me, don't you think that your angels are a little stiff in their attitudes?"

"No, sir; not for angels. When I deal with mythological subjects I would never put my figures in natural attitudes; it would be inharmonious. A natural angel would be out of keeping with the rest of the work."

To which my father replied that it was quite likely that such would be the case. "But why have you made Handel and Beethoven frown at each other? They are not mythological subjects."

"No, no," said the painter. "But they are musicians, you know; and great musicians always quarrel, eh? Ha, ha!"

"Yes," said my father; "but as Handel died before Beethoven was born, I don't see how any coolness could have existed between them."

The foregoing dialogue, while it way not be verbatim, is at least in the spirit of the original. I could not possibly remember the exact words of the different conversations that will naturally occur through these chapters; but I have placed them in their present form, as I believe it is the clearest and most effective way to tell the story. Many of the conversations and incidents are traditional in my family; I have good reason to take them for granted, and I must ask the reader to share my confidence.

The greenroom was a perfect gem, with a three-foot wavy mirror and cushioned seats around the wall—traps under the stage so convenient that Ophelia could walk from her grave to her dressing-room with perfect ease.

With what delight the actors looked forward to the opening of a new theatre in a new town, where dramatic entertainments were still unknown—repairing their wardrobes, studying their parts, and speculating on the laurels there were to be won! . . .

67. NEW AMERICAN THEATRE
New Orleans, Louisiana
Opened November 10, 1840

Sol Smith and Noah M. Ludlow had entered into a partnership as theatrical managers and had widespread interests along the Mississippi River valley. In 1840 they opened a theater in competition with James Caldwell and named the playhouse the New American Theatre. Smith, in his memoirs, tells of the enterprise and its success.

67:1   On Poydras Street, between St. Charles and Camp Streets, and on the site of an old cooper's shop, there was in the course of erection a large stable and circus by Messrs. Dubois & Kendig. Taking a look at it, I found that, with certain alterations which could easily be made, a tolerably commodious theatre could be formed out of this building. I sought the

67:1. Sol Smith, *Theatrical Management in the West and South for Thirty Years* (New York: Harper & Bros., 1868), pp. 154–55.

proprietors, had a talk with them, and a consultation with a few friends, and before any dinner went into my mouth that day a contract was made for the erection of a theatre, of which I was to be the lessee for five years at $10,000 per year. I took it in my individual name, not feeling that I had a right to involve my partner in the speculation, he being at the time 1200 miles away, but reserving for him the right to become joint lessee with me if he should elect to do so, thus making what I call something of a Christian return for his conduct in regard to the Mobile Theatre in the fall of 1834, when he leased that house *on his own account,* excluding me from a participation in the business of that season, in violation of an understanding that we were to join our forces and become joint managers.

Next morning the lease was duly executed; and this was the way there came to be a new American Theatre in New Orleans in 1840.

The theatre on Poydras Street, corner of St. Francis Street, New Orleans, I named the NEW AMERICAN. During the summer a very excellent dramatic company was engaged, and a circus company, under John Robinson, besides. The parquet seats were so arranged that they could be taken up in a couple of hours, and replaced in three or four hours; so that, if it was desirable to exclude the equestrian performances any night, no one, on entering the house, would suppose from its appearance that any *saw-dust* had ever been there. While this theatre was being built, Mr. Caldwell was pushing ahead his new theatre in Mobile, and opened it during that fall. It gives me no pleasure to write that he never made any money there.

The New American opened for the season on the 10th of November, 1840, and the receipts on the first night were $981.25. On the second night they fell down to $179! The circus company was brought in on the 19th (together with dramatic entertainments), the receipts on that occasion being $624. The business was almost universally good the whole season, particularly so during the engagement of that charming actress, Mrs. Fanny Fitzwilliam, and that capital comedian, Mr. Buckstone, who played about fifty nights, the horses being, of course, dispensed with during their engagement. TIMOUR THE TARTAR, MEZEPPA, the FORTY THIEVES, EL HYDER, and CATARACT OF THE GANGES were the "horse pieces" produced. The great feature of the circus company was a little boy, adopted son of our equestrian manager, whose name I changed from Jimmy Robinson to Juan Hernandez. He was a wonderful child, not over eight years of age, and could execute the most difficult and dangerous equestrian feats, besides singing comic songs and acting children's parts on the stage.

I mention, as a great error in management, the engagement of Fogg and Stickney's company and stud of horses for three months of this season, paying them $9300, which might just as well have been saved. They attracted not one person to the house, as I verily believe, and the expense of keeping an extra stud of useless horses was a considerable item in the outlays from the treasury.

On July 30, 1842, the New American Theatre burned. Ludlow reveals the difficulties faced by the two managers in finding another theater in which to play the coming season. Stars had been signed, and it was imperative that a new house be found immediately.

67:2   This same year of 1842 I have set down in the calendar of my theatrical life as the most disastrous one in the eighteen managerial years of Ludlow & Smith. On the 30th of July, 1842, our theatre, the American, standing on Poydras Street,

67:2. Noah M. Ludlow, *Dramatic Life As I Found It* (St. Louis: G. I. Jones & Co., 1880), pp. 551–54.

New Orleans, *was burned to the ground!* This was a sudden and heavy blow to us,—especially heavy because of our situation at the time, following immediately on the heels of a very unfortunate year for us, financially. We had just made engagements East with a number of "stars" for the coming New Orleans season, and had increased our stock company for that city, and all of a sudden we found ourselves without a theatre there in which we could fulfill our engagements thus made.

As soon as I heard of the disaster, I wrote immediately to my partner on the subject, who received my letter in Baltimore, Maryland, and desired him to come immediately to St. Louis, feeling there would be a necessity for one of us to go to New Orleans without delay. I wrote also to Messrs. Dubois & Kendig, at New Orleans, to know what they intended to do in regard to rebuilding the theatre. I endeavored to see Mr. Dubois, whose family residence was in St. Louis, and who generally passed his summers in that city. He was, when I applied, temporarily absent; but in a few days he returned, and we met and had a conversation on the subject of the theatre. He told me that he had received letters from his partner, Mr. Kendig, at New Orleans, and that from the tenor of them, and their perfect unison with his own views, he thought there was scarcely a doubt that they would immediately commence the work of rebuilding the theatre; and concluded by saying, that unless some unlooked-for disaster interfered with their work, we might rest assured that the house would be ready for us by the middle of November ensuing, when we could take possession and proceed under the lease as though no fire had occurred.

My partner having returned from the East, I informed him of the conversations had with Mr. Dubois; and that gentleman shortly after meeting with Mr. Smith, the same assurances were made to him that the theatre would be ready for us in the following month of November. Under the conviction that all was understood and going on as we wished, we went to work in making preparations to get new scenery ready for the then progressing building.

Our losses by the burning of the theatre, in the way of scenery and other property owned by us and remaining there when we closed our previous season, we considered as having cost us from ten to twelve thousand dollars. We were never able to ascertain positively in what manner the theatre had been set on fire,—for that it had been purposely fired there was no kind of doubt. It had not been occupied in any way for over a month, and the last person that had access to the interior of it was a stage-carpenter named C----, whom, through our agent, we had put out of the occupancy of a room within it, for a beastly and outrageous piece of conduct too disgusting to be mentioned. This man had been heard to say he "would be even with us!" While we were endeavoring to obtain sufficinet evidence to convict, he was arrested for a repetition of the same crime, tried, convicted, and sent to the State penitentiary, where I was told he died after two or three years of incarceration.

About the middle of September, a clerk of Messrs. Dubois & Kendig arrived in St. Louis, and we were told by him that the theatre was progressing rapidly, and would certainly be ready for us early in November; and this was again repeated by Mr. Dubois, and with full assurances that we might depend upon it. About the 1st of October, we received a confidential letter from a friend of ours in New Orleans, setting forth circumstances which led him to believe that there was some underhand work going on in that city by certain individuals which would prevent our getting possession of the new American Theatre, then in a very forward state towards completion. This was to us a most unlooked-for and confounding statement, but one that produced grave evidences of a sound judgment and a warrantable conclusion. Mr. Dubois was again interviewed in reference to the theatre, and although he seemed in some measure embarrassed by our questionings, yet he persisted in assuring us that the theatre should be ready for us to occupy in November, and concluded his remarks by saying he was about to start for New Orleans to look into the progress of the business.

On consultation, it was agreed by my partner and myself that he should proceed to New Orleans without delay, with the view of looking after our interests in that city. He, being the one who made the original contract with Dubois & Kendig, was best acquainted with all the particulars, unwritten as well as written, connected with the transaction thereof; while I, who had been managing the affairs of the company during the existing summer, was so blended with the concluding business of it as to make my presence absolutely necessary in St. Louis.

About the middle of October, Mr. Smith embarked on a steamer for New Orleans, with Mr. Dubois for a fellow-passenger. On the 20th of the same month, they arrived in the "Crescent City," and in a few hours after found out that all which had been reported to us was but too true,—Mr. Kendig had leased the new American Theatre to James H. Caldwell,—and that Ludlow & Smith, within a month's time of their expected opening, had no theatre. The situation may easier be conceived than described.

In regard to the burning of the American Theatre, and the perplexities and embarrassments in consequence thereof, I shall say but little more. My partner, Mr. Smith, in his book, published in 1868, has given a full account of the particulars; and those who feel any desire to be acquainted with them, are referred to that book. I would wish it to be understood that my individual opinion is in perfect unison with that of my partner, that Mr. Dubois was not a willing accessary of his partner's treachery. Of the machinations of Mr. Caldwell and the duplicity of Mr. Kendig, it is my opinion Mr. Dubois was not assured until his partner had so far involved the firm that a dissent on his part would have produced a rupture of their entire affairs. While this fraud was being perpetrated, Mr. Dubois was with his family in St. Louis, where I often met him, and was always unequivocally assured by him that the theatre was in progress of erection in accordance with the understanding existing between us, and would be ready for us to commence our season by the middle of the ensuing November.

And now, just here, I desire to record, without disguise, hypocrisy, or any other feeling but that of candor, my unqualified admiration of the tact, judgment, skill, and energy exhibited by my partner in the treatment of the various and complicated difficulties that arose out of the burning of the American Theatre.

In 1835, when James H. Caldwell built the St. Charles Theatre, it was understood, at the time, that he obtained a large sum of money from the Gas Bank of New Orleans, to aid him in erecting that building, giving the bank, as security, a mortgage on the ground, which he then owned, and on the building which he was about to erect on it. After the theatre thus erected was burnt, in March, 1842, Mr. Caldwell transferred the ground and the ruins on it to the Gas Bank, in settlement of its claims against him. I mention this, merely that the reader may understand what follows.

My partner, Mr. Smith, had been in New Orleans only about a week, when he wrote to me at St. Louis that he had made an arrangement with the Gas Bank

of that city for a lease of the lot on which the late St. Charles Theatre had stood, and had obtained also a promise from that institution of financial assistance. He further stated that he was going to work immediately to see what could be done with contractors and builders, for the erection of a theatre in the shortest possible time. It was not long before I received another letter from him, stating that he had succeeded in finding an architect, carpenter, bricklayers, and others who would undertake the erection of the theatre, receiving a portion of their money during the progress of the building, and giving us time for the payment of the remainder. He further said he had obtained a lease of the ground for five years, renewable for five years more, at our discretion. I need not say, perhaps, that the intelligence was to me highly gratifying.

68. NEW ST. CHARLES THEATRE
New Orleans, Louisiana
Opened January 18, 1843

The new St. Charles Theatre was opened in January 1843, approximately nine months after the old St. Charles had burned to the ground. The lessees were Ludlow and Smith, and Ludlow retells the circumstances surrounding the opening.

68:1　During the last week of December I received a letter from my partner, dated on Christmas Day, wishing me "a merry Christmas and a happy new year," and conveying the pleasing intelligence that the new St. Charles Theatre would be ready to open between the 10th and 15th of the ensuing month, and requesting me to hold myself in readiness accordingly. This was as unexpected as it was gratifying; I could hardly believe it possible, although I was fully persuaded that great

68:1. Noah M. Ludlow, *Dramatic Life As I Found It* (St. Louis: G. I. Jones & Co., 1880), pp. 557–58.

150

efforts had been made towards a speedy accomplishment of this great necessity.

I went to work immediately to close up the season in Vicksburg, and in doing so gave a few benefits that had not been promised, in order to compensate certain married persons for the unexpected disturbance of their family arrangements by this flying visit of the company to Vicksburg.

Before proceeding to make any mention of the opening of the new St. Charles Theatre, I desire to make a statement of facts that will show that Mr. James H. Caldwell had not abandoned his *crushing system,* declared to me in 1824. As soon as Mr. Caldwell became assured that Ludlow & Smith would get the St. Charles Theatre erected, he commenced a process by which he thought he could prevent their opening it, crush them completely, and stamp them out forever. The reader may remember that I have previously stated that Ludlow & Smith had given to Dubois & Kendig a note for $2,400 in the spring of 1842, falling due in January, 1843. This note Caldwell had become the owner of, in the arrangement with Kendig for the American Theatre, and had obtained a subrogation, or transfer, of the judgment to him, that had been by us confessed when the note was given. Supposing we could not pay the note, from the fact that we were building a theatre that he thought must undoubtedly have involved all the resources we possessed for raising money, he advertised the new St. Charles Theatre to be sold at public sale, to pay a judgment which he held against the firm of Ludlow & Smith. But the smartest men very often find their plans thwarted at the very moment they deem their success most certain; and thus it happened with Mr. James H. Caldwell. Mr. Smith chanced to find a person in New Orleans who had purchased of the lamented Tyrone Power notes of James H. Caldwell, given Mr. Power for unpaid amounts due him

by Mr. Caldwell on his engagement of twenty-five nights in the St. Charles Theatre during the season of 1841–2. These notes were largely in excess of the amount of the judgment held by Caldwell against Ludlow & Smith, and these notes the holder of them thought it most conducive to his interest to place at the service of Ludlow & Smith; and these notes were used by them to satisfy the *crushing* judgment obtained by James H. Caldwell. How true are the words that "man proposes, but God disposes." In all instances where men permit their rancorous feelings to urge them to commit acts of injustice to their fellow-men, "their evil deeds return to plague the inventors."

Sol Smith, in his autobiography, relates the story of the New St. Charles and the difficulties he and his partner experienced with Caldwell.

68:2   Mr. Caldwell had endeavored to raise means for rebuilding the splendid St. Charles, and failed. Dubois and Kendig commenced rebuilding the American very shortly after its destruction. In September or October, an agent of theirs went to St. Louis and informed us that the house was nearly covered in, and advised that we should begin to prepare the scenery for it, which we accordingly did. The agent had not been long returned to New Orleans before reports came that *the American had been rented to Mr. Caldwell!* Mr. Dubois, who was in St. Louis, stoutly denied the truth of this report, and said there was no doubt about our going on with our lease, as if no fire had happened. I resolved to go to New Orleans at once. Dubois said he would go with me, and we went down on the same boat. Arrived in the Crescent City (on the 20th of October), my worst fears were realized; Mr. Caldwell was in

68:2. Sol Smith, *Theatrical Management in the West and South for Thirty Years* (New York: Harper & Bros., 1868), pp. 166–68.

possession of the new theatre sure enough, and was preparing scenery and decorations for an early opening. Upon consultation with friends, I found there existed a general desire that we should not "give it up so," but that *another* new theatre should be built, and that immediately. On the 21st I wrote the following statement, which appeared in the *Picayune* of the next day:

"THE AMERICAN THEATRE.

" *'Where the offense is, let the great axe fall.'*

"We have never obtruded our private affairs upon the attention of the New Orleans public. An excuse for making the following statement, it is believed, may be found in the fact that we have been connected, in the responsible capacity of managers, with a *public institution* which has been sustained and fostered by our *'resident population,'* as well as by the numerous residents of other parts of our country, who pass a part or the whole of the winter in this southern emporium, and in the other fact that by no fault of ours *our connection with that institution has ceased.*

"We have no wish to excite sympathy. Since 1837, blow after blow has fallen heavily upon us. We have been constrained to abandon one of our strongholds (Mobile) for want of means to compete with a powerful professional contemporary, who, 'with appliances and means to boot,' has for many years aspired to control the destinies of the Drama in the entire South and West. In St. Louis we were enabled to maintain our position, the stockholders having refused to listen to his propositions for a lease of their splendid temple.

"We came to New Orleans as to a place of refuge. Although it appeared plain to us that we could not compete successfully with the theatre then building in Mobile by Mr. Caldwell—our last theatre in that city being in a compara-

tively bad location—we thought that *here* two theatres *might* be sustained. We opened the American. To the threats of our contemporary that he would *shut us up in a month* we made no answer; his sneers at our humble temple, which he endowed with the classical appellations of a 'dog-pit' and a 'shanty,' we heeded not; his statements in the public newspapers that 'the expenses of his orchestra alone exceeded those of our whole establishment,' we noticed not, though, at the time that statement was made, our orchestra contained *ten* more musicians than his, and our dramatic company was superior to his, both in number and talent, to say nothing of two *equestrian companies* which were attached to our establishment, and which certainly did not *lessen* our expenses. We pursued the 'even tenor of our way,' satisfied that our exertions were appreciated by the public and munificently rewarded. Affairs are changed; both theatres have been destroyed by fire. One (the 'Little American') is being rebuilt, and as the time approaches when we expected to resume our professional operations, we find our 'shanty' in possession of James H. Caldwell! And that is not all; he has managed, hard as the times are, to find means to *purchase a judgment,* which he holds *in terrorem* over our heads! We repeat, we do not wish to excite sympathy; we trust we have sufficient energy remaining to enable us to rise even from this last blow. We shall at least *make the attempt.*

"STATEMENT.

"On the 14th of January, 1841, we leased of Messrs. Dubois and Kendig, for the term of five years, computing from the 1st of July, 1840, all and singular that portion of ground situated on Paydras Street, in the second municipality of this city, which was leased by Dubois and Kendig from George Morgan and others, by an act passed before H. B. Cenas, a notary public in this city, on the 4th of May, 1840, together with all the buildings and improvements thereon, known as the American Theatre.

"A clause in the lease provides that, *'in case of the destruction of the said premises by fire or otherwise, the rent shall cease and be no longer payable.'*

"In virtue of this agreement of lease, we occupied the premises two seasons. On the 30th of July last the premises was set on fire by an incendiary, and burned to the ground, together with all our theatrical property in New Orleans, consisting of scenery, furniture, machinery, gas fittings, and properties of every description pertaining to a well-regulated theatre, and which cost over twelve thousand dollars. We were the only parties interested, who were utterly uninsured. When the intelligence of the destruction of the theatre reached St. Louis, one of our firm was in New York making engagements for the ensuing winter campaign; the other immediately communicated with Mr. Dubois, then at St. Louis, and it was distinctly agreed between them that if the theatre could be rebuilt with the insurance money, a contract would be made to that effect immediately, and we were to continue to occupy it until the close of the term of our lease. Neither party being in possession of a copy of the lease, neither was certain what stipulation it contained in regard to the contingency which had occurred; but Mr. D. observed that, whatever the stipulation might be, they should feel themselves *morally* bound to rebuild, if they had the ability so to do, and he considered we were *morally* bound to go to work with our occupancy; and Mr. Dubois departed for New Orleans. On his return he said he had not made himself acquainted with the 'stipulations in the lease,' considering it quite unnecessary to do so, as the rebuilding was contracted for, and we were to have the theatre as a matter of course. He said *an application had been made, immediately after the burning,* for a lease of the American, should it be rebuilt; but he laughed at the idea of any one supposing it could be taken out of our hands, after the great loss we had sustained. It being clearly and distinctly understood that the lease was to be held good by both parties, the partner in New York was so advised, and, placing implicit confidence in the honor of our old friend Dubois, we felt no uneasiness on the subject. The theatre was to be ours beyond a doubt.

"On the strength of this understanding, and without a suspicion of bad faith any where, we proceeded to make our arrangements for the ensuing winter—engaged performers, orchestra, artists, and machinists—commenced preparing scenery and fixtures—applied for gas fittings, and expected to commence business in the new house about the 20th of November.

"On the 24th of September the Commercial Bulletin contained the following editorial article, founded, as we have since learned, *upon information furnished by Mr. James H. Caldwell himself:*

" 'We hear that Mr. Caldwell has leased the American Theatre, Poydras Street. There was a clause in the late lease by which it was stipulated that, in case the building was burned, the lease should end.'

"This article was republished, in substance, by nearly all the city papers, and in the papers of the Eastern cities, much to our injury, as we believe—though we most cheerfully acquit the Bulletin of any intention to injure us—holding out to professional people at the East who might be engaged to come to us the supposition that we should have no theatre at which to receive them. Seeing this paragraph in the newspapers, we had another interview with Mr. Dubois, and he assured us he knew of no such proceeding as the one spoken of, and *placed no reliance whatever on the report.*

"A confidential clerk of Messrs. Dubois & Kendig had been to St. Louis a few days previous to the above paragraph meeting our eye. He had two or three interviews with us, and did not say a word about any intention to lease the theatre to Mr. Caldwell or any one else. On the contrary, our conversation was exclusively confined to the progress of the new building; the preparations we were making to carry down scenery from St. Louis; the necessity of one of us proceeding to New Orleans in the course of a few weeks; and, finally, he promised to write us immediately on his arrival, and advise us of the state of the building, and when it would be necessary for us to commence work on the stage and machinery. Mr. Dubois informed us that the clerk had visited him for the purpose of raising means to go on with the building, in case one of the insurance companies should fail, as he feared it would, to meet the payments which would be due the contractor. He added that he had given the clerk authority to raise means from his personal friends, if they could be so raised, and if those means failed and the insurance company did not come up to the mark, he feared the *building must stop,* but said not a word about transferring the house into other hands.

"On the 9th of the present month we received intelligence that the new building had certainly been leased for our unexpired term to Mr. James H. Caldwell, and that he had obtained control over a judgment for $2418, which we had confessed in favor of Dubois & Kendig for a balance due on last year's rent. In short, we received the assurance that we had been 'headed' by Mr. Caldwell, trifled with by Mr. Kendig (for to this day we sincerely believe Mr. Dubois was no party to the transaction, and knew not of it; he assured us so himself, and our company, orchestra, artists, machinists, and all others who had formed engagements with us for the coming season,

numbering nearly one hundred persons, were thrown on our hands, and we without a place to employ them in!

"One of us is here, and, to save the time and trouble of answering questions —for there does appear to be considerable curiosity to know the particulars of a transaction by which we have been thrust out of the American Theatre— this statement is thus publicly put forth. The community may think we have received ill treatment; indeed, we believe there will be but one opinion on the subject. We shall not occupy our time in useless complainings, but act. If our courts will afford a remedy for the injuries we have sustained, they may be appealed to, when leisure will permit us to 'wait the law's delay;' at present a new theatre must be prepared for the reception of our company. We shall exert every faculty and use every honorable means to resume the position from which we have been ejected by incendiarism, intrigue, and treachery. Notwithstanding the untoward circumstances in which we are temporarily placed, we confidently expect to be able to fulfill every engagement made for the ensuing winter.

"[Signed in the name of the firm.] "New Orleans, October 22, 1842."

The New Orleans *Times-Picayune* described the new theater.

68:3   We are sure we shall be fully borne through by popular sentiment in the favorable opinion we have expressed regarding the interior design of this new structure. It opens this evening, when patrons and connoisseurs of the drama will see and judge for themselves, and in the meantime we will give our readers here and abroad some idea of what the building is.

The front upon St. Charles street is seventy-nine feet eight inches, by a depth

68:3. New Orleans *Times-Picayune*, Jan. 18, 1843.

of the house, running between parallel lines, of one hundred and forty-nine feet four inches. These dimensions are inferior to the great pile that was consumed, but upon entering, the audience section of the house it is discernible that little is left to be desired in the way of ample and convenient room. The same doorways through which we have all passed (for the front wall of the old theatre has been used, as well as other portions of the substantial brick work) admit us to a neat vestibule, thirty-four feet by twenty-three, from which arises a double flight of geometrical stairs, conducting the visitor to the lobby of the first circle. This part of the house we most admire, inasmuch as the persons seated anywhere in the tier are brought nearer the stage, and with a clearer view than we have ever known in so large a theatre. This will be understood when we describe the shape of the pit as a complete semi-circle, the outside railing of the orchestra forming the straight line. The upper tiers, of course, have the same advantage.

The depth of the boxes in front, from the rear seat to the balustrade, is twenty-one feet, and from the centre box to the footlights is thirty-one feet, leaving a depth of stage behind of sixty-one feet by a width of seventy-one in the clear. The proscenium presents an elevation of thirty-nine feet eight inches, with a width of fifty. From this the size of the new theatre may be seen.

In place of the old fashion of painted ornaments around the fronts of the boxes, we have here an open white balustrade, producing an effect quite new and beautiful upon the eye.

The dome is ornamented by the scenic artist with sunken panels of salmon ground with white scrolls and other emblematical devices. A golden fringed national drapery falls from the proscenium, showing in the centre an allegory. The arms of the Union form the lower object, and above Shakspeare is seen, borne

in a halo of light upon the pinions of America's eagle. Fame is there, too, darting with his trumpet through the sky, and triumphantly heralding the drama on. Four columns sustain the ornamented entablature above, composed of a mixed style of architecture, and copied after those of the celebrated Benares.

Such is the New St. Charles, as we have hastily sketched it; go tonight and see the opening.

69. RICE'S THEATRE
Chicago, Illinois
Opened June 18, 1847

The Rialto Theatre had closed its doors in 1840 and there was no permanent home of the drama until John Rice opened his theater on June 18, 1847. This milestone in Chicago theatrical history is chronicled in Andreas's *History of Chicago*.

69:1   The year 1847 makes an epoch in the dramatic history of Chicago, for then it was that John B. Rice decided to return to theatrical management, and adopted Chicago as his future home. While to Isherwood, McKenzie and Jefferson belongs the honor of introducing the drama in its peripatetic form, yet to John B. Rice is due the credit and distinction of giving to this noble art a local habitation and a name. The former men were the precursors of the great results, which now are one of the chief badges of Chicago's metropolitanism, but the latter is the man to whom must be accorded the title of founder of the drama as a distinctive feature of the city's greatness.

Mr. Rice had determined to retire from the stage, with which he had been identified in the East, when his attention was directed to this place, by a sanguine friend. He concluded to investigate the field, and with that purpose in mind, came

69:1. A. T. Andreas, *History of Chicago*. 3 vols. (Chicago: A. T. Andreas Co., 1884–86), 1:484–85.

to Chicago in the spring of 1847. So favorably was he impressed with the prospect, and so firmly convinced of Chicago's future development, that he at once arranged for the construction of a theater building. The Democrat of May 11, 1847, said:

"Mr. Rice, of Buffalo, has contracted with one of our oldest and most respected mechanics, Alderman Updike, to erect a frame building, forty by eighty, on the corner of Dearborn and Randolph streets. Mr. Rice comes here with an excellent reputation as a theater manager. There is no doubt now but Chicago will have a theater."

The site chosen was not upon the corner of Dearborn and Randolph streets, however, but on the south side of Randolph, one or two lots east of the southeast corner of those streets. . . .

. . . we discover that six weeks have sped by, since the announcement was first made. The little theater has assumed the form and dimensions of an imposing edifice to our retrospective eyes. We saunter into a neighboring hotel, and, picking up the Democrat of June 22, read: "The new theater building on Randolph Street, which is now nearly finished, is worthy a visit. The economy of the interior arrangement is excellent, the stage is roomy and well-designed for its purpose, the pit will be a very comfortable and convenient place to spend an evening there." Piqued with curiosity, we are about to visit the inviting place, when other duties interpose. The days fly by. Again the Democrat appears. We learn with pleasure that "Mr. Rice will open his theater on the 28th day of June. The internal arrangements of the new theater, now nearly completed, are admirable. A full view of the stage can be obtained from every part of the house, and the plan of the old Coliseum has been followed. The boxes are elegantly furnished and fitted up with carpets and settees, rather resembling a boudoir, or private sitting-room in a gentleman's house, than

an apartment in a place of public resort. The building has been completed in six weeks. A new era is unquestionably dawning in the theatrical world, and under the efficient management of Mr. Rice, assisted by his talented corps, we shall always have, in the rich language of Dan Marble, 'Something new, something rich and something rare.' The scenic accompaniments are said to be beautiful, being the joint production of two distinguished artists."

The company engaged by Mr. Rice consisted of Edwin Harris, leading man; Mrs. Hunt (now Mrs. John Drew), leading lady; James Carroll, G. W. Phillimore, George Mossop, Mr. Meeker, Jerry Merrifield, proficient as a dancer; for at that time, and for many years later, the public demanded a divertisement of this sort between plays. The scarcity of actors and the limited revenue of the little theater caused an amusing doubling up of parts, at this early period of the drama, and it was no uncommon thing for one actor to assume several characters in the same play. The Common Council imposed a license fee of $25 per month upon this theater.

On the evening of June 28, 1847, the opening performances at Rice's Theater took place. The play given was the ever-popular one called "The Four Sisters," in which Mrs. Hunt impersonated the quadruple role. Dan Marble was engaged as the "star" attraction, and carried the leading male part. Of this eventful night the Journal said, in its issue of June 29:

"The new theater last evening was crowded with a large and delighted audience. Mrs. Hunt never played better. Dan Marble never gave greater satisfaction. The performance, and the good order preserved, was just what could be expected under the efficient management of Rice. The numbers that could not gain admittance last evening will be pleased to see by the announcement that Mrs. Hunt and Mr. Marble appear again this evening; and if they be not both complained of today, for the injuries occasioned by throwing last night's audience into convulsions, we apprehend the friends of the parties will be there to know the reason. . . ."

The Democrat of June 29 said:

"Last night our theater opened with a rush. Those who were late needed a pilot to get through the crowd. If Mr. Rice intends keeping his present company, the large new building, so honorably and so enterprisingly erected, will have to be enlarged. Our city is under great obligation to Mr. Rice for his enterprise. The dress circle was the most brilliant ever brought out by any entertainment in our city. Dan Marble is here, and everybody knows him. Mrs. Hunt made herself known last night, and will never be forgotten. Rice proved himself a splendid actor, as well as theater builder. In fine, Chicago can boast of being ahead of any city of twice its size in the theatrical line. . . ."

The popularity of Rice's Theatre was unexcelled in Chicago in the decade of the 1840s. The popularity, however, was to be cut short because of the great theater hazard, fire. Andreas wrote:

69:2   The evening of July 30, 1850, was the most startlingly memorable in the history of this theater. A company composed of Miss Eliza Brienti, Miss Helen Mathews, Mr. Guibelei, and Mr. Manvers and a home-chorus, aided by a local orchestra, introduced opera for the first time in Chicago. The event was one, however, which did not call forth a large audience. The little theater was far from being crowded. The curtain rose upon the pleasing scene of "La Sonnambula," and all went well, promising a most satisfactory inauguration of the opera, however, the appalling cry of fire rang through the house. The audience started to their feet

69:2. A. T. Andreas, *History of Chicago*. 3 vols. (Chicago: A. T. Andreas Co., 1884–86), 1:189.

in terror. No signs of disaster were discernible, and for an instant it was believed the alarm was false. A moment later the warning cry was heard again and serious injury to many might have ensued, had it not been for the presence of mind evinced by Manager Rice. "Sit down! Sit down! Do you think I would permit a fire to occur in my theater? Sit down!" and, obedient to his command, the panic-striken people, paused, half-assured by the peremptory tone that all was safe. But, while Mr. Rice was standing on the stage, some one from the prompter's box said, "Mr. Rice, the theatre is on fire?" The alarm spread, and soon the building was cleared of its audience. J. H. McVicker was on the stage at the time. He began to pull down scenery, hoping to save something; but the flames spread so rapidly that everybody was driven away. Mr. McVicker hastened to his rooms, a few doors from the theater. Before he could reach there, that building was also on fire, and he was compelled to go to the Sherman house in his stage costume. He lost everything except the clothes then worn by him.

The cause of the alarm was the burning of stables on Dearborn street, in the rear of the theater, owned and occupied by J. T. Kelley. So rapid was the progress of the fire that the audience was scarcely in the street before the stage of the theater was enveloped in flames. The firemen labored bravely to suppress the fire, but did not gain mastery over it until one-half the block was laid in ruins. The theater was totally destroyed, involving a loss of $4,000 to Mr. Rice. Added to this material annihilation of his property was the interruption of business, and although the sum named seems inconsiderable at the present day, its real character is better understood when we take into account the fact that all things are relative. The disaster was a serious blow to Mr. Rice. It checked a prosperous career by summarily closing the season and disbanding the company in his employ. . . .

70. EAGLE THEATRE
Sacramento, California
Opened October 18, 1849

The discovery of gold in California in 1849 caused a massive migration westward. Towns were rapidly established and some men made huge fortunes. Prices soared to become the highest the nation had ever known, but money seemed to be plentiful in the mining towns, and the men apparently did not object to the outrageous prices of five dollars for a seat in one of the boxes or three dollars for a place in the pit. Thes men were starved for entertainment, and the theatres were erected rapidly to meet the demand.

The first of these playhouses was the Eagle Theatre in Sacramento. Bayard Taylor, writer, adventurer, and traveler, was in California at this time, writing about the Gold Rush for the New York *Tribune*. In his book *Eldorado* he describes this primitive frontier theater:

70:1   At the time of which I am writing, Sacramento City boasted the only theatre in California. Its performances, three times a week, were attended by crowds of miners, and the owners realized a very handsome profit. The canvas building used for this purpose fronted on the levee, within a door or two of the City Hotel; it would have been taken for an ordinary drinking-house but for the sign: "EAGLE THEATRE," which was nailed to the top of the canvas frame. Passing through the barroom, we arrive at the entrance; the prices of admission are: Box, $3; Pit, $2. The spectators are dressed in heavy overcoats and felt hats, with boots reaching to the knees. The box-tier is a single rough gallery at one end, capable of containing about a hundred persons; the pit will probably hold three hundred more, so that the receipts of a full house amount to $900. The sides

and roof of the theatre are canvas, which, when wet, effectually prevents ventilation and renders the atmosphere hot and stifling. The drop-curtain, which is down at present, exhibits a glaring landscape, with dark-brown trees in the foreground, and lilac-colored mountains against a yellow sky.

The overture commences; the orchestra is composed of only five members, under the direction of an Italian, and performs with tolerable correctness. The piece for the night is *The Spectre of the Forest,* in which the celebrated actress Mrs. Ray, "of the Royal Theatre, New Zealand," will appear. The bell rings, the curtain rolls up; and we look upon a forest scene, in the midst of which appears Hildebrand, the robber, in a sky-blue mantle. The foliage of the forest is of a dark-red color, which makes a great impression on the spectators and prepares them for the bloody scenes that are to follow. The other characters are a brave knight in a purple dress, with his servant in scarlet; they are about to storm the robber's hold and carry off a captive maiden. Several acts are filled with the usual amount of fighting and terrible speeches; but the interest of the play is carried to awful height by the appearance of two spectres, clad in mutilated tent-covers, and holding spermaceti candles in their hands. At this juncture Mrs. Ray rushes in and throws herself into an attitude in the middle of the stage; why she does it, no one can tell. This movement, which she repeats several times in the course of the first three acts, has no connection with the tragedy; it is evidently introduced for showing the audience that there is, actually, a female performer. The miners, to whom the sight of a woman is not a frequent occurrence, are delighted with these passages and applaud vehemently.

In the closing scenes, where Hildebrand entreats the heroine to become his bride, Mrs. Ray shone in all her glory. "No!" said she, "I'd rather take a basilisk and

70:1. Bayard Taylor, *Eldorado, or, Adventures in the Path of Empire.* 2 vols. (New York: G. P. Putnam & Sons, 1850), 2:29–31.

67. New American Theatre, New Orleans. Engraving, published in Pitt and Clark's *New Orleans Directory* (1842). Courtesy of the Rare Book Room, Special Collections Division, Tulane University Library.

70. Eagle Theatre, Sacramento, Calif. From a mural by Frank Tenney Johnson, 1926, in the Cathay Circle Theatre, Los Angeles; based on a 19th-century sketch by E. Wyttendach. Courtesy of the California State Library.

SAINT CHARLES THEATRE, NEW ORLEANS

LUDLOW & SMITH PROPRIETORS & MANAGERS

68. Interior, New St. Charles Theatre, New Orleans. Lithograph and drawing by G. Tolti. Courtesy of the Louisiana Collection, Special Collections Division, Tulane University Library.

wrap its cold fangs around me, than be clasped in the hembraces of an 'artless robber'." Then, changing her tone to that of entreaty, she calls upon the knight in purple, whom she declares to be "me 'ope—me only 'ope!" We will not stay to hear the songs and duets which follow; the tragedy has been a sufficient infliction. For her " 'art-rending" personations, Mrs. Ray received $200 a week, and the wages of the other actors were in the same proportion. A musical gentleman was paid $96 for singing "The Sea! The Sea!" in a deep bass voice. The usual sum paid musicians was $16 a night. A Swiss organ-girl, by playing in the various halls, accumulated $4,000 in the course of five or six months. . . .

In 1880 the *Illustrated History of Sacramento City and County* was published and included a description of the theater as well as a reproduction of the opening night's program.

70:2   The subject of amusements, while not affording much scope for the pen of the historian, may form an interesting topic for the pioneer and others to look back upon: recalling, as it must, the many comical occurrences that they have seen, as well as those which are more serious. The following article, descriptive of the first performances at the Eagle Theatre, is mainly compiled from articles by J. E. Lawrence and J. H. McCabe, who were eye-witnesses and participants in the scenes they describe:

"Sacramento, the earliest and richest birth of the golden age of the Pacific, enjoys the honor of dedicating the first structure to the purposes of the drama in California. The Eagle Theatre opened October 18, 1849, the bill for the occasion making the following announcement:

70:2. Thomas Hinckley Thompson and Albert Augustus West, *Illustrated History of Sacramento City and County* (Sacramento: Thompson & West, 1880), pp. 119–21.

"EAGLE THEATRE

"L. Hubbard & Co......Proprietors
"Charles P Prince.........Manager
"V. Bona (of N.Y. Theatre)........ Leader of Orchestra

"The manager takes pleasure in announcing to the citizens of Sacramento, also of Sutter and the mining districts, that this establishment is completed, and will open for the first dramatic representation on Thursday, October 18, 1849.

"Box Tickets ..... $5, Pit $3

"The evening's performance will commence with an overture by the orchestra, to be followed by the beautiful drama called the

"BANDIT CHIEF;
or, Forest Spectre.

"Hildebrand......... Mr. Atwater
"Herbert............. C. P. Price
"Carmelo................. Harris
"Baptisto.................... Ray
"Valletto................... Daly
"Lucille...............Mrs. Ray

"Overture by the Orchestra
"To conclude with the petit comedy of

"LOVE IN HUMBLE LIFE.

"Rouslans............Mr. Harris
"Carlitz.................... Ray
"Brandt.................... Daly
"Christine.............Mrs. Ray

"Doors open at 6½ o'clock; performance to commence at 8 o'Clock. Tickets may be procured at the saloon in front of the Theatre."

Thus did the City of the Plains obtain a precedence in the formation of the Arts on the western shores of the Union, which the liberal taste and refined social culture of the inhabitants still promises to maintain. The Placer Times, of October 20, says:

"EAGLE THEATRE.—This house opened to a full, and we may add, fashionable house, for the dress circle was graced by quite a number of fine-looking, well-costumed ladies, the sight of whom was revivifying. Of the performance, we have no room to speak in detail, nor point out many imperfections, which, no doubt, will be corrected after a few representations. Messrs. Hubbard, Brown & co. deserve the patronage of the theatre-going public for building such a comfortable and well-arranged house."

The season of the Eagle Theatre lasted over ten weeks, the performance being given generally three times a week, with two or three interruptions, not exceeding a fortnight in the aggregate. Not less than eighty thousand dollars was expended in the erection of the theatre, including the saloon in front. Its size was thirty by sixty-five feet, and the lumber of which the frame was made cost from six hundred to seven hundred dollars per thousand feet. The roof was covered with sheet iron and tin, and the sides with canvas, costing one dollar per yard, and sewed at the expense of sixteen dollars per day paid to each man employed on the work. Pieces of packing boxes served for constructing the stage, which was sixteen feet deep, and a large box placed upon it did for a trap, in such pieces as the "Floating Beacon," and "Lady of the Lake." George Wilson, who came out in Graham's command, painted the drop-curtain, representing an incident in Texas during the Mexican war. The drop furnished a wood, street, and interior view. As an entrance to the second tier, a step-ladder was provided on the outside of the building, and, in deference to the ladies, canvas was nailed beneath it. In the parquet, the seats were of rough boards, the ground serving for a floor. Visitors purchased their tickets in the saloon, generally pouring out a quantity of dust in the treasurer's scales, who took down weight at twelve dollars to the ounce. The theatre held, when full, about eight hundred dollars. It was common, between the acts and pieces, for parties in the pit to indulge in a game of mone, using their seats to make their lay-out upon. . . .

One incident shows the difficulties under which they (the actors) labored. A benefit was given to J. H. McCabe, a member of the company, at which "Douglas" was produced. All the in-door elements predicted a triumphant result, but storms and floods willed it otherwise. The water rose inches deep in the pit before the doors opened, and the play had progressed but an act or two when the benches ceased to afford a dry foundation. At last the water rose over the tops of the parquet seats nearest the stage. Some of the miners took great pleasure in wading along the seats covered with water and sitting on the railing around the orchestra. Occasionally, one would appear to be roused to enthusiasm, and while shouting his approbation, would throw out his arm, and, striking his neighbors on either side, would precipitate them into the water. This sometimes caused a laugh, but always interrupted the performance for a while.

Half the town was submerged and the few second floors then to be found in the city of canvas afforded sleeping apartments for but a few of its unhoused inhabitants. Fortunately, the actors were better bestowed, and the stage was their domicile by day and night. . . .

The first flood which submerged Sacramento caused the Eagle Theatre to close on the night of January 4, 1850, and the company, under the direction of Mr. Atwater, proceeded to San Francisco. . . .

71. JENNY LIND I THEATRE
San Francisco, California
Opened October 30, 1850

By 1850 San Francisco had developed into a boom town with new settlers pouring in —settlers who were looking for diversion in the evening. Thomas Maguire, who had been a hack driver in New York, was ready to help supply the entertainment they craved. He started with a gambling and drinking saloon, but soon entered the field in which he was to be a driving force, for many years to come, as a theater owner and impresario.

His first venture was the Jenny Lind I Theatre, named for the Swedish Nightingale, although she never sang there. Maguire merely made capital use of her name. The first Jenny Lind Theatre was located over the Parker House Saloon on Kearny Street. Unlike the other crude San Francisco "theaters," the Jenny Lind was ostentatiously ornamented in white and gold gilt and rose panels and seated nearly 800 persons. The *Alta California* made mention of the new playhouse.

71:1   JENNY LIND THEATRE

This is the name given to an elegant, spacious saloon fitted up in the newly completed Parker House, on the easterly side of Portsmouth Square. It has a neat and pretty stage and an auditorium fitted up with commodious settees, capable of holding probably five hundred persons with ease. The walls and ceilings are handsomely painted in fresco. The proprietors contemplate opening tomorrow evening with a musical olio and feats of legerdemain. The principal attraction is Madam Van Calpin Korsinski, who is said to be an admirable vocalist. We trust that the managers will be able to secure a succession of attractions that will ensure to them a liberal share of public support.

The playhouse did not open the following day, as the article announced, but on October 30. Maguire leased the theater to James Stark and Sarah Kirby, who booked dramatic performances into the playhouse, mingling Shakespeare with the kind of melodrama that was so popular with the frontier crowds.

The theater continued to be a successful one until May 4, 1851, when it and the Parker House Saloon burned to the ground. Maguire immediately announced his plans to build a

bigger and better Jenny Lind Theatre, and the plans were reported in the *Alta California*.

71:2   The proprietors of the Parker House are pushing on and upward the walls for their new theatre, which is to occupy nearly two-thirds the front breadth of the old Parker House, with a depth of one hundred and fifty feet. The walls are brick. It is to be fireproof. It is intended to make it worthy of California, beautiful, airy, commodious and safe. The stage will be seventy-five feet deep, and the theatre of a capacity to seat three thousand persons.

72. BATES THEATRE
St. Louis, Missouri
Opened January 9, 1851

In 1851 theatrical activity in St. Louis increased with the opening of the new Bates Theatre, which was built by John Bates, who also owned another playhouse in Cincinnati. A history of St. Louis written in 1883 tells something of the history of this theater.

72:1   Bates' Theatre.—On the 9th of January, 1851, a new theatre, known as Bates' Theatre, situated on Pine Street near Fourth, was opened by John Bates, the play being the "Honeymoon," with the Raymonds, Mr. Fleming, Miss Maywood, and others in the cast. Before the play Mr. Fleming delivered the opening address, which was written by Edmund Flagg, of St. Louis. The movement for the erection of the theatre began about May, 1848, and was prosecuted vigorously by Mr. Bates, who already owned a theatre in Cincinnati. The building, which was eighty-four by one hundred and thirty-one feet, was erected on the north side of Pine Street, about midway between Third and Fourth Streets. The manager was Mr. Bates' son, James W.

71:2. *Alta California*, May 31, 1851.
72:1. J. Thomas Scharf, *A History of St. Louis City and County*. 2 vols. (Philadelphia: Louis H. Everts & Co., 1883), 1:977–78.

71:1. *Alta California*, Oct. 27, 1850.

Bates, and the stage manager, R. Malone Raymond. J. W. Bates continued to manage the theatre until his death on the 11th of February, 1853, from the effects of an accidental fall on the pavement. Mr. Bates, who was about thirty-five years of age, was his father's only son, and had assisted his father in the management of theatres at Cincinnati and Louisville. Shortly after his death his father relinquished the management of the theatre in St. Louis, which he finally sold. Among the actors who appeared at the theatre were Charlotte Cushman, J. Wilkes Booth, Maggie Mitchell, who made her first appearance as *Fanchon* there; J. K. Emmet, Thomas Connor, Ristori, James Anderson, the English tragedian; Charles Matthews, Edwin Adams, James E. Murdoch, Charles Kean and Ellen Tree, Madam Celeste, James Wallack, Rogers and Shelly, G. V. Brooks and his wife, Avonia Jones, daughter of the eccentric Count Johannes; James Wallack, Jr., E. L. Davenport, the Raven family, and many others.

Among the vocalists who sang at the theatre were Madame Nilsson, Pauline Lucca, Parepa Rosa, and Louisa Pyne. Mrs. Blanche De Bar made her *début* there as *Miss Hardcastle* in "She Stoops to Conquer," and Ben De Bar and Mark Smith often appeared on the stage together. It was on the same stage that William J. Florence and Barney Williams secured their first successes in the West, and Lotta her first "hit" east of the Pacific Slope. What came very nearly being a terrible catastrophe occurred in Bates' Theatre in 1853, while the famous Ravel family were playing an engagement. After the theatre was closed and locked up the ceiling fell with a terrible crash. Had there been an audience present many lives would have been lost.

Ben De Bar became manager of the theatre in 1856, having purchased it from Mr. Bates for fifty-six thousand dollars, and its name was changed to the St. Louis Theatre, and in 1860 to "De Bar's Theatre." Adah Isaacs Menken made her last appearance in *Mazeppa* in St. Louis at De Bar's. The theatre was the scene of two murders,—the killing of Mabel Hall, a ballet-dancer, by Edgar Moore, and the murder committed by William Wieners. About 1874 the property was leased to William Mitchell, who changed the name to "Theatre Comique." Ben De Bar died in the summer of 1877, leaving the property as a part of the estate, and appointed John G. Priest as executor of his will. Some time prior to his death Mr. De Bar gave a deed of trust on the property, and under this deed of trust it was sold to George Fales and Alfred G. Baker, of Philadelphia.

Mr. Mitchell leased the theatre for six years, and during the latter portion of that period the manager was William H. Smith. The building was destroyed by fire on the 9th of December, 1880.

The *Missouri Republican* covered the opening of the Bates Theatre.

72:2 The theatre of Mr. Bates, on Pine street, was opened for the first time last night, to a very numerous audience. The performances gave satisfaction, as was evinced by the marked attention and order which prevailed throughout. From what we can judge, after so short an acquaintance with the stock company, we incline to believe that they will generally become favorites in their various departments, and that—with always at least one or two "stars" to sustain principal characters—they will remain in high favor with the public. Mr. Fleming, Miss Maywood, the Raymonds, and the best of other artists, acquitted themselves creditably in the comedy of the *Honey Moon*. Mr. Fleming delivered the opening address with effect. This address is from the pen of one of our townsmen— we give it our readers:

72:2. *Missouri Republican,* Jan. 10, 1851.

With the internal arrangements of the Theatre building, we were, in common with hundreds of others, agreeably surprised. Every portion teems with elegancies and conveniences. With well carpeted floors and comfortably cushioned seats; with a splendid salon to each tier, where parties, between the acts, are furnished with creams, fruit, and all varieties of refreshments, with well-organized anterooms for storing away cloaks, over shoes, etc., nothing has been forgotten or omitted which can tend to the convenience of the audience. The building is, moreover, well lighted, and so well heated that it may be rendered comfortable in the coldest weather. In the matter of elegance of decoration, the interior of the house exceeds anything we have ever seen before in this city. The figures on the dome, the carving and gilding on the boxes are, with all else, in excellent taste.

We can but repeat our admiration of everything disclosed at the opening of the new Theatre, and re-echo the wishes of many others for its success.

A few days later, however, in a review of a performance at the theater published in the *Missouri Republican,* the critic voices the need for some changes in the physical comforts of the playhouse.

72:3 We confess that we do not clearly see, and that we cannot at all appreciate the beauties of the "celebrated" tragedy of Adelgitha, performed last evening at the new Theatre. It is altogether too terribly tragical in sentiment, and further is somewhat incorrect, we believe, in some of the moral lessons it proposes to convey. Nevertheless, it afforded us another opportunity of witnessing the fine acting of Miss Logan, and for this reason was at intervals a passable entertainment to the audience. The beautiful Miss Louisa Raymond was warmly applauded in the song, "Mary of Argyll." She is rapidly

72:3. *Missouri Republican,* Jan. 16, 1851.

gaining the favor of our theater-going community.

Before closing our notice we ask leave to make one of two suggestions, an attention to which we believe would conduce materially to the comforts and enjoyment of the Theatre. The first is to increase the number of passage ways between the seats, in the first and second tiers. These seats, as it is now, are very long and very near each other, so that at every new arrival of a person who wishes to reach a vacant place in the middle, the occupants at one or the other end must all rise and walk out to let him reach it. The annoyance caused by these occasional disturbances in the progress of the play, has already been experienced by many. Our second suggestion is to increase the light at the rear of the dress circle. This could be easily effected by lowering the burners attached to the tier above, so that they may project an inch or two below the dress circle ceiling, or better still, probably by placing a few additional lights at the rear of that tier.— That portion of the house is, of course, sufficiently lighted to allow visitors to walk in safety to their seats, but this is not enough. The internal fittings and decorations of the Theatre are such as show to a better advantage where every portion is lighted very brilliantly; and, moreover, the fact should be remembered, that every aspiring belle, who visits the Theatre, carries with her a longing desire "to see and be seen,"—the hint, we trust, will be considered. Rome was not built in a day, however, and with every desire to see Mr. Bates supply the deficiencies in his elegant building, we are quite willing, with his other well-wishers, to accord him time to do it in.

73. JENNY LIND II THEATRE
San Francisco, California
Opened June 13, 1851

The destruction by fire of the first Jenny Lind Theatre seemed to be a blessing in disguise for Thomas Maguire, since his plans were to build a new playhouse that would increase seating capacity by more than two and a half times and be completely fireproof. The *Alta California* recounted the brief history of drama in California and mentioned this ill-fated house.

73:1 . . . On the 4th of July, 1850, Messrs Robinson and Evard opened the little Dramatic Museum in California street above Montgomery. This little establishment had a tremendous run until September, when the original Jenny Lind was opened over Mr. Maguire's Parker House saloon on the Plaza. Mr. and Mrs. Stark played here through the fall and a portion of the winter. In the fire of May, 1851, the building was destroyed, and at the same time the Dramatic Museum of Messrs. Robinson & Evard, which had been enlarged, was also destroyed by fire. Immediately after the fire of May, the foundation of a theatre was commenced on the ground where the present Jenny Lind now stands, and a temporary wooden building, with a theatre in the upper story, erected where Maguire's saloon now is. A company had just commenced playing in this, which had been in operation but a few nights, when the fire of June came and again swept the whole building. . . .

The fact is that the Jenny Lind II had been a temporary building, opened hastily because of the advent of a small new theater named Temple of the Arts. The edifice was scarcely fireproof, but was only a rapidly constructed building in which to present theatrical performances. Short notices in the *Alta California* over a three-week period tell of the rise and fall of the Jenny Lind II.

73:2 THE THEATRE.—Rapid progress is being made in the building on Portsmouth Square, on the site of the old Jenny Lind,

and intended as a temporary theatre to be used until the large and elegant one to be built on the next lot is completed, which will be in the course of six or eight weeks. It is understood that Mr. C. R. Thorne will open with his company in about eight or ten days.

73:3 THE JENNY LIND.—The opening of this establishment has been postponed from Monday to Thursday evening, in consequence of the impossibility of Mr. Thorne's coming to the city with his company before that time.

73:4 THE JENNY LIND.—This new theatre, together with the whole house of Mr. T. Maguire, upon the Plaza, will be opened on Thursday evening. The theatre is a neat little place, and will answer a very good purpose until the magnificent one to be erected on the next lot is finished. On the ground floor is the saloon containing four fine billiard tables, and below is a spacious room containing six splendid bowling alleys. Altogether, this house will be one of the finest in San Francisco.

73:5 JENNY LIND THEATRE.—The new Jenny Lind Theatre was opened last night by a portion of the company of Mr. Stark and Mrs. Kirby. A very good audience attended, and the performances went off very well. The house is neatly and tastefully fitted up, is commodious, and will doubtless be liberally patronized.

73:6 JENNY LIND THEATRE.—This establishment is becoming as popular as it formerly was. The managers are presenting only those light and interesting pieces which have a tendency to drive away the blues and give a man a better opinion of the world. This evening will be presented the petite comedy of Love in Humble

73:1. *Alta California*, Oct. 24, 1851.
73:2. *Alta California*, May 29, 1851.

73:3. *Alta California*, June 8, 1851.
73:4. *Alta California*, June 10, 1851.
73:5. *Alta California*, June 14, 1851.
73:6. *Alta California*, June 15, 1851.

Life, The King's Gardener, and the Widow's Victim.

73:7 JENNY LIND THEATRE.—This evening will be presented the laughable farce of the "Man About Town," "Widow's Victim," and "Crossing the Line," with dancing by Senorita Abalos. Tomorrow evening Messrs. Barry and Daly, and Miss Montague will make their re-appearances.

73:8 ANOTHER TERRIBLE CONFLAGRATION . . . After the fire reached Washington street, the California Restaurant, which adjoined the Alta California office, was blown up, but it did not stop the flames. The Jackson House and Lafayette Restaurant and buildings in the rear, were all on fire at once, and the flames were at the same time enfolding the building formerly called the St. Charles, which stood between the Alta office and the fire proof Bella Union. Thus surrounded and enveloped in flames, all our efforts to beat back the destroyer were in vain. With a plentiful supply of water and a fire engine, in addition to two force pumps of our own, we were perfectly powerless. Yet a dozen men contended long and manfully, risking their lives and doing all that men could do, but in vain. Then, and not till then, they left, when they could no longer breathe within the building, and rushed through cinders, sheeted flames and dense smoke to the Plaza. Here most melancholy sights met the view. A large portion of the goods removed there for safety were on fire and were totally consumed. Among them was our own stock of stationery and material. But more horrible than all, two or three corpses, one of a man who was moved on account of sickness, in his bed, to the Square, and there died while the fire was raging.

Another was the trunk of a man burned to death and partly consumed. The new Parker House, nearly finished outside, containing the new Jenny Lind Theatre,

73:7. *Alta California*, June 22, 1851.
73:8. *Alta California*, June 23, 1851.

which had been built since the fire of May 4th when the fourth Parker House was burned, went with the rest. This was the fifth burn down since December 24th, 1849. Our own office is merely ruins, only a portion of the walls remaining. Fortunately the Amphitheatre or Circus on the west side of the square had been torn down a few days before, which was the means partially of saving the old zinc custom house building on Clay street, and a few adjoining small wooden houses, and preventing the fire crossing Clay street above the plaza. The old "adobe" on the plaza, in which was the office of Burgoyne & Co., and several, shared the fate of others—It was completely burned. Thus about the last relic of the Feudal age of San Francisco has been blotted out. So our poor city is again in sackcloth and ashes. Our community are blank. For although but few heavy stocks of goods or fine buildings have been consumed, yet the blow is felt very severely, for most of the buildings were occupied as dwellings and lodgings. It is too soon to speculate particularly about the effects, except as to general results. Thousands of our people are homeless. We are sick with what we have seen and felt, and need not say more.

The fire that destroyed the Jenny Lind II was the work of an incendiary, as were so many of the fires San Francisco experienced at this time.

74. JENNY LIND III THEATRE
San Francisco, California
Opened October 4, 1851

The Jenny Lind II Theatre, the third playhouse to bear that ill-fated name, opened just three and a half months after the destruction of the Jenny Lind II. This time Maguire did make good his promise to build a more substantial building, one of which San Francisco could be justly proud. Soulé's *Annals of San Francisco* tells a little of the history of this building.

74:1   NEW JENNY LIND THEATRE
         SAN FRANCISCO

October 4th. (1851). Opening of the new Jenny Lind Theatre on the Plaza. This was a large and handsome house. The interior was fitted up with exquisite taste; and altogether in size, beauty and comfort, it rivalled the most noted theaters in the Atlantic States. It could seat comfortably upwards of two thousand persons. The opening night presented a brilliant display of beauty and fashion, and every part of the immense building was crowded to excess. A Poetical address was delivered on the occasion by Mrs. E. Woodward. A new era in theatricals was now begun in San Francisco; and since that period the city has never wanted one or two first class theatres and excellent stock companies, among which "stars" of the first magnitude annually make their appearance. Before this date there had been various dramatic companies in San Francisco, but not before had there been so magnificent a stage for their performances. The "Jenny Lind" did not long remain a theatre. The following year it was purchased by the town for a City Hall for the enormous sum of two hundred thousand dollars. The external stone walls were allowed to stand, but the whole interior was removed and fitted up anew for the special purposes to which it meant to be applied.

The Jenny Lind was a large theater and quite elaborate for the time.

74:2   Being built by Tom Maguire, the Jenny Lind III was of course to be like

nothing ever seen before. And it was. Its size was tremendous for the time, with a frontage of seventy-five feet, a height of sixty feet and a depth of one hundred and forty feet. The stage itself was fifty feet deep by forty-one wide, enough room in which to drill a regiment. There was of course a handsomely painted curtain, representing a scene from *The Bride of Abydos* and, what was more novel, an ingenious ventilating system whereby air was admitted through a cupola in the center of the ceiling. The cost of the Jenny Lind III was estimated at $150,-000.

SEVEN DOORS TO PARADISE

Inside and out the admiring populace walked around and held its breath. The massive front was composed of a creamy white sandstone imported from Sydney, Australia, and, lighted up at night, must have had somewhat the effect of a white shirt-front gleaming out of the dull black of a dress suit. There were seven arched doors through which to enter and, once inside the vestibule, seven more through which to reach the inner sanctuary. On the second and third stories there were seven windows reaching from floor to ceiling. It was all very classical.

But one can imagine a newly arrived miner sloshing up Kearny Street and wonder how it would strike his already fogged brain to be confronted with this gleaming pearl of the desert. All around him were muddy streets and squalid ramshackle buildings, and here before him suddenly loomed a white palace—a mirage no doubt. There would be but two courses open to him: to shake his head and turn into the nearest saloon, or, more manfully, to brace his shoulders and march through two of the fourteen doors, look around at the white and gold walls, at the Bride of Abydos on the curtain, look up at the Muses and Apollo painted on the ceiling, wonder if the chandelier would fall on him if it fell,

74:1. Frank Soulé, John H. Gihon, and John Nisbett, *The Annals of San Francisco* (New York and San Francisco: D. Appleton & Co., 1855), p. 353.

74:2. "Theatre Buildings," San Francisco Theatre Research, vol. 15, pt. 1, mimeographed (sponsored by the City and County of San Francisco, 1939), pp. 53–54.

settle down in one of the handsome plush chairs and blissfully go to sleep. . . .

The critic for the *Alta California* was suitably impressed on opening night.

74:3 THE OPENING OF THE JENNY LIND.—Last evening the elegant theatre on the Plaza, that has already, during the process of construction, attracted so much public attention, was thrown open to our citizens. It was of course crowded, a goodly number of ladies gracing the dress-circle. In the interior, it is a most chaste and finished piece of workmanship. The prevailing color is a light pink, rendered brilliant and tasteful by gilding most tastefully applied. The style of decoration harmonizes most admirably with the architecture of the interior, which is light and airy. The act-drop is a rich fancy sketch, in which a picturesque ruin is the leading feature. We cannot but regret, however, that some actual scenes in California, in the Sandwich Islands, or somewhere on the Pacific coast had not been selected as a subject for the painter's pencil. The proscenium boxes are richly decorated, and in fact the whole affair reflects great credit on Mr. Maguire, whose repeated efforts to rear a temple of the Muses which shall be a lasting ornament to California, we may trust are finally crowned with success. The front will at least present an imposing appearance, and as there is to be no ingress left open for the flames to enter, the only danger to be feared is from internal fire. . . .

During the summer of 1852 there was a surprise announcement that the Jenny Lind III had been purchased at the enormous price of $200,000 by the city of San Francisco for use as a city hall. Suspicions were raised that skullduggery was afoot, but nothing was proven, except that Thomas Maguire had made a very handsome profit on his major theatrical venture.

75. AMERICAN THEATRE
San Francisco, California
Opened October 20, 1851

Sixteen days after the opening of the Jenny Lind III, a formidable rival, the American Theatre, opened its doors. The new playhouse was built on recently filled-in land on what had been nothing more than tidal flats. The American Theatre was to be one of the reasons for the sale of the Jenny Lind III by Maguire. The first mention of the new playhouse appeared in the *Alta California*.

75:1 THE AMERICAN.—Among the remarkable events happening in our city, none deserves mention more than the celerity with which the new American Theatre is being erected. Very much as it was with the building of the Jenny Lind, everything is going on at the same time. Masons are clicking the bricks and spreading the mortar, carpenters are pounding at the beams, joiners are tacking on the mouldings and lighter work, roof layers are spreading the huge iron sheets upon the rafters, while painters, upon rope-suspended platforms, just large enough to sit on, are plying the brush. We stepped in for a moment last evening, and found all these occupations going on at once. Scene painters were upon the stage, with their huge canvas stretching above and on each side of them, while they were attacking it skillfully with broom-handled paint brushes. We wonder if Titian ever tried his arm and back at scene painting. O there is a grandeur about those paint streaks and this scene painting! It is like a ship building—rib by rib, and shear plank by shear plank. The work goes bravely on!

The proscenium boxes are in an advanced stage of preparation. The first

74:3. *Alta California*, Oct. 5, 1851.

75:1. *Alta California*, Oct. 9, 1851.

tier will be festooned with sofas, and every care will be taken, and no expense spared to render the theatre, for comfort and elegance, unsurpassed. We are informed that the opening will be on Monday evening.

Work on the new playhouse did not proceed as rapidly as the owners hoped, however, and another announcement appeared in the *Alta California*.

75:2 THE AMERICAN.—The proprietors of the American find that they can not push matters sufficiently to be enabled to open their theatre this evening as they had planned. The play for the opening night is not announced yet, but the opening address to be delivered was written by a member of the company. Last evening the building was lighted up and presented inside a most brilliant appearance. The lights are arranged so as to extend from the two circles, there being no chandelier. On each side of the curtain and over the proscenium boxes two hanging lamps were suspended, each held up by an eagle's beak. The harmony between the gilding and the prevailing colors of the house, the richness of the dome, with the pendant brilliancy of the centre piece, the warmth, comfort and at the same time aspect of drawing-room elegance which the coverings of the seats give to the interior, all make the American an exceeding pretty little theatre. We almost anticipate that it will possess that air of cheerfulness and sociability which made the Dramatic so popular before the 4th of May last.

By October 20 the house was fully ready for the opening, and an announcement to that effect appeared in the *Alta California* on that day.

75:3 AMERICAN THEATRE.—This splendid establishment which, within a little more than a month from the date of its commencement, has been completed, will be opened to-night. It has been fitted up and decorated in a style that would do credit to any city in the world, and is as commodious as it is beautiful. The company is a strong one, and embraces many old and well known favorites, among them Mr. and Mrs. Stark, the Chapman Family, Mr. Barry, Mr. Downey, Mr. Johns, Mrs. Berrill and Miss Edwin. The bill for the opening night is Mrs. Anna Cora Mowatt's play of Armand, and the amusing afterpiece of "A Day in Paris," with a variety of other performances. An opening address, written by a gentleman, will be delivered by Mrs. Stark. There will of course be a tremendous house to-night.

The next day the *Alta California* reported that more than two thousand persons had attended the opening, which the critic termed "brilliant."

A young French newspaperman, Albert Benard de Russailh, kept a journal of his experiences in San Francisco in 1851, and wrote of the American, Jenny Lind, and other theaters.

75:4 The theatres and gambling houses are the only places where one can spend the evening. On clear nights when the moon lights the dark city, one can stroll along the shore of the bay and on the wharves, and breathe a little fresh air; but I must add that such weather is rare, for it either rains or its cold, and walking is usually unpleasant. Moreover, if you stay too long enjoying the moonlight on the bay the chances are that on the way home you will be held up by some of the escaped bandits from Sidney, who live in the cheap hotels along the waterfront. To get a few cents, they will slug you and drop your body into the bay. After eight

75:2. *Alta California*, Oct. 18, 1851.
75:3. *Alta California*, Oct. 20, 1851.

75:4. Albert Benard de Russailh, *Last Adventure, San Francisco in 1851.* Tr. by Clarkson Carne (San Francisco: Westgate Pr., 1931), pp. 17–20.

72. Bates Theatre, St. Louis, 1851. Lithograph. Courtesy of the Missouri Historical Society.

Jenny Lind Theatre.

74. Jenny Lind III Theatre, San Francisco. Wood engraving, published in Frank Soulé, John H. Gibon, and James Nisbet, *The Annals of San Francisco* (New York, 1855). Courtesy of the California State Library.

76. St. Louis Varieties Theatre, St. Louis, ca. 1866. From a stereograph by Hoelke and Benecke. Courtesy of the Missouri Historical Society.

o'clock in the evening it is hardly ever safe to walk alone on the wharves, and even if you go with a friend, you must be sure to carry a revolver. Murders are very common, and it is always unwise at night to go beyond the two or three busy streets where there is no danger. But how about the police? you ask. I shall devote a separate section to them. For the moment we are dealing with the theatres, the only civilized distraction in this new city.

San Francisco has three theatres and a circus. Two of the theatres are American, the Jenny Lind, and the American, the third is French, the Adelphi. The circus is essentially American. When I was a newspaperman, I was fortunate enough to have quite a few privileges, . . . a box in every theatre. . . .

When I had nothing better to do in the evening, I used to stroll around after dinner, and about seven o'clock I often dropped into the nearest theatre, but I always preferred the American, which is extremely agreeable. It has two balconies and a gallery, a dress-circle, orchestra seats, and several stage boxes. There is a great deal of typical English or American comfort. The carpets are think and soft, and deaden your footsteps so that you can walk peacefully through the lobby and glance into the boxes without disturbing the audience. The house is nicely decorated with paintings and gilt-work. The boxes have red velvet curtains and the seats are upholstered in red plush. In many ways the luxury and good taste of this little theatre remind one of the *Opéra Comique*. The company is directed by two intelligent and capable men, Mr. Robinson and Mr. Evrard. One of the most popular actresses is Miss Carpenter. She is attractive and versatile, and San Franciscans always applaud her with enthusiasm. Miss Woodward may not be pretty but has a great deal of charm. She is slight, and one is surprised by the unexpected warmth and power of

her acting in Shakespeare, especially in the tragedies of King Lear and Macbeth, which are her best plays. The company as a whole is not remarkable, but the public finds it adequate and shows its affection for the actors by filling the house every evening. The orchestra is well-conducted and fairly large, and during intermissions plays all the quadrilles, waltzes, and polkas that were popular in Paris some years ago.

The fire of May 4 destroyed the first Jenny Lind Theatre. The house was rebuilt with amazing speed, and just two days after the formal opening the June fire burned it down a second time. The theatre is now completely restored and is a handsome building of brick and stone, with a balcony and three galleries, a parterre, orchestra stalls, a dress-circle, and a few boxes behind the seats of the balcony. The walls are unpapered, without hangings or decorations, which makes the atmosphere of the hall a bit chilly; but the house is sold out every evening. . . .

76. ST. LOUIS VARIETIES THEATRE
St. Louis, Missouri
Opened May 11, 1852

Within a year and a half of the opening of the Bates Theatre, another major playhouse opened its doors to the St. Louis public—the Varieties Theatre, under the direction of J. M. Field. Noah Ludlow, who with his partner Sol Smith had operated the St. Louis Theatre, mentions the new playhouse in his book.

76:1 . . . During the summer of 1851, a new theatre had been commenced in St. Louis, of which Mr. J. M. Field was the lessee. It was built by a stock company of gentlemen living in St. Louis. The shares were five hundred dollars each, and a

76:1. Noah M. Ludlow, *Dramatic Life As I Found It* (St. Louis: G. I. Jones & Co., 1880), pp. 716–17.

169

very fine building was erected. Its location was on the south side of Market, midway between Fifth and Sixth streets. It would seat eleven or twelve hundred persons. It was erected on ground leased from Thomas S. Rutherford, for thirty years from the 1st of January, 1851; the ground was then to revert to the lessor, and the building to become his property. This theatre was called the Varieties, and was opened with a good stock company, under the management of Mr. J. M. Field, on May 19, 1852. . . .

This theatre was a very good building, handsomely decorated and furnished, but not so large and comfortable for a summer theatre as the St. Louis Theatre, recently given up by Ludlow & Smith. . . .

The background of the Varieties Theatre is given by Scharf in his *History of St. Louis City and County.*

76:2   Grand Opera-House.—On the 15th of September, 1851, the old St. Louis Theatre was reopened for a brief period by J. M. Field, with a company from the Varieties Theatre, New Orleans, then under the management of Thomas Placide, which included W. H. Chippendale, George Holland, Mr. and Mrs. J. M. Field, and others. As the St. Louis Theatre was about to be torn down, Mr. Field had already determined to procure the erection of another theatre, and on the 2d of May, 1851, had published an announcement of his scheme, in which he proposed that the theatre be built by subscription, and that certain privileges be extended to the stockholders, among them being a free admission to the theatre, "the accommodation of a reserved portion of the front of the house, box, or parquet," the use of "an elegant saloon or club-room," and the right to sell their stock should they desire to do so. Mr. Field also proposed to repay the amount

76:2. J. Thomas Scharf, *A History of St. Louis City and County.* 2 vols. (Philadelphia: Louis H. Everts & Co., 1883), 1:979–80.

of the capital stock to the holders in ten annual installments, with the understanding that the annual payments should constitute a fund with interest accumulating for ten years, which fund should stand as an insurance upon the building, to be drawn upon in case of fire, in which event a renewal of the ten years' contract was to be permitted.

At the end of the ten years the capital stock, with the accumulated interest, was to be divided among the subscribers, and the property was to belong to Mr. Field. It was proposed, also, to so construct the theatre as to permit its conversion, by raising the flooring of the parquet to a level with the stage, into a ballroom, the stockholders to have the right to avail themselves of its use for dancing assemblies once in every month. The project was taken up by the Varieties Dramatic Association, an organization that had its beginning in a social club. The first formal meeting of the Varieties Dramatic Association was held June 10, 1851, at the Planters' House. There were present Messrs. C. P. Chouteau, Sanford J. Smith, B. W. Alexander, Peter Brooks, and J. M. Field. Mr. Chouteau was elected president of the association, Mr. Smith vice-president, and Mr. Anderson secretary and treasurer. The erection of the theatre having previously been agreed upon, a building committee was appointed, to consist of Messrs. Chouteau, Field, and Alexander, and resolutions were adopted appointing George I. Barnett the architect of the new theatre and calling for the payment of subscriptions as follows: Twenty per cent. on August 15th of that year, twenty per cent. on September 15th, twenty per cent. on October 15th, twenty per cent. on Jan. 1, 1852, and twenty per cent. on March 1, 1852. C. P. Chouteau was chairman of the Planters' House meeting, and J. M. Field secretary. Treasurer Anderson at once issued orders for the payment of one hundred dollars on each subscription on the dates designated, which showed that the amount of a single subscription was five hundred dollars. The articles of the association adopted by these gentlemen set forth that the stock of the association was to be twenty-five thousand dollars, in shares of five hundred dollars each.

A lot on the south side of Market Street, between Fifth and Sixth Streets, was leased from T. S. Rutherford for thirty years, as the site of the new theatre, which was to be known as the "Varieties Theatre." The lot had a frontage of seventy-two and a half feet, and a depth of one hundred and thirty-eight feet, and on it was erected a handsome building, "with many novel and important improvements adopted from the designs of Barthelemy's Theatre, lately erected in Paris and now attracting wide attention in Europe." The corner-stone was laid on the 18th of August, 1851, by Sol Smith, "the oldest man of the theatrical profession in St. Louis," the orator of the occasion being Uriel Wright. The following articles were deposited in the cornerstone:

A copy of several morning city papers, both English and German.

A full account, from the *Missouri Republican,* of the Pacific Railroad celebration.

A memoir of the association concerned in the theatre enterprise, with the names of the subscribers, officers, and architect, and the city officers.

Daguerreotype likenesses of Uriel Wright, orator of the day, and J. M. Field, manager.

Lithograph of the St. Charles Theatre, New Orleans, with portraits of its managers, Sol Smith and N. M. Ludlow.

A proof copy of Mr. Wright's speech, and the various American coins of the year 1851.

The theatre, was was known as the Varieties Theatre, opened with a per-

formance of a good stock company, under the management of J. M. Field, on the 10th of May, 1852. The first piece on this occasion was a prelude entitled "You Can't Open," written by Edward W. Shands, of St. Louis, which was followed by the comedy "When There's a Will There's a Way," in which Mr. and Mrs. J. M. Field played the leading parts, assisted by C. L. Stone and Miss M. A. Hill. After the comedy Madame Ciocca, Mlle. Baron, Mons. Espinosa, and others executed a number of dances, and the entertainment concluded with the farce "The Good for Nothing," with Annie Lonsdale (her first appearance in St. Louis) as *Nan the Good for Nothing,* supported by W. H. Chippendale. Mr. Field offered seventy-five dollars for the first and fity dollars for the second best poem to be delivered as the opening address, which "must be written by a citizen of St. Louis and presented by the 30th instant;" but whether a prize was awarded to any other competitor than Mr. Shands does not appear. The new theatre was a handsome building, finely decorated and furnished, but Mr. Ludlow tells us "not so large and comfortable for a summer theatre as the St. Louis Theatre." The season, which terminated on the 13th of June, 1852, was not remunerative to Mr. Field, who retired a year later.

The theatre remained closed for two years, after which Dr. Henry Boernstein, a prominent journalist of St. Louis, opened it with a German theatre company. He failed after a brief season, and it was again closed.

For a time the building was used as a club-house, and in 1865, Messrs. George Deagle and George D. Martin took the house and restored its name, Varieties Theatre. After several successful seasons under their management, it fell into the hands of A. B. Wakefield and Stilson Hutchins. The name was then changed to Wakefield's Opera-House. The theatre was remodeled, and the opening performance was given in the fall of 1872. A year later Ben De Bar took possession, and it was thereafter known as De Bar's Opera-House. . . .

The drama critic for the *Missouri Republican* wrote about the opening of the new playhouse.

76:3 FIELD'S VARIETIES.—The opening last evening was an event in the history of theatricals in St. Louis.—Only a short time after 11 o'clock in the forenoon, every choice seat in the building had been retained—indeed, it was with difficulty that even at that hour, tickets could be secured for the dress circle or parquette. At night the house was literally jammed, the test to which it was subjected dispelling completely the ridiculous doubts which always attend the *first night* of a building devoted to public amusements. The array of beauty and fashion present, we have never seen excelled. The audiences of Jenny Lind, a few months since, alone equalled it. While we must give the performances their proper credit, we must say that in admiring the exceeding beauty of the proportions, decorations and finish of the house as in the brilliancy of the audience leading a rare eclat to the whole, we enjoyed ourselves full as well as otherwise. We were not alone in our satisfaction—the general expectation has been fully met, as we could judge from the conversations at every side.

To the performances we have barely time to allude. A laughable introduction from the pen of our humorous and talented fellow citizen, EDW. W. SHANDS, Esq., allowed the members of the new company a chance for a debut. Field, Chippendale, M. Smith, Waldauer, and a host of other talented artists were in turn received with shouts of applause. Afterward, the admirable actress, Miss LONSDALE, the pretty and graceful Ciocca,

76:3. *Missouri Republican*, Sept. 16, 1851.

the accomplished Baron, the irresistible Espenosa were as enthusiastically received. We will give a more detailed notice hereafter, and will, from time to time, particularize the merits or demerits of the performers as they impress us. In the meantime it will be borne in mind that the programme for to-morrow is for the gratification of those who were unable to obtain seats last evening—in a measure unchanged.

77. METROPOLITAN THEATRE
San Francisco, California
Opened December 24, 1853

In 1853 the first woman theater manager in San Francisco opened the new Metropolitan Theatre. She was Mrs. Catharine Sinclair, an actress of some ability who had been married to the great tragic actor Edwin Forrest. Their divorce had been a particularly bitter one, and she gained much notoriety from it. She had originally come to San Francisco earlier in 1853, playing an engagement at Maguire's theater in May.

Her management of the Metropolitan proved to be excellent and the theatre prospered. The playhouse opened on Christmas Eve, 1853. Details of the opening appeared in the *Alta California*.

77:1 OPENING OF THE NEW THEATRE.—The new San Francisco Theatre was opened for the first time last evening. Long before the doors had opened, a crowd gathered around, waiting for admittance, and a few minutes after the opening the house was well filled. The interior decorations are not yet completed, and many of the arrangements are in an unfinished condition, but still the theatre presented an elegant appearance. It is one of the best arranged, as it will be when completed, one of the handsomest theatres in the United States. The lower tier was filled with a very fashionable assemblage, —among whom were many ladies,—and

77:1. *Alta California*, Dec. 25, 1853.

the upper tiers, parquette, and private boxes, although not crowded, were well filled. After an excellent overture, the the curtain rose for the performance of Sheridan's Comedy of the *School for Scandal*. This is one of the most perfectly written stage pieces ever presented. Every character stands out prominently, and may be worthily played by the most superior actors, in their particular lines of business. Mrs. Sinclair made her debut upon the stage in the character of Lady Teazle, and it is one to which she had evidently devoted a great deal of study. If there is any fault in her performance, it is that it is too studied, and that she neglects a little that identification of herself with the part she is playing, in the care which she bestows upon the text. This, however, is a pardonable fault, and we must say, that on the whole, we were highly pleased with Mrs. Sinclair's performance. . . .

The playhouse, which was one of the first theaters in San Francisco to be lighted with gas, was a well-appointed house with excellent furnishings, three tiers of boxes, and sumptuous decorations for that time in San Francisco. The theater burned in 1857 but was rebuilt on the same site and reopened in 1861.

78. MAGUIRE'S OPERA HOUSE
San Francisco, California
Opened November 29, 1856

Thomas Maguire, who had built the various Jenny Lind theaters, started his most ambitious project to date when, in 1856, he built Maguire's Opera House, the most elegant and up-to-date theater in San Francisco. The playhouse was completely lighted by gas, even to the huge chandelier suspended over the auditorium. The seating capacity was rather small when the house opened—only 1,100—but this was corrected a few months later, when Maguire enlarged the seating potential to 1,700.

On November 28, the day before the opening, Maguire held a preview for the press. The reporter for the *Daily Evening Bulletin* write a description in his column that evening.

78:1   MAGUIRE'S NEW OPERA HOUSE

The great success with which the popular troupe known as the "San Francisco Minstrels" played in this city for a long succession of months, and the too limited capacity and accommodations of the old San Francisco Hall, have induced Mr. Thomas Maguire, the proprietor, to tear down the old building, and erect on its site a beautiful, capacious, and highly ornamental new building. The structure, which is situated as is well known on the North side of Washington street, between Montgomery and Kearny streets, is to be known hereafter as "Maguire's Opera House." The work upon it was commenced about the 15th of October last, under the charge of Mr. Stebbins, master mason; Stockhouse and Torrence, carpenters and machinists; Fairchild and Rogers, scenists; and Lubey, upholsterer.

The new house, which has an ornamental front, is 55 feet wide, 137 feet deep from the front wall to the back of the stage; and 50 feet high, from the parquette floor to the ceiling of the dome. The stage is 35 feet deep. There is a large orchestra enclosure in front. On each side of the drop curtain, or at the proscenium, there are two large private boxes, constructed in the style of those in the Metropolitan Theatre of New York. They are placed one above the other, and are highly ornamented with gilded mouldings and rich hangings of crimson and gold. The drop curtain, a very large and fine one, represents the sea-born city of Venice, with its domes, towers and palaces. One of the great canals is seen in front, with barques and gondolas floating upon it. In the foregoing is the marble porch of a palace, with columns

78:1. *San Francisco Daily Evening Bulletin*, Nov. 28, 1856.

and tapestries; and there are not wanting the figures of high born ladies and gallant chevaliers. The view of the stage is very pleasing. When the curtain is up, the spectator looks upon the scenes, which are all new, through a rich frame work, as it were, of golden mouldings and decorations of crimson.

The body of the house is spacious. It is unbroken by columns, except such as support the dress circle tier, or gallery. The whole floor of the house, in front of the orchestra, is occupied by the parquette, which contains seats for over 700 persons. There is but one tier or gallery in the house, raised upon columns, ten feet above the parquette, and constituting the dress circle. Its front or rim runs with a graceful curve around the house, in the manner of the tiers in ordinary theatres; but there are no columns reaching from this tier to the ceiling, and its extent from front to back is much greater. As it recedes from the front, it rises, and the rows of seats are considerably elevated, one behind the other, so that there is a perfect, complete and uninterrupted view of the stage to be had from every part of it. The seats in this part of the house, which are capable of accommodating over 400 persons, are cushioned with new and bright colored materials, and divided off by various aisles. The dress circle is reached by a wide flight of ascending stairs, immediately after leaving the vestibule at the front door; and at its sides are the descending stairs to the parquette. In every part of the house there are gas-lights. A splendid chandelier, containing twenty burners, which has been sent for to New York but not yet arrived, is to depend from the centre of the dome, or arched ceiling. Two windows, high up in each of the sidewalls, are intended for the purpose of ventilation; it having been found by experience, as is said, that a large ventilator in the ceiling, is unfavorable to a house devoted to music and song.

Taking a view of the whole—the pure white walls and the high extensive dome over head—the spectator is struck with the airy appearance of everything about him. As he casts his eyes forward towards the stage, he must be pleased with the crimson and gold in contrast with the white, all glittering in the gas-light. How all these may stand the test of time and familiarity we do not know; but they certainly look very fine as they have come from the hands of the workmen, and we think that great taste has been displayed throughout, particularly upon the proscenium.

The house will open this evening for the inspection of visitors; and to-morrow evening, with the original San Francisco Minstrels, and several valuable additions from the troupe lately known as the Backus Minstrels. The whole company will consist of about fifteen persons. They will continue to be a standing institution in San Francisco.

Two days later, on November 30, 1856, the *Alta California* reported the opening of the new theater.

78:2   OPENING OF
MAGUIRE'S NEW OPERA HOUSE

Last evening, this elegant establishment was opened to the public, and, of course, was crowded almost to suffocation. There was not standing room, and the seats in the dress circle and boxes were filled with ladies. The San Francisco Minstrels, ever favorites with our citizens, were received with great enthusiasm, and their songs, duetts, burlesques, etc., excited more admiration than ever. The burlesque on the Hutchinson Family made the house fairly quiver with laughter and applause. Schemerhorn's Boy, in which the inimitable Billy Birch appeared, closed the entertainment.

78:2. *Alta California,* Nov. 30, 1856.

77. Metropolitan Theatre, San Francisco, 1865. Published in John P. Young's *History of San Francisco*, (San Francisco, 1912). Courtesy of the California State Library.

78. Maguire's Opera House, San Francisco. Courtesy of the California State Library.

79. McVicker's First Theatre, Chicago. Lithograph, after a drawing by Louis Kurz; published in James W. Sheahan, *Chicago Illustrated*, part 10 (Chicago: Jevne & Almini, October, 1866). Courtesy Chicago Historical Society.

79. McVICKER'S FIRST THEATRE
Chicago, Illinois
Opened November 5, 1857

John H. McVicker, who became the greatest theatrical manager in Chicago in the nineteenth century, began his career in the theater as a call boy at the New St. Charles Theatre, New Orleans, when it was under the management of Noah Ludlow and Sol Smith. His first experience as a stage manager came several years later in St. Louis, where he was assistant to the manager of the People's Theatre. Later he toured in the United States and England as an actor, returning to Chicago in 1856 to build a major playhouse on Madison Street near State.

Andreas's *History of Chicago*, published in 1885, told something of the background of this theater.

79:1   During 1857, the construction went on, until it was opened on November 5. When it is remembered that, up to that period, the best theatre in Chicago was, at its best, but a modest affair, involving an expenditure of but a few thousands, there is reason to believe the people were proud to see an edifice which cost $85,000, contributing to their delight in the perfect presentation of standard plays. It was the most substantial, convenient, safe and costly theater building then standing in the West, and had a seating capacity for two thousand five hundred persons. The acoustic properties were very good, and the stage had an area of eighty by fifty-three feet. The scenery and properties were the most extensive, and the finest in quality and finish, then seen at any Western place of amusement. The drop curtain was esteemed a work of art, and represented the cities of Rock Island and Davenport connected by the railroad bridge. . . .

The Chicago *Tribune* was ecstatic in its praise for the new theater and for McVicker himself.

79:2   Last evening was an era in the dramatic history of our city. For the first time since Chicago took rank as one of the first cities of the Union, she has a Theater worthy of her citizens who patronize the Drama. Mr. McVicker has labored against a host of adverse circumstances. He has overcome a succession of obstacles which were sufficient to have overcome ordinary men, and last evening he opened to the public, if not one of the largest, certainly one of the finest and most comfortable Theatres in the country.

The exterior of the structure is plain but exceedingly tasteful and an ornament to the street in which it is situated. The front, when completed, will be occupied for stores and offices. The rear of the building is the Theatre, which is approached from the street by a spacious and well-lighted hall.

The Theatre itself is neither remarkable for brilliancy of decoration or grandeur of design, but it is beyond question exceedingly graceful. The auditorium is reached by two broad flights of stairs leading from the main hall to the dress circle and parquette and by stairs leading directly from the alley to the gallery. Eight large windows on each side give ample ventilation. The dress circle is surrounded by a roomy lobby handsomely carpeted. The seats are particularly comfortable and so arranged that one can see and hear distinctly from every portion of the house. The principal decorations are white and gilt with crimson and white lace draperies and are all in excellent taste. The auditorium is 60 by 97 feet.

The stage is 60 x 80 feet, with a proscenium of 33 feet in height. The scenery is of the very best description, and the stage furniture, costumes, etc., all that can be desired. . . .

79:1. A. T. Andreas, *History of Chicago*. 3 vols. (Chicago: A. T. Andreas Co., 1884–86), 2:598.

79:2. Chicago *Tribune*, Nov. 6, 1857.

The theater was the most popular one in Chicago until it was destroyed in the great fire of 1871.

80. PIKE'S OPERA HOUSE
Cincinnati, Ohio
Opened February 22, 1859

Pike's Opera House, which was built in 1859, was the finest theater ever built in Cincinnati until that time. Samuel Pike, who was a wealthy liquor dealer, had built the playhouse to provide a worthy setting for the voice of Jenny Lind, "the Swedish Nightingale," who did perform there a few years later.

The Cincinnati *Daily Commercial* gave the following glowing account of the opening of the theater:

80:1   THE GRAND INAUGURAL FESTIVAL
BRILLIANT DISPLAY
Congress of the Fashion of the West
DESCRIPTION OF THE INTERIOR
Emporium of Elegance,
Refinement and Art
A Temple Worthy of the Muses
The brilliant fete that inaugurated the beautiful temple, henceforth to be dedicated to the fair Euterpia, is over, and the many bright eyes which flashed in responsive sympathy to the sunny influence of the scene, are closed in sweet but dreamy slumber, for wakeful fantasy will yet again enact the joyous revel of the night, and tinge the golden dawn with a vision of roseate hue mingled with the liquid fall of fading music, and sweet as the fragrance of an Arcadian breath.

To do justice to the rich and glowing scene as we beheld it, real and palpable, and as it will in years to come float upon our memory in "faint fair hues," were a task which should be delegated to a more potent and poetic pen. The classic temple in which was assembled the *creme de la creme* of the crimson West, was worthy of its guests, for never did the voluptuous

Goddess of the Dance receive the homage of a more gay and brilliant throng.

The night was clear and balmy, and Winter appeared absorbed by the genial influence of Spring. In short, everything appeared to smile propitiously upon the event, and, so far as our observations extended, nothing occurred to mar the harmony, or to cast a shadow upon the happy inauguration.

SCENE AROUND THE OPERA HOUSE
Shortly after the lamps were lit, the crowd of curious spectators began to assemble in front of the building, attracted by the interest excited in the brilliant *cortege*, which, in accordance with the program, entered the Block from the West, and as in rapid succession the drivers set down their freight in front of the principal entrance, again drove on, proceeding in regular order to the East. By this arrangement, the confusion, which under other circumstances, would have been inevitable, was avoided, a system was established, and collisions with their accompanying inconveniences, were avoided.

THE RECEPTION ROOMS
Very richly carpeted, and for the first time in this city our fair ladies were enabled to comprehend the luxurious appurtenances belonging to a first class Opera House. They were brilliantly illuminated from costly chandeliers, and bronzed and gilded brackets, while the furniture was in like superb and classic style with the remainder of the decorations. In the center of the grand promenade hall, to the right of the main hall, hung a chandelier, richly gilt, and upon the walls were fifteen brackets, bronzed and gilded in the same elaborate style, the whole emitting a jetty splendor, which in turn was flashed back from the myriad of brilliant eyes of the fair promenaders beneath. Through a richly carpeted side entrance, we enter the

GRAND HALL,
Or ball room: and here a scene of

80:1. Cincinnati *Daily Commercial*, Feb. 23, 1859.

176

80. Pike's Opera House, Cincinnati, ca. 1859. Lithograph. Courtesy of The Cincinnati Historical Society.

INTERIOR PIKE'S OPERA HOUSE

80. Interior, Pike's Opera House, Cincinnati. Engraving. Courtesy of The Cincinnati Historical Society.

82. Piper's Opera House, Virginia City, Nev., ca. 1958. Courtesy of the Nevada Historical Society.

dazzling brightness met the gaze, which came as near the idea of Fairyland as even an oriental imagination might conceive. From the proscenium, including the stage, was represented a graceful tent of drapery canopies with festoons of red and blue. At the rear the art of the painter had been evoked and a fair palatial scene was visible in the distance, in front of which was a promenade balcony, approached by two capacious flights of steps, the entrance to each flight ornamented with life-size statuary. In the front center of the balcony, and between the stairways, was a grotto fountain, furnished by Gibson and Co., clustered around were choice evergreens and gaudy flowers, arranged by Mr. Palmer, and from the nursery of Messrs. Fifer & Palmer. Within this tent, which, in its pure and spotless proportion, and airy beauty, might serve as the winter palace of Titania and her court, hung pendant five chandeliers, tastefully arranged, beneath which a portion of the gay revelers sacrificed to the supreme Goddess of the Night, the tender Saltatrix, the inventor of the classic dance. The great body of the hall was comprised within the auditorium, and here, too, a scene of splendor was revealed to the charmed sight, which might well carry out the dream of Fairyland and enchantment. Myriads of jets illuminated the vast structure, and cast their mellow radiance alike upon the richly ornamented and pictorial dome and ceiling, and the brilliant throng who moved gracefully through the mazy dance, their motions swaying in easy measure to the richly swelling strains of a double Orchestra of fifty-five musicians, who, ranged in two temporary orchestras on each side of the second tier, under the direction of Mr. Harry Jones, filled every crevice of the vast structure with entrancing harmony.

Monsieur Ernest presided as the Master of the ceremonies, and it was in this connection, superfluous to add, that his arrangements were perfect. In truth, Cincinnati like the Belgium Capital, had gathered round

"Her beauty and her chivalry, and bright
"The lamps shone o'er fair women and brave men:
"A thousand hearts beat happily; and when
"Music arose with its voluptuous swell,
"Soft eyes looked love to eyes which speak again,
"And all went merry as a marriage bell."

It was, in truth, a memory for a life time.

A crowd of elegantly dressed ladies and gentlemen, who either did not participate in the dance, or sacrificed but briefly to the presiding Deity, crowded the first and second tiers, spectators of the "gay and festive scene." Among these were many of the old and stable citizens, who have grown with our beautiful emporium of the West, and witnessed its rapid transition from a backwood settlement to a metropolis in which commerce and the fine arts hold mutual sway. They were there to countenance by their presence the successful inauguration of an enterprise the most spirited and stupendous ever undertaken and brought to a successful issue by one energetic individual.

THE SUPERB

This most important part of the arrangement was under the superintendence of Messrs. Johnson and Morris, who proved themselves excellent caterers, in the delicacy, variety and abundance of luxuries provided for the guests. In accordance with the advertised arrangement, the supper room was thrown open from ten until two, so that any unpleasant jam was avoided by those whose appetite induced them to participate in the somewhat unpoetical business of discussing the viands so temptingly spread, and which appeared to have full justice bestowed upon them, by even the sylphlike portion of the assembly, to whom the brisk exercise of the dance had, in spite of their romantic temperament, given a very matter of fact appetite. The promenade hall of the second tier was thus appropriated, and in its size and extent admirably suited to the purpose.

GENERAL APPEARANCE OF THE GUESTS

As near as we could judge there were over two thousand of the cream of Western society present at the Festival, and certainly a more brilliant gathering never assembled in this or any other city of the continent. The toilet of the majority of ladies was superb, and were other evidence of the luxury of a metropolis wanting, the costly attire of the fair creatures would alone have sufficed to prove our rank in the race of fashion and progress. As we have observed, the guests were worthy of the temple, and the temple the guests, and both were in magnificent and harmonious keeping. The architect, Mr. J. M. Trimble, has witnessed under his supervision thirty-two fair and palatial structures arise; the present and last, he esteems his crowning triumph.—When it is next thrown open to the public, its legitimate guardian, Euterpia, will be in the ascendant, and the classic and refined opera the rage.

The Opera House had thirteen entrances, a black and white marble lobby, and seats for two thousand people. The following account, supplied from an unknown source by the Cincinnati Historical Society, tells more about the edifice:

80:2 . . . This splendid building reflects the highest credit on the enterprise of Mr. Pike, the proprietor, and on the skill and taste of the architect, Mr. J. M. Trimble. It would be an ornament to any city in the world. The architecture is rich and

80:2. Unidentified newspaper clipping, Bliss Fund Collection, Cincinnati Historical Society.

ornated, without being tawdry, and the vast extent and height of the facade, give it a truly imposing aspect. We are indebted to the kindness of R. Delavan Mussey, Esq., of the Cincinnati Gazette for some interesting details respecting the interior of the opera house, which will be inaugurated by a splendid ball on Washington's birthday. The hall proper is only one of several spacious rooms in the building. There are four very large stores on the first floor, two fine dancing, concert or lecture rooms, and a profusion of offices. The opera hall is situated in the second story back. In front of it are corridors, approached from the street by three stairways. The auditorium of the hall is divided into parquette, parquette slips in the rear of the parquette; above these slips the balcony, and above the balcony the upper boxes or amphitheatre. The auditorium is about twenty feet less in depth than that of the New York Academy of Music, and about fifteen feet wider. The result of this proportion is to bring the audience nearer the stage. The auditorium is so constructed that all of the seats in Pike's Hall have good views of the stage. The stage is very broad and deep; the proscenium opening being 54 feet high by 50 feet wide, and the stage deep in proportion to its width. There are three proscenium boxes on either side, the proscenium being 22 feet deep. There will be ample room upon the stage for grand scenic effects, and liberal accommodations for machinists, carpenters and painters. The proscenium boxes are also on a magnificent scale. They will hold about twenty persons each. The hall is lighted by a row of gas lights about the dome, and below the windows above the amphitheatre, thus avoiding the distressing glare that comes from chandeliers and box lights in ordinary theatres. The ceiling is painted in fresco, by Signor Guidocci, an Italian artist, who fancy has revelled in the delineation of allegorical figures, and graceful devices. As we have before remarked, the opera house will be inaugurated by a ball on the 22nd, on which occasion the parquette will be entirely boarded over, making, with the stage, a grand dancing floor like that of the Parisian opera during the carnival. Next month Stakosch's Italian opera company will take possession of the hall, and in June the Ravel troupe will probably perform there. We congratulate our Cincinnati friends on the consummation of this brilliant enterprise, for we are perfectly cosmopolitan in our feelings, and feel the sincerest pleasure in recording every triumphant step in the progress of the arts and of civilization. In these respects the West is moving on as surprisingly as she has done in all the avenues of business and commerce.

The Opera House burned on March 22, 1866, was rebuilt in 1867, and burned again on February 25, 1903.

81. SALT LAKE CITY THEATER
Salt Lake City, Utah
Opened March 5, 1862

One of the most remarkable theaters built in America during the period preceding the Civil War was the Salt Lake City Theater. The trek of the Mormons from western New York State across the Great Plains to the valley of the Great Salt Lake is one of the most exciting yet heartbreaking stories of nineteenth-century America. Persecuted and driven from place to place, the Mormons endured incredible hardships before approximately two thousand men, women, and children reached their promised land. Nearly eighty thousand members of the Latter-Day Saints reached Salt Lake City by 1869. Here they literally carved their Eden from a wilderness.

The story of the building of the Salt Lake City Theater was related by Hiram B. Clawson in a speech before a meeting of the Daughters of the Pioneers in Salt Lake City on March 20, 1907.

81:1   After Johnston's Army had wintered in Ham's Fork, the United States Commissioners consulted with the authorities and the army was moved to Camp Floyd. Here it later disbanded with a large stock of supplies on hand. These the government ordered sold to the highest bidder. Notice was given of the sale, and President (Brigham) Young sent me with $4,000 in gold to buy the things we most needed. I found building materials, glass, nails, tents, sugar and other groceries, and many necessities. I was cordially received and favored by the officers. The following incident will illustrate the cordial feeling that existed between the officers and President Young: One evening, while sitting in front of the general's tent, I was attracted by a beautiful flag and staff and I was asked by the commanding officer, if I thought President Young would accept it. I assured him that he would not only accept it, but place it on his Salt Lake home, the 'White House', and that on all national occasions the flag would be unfurled. They presented it; it was accepted and placed as stated.

I made my purchases as instructed. Tents with cook stoves that sold in New York City for $12 or $15, I bought for $1, nails worth $40 a box for $6, and other things in proportion. From the sale of a part of the things that I purchased, which realized $40,000.00, and with nails, glass and other building material, so conveniently provided, the building of the Salt Lake Theater was made possible. This building was thought by some to be much too large, and President Young was urged to build a smaller house, but with his great wisdom and foresight, he insisted that time would prove he was right. After it was finished, it was found that the acoustics were not good. A large dome was in the center of the theatre,

81:1. George D. Pyper, *The Romance of an Old Playhouse* (Salt Lake City: Seagull Pr., 1928), pp. 75–77.

179

which I believe interfered with the acoustic properties, and at my suggestion, a ceiling was built over it with the desired result.

After the plans of William H. Folsom, the architect, were approved, work was at once started with Joseph A. Young, as superintendent of supplies. May 6, 1861, arrangements for making 250,000 adobes were completed. The first rock was hauled June 20, and the building was started the first of July. By August 21 the following workmen were at work on the building: sixteen diggers under William Wolstenholm; eight stone cutters, under Alexander Gillespie; three millwrights under Joseph Schofield. At this time the water table was up and the stone work four feet high. The power for hoisting the rock and timber was supplied by an undershot wheel placed over the water ditch. This wheel connected with a shaft and gearing.

By the time the walls were up, E. L. T. Harrison, an architect from London, who had been trained in the very best schools, arrived in Utah. He saw the distinctive possibilities of the Theatre, and being an admirer of Drury Lane, was anxious to apply some architectural treatment to the interior. His coming at this opportune time was like an inspiration. He was at once associated with Architect Folsom and designed much of the interior. The galleries, the elaborate ceilings, the boxes with their lacy filigree and the proscenium are examples of his masterful work.

Ox teams brought to the 'Valley' another much needed man, 'just in the nick of time'. This was George Martin Ottinger, the gifted artist. He was at once set to work painting the stage scenery, and made the first scenery used in the theatre. For four years, assisted by Henry Maiben and William Morris, a decorator from London, he painted scenes. Later our artist-poet, Alfred Lambourne, author of 'The Playhouse', was painter for this historic building. . . .

William Folsom, the architect of the building, presented the following description to President Young on completion of the theater:

81:2   It was commenced July 1, 1861, and completed for temporary use March 5, 1862. The building is situated on the corner of the State Road and First South street. The size of the building on the ground is 80 by 144 feet, 40 feet high from water-table to the square of the building. The roof is self-supporting and hipped all around, with a promenade on top 40 by 90 feet. The south main entrance has an opening 32 by 20 feet, supported by two Grecian Doric columns. The exterior of the building is Grecian Doric. The auditorium has a parquette and four circles, 60 feet on the outer circle, 37 feet on the inner, and covered with a circular dome in ogee or bell form. In the interior, the stage has an opening at the drop curtain of 31 feet front by 28 feet high, shows 27 feet in flats and 62 feet deep from footlights, 10 feet proscenium and 40 feet high from stage floor to ceiling. The building is still in progress and will probably be completed the present season.

An English writer and traveler, William Hepworth Dixon, visited the Salt Lake City Theater in 1866 and wrote of the experience in a two-volume book, *New America*.

81:3   The playhouse has an office and a service in this Mormon City higher than the churches would allow to it in London, Paris, and New York. Brigham Young is an original in many ways; he is the high-priest of what claims to be a new dispensation; yet he has got his theatre into perfect order, before he has raised his Temple foundation above the ground.

81:2. George D. Pyper, *The Romance of an Old Playhouse* (Salt Lake City: Seagull Pr. 1928), p. 77.
81:3. William Hepworth Dixon, *New America* (London: Hunst & Blackett, 1867), 1:198–204.

That the drama had a religious origin, and that the stage has been called a school of manners, every one is aware. Young feels inclined to go back upon all first principles; in family life to those of Abraham, in social life to those of Thespis. Priests invented both the ancient and the modern stages; and if experience shows as strongly in Salt Lake City as in New York, that people love to be light and merry—to laugh and glow—why should their teachers neglect the thousand opportunities offered by a play, of getting them to laugh in the right places, to glow at the proper things? Why should Young not preach moralities from the stage? Why should he not train his actors and his actresses to be models of good conduct, of correct pronunciation, and of taste in dress? Why should he not try to reconcile religious feelings with pleasure?

Brigham Young may be either right or wrong in his ideas of the uses to which a playhouse may be turned in a city where they have no high school and colleges as yet; but he is bent on trying his experiment to an issue; for this purpose he has built a model theatre, and he is now making an effort to train a model company.

Outside, his theatre is a rough Doric edifice, in which the architect has contrived to produce a certain effect by very simple means; inside, it is light and airy, having no curtains and no boxes, save two in the proscenium, with light columns to divide the tiers, and having no other decoration than pure white paint and gold. The pit, rising sharply from the orchestra, so that every one seated on its benches can see and hear to advantage, is the choicest part of the house. All these benches are let to families, and here the principal elders and bishops may be seen every play-night, surrounded by their wives and children, laughing and clapping like boys at a pantomime. Yon rocking chair, in the center of the pit, is Young's own seat; his place of pleasure, in the midst of his Saints. When he chooses to occupy his private box, one of his wives, perhaps Eliza the Poetess, Harriet the Pale, or Amelia the Magnificent, rocks herself in his chair while laughing at the play. Round about that chair as the place of honour, cluster the benches of those who claim to stand nearest to their prophet; of Heber Kimball, first councillor; of Daniel Wells, second councillor and general-in-chief; of George A. Smith, apostle and historian of the church; of George Q. Cannon, apostle; of Edward Hunter, presiding bishop; of Elder Stenhouse, editor of the 'Daily Telegraph;' and of a host of less brilliant Mormon lights.

In the sides of the proscenium nestle two private boxes; one is reserved for the Prophet, when he pleases to be alone, or wishes to have a gossip with some friend; the other is given up to the girls who have to play during the night, but who are not engaged in the immediate business of the piece. As a rule, every one's pleasure is considered in this model playhouse; and I can answer, on the part of Miss Adams, Miss Alexander, and other young artists, that this appropriation to their sole use of a private box, into which they can run at all times, in any dress, without being seen, is considered by them as a very great comfort.

Through the quick eye and careful hand of his manager, Hiram Clawson, the President may be congratulated on having made his playhouse into something coming near to that which he conceives a playhouse should be. Everything in front of the footlights is in keeping; peace and order reign in the midst of fun and frolic. Neither within the doors nor about them, do you find the riot of our own Lyceum and Drury Lane; no loose women, no pickpockets, no ragged boys and girls, no drunken and blaspheming men. As a Mormon never drinks spirits, and rarely smokes tobacco, the only dissipation in which you find these hundreds of hearty creatures indulging their appetites, is that of sucking a peach. Short plays are in vogue in this theatre, just as short sermons are the rule in yon tabernacle. The curtain, which rises at eight, comes down about half-past ten; and as the Mormon fashion is for people to sup before going out, they retire the moment they get home, never suffering their amusements to infringe on the labours of the coming day. Your bell rings for breakfast at six o'clock.

But the chief beauties of this model playhouse lie behind the scenes; in the ample space, the perfect light, the scrupulous cleanliness of every part. I am pretty well acquainted with green-rooms and side wings in Europe; but I have never seen, not in Italian and American theaters, so many delicate arrangements for the privacy and comfort of ladies and gentlemen as at Salt Lake City. The green-room is a real drawing room. The scene-painters have their proper studios; the dressers and decorators have immense magazines. Every lady, however small her part in the play, has a dressing-room to herself.

Young understands that the true work of reform in a playhouse must begin behind the scenes; that you must elevate the actor before you can purify the stage. To this end, he not only builds dressing-rooms and a private box for the ladies who have to act, but he places his daughters on the stage as an example and encouragement to others. Three of these young sultanas, Alice, Emily, and Zina, are on the stage. With Alice, the youngest wife of Elder Clawson, I have had the honour to make an acquaintance, which might be called a friendship, and from her lips I have learned a great deal as to her father's ideas about stage reform. "I am not myself very fond of playing," she said to me one day as we sat down to dinner—not in these words, perhaps, but to this effect—"but my father desires that my sisters and myself should act

sometimes, as he does not think it right to ask any poor man's child to do anything which his own children would object to do." Her dislike to playing, as she afterwards told me, arose from a feeling that Nature had given her no abilities for acting well; she was fond of going to see a good piece, and seldom omitted being present when she had not to play. Brigham Young has to create, as well as to reform, the stage of Salt Lake City; and the chief trouble of a manager who is seven hundred miles from the next theatre, must always be with his artists. Talent for the work does not grow in every field, like a sunflower and a peach-tree; it must be sought for in nooks and corners; now in a shoeshop, anon in a dairy, then in a counting-house; but wherever the talent may be found, Young cannot think of asking any young girl to do a thing which it is supposed that a daughter of his own would scorn. . . .

82. PIPER'S OPERA HOUSE
Virginia City, Nevada
Opened July 2, 1863

The opening of the Comstock Lode in Nevada caused a great rush for land and riches and the creation of many fairly sizable towns. Virginia City was foremost among these new communities, and it was here that Thomas Maguire, the theater impresario from San Francisco, opened a new opera house in July 1863. A description of the town and the opening of the theater are written by Walter M. Leman, whose autobiography, *Memoirs of an Old Actor*, gives some fascinating insights into the theater of the West in the latter part of the nineteenth century.

82:1   Our prosperous season terminated about the middle of April, and on the twenty-second of that month (1863) we crossed the Sierra Nevada Mountains to

82:1. Walter M. Leman, *Memories of an Old Actor* (San Francisco: A. Roman Co., Pub., 1886), pp. 293–97.

Carson City, via Placerville, over the grade that Hank Monk made historic when he let out the lines over his six-in-hand, and assured Horace Greeley that if he'd "hold on" he'd have him in Placerville "on time."

At Carson, Silver City and Gold Hill we filled up the time until the 10th of May when we got into Virginia City. This was in the flush times of the "Comstock," and the wild town on the slope of Mount Davidson was crowded with men who were there to make their fortune—or had made it, in "feet." From the edge of Carson Valley, up through Silver City and Gold Hill, over the ridge between the latter place and Virginia, where sometimes the "Washoe Zephyrs" blew with sufficient strength to overturn a stage-coach, along the whole line of the city to far north of the Ophir Mine, was, or was supposed to be, one vast repository of gold and silver, and from North, South, East and West the seekers for wealth had come to get it.

The wonderful produce of the "Gould and Curry," the "Imperial," the "Ophir" and other leads that had then been opened, had made men wild, and holes in the ground were dug and "salted" and new "leads" discovered every day, which, with all their "dips, spurs and angles," were put on the market; and men with mining "shares" in their pocket representing a value of $50,000 would frequently borrow four bits, if another equally wealthy friend had it to lend, to get a dinner at the restaurant. It was the commencement of the wild game of speculation which, at a later day, was transferred to San Francisco, making a few rich and beggaring thousands.

Our first performances were given in a hall, the name of which I forget, and we had powerful rivals in the minstrel and hurdy-gurdy establishments. But a fair patronage was secured. The ground had been obtained for the erection of a new theatre, which was commenced soon

after our arrival, by Mr. Thomas Maguire, and rapidly hurried to completion. Our company formed the nucleus of a new organization, which was filled by additions from the Bay City, and on the evening of July 2, 1863, the new theatre was opened with Bulwer's Comedy of "Money," preceded by an opening address by Walter M. Leman, spoken by Mrs. Julia Dean Hayne.

In speaking of that first night, the *Territorial Enterprise* said: "There was scarcely space to move throughout the theatre, it was so densely filled. A strong wind blew during a portion of the evening and there was considerable agitation visible in the fairer portion of the audience; the most decided sensation of the evening was produced on Mrs. Hayne—by a mild shower of gravel-stones, which rained upon the building. Large as was the audience, its magnitude was surpassed by its beauty and manliness. Well, we'll just bet, that if there's a marriageable actress in the company with winning graces and matrimonial inclinations, she never goes over the mountains unwedded. . . ."

The "mild shower of gravel stones," of which the *Enterprise* speaks, not only produced a sensation upon Mrs. Hayne, but upon every one in the house; I am sure it did upon me. When the "Washoe Zephyr," sweeping up the cañon, "rained" that stony artillery upon the rear of the new building, which creaked in the tempest like a ship at sea, I thought for a moment that the opening and closing of "Maguire's New Opera House" would occur on the same evening, but it was reserved for the *usual* fate, which befell it years after; it went up in a cloud of fire, and took a good portion of the city along with it.

Virginia City was rather a wild "metropolis" in those days—"new discoveries" were reported every day, and speculation ran mad. There were two stock boards in operation, and it was only necessary to dig a hole, "salt" it a little, and put the "shares" on the market to become a capitalist or a beggar in four-and-twenty hours, dependent upon whether one *bought* or *sold*. . . .

A history of Maguire and Piper's opera house was written in 1952 by two residents of Virginia City, and in this short account they were able to capture the spirit of the times and the difficulties encountered by the players in Virginia City a century earlier.

82:2   The arrival by stage of a theatrical troupe, its duelling swords, silk tights and daring sundries lashed overhead in Saratoga trunks, was one of the surest signals that a frontier mining camp's diggings had destiny.

Along with the establishment of Wells Fargo offices, the importation of back bar mirrors big as barns, and a murder or two, the opening of the first theater was tonic indication that rich rumors were fact and bonanza days had romped round the corner.

In the case of Virginia City, Queen of the Comstock, Empress of all the far-flung, fabulous Western mining operations, from Colorado to California, the first stage show was presented in 1860 at the Howard Street Theater when the town population was little, if any, more than 1000. It was titled "The Farces of Toodles and Swiss Swains." No ladies admitted.

"Toodles" was a modest preface to the grand and racy chapter of Virginia City's theatrical history that really began with the opening of Maguire's Opera House in July, 1863. Maguire's—of which the present Piper's Opera House is the lineal descendant—was a true expression of the opulence that had smote the town with the discovery of riches in silver and gold beyond the dreams of avarice, and proof

82:2. Katherine Hillyer and Katherine Best, *The Amazing Story of Piper's Opera House in Virginia City, Nevada* (Virginia City: Enterprise Pr., 1953), pp. 3–20.

that the population had jumped to 15,000 amusement-hungry people.

Maguire, San Francisco impresario, built bigger and finer than any theatergoer west of the Hudson had ever clapped eye upon. It was gaslit, from footlights embedded in green cabbageleaf sconces, to the crystal chandeliers that hung in dazzlement from a ceiling that neither leaked nor threatened to blow away in the locally ungentle winds known gently as Washoe zephyrs. There were carpets instead of sawdust on the floor; gilt chairs and velvet railings in the boxes; a curtain that for sheer novel refinement surpassed anything saloon art patrons had ever seen before. It was a picture of Lake Tahoe. It was done by an itinerant to help pay his hotel bill, though of course it was billed as an item imported at vast expense from Italy.

Both literally and figuratively, opening night got off with a bang, or, rather, several bangs. The house was packed. In those electric moments just before curtain time, when the crowd was growing silent, one Howard, a trigger-happy individual with seven nicks in his gunbutt, spotted ancient enemy Jack McNab in a dress circle seat directly across from him, and started firing. With the first shot from Howard's big "Navy", McNab's hands were up to signify he was unarmed, while folks in his vicinity scattered like chicks in a hail of hawks. On the second shot, McNab vaulted the footlights, and by the third or fourth had disappeared through the curtains. Except for slight damage to the woodwork here and there nothing was permanently harmed and the curtain rose on "Money," with Walter Leman and Julia Dean Hayne in the leading roles. A Washoe zephyr that whipped down the mountain with such fury that the sound drowned out the actors' voices was considered tame to the point of anticlimax.

There was never anything tame or lace-valentinish about the tastes of Maguire's patrons, who cut their amusement teeth on the divertissements of the hurdy-gurdy girlies dancing the shoofly and can-can in the saloons, bet vast sums on cockfights in their clubs, and attended hangings with the merriment generally accorded the arrival of Santa in a poorhouse.

Neither the surroundings of plush and ormolu nor the grand little "Opera House" deterred Maguire from catering to these robust appetites. Miners and gentry, assorted millionaires flocked in by foot and silver-spangled broughams to huzzah and burst the seams of their 12-button gloves in forthright approval of everything from animal fights to Hamlet. After Lotta Crabtree, the virginal teenage lark of the day, had picked up the showers of gold and silver coins a delirious audience had flung over the footlights, and departed, the next billing was likely to be a minstrel show; and after a run of Shakespearean repertory something earthy in the way of a bear and/or wildcat vs. bulldog rowdy-dow was sure to follow. A critic for The Territorial Enterprise, reporting on one night's trio of cougar and dog fights, tells how they were done:

"The great wildcat and bulldog fight came off at the Opera House last night according to programme and was witnessed by a full and excited house. . . . There was rigged up on the stage a large cage. Toward the roof of the cage, placed so as to perfectly light up the interior, were eight gas jets. All being in readiness, Fight No. 1 took place. The smallest cat was let into the den and shortly afterward Mr. Gage's white bulldog, "Hero." He went after that cat 'thar and then.' The cat stood his first charge and then began to want to leave. After a few wild plunges about the cage the dog got a square hold on the beast and promptly killed it."

A cat won the second contest; a dog the third in what was really "a terrific battle. The cat now for the first time found it necessary to use her teeth as well as her claws. Over and over again they rolled, fighting so rapidly that it reminded one of a big bunch of firecrackers exploding and whirling about. . . . The fight lasted over twenty minutes, and finally the dog was victorious, not only whipping but killing the cat. The little bulldog was cheered by the crowd and all dispersed declaring the new Opera House troupe a decided success."

It is doubtful whether any one of the three big guns on the Territorial Enterprise—Joe Goodman, Dan De Quille, Mark Twain—covered cat and dog fights. The big three reserved their criticisms for capitol A Art, sitting in a row of free seats marked Enterprise provided up front by the management. At show's end they would all retire to the office, write a review apiece and then, if in agreement, blend the best parts of each one into one fine review. If they didn't agree, three separate reviews were run.

This, at least, was their custom until Adah Isaacs Menken appeared in "Mazeppa," and the trio of journalistic giants unexpectedly fell so flat on their hearts at her performance that they held a contest to see who could produce the most lyrical prose on her behalf. In the end, no man would give up a quarter of an adjective of his prodigal praise and all three lengthy reviews were set forth in type—an act that caused an explosion heard half-way around the theatrical world.

It was purely unintentional. Messrs. Goodman and De Quille and Twain had heard of The Menken, as who hadn't in the 1860s? Her gaudy lovelife was keeping the gentlemen of two nations in a state of perpetual emotions, and every now and then she would marry someone interesting like Benecia Boy Heenan, a prizefighter who taught her how to box. Wherever she went there was tumult! She was "Queen of the Plaza" in Havana, the "Frenzy of Frisco" in San Francisco. In

Texas, she was captured by Indians, rescued by Rangers and taught to ride like a circus acrobat. In the finale of "Mazeppa," as everyone in the Comstock knew from the giant playbills that were plastered all around the town, The Menken would thunder up a mountain and off-stage lashed to the back of a big, black stallion. Her costume was bold for the times: flesh tights and bloomers topped by a filmy blouse.

The staff of The Enterprise regarded The Menken the way present-day drama critics look upon burlesque strippers. She was merely "a shape," and they went to her show just for chuckles. Boy! The lady, as the saying goes, knocked them clean out of the ballpark.

No other actress, before or since, has received such notices, and the rest of the cast, which might have been non-existent so far as The Enterprise was concerned, was miffed, to put it mildly. That night they garnished their regular lines with asides reflecting upon the intelligence, integrity and literary abilities of Reporters Goodman, Twain and De Quille. Menken stopped the show to demand an apology from Maguire and company that was not forthcoming. She continued the run the following night only because her gentlemen journalistic friends begged her to do so.

An uproarious couple of weeks followed. The Menken boiled an egg in the scalding waters of underground diggings; she nightly bucked the tiger at the gaming tables; she rode out on Forty Mile Flat with the Fire Chief, flung herself from her horse to cry "I was born in that yellow sand once, sometime, somewhere." At the Sazarac, she put on the gloves to box "Joggles" Wright, mine superintendent, and knocked him cold. The fire laddies elected her an honorary member and gave her a red morocco belt with the company insignia embossed in silver bullion; a street was named for her; a new mining district was called "The Menken." Of the latter, one newspaper's facetious comment was: "We suppose the first work done in that district will be to 'strip all the ledges.'" When she departed, the miners presented The Menken with a bar of silver bullion worth $2000 and a Wells Fargo stage had to be reinforced with special braces to transport it down below!

As soon as Menken left, the feud between Opera House and Enterprise resumed. Maguire withdrew his advertising from the paper and cancelled the staff's free ducats. The Enterprise then entered into a thoroughly enjoyable phase of reporting that was to last for months until a ferociously beaten Maguire was to meet its demands that the stage manager be fired, the paper's courtesy seat privileges restored and a public apology made to the staff by the management.

The paper's plan was simple. Good shows were ignored; bad shows were taken apart in gruesome detail. In consequence, Virginia City's reputation as a profitable fun-town to play changed; it became the terror of the theatrical world. Walter Montgomery, an English tragedian, took one look at the reviews (three stinkeroos) of his Hamlet and left the same day. So did Emily Thorne, a beauty who made the mistake of bringing Mazeppa back to the mountaintop. There were others, until finally Maguire couldn't get bookings, the house was closed and he was forced to meet The Enterprise's humiliating terms.

Mark Twain left the Comstock before the battle ended, but not before hoisting a few at John Piper's saloon, closest thirst quenchery to the Opera House and a notable hang-out for players and newspapermen. Whether it was simply a matter of proximity or something else, Saloonkeeper Piper had got bit by the greasepaint virus and started buying into the Opera House. By 1868 he had the controlling interest and began a career that for thirty years would dominate theatrical activities in the region. His first booking was Aimee and her French Opera Company, the first opera to be sung on the high Virginia range. He changed the name of the house to Piper's.

John Piper had a snug method of operation. He retained many members of Maguire's stock company—among them such celebrated personalities as Annie Adams, mother of Maude Adams, and Frank Mayo. Fresh talent was captured and kept by the simple process of advancing $1500 to each actor, then withholding all salary until the debt was worked off. The combination of high living expenses and gambling losses assured Mr. Piper of a minimum turnover in cast.

One notable captive was the late, great David Belasco who was 20 years old when he arrived in Virginia City after an engagement at Gray's Opera House in San Francisco. In his almost instantly impoverished condition Belasco hated life on the Comstock, yet he was forced to stay long enough to fulfill five engagements. Once, in an attempted get-away, he managed to get as far as Reno before the sheriff caught him and returned him to Piper.

Later, reflecting on this period of his career, Belasco declared that all the shootings and hangings he'd seen in Nevada made him "all the more particular in regard to the psychology of dying on the stage. I think I was one of the first to bring naturalness to bear in death scenes and my varied Virginia City experiences did much to help me toward this." . . .

The Yellow Jacket fire took place in 1873, one of the many conflagrations that took a fearful toll of lives and property both above and underground. It was one of the worst, until, on the morning of October 26, 1875, fire—"The Great Fire" —broke out at the corner of B and Taylor Streets, with the wind from the southwest. Desperate fire-fighters dynamited buildings in an attempt to stop the flames. Piper's was one that went up in a boom, but still the flames swept on. When it was over most of the city was in ashes.

John Piper lost both his Opera House and his saloon and was stony broke. He turned to Maguire for help and between them they raised $50,000 for a new establishment that was to stand at the corner of Union and B Streets, the present location of the third and final Piper's. It opened in 1878 with a seating capacity of 900, a stage 54 feet wide and 38 feet deep. . . .

The Opera maintained its own orchestra, the personnel of which varied. One of the early premier violinists was William Withers, Jr., who came in the early 70's from Ford's Theatre in Washington, D.C., where he'd gotten stabbed trying to intercept the assassin of President Abraham Lincoln. The merits of Wither's fiddle playing are lost in the bygone mists; it was sufficient recommendation for Virginia Citians that he had a story of violence to tell.

After the fire of '75, Louis Zimmer arrived in Virginia City with his violin and it wasn't long before Piper put him in charge of the orchestra. Zimmer married Piper's daughter Lulu, and their son, Ed. Zimmer, grandson of John Piper, is the owner now of the old Opera House.

Opera House receipts often were better than a thousand dollars a night, yet whether or not a specific performer failed to pull a good gate, Mr. Piper knew that everything was hunky-dory. Bonanza King Mackay, patron of the arts and richer than all get-out, had been inspired to back him in one of the sweetest financial deals of all time. The arrangement was that John Mackay would make up all deficits incurred; all profits went to John Piper. In return, if it can be called return, Piper gave Mackay a box FREE. . . .

If it hadn't been for Mackay, Piper might well have foundered on the financial rocks. Expenses of importing celebrities from the East were enormous. Sometimes, in the afternoons and on free evenings he would open the doors to roller skates. . . .

On March 12, 1883, Piper gave a Grand Ball, by invitation only, to the aristocracy of the town. According to The Territorial Enterprise on March 14th, Piper stayed awake an hour after everyone left to make sure no burning cigars were left about the building. He then retired to his bed above the box-office. At five a.m. an old retired sailor named Dave, just off duty from his job at The Delta saloon, spotted smoke coming from the Opera House and raised the alarm. John Robertson, watchman at the California and Nevada Banks, remembering that Piper slept in the building, rushed to rouse him and drag him to safety. By the time firemen reached the scene, it was too late to save the building and they concentrated on saving the town. It was a damp, windless night, with some sleet, so a holocaust was avoided. Only Piper's and several buildings to the West and North were burned.

Again John Piper was a ruined man. But only temporarily. His personal popularity was his ace in the hole and the townspeople came to his rescue. All kinds of public subscription parties, testimonial dinners and benefits were given for him during the next few months. And within a day of his disaster he had leased Cooper's Hall on B Street, had it fitted with seats and a stage. On March 15, just three days after the fire, Miss Alice Harrison, singer, opened at the temporary Opera House.

The new and present Opera House is built on the ashes of the old one, with lumber that came from old mining buildings, supplemented with material from the Great Fire of '75. Use of such material meant that walls and ceilings were sooted and scorched, but Piper had them covered with muslin, and finished with ornate rose and gold wallpaper. And while the new building couldn't boast of such things as maple flooring shipped around the Horn, it could boast a whole breathtaking bevy of modern styling.

Its balconies are suspended from the ceiling; their railings came from a drug-store balcony which had at one time been used for the projection of stereopticon slides. The floor has springs under it, on the theory this would make it easier on the feet of dancers and Piper planned to intersperse his theater bookings with balls, levees, hoedowns and suchlike. Two types of double coil springs under the floor may not have helped anyone trip the light fantastic, but there was sheer magic in in them: a ball placed in the middle of the floor would roll toward any weight placed along the wall.

The stage is 32 feet deep and 50 feet wide, with a proscenium opening 30 feet wide and 20 feet high. Overhead a charcoal portrait of William Shakespeare by Piper's artist son George, executed in 1885, has miraculously escaped the stains of rain that washed in until a new roof was put on in 1942. The auditorium floor is 50 feet wide and 80 feet long, and the wooden chairs that remain in it are the originals. Instead of a sloping auditorium as today's theaters have, Piper's has a rake stage that slants upward from the footlights; thus patrons, seated on the flat could see the feet of the performers. It is one of the few such left in the U.S.

The official opening of Piper's third and last Opera House took place, after a final magnificent ball in his benefit had been given, on March 6, 1885, with all the nabobs and their ladies in attendance. The production was, of all things, Peck's Bad Boy. . . .

Piper's Opera House was condemned and closed for performances in 1920, but was reopened in 1940 as a museum.

83. CROSBY'S OPERA HOUSE
Chicago, Illinois
Opened April 20, 1865

By 1865 Chicago had grown into a thriving city, and one with a great need for entertainment. McVicker's Theatre was this time without a rival—until the opening of the new Crosby's Opera House at Washington and

SALT LAKE THEATRE—Salt Lake City.

81. Salt Lake Theatre, Salt Lake City, Utah, ca. 1902. Courtesy of the Utah State Historical Society.

81. Interior, Salt Lake Theatre, Salt Lake City, Utah, ca. 1900. Courtesy of the Utah State Historical Society.

83. Crosby's Opera House, Chicago. Lithograph, after a drawing by Louis Kurz; published in James W. Shea-han, *Chicago Illustrated*, part 3 (Chicago: Jevne & Almini, March, 1866). Courtesy Chicago Historical Society.

Dearborn streets. Unfortunately, Crosby's had planned to open on April 17, but cancelled the plans when the news of Lincoln's assassination became known, and opened instead on April 20. The following account is from the Chicago *Tribune*.

83:1　　OPERA HOUSE IS OPENED
———————————
INAUGURATION NIGHT

The Opera House is opened. The event long expected, much contemplated, anxiously awaited, some time deferred on account of the national bereavement came off last evening; the grand Temple of Music erected by Crosby was opened up to the world by Grau; the event was a triumphant success.

We have previously announced that every seat in the house was taken long before the time came for occupying them; it only needs to say now that the miserable weather of last evening did not deter the holders of tickets from honoring the manager with their presence, nor did it in the slightest degree detract from the character of the audience. The skies without were dark, the rain fell heavily and the loud thunder pealed across heaven's archway, making it any thing but "comfortable," out of doors. But inside the hall there was nothing to remind us of the war of the elements. The building was dedicated to the Goddess of Harmony (or a twin sister) and nought interfered to mar the splendors amid which her gentle reign was inaugurated. Cloaks and jewels were numerous, as though the sun had shone out brightly. The only difference was, perhaps, that the call for carriages was greater than it would otherwise have been. Such a gathering of vehicles has certainly never before been seen in Chicago. Long lines stretched all along Washington and Dearborn streets and wound sinuously far into the adjacent thoroughfares. It is fair to presume that private and public stables were alike

83:1. Chicago *Tribune,* Apr. 21, 1865.

emptied of their equine denizens for the grand occasion.

A description of the building has already been given. Those who had the good fortune to be present last evening will agree with us that the published descriptions were far too tame expressions of the reality. The *tout ensemble* is vast, complete, magnificent, with scarcely a single fault in detail to mar the general effect. Prominent among the little offenses are a disproportionate size of the brackets which support the soffit of the proscenium arch, and a rather unpleasant draft in the aisles, the result of a somewhat too vigorous ventilation—it strikes us that this might be easily remedied; it is sufficiently unpleasant to those seated within its range to make it worth an effort.

A very striking point in the general look of the auditorium is the tone and harmony of the coloring. All is quiet, subdued; very favorably contrasting with the glaring reds, whites and yellows of most public structures. There is nothing to offend or fatigue the eye. The general work of the furniture is blue, a very mild color; it is just sufficiently relieved to avoid monotony without gaining by the undue use of pigments. The lighting arrangements aid this materially; the spectator has not to look at and through a blaze of gaslights; these are all far enough removed from the ordinary range of vision. Look upward to the dome, and you see a blaze of light which may recall ideas of the midday sun; but the gaze averted from the ceiling meets nothing but a mild reflection of the rays shorn of all their actinic properties.

The acoustic qualities of the hall are all that could be desired. The greenness of the walls and the dampness of their paint coatings, combined with a very unfavorable atmosphere last evening, caused a lack of that full mellowness of sound we may expect to find in the future; but in this respect it was far less disagreeable than we anticipated, while in the point of distinctness the acme of perfection has been attained. Every sound was equally audible in the farther part of the galleries as from the orchestra chairs; not a note or articulation was lost to anyone. Those who failed to hear Mr. Crosby from the ultimate parts of the house may rest assured that the failure was owing to his extreme modesty; he was scarcely audible to those sitting immediately in front of the stage.

And then the scenery and stage fittings: well, we can only say that they would do honor to any theater in the Old or New World. We cannot imagine an improvement in the paintings, and the working was admirable. We presume that there were few in the audience but expected to see trouble in the shifting of scenes. There was not an iota. Everything worked as smoothly and with a complete absence of noise as if the scenes had been trained to run in these grooves for half a century. A few new features were introduced in stage management, not necessary to particularize, which might with advantage be noted by other parties.

We must not omit to speak of the admirable arrangement for the conduct of members of the audience to their seats. There was no confusion, notwithstanding the rush. The seats were apportioned into sections, and sufficiently large and drilled corps of ushers were in attendance to indicate locations. They were dressed neatly and wore white kids; but what is better, they understood and did their duty well. The chief of staff, Mr. John Newman, late of the Museum, is entitled to mention for his efficient supervision of these details. . . .

Chapter 4

Playhouses in
New York City, 1865-1899

Although there were now many playhouses in San Francisco, Boston, and Chicago, New York City had gained supremacy early in the nineteenth century as the theater center of the United States. Following the Civil War an increasing number of theaters were opened.

During this period stock companies became practically nonexistent, with only a handful of theaters in New York City maintaining this system. Daly's and Wallack's companies became two of the outstanding repertory companies in American theater history, and particularly in the person of Augustin Daly we see the rise of the strong producer-director, a phenomenon that was being paralleled in Germany, France, England, and Russia at this time.

Daly began his theatrical career as a drama critic for several important newspapers. During this period he also began to write plays, at least one of which, *Under the Gaslight,* became a success. In 1869 he became manager of the Fifth Avenue Theatre, and in this and subsequent playhouses under his management he gathered together a distinguished company of actors, alternating performances of the classics with some contemporary melodramas.

Wallack's Theatre became an institution in New York, maintaining the outstanding repertory company in the city. The Wallacks—Henry, James W., Jr., and Lester—specialized in revivals of Shakespeare and the classics that won the praise of the critics and proved popular with the public.

One other theatre manager of the period should be mentioned—Edwin Booth, the great Shakespearean actor. Booth was a stellar stage attraction and traveled throughout the country playing those roles that had made him famous. When acting in New York City, he generally presented his plays at the old Winter Garden Theatre, a playhouse that saw many of the outstanding stars of the period in some of their most famous roles. On March 23, 1867, the Winter Garden burned and Booth was without a theater home.

This seemed to be a propitious time for Booth to open his own theater and, with financial aid, he built the most advanced playhouse yet seen in New York. Booth's Theatre opened on February 3, 1869, with Booth in *Romeo and Juliet,* and there followed a number of excellent plays. Booth, however, was not a good business manager and soon was forced to withdraw from the management of the theater. The standards of production he set at his theater were of the highest order.

The playhouses built in New York at this time were becoming more ornate, more comfortable, and more elaborately equipped for scenic effects. The introduction of electric lighting, hydraulic lifts, three-dimensional scenery, and historically accurate costuming brought about revolutionary changes in the American playhouse. Some of the theaters built during this period were to be in use for the next fifty years. Others, because of poor management, unfortunate location, or financial difficulties, would soon close their doors or be burned and never rebuilt.

This period in New York theater history culminates in 1895 with the opening of the first New York theater complex, Hammerstein's Olympia. It was the dream-child of Oscar Hammerstein, cigarmaker turned impressario and theater manager. The Olympia contained four theaters in one building, including a roof-garden theater. The fact that the playhouse was located on a prime site on Broadway between Forty-fourth and Forty-fifth streets showed that the forward-looking Hammerstein sensed the northward drift of the theatrical section of the city. The popularity of this enterprise, which presented many great stars, proved Hammerstein to be a man in advance of his times.

84. TONY PASTOR'S OPERA HOUSE
New York City
Opened July 31, 1865

Tony Pastor has been called the father, or the godfather, of vaudeville. Whether or not this is true may be open to debate. What is true, however, is that he did more to dignify and to make socially acceptable this form of entertainment than anyone else in his era.

Pastor, who was born in New York City in 1832, made his professional debut in 1846, when he joined the minstrel show at Barnum's American Museum as a singer and tambourine player. During his years as an entertainer he sang, wrote hundreds of songs, and at one time

was even a circus clown. While with the circus he also tumbled, danced, and acted as ringmaster.

In 1860 he began acting as a variety entertainer, taking a job as comic vocalist at the Broadway Music Hall in 1861. He was appalled by the crudity and obscenity of the variety entertainment of the day and determined to reform it if he had the chance, so that women and children would find it socially respectable to attend. His first attempt at management was at 444 Broadway, and here he was such a success that he decided the time had arrived to try his ideas about variety entertainment on a much larger scale.

Entering into partnership with a friend from his minstrel days, Sam Sharpley, he rented a theater at 201 Bowery, which he renamed Tony Pastor's Opera House. The original rental agreement was for only two weeks, since Pastor and Sharpley did not know whether their experiment would succeed. Succeed it did, and Pastor bought a lease on the property.

The policies Pastor instituted were unheard of in a variety house: no drinking, smoking, foul language, or obscene entertainment. This was a house to which a gentlemen could bring a lady without embarrassment and be rewarded by first-class variety entertainment. Pastor encouraged attendance of women and children by offering candy, prizes, and Ladies' Nights with free admission if accompanied by a gentleman. The women stood in line to gain admittance and Pastor's Opera House was a huge success.

A writer for the *Herald* wrote about Pastor's Opera House:

84:1 TONY PASTOR'S OPERA HOUSE.—The entertainments given at this establishment are winning for it a well deserved popularity. They embrace both the features of the minstrel hall and the arena, and are first class in their character. It is precisely such a combination as was needed for the part of the town where

84:1. New York *Herald*, Sept. 26, 1865.

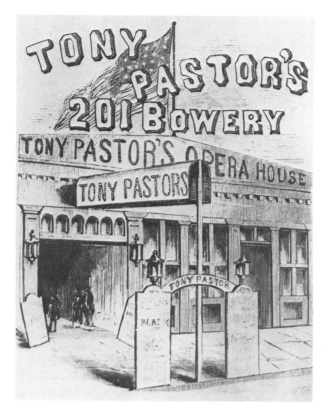

84. Tony Pastor's Opera House, New York. Courtesy of The Hoblitzelle Theatre Arts Library, The Humanities Research Center, The University of Texas at Austin.

84. Tony Pastor's Opera House and Tammany Hall, New York, 1904. Courtesy of the New-York Historical Society, New York City.

85. Barnum's American Museum, New York. Engraving by Avery, after a drawing by Chapin; published in Gleason's *Pictorial Drawing-Room Companion* (Jan. 29, 1852). Courtesy of The Hoblitzelle Theatre Arts Library, The Humanities Research Center, The University of Texas at Austin.

85. Interior, Barnum's New Museum, New York. Engraving on playbill, ca. 1865. Courtesy of The Hoblitzelle Theatre Arts Library, The Humanities Research Center, The University of Texas at Austin.

87. Daly's First Fifth Avenue Theatre, New York. A cigar card, "Between the Acts." Courtesy of The Hoblitzelle Theatre Arts Library, The Humanities Research Center, The University of Texas at Austin.

this house is situated. The success proves the success of the axiom that where there is a want there is always a way of filling it. We are glad to see the management is bestowing as much attention upon the audience part of the house as upon the stage arrangements. The strict surveillance exercised over it has resulted in excluding rowdyish and troublesome elements, and in attracting crowds of ladies and children. As a place of family resort we know no nicer or pleasanter place of amusement in the whole metropolis.

A few days later the *Herald* again lauded Pastor's.

84:2 The East end has its peculiar tastes in dramatic and operatic art, and the people of that region—which equals at least, if it does not exceed, any other district of the city in the number of its theatrical establishments, where fixed rules of etiquette, hackneyed old plays and flat new ones, often represented by worn out stock companies, would be but small attraction to them. They want something hearty, genial, racy, and, above all, varied in its character, such as they find, any apparently appreciate at Tony Pastor's Opera House, in the Bowery. The drama, whether legitimate or absurdly sensational, such as the theatres produce, is not the kind of performance best suited for the class who frequent the Bowery establishments. They require something congenial to their own natures, which love mirth in its broadest phases and passion delineated by its strongest dramatic agencies. The patrons of Bowery amusements have little time for sentiment, but just enough time for fun and that relief from the exacting obligations of everyday life which an establishment like that of Tony Pastor affords them. Variety, above all things, is a necessity with this class. They must have histrionic art, and music, and the ballet combined, in order to spend an

84:2. New York *Herald,* Oct. 2, 1865.

evening profitably, for they have neither the leisure nor the means to enjoy them in any other way. It is by this combination that the Opera House of Tony Pastor has attained its great success. The good order observed and the absence of peanut feasts and boisterous applause, which have become traditionary with Bowery establishments, can, no doubt, in a great degree account for the respectable character of the audiences which attend there. The bill of Pastor's Opera House this week is entirely new, as are also some of the actors —Misses Jennie and Hattie Engel—who appear this evening for the first time, with the clever Fowler Sisters and other favorites of the company. The Bowery Opera House is rapidly becoming the select resort of the East end theatre goers.

85. BARNUM'S NEW MUSEUM
New York City
Opened September 6, 1865

Of the various theatrical managers, impresarios, and showmen of nineteenth-century America, none gained more fame than Phineas Taylor Barnum, showman extraordinary. Barnum was born in Danbury, Connecticut, in 1810, the son of a livery stable owner. After trying various trades, including that of newspaper editor, he finally discovered his forte as a purveyor of hokum. In 1835 he bought an old Negro slave and introduced her to the public as the nurse of George Washington and the oldest living human being. She caused a sensation.

Later Barnum bought a riverboat and plied the Mississippi River with a theatrical showboat. Firmly launched in the theatrical business, Barnum returned to New York and purchased Scudder's Museum, with all its curious relics, and added many more curiosities of his own. He opened Barnum's American Museum at Broadway and Ann Street. In addition to his exhibits Barnum gave dramatic performances in the "Moral Lecture Room." These performances were continuous and set the format for the techniques of presentation in vaudeville.

Sometimes as many as ten or twelve performances were given each day. The most famous play presented by Barnum at this time was *The Drunkard*, a temperance melodrama.

In July 1865, Barnum's American Museum burned, but he quickly leased the old Winter Garden Theatre and continued his performances there until he could open a new museum. On July 21, 1865, a great benefit performance was given for the people who worked at Barnum's.

85:1   BENEFIT OF BARNUM'S
              ATTACHES AT THE ACADEMY
                  OF MUSIC

The double performance—afternoon and evening—yesterday for the benefit of the attaches of Barnum's Museum, who have suffered severly by the late fire, was a decided success. The most pleasing feature in the entertainment was the spontaneity with which all the artists, musicians, and even the carpenters and machinists, volunteered their services, showing that an *esprit de corps*, as well as instinct of charity,. animates the theatrical profession. The characters of the performances selected is an evidence of the good judgment of the managing committee. It was light and varied. Nothing heavy or imposing upon the patience of the audience was inflicted, which would have been a severe trial, considering the weather of yesterday. People laughed so much at the combination of fun and humor presented to them that they forgot the range of the thermometer outside. The returns for the benefit of the sufferers by the destruction of the Museum must have been very handsome, considering that nothing was paid for except the rent of the Academy—the inexorable rule of the inflexible directors forbidding a donation of that in situation even in response to the voice of charity. Mr. Barnum addressed the assembled crowd at both performances. He

85:1. New York *Herald,* July 22, 1865.

said that he regarded the destruction of the Museum not as an accident, but as a dispensation of Providence. His name had been associated for some years with that of humbug, and perhaps the conflagration was designed to fumigate and burn up and evaporate the stench which had eminated from the name which he himself, as well as others, had allied with his name and his Museum. When he wrote a book he knew that people expected that humbug would be thrust forward prominently, or they would not consider that they had got their money's worth, and so he gratified the public. He said that he cared nothing for the loss of money, because, thanks to the public patronage, he was above want; but he had pride in restoring the old establishment on a better basis as a means of amusement and instruction to the young, and if the feeling now demonstrated towards him continued he might one day erect a magnificent building. Governors of states and the federal government at Washington had offered him assistance in supplying valuable relics, as had also many private individuals, but what was a greater stimulation than all, he had received upwards of fifty letters from children begging him to build a new Museum, and if he lived he would attempt it before twelve months. Meanwhile, he was about to fix up the Chinese Assembly Rooms as a Museum for the next twelve or eighteen months. His pantomime company would, for the present, appear at the Winter Garden. Mr. Barnum was greeted with much applause during the delivery of his remarks, which he interspersed with characteristic anecdotes and the development of a philosophy strictly of the Barnum school. A noticeable feature of the evening's performance was the appearance of the Hanlon Brothers, who had just arrived from Havana, and upon hearing of the disaster at once offered their services. Their acts upon the trapeze were perfectly astounding, the ropes being attached to the summit of the proscenium, at an immense elevation from the stage.

Barnum and his public did not have to wait twelve or eighteen months for a new Museum, for the work went very quickly, and Barnum's New Museum was ready for its premiere on September 6.

85:2 BARNUM'S MUSEUM.—Mr. Barnum's new and singularly bright establishment opened yesterday, when the energetic and deserving manager address his audience in a short *extempore* speech. It said little more than is known, but dwelt with fondness on the future: on that perfect Museum which Barnum intends to establish and bequeath to the nation. The dramatic performances were very good, and the dresses particularly brilliant,—an advantage gained by the fire. The attendance was somewhat injured in the afternoon by the rain, but in the evening the ample and elegant "lecture hall" was crowded.

Barnum's opened with *The Children of Cyprus,* which is listed on the opening night's program as "the Grand Oriental, Fairy, Spectacular Romance."

86. BOOTH'S THEATRE
New York City
Opened February 3, 1869

One of the most eagerly awaited theatrical events of the post-Civil War era was the opening of a new theater by the famous tragedian, Edwin Booth, who had been acclaimed as one of the greatest Shakespearean actors America had produced. The new playhouse, which was built on the corner of Sixth Avenue and Twenty-third Street, was one of the best-equipped theaters of the day, employing the most up-to-date methods available at that time.

The critic for the New York *Tribune* was so excited about the prospects of the new playhouse that he wrote a lengthy description of it more than two months before it opened.

85:2. New York *Times,* Sept. 7, 1865.

86:1   EDWIN BOOTH'S THEATER

When the Winter Garden was burned, Edwin Booth was left without a theater and Tragedy was left without a home. It is, however, as the wise old proverb affirms, an ill wind which blows good to nobody. Edwin Booth had long entertained the desire and the design of building a theater in New York, in conformity with his own ideal. His design, though, might long have slept, and, perhaps, might never have awakened to fulfillment, had not the Winter Garden catastrophe supplied both the freedom and the motive for new and vigorous enterprise. The occasion thus offered was promptly improved. During the Spring of 1867, Mr. J. H. Magonigle, the business representative of Mr. Booth, made a thorough investigation of all the building sites in the city that were deemed eligible for a theater, and finally selected the lot of land on the south-east corner of Twenty-third-st. and the Sixth-ave. This choice was approved by Mr. Booth and by all concerned in the enterprise; the property was purchased; and on the 1st of July, 1867, work was commenced on the new enterprise. The buildings that stood upon the land had first to be removed. This was soon done. Their removal, however, disclosed a foundation of solid rock. Part of this it was found necessary to blast away, and the work of blasting somewhat tedious. But no time was lost; and on the 8th of April, 1868, the labor of construction was so far advanced that the cornerstone of the theatre was laid. It is the great granite block, at the base, on the east end of the building. It was laid, on a cold and blustering day, in the presence of only a few persons. Mr. James H. Hackett, the veteran comedian, the best living representative of *Falstaff,* and one of the most devoted and affectionate students of Shakespeare, performed the official ceremony, and pronounced a brief address.

86:1. New York *Tribune,* Nov. 18, 1868.

Some words were also spoken by Judge Daley,* who said that the drama was cradled in a booth, and that by a Booth it would be perpetuated. From that day to this the hand of labor has never stayed nor faltered; and now the strong and stately edifice—close upon completion—rears its noble front to all, a beautiful monument of pure taste and skillful labor. It is built of granite, the stone that best typifies solidity, in that graceful style of architecture that is known as the Renaissance. This rugged material, so wrought together, becomes a truly poetic emblem of blended strength and beauty. Fair in proportion, true in substance, wisely planned, and excellent in all details, Edwin Booth's new theater is one of the most magnificent buildings on the American continent. Let us come to particulars, and try to show this in description. The front of the structure, on Twenty-third-st., is 184 feet in length, the theater front measuring 150 feet. The other 34 feet is the width of a wing of the main building, which abuts upon its west end, and has frontage of 76 feet on the Sixth-ave. The lower part of this wing is arranged for stores, while the upper part contains offices, studios, miscellaneous rooms, and rooms for a Masonic Lodge. The theater is 100 feet deep, from north to south, and 120 feet in height. The main entrance opens from Twenty-third-st., but there is another large entrance opening from the Sixth-ave. At the east end of the front is a great door to the stage, corresponding in size and style, with the main entrance to the auditorium. Between these are three smaller doors, which are to be used as a means of exit. Three large panels surmount these three doors, which are to contain sculptured bas-reliefs. All the doors are arched. Higher up, and placed equi-distant along the front of the theater, are three large alcoves, framed in Ionic pillars, which are

*Judge Joseph Francis Daly, brother of Augustin Daly, and also his collaborator and biographer.

to contain enormous statues in white marble. Shakespeare will stand in the central arch, and Tragedy and Comedy will occupy the others. There are four large and handsome windows on a line with these alcoves. Above runs a beautiful cornice, and above this the side slopes inward to meet the roof, which is surmounted by three short towers. In the front of each tower there is an oval window, surrounded by elaborate carvings. A flag staff rises from the center of the flat roof. Around the summit of each tower runs an ornamental trellis-work of iron, and, artfully placed on the lightning rods which trail over towers and roof, are gilded stars and cresents. Entering at the principal door, the visitor will find himself in a commodious vestibule, paved with Italian marble tiling, and lined with Italian marble cement—the ceiling being frescoed. This vestibule extends in a semi-circle along the rear of the auditorium, to which entrance is afforded by three arched doors. The lower floor of the theater comprises the divisions of parquette and orchestra. A spacious stone staircase, at the south end of the vestibule, leads to the balcony, in the rear of which provision has been made for a commodious promenade. Above the balcony is the second gallery, and above that is the amphitheater, which is to be reached by a stone staircase from the vestibule within the Sixth-ave. entrance. There are ten proscenium boxes—five on each side of the stage—and the house will afford comfortable seats for 1,700 persons, besides standing room for at least 300 more. In shape, the auditorium follows the old horse-shoe model, only that it has been skillfully modified as to result in a shape of delightful symmetry. From every part of the theater the entire stage can be distinctly seen. As yet the chairs have not been put in, nor have the walls been decorated; but the former are to be of a new design, especially provident of the sitter's comfort, and the latter are to be lined, near the floor, with Italian marble cement, and richly ornamented above in white and gold. On the ceilings bright frescoes are already beginning to shine forth. A vast chandelier will depend from the center of the roof, and this, together with all the other lights in the building, will be lit by electricity. The ornamenting of the proscenium will be simple and beautiful. Marble pillars, adorned with statuesque figures, will arise on either side of the boxes. In the center of the arch above, a massive statue of Shakespeare will be placed—the work of Turini, an Italian artist. It reperesents the poet meditating and in act to write. Other statues and emblematic devices will surround this figure and complete the decoration of the arch. There is a neatly designed pit for the orchestral performers, sunk below the front of the stage and below the level of the main floor, so that neither the performers nor their musical instruments can obstruct the view of the stage from the auditorium. The reader will perceive that we speak of a perfectly devised theatrical interior. It will be easy alike of access and of egress. It will be superbly lighted. It will please the eye with the symmetrical shapes and harmonious colors. It will afford luxuriously comfortable accommodation. It will be so thoroughly and so artfully heated and ventilated by hot-air pipes that run beneath the floors and distribute their warmth equally, and by masked ventilators up beneath the roof, that the atmosphere will be kept, as far as that is possible in a public building, wholesome and pleasant. More than this could not reasonably be desired, and more than this certainly has never been attained. Passing to the stage, the visitor finds that this is not less excellent than the auditorium. The distance from the footlights to the rear wall is 55 feet, and the stage is 76 feet wide. Beneath it is a pit 32 feet deep, that was blasted out of solid rock. This useful chasm is neatly paved with brick. An entire scene can be sunk out of sight. On the stage, as in every other part of the theater, double floors are laid, and the flooring of the stage is secured entirely by screws—not a single nail being driven. In each of the rear corners of the stage is a spiral staircase, which leads to the fly-galleries, high beneath the roof. These galleries are four in number, two upon each side. Between them, up aloft, depends the complex machinery requisite for lifting and lowering the scenes. There are no obstructions upon the stage, no dressing rooms there, none of those dirty and mysterious burrows which make many other stages look like slices out of chaos. Ample space on the contrary is afforded, every particle of which ripe skill has utilized, and over which the great instinct or order imperiously presides. At the south side of the stage is a scene room already well-stocked with scenery (for the painting, under the direction of the scenic artist, Mr. Witham, has been going on since August of last year). Above this is the paint room, 57 feet by 16, in which a flat 50 feet high, or more, can easily be stretched and painted. Also at the south side of the theater are five stories of rooms, approached by a convenient staircase, including the green-room, a fireproof room for the wardrobe of the theater, Mr. Booth's private apartments, and almost thirty dressing-rooms. Each of the latter is lighted by two gas-jets and supplied with water, which flows into and out of a marble basin. Neatness and order everywhere prevail. The green-room is a large and handsome apartment on the second floor. As yet, of course, these rooms have not been furnished, but no actor will miss any requisite comfort when at length they are made ready for occupation. It is easy to see that they, no less than the adjuncts of the stage, have been planned by an actor of the largest experience and the most considerate nature. Every inch of space, as already said, has been used. From the vault beneath stage passages conduct into vaults beneath the auditorium, and also into those beneath the contiguous side-walks. As the visitor walks through those strange caverns he is impressed anew with a sense of the solidity of this splendid structure. Here is seen the foundation, which is of solid rock. Here are the supports—stone pillars nearly three feet square. The front wall is nearly five feet thick, and the thickness of the other walls is upward of two feet. Under the side-walk in Twenty-third-st. is the carpenter shop of the theater, in a large dry vault; and under the side-walk in the Sixth-ave. are two large boilers which are to supply the theater with heat, and possibly to impel certain machinery which is being effected for the working of the stage; for it is Mr. Booth's design to supersede, as far as may be possible by scientific means, the necessity of manual labor. These boilers have been tested, and have been pronounced the best ever inspected in New-York. They are perfectly safe, and so, indeed, is every part and accessory of the theater. One fact, in this respect, may speak for many. Not a rope is to be employed on the stage; its place will be supplied by wire cable. All these details will enable the reader to form something like an adequate idea of the beauty and finish that characterize Edwin Booth's new theater. To our mind they combine into a perfect whole, and constitute the fullfillment of an exalted ideal. On the floor of one of the vestibules, deftly fashioned in multiudinous little stones, many-colored and beautiful, will be seen the figure of Apollo, standing erect in his chariot and borne onward in swift triumph by his fiery steeds. It is a fit emblem of Edwin Booth's honorable ambitions. May it prove also the auspicious augury of his great success.

The actual opening of the theater took place on February 3, 1869.

86:2   OPENING OF BOOTH'S THEATRE
Mr. EDWIN BOOTH'S Theatre, on the south-east corner of West Twenty-third-

86:2. New York *Times,* Feb. 4, 1869.

street and Sixth-avenue, was opened to the public last evening, and was very extensively occupied by the many-headed monster. The establishment is one of the most important ever dedicated to the art. Its exterior grandeur is only equaled by the beauty and brightness of the interior decorations. It lacks, however, the spacious freedom of the Grand Opera House, and is particularly deficient in lobby room. Ladies' dresses were rent and disordered last evening in a way that will bring a powerful interest to bear against the theatre. It is only under certain conditions that the sex permits itself to be crowded. As a rule, it is best not to step on a woman's dress, unless, like poor *Mercutio,* you wish to be "scratched to death." What would have become of the attendance last night had an alarm of fire taken place, it is dreadful to think of. The alarm of water —and the skies were plenteous in their gifts—congested the little lobby, and made egress almost impossible. Mr. BOOTH can remedy this by having additional wickets, and will, no doubt, do so. Where so much has been done, it is hardly vain to look for more. At all events it is natural to do so.

The play selected for the evening, as our readers are well aware, was "Romeo and Juliet." Ere the tragedy had commenced Mr. BOOTH made his appearance before the audience, and in a few well-selected remarks referred to the calamity which nearly two years ago deprived the community of his services, and of his subsequent resolve to build a theatre worthy of the Metropolis and the drama. He then retired, changed his dress and the piece proceeded. Of this everything remains to be said. The waits which are inevitable on first nights, although never prolonged to the point of exciting inquietude or displeasure, led the performance into the most advanced stillness of the night. They who could remain were doubtless rewarded for their pains. Most certainly the early acts were the most marvellous specimens of stage production ever witnessed here. The scenery is absolutely perfect, and the proportions of the stage enable it to be worked also to perfection. There were "sets" last night which could not even be attempted at any other establishment, such, for instance, as the banqueting hall in *Capulet's* house and the celebrated Balcony scene. But to these and cognate topics we must hereafter refer, our habit being not to write a column before breakfast on the day of the performance, and to insert a comma by way of comment after supper. The opening was a success worthy of the gravest attention, and trivial generalities and shimmering verbiage are hardly appropriate for the occasion. We may say hurriedly that Mr. EDWIN ADAMS seemed to divide the favor of the audience with Mr. BOOTH. He was called out (would that it were always possible) after the death and appeared to be breathing quite freely. The fighting be it observed was furious on all sides. Miss McVICKER'S *Juliet* was perhaps marred by timidity. Under any circumstances it is a proper subject for further comment, if not much study. Much credit is due to Mr. MARK SMITH, not only for his excellent performance of *Friar Lawrence*, but for the general completeness of the stage arrangements. The new ropes and pullies, and machinery and mechanics led to occasional delay, but never to disaster. The play was perfectly well studied, and followed the text of SHAKESPEARE more closely than usual.

87. FIFTH AVENUE THEATRE
New York City
Opened April 16, 1869

Assumption of the management of the Fifth Avenue Theatre by Augustin Daly signified an important event in the history of the American theater, for Daly became a major force in quality theatrical performances for more than thirty years and dominated the professional theater. He was certainly one of the first *régisseurs*, those all-powerful producer-directors who were to mold the modern theater.

The playhouse had been built on Twenty-fourth Street near Broadway and had opened on September 2, 1867. The early years of the playhouse were singularly undistinguished, with the exception perhaps of a performance of John Brougham in January 1869 in one of his own plays. Daly took over the management of the playhouse, opening with Tom Robertson's comedy, *Play*. A review of the opening appeared in the New York *Times*.

87:1 FIFTH-AVENUE THEATRE

This theatre was opened for the season last Monday evening under the management of Mr. AUGUSTIN DALY. The audience, though unaccountably small, was cordially disposed, and welcomed the various members of the company with a heartiness that in particular cases—notably that of Mr. GEORGE HOLLAND—rose to positive enthusiasm. The general performance was also received with great consideration, certain brilliant effects of scenic decoration and artistic grouping being recognized with an evident determination to show all possible favor to the new enterprise. That the success of the occasion was not as complete as could have been wished for cannot, therefore, be attributed to any spirit of coldness or indifference on the part of the public. The fact is that the entertainment in many important respects was a disappointment. A comedy, new to this City, by Mr. T. W. ROBERTSON, was announced, and the character of that gentleman's contribution to dramatic literature is now so well established and so universally understood that any direct deviation from his methods is liable to be looked upon with suspicion, and to create the impression either that he has been careless of his own fame or that his work has been tampered with. In

87:1. New York *Times,* Aug. 18, 1869.

the present instance it is admitted that "Play" has been remodeled, and to some extent rewritten, by Mr. DALY, the manager. Nothing could be more presumptuous than for a dramatic writer of questionable ability and inferior reputation thus to rearrange, under whatever pretence, the production of an author whose good taste in construction is hardly less conspicuous than his rare felicity of expression. "Play" may not be Mr. Robertson's best comedy, but like all his compositions, it at least possesses a distinct literary value—a quality for which Mr. DALY'S pieces, so far as we are aware, are not distinguished. The result of his effort to improve the English dramatist is as unfortunate as might have been expected. Passing over the injury to one or two interesting scenes occasioned by certain excisions and colloquial changes, we find that the entire design of the last act is perverted by the substitution of an unnatural exhibition of melodramatic bombast for the original quiet and simple gathering together of the threads of the story. In consequence of this error one of the chief purposes of the comedy—one, indeed, which Mr. ROBERTSON appears always to have in view in his more ambitious works—the consistent illustration of society as it actually exists, and not as theatrical imagination pictures it, is as good as lost. Perhaps it is too much to expect from imperfect human nature that a manager who is also a writer of plays should refrain from occasionally offering the public specimens of his own work; but after this unsatisfactory experience we may trust that such inharmonious combinations as that witnessed in "Play," as it now stands, will not be attempted in the future. There are dramatic extremes which will not meet, and never can be made to meet, on equal terms.

The representation, on Monday evening, was not without good points. The chief defect in the general action was a want of the promptness and directness es-pecially required in Mr. ROBERTSON'S pieces, to preserve the unity of effect. This, undoubtedly, will be less perceptible hereafter. The principal characters were sustained with very different degrees of merit. No pleasanter success has been witnessed in many seasons than that achieved by Miss AGNES ETHEL, in the part of the fresh-hearted, ingenuous and affectionate young English girl, *Roxie Fanquhere*. Her unaffected and apparently artless grace in every scene called to mind some of the daintiest performances of the same class upon the French stage. On the other hand, the impersonation of her immediate companion and follower, *Frank Price*, by Mr. J. B. POLK, was correspondingly bad, the gentleman acting upon a sort of theory that angular awkardness and agile avoidance of easy posture were necessary to express the bashful timidity with which his young lover is oppressed. His fantoccine skippings and twirlings reduced the lively and sometimes delicate scenes in which he participated to the last condition of absurdity. If his singing we say nothing, as we take for granted it has already been dispensed with. Mrs. CLARA JENNINGS displayed her usual intelligence and cultivation in the character of the neglected wife, *Amanda*, and the icy cruelty of her husband, the *Chevalier Browne*, was forcibly depicted by Mr. *GEORGE CLARKE*. Mrs. G. H. GILBERT and Mr. GEORGE HOLLAND, as a couple of English tourists of the type which annually spreads terror throughout continental watering places, were abundantly rewarded for their endeavors to enliven less important scenes. A new proof of an old theatrical fact—that if the impossibility of even the best among actors to advantageously appear in parts totally unsuited to them—was afforded, we regret to say, by Mr. E. L. DAVENPORT. In appearance and in manner, alike, he failed to realize the idea of the cool and practical adventurer, *Bruce Fanquhere*. Messrs. DAVIDGE and BEEKMAN contributed to the mirth of the evening by their humorous representation of two hot-headed Prussian officers. Their uniform, by the bye, was incorrect, but that is a matter about which the public cares little.

The scenery prepared for "Play" is charming. The opening picture of the valleys and hills of Baden, and the view of the ruined castle, are as picturesque and romantic as travelers are apt to find in their European wanderings. They are not like anything in Baden, to be sure, but they are admirable all the same. The music, what there is of it, is excellently managed by Mr. ROBERT STOEPEL. We presume he is not responsible for the mistake, during the second act, of producing progressive chords from an AEolean harp.

"Play" is announced for repetition every evening, and on Saturday afternoons, until further notice.

One of the best contemporary descriptions of this theater was written before the playhouse was taken over by Augustin Daly.

87:2 Seldom has space been so economized as in this new house of mirth. The house, to the outside gazer, looks painfully narrow, but the happy idea of a genius in having the side walls of the interior plated with mirrors, affords a most agreeable illusion of immensity to the seated audience. These mirrors line the walls of the parquette and the dress-circle. Upon the walls of the gallery the pervading tint of the house prevails. This is blush-rose, neatly framed in white, with delicate boundaries of gold. The lower floor of the house is not divided, as in other theatres, into parquette and balcony circle, but is furnished with the convenient iron chairs now so popular, and is devoted to the orchestra reserves. Above these rises the balcony, with its boxes at either end much

the same as at Wallack's, only here again the iron chairs are wholly used in lieu of sofas. There are also two rows of these chairs in the balcony circle, which is the only other division of the house. A neat vine, in iron-work, painted white and flected with gold, fronts these two circles. The descent from the back to the front in both is rather precipitous, and calls for the nimbleness of the lively chamois in those who would make the passage to the foremost seats in safety. Nine hundred persons, it is stated, can be seated comfortably, and a thousand persons may be crowded into the place. . . . On account of the presence of the mirrors fewer gas jets are required to light the theatre, but the necessary illumination is furnished by a tasteful chandelier, suspended from the dome, modeled to represent circles of wax candles, and from half a dozen bunches of similar lights placed at intervals in front of the first circle. The boxes, of which there are four, are not permitted to obtrude the stage, but, as we have already stated, like those at Wallack's, are reserved from the body of the house. The proscenium is formed by a slender column, and is considerably higher than wide; indeed, on account of the limited space from wall to wall on the stage, everything had to be built above or below, and for this reason so little of the old-fashioned, entangling machinery has been employed, that there is probably more room in this tiny dramatic parlor than may be found in many a larger concern. A new drop curtain by the veteran Russell Smith . . . represents, within a clear ring broken here and there by a fold of drapery, a pleasant rural prospect of mountain and valley country. The first curtain is a heavy drapery of dark reps, with broad stripes of a lighter ground and figure; at the bottom a deep fringe adds weight and rich effect to this.

87:2. New York *Times*, Jan. 25, 1869.

Daly's Fifth Avenue Theatre burned on January 1, 1873, and the company moved to temporary quarters at 728 Broadway.

88. UNION SQUARE THEATRE
New York City
Opened September 11, 1871

The Union Square Theatre, which was located on the south side of Union Square, was opened on September 11, 1871, as a variety theatre. Its greatness as a playhouse, however, began when A. M. Palmer bought the theater and made it into one of the most respected in New York. The original opening was covered by both the *Tribune* and the *Herald*.

88:1   UNION SQUARE THEATER

Mr. R. W. Butler opened the Union Square Theater last evening. The new establishment succeeds what was formerly known as the Union Place Hotel. Its front doors open upon the Square and the Washington Monument. Its rear wall stands within a few feet of the side wall of Wallack's. It manifestly occupies an excellent position. Its manager offers a various entertainment. The elements of this are burlesque, ballet, comedy, and pantomime. Varieties are commingled, but refinement prevails in their presentation. Upward of fifty performers have been engaged, each of whom is to offer a specialty of some kind. The plan commends itself to approval. The success of one really elegant variety theater—which should, of course, exclude the obnoxious features—would meet a requirement of the time, and serve to keep variety shows out of theaters that ought to adhere, through all sorts of weather, to the legitimate drama. Also it might contribute toward shutting up the concert cellars, and thus abating a public nuisance. The current of affairs at the Union Square Theater is sure to be observed with attention and interest.

There was a considerable crowd in front of the doors, last night, before they were opened; and when at last the throng gained access to the new auditorium, it was speedily filled. There is a cheerful and commodious entrance. The vestibule stretches from beneath spacious porticos, and is brilliantly frescoed, in green and red, and brilliantly lighted. The name of the new theater appears, in letters of fire, above the portal. The interior arrangements have been made with due regard to comfort and beauty of aspect. There is a great deal of gallery room. Seats are afforded for—we should estimate—about 1,200 persons. The prices for admission and seats are arranged according to the scale in use in the first-class theaters of the city—a fact which seems to denote the intention to vie with those theaters in refinement, elegance and worth of performances, and the assemblage seems to enjoy all that was presented. Several familiar faces were once more welcomed—among them Bonfanti, Miss Belle Hewitt, Miss Lizzie Willmore, and Mr. Felix Rogers. It is sincerely hoped that the Union-square Theater may ripen into a worthy institution which it seems designed to be. There is no reason why the thistle-down of entertainment should not be made to float in a clean and pure air.

88:2   THE UNION SQUARE THEATER opened on Monday evening, under the management of Mr. Robert W. Butler. About three months have been occupied in the erection and fitting up of this theatre, which is one of the prettiest and costliest in the city. This house is not large, and probably will not seat more than fifteen hundred people, but it possesses the advantages of allowing every one an excellent view of the stage. Owing to the smallness of the plot upon which the theatre has been erected the house is built very high, and the appearance of the family circle, which rises tier above tier, is exceedingly stiff-backed. But, in spite of this, the house has a compact, comfortable look about it that impresses one

88:1. New York *Tribune,* Sept. 12, 1871.

88:2. New York *Herald,* Sept. 13, 1871.

rather favorably. In point of arrangement and decoration there is nothing to complain of. Not to hurt the susceptibilities of the upper ten thousand, as well as for the sake of convenience and safety, there is a distinct entrance to the family circle on Fourth avenue. The house is divided into parquet, dress and family circles. The seats in the latter resemble the wooden pews of a church arranged in tiers; but when occupied their bareness and somewhat rough appearance is not visible. In the other parts of the house the audience is accommodated with iron chairs painted white, the seats being covered with mareen-colored leather. With a view to afford a pleasant, easy view of the stage to those seated in the back of the dress circle the horseshoe curve of the rail has been made to descend towards the edge with a graceful sweep. Six light and elegant cast iron pillars, with nondescript caps, the whole painted white and decorated with circular gold-fluting, support the dress circle, and are so arranged as to offer very little obstruction to the view. Six similar pillars support the family circle. The rails of the circles and of the lawer stage boxes are covered with crimson velvet, which gives a very rich effect. On either side of the stage boxes are pillars, which have been painted a very faint sky blue and decorated with gold. In front the boxes are ornamented with curious intricate work in the Byzantine style, and delicate blues and pinks are made to harmonize agreeably with the lustrous gilding. Art, too, has been called in to aid in making the Union Theatre a fit temple for the muses. We cannot say that the art is of a very high quality, but in view of the very low state of decorative painting in America, it is not, perhaps, fair to be over fastidious. We must, therefore, accept the will for the deed, and, shutting our eyes to the defects of the frescoes from an art point of view, applaud the taste that imagined this form of decoration, while regretting our want of power to produce something more worthy of the great republic. Notwithstanding the bad figure drawing the effect of the decoration of the ceiling is very pleasant. Immediately over the stage there are two large female figures painted over life size. One, in the act of removing a mask from her face, represents Drama, and the other, with harp, typifies Music. Two other figures, representing Tragedy and Comedy, are painted on the right and left of the dome, but are not visible from the lower part of the house. A number of little Cupids are scattered above the dome, bearing wreaths of laurel, ready to shower them down on the successful actors. Interspersed from distance to distance are a number of curious dragons with the head of a bird rising from suits of Roman armor, painted in black and white. The *fond* of the ceiling is painted in a very light distemper and is artistically relieved by the tasteful introductions of fanciful, intricate work of the Byzantine order, painted in a delicate rose pink and relieved by gold. This part of the decorative work has been excellently done, and displays correct feeling for harmonious color. Festoons of flowers are painted round the large sunlight which occupies the centre of the dome. These garlands are thin and poor, and look flat and stringy. Instead of increasing the beauty of the sunlight in the dome they interfere with its effect. A large sunlight in the dome, supplemented by a number of chandeliers axed in the walls and in front of the house, sheds a soft and brilliant light over the house. Each chandelier has three jets and is surmounted by a little brazen figure. The branches are burnished, and inlaid to represent blue enamel. Immediately over the stage there is an allegorical painting of Apollo in the chariot of the sun, holding in his left hand a lyre. The composition is spirited, but not original; otherwise the execution is poor enough. Four horses are yoked to the chariot, and Apollo stands up nobly, like a child of genius, and drives his snorting steeds through space. He is coming out in the direction of the audience, but his presence in no way seemed to create any alarm. The proscenium is painted to represent a mass of maroon-colored drapery, with deep gold edging. A special order was given for a new drop, and the artist selected for his subject an imaginative Italian scene; but the result does not speak well either for his skill or the richness of his imagination. In a deep valley we see a strange jumbled-up structure, which it is charitable to believe was meant for a castle, but of what style of architecture one would be sadly puzzled to decide. On the right dark mountains loom up in the background, but with as little pretension to hill form as a mountain may have. In the foreground, on the left, some trees occupy a sloping ground, and are somewhat more naturally painted. Owing to the great height of the theatre the decorations on the dome, and even those over the proscenium, are scarcely visible from the parquet. . . .

89. SECOND FIFTH AVENUE THEATRE
New York City
Opened December 3, 1873

Following the destruction by fire of Daly's first Fifth Avenue Theatre on New Year's Day, 1873, his company took up temporary quarters in a theater at 728 Broadway. In the meanwhile, Daly took a lease on a theater on Twenty-eighth Street near Broadway and promptly labeled it "The New Fifth Avenue Theatre" because it indicated a continuity with the old establishment, even though the playhouse was no longer near Fifth Avenue. The venture was not a very successful one for Daly, who lost a lot of money on the theater—so much that he was forced to give up the playhouse in 1878.

The opening was a particularly auspicious one, featuring an address written by Dr. Oliver Wendell Holmes. The play for the evening, however, was a complete failure.

89:1

MR. DALY'S NEW THEATER
OPENING NIGHT AT THE NEW
FIFTH AVENUE—
MR. ALBERRY'S FORTUNE

Mr. Daly's new Fifth Avenue Theater —the third and the most luxurious of all —was dedicated last night, in fog and mist, but under many circumstances both brilliant and auspicious. It was crowded with people, and the assemblage was characterized, in an unusual degree, by sparkling intelligence and fastidious refinement. It presented in adornment, color, light, and stage adjuncts, a scene of rich and impressive magnificence. It is a very handsome theater. The frescoes upon its ceiling, done by Gariboldi, are genuine works of art, beautiful, original, and rarely fine. The prevalent colors upon the walls are French gray, light green, and sea-shell pink. The hangings are of crimson silk. Mirrors upon the walls are framed in walnut and crimson satin. There are twelve proscenium boxes. There are two galleries. The house will seat about 1,500 persons, and will contain about 2,000. The lighting is from above. The drop-curtain is of crimson rep and silk, and parts in the center, so that its folds droop gracefully over each stage picture. The miscellaneous decorations are of black and gold. There are six cosy boxes at the back of the parquette. The floors are softly carpeted; the chairs are comfortable. Above the auditorium there is an aerial dome. Altogether it is a place for pleasure and comfort. It was dedicated with such exercises as are usual upon such occasions. Excellent music, by Mr. Dodworth's band, was the prelude. Miss Fanny Morant then came before the curtain and spoke the first half of an original address, written for this occasion by Dr. Oliver Wendell Holmes. At a certain point the curtain parted, disclosing the entire company—excepting Mr. James Lewis,—ranged upon the stage; and Mr.

89:1. New York *Tribune*, Dec. 4, 1873.

86. Booth's Theatre, New York. Courtesy of The Hoblitzelle Theatre Arts Center, The Humanities Research Center, The University of Texas at Austin.

86. Interior, Booth's Theatre, New York. Engraving, published in *Harper's Weekly* (Feb. 27, 1869). Scene shown is from Booth's production of *Romeo and Juliet,* with Booth as Romeo and Mary McVicker as Juliet. Courtesy of The Hoblitzelle Theatre Arts Library, The Humanities Research Center, The University of Texas at Austin.

88. Union Square Theatre, New York. Published in *The Theatre* (Mar. 1903). Courtesy of The Hoblitzelle Theatre Arts Library, The Humanities Research Center, The University of Texas at Austin.

89. Fifth Avenue Thea-
tre, New York. Engrav-
ing. Courtesy of the
Museum of the City of
New York.

89. Interior, Fifth Avenue Theatre, New York. Photograph by Byron. Courtesy of the Byron Collection, Museum of the City of New York.

Daly came forward and bowed in acknowledgement of the vociferous call and the hearty public plaudits. The other half of Dr. Holmes's address was then spoken —and that with excellent spirit and discretion—by Mr. Frank Hardenburgh. The assembled company, a noble and interesting group, received emphatic recognition and welcome. There were twenty-eight persons upon the stage, conspicuous among whom may be named the stately and courtly Charles Fisher and the quaint and thoughtly William Davidge. Of the roses and lillies of feminine loveliness it is needless to say that there was a perfect garden. After more music came the play. It was a new comedy, by Mr. James Alberry of London, written expressly for this theater. It is in five acts and is entitled "Fortune." It was set upon the stage with unusually rich furniture and fine scenery and costumes. They did not save it: they did not even palliate its hopeless stagnation. There may be something in this world that is heavier than the respectable dullness of a clever man; but, if there be, we know not what it is. Mr. Allberry's "Fortune" is an indescribable mass of incoherent stupidity. We shall not inflict it at second hand upon the readers of this journal. It has caused suffering enough already. Two or three facts about it will here suffice. It apparently tries to deal with the subject which Bulwer treated so well in "Money." In its first act several people prattle and sit down to dinner. In its second act an old lady sits in a garden and says that English proverbs are vulgar, and asks her acquaintances to strike upon a gong. In its third act three girls and two young artists—bad copies of Clive Newcome and J. J. Ridley—gabble together in a studio. These three acts were seen between 8 o'clock and half-past 11; and we could endure no more. There is no need to eat the whole of a cheese in order to find out if it be moldy. Persons who remained till breakfast may have discovered what it was all about. To us it was a weak and tedious imitation of Robertson, without his point, his vigor, his use of contrast, or his delicious semi-sadness of philosophy: and this we think it will be found to be. A spice of epigram occurred here and there, but the wit was mostly harsh and impertinent; and, in the first act, the Joe Miller jokes were so ancient that the band played Auld Lang Syne, in delicate recognition of their antiquity. Among the players Mrs. Gilbert did the best acting and Mr. Harkins got the most enthusiastic reception. Miss Davenport was interesting, droll and clever, in a diluted mixture of *Letitia Hardy* and *Sophia.* Mr. Harkins seemed now and then on the verge of a whimper, in his sentiment; but he suggested a gentle and cheerful nature with fineness of motive and feeling and good effect. Miss Minnie Conway, a charming girl and a promising, though now rough and crude actress, made a first appearance and was creditably successful. The part assigned to Mr. James Lewis, who is ill, was played by Mr. Owen Fawcett. Mr. Daly is too discreet a manager to tie his fortune for very long to that of Mr. Alberry. . . .

90. NEW PARK THEATRE
New York City
Opened April 13, 1874

This playhouse, which had a rather short life, was built expressly for the very popular playwright, Dion Boucicault, but difficulties arose and Boucicault severed his connections with the management of the theater. The opening finally took place on April 13, 1874, after many postponements, with the famous French actor Charles Fechter playing his last stage role and serving as manager of the company. The play was *Love's Penance,* which had been adapted by Fechter from a French work.

Later, in 1876, Henry E. Abbey took over the management of the theater, and the name was changed to Abbey's New Park Theatre. He was very successful and remained in charge until 1882, when the theater burned.

The following opening-night review is from the New York *Times:*

90:1
THE NEW PARK THEATRE
OPENING NIGHT—MR. FECHTER
IN "LOVE'S PENANCE."

After many delays, more than one postponement, and much anxiety, Mr. (William) Stuart's Park Theatre was thrown open to the public on Monday night. As might be supposed, an occasion like this called out an exceptional audience. The theatre was filled not only by the representatives from the fashionable world, such as usually make a "first night" attractive, and that mixed assemblage found within the walls of most theatres, but members of the literary and artistic and even political worlds were to be seen, and made altogether one of the most notable gatherings we have ever beheld in a place of public amusement. So much has already been written about the Park Theatre in these columns that little is left to be said at this moment. The general appearance of its interior is not likely to impress the auditor immediately. There is an absence of bright colors, of gorgeous upholstery, and elaborate fresco such as we are little accustomed to in our City theatres. Nothing could be more simple and, at the same time, so chaste as the design of the auditorium. The softest pink, with white and gray prevail throughout. Where there is any gilding it it done with a sparing and tasteful hand. The proscenium arch is quite a revelation in its simplicity and beauty, and the few bits of color, as in the design on the ceiling, the drapery of the boxes, and the charmingly painted drop-curtain, are welcome to the eye without offending any sense of symmetry or harmony. Although we have just reason to be proud of our New-York theatres, the Park Theatre, in this modesty of decoration, offers an example we should like to see followed. Theatrical frescoers and upholsterers too often forget that the gorgeousness of the auditoriums of most of our theatres almost invariably detracts from, and in some cases, spoils, the general effect of the spectacular efforts on the stage. While the style of decoration adopted here is an agreeable reform upon this too general error, it must not be supposed that any tameness or lack of what is essential in the upholstery of the theatre is visible. On the contrary, this department was, we understand, placed in charge of Messrs. Lord & Taylor, and the result was, the appointments, both of the auditorium and the stage, were admirable. The unfortunate orchestra, which once proudly reared its many heads above the stage, is in the Park Theatre sunk completely out of sight. Not only this, but the time-honored orchestral-box is dispensed with, and, from an insignificant hole in the stage, visible to the dress circle and gallery only, comes all the music, whether it be to while away the tedious waits or to lead up the pathetic and striking situations. This is a great innovation, but one which we think no one will quarrel with, except, perhaps, the musicians in hot weather.

The drama chosen by Mr. Stuart with which to open his theatre, is one of the best specimens of superior French melodrama we can remember. On the English stage it might be called a domestic drama, but the almost tragic strength of its theme lifts it beyond this class of play. The story upon which "Love's Penance" is founded was the work of Count D'Avrigay, and some years ago furnished M. D'Ennery with the subject of his very successful play of "Le Medecin des Enfants." Mr. Fechter's adaptation of the very touching story, while differing from "Le Medecin des Enfants" in many material points, is quite as strong as that drama. It is written in smooth, flowing English, and what little eloquence there is in the dialogue comes, happily, from its comparative brevity, the determination of each speaker to avoid circumlocution, and the, to us,

90:1. New York *Times,* Apr. 15, 1874.

welcome avoidance of the far-fetched metaphor with which this sort of play is usually encumbered. There is no underplot to the story, and the incidents seem briefly thus: About the year 1785, in provincial France, a young lady was forced into a marriage *"de convenance,"* with a *Count Rocklane,* a man very much her senior. A few weeks after the bridal, the *Count* was sent abroad by his Government, in command of a scientific expedition. Before the young lady has been three years a wife she is officially informed of her husband's death. During his absence she had made the acquaintance of one *Karl,* a young medical student. A strong attachment springs up between the two young people, but bound as they are by ties of honor, each remains silent on the subject. When the young lady becomes a widow, *Karl* reveals his love, and after mourning for a year, she accepts him, and they are united. Before the first year of her second marriage had expired, the dreadful news reaches the young couple that the *Count Rocklane* is alive and is on the way home. In this dilemma they take refuge in flight, and settle in an obscure village on the Swiss frontier, where we find them as the prologue to the drama opens. The curtain rises on the interior of the village inn, and we find *Dr. Karl* prescribing for the sick gratis, and feeding the poor from his own hands, thereby gaining great popularity from the disinterested and enthusiastic peasants. *Shambear,* (Mr. *Lamb,*) accompanied by a mysterious traveler, enters shortly after the rising of the curtain. *Shambear* has an interview with *Dr. Karl,* (Mr. Fechter,) from which we learn the incidents already narrated, and also that the doctor's wife, *Clarisse,* (Miss Geraldine Stuart,) is the mother of a daughter, now two years old, and that the happiness of the pair is only interrupted by fears of the *Count's* discovery of their retreat. *Shambear,* it seems, has been seeking *Karl,* at the request of *Karl's* mother, and now urges

him to return home. *Clarisse* at this moment enters and seconds *Shambear's* entreaties. It is at length decided that they shall all go, and to accomplish this *Shambear* purchases a wagon in which he places the child. When the preparations are all completed and the party is on the point of leaving, the mysterious traveler enters, reveals himself as *Count Rocklane,* (Mr. Studley,) informs the bewildered pair that their child has just been driven to his home, and commanded *Clarisse* to follow him. A very powerful scene ensues, in which *Rocklane* informs *Karl* that by the laws of France the child is his, that he means to preserve the honor of his name untarnished, and to this end the real parentage of the child will always be kept secret. The emotion and excitement are too much for *Clarisse,* and she falls dying on the floor as the stern *Count* retires. *Karl* leaves the pursuit of his child to save his wife. She dies in his arms as the curtain descends upon the prologue. After a lapse of fifteen years the drama proper opens at the chateau of *Count Rocklane,* where we find the child of the prologue grown into a girl of seventeen, living as the *Count's* daughter and under the guardianship of *Shambear.* The *Count* is supposed to have seen her but thrict during these fifteen years, and *Clara,* as she is called, rather fears than loves him. We also here make the acquaintance of *Frank Manbe,* (Mr. Dalton,) a young artist, who has painted *Clara's* portrait as a birthday present. Of course, the artist is in love with *Clara,* and the love is reciprocal. *Old Shambear* is anxious to see them wedded, but his amiable design is frustrated by the arrival of the *Count,* who informs him that he has already disposed of *Clara's* hand to a noble *Marquis.* This complication is heightened by the appearance of *Karl,* under the name of *Dr. Hartreck,* who has been invited by *Frank Manbe* to the village to prescribe for some of *Clara's* little patients. He is left alone with *Clara,* without in the least suspecting her identity, when her voice, her portrait on the table, and the appearance of *Old Shambear* reveal it to him. The *Count* enters and orders him to quit the house. He refuses, and the act terminates with a very strong situation. The second act shows us the fruitless efforts of the *Doctor* to gain the *Count's* consent to *Clara's* marriage with the young artist. The *Count* is obdurate, and when *Frank* enters and asks the hand of *Clara,* he looks upon his conduct and that of the *Doctor* as a scheme. A violent scene ensues. The *Count* insults *Frank,* who challenges him. The *Doctor* interposes, urging that *Frank's* life belongs to *Clara.* He will fight for him, whereupon he strikes the *Count,* and both rush off the stage. A report of pistols is heard. The *Count* returns with his discharged weapon in his hand: to find *Clara* lying senseless on the ground, and the curtain falls. The last act is very brief. *Clara* is supposed to be dead, and the *Count* is in a state of deep penitence. The *Doctor* has been mortally wounded, and comes into the room to take a last farewell of his child, supposing she is still alive. The girl's body, ready for interment lies upon the bed, and her appearance is the first intimation he receives of her supposed death. His medical skill, however, informs him that she is not dead. He is himself dying, and he devotes his last moments to saving his child, without revealing his relationship, and to extracting from the *Count* his promise to unite Clara with her lover. All this being accomplished, the curtain falls, for the last time, upon the two groups. *Clara* on her couch, with her future husband by her side, the *Count* and *Shambear* concealing the dead body of the heroic and long-suffering *Doctor,* lest it might darken the happiness of her for whom such sacrifices have been made.

The story, as we have intimated, is told in a coherent and simple manner. It furnished little opportunity for the display of good acting, except upon the part of Mr.

Fechter. On his shoulders fell the burden of the piece, and with the public's knowledge of Mr. Fechter's great powers, it is unnecessary to say that upon few actors could such a responsibility lie more gracefully. . . . Despite the long waits and the few unavoidable hitches of a first night, "Love's Penance" may be safely pronounced a success and the opening of Mr. Stuart's treatre one of the most gratifying events of this exceedingly eventful theatrical season.

91. DALY'S THEATRE
New York City
Opened September 17, 1879

Augustin Daly, who had lost his Fifth Avenue Theatre because of financial difficulties and later, in 1877, announced his retirement, reentered the theatrical scene in 1879. He bought, and completely remodeled, the old Broadway Theatre at Broadway and Thirty-ninth Street, renamed the house Daly's Theatre, and started the most distinguished era of his career as a theatrical manager. With the opening of the playhouse a new and important chapter was begun in the history of the New York theater.

The newspaper accounts of the opening are of particular interest.

91:1   DALY'S THEATRE

The proceedings of Mr. Augustin Daly are always interesting—for Mr. Daly is one of those alert and agile spirits that are never content with themselves, and never at ease, except it be when in some way or another, they are troubling the waters of public attention. This truth was long ago illustrated by Mr. Daly, in his management of his several Fifth Avenue Theatres, and more recently by his sudden though transitory apparition astride of the washing-tubs in "The Assomoir." He has now opened a new treatre. It bears his own name, and it stands on the site

91:1. New York *Tribune,* Sept. 19, 1879.

90. New Park Theatre, New York. Courtesy of The Hoblitzelle Theatre Arts Library, The Humanities Research Center, The University of Texas at Austin.

90. Interior, New Park Theatre, New York. Engraving by "CFR." Courtesy of The Hoblitzelle Theatre Arts Library, The Humanities Research Center, The University of Texas at Austin.

91. Interior, Augustin Daly's Theatre, New York. Engraving. Courtesy of the Cooper-Hewitt Museum of Decorative Arts and Design, Smithsonian Institution.

91. Augustin Daly's Theatre, New York, ca. 1894. Courtesy of the J. Clarence Davies Collection, Museum of the City of New York.

where once the intrepid Colonel Lilliendahl led the hippopotamus, while the gentle George Wood frowned upon the expensive tiger. In other words, what was once Wood's Museum, and then became Broadway, is now Daly's Theatre; and last night it was opened. The house has ben greatly changed, and the changes are greatly for the better. It is, indeed, a very handsome theatre—and this, notwithstanding that the decoration of it is, just a little, both incongruous and sombre. The seats are comfortable. The light falls from above and behind. The walls gleam with dark gold and various tints of gray. Brasses appear in various spots, relieved against red velvet. The ceiling is ribbed and daintily painted. The proscenium is a golden band. The carpets are soft and delicate. The entrance is imposing with Ionic pillars, and the porches and halls are gay with painted glass and oriental emblems. There has, evidently, been a mixture of tastes, and the result is complex; yet it pleases. The stage, likewise, seems to be well appointed. There was not a large attendance, last night, but the assemblage included many representative persons, and its demeanor was that of kindly good-will. . . .

91:2   DALY'S THEATRE

Mr. Daly's new theatre was formally opened last evening, and its novel, yet rich and tasteful, decorations were freely admired. Such an attractive house should become, under wise management, one of the favorite resorts in our City. Mr. Daly has had vast experience; he has done much for which he will be gratefully remembered, and he has also done much to injure the drama and the stage; but his past mistakes should be spurs to his present ambition, and now that he has his opportunity, we hope that he will make the most of it. The company which he has gathered about him, so far as can be

91:2. New York *Times,* Sept. 18, 1879.

judged, embraces many elements of talent and strength, and youth figures in it prominently. Bright faces and fresh voices there were in abundance last night on Mr. Daly's stage. It is, therefore, unfortunate that the performance with which the new theatre opened was, to speak plainly, most unworthy of praise. This performance consisted of two pieces, both new, one a little comedietta entitled "Love's Young Dream," by Mr. Joseph Francis, and the other a "farcical comedy, in three acts, by an American writer residing abroad," and called "Newport"—a title which naturally suggests the popular "Saratoga," one of Mr. Daly's Fifth-Avenue successes. The first piece, "Love's Young Dream," is a rather pretty story, but it is written without the least spark of wit or humor. It is, besides, much too long. However, it is neatly acted by Messrs. Charles Fisher, George Parkes, Henry Lacy, E. P. Wilkes, and Misses Ada Rehan and May Fielding. The latter is new to the stage, and will prove, we think, an interesting member of Mr. Daly's company; she has one of these blonde, Madonna-like faces which seem to indicate a nature full of softness and gentleness. Her face does not belie her actions, for these are singularly gentle and graceful—while her voice is pure music. She is a good singer, and is evidently meant to occupy a leading place as vocalist. Of the second piece on the programme, "Newport," Mr. Daly announced that it was the work of "an American writer residing abroad." This is only partially true, since it is based upon a French farce, "Niniche." Perhaps the author of "Surf" may aspire in this case to the honor of the adapter. "Niniche" has already been played in England and in Boston under the name of "Boulogne." Its aim is not to depict the intrigues and eccentricities, not to speak of the little peccadiloes and immoralities of life by the sad sea waves. "Newport" is proper enough, however, as proper, indeed, as it is stupid—and this is saying a great deal. There are bright suggestions in it, which become apparent at rare intervals, but they are the sputterings of a candle set in a draught. It is full of incidents, so full of them that one is at a loss to account for their being; each incident seems to be a little play by itself, and one's patience is exhausted before its relationship is discovered. In fact, we have seldom seen a more startling specimen of utterly crude and illogical construction than this unfortunate "Newport." Its characters, we may add, are numerous, but, as a rule, they seem to know as little of their own actions as the author who evolved them did. They are merely absurd, without being in the least amusing. Even the grace, beauty and sparkle of Miss Catherine Lewis—a pleasing singer and a bright actress—failed to infuse life into this laborious structure of triviality. Miss Lewis rendered several songs in a piquant style, but only one of these, "Crutch and Toothpick," was really gay. Mr. Charles Leclercq, Mr. Davidge, Mr. Hart Conway, Mr. George Parkes, Mrs. Poole, and other excellent actors, not to speak of a small host of pretty girls, also appeared in the piece, and did their best to make it interesting, but the effort was useless. How Mr. Daly came to produce anything quite so bad as "Newport," it is hard to understand. Perhaps, however, in his eagerness to introduce his new plans for a genuine vaudeville theatre, he overshot the mark: be this as it may, he should recognize his mistake without delay, and correct it. He possesses too much good material in his company to squander it without profit. It is announced, we may add, that a series of midweek afternoon performances will be given at this theatre, commencing on Oct. 1, which will be devoted to dramas already favorably known. "Divorce" will be the first of this series.

After a rather slow start with this first bill of plays, Daly's Theatre became known as the best and most popular theater in New York for the next twenty years, until Mr. Daly's death in 1899. After that time the theater was used for variety, burlesque, and motion pictures until it was torn down in 1920. At the time of its demise, the New York *Times* had a special feature article on the playhouse.

91:3   THE PASSING OF DALY'S

So Daly's also is to be demolished, giving place to a steel construction office building. Lovers of the theatre had better not go to see it. Its mid-century brick walls and mansard roof are inescapably ugly. The spacious entrance, once thronged with beauty, the wit and social grace of Manhatten, is now plastered with crude posters advertising a neighboring vaudeville and moving-picture house. Nothing is so dingy, so heart-breaking to the sentimentalist, as quondam glory in decay. Long decades were needed to bring even Sheraton and Chippendale into their own again. All that remains of the real Daly's is a distant memory that still fondly lingers but eventually must pass.

The era of DOUGLAS and MARY will doubtless never realize how inferior it is in opportunity to the era of ADA and JOHN. A generation inured to the dimpling knees of the Winter Garden would be amazed if it could know the mad thrill which swept the youth of the city when Miss REHAN appeared in satin knee breeches in "The Country Girl"—that romping comedy which the magic of AUGUSTIN DALY Victorianized from the Restoration naughtiness of Wycherley's "Country Wife." But the greater, the more incommunicable marvel lies in the fact that dramatic art was then a mystery of the spoken word. Every wrinkle in those bewitching sky blue small-clothes is indelibly stamped in memory, but they still stand out less vividly than the sparkling with a verve of the dialogue, the abounding nature and vivacity of every character and situation in the play. It is only those who have known the richness

91:3. New York *Times*, Aug. 1, 1920.

and variety of spoken comedy at its best who really suffer from the narrow range and stereotyped dullness of modern character and plot.

Then there was the Shakespearean repertory. Miss REHAN'S Viola and Rosalind were perhaps a trifle hoydenish—lacking in the delicate, peachlike bloom and poignant tenderness of the true Shakespearean girlhood; but what a rush of sheer spirit, what an overflowing of divinely potent comedy! Her Kate the Shrew was a towering monument of rage and scorn, lifting the boisterous Elizabethan action to the plane of character comedy, yet always finely emphasizing the essential farce of the situation. Her Portia in its serious moments, as in the "quality of mercy" speech, had a cathedral authority, a majesty of spirit, that suggested possibilities of tragic acting destined never to be explored. In the makeup of his companies, AUGNSTIN DALY was always a feminist and essentially an exploiter of what was beginning to be denounced as the "star"; yet others of his household were no less artists and comedians. Mrs. GILBERT and JAMES LEWIS, the brothers HOLLAND, and a score of others, were perfection itself. In OTIS SKINNER and JOHN DREW the value of the old stock company training is still manifest for those who have eyes to see.

Art at Daly's was Victorian in the best sense of the word, as in the second best. During a brief stay in the company MAY IRWIN had the part of a young housewife who smelled the burning of fish in her drawing room and "exited" to the kitchen. In the rehearsal, Miss IRWIN gave one sniff, threw up her hands and bolted through the door. The horrified Mr. DALY led her "down centre" and told her to sniff more gently. Then he led her to the white marble Vestal Virgin pillared in one corner and to the Rogers Group that dispensed native humor in another, bidding her to sniff in each place. Then he led her to the register (an antique de-

vice well known to archaeologists), where he told her to sniff mightily if she must, but not to forget how a gentlewoman quits her drawing room. Miss IRWIN sniffed mightly, as the story goes, but not at the register. "If I smelled my dinner burning," said the unterrified modernist to the Victorian genius loci, "do you suppose I'd have to consult the Rogers Group to find out it was the kitchen?" Art in these latter days may be many things, but it is no longer deliberate, measured and canonical.

In his Shakespeare productions DALY followed the Victorian scenic tradition as unhesitatingly as did HENRY IRVING and BEERBOHM TREE in London. His greatest triumph was "A Midsummer Night's Dream," in the staging of which in 1888 he used to the full the novelty of electric lighting. In a monograph on the several productions of the play on the New York stage, Professor G. C. ODELL of Columbia gives an admirably detailed record of the production and sets down his own impressions of it in a vein of lyric fondness. In the way of scenic production it was, indeed, as perfect as it was in the acting. This result was almost certainly due, however, to the fact that the play happens to lend itself to pictorial investiture with a minimum of "cutting" the lines and transposing the scenes to fit the scenery. When DALY applied the same method to "The Tempest," the result was disaster. Prospero's magic, for a ready belief in which SHAKESPEARE trusted largely to the magic of his lines and his characterizations, became ridiculous when executed by carpenter, mechanician and scene painter. The two passages in which Shakespeare used mechanical effects, Caliban's "rock" and the melting of Prospero's Masque "into thin air" went hopelessly wrong—probably because the Victorians knew less than nothing of the resources and methods of the Elizabethan stage. Added to this, essential passages of the text were cut and whole scenes transposed, so that the force of the narrative was lost and the entire play became unintelligible. After thirteen performances the production gave way to a musical comedy from London.

Within the sphere of his age, however, DALY was an artist of the first order, and his equal has never since appeared. Seldom in any age has a playhouse been devoted more loyally to the spirit of wholesome beauty and the flush, warm splendor of romantic comedy. It is only a little over twenty years since he last faced the applause of an audience. He stood erect and gravely smiling, clad in a black sack coat that showed a streak of dust at the shoulder—doubtless the result of lending a hand to the scene shifters.

92. MADISON SQUARE THEATRE
New York City
Opened February 4, 1880

One of the most publicized theatrical events of 1880 was the opening of the Madison Square Theatre under the management of Steele MacKaye. The playhouse on West Twenty-fourth St. was filled with new inventions of MacKaye, including a double stage, which permitted a complete change of scenes in just seconds. Other inventions controlled the heating and ventilation of the building. The dramatic critic for the *Spirit of the Times* called it "the most exquisite theater in the world."

The New York *Dramatic Mirror* critic wrote of the theater:

92:1   MADISON SQUARE THEATRE
THE UNION OF THE CHURCH, THE STAGE,
AND J. STEELE MACKAYE.

The Madison Square Theatre is ready for its reopening, under the management of Mr. J. Steele MacKaye, and our readers are already familiar with the elevator stage, the ventilated seats, the orchestra over the proscenium, and the other devices and inventions which are to render the thea-

92:1. New York *Dramatic Mirror*, Jan. 31, 1880.

tre unique. But the most peculiar feature of the new theatre is the fact that the Messrs. Mallory, a pious firm of religious persons who issue Christian periodicals, are the capitalists who back the enterprise and engage Mr. MacKaye upon a salary to conduct it for them. These gentlemen believe, not only that a good theatre is a profitable speculation, financially, but that it is an important moral factor, and may be run in connection with the church and their church papers, so as to be mutually advantageous. Upon both of these points, it need hardly be said, we thoroughly agree with the Messrs. Mallory. They have selected and engaged a very strong company; they have poured out their money like princes to enable Mr. MacKaye to realize his ideas, and we hope that they will meet with a fair field and plenty of favor when it comes to be judged by the critics and the public.

J. Steele MacKaye has had a remarkable record, which we do not care to exploit at present; but it is not until recently that he has displayed that art of attending to his own business which marks the competent manager. When he first took charge of the Madison Square Theatre, he went astray in a manner which delighted his enemies and alarmed his friends. Allying himself with the worst and most contemptible clique of ruffianly blackmailers that ever befouled the press of New York, he was praised and petted in their paper, for which he went so far as to promise a series of articles upon his Delsartean system. Thoroughly in the hands of these villains, he engaged as his leading actress an almost unknown amateur, who at that time was the mistress of one or more of the gang. But his disenchantment came quickly and was quite severe. Alfa Merrill, dragged into court by her outraged husband as an adulteress, was convicted of the crime in connection with Byrne the Blackguard, one of the lowest and foulest of the horrible nest of vipers, and Mr. MacKaye was forced to dismiss her from his company. Thereupon, the very columns that used to reek with his praise, were loaded with abuse of himself and his projects, and all the confidential information which he had imparted to the gang was vomited forth to shock the prejudices of his pious backers. We have reason to believe that Mr. MacKaye repented sincerely and in tears of the filthy affiliations that had cost him so dearly. The fact that the Messrs. Mallory restored him to their confidence, and permitted the theatre to proceed, is a proof that his repentence was not a mere form.

Since then the Madison Square project has thrived upon the attacks of the degraded gang that formerly praised it, and the Messrs. Mallory, who are shrewd business men as well as good Christians, have discovered that the enmity of the wicked is the best guarantee of the favor of the public. That these gentlemen are new to the theatrical business is evident; but men of their character are always welcome to the profession, and the money they have lost learning the details of the business is not too high a price to pay for the privilege of dispensing with the ordinary course of apprenticeship. For instance several actors and actresses have been under salary for many months, awaiting the opening of the new theatre, and a large traveling company has been sent about the country, often at a loss, rehearsing the Iron Will, by Mr. MacKaye, which is to form, under another title, one of the principal performances of the season at the new house. These proceedings look like a waste of money, and the Messrs. could have saved many hundreds of dollars by consulting an experienced theatrical agent, who would have placed the actors and actresses so that they would not have been a drag on the treasury, and would yet have been ready for duty when the theatre was ready to open. But money lost in preparation and rehearsals is saved to the profession, and indirectly benefits the public, and we should rather applaud the Messrs. Mallory for their pluck and liberality than laugh at them for their mistakes and inexperience.

The company engaged for the Madison Square Theatre is remarkably strong, and is in some respects superior to any outside the Union Square Theatre. Its principal members are:

Rose Coghlan	C. W. Couldock
Effie Ellsler	Thomas Whiffen
Gabrielle Du Sauld	Dominick Murray
Cecile Rush	Eben Plympton
Blanche Galton	B. T. Ringold
Agnes Loring	Edward Coleman
Annie Ellisler	Frank Weston
Josephine Craig	Richard Brennan
Ada Gilman	J. Barton

For such a company it will be easy to find good plays that will draw even without the assistance of the patent elevator stage. But our public novelties, and there will be a rush to see the stage that works up and down, and "the area of repose," and all the other nicknackeries which Mr. McKaye has provided to tantalize theatregoers. The real drawing power of the stage, however, is not the way it works up and down, but what the manager puts on it, and should Mr. MacKaye's own plays fail to please the public, he has, with the strong company engaged, an immense repertoire of old and new pieces from which to select. Bartley Campbell has written too many plays for Effie Ellsler not to have a new part ready for her in his teeming brain; and, from Shakespeare to Tom Robertson, there are plenty of pieces which such an aggregation of talent as Rose Coghlan, C. W. Couldock, Miss Du Sauld, Dominick Murray and Mr. and Mrs. Tom Whiffen could not make profitable to the management.

Good luck, then, to the new theatre, the new company and the new management! We do not place much dependence of the new-fangled notions which Mr. MacKaye has introduced, except as a

213

means of attracting public attention to the enterprise; but we rest our calculations upon the old solid ground company, all able and experienced enough to go anywhere and play anything. Mr. MacKaye is erratic and may lead the whole company astray by some of his strange whims and caprices; but he has had a bitter lesson, and as his wanderings are the only dangers to be feared, we presume that the Messrs. Mallory will try to keep a strict guard upon him and hold him steadily to his work. Rehearsals have been conducted at the theatre during the past week, and the public may be assured of a complete performance whenever Mr. MacKaye raises the drop-curtain. There is room for another stock theatre in New York since Wallack's is soon to be given over to stars again, and the Union Square and Daly's will be left alone in the field. We would ask for the new house an unprejudiced judgment; but at present the prejudice seems to be altogther in its favor, since no theatrical event for many years has so excited the fashionable circles of New York as the announcement that the Madison Square Theatre is at last ready for its opening performances next week.

The principles of the new stage were explained in an article appearing in *Scientific American*.

92:2   MOVABLE THEATRE STAGES.

For a few years back, or since Richard Wagner first brought out the Niebelungenlied at Bayreuth, the tendency in first class theaters and opera houses has been to greater elaboration of the scenic details, the more vivid representation of the surroundings connected with the plot of the play or opera. It was on this account that a temple was specially built in which to present the best illustration of the "music of the future." Thus also has Mr. Henry Irving obtained phenomenal success in

92:2. "Moveable Theatre Stages," *Scientific American*, 50:207 (Apr. 5, 1884).

England, and won great favor here, by the hard study and unstinted labor he gives to the perfecting of the scenery and stage equipments for the setting of his plays. Yet in all of the additional work now demanded of stage managers, there has been but little aid extended by inventors, and but few theater appliances patented. The illustration we herewith present, however, affords a view of an improvement practically tested at the Madison Square Theater in this city, which has not thus far been put in operation in any other theater, and which would seem to afford every facility for the elaborate setting and changing of scenes without necessitating long "waits" on the part of the audience.

Our illustration affords a view of two theatrical sages, one above another, to be moved up and down as an elevator car is operated in a high building, and so that either one of them can easily and quickly be at any time brought to the proper level for acting thereon in front of the auditorium. The shaft through which this huge elevator moves up and down reaches 114 feet from the roof to the bottom of the cellar below, and the stages so moved up in a compact, two-floored structure of timber strapped with iron, knitted together by truss beams above and below, and substantially bound by tie and tension rods. The whole makes a structure fifty-five feet high, twenty-two feet wide, and thirty-one feet deep, weighing, as stated by the management, forty-eight tons, and having a vertical movement of 25 feet 2 inches at each change.

This immense contrivance is suspended at each corner by two steel cables, each of which would be capable of sustaining far more than the whole load, and these cables pass upward over sheaves or pulleys set at different angles, thence downward to a saddle, to which all are connected. Connected to this saddle is a hoisting drum, by the rotation of which the stages are raised and lowered. Practically, only forty seconds are required to raise or lower a stage into position, and four men at the winch are as much as ever required. This movement is thus easily effected, without sound, jar, or vibration, from the nice balancing of the stage and its weight with counterweights, which are suspended from the saddle to which the cables supporting the weight of the stages are attached.

In combination with each of these movable stages are borders and border lights arranged to throw light down upon the stage, and so connected with flexible gas tubes as to be readily turned on and off; each stage has its trap floor, with traps and guides and windlasses for raising the traps—the space for this, and for operating the windlass under the top stage, being about six feet. Our illustration shows that, while the play is proceeding before the audience, another scene is being arranged by the assistants on the upper stage, to be followed, when this is lowered, by similar prepreparations for the succeeding scene, should this be necessary, on the stage that will then be twenty-five feet below.

Independent of the peculiarity of the movable stages, there were many innovations on former practices in the fitting up of this, one of the pleasantest of New York's theaters, some four years ago. Fresh air is forced over steam radiators and through pipes to every part of the auditorium, or it is cooled and sent through the same pipes in the summer, but under such a system that it can conveniently at any time be shut off from any section; there is also a ventilating shaft in the roof through which the vitiated air is carried off, so that the whole atmosphere of the house is renewed, it is claimed, six times in every hour [The whole matter of the ventilation of the Madison Square Theater was fully explained, with illustration in SCIENTIFIC AMERICAN SUPPLEMENT, No. 250.] Another noticeable feature is

that the orchestra, instead of occupying the usual position just below and in front of the stage, is placed in a balcony at the top, just over the stage opening, in the proscenium arch, thus keeping the view of the stage from the parquette unobstructed.

Not a little fun was made of Mr. Steele MacKaye, in 1879, when he obtained his patent for and proposed to build the first movable stage, as here represented. The details of Mr. MacKaye's patent were not as completely worked out, although the idea was there, as they subsequently were by Mr. Nelson Waldron, the sage machinist, who elaborated the system and obtained a subsequent patent therefor, under which these movable stages have since been so successfully and satisfactorily operated at the Madison Square Theater.

The architecture of this theater, by Messrs. Kimball and Wisedell, and the decoration, by Mr. Louis C. Tiffany and Mrs. Wheeler, have received wide and deservedly high praise; many features were novelties but there was nothing inappropriate or commonplace.

The following review of the opening is from the New York *Times*:

92:3   THE MADISON-SQUARE THEATRE.
Last evening the above-mentioned theatre opened under all the conceivable circumstances likely to put an audience in good humor with itself and with the drama which was to be presented. The announcements which Mr. MacKaye, after long and arduous labor, had made with regard to the structure and appointments of the theatre were found to be literally truthful. Originality of taste and fancy was particularly manifest in the decoration of the auditorium, which, having previously been described in this journal need not be now dwelt upon at great length. The prevailing sombre hue was sufficiently relieved

92:3. New York *Times,* Feb. 6, 1880.

by bright-colored draperies, which repeated themselves infinitely in opposite mirrors, that seemed also to reflect the vivacious occupants of the private boxes. A curtain bearing some resemblance to an idealized blanket, met the eye's first glance at the stage; but the object of this excessive plainness was revealed when the drapery was raised and brought to view a veil of the most delicate colors most harmoniously blended. The orchestra occupied their little gallery above the stage, and were as carefully secluded as Oriental houris, and the double stage performed its necromantic movement faithfully within the moments advertised by the management.

This brief reference is due to the successful pains which Mr. MacKay has taken to be both original and artistic. The result is that he has an exquisite little theatre, which in appearance and mechanical contrivances is unique in New-York. In regard to the more important matter of the play, it is impossible to continue in this complimentary strain, although we should be glad to do so should the facts permit. "Hazel Kirke" is identical with "An Iron Will," written by Mr. MacKaye and performed for several months in the United States. Its merits are not so great either in quantity or quality as to demand long discussion. It is the story of a girl who was apparently entrapped by a nobleman into a Scotch marriage on English soil, who afterward fled from him to her own home upon his supposed villainy being revealed to her by her mother, and who, after suffering much from complicated disaster, attempted suicide, and was rescued by the slandered man, who, it appears, had been legitimately married to her according to his intention and supposition. This story gives rise to several situations which have a certain degree of pathos and power, but which would have had more could they have been accepted as possible. . . .

93. BIJOU OPERA HOUSE
New York City
Opened March 31, 1880

This playhouse was originally built as a variety house called the Brighton Theatre and opened on August 26, 1878. It was on Broadway between Thirtieth and Thirty-first streets and was one of those houses that changed managements and names frequently. After several of these changes the management was assumed by two men, Charles E. Ford and John A. McCaull, who changed the name to the Bijou Opera House and made it into a respectable theater.

A review of the new theater and its opening night appeared in the New York *Tribune:*

93:1   THE BIJOU OPERA HOUSE

This charming little theatre, lately known as the Broadway Opera House, was opened last evening in the presence of a large, brilliant and sympathetic audience, with the production of two operettas, one by Frank Clay, the other by Alfred Cellier, who has become known to this public during the past season as the conductor of the "Pirates of Penzanze" company at the Fifth Avenue Theatre. No other place of public amusement in this city has gone through greater vicissitudes than this. By turns an eating-house, a billiard-room, a concert hall, and a variety theatre, it has at last become the home of "Opera di Camera," a musical and dramatic entertainment of the kind that Mr. and Mrs. German Reed long ago made so perfect in London. The little theatre has been completely renovated. It has been decorated lavishly, yet in the most admirable taste, and in all its appointments is one of the most complete and pleasantest of the small theatres in the city. "Ages Ago," by Gilbert and Clay, which opened the performance, was given here several years ago in private by a company of amateurs. The story is a feeble one, and Mr.

93:1. New York *Tribune,* Apr. 1, 1880.

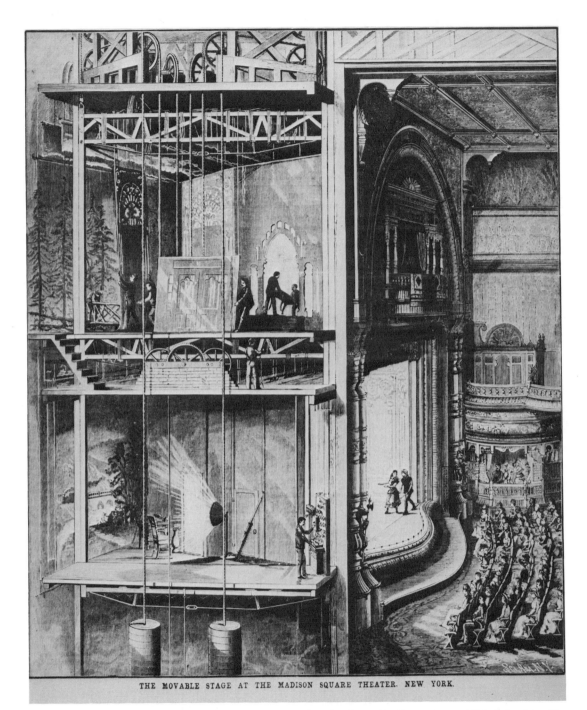

THE MOVABLE STAGE AT THE MADISON SQUARE THEATER. NEW YORK.

92. Double stage, Madison Square Theatre, New York, 1884. Engraving, published in *Scientific American* (Apr. 5, 1884). Courtesy of the Museum of the City of New York.

93. Bijou Opera House, New York. Courtesy of The Hoblitzelle Theatre Arts Library, The Humanities Research Center, The University of Texas at Austin.

94. New Wallack's Theatre, New York, 1890. Courtesy of The Hoblitzelle Theatre Arts Library, The Humanities Research Center, The University of Texas at Austin.

Clay has set the libretto to some very excellent music. It is smooth and graceful, not vigorous nor of the sort that the town will be whistling in a week, but good and musicianlike, and having, oddly enough, here and there in the lovelier numbers, a strong flavor of Offenbach. One song, indeed, might have come bodily out of "Orphée aux Enfers." The performance was not quite smooth, and though the piece was kindly received, it will create a much better impression when the singers shall have learned their parts. Mr. Cellier's piece, "Charity Begins at Home," is shorter than Mr. Clay's, and much more jolly. It is simply a rollicking piece of nonsense, containing some extremely pretty music, and giving an opportunity for some rather clever acting. Mr. Cellier's songs and concerted pieces are all bright, sparkling and original, and they were received with great favor. Almost every number was encored, and a dainty little quartette, "Twinkle, Twinkle, Little Star," had to be repeated three times. The singers, among whom Miss Barton and Mr. Courtney deserve especial praise, seemed to be much more familiar with this work than with the other, and it went off smoothly and with spirit. It received and deserved an unquestionable success. The season at the Bijou Opera House opened with the most favorable prospects, and it is to be hoped that this pure, refined and delicate entertainment will meet with the support that it deserves.

94. NEW WALLACK'S THEATRE
New York City
Opened January 4, 1882

The second Wallack's Theatre had been built in 1861, and from the early 1870s began to feel stiff competition from Booth's and Daly's. The playhouse was rather dated in its accommodations, and even the redecoration in 1880 failed to answer the problem completely. In 1881 Lester Wallack closed the theater known as Wallack's (although the playhouse continued under the name of the Star Theatre), and concentrated on a new, magnificent theater at Broadway and Thirtieth Street.

The New York *Times* was particularly enthusiastic about the new playhouse and reviewed briefly the history of Wallack's as an institution of the New York theater.

94:1   A NOTABLE FIRST NIGHT

WALLACK'S NEW THEATRE
OPENED TO THE PUBLIC.

A Large and Brilliant Audience—The House, The Play, The Actors, And The Performance—How The Artists Were Received.

The new Wallack's Theatre, the third playhouse in this City bearing that name, was given to the public last evening, and the public, clad in fine clothes donned for the purpose, entered and took possession of it. After many months the theatre had been completed, and the announcement was made that the doors would be opened at 7 o'clock last night. At that hour awnings were stretched from the three doors leading to the vestibule to the sidewalk curb, and a long line was formed of men, whose swallow-tailed coats and wide shirt-bosoms were concealed beneath ulsters, and who chaffed each other as they pushed forward to the ticket-taker's window. The box-office was not opened, however, until 7:15, when the men in the line grabbed tickets of admission as quickly as they could be delivered, and rushed forward through the curtained doorway into the auditorium. In a very short time the space back of the stalls in both the parquet and balcony was jammed, and the ushers had no little difficulty in escorting the ladies and gentlemen who arrived later to their seats. The house filled slowly, and it was noticeable that a great majority of the ladies wore bonnets, in spite of the largest size, although some of the first ladies to be seated in the stalls wore head-gear

94:1. New York *Times,* Jan. 5, 1882.

that approached the formidable. Most of the gentlemen wore the regulation full dress. The stalls were not filled when the curtain rose, somewhat after 8 o'clock, and the first act was presented to an unsettled audience.

The family circle, which is reached by a separate entrance, was soon completely filled. Most of the seats held by the few speculators about the doorway were in this part of the house, and they asked $2 and $3 for them. A few seats remained on sale at the box-office early in the evening, but they were speedily disposed of. When the house was finally filled in it presented a very brilliant appearance. The performance was announced to begin at 7:45 o'clock, but it was long past that hour when the gas was turned on full, and Mr. Herman Brode, the successor of Mr. Thomas Baker as director of the band, took his seat amid a murmur of applause. Mr. Brode's hair is black and covers his head, and the shiny pate of Mr. Baker is a departed glory of Wallack's. While the orchestra played its first selection the green curtain separating the stage from the audience was displaced by a new act drop painted by Mr. Philip Goatcher, representing a heavy curtain of blue satin, beneath which is a marble floor partly covered by a handsome rug. The act drop received cordial approval, and the audience, having already inspected the elaborate decoration of the new theatre, directed their attention to the bill of the play. For the ladies a simple white card, with gilt-beveled edges on which was printed the cast of the comedy, was provided. There was also a four-sheet bill of heavy tinted paper, which sustained not only all the announcements relating to the opening of the house and the cast of the play of the evening, but, in addition, the playbills of the first nights at the two former Wallack Theatres.

The house at the corner of Broadway and Broome street was opened on the 8th of September, 1852. On the bill Mr. Wallack was announced as lessee, Mr. John W. Lester as stage manager, and Mr. Charles Wallack as Treasurer. The plays of the evening were the comedy of "The Way to Get Married," and a farce called "Boarding School," which, according to the bill, had an uninterrupted run of 100 nights in London. That was in 1852, when it was not common for plays to be performed consecutively for more than three months, even in London. Blake, Walcot, Lester, Brougham, Chippendale, Mrs. Blake, and Mrs. Brougham took part in these pieces. During the evening Mr. Wallack had the honor to address the audience, and Mlle. Malvina danced a "picturesque pas seul." The second theatre, at Broadway and Thirteenth-street, was opened Sept. 25, 1861. Mr. Wallack was announced as proprietor and manager, Mr. Lester Wallack as stage manager, and Mr. Moss as Treasurer. The piece was a new comedy by Tom Taylor called "The New President." Mr. Wallack had the honor of addressing the audience after the performance of the "Grand National Union Overture," composed by Mr. Robert Stoepel.

The piece selected for the opening of the third house, at Broadway and Thirtieth-street, was Sheridan's "School for Scandal." The performance was witnessed as has been intimated, by an immense audience. All the seats were filled, and all the habitual first-nighters were present. There was the large proportion of elderly gentlemen and ladies customary in Wallack audiences. The eight proscenium boxes were occupied by Mr. William H. Vanderbilt, Mr. W. R. Travers, Mr. T. B. Musgrave, Mr. Cornelius Fellows, Mr. Albert Weber, Mr. William H. Tyler, and the families of Mr. Wallack and Mr. Theodore Moss. Vice-President Blanchard of the Erie Railway; Mr. W. R. Fletcher, Mr. Stacy Charlier, Col. B. T. Morgan, Herman Aldrich, James Barton Key, H. K. Enos, and John H. Draper were among the audience, and all the newspaper critics were present. The distribution of the parts last evening in Sheridan's masterpiece is printed here as a part of the record of a noteworthy dramatic event:

Sir Peter Teazle ..... Mr. John Gilbert
Sir Oliver Surface .. Mr. Harry Edwards
Charles Surface .... Mr. Osmond Tearle
Joseph Surface ...... Mr. Gerald Eyre
Sir Benjamin Backbite . Mr. F. V. Sinclair
Crabtree .... Mr. D. Leeson
Moses .... Mr. W. Elton
Careless .... Mr. Wilmot Kyre
Rowley .... Mr. H. Gwynnette
Trip .... Mr. C. F. Edwin
Sir Harry Bumper, with song . Mr. Taylor
Snake .... Mr. W. H. Pope
Sir Toby .... Mr. F. G. Kerr
Joseph's servant .. Mr. Harry J. Holliday
Lady Sneerwell's servant ...... Mr. H. Pearson, Jr.
Lady Teazle ...... Miss Rose Coghlan
Mrs. Candour .... Mme. Ponisi
Maria .... Miss Stella Boniface
Lady Sneerwell .... Miss Agnes Elliott

When the band had finished the overture the drop was lifted, displaying the reception-room of Lady Sneerwell, a gorgeous apartment in which green, buff, and gold were the predominating colors. Lady Sneerwell, seated at a table, discussed with Mr. Snake her plans for the dissemination of scandal. The scene and Miss Elliott's garments were both warmly applauded. Mr. Surface was announced, and Mr. Eyre, handsomely attired in coat, waistcoat, and breeches of dark satin, was obliged to bow his acknowledgments of a hearty reception before he began to give expression to his sentiments. Miss Boniface, who entered immediately afterward, received a greeting that would be calculated to turn the head of a young actress not under such wise influence as prevails at Wallack's Theatre, and when Mme. Ponisi, dressed in crimson satin, flounced upon the stage as Mrs. Candour, and began to defend the reputation of her acquaintances, the house fairly rose to her. But, after all, that reception was merely nothing in the matter of noise to the one accorded to Mr. John Gilbert, when the room at Sneerwell's was closed in by a front scene, representing a corridor at Sir Peter Teazle's, and Sir Peter, with his most distinguished gait, entered, snuff-box in hand. The spectators began by clapping their hands, but somebody upstairs shouted "Bravo," and the whole house took it up, until the building thundered with the echoes. The veteran bowed, and bowed again, in stately fashion, and, at last, after it was all over calmly took up his part, remarking: "When an old bachelor marries a young wife, what is he to expect?" Miss Coghlan's entrance as Lady Teazle at the beginning of the second act, was the signal for audience outburst. A bouquet was thrown to her from one of the boxes, and the men cheered while the women clapped their hands. The popular actress was as charming as ever, and the ensuing scene between the husband and wife was one of the brightest bits of the performance. Mr. Edwards, who presented an imposing picture as hearty Sir Oliver and Mr. Elton as Moses were also warmly welcomed, and the handsome views of the "room full of ancestors" and Joseph's library were much admired.

Mr. Wallack had the honor to address the audience between the third and fourth acts. The drop was pulled up showing again the hallway at Teazle's, and there stood the distinguished manager, with a huge floral trophy on either side of him. When the plaudits had subsided Mr. Wallack stepped forward and remarked that it would probably seem ungrateful for him to acknowledge that he could not repress, in spite of the warm greeting given to the new Wallack's Theatre, a feeling of sadness. He recalled the opening of another Wallack's Theatre, 21 years before, when another than himself had addressed the audience. The new house had not been built upon any fanciful artistic plan, nor to satisfy any pet fashion; it was designed simply to be a comfortable, warm and cheerful theatre, and he thought the design had been carried out. (Applause.) He would not dwell upon any announcement of the plays to be produced in the new house, as he was confident that his past would be a sufficient guarante of his future. (Applause.) He thanked the audience for their generosity, and retired in favor of Sheridan. After Mr. Wallack's speech, Mr. Gilbert was summoned forth to say a few words, and afterward the play proceeded to the end.

It was quite appropriate that "The School for Scandal" should have been selected by Mr. Wallack for the opening play. The work is identified in this country with his name as an actor and as a manager, and it typifies a broad class of dramatic effort which has added permanent honor to the stage. All kinds of plays, differing widely in purpose and merit, have been provided by the management of Wallack's since this institution came into life, 30 years ago; but thoughtful and careful revival of English comedy from year to year has been the basis of its reputation. This has not, perhaps, served as the largest source of profit to the theatre; but it has been its chief and lasting claim to public consideration; it has placed at least one theatre somewhat—however slightly—beyond the now sure divorce between literature and the stage. "The School for Scandal" is, without doubt, a brilliant example of its class, and it has been seen frequently by the present generation at the second Wallack's Theatre with various and notable casts. The performance of it given last night was viewed under peculiar and sparkling conditions. The same performance was witnessed last year, and was then felt to be somewhat inferior to other and recent representations

of the play; a few of the characters were not in the strongest and most skilled hands, and the merit of the acting was found principally in individual beauties, not in a round, equalized, and sustained illusion. The glamour thrown over the occasion last night gave, unquestionably, a certain extraneous brilliancy to the work of the players. . . .

THE BUILDINGS AND DECORATIONS

If anything were needed to prove that in America and even in New-York the theatre is a plant of recent growth, it would have been afforded last night by the sight at the new theatre of Mr. Lester Wallack's company. The audience was in irreproachable attire and most benevolently disposed. But it lacked entirely the intelligent enthusiasm, more particularly, however, the air of being at ease with the opening of a new theatre, which one finds in the capital of a great theatre-loving nation across the water. There has been a great deal of excitement manifested in some quarters about the new theatre, if prices paid for boxes denotes excitement. The public, also, is certainly interested in the appearance of the edifice to which the greater number of persons of moderate means is likely to make at least one visit. How does it compare with the old quarters? What have the actors and audience gained by the transfer from Thirteenth to Thirtieth street?

As one enters from Broadway nothing remarkable appears. There is room enough for a discreet "queue" of buyers at the wicket. Some hesitation will occur to decide what door is to be tried, for the paneled Queen Anne double doors are close to one's face and no signs are up. But, though the space is narrow, these doors can be slid bodily aside at any moment and leave an open exit to the audience of balcony and parquet. The entrance does not differ noticeably otherwise from that of the Academy of Music.

In the lobby the floor is of bright tiles, and the walls are stretched with stuffs of good selection that have a comfortable look. To the right and left are the stairways leading to the balcony; separate stairs with separate doors on Broadway receive the audience of the family circle. The arrangements as to stairs are thus of the simplest, and so far as the emptying of the houses on the Broadway or auditorium side is concerned may be considered quite safe. The only possible question would be the emptying of the family circle, always the least protected, most crowded, most distant, and most exposed portion of a theatre. The auditorium itself at the balcony is exactly a horseshoe with a blunt toe. The parquet is the same, only deeper and broader. The system is neither that of the ancients, who made the auditorium the greater portion of a true circle, nor that of later inventors, who have sometimes attempted an oval. Consequently, and also because the theatre is small, the voices from the stage reach every part well, and are particularly loud in the family circle, where the concave roof with the well of the cupola, sends the voice back and downward again. The roof appears to be supported on columns with Corinthian capitals almost entirely engaged in the walls. The mouldings of these capitals have as ornaments a pair of masks— comic and tragic. Above each capital on the molded architrave is a trophy consisting of a lyre and oak leaves. From the heads of the capitals spring arches, in low relief, which appear to support the architectural paintings of the ceiling. These stimulate bold arches supporting the central lantern. From the well of this lantern falls a great chandelier, with jets of gas not too frequently disposed, and forming with its complicated trace-work a brace of fantastic dragons, as well as festoons, bands and balls. At points on the stem of this huge chandelier there are painted china globes after the fashion common in lamp shops that sell to fur-

nishers of hotels and the palaces of "merchant princes." The other gas-lights are in a similar style of questionable taste.

The ceiling is treated with forbearance so far as color is concerned. The decorator has known too much to repeat the enormous gilt figures of the Opéra in Paris —perhaps the cost may have had something to do with it, too. Comparisons are inevitable between New-York and Parisian theatres, yet they are from the start unfair in this respect: New-York builds with private funds; Paris with the public. Mr. Wallack's company, although in some respects the first in the United States, has to be always managed on an economical basis. It must pay for itself or disband. There is no fat treasury to draw from; no legislators who considere the theatre one of the necessary baits of the public, if not one of the props of the State. And it must be confessed that neither as to ediface nor as to decoration is there anything extraordinary about the present theatre. It is no better situated than the old, so far as exits are concerned. Indeed, it may be questioned very seriously whether, in case of fire on the stage, the actors would not be in great danger. Its decorations are in fair taste; without being brilliant, they are on the safe side—they are passable. Its seating capacity is not very large; its ceiling not a wonder of art; its curtain, that favorite butt of audiences who have to stare at it alone during many a bad quarter of an hour, is less than mediocre.

Nevertheless, it should be understood that Wallack's new theatre, while in the main much what the old was, offers minor points of excellence. The red velvet used profusely in the chairbacks and curtains of the boxes, the dark-red carpets, the glittering silver and gilt decorations of the faces of balcony and scenic arch, give a much gayer, more festive look to the auditorium than was the case in the former theatre. The paintings of Muses and others, (there are 14 of them, and some are presumably nymphs of less definite meaning than the nine Muses,) are a great advance on the usual flat fresco work by Italian decorators. They recline on clouds under the arches afore mentioned, which appear to support the roof, and are only to be seen well from the family circle. Some of the walls stretched with "art-stuffs," both on the stairways leading to the balcony and the upper lobby, which may be called the foyer, are agreeable to the eye. There is some want of unity of taste and design throughout the building, as if several persons had had a finger in the decorative pie. The foyer and staircases have heavy, soft carpets. A lady's boudoir is railed off from it by heavy dark-blue curtains, and opposite is an "art-decorative" drawing-room—small and supplied with one or two paintings. All these arrangements indicate good taste up to a certain point. They are not the result of unusual artistic force; neither can any of them be termed vulgar. What is vulgar, however, is the presence in the foyer and the auditorium of little portable fountains of perfume. And to make this perfumery unavoidable, boys were occupied in throwing spray from the fountains through "atomizers," until the foyer was unbearable. It is to be hoped that this is a special feature not to be repeated.

The change to Thirtieth-street has brought Wallack's Theatre again into the centre of the theatre-going population and into the neighborhood of the Fifth-Avenue Hotel, that caravanserai of caravanserais. In this fact we must recognize the only really important gain from the removal. It is a pretty, light, gay little theatre, exactly suited to the quality of drama for which its company has been famous hitherto. One can hardly associate a real tragedy with its red plush seats, red velvet curtains to the boxes, and glittering ironwork on balcony, and pillars, and on the composite columns of the arch of the stage. The upper part of this arch is one of the best things in the theatre, by the way, for it has an air of originality, it makes itself felt, and yet is neither too heavy, nor too loaded, nor too severe. The ceiling does not entirely harmonize with the other decorations. The main painting is of a chocolate, with green spaces between the architectural fresco. And, speaking of paintings, a peculiar arrangement is the panel of flowers in water-color, protected by glass, which decorate the two main stories. They are delicately done and very much superior to the ordinary work of decorators. The water-colorist Stlepevich is said to have done them. The outer walls of the proscenium boxes, of which there are only eight, have these water-color decorations of large size under glass; with their plain walnut frames they look like pictures let into the wall. The main wall of the whole theatre, where it shows near the tops of the columns, is treated in a mixed brownish color which contrasts, not too well, with the inner walls of balcony and parquet. The theory doubtless is that when, as in our democratic theatres, the boxes are more and more removed, the rear walls of balcony and parquet are merely the walls of one common box, open in the entire circuit of the theatre, and therefore to be treated like the rear walls of the several boxes which it has displaced. It may be questioned whether this is worth while. For when one stands near the orchestra and looks up from balcony to family circle, the changes from the bright red of the balcony to the dull tones of the main walls in the circle is not pleasing. Better taste shows in the different colored stamped stuffs with velvety pile that take the place of paper or paint on many of the wall spaces. The plainer ones on the main staircases are particularly neat, although now and then one catches a gaudy effect from defective calculation of their ultimate effect one on the other when all are in place. Were one to ask what the keynote of color in the whole building was it would be difficult to say. In the auditorium it may be said to be deep red; in the foyer, dark blue. In the latter the large embroidered curtain of the ladies' room holds the attention, assisted by a highly gilt and carved super-structure. In the auditorium the effect is much more scattered. Nothing dominates; nothing is absolutely bad; nothing is strikingly and certainly fine.

Several really meritorious points should not be overlooked, even in this hasty sketch. There are no shops and restaurants connected immediately with the theatre and forming part of its plan, as is the case too often in Paris. For example, the little Theatre de la Renaissance was hoisted dangerously in the air in order to give room on the ground floor to a beer-saloon and a café. Considering the size of the theatre, the space allowed for the main stairways is ample, and the effect on the stairs and in the lobby good. On the whole, while the theatre may not come up to the expectations which the public was allowed to form, it is certainly an improvement on the ordinary building of the kind. The science of theatre building and theatre decoration is one of the most difficult in architecture. It belongs to the special needs of modern life, and has not yet found a real master in the profession. As the taste for the drama grows here we may look for startling innovations on the good old rules handed down from the ancients that do not always meet the complications of today. The laws of sound are not yet settled. A writer of the last century claimed that no auditorium should be fitted with any other material than wood, and that should be thin, dry and resonant. Vitruvius advocated brazen vases hidden under the seats with their mouths toward the stage. We have much greater difficulties to solve than he had, yet we are no further on in the true understanding of such matters than were the Romans.

95. CASINO THEATRE
New York City
Opened October 21, 1882

The Casino Theatre, which opened in 1882, became one of the most successful and distinguished playhouses in New York City over a fifty-year period of specializing in the production of musical comedies. It was at Broadway and Thirty-ninth Street. The auditorium, which was reached by two flights of stairs, seated 1,300 persons and was decorated in Moorish style.

When the theater opened its doors originally on October 21, 1882, it was in such an unfinished state that it was closed a week later and not reopened until December 30. The New York *Tribune* of October 23 carried the following review of the first opening.

95:1   THE NEW CASINO OPENED

"THE QUEEN'S LACE HANDKERCHIEF" PERFORMED ON SATURDAY NIGHT—THE BUILDING FAR FROM FINISHED.

The Casino, at Broadway and Thirty-ninth-st., was opened to the public on Saturday night by a performance of Strauss' operetta, "The Queen's Lace Handkerchief" by the McCaull Opera Comique Company. Notwithstanding the frequent postponements had for the purpose of enabling the contractors to finish the building, Saturday night found it in a very incomplete state. Great stretches of unbleached muslin, draperies of the National tri-color and frowzy hangings concealed gaps in the walls and did service for partitions, but marred sadly the picturesque effect presented by the ceiling and proscenium and the general design of the exterior of the house. Besides these offenses to the eye and the masses of rubbish which littered the place the comfort of a large audience was destroyed by cold blasts of air that came from thousands of crannies.

Under the circumstances it would be difficult to form anything more than a general idea of the appearance of the Casino as it will present itself on the com-

95:1. New York *Tribune*, Oct. 23, 1882.

223

pletion of the building. Novelty in design and execution are its most striking characteristics. The architectural forms are Moorish, and the soaring round towers and bold outlines of the exterior are sure to strike the eye of all visitors to the vicinity of Broadway and Thirty-ninth-st. What the vestibule, staircases and lobbies will look like remains to be seen. The intention here, as elsewhere, seems to have been that harmony should be preserved throughout between the Moorish forms and the decoration. Walls and ceilings, so far as they have been finished, show no wood of any kind, but, instead, plaster moulded into ornamental forms. Most of it on Saturday night was of a dirty white color, but where it had received its coat of paint and bronze it was gorgeous and showy. The curtain of blue, dead-gold, yellow and brown velvet, with a central ornament, studded with paste jewels and heavy fringes, carries out the Oriental idea of the whole design.

The performance of the operetta was the first in this country, and was attended by other embarrassments besides an ill-fitting curtain which revealed the feet and ankles of the performers before they had formed their positions on the stage. For a time on Saturday, it seemed as though a legal difficulty wouldl compel another postponement. Leo Goldmark, the original owner of the right to produce the operetta in the United States, sold the right under contract to Townsend Percy and others for $3,000, of which sum one third was paid in cash, while promissory notes were given for the balance. In an application for injunction made to Justice Dononne, Mr. Goldmark claimed that the condition of sale was that if the notes were not paid when they fell due the sale should be void. Mr. McCaull obtained a license from Mr. Percy to perform the operetta on the payment of a royalty. One of the notes fell due a few days ago and was protested. Mr. Goldmark, claiming that the title had reverted to him, secured a temporary restraining order, but afterward arranged to permit the performance to go on condition that Mr. McCaull should pay the royalty to A. J. Dittenhoefer, instead of Percy and others, its trustee for the persons who shall establish a right to it in the injunction suit.

The playhouse was closed on October 28 until completion of the premises, but was reopened on December 30, which was declared the official opening date. The same operetta was presented at this performance.

95:2   THE CASINO OPENED

The new Casino was formally opened to the public last evening with the production by the McCaull Opera Comique Company of the English version of Johann Strauss's operetta, "The Queen's Lace Handkerchief." The beautiful little theatre, whcih is one mass of gold and silver colors, was filled with an appreciate audience, and from the raising of the curtain until the final chorus in the third act of the operetta the applause was continuous and enthusiastic. "The Queen's Lace Handkerchief" since its first production at the Casino has been judiciously cut by the stage manager, so that all the dullness of the libretto has been dispensed with, and nothing remains but the sparkling music of Strauss and a dialogue in which the audience can recognize something like a regular plot. The reception of the operetta last evening was such as to warrant the prediction that it will enjoy a profitable run at the new temple of opera comique. At the end of each act the curtain was rung up in response to an encore, and several of the choruses had to be repeated to satisfy the demands of the audience. Miss Matilda Cottrelly as Donna Irene, the Queen's confidante, carried off the honors of the evening, and Miss Louise Paullia, Miss Lily Post, Signor Perugini, Mr. Standish, and Mr. J. Taylor are to be credited with spirited

95:2. New York *Times*, Dec. 31, 1882.

Casino Theatre, New York, 1896. Photograph by Byron. Courtesy of the Byron Collection, Museum of the
y of New York.

97. Garden Theatre, New York, 1900. Photograph by Byron. Courtesy of the Byron Collection, Museum of the City of New York.

work. The chorus was efficient, and the whole performance left an agreeable impression. The first Sunday night concert, under the direction of Mr. Rudolph Aronson, will be given next Sunday evening by an orchestra of 50 pieces.

96. NEW LYCEUM THEATRE
New York City
Opened April 6, 1885

The New Lyceum Theatre was built by Steele MacKaye as another of his interesting experiments. This time it was to give New York a school of acting to be run by MacKaye. The playhouse, which was on Fourth Avenue between Twenty-third and Twenty-fourth streets, was not a success under MacKaye's management. He retained the managership until May 23, when the reins of leadership were taken over by Daniel Frohman.

T. Allston Brown gave some of the pertinent information about the New Lyceum.

96:1   To the late Steele Mackaye we owe the existence of this unique little playhouse known as "THE LYCEUM THEATRE." It occupied a lot, fifty feet in width, on the west side of Fourth Avenue, between Twenty-third and Twenty-fourth streets, adjoining the Academy of Design. In January, 1884, William Y. Mortimer leased the ground to Philip G. Hubert, Chas. W. Clinton, and Michael Brennan for twenty-one years, from May 1 of that year, at a yearly rental of $4,000.

It was the original intention to use it for the Lyceum School of Acting, an institution of which Steele Mackaye, Gustave Frohman, and Franklin Sargent were associate managers. The theatre was leased by Mr. Mackaye and Mr. Frohman for ten years from February, 1885, for $12,000 for the first three years and $15,000 a year for the remaining seven years. The theatre was three stories high,

96:1. T. Allston Brown, *A History of the New York Stage from the First Performance in 1732 to 1901.* 3 vols. (New York: Dodd, 1903), 3:419–20.

of finished brick, with freestone trimmings. It cost $50,000. The house consisted of a parquet and one gallery, which was entered from the centre. The auditorium was 75 feet deep by 48 feet 6 inches wide. The seating capacity of the house was: boxes, 88; parquet, 344; dress circle, 172; balcony, 123. The musicians occupied a frame or box about 5 feet deep and reached entirely across the stage. They were not visible to the auditors until the double curtains, crossing each other, draped themselves and disclosed the band apparently occupying the whole stage. When the overture was finished the curtains closed again and the frame and the musicians were hoisted on the automatic elevator clear into the flies, where the bottom of the car made the top part of the proscenium frame. This car was removed during the summer of 1886. The initial performance of the Lyceum Theatre was April 6, 1885, with the first production of "Dakolar," by Steele Mackaye (the first two acts partially suggested by George Ohnet's novel "Le Maître des Forges"). The cast:

Dakolar . . . . R. B. Mantell
Duc de Villaflor . . . . J. B. Mason
Noel . . . . Jos. Frankau
Kerouac . . . . A. Lindsay
Pierre-Kadoc . . . . Jos. Adleman
Taloche . . . . C. H. Canfield
Dennis . . . . F. E. Stoddard
Sagot . . . . Walter Clark Bellows
Potin . . . . C. H. Welsh
Madeleine . . . . Viola Allen
Sophie . . . . Sadie Martinot
Marquise . . . . Blanche Gray
Minerva . . . . Maude Banks
Gillome . . . . Emma Sheridan
Nanette . . . . Laura Johnson
Yvonne . . . . Mary Saunders

This was the professional début of Maude Banks and Emma Sheridan, pupils of the Lyceum school.

The prices of admission were: the first two rows (36 seats) in the balcony, $2.50 each; the next two rows (32 seats), $2; the five rows next succeeding, $1.50; the few remaining back row seats in the balcony, $1; the parquet front row seats, $2; and the other orchestra chairs, $1.50. A change was made in the scale of prices soon after the opening, the two front rows in the balcony being sold at $2. In consequence of a misunderstanding Viola Allen refused to play; the house was closed evening of April 15. On April 16 Kate Forsythe read the part of Madeleine. E. J. Buckley appeared April 20 as Duc de Villaflor. The house was closed May 23. The next lessee was Daniel Frohman. The season opened Sept. 15, with, for the first time on any stage, Steele Mackaye's version of Sardou's "Andrea," to which he had given the title "In Spite of All."

The New York *Times* described the opening.

96:2   THE LYCEUM THEATRE

Mr. Steele MacKaye has given New-York a comfortable and attractive little playhouse, a trifle strange in its appointments and in the conglomerate character of its decorations, but on the whole one that pleases the visitor, after he has become used to it. Many singular devices Mr. MacKaye thought of putting into here have been abandoned; one who wishes to enter receives a ticket from the box office or the ubiquitous speculator, which is taken from him at the door of the auditorium; the audience are not compelled to wear badges, and the play bills, although unusually handsome, are printed from type on paper. The musicians do not wear knee breeches and powdered wigs, but these gentlemen do sit in a pavilion upon the stage while they play, and the pavilion, musicians and all, disappears while tapestry curtains are drawn slowly in front of

96:2. New York *Times*, Apr. 7, 1885.

the stage, leaving in its place the picture belonging to the play. A large audience attended the opening of the Lyceum Theatre last evening, and sat with cheerful faces during the presentation of the new play, which began at 8:30 o'clock and continued until after midnight. Mr. MacKaye has plumed himself much in advance of its opening upon the beauty of his new theatre and the ingeniousness displayed in the arrangement of its stage and audience room. But Mr. MacKaye, we have reason to believe, does not overestimate the value of these things; he understands fully that scenic magnificence and luxurious furniture will not serve to make a bad play good, that the object of drama is to illustrate huamn life and character, and that a mass of dull conversation studded with dreary platitudes and combined with a few startling "situations" does not make such a play as this public had the right to expect in the first production of the much-trumpeted Lyceum Theatre. Mr. MacKaye has posed during the past Winter as a trainer of actors and a Professor of the art of acting; he has thus led people to expect more than was forthcoming last evening. . . .

The playhouse was demolished in 1902.

97. GARDEN THEATRE
New York City
Opened September 27, 1890

The building of Madison Square Garden had a special dividend for theater-lovers—the Garden Theatre. This 1,200-seat playhouse was on the ground floor of the Garden, and for thirty-five years housed some of the leading productions to be seen in New York City, including performances by Sarah Bernhardt in the play *Tosca*. In 1919 the playhouse became known as the Jewish Art Theatre and presented Yiddish drama.

A brief description of the Garden Theatre appeared in the New York *Times*.

97:1   THE HANDSOME GARDEN THEATRE

DECORATIONS OF THE NEW PLAY-HOUSE
AT THE MADISON SQUARE GARDEN.

The new Garden Theatre is so nearly finished that there seems to be no doubt of its being ready for the opening with "Dr. Bill" next Saturday evening. It was lighted last night for a private inspection of the decorations and the arrangement of the house. The result was extremely satisfactory, everybody agreeing that the house was comfortable and convenient and remarkably pretty. It has a seating capacity of about 1,200, and the lines of sight are excellent, almost every seat affording a good view of the stage. The stage is low, so that people sitting in the front rows can see the floor of it. The orchestra is to be placed under the stage, the enclosure for the musicians being modelled after that at Bayreuth. The stage is a wide and convenient one, with ample provision for working scenery both above and below.

The walls of the theatre will be hung with silk, and the prevailing colors in the rest of the decorations are white, light-brown and gold. The balcony fronts represent curtains and cords with tassels. At the right of the orchestra floor is a little colonnade affording good standing room, and there is another above the gallery on the same side. It may be remarked in passing that the decorations of the gallery are as rich as those of any part of the house. The ceiling has a handsome dome, with a large ventilator and a brilliant cluster of lights. The floor is carpeted with red, and the upholstery of the seats is of the same color.

The proscenium is especially rich and handsome in effect. The arch is broad and rests on four tall pillars, which form the corners of the box fronts. These columns are adorned with twining garlands and the lower parts of them are of marble. The box fronts are also hung with garlands. The proscenium frame is heavily gilded, and above it is a rich frieze, which extends across the tops of the highest boxes. The arch itself is divided into small panels, and within the arch, above the frame, is a high relief, representing the Angel of Fame, with spreading wings, bearing a wreath and a palm branch and surrounded by a group of Cupids. The act drop, painted by Henry Hoyt, of the Metropolitan Opera House, is a copy of Boldini's picture of the park of Versailles in the time of Louis XVI, and is quite in harmony with the rest of the house.

Much care has been taken to make the house fire proof. There is an asbestos curtain, and there are fourteen exits, with communication with the roof garden, which is intended to open next summer. The architects are McKim, Mead & White.

98. NEW FIFTH AVENUE THEATRE
New York City
Opened May 28, 1892

The Fifth Avenue Theatre that Augustin Daly had originally opened in 1873 burned to the ground on January 2, 1891. Plans were drawn immediately for a new playhouse, which was opened a year and a half later, in May 1892. The theater was well-designed architecturally, as will be seen from the architectural description by William H. Birkmire.

98:1   THE FIFTH AVENUE THEATRE
OF NEW YORK.

This splendid example of modern architecture, the fourth playhouse that has borne that name, is situated upon the north side of West Twenty-eighth Street, a few feet from Broadway, on the site of its namesake, which was burned on January 2, 1891. The Twenty-eighth Street

97:1. New York *Times,* Sept. 21, 1890.

98:1. William H. Birkmire, *The Planning and Construction of American Theatres* (New York: Wiley, 1901), pp. 16–20.

227

front, which is the broadside of the building, is in the style of the Italian Renaissance, very elaborate in the detail of its ornamentation, in which free use has been made of the emblems of the drama.

The columns of the portico, and the iron structure of the first story back of the portico, are relics of the former building, and were retained by Mr. Francis H. Kimball, the architect, in their original positions, but the cornice and balustrade of the portico are parts of the new work. Above the first story of the new theatre all the ornamental features and cornices are wrought in white terra cotta. The exterior, so elaborate, on the whole, on account of the employment of this medium of terra cotta, while maintaining the exquisitely delicate and graceful characteristics of the period which it represents, expresses in all its constructive details the continuity of an idea strictly in harmony with the purpose of the building.

In a word, it embodies in itself the most appropriate suggestion of the uses of the interior; the grand divisions or principle parts of a theatre, namely, the auditorium and the stage, being illustrated most effectively in the architectural composition, the more elaborate portion representing the auditorium, and the plainer section the stage.

The richness and minute elaboration that such a treatment is susceptible of in clay were never more apparent than in this illustration.

On either side of the central feature of the balcony foyer are windows, with ornamental terra-cotta panels between, the one denoting comedy, the other tragedy.

Again, the mullions of the windows of the gallery foyer are in the form of caryatides supporting the main cornice, and in the panels of the larger piers are bas-reliefs representing dancing and singing figures, all of these being in terra-cotta.

The leading architectural lines of the Twenty-eighth Street side are carried throughout the entire front, and the stage portion is less elaborate than that of the auditorium just described, calling for but little decoration, comparatively, in terra cotta.

There are two principal entrances to the theatre, one of which is sheltered by the portico and opens into the main foyer, an apartment 40 feet long and 13 feet wide, and from which a wide marble stairway leads to the upper boxes and balcony.

This entrance to the auditorium is no insignificant subject for decorative treatment, and in its treatment the architect has kept well in mind that the "first impressions are everything." The illusion is complete, as this hall in itself has no great length; though well proportioned, it appears twice as long as it otherwise would, had not the mirrors placed there against the east wall been adopted.

The other entrance is through a lobby 50 feet long and 12 feet wide, which leads from Broadway to the rear of the parquette.

Both the entrances are paved with perfectly white Vermont marble, with Tennessee marble borders and plinth under-columns and pilasters, and the walls are divided into panels by pilasters and columns of Mycenium marble.

There is another marble staircase from the parquette to the balcony on the north side of the theatre, and one immediately under, to the smoking-room and gentlemen's toilet under the auditorium.

Entering the theatre by the regular Broadway entrance, it will be noticeable that the style of the exterior is adhered to throughout entrances, foyers, and auditorium in all its elaborateness. The pilasters along the walls of the entrance represent Sienna marble with capitals of ivory and gold, and the ceiling overhead is vaulted in tile, on which are decorated ribs in plaster relief, the subject of the ornamentation being fruits and flowers, and on the plain surfaces of the walls and ceilings are frescoed ornaments in color and gold. There are three divisions combined in this entrance: the outer lobby next to the street, with iron enclosing gates, then the box-office lobby, and an inner lobby next to the theatre; the purpose of which divisions being to control the rush of cold air into the theatre when the outer doors are opened.

The main decorative feature of the Twenty-eighth Street foyer is the beautiful coloring which the marble columns and marble wainscoting give that superb wall; and when this is contrasted with the ceiling and side walls, in white and pale pinkish terra cotta, the composition is impressive in its fullest sense.

On entering the auditorium from the foyer of the Fifth Avenue Theater we are impressed with its cosey and comfortable appearance. The parquette seats 600 people, and the entire seating capacity is 1400.

Growing out of the proscenium boxes of the theatre is the great splay of the proscenium arch, itself panelled and enriched with Italian ornamentation, and from this springs the dome, beginning from a heavy cornice as a base and supporting heavy ribs arranged in pairs. Among the most charming decorative features of the auditorium is the drop-curtain, part of which is shown, painted by H. Logan Reid, after the original by Cottazzo, "The Crowning of the Bride," described and illustrated by Henry M. Stevens in an article entitled "The Fifth Avenue Theatre," published in the *Scientific American,* July number 1893. Mr. Stevens says it is "A souvenir of the happy days of Louis XVI. The scene itself is one of considerable magnitude and introduces a large number of figures. The atmosphere of old French court life, and the simplicity of the country custom of the time, in which a provincial bride and groom seek distinction at the hands of Louis and his beautiful consort, Marie Antoinette, through a graceful ceremony of this coronation, are most attractively and truthfully portrayed."

By taking another glance at the auditorium we see the same general idea of design and tints displayed with equally good taste throughout the minor details. The acoustic properties are perfect and the lines of sighting of the parquette and upper tiers are carried out in the same manner as described under the remarks upon these subjects hereafter.

Symmetrical planning is to our mind the first necessity for any theatre that is to be a safe one. The position of all passages and staircases, the nearnes of all exits to these essential parts and to the outer air, are all-important. The front of the site, as well as the sides looking on the thoroughfare, is of course a great advantage. In this particular but a few feet separates the auditorium from the street, and the building, in case of any emergency, could be emptied of its audience in at least two and one half minutes, even that portion occupying its farthest seats.

The Fifth Avenue is about the size of the Empire Theatre, but adjoining its 1400 seats plenty of room is allowed for aisles and passages. The seats are comfortable and elegantly upholstered.

The stage occupies a space 35 feet wide by 80 feet long upon the main floor, and adjoining is one dressing-room, the manager's room, and a large passage leading to Twenty-eighth Street (the other dressing rooms are above the stage). There are eight boxes, a balcony, and a gallery extending well forward.

The auditorium is 68 feet wide by 64 feet deep and 65 feet to the dome.

The stage is also entered upon the right through an open court, containing fire-escapes, and balconies built of iron, which extend to the upper tiers and in case of emergency are used as exits leading to Broadway through a wide passage. The theatre is fully equipped with approved fire-apparatus, the construction throughout is of iron and steel with Guastavino arches in the floors, and the building is lighted by electricity.

As in the old system of lighting a stage by gas a gas-plate was needed, with the taps labelled as to the portion of the system they governed, so for the electric system a switchboard is used, containing all the necessary switches, cut-outs, and other fittings for the control and regulation of the stage-lighting. This switchboard is fixed in a convenient position overlooking the stage, and is accessible only to the person employed to operate it.

The entire scenery has been treated by the "Martin Process" of fireproofing, a description of which will be given later on.

The New York *Times* drama critic made brief mention of the new playhouse in his review of the opening day.

98:2   THE NEW THEATRE

OPENING OF THE FIFTH AVENUE
WITH A NEW OPERETTA.

The opening of a new theatre is regarded as an event of importance among the myriad lovers of dramatic and lyric art and is certain to attract a large audience. Those who attended the opening of the new Fifth Avenue Theatre, at Broadway and Twenty-eighth Street, last evening were rewarded by a view of one of the most inviting places of amusement in the city. The new house is a commodious and handsome building, and the promise of the handsome facade on Twenty-eighth Street is well carried out by the warm and tasteful decorations of the interior, in which the delicate cream color of the walls and the rich crimson of the upholstery and hangings combine with delightful effect. This is not the place for a detailed description of the theatre, and it will suffice to say that Mr. H. C. Miner, the manager, is to be congratulated on possessing one of the most attractive playhouses in a city which is well provided with such resorts. . . .

98:2. New York *Times,* May 29, 1892.

99. MANHATTAN OPERA HOUSE
New York City
Opened November 14, 1892

A colorful impresario and theatrical manager appeared in the person of Oscar Hammerstein, a cigarmaker and opera buff, who built a number of theaters in New York and Philadelphia, made fortunes and lost them, and gave the new Metropolitan Opera Company the stiffest competition it ever faced. Hammerstein built theaters, but the theaters were constructed to be opera houses, for opera was Hammerstein's greatest love, even though he was constantly told there was no money in that art form.

The Manhattan Opera House is a case in point. It opened as a playhouse, but soon reverted to opera.

99:1   ANOTHER FINE THEATRE.

THE NEW MANHATTAN OPERA HOUSE

MRS. BERNARD-BEERE TO APPEAR AT THE
OPENING TO-MORROW NIGHT.

One of the handsomest and most commodious theatres in the city of New-York will be opened to the public for the first time to-morrow evening. It is the Manhattan Opera House, in Thirty-fourth-st., a few doors west of Broadway, built and owned by Oscar Hammerstein, the proprietor of the Harlem Opera House and the Columbus Theatre. A good description of the house has already been given in The Tribune, but the approach of the opening makes some additional account appropriate.

The house is a large theatre with the appearance of a small one. That is to say, it has a considerable seating capacity, about 2,000, while the architectural plan is such that the seats are completely arranged and brought nearer the stage than is common when there are so many. The building runs quite through the block from Thirty-fourth to Thirty-fifth-st., the wall

99:1. New York *Tribune,* Nov. 13, 1892.

in the latter street forming the back of the stage and the main entrance being in the former. The building has a frontage of 100 feet, with a wall about ninety feet high of pressed brick and Indiana limestone, with a portico of red Scotch granite and iron.

In the entrance and main lobby is a base of rich Italian marble blocks, with twelve pillars resting upon it and supporting a cornice, the whole being decorated in white and gold. The box-office is on one side and two elevators are on the other. These are to carry passengers to the balcony and to the roof garden, which will cover the whole space of the roof of the building. It will naturally not be opened at present. Swinging doors of dark red plush separate this lobby from the auditorium. As one enters the latter from the front of the building no balconies are seen, only the back of the front row of boxes, with a little gallery, by which, together with the two broad and handsome marble staircases at the sides, the boxes are to be reached. The circle of boxes does not skirt the wall of the room, as is usual in opera houses, but extends across the middle of the orchestra floor, from side to side, like a bridge, bringing the boxes much nearer the stage than could be done by the usual plan, and yet not interfering with the view of anybody in the seats below. Above this is another tier of boxes arranged in the same way, but approached from the upper foyer instead of from a gallery. Extending back from this second row of boxes, and above it, is a broad balcony, and above this again is a gallery.

The foyer which gives access to the second tier of boxes is a beautifully and richly decorated room. At the back of it is another large and handsome room for promenading, situated at the front of the building, over the entrance. These will afford space enough for the whole audience, if necessary, to walk about and rest between the acts. The floor of Italian marble, the ceiling of quilted stucco relief,

the pillars, the staircases leading still farther up and the huge candelabra are all rich, costly and artistic. There is a smoking room adjoining, and there is yet another foyer connected with the balcony above which will be used later for a cafe.

The decorations of the auditorium are chiefly of light blue and gold, and the curtains, hangings and upholstery are of dark blue plush. There are fifty-two boxes, some of which are large enough to be divided, so as to make over seventy in all. The most of them have separate anterooms. They are hung with the prevailing dark blue plush, and the rails in front are upholstered with the same. All the boxes have separate rounded fronts, and these, like the front of the gallery above, are decorated in high relief and the prevailing colors. Each of the boxes, except those of extra size, holds six people.

The proscenium opening, measuring forty-two feet in width and fifty feet in height, is surrounded by masses of columns, caps, arches and recesses, with scroll and fluted relief work. Above it is a large allegorical painting, while above this still more arches reach up to the ceiling. This is also extremely handsome in decoration, and about 500 electric lights are arranged over it. There are altogether some 2,300 electric lights in the building. They are everywhere, and always enter into the scheme of decoration. The stage has a fire-drop of asbestos and iron composition, and also a curtain of blue plush, draped in heavy folds, and trimmed with nettings of white silk cord and tassels.

The stage itself is large and conveniently arranged, and any dramatic event of operatic performance that can be done anywhere can be done on it. The dressing-rooms and all the other rooms for the purposes of the stage management are in a separate building, where there are accommodations for 500 people. In the basement of this building are the boilers, the electric light plant, the heating and ventilating machinery and the fire pumps.

The cost of the whole theatre is said to be about $500,000. . . .

100. EMPIRE THEATRE
New York City
Opened January 25, 1893

In 1893 a new theater featuring a stock company under the direction of Charles Frohman was opened at Broadway and Fortieth Street. Christened the Empire Theatre, it was to have a distinguished history during the next sixty years, until it was demolished in 1953. It opened with David Belasco's *The Girl I Left behind Me* and later featured such performers as Maude Adams, Katharine Cornell, John Drew, John Gielgud, Nazimova, and many other famous stars. The theater played host to the famous long-running production of *Life with Father*.

The playhouse was built by Al Hayman and Frank Sanger and leased by Charles Frohman and William Harris. The New York *Times* trumpeted its opening:

100:1   A NEW AMERICAN DRAMA

THE EMPIRE THEATRE BEGINS ITS
HISTORY WITH TRIUMPH

Franklin Fyles and David Belasco's New Piece, "The Girl I Left Behind Me" Will Be Deservedly Popular—A Strong, Spirited, and Well-Constructed Melodrama.

The Empire Theatre, at Broadway and Fortieth Street, was opened to the public last night, with no accidents and no pretentious fuss. It is a handsome, well-appointed house of moderate size, so well constructed that any play may be presented on its stage and thoroughly enjoyed by the audience, for the architectural lines of the auditorium are so perfect that every spectator is near enough to the stage to be in sympathy with the actors, so that the most delicate comedy would not fail of effect, while the stage is broad and deep enough for any scenic or purely mechanical effects required in melodrama.

The decorations of the interior are handsome and tasteful, and the general effect reminds one of the Broadway Theatre across the street designed by the same architects. The prevailing tints are a subdued red, terra cotta, cream, and a dull green. The arrangement of the electric lights is most happy. There is, happily, no pretentious, ill-painted set drop, such as disfigures several otherwise handsome theatres in New-York. The curtain is one of embroidered cloth. An unusually capable band, under the baton of W. W. Furst, is suitably placed near the front of the stage. The house is said to be absolutely fireproof, and the means in ingress and egress are ample. The rows of seats are entirely too close together for perfect comfort, but that is a fault common to most theatres.

This handsome new house is controlled by Charles Frohman, a remarkably energetic young manager, who has already gained the esteem of the multitude, and we may expect to see there new plays designed to amuse and satisfy the larger public which cares very little for either poetry or satire, which is never pessimistic, and is restless under the influence of literary hair-splitting, but which, in this big town, is not very easily pleased for all that. The play chosen to begin Mr. Frohman's new term, and acted by his competent, well-balanced stock company, with a fine pictorial background, may be taken as a fair sample of the kind of plays likely to be popular at the new theatre. Its effects are large, its situations elemental, its sentiment simple, the humor juvenile and innocent, its characterizations plain, understandable, free from all complexity.

"The Girl I Left Behind Me" was received last night with acclaim. No one could doubt the honesty of the praise freely accorded to it. No one not afflicted by billious distemper could honestly object

100:1. New York *Times,* Jan. 26, 1893.

96. New Lyceum Theatre, New York. Courtesy of The Hoblitzelle Theatre Arts Library, The Humanities Research Center, The University of Texas at Austin.

99. Manhattan Opera House, New York, 1907. Photograph by Byron. Courtesy of the Bryon Collection, Museum of the City of New York.

100. Empire Theatre, New York, 1915. Photograph by Byron. Courtesy of the Byron Collection, Museum of the City of New York.

to the public verdict spoken loudly by the representative audience that crowded the theatre.

All successful plays of this description resemble one another in certain essential traits. The human heart does not change through the ages, and the common kind of to-day cherishes the same ideals as those cherished by our forefathers and their ancestors. The hero of successful melodrama is always a man of invincible courage and unswerving loyalty. He always loves, devotedly, unchangingly, the same woman that the villain loves, and the villain is always a coward and a liar.

People who have lived long in this world, and have the capacity to understand human nature, know that many men are villains who are much braver than the purely fictitious lions of legend, and who would not tell a lie except upon great provocation. But the great public that supports the popular theatre will not believe that. If Lieutenant Milton Parlow, the villain of "The Girl I Left Behind Me," was not afraid to ride forward under orders and warn the scouting party at Flagstaff Rock that the savages are out in warpaint it would be hard to convince nine-tenths of the spectators that he is really the cowardly destroyer of his family honor that the fine old Major is looking for.

Messrs. Franklin Fyles and David Belasco, the authors of "The Girl I Left Behind Me," have chosen for the scene of their new play the Western American frontier in the year 1890. The action passes at a remote army post in the Blackfoot country of Montana, and is transferred thence, for the denouement, to Fort Assinaboine. The play is in four acts, and introduces seventeen personages. The daughter of General Kennlon and other ladies are at the post to celebrate the Fourth of July. The Indians, led by an educated demon named Ladru, are angry because the soldiers interfere with the performance of their ancient rite, the sun dance. Failing to overcome the military resistance by parley, they cut the telephone wires connecting the Post with Assinaboine and surround the stockade. It becomes the hero's duty to ride through the savages to the Fort and bring aid to the Post. He has been accused falsely by his rival in love of cowardice. He accomplishes his mission and returns in time to save the lives of his fellow-officers and the honor of the women.

The situations developed from this simple, but serviceable, dramatic scheme could not possibly be elementally new to the stage, nor would it be possible in thus adapting the routine of the life of a West Pointer in the Indian country to the necessarily conventional requirements of romance and drama to stick closely to the dry facts of history and geography.

We all know perfectly well that a dead Indian is the best kind of Indian. We have read about the Custer massacre, and the horrible tortures to which the savages often subject their prisoners. We know the life of an army officer in the far West is not free from peril and privation. We know that young West Pointers frequently fall in love and marry. We know that the course of true love does not invariably run smooth. And we know that a General's daughter and a handsome Lieutenant's sister were apt to be comely, grave girls, who would make good wives.

The authors have builded their play carefully, introducing the personages and foreshadowing the plot clearly in Act I, and beginning in Act II the suspense which is sustained with cumulative effect till the curtain falls in Act III. The incidents of the mishap of the scouting party and the beginning of the uprising, are felicitously used. The language is simple and direct, and the sound of gayety in the barracks where the cavalry ball is going on lends the desired effect of contrast. The scenes and incidents in the stockade, while the Indians are preparing for their last attack and the hopeless garrison is waiting to die bravely, are strongly and simply set forth.

The daughter's frenzied appeal to her father to kill her before she falls into the hands of the savages, who have declared their purposes not to kill her, and his determination to thus preserve her from shame, naturally reminds one of "Virginus," just as the peril of the garrison and its rescue at the last moment inevitably recalls Boucicault's "Jessie Brown; or, the Relief of Lucknow." The great scene in every play of this class is founded on exactly the same principle. The rescue of Eliot Grey and the child by the lancers in "Rosedale," the rescue of Snorkey from the railroad track in "Under the Gaslight," the rescue of the hero from the moving saw log in "Blue Jeans," are elementally and technically the same as the stockade scene in "The Girl I Left Behind Me."

The authors, however, have most deftly used the old situations. Their atmosphere is their own; the details of the story are their own; their deadly educated savage, one of the most impressive of the many Indians of the stage, is their own. More forcible, moving melodrama than the second and third acts of this new play we have never seen. The illusion is perfect, and the thrill of the suspense never lacking.

In their humorous moods the authors err, perhaps, in giving a little too much prominence to the petticoat in preference to any other article of feminine apparel. But this is harmless and seems to please. Of course, as Mr. George Sampson remarked, we all know the ladies wear them. . . .

101. AMERICAN THEATRE
New York City
Opened May 22, 1893

A new playhouse, which the New York *Times* called "fit for the noblest plays and the best audiences," opened on May 22, 1893, but the theater underwent many managements and had many kinds of entertainment, including burlesque, before being demolished in 1932. At the time of its opening, however, the playhouse was hailed as an architectural gem. It was described architecturally by William H. Birkmire.

101:1   THE AMERICAN THEATRE.

The American Theatre, situated on the southeast corner of Eighth Avenue and West Forty-second Street, New York City, as designed and constructed by Charles C. Haight, architect, presents to us an example of the newest of the great places of amusements in which New York delights.

It was opened for the first time in 1893, and attained at once great popularity.

The theatre proper covers a plot of ground 100 feet by 98 feet 9 inches, with three fronts upon three different streets. The photo-plate shows the Forty-first Street front with entrances to the foyer, balcony, gallery, and stage. The other two fronts face Eighth Avenue and Forty-second Street respectively, and are used also as entrances to the foyer. The Forty-second Street entrance contains stairways leading to balcony and gallery. The architecture of the exterior is simple and effective, showing at once that the design has been well studied, and carried out with neatness and precision.

In the decoration of the auditorium and throughout the interior of other portions of the building the same taste has been exercised as in the front, the colors of which are in warm tints.

In the construction of the auditorium particular care has been taken to provide a system by which each spectator commands a good view of the performers.

Some of the important provisions for the safety of the public against fire are wide and easy staircases, large outside fire-escapes, open courts, and an abun-

101:1. William H. Birkmire, *The Planning and Construction of American Theatres* (New York: Wiley, 1901), pp. 22–31.

dance of exit doors; fire-extinguishers, fire-curtain, and skylights constructed to fly open automatically. Iron and concrete enter largely into the entire construction of the building.

A feature of the American Theatre is its roof-garden, which is constructed upon heavy iron girders over the auditorium, where in hot weather one may partake of refreshments and listen to the orchestral music.

The garden, as well as the rest of the entire building, is brilliantly lighted with electricity, and is reached by elevators and stairways.

The elevator-shafts are constructed of solid masonry walls, having openings leading into the different galleries, the auditorium, and foyer. The elevators are used by the audience at the beginning and close of each performance.

The auditorium will accommodate, in seats which are comfortably arranged, about 2500 persons.

The ground-floor plan clearly shows the entire arrangement of the entrances and lower portions of the building. The passage from Eighth Avenue is 19 feet 8 inches wide, and that from Forty-second Street 15 feet 8 inches; the lobby at the end of these two passages being 18 feet 6 inches in diameter.

The foyer is 14 feet 6 inches wide at its narrowest part, by about 60 feet long.

The distance from the curtain to the rear is 74 feet 6 inches by 74 feet 5 inches wide, and the height of the auditorium from the stage level to the top of the dome is about 70 feet.

From a point on the centre-line, 7 feet 4 inches from the curtain, a radius of 34 feet describes the rail which separates the parquette from the parquette circle. Each successive row of seats in the circle, 2 feet 7 inches wide, is described from the same point, allowance being made for an aisle 6 feet 3 inches wide at the back.

The steppings of the parquette are described by a radius of 31 feet 8 inches to a point on the centre-line back from the curtain, each row being the same width as those of the circle.

In addition to the main entrances to the foyer there are in this portion of the house four exits on each side, two leading to an open court and the other two leading to Forty-first Street.

The stage with its galleries, and the proportions of the auditorium, are shown in the section.

The proscenium opening is 39 feet wide by 39 feet high. The stage is 43 feet 4 inches deep by 77 feet 9 inches wide, and 73 feet 6 inches to the gridiron.

There are seven small dressing-rooms, fitted up with toilets and every convenience, opening upon the stage level, two of which are for star actors.

Directly back of the stage is placed the scene-dock, 11 feet 4 inches wide by 25 feet 8 inches clear height, for the storage of scenery used in large spectacular plays.

Under the entire stage and not shown in any of the illustrations are spacious rooms used for various purposes, such as bill-rooms, toilets for stage hands, orchestra, etc.

The balcony, being directly over the parquette circle, is somewhat similar in plan, with the exception that the four rear rows of seats are raised above the balcony-level.

The four emergency exits shown upon the plan lead to the outside fire-escapes. All the dressing-rooms above the stage-level, some of which are also shown in the plan, are reached by iron and slate stairways.

The height of the balcony is 21 feet from the foyer floor-level, being 9 feet 1½ inches to the first stepping; eleven steppings take up the remaining height of 10 feet 10½ inches.

The first fly-gallery is 8 feet 9 inches from the stage, the second 7 feet 9 inches, and the third 7 feet 9 inches from the second.

The front of gallery and stepping as shown by the plan of gallery are described by a radius of 38 feet 10 inches from a point on the centre-line 5 feet 4 inches from the curtain. The steppings are all 2 feet 6 inches wide, the height of the first being 17¼ inches, the second 18¼, the last at the gallery-level, 20¼ inches, making 14 feet 6⅜ inches, or 16 feet from the balcony level.

From the 16-foot level at the back of the gallery there is a passage 6 feet 4 inches wide, and placed above this passage there are six rows of seats 2 feet 6 inches wide, from 18⅞ to 20⅞ inches in height.

The halls of this gallery leading to the main stairways are 8 feet 6 inches wide, and the doors leading to the fire-escape stairs are 6 feet wide.

It is also possible, by the arrangement of steppings, to reach the lower floor by the circular stairs at the rear of the six boxes.

The stage side of the auditorium at the gallery-level contains the paint-bridge, the two large fly-galleries, and the carpenter-shop.

All the heating, ventilating, and lighting appliances known to the mechanic's world are placed in this theatre. In designing the ventilating plant no expense was spared to make the system a perfect one.

The theatre is heated mainly by the indirect system, while a few direct-heating radiators are placed in the dressing-rooms, lobby, and the rear of the stage, where the heated air that is blown into the body of the theatre would not be liable to penetrate.

There are about 1400 square feet of heating surface of direct radiators in the building, and about 2500 square feet of heating surface in especially designed coils for the heating-chamber in the basement. About 2,000,000 cubic feet of air per hour is drawn from the heating-chamber by the fan and forced into the theatre, thus giving about 660 cubic feet per person per hour, assuming the theatre to hold 3,000 persons.

The fresh air for the indirect system enters by a loggia or open gallery near the roof, and descends to heating-chamber in the basement by means of an 8½′ x 3′ duct. An iron damper, placed in the duct and controlled from the heating-chamber, prevents an upward current when the fan is at rest.

The air enters at one end of the chambers near the floor, and, rising, passes between the inclined coils to the fan.

There is, however, an unobstructed passage at one side of the coils, which allows the greater part of the air to pass directly to the fan. This passage can be closed by a switch-valve or door swinging on a vertical axis, and by the partial opening or closing of this door the temperature of the air entering the theatre can be regulated.

The coils also being in separate sections, each controlled by a valve, allows the operator to use any number at a given time. An opening through the wall of the coil-chamber allows the passage of air to the plenum-chamber.

A cone-wheel fan 8 feet in diameter is placed opposite the opening above mentioned, the shaft carrying the fan being supported by a pillow-and-spider bearing, the fan being driven by a belt from a 9″ x 10″ engine.

The plenum-chamber, as shown on the section, occupies all the space in the basement under the auditorium, the air being delivered to the parquette and circle by means of 341 openings under the seats, the same method being used for the balcony. These openings are approximately under every seat in the lower floor and every third seat in the balcony, a hood being placed over each opening to diffuse the air for the comfort of the occupant, each opening having a sectional area of seven square inches. The air is carried to the balcony from the plenum-chamber by vertical ducts built in the walls of the auditorium, the largest of which has a sectional area of 16 square feet, and also supply fresh air to the main halls. Radiators, or what may be termed secondary coils, are placed in branch ducts to increase the temperature of the air supplied to the halls.

The foul air is taken from under the galleries by horizontal ducts leading to vertical ones, and finally combine and form one circular flue 30 inches in diameter.

The greatest volume of foul air from the auditorium ceiling-bell is carried by a horizontal duct leading to a vertical flue having a sectional area of 24 square feet, supplied with damper and controlled by the engineer.

HEATING AND VENTILATION.

Heating and ventilation are branches of science which have received thus far a general acknowledgment, embodying principles of the greatest importance.

The ordinary comprehension of ventilation as applied to theatres is the introduction of fresh air and the simultaneous removal of vitiated air. Air when once passed through the human system is unfit for reinspiration, that portion which is emitted being not only useless, but deleterious to health. On this account it becomes necessary to remove this vitiated air and to substitute fresh air, which should be at a temperature of 60° to 65°. The vitiated air on being exhaled has a temperature between 80° and 90°, and, being thereby rarefied and rendered lighter has a tendency to rise.

The fact is, of course, a constant continuous mingling of the vitiated and the fresh air, depending somewhat on their relative temperatures and densities, but mainly on the absolute motion of the air in the room. A process of dilution of the vitiated air exhaled by man and the air in the room is constantly going on, and the fresh-air supply must be adequate to keep the air breathed by the inmates at a proper standard of purity.

We have no mode of measuring the mixed quantities of impurities in the air with precision. To come to any near approximation we must first calculate the amount of carbonic acid contained in the air, and allow that the *quantum* of the organic impurities are proportional to it.

We are informed by the best hygienists that a room to be properly ventilated not exceed by volume 6 to 8 parts of carbonic acid in the air. When the proportion rises above six—possibly eight—the disagreeable odor experienced by every one who, coming from the fresh external atmosphere, enters a crowded and inadequately ventilated room becomes perceptible.

We are also informed that although, in poorly ventilated quarters the proportion rises as high as 80 parts in 10,000 no room is properly ventilated in which the proportion is higher than 6 in 10,000, or sometimes 8.

Mr. A. R. Wolff, M.E., states in his treatise on ventilation that an ordinary man exhales .6 of a cubic foot of carbonic acid per hour. New York gas gives out 0.75 of a cubic foot of carbonic acid for each cubic foot of gas burnt, or for a 4½-foot burner 3⅜ cubic feet per hour. An ordinary lamp gives out 1 cubic foot per hour. An ordinary candle gives 0.3 cubic foot per hour. To express it mathematically, one ordinary gaslight equals in vitiating effect about 5½ men, an ordinary lamp 1⅔ men, and an ordinary candle 1 man.

To appreciate the importance of this it is but necessary to recognize that an air-supply ample for six men when there is no lighting, would be sufficient for one man when the room is lit by a single gas-burner.

And furthermore, the value of an incandescent electric light as an illuminant, in which no vitiation of the atmosphere is caused, is at once evident.

Pure country air contains about 4 parts of carbonic acid in 10,000. Hygienists calculate that 3000 cubic feet of fresh air should be supplied by systematic ventilation per hour to each person. In theatres and large auditoriums, in which the cubic space per individual is great, this may be considerably reduced.

Pure air penetrates in many ways. Windows, doors, and even brick walls, all permit the entrance of the external air, and thus without a systematic air-supply a large amount of external air enters to purify the air in the room.

In theatres where the air enters through the steppings of the galleries and auditorium, and where it can be made to enter through apertures in the decoration, it is a comparatively simple matter to supply from one to two thousand feet per hour to each person at a low velocity, the quantity of fresh air supplied being conditioned on the removal of the same amount of air from the building.

The most active circulation and removal of air by vent-ducts are produced by exhaust fans and blowers. Indeed, for theatres especially, reliance should be placed either on bringing in the fresh-air supply under pressure by means of blowers, or by attaching exhaust fans to the vent-ducts to create a current within them, or a combination of both systems may be arranged.

The ordinary ratings of blowers supplied by the trade range from wheels 4 feet in diameter, with 350 revolutions per minute, and 10,635 cubic feet per minute, to wheels 15 feet in diameter, with 100 revolutions and 160,000 cubic feet per minute.

The new playhouse was opened on May 22, 1893, with the first American perforance of a new English melodrama, *The Prodigal Daughter,* by Henry Pettitt and Augustus Harris. The New York *Times* labeled the play "the most successful of the recent English melodramas" and went on to comment that there was "no better play of its kind . . . brought across the Atlantic since 'The Silver King.' . . ."

102. ABBEY THEATRE
New York City
Opened November 8, 1893

Henry Abbey was one of the most successful theatrical managers of the latter part of the nineteenth century, managing both theatrical and opera companies. It was he who persuaded Sarah Bernhardt to act under his aegis on her first tour of the United States. He had been manager of the New Park Theatre until its destruction by fire in 1882. The new playhouse, which bore his name, remained under his direction until his death in 1896, when it was bought by Al Hayman and renamed the Knickerbocker Theatre, the name it retained until its demise in 1930.

The opening performance was a particularly important occasion, since Sir Henry Irving and his London repertory company, including Ellen Terry, had a six-weeks engagement there. The opening play was Tennyson's *Becket.*

102:1   MR. IRVING AS THE PRELATE

BRILLIANT OPENING NIGHT AT THE
NEW ABBEY'S THEATRE.

A Great Throng To Welcome Mr. Irving and Miss Terry on the Fourth Visit to New-York—The New Theatre Handsome, Well Appointed, and Comfortable Except for the Lack of Lobby Room—Irving's Martyred Archbishop a Flawless and Memorable Piece of Acting.

Abbey's Theatre, one of the costliest and best-appointed playhouses in the metropolis, was opened to the public last night, when Henry Irving and Ellen Terry appeared there in Tennyson's sombre and tragic dramatic piece called "Becket." The recital of these facts is a needful part of the day's news chronicle, but the element of novelty is not permitted in these times to any theatrical event of so much importance.

The readers of this newspaper already know all about Abbey's Theatre, what its seating capacity is, and how many incandescent lamps illuminate its interior; the

102:1. New York *Times,* Nov. 9, 1893.

dimensions of its stage, and its architectural peculiarities.

The first impression of the new house is most agreeable. It is handsome, tasteful, and comfortable. Every material used in its construction and furnishing seems to be of the best possible quality. The slope of the orchestra floor is just right for the vision, the curve of the balconies is symmetrical, and the occupants of those divisions of the auditorium seem to be brought closer to the stage than they are in most of the city theatres.

The stage is said to be comparatively small, but the fact was made manifest last night that the scenic effect of distance can be easily secured upon it, and that a large body of supernumeraries can be marshalled within its compass. But it is also well devised for performances of conversational comedy. The plays in which Coquelin and his French associates appear there in January will be as enjoyable as the larger and more spectacular productions such as Irving's.

The chief fault of the house, which will not be noticeable or a source of discomfort, except on rare occasions, like last night, is the lack of the spacious lobbies such a theatre ought to possess. Carried in the crowd through a small outer vestibule, the visitor is precipitated into a narrow aisle at the back of the orchestra chairs. From this aisle stairs ascend to the balcony. The aisle was jammed by men, pushing and shoving their way about in the entre-actes. But, of course, the new theatre is plentifully supplied.

Much novelty is not attached either to Tennyson's "Becket" or Mr. Irving's fine production of it. The play has been included in the later editions fo the laureate's works, and has been read as generally as any of his plays; and the voice of praise in London, when the tragedy was acted at the Lyceum, was heard plainly on this side of the Atlantic. Since they came to America, for the fourth time, in

September, Mr. Irving and Miss Terry have acted Becket and Fair Rosamund in San Francisco and Chicago, and the opinions of the judges of acting in those cities have reached us here.

These opinions will not be reversed. Irving's portrayal of Becket is one of his finest achievements. Miss Terry, though the sunshine in her nature is always under a cloud in the role of Rosamund, has never seemed more beautiful to the eye than she does in the few scenes in which that personage figures. The production of the play, in a scenic sense, is in keeping with Irving's fame. . . .

A detailed architectural description of the theater was written by William H. Birkmire.

102:2   THE ABBEY THEATRE.

The Abbey Theatre, corner of Broadway and Thirty-eighth Street, the newest of the places of amusement for which New York is noted, combines in its planning and decorations all the comforts and beauties required by the theatre-going public.

The seating capacity is 1450.

The work of demolishing the old buildings upon which the new structure stands was commenced May 1, 1893; in the short space of 6 months and 8 days the new theatre was opened by Henry Irving and Ellen Terry in Lord Tennyson's play *Becket*.

This theatre is one of the first to be completed since the enactment of the new law relating to the building of theatres. The law is stricter than any of its predecessors, and in the case of the Abbey Theatre has been rigidly enforced. The exterior of the theatre presents a six-story office building of light stone.

A new feature in regard to the exits has been introduced. All the doors are controlled by electric openers; by pressing a

102:2. William H. Birkmire, *The Planning and Construction of American Theatres* (New York: Wiley, 1901), pp. 16–20.

button on the stage, or from either of two stations on each tier, in the manager's office or box-office, all the doors will fly open.

It is calculated that a large audience can get out of the theatre in a minute and a half by using the various exits.

To prevent fire that might arise on the stage from extending into the auditorium the *asbestos* curtain demanded by law has been provided, and as a further precaution two large windows or skylights have been placed on the roof over the stage, and so built that when not pressed down they will fly open. A light rope has been attached to each and carried down to the stage. By applying a match or using a penknife these ropes are loosened, whereupon the windows will fly open. In case of fire upon the stage—the asbestos curtain being down—the draught would all be directly through the windows, and it would be impossible for the flames to go in any other direction than upward. Every precaution has been taken to guard against fire, and the entire building is as nearly fire-proof as possible. The heating is by an indirect-blower apparatus, and the lighting is by electricity furnished by a special plant under the sidewalk.

The lights can be absolutely controlled, and can be raised or lowered as perfectly as gas. The wires are insulated, and carried through the building in brass tubes.

For a modern theatre a suitable site is the most important. If on the inside lots of a city block between streets, 10 to 12 feet should separate a theatre from contiguous buildings. The corner site is to be preferred. To successfully design a plan, a general knowledge of the internal workings of such buildings must be first acquired. The representative of each department should be consulted.

The plans should be such that masonry walls separate the auditorium, entrances, staircases, stage work-shops, and dressing-rooms, and when practicable these walls should be carried up through the roof. In the case of the proscenium wall this is imperative.

Construct all roofs as flat as possible, connected with flights of iron platforms and stairways. The most approved plan should be lighted by means of windows in every part.

The auditorium, stage, and dressing-rooms should be sufficiently lighted from the outer air to conduce to ventilation and cleanliness.

Entrances and exits are all-important.

The safety of an audience depends more upon judiciously arranged means of egress than upon any precautionary system of fire-appliances or fire-resisting construction.

Panic may develop itself at any moment without adequate cause; consequently there should be means of escape from the building sufficient to withstand the sudden and extraordinary pressure of a stampede without the exits becoming congested. With this in view it seems that the present New York Building Law has been well considered. . . .

In the Abbey Theatre, Broadway and Thirty-eighth Street, the parquette and circle are arranged upon the same general plan as the Empire, with some slight differences . . . the proscenium opening is 35 feet wide and 34 feet in height. The auditorium is 79 feet in depth from curtain-line by 70 feet 9 inches in width, from which it has been deducted 10 feet in the depth for the promenade and stairs to balcony, and in the width for aisles.

There are in this theatre three exits on the left of the auditorium, opening into the open court which leads to Broadway, and upon the right side three, two of which are to be used in case of emergency —through the ladies' parlor—the other as an entrance for those persons arriving and departing in carriages. The stage of the Abbey Theatre is 40 feet by 65 feet 7 inches, and the Empire 30 feet by 67 feet. . . .

All measurements of heights are taken from the stage-level, the longitudinal measurements from the curtain-line. The parquette floor is 3 feet 9 inches below the stage and starts 10 feet from the curtain line. For a distance of 38 feet 8 inches there is an upward pitch of 12½ inches to the first stepping of the parquette circle, which step is 3 inches.

The other steppings are in the following order: the second step 3½ inches, third 4 inches, fourth 4½ inches, and continue in successive half-inch increases until the next to the last of 7 inches, which is the foyer-level, 20 inches above the stage.

There is an additional step of 8 inches by 2 feet 7 inches wide raised above the foyer-level. All these steps except the last mentioned pitch down toward the sides of the auditorium 6 inches.

The parquette floor gradually rises toward the boxes at the orchestra to meet the lowest step at that point.

The height of the balcony floor above the foyer-level is 18 feet, the lowest step 8 feet 7 inches above the same point. The lower step of the balcony descends 20 inches from the centre toward the boxes; consequently, the top step being level, this 20 inches is divided among the various steps at the wall-line.

The gallery-floor is 16 feet 4 inches above the balcony, and 4 feet 4 inches at the lowest step. The upper step is level, and the first step descends 2 feet 10 inches toward the boxes; the difference of height is made up in the various number of steppings, as explained for the balcony.

The flat roof, 14 feet above the gallery, is constructed of steel beams and filled between with flat terra-cotta arches. The hanging ceiling under the same is constructed of 1 1/2″ x 17₂ x 3/16″ angles supported from the beams, curved at the intersection of the wall and truss, and covered with wire lath and plaster.

This section shows the bottom chords of the trusses supporting the main roof of the auditorium, which are 47 feet 8 inches above the stage-level, and also clearly shows the north interior view of the stage. The large door upon the stage leads to the scene-room. The first set of flies is 28 feet above the stage, the second 52 feet, and the gridiron 69 feet. The paint-bridge is at the rear of the stage, connected to the first set of galleries. . . .

103. HERALD SQUARE THEATRE
New York City
Opened September 17, 1894

The Herald Square Theatre was not a new playhouse, but a completely remodeled older one. It was originally built in 1874 as the Colosseum Theatre, but later bore the names Criterion, Harrigan's Park, and, in 1889, Park Theatre. As the Herald Square Theatre it was reopened on September 17, 1894, and remained an important theater until it burned in 1908. The opening performance was of George Bernard Shaw's *Arms and the Man*, starring Richard Mansfield, one of the favorite actors of the day. The New York *Dramatic Mirror* gave good coverage to the opening and provided some information about the playhouse.

103:1   The Herald Square Theatre was opened last evening with Richard Mansfield in Arms and the Man. This is the play that created so much discussion on the original production in London. It was billed as a "Romantic comedy." But some of the critics persisted in their belief that the author, Bernard Shaw, was simply satirizing the weakness of the conventional drama. . . .

The remodeling of the former Park Theatre has proved most effectual in every respect. The white brick walls have been replaced by a tasteful facade in the style of the Italian Renaissance. A striking effect is produced by the colonnade that supports the balcony, and a number of arched windows, the entire exterior being

103:1. New York *Dramatic Mirror,* Sept. 22, 1894.

illuminated at night by innumerable electric lights under the cornices.

The decorations of the interior are fashioned after the rocco style. The colors are pink, blue, green and gold. The doors and screens are provided with glazed art glass. To the right of the lobby is a café, also decorated in light shades of the French school. The open space from the lobby to the foyer is furnished with comfortable divans and couches. The carpeting is in maroon and black.

The seats in the auditorium have the latest improvements. The stage is unusually large, and taken all in all, the present manager, Charles E. Evans, has in the Herald Square Theatre an enviable house for metropolitan productions. . . .

104. GARRICK THEATRE
New York City
Opened April 23, 1895

Richard Mansfield, who had opened the Herald Square Theatre in Shaw's *Arms and the Man*, took a lease on this theater, which had been built in 1890 as Harrigan's Theatre. After a redecoration of the house, he opened it as the Garrick Theatre on April 23, 1895, again with a performance of *Arms and the Man*.

Although Mansfield was not a particularly successful manager, the theater did house some very important productions until it was demolished in 1929. Among them were William Gillette in *Secret Service* and the young Ethel Barrymore in Clyde Fitch's *Captain Jinks of the Horse Marines*. In 1919 the theater was taken over by the Theatre Guild, which used it for the next six years. One interesting fact is that this theater housed the last production of the Provincetown Players.

Brief comments on the renovation of the theater were included in the review of the opening by the New York *Times*.

104:1   MR. MANSFIELD'S THEATRE
——————
A BRILLIANT OPENING NIGHT AT THE
NEW GARRICK

104:1. New York *Times*, Apr. 24, 1895.

ARMS AND THE MAN
——————
AGAIN EVERYBODY LIKES THE BEAUTIFUL
THEATRE, AND THE POMPEIIAN
REFRESHMENT ROOM SEEMS TO BE
POPULAR ALREADY

A great crowd assembled at the opening of the Garrick Theatre, in West Thirty-fifth Street, last night. The audience which filled the theatre was of an unusually fine quality, too. The beautiful new decorations were admired without reserve, and the wonder that this was Harrigan's—or had been a month before—was freely expressed. As a matter of fact, the house the McElfatricks designed and built for Harrigan has always been one of the best appointed in the country. The acoustics are good, the means of entrance and egress ample, the stage sufficiently broad and high for any dramatic purpose, and the lines of the audience room correct and beautiful.

By his contract with Harrigan, Mr. Mansfield came into possession of a modern fireproof playhouse, which, with the liberal expenditure of money and the exercise of his good taste, he has now made one of the most inviting theaters in the world. The seating arrangements have all been changed, and the orchestra and balcony stalls are now roomy, high-backed, and luxurious. The electric-lighting apparatus is also new and of the most improved kind. But the great change has been made by the recoloring of the house, which is now rich Pompeian red, relieved by gold and bronze, and shading under the balconies to rose-color. The proscenium arch is bronze, the curtains are of red velvet, while the act drop is a beautiful landscape by Mr. Physioc, the scenic artist of the theatre. There were many rich toilettes in the house last night and they were seen to advantage with the dark-red background.

The Pompeian refreshment room, approached from the outer lobby by a flight of stairs lined by original Hogarth plates

102. Abbey Theatre (renamed Knickerbocker Theatre), New York, ca. 1910. Courtesy of The Hoblitzelle Theatre Arts Library, The Humanities Research Center, The University of Texas at Austin.

103. Herald Square Theatre, New York. Courtesy of The Hoblitzelle Theatre Arts Library, The Humanities Research Center, The University of Texas at Austin.

105. Hammerstein's Olympia Theatre, New York, ca. 1895. Photograph by G. P. Hill. Courtesy of The New-York Historical Society, New York City.

in oak frames, was crowded in both entre-actes. The buffet there is in charge of Maillard. Girls from Thorley's have flowers to sell at the door. The refreshment room, lined with high-backed, red velvet sofas, in a novelty. As a novelty it was liked last night, but it is still a problem whether a buffet will be profitable in a New-York theatre. . . .

105. HAMMERSTEIN'S OLYMPIA
New York City
Opened November 30, 1895

It was left to Oscar Hammerstein to open the largest and first real theater complex in New York City. Called "The Olympia," the complex consisted of four theaters in the same building. It was on the east side of Broadway between Forty-fourth and Forty-fifth streets. Hammer-stein had the theaters designed by the McElfat-rick firm and planned for the enterprise to have four connected theaters: the Olympia Music Hall, containing seating for 2,800 persons; the Concert Hall; the Lyric Theatre; and the Roof Garden.

The New York *Dramatic Mirror* com-mented on this huge entertainment palace:

105:1   OLYMPIA OPENED.

OSCAR HAMMERSTEIN'S GREAT
AMUSEMENT ENTERPRISE ON
LONG ACRE SQUARE.

Hammerstein's Olympia had a rousing housewarming last night. So great was the crowd and so eager were the people to get inside the building, that one literally had to fight one's way in. Such a struggle of modish people to get into a theatre has seldom, if ever, occurred in New-York. To add to the confusion and excitement, the ushers were unfamiliar with the house, and all those who held seat coupons were not seated until after the curtain was raised. Once comfortably ensconced in the beauti-ful new theatre, however, the audience for-got the early discomfort of the evening and

105:1. New York *Dramatic Mirror,* Nov. 30, 1895.

enjoyed the manifold charms of Excelsior, Jr., to the utmost.

Hammerstein's Olympia does honor to New York. Twenty years ago the construc-tion of such a mammoth building for theatrical purposes would have been re-garded as a madman's enterprise. It is perhaps the largest building in the world devoted to purely theatrical entertain-ments.

And it is as beautiful as it is big. The three auditoriums spanned by the one roof are all of them models of architectural beauty and luxurious appointments. It is Mr. Hammerstein's intention to give en-tertainments nightly in each of these halls. There is also a roof garden, with a level floor space almost equal to the surface dimensions of the building, and capable of seating several thousand persons. Be-low the street level there will be, when completed, apartments for cafés, billiards, and bowling.

The Olympia is located on the east side of Broadway, occupying the entire block-front between Forty-fourth and Forty-fifth streets, 203 feet in length, 154 feet deep on Forty-fifth Street and 101 feet on Forty-fourth Street. Mr. Hammerstein purchased the ground last January. He says that the entire cost—ground and building together —represents an investment of between two and three million dollars.

The music hall, which is the largest of the three auditoriums, is in the style of Louis XIV. It is immeasurably superior to the English Palace, formerly the Royal Opera House, which Londoners regard as the finest music hall interior in the world. There are six tiers of proscenium boxes and five tiers of mezzanine boxes, making a total of 124 boxes, the largest number under the roof of any existing place of amusement.

The theatre, which occupies the Forty-fourth Street end of the building, is in the Louis XVI style. The decorations are in light and dark blue. There are eighty-four boxes, more than in either Metropolitan Opera House or in Carnegie Hall.

The concert hall, which occupies the centre of the building, is in the style of Louis XV. The four walls are surrounded by a balcony which is approached from the second tier leading from the music hall and theatre. Here there will be no reserved seats, as the room is to be devoted solely to promenade concerts. . . .

The architectural dimensions and description of the Oympia are furnished by Birkmire in his book:

105:2   HAMMERSTEIN'S OLYMPIA.

In the short space of ten months, beginning with February 1895, the large and magnificent amusement palace situated at Forty-fourth street and Broadway, New York, was opened to the public on November 25th.

The building has a frontage of 203 feet on Broadway, 156 feet on Forty-fifth Street, and a little less on Forty-fourth Street. The greatest height of the building is 96 feet at the centre of the Broadway side. The architecture follows the lines of the French Renaissance period.

"Olympia" comprises three spacious auditoriums, as shown by the plans, under one roof, known as Olympia Music Hall, Olympia Concert Hall, and Olympia Theatre, where three distinct entertainments are given nightly, one admission-fee admitting to all.

In addition to the above auditoriums there will be a roof-garden with complete stage appointments and a level floor-space almost equal to the surface dimensions of the entire building and capable of seating several thousand persons.

Below the street-level there are cafés, billiard-rooms, bowling-alleys, and Turkish baths.

The edifice is fire-proof and strictly complies with the laws of the Building and Fire Departments.

No wood or inflammable material has been used in the structural portion, excepting in some parts over concreted floors. It is provided with ample means of escape in case of fire or panic, and has numerous exits on every floor front and back of the curtain-line. Automatic sprinklers are distributed over all the auditoriums, stages, fly-galleries, and dressing-rooms, and at any point the building can be deluged should the temperature reach an abnormal degree.

The building is heated and ventilated by the rotary-fan process, which forces hot and cold air through ducts, and permits an even temperature at all times, no matter what the climatic conditions may be or how densely the auditoriums may be crowded. The same process drives impure air from the various auditoriums through the openings placed above the ceilings.

Olympia is lighted by electricity supplied by four large dynamos operated from vaults underneath the sidewalk.

The music hall is on the Forty-fifth Street side, occupying a frontage on Broadway of about 75 feet; the concert hall is in the centre, and the theatre is on the Forty-fourth Street end. The main entrance to the three auditoriums, as shown by the plan, is through two massive carved doorways on the street-level in the centre of the Broadway front, leading to the marble foyer. In the centre of the foyer there are two immense passenger-elevators, which run to the upper floors and the roof-garden. To the right and left are marble staircases leading to the balconies and box-tiers of the music hall and theatre.

The dimensions of the music hall are: auditorium, 10 x 100 feet; stage, 43 x 70 feet; proscenium opening 36 x 36 feet; height to rigging-loft, 80 feet; height to fly-gallery, 30 feet.

The stage is well stocked with scenery calculated to meet all requirements.

The dressing-rooms are numerous, well lighted, heated, and ventilated, and are a luxury compared with those usually provided in the average playhouse.

105:2. William H. Birkmire, *The Planning and Construction of American Theatres* (New York: Wiley, 1901), pp. 41–47.

Ample provision has been made for seating in the music hall. There are six tiers of boxes and five tiers of mezzanine boxes, making a total of 124, the largest number known of any single place of amusement. The box-tiers and balconies, while not too far removed from the stage, do not overshadow the orchestra, and are so encircled as to allow freedom of space in the auditorium, which cannot fail to be agreeable to the occupants of boxes, as well as those in the chairs below. The concert hall is 85 feet long, 43 feet wide, and 45 feet in height. It is the centre between the music hall and theatre, separated by courtyards, and is on a level with the first balcony tiers.

The theatre, situated at the south end, has a seating capacity less than the music hall, although it contains eighty-four boxes.

The decorative scheme is blue and gold, in the softest tints and most delicate color effects. Carpets, chairs, and hangings are all blue.

Back of the footlights everything is as complete as human ingenuity could make it. The dimensions of the theatre are as follows: auditorium, 60 x 68 feet; proscenium opening, 32 x 32 feet; stage, 31 x 60 feet; height to rigging-loft, 80 feet; height to fly-gallery, 30 feet. The general arrangement of the different balconies is shown by the section.

The stucco work used in the interior decoration of the entire building is one of the beautiful and artistic features of this immense amusement temple. The sculptural groups, figures, and designs which decorate the boxes and prosceniums in the various auditoriums make the interior appear very attractive.

The designs were made after the style in vogue during the reigns of Louis XIV., Louis XV., and Louis XVI., and living models were employed for the life-size groups and figures. In the decorative scheme that has been followed the music hall is Louis XIV., the concert hall Louis XV., and the theatre Louis XVI.

The music hall is highly decorated. The walls and ceilings are rich in panels of beautiful designs. A massive chandelier depends from a rosette surrounded by dancing cupids. A heroic female figure upholds the forty-eight boxes, which are all different in design.

The proscenium panels, as technically described by decorators, are round form at top and bottom, with a slight square break, with motifs in relief ornamenting the base, the middle and top having a bold cartouche with hanging laurel pendants at either side. The carved and undulating Louis XIV. lines are easily recognized in the lyre crossed by two flutes which appear to grow from the top of the cartouche.

The base is decorated with a rich design, a semi bas-relief, consisting of an ornamental pedestal on which rests a vase with dolphin handles. Japanese dragons crouch at each side of the base.

The panel is surmounted with a female head at the top, decidedly "French" in its expression, on whose forehead rests a star, with festoons of flowers hanging at either side. Below this will be found suspended by cupid's chains an emblem, of which a classic shield, cupid's bow, arrows, etc., form its composition. Its alternate strong and low reliefs and soft lines, with plain grounds well distributed, at once betray to the layman the quality of its execution. The main group over the procenium arch represents Poetry and Prose being crowned by the goddess Fame. Its dimensions are 24 x 10 feet.

A panel of cupids forms the frieze extending all around the concert hall. In the decorative scheme here cupids, lutes, lyres, etc., all figure prominently. At the corners of the hall are four female figures, twelve feet in height, with arms extended, each supporting a large crystal chandelier.

Four large mirrors are set in the sides between the pilasters, and the ceiling is elaborately decorated in floral designs.

The theatre is in white and gold, also elaborately decorated in floral designs and ornamented with statuary and relief figures representing the muse of the drama. The walls of the theatre are covered with ornamental designs in medallions and panels.

The base of the proscenium arch in the theatre, style Louis XVI., is modelled on a convexed surface, inclosed on the one hand by a rich old-gold leaf-moulding and bead, on the other by a flower-band standing out almost free, which run up on each side of the arch to a point in the middle of the top.

Motif composed of classic Louis Seize vase in bas-relief, in which kneels a cupid in perspective; a dove, drapery, and a liberal quantity of flowers finish the whole.

The music hall has a seating capacity of about 1625, in seats arranged as follows: first floor, 576 chairs, 16 boxes; first box-tier, 32 boxes, 160 people; second box-tier, 32 boxes, being similar to the first box-tier; balcony, 210 chairs, 40 boxes, 410 people; gallery, 165 chairs, 12 boxes, 225 people. In addition to the above there is 934 square feet of standing-room. The steppings of the first-floor plan are arranged somewhat differently from those of any theatre heretofore illustrated, in that those in the centre, or parquette circle, are described from a point on the centre-line,

37 feet 6 inches from the curtain-line, while those right and left of the centre are described by a line extending from the same point 13 feet 8½ inches distant, 11 feet 4 inches back on the centre-line, and 7 feet 4 inches right and left of the centre-line.

The steppings of the parquette and circle are 3 feet 4 inches wide.

The seating capacity of the theatre is about 1000, in seats as follows: first floor, 371 chairs, 6 boxes, 401 people; first and second box-tiers, 22 boxes each, 110 people each; balcony, 106 chairs, 28 boxes, 248 people; gallery, 77 chairs, 8 boxes, 117 people. In addition there is about 900 square feet of standing-room. The steppings of the different tiers are about 2 feet 8 inches wide.

The stairways connecting the first and second balconies in both buildings are easy and about 6 feet 6 inches wide, placed as shown upon the plans, and are not included in the square feet of standing-room mentioned above.

There is no standard in this country by which the Olympia can be measured. No theatrical management ever before offered the public such a diversified scheme of amusement in such a building as this.

Chapter 5

Regional Playhouses, 1865-1899

The period following the Civil War was one of consistent growth for playhouses in various parts of the country. The stability of these theaters was aided by the development of rail transportation, which made it possible for shows to travel more easily. No longer was it necessary for stars to make a long and hazardous journey by sea or uncomfortable overland coach to reach inland or California theaters. The train would take them in comparative comfort. And when they arrived at their destinations, they could expect to find theaters comparable to or even better than those in New York City. This was especially true in population centers such as Chicago, Denver, and San Francisco.

Wade's Opera House and Baldwin's Academy of Music in San Francisco, the Tabor Opera House in Denver, and certainly the giant Chicago Auditorium were matches in luxury of appointments for almost any of the playhouses to be found in New York City. And the greatest theatrical venture of the century, Steele Mac-Kaye's Spectatorium, was planned for the Chicago Exposition of 1893.

Perhaps the most important theatrical development of this period for the regional theater was the use of the "package show." Instead of a touring star acting with the permanent stock company of a theater, an entire production was mounted, all the parts were cast, and the whole company toured throughout the country taking with them their costumes, scenery, and properties. As the century drew to a close, a theatrical syndicate was formed that held complete power over the theaters "on the road," guaranteeing them quality bookings every week in return for a monopoly over the theater's scheduling. The members of the syndicate were Abraham Erlanger, Charles Frohman, Al Hayman, Marc Klaw, Sam Nixon, and J. Fred Zimmerman.

Innovations in technical theater included the adoption of electrical lighting systems by many theaters, the use of the box set, improved methods of stage rigging that facilitated the changing of scenery, and greater authenticity in costumes and scenery. This latter innovation reached its zenith in the productions of David Belasco.

The regional playhouses of the period were, for the most part, planned on a large scale, as various theater owners vied with one another to see who could build the largest theater. The battle was won by Chicago with the building of the magnificent Auditorium, which seated more than 5,000 persons.

106. CALIFORNIA THEATRE
San Francisco, California
Opened January 18, 1869

The California Theatre was built by William Ralston, president of the Bank of California, for two outstanding young Irish actors who earlier had won the hearts of the San Francisco theatergoing audience—Lawrence Barrett and John McCullough. The playhouse was to be the home of serious drama in San Francisco and was to reflect in its aspect the high caliber of its dramatic presentations. The total cost of this venture was estimated at $150,000, quite a princely sum for that time. A reporter for the San Francisco *Daily Evening Bulletin* gave an elaborate account of the new playhouse:

106:1   CALIFORNIA THEATRE.

—————————

Description of the Edifice—
Its Capacity, etc.

—————————

This magnificent building at once the pride and latest boast of the Pacific Coast, is rapidly approaching completion, and is the astonishment and delight of all who view it. No theatre on this continent has been fitted up with more elegance and regard for the convenience of the general audience and none in Europe excel it in comfort. The exterior and general form of the building have been already described in the *Bulletin*, and we need now only recapitulate the heads before proceeding to describe the interior. The building occupies a lot on the north side of Bush street, between Kearny and Dupont, and has a frontage of 165 feet on Bush street by 137½ feet deep. Abutting on the latter street, besides the various entrances, are four handsome stores, and over them is a lofty music hall, 100 feet by 51, and a smaller hall of 50 feet by 50, opening from it. These halls are not yet finished, and will be described at some future time.

106:1. San Francisco *Daily Evening Bulletin*, Jan. 8, 1869.

THE EXTERIOR AND ENTRANCES.

Walking up Bush street from Kearny, the first opening reached is the doorway, 9 feet wide, and staircase, leading to the upper circle and gallery. Adjoining it is the entrance to a chamber, running back some 50 feet, which will probably be let as a saloon. Next beyond that, and divided into three compartments by two stout Corinthian pillars of cast-iron, is the main entrance, 28 feet wide. The next opening leads to a staircase, running up to the square or smaller hall; then come the stores; next the main staircase to the music hall, and opening from the lobby leading to the staircase is a side passage, running to the stage of the theatre, for the ingress and egress of performers. At the Dupont street end of the building is the stage entrance, 17 feet wide and upwards of 50 feet long, leading to the rear of the stage. The main entrance of the theatre, leading to the parquette and dress circle, and the entrance to the large music hall are each marked by two very massive iron street lamp pillars, with large lanterns of plate glass, containing three large argand burners each.

THE MAIN ENTRANCE.

Passing from the street by the main entrance the visitor finds himself in a large hall, 50 feet by 30. On his left is a handsome office built out from the walls, with openings for three or four ticket clerks if necessary, and thus avoiding any necessity for crushing and pushing, in purchasing tickets. After obtaining his ticket the visitor will pass through one of the several green doors, which occupy the spaces between the second row of iron columns, and lead him into the lower promenade hall. This hall is the full width of the theatre building—82 feet. On the right, are two noble staircases leading to the upper hall and dress circle. This hall will be furnished in drawing-room style, complete with walnut furniture, pictures, etc., except that the floor will be cocoa matting, and with its bronzed statues, etc., will have a very striking effect on the beholder. On the left will be the several entrances into an inner semi circular corridor, which runs around the outer wall of the parquette. On each side of the auditorium, the corridor extends itself into wings, gradually narrowing until it reaches the proscenium wall. At the end of each of these wings is a staircase leading to the upper circle, and also a wide entrance to the orchestra stalls. Going back to the entrance from the outer hall, the visitor, if a gentleman, will find on his right, as he enters the main hall, a commodious square compartment, fitted up for a smoking room, and open on one side to the promenade hall. Here the gentleman visitor will find files of the daily and Eastern papers, easy chairs, and a floor covering that will not take fire if he should drop his cigar. If our gentleman visitor has brought a lady with him and has arrived too early, or wishes to converse with a male friend before taking his companion to her seat in the auditorium, he can lead her to the ladies' withdrawing room, a chamber 18 feet by 30, occupying the space between the two principal staircases. This room is richly carpeted, and contains an elegant set of drawing-room furniture, paintings on the walls, bronze statuettes, a handsome gaselier pendant from the centre of the ceiling, a carved table, bearing a beautiful flower vase, imported for the purpose, ice water vessels, settees, easy chairs, lounges, etc., and opening from each side are toilet rooms. Further on, and in the space corresponding to that devoted to smokers is the Director's office. In the centre of the floor, but near the further end, will be the flower stall, and the stand for the sale and loan of lorgnettes. Over the chief entrance to the parquette will be a bronze figure of Falstaff, bearing a clock, and in his right hand a small bell, which will ring for one minute before the rising of the curtain, and serve to recall the promenaders to their seats.

The main staircases to the upper corridor and dress circle are very handsome;

the balusters are California laurel, polished, and the rail is black walnut, 6 inches in the square, and handsomely moulded. The balusters run up the stairway, around the aperture, and return to the back wall. The newel posts at the foot are remarkably handsome, of California laurel overlaid with black walnut. On each will be a bronze Oriental figure, about 4 feet high—one male, the other female—each surmounted by a lamp. These statues were imported from Paris, by Haughwout & Co. of New York, especially for the California Theatre. The upper corridor, like the lower hall, will be covered with cocoa matting, but otherwise furnished in drawing-room style, with settees, chairs, paintings, etc. The furniture for this portion of the house is of oak. The dress circle opens directly from this corridor, without an intervening circle, as on the floor below. The corridor also runs into wings on each side the auditorium, and at the termination of these wings will be found the entrances to the open and balcony boxes, and stairs, as noticed before, for going below to the orchestra stalls.

THE AUDITORIUM

The height of the building (the outside walls) is 65 feet, and the height from the orchestra floor to the ceiling is 51 feet. The length of the house from the curtain to the wall at the back of the gallery is 30 feet, and from the curtain to the centre of the curve of the front rail of the dress circle is 47 feet. The proscenium opening is 45 feet wide and 40 feet high, and the moulding and decoration of the arch is that of a picture frame, and has been carried out from a suggestion of John Torrens. On each side is a fluted column, gilt and white, rising out of a carved pedestal, gilt and tings on a solferino ground, and surmounted by a Corrinthian capital, white and gold. These columns stand on a base eight feet high, the lower part being an imitation of green marble and the upper of sienna. The inner arch has two beads of bronze running around it, the ground work between is lilac ting. The spandril of the area are filled with gold, white and tinted scroll work on pale blue ground.

THE CURTAIN, ETC.

The green curtain, instead of baize, is green repe, striped with gold and crimson, and will itself be a very handsome feature in the *tout ensemble* when down.

The drop curtain has been painted by W. Denny, the well known marine painter. The subject is the Golden Gate. The spectators are supposed to be standing on an imaginary balcony at Lime Point, and the view embraces the opposite coast and channel from the Cliff House to the city. Prominent in the picture are the ship *Challenge* going into port under full sail; the pilot boat *Fanny* sailing out in tow of a steam tug; the P.M.S.S.Co.'s steamer *Golden City* coming in; the yacht *Restless* and several fishing boats cruising about. Underneath the main picture, and in the center of the flowing drapery and painted scroll work which surrounds it, is a medallion picture of a scene on the Central Pacific Railroad. In the foreground is an Indian boy, the village in a distance, watching a locomotive and train of cars rounding the rocky point known as Cape Horn, and thinking if not saying "What next?" The work is considered the best performance ever achieved by this artist.

Two borders have also been painted for this theater by Mr. Denny, one of the usual crimson drapery for ordinary use, and one green, to be used with forest or any other rural scenery.

VIEW FROM THE FOOTLIGHTS

The general color of the walls is French gray, and the ceiling is perfectly plain, except such relief as comes from a large, fan-shaped ventilator in the centre and nine smaller ventilators shaded from deep brown to a golden tint.

The plain wood-work of the auditorium throughout is California laurel, or California laurel and Port Oxford cedar, alternated in stripes. Immediately in front of the footlights is the orchestra, extending the whole width of the stage and with sufficient space for thirty or more musicians. Beyond that is the parquette or the orchestra stalls. This part of the house has communication with the corridors and thence freely with the street by wide entrances on each side near the proscenium, by a double "steamboat" stairway at the back of the parquette, and coming up from under the dress circle, and by two tiers of steps descending from the dress circle.

The dress circle in the rear of the parquette, is just elevated enough to allow headway for those entering the parquette from the lower corridor, and is 33 feet deep in the centre. On each side of the house between the proscenium and the dress circle is a large balcony box capable of accomodating five or six spectators. A little nearer the circle, and on some two or three feet higher level, is another balcony box a little smaller in size. Beyond and below these, but raised three feet or so above the ordinary level of the dress circle, from which they are taken, are on each side, three open dress boxes, separated from each other by low rails and each connecting with the corridor in the rear by a handsome arched entrance. Over the dress circle is the upper circle, containing five circles of chairs, and opening into wings on each side, running over the balcony boxes, where spectators standing can see the whole of the house and command at the same time a view of all the front of the stage and two-thirds of the back. These wings, or slips, are each faced by seven arches, of which the three nearest the stage open on to balconies similar to those of the balcony boxes. At the back of the upper circle and raised above it, as the dress circle is raised behind the parquette, is the gallery.

ORNAMENTAL WORK

On the flat wall between the proscenium arch and the first balcony box, on each side of the theatre, is a magnificent mirror, with a plate of California glass 96 inches by 150. This is surrounded by a deep, massive frame of carved and composite work. On the two lower corners of the frame are cornucopeas, from which up the molded sides rise gigantic stalks and ears of wheat and other California grain. The upper corners are enriched with carvings of two California grizzlies, and the whole is surmounted by a lofty trophy of California fruits, with their foilage, tinted to nature. The mirrors, with their frame, measure 9 feet by 6 inches by 17 feet high. By the aid of these mirrors, those who are seated on one side of the house or in front, can see and recognize all who sit behind or on the same side of the circle as themselves as easily as if they were opposite them.

The balcony boxes have white balustrades on green ground, surmounted by a black walnut rail. The open dress boxes have laurel wood balustrade, tinted and gilded, with walnut rail, against panelling of cedar. The front of the dress circle is very chaste; the balustrade is white, tipped with Solferino and gilt, against lilac ground; the rail is polished laurel. The bronze gas brackets are double, of a gothic pattern, and are capped with minute busts of Milton.

The front of the upper circle is divided into panels, in each of which a beautiful view in oil colors has been painted by Mr. Denny. Beginning at the spectator's right, if he stood with his back to the stage, is a view of Clear Lake; then of Fort Point, looking into the bay; then of Diamond Head, at the entrance of Honolulu harbor; then of Fort Point, looking out, at sunset; then of Sutter's Fort; then of the Pacific railroad, and a train crossing the Salt Lake Valley; then of the steamer *Capital*, bound up the river and entering the Slough—showing the Sacramento river; then the Gould and Curry Quartz Mill, Virginia City; then the Chemical Works, erected by Mr. Wakelee at Mission Bay; then Columbia River bar, with a steamer entering the river; next the Cliff House, from the sea—by moonlight—a beautiful view; and, lastly, Lake Bigler, completing the circle. The wood-work of this circle is similar to the lower circle. The gaseliers are similar in design except that they have three branches instead of two, and are surmounted by busts of Shakspeare instead of Milton.

The front of the gallery circle, behind the heads of those sitting in the upper circle, contains ten panels also filled with paintings from local subjects, by the hand of Mr. Denny. Besides these paintings, and conspicuous in front of the house, there are on each side the three balcony panels above the boxes, on the same tier as the upper circle. On the right hand, the first represents a swamp on the Isthmus; the next the California, Oregon and Mexico S.S. Company's steamer *Oriflamme* at sea, bound up from the south; then a view of the rich verdure of the coast of Lower California near where it is first sighted by the steamer coming north. On the opposite side, and corresponding, is, first, a view of the San Joaquin river; next a sunset view on the Sacramento river near Rio Vista, and, lastly, one of plains above Marysville.

SEATS—SEATING CAPACITY—
EXITS AND ENTRANCES.

The seats in the parquette and dress circle are, without possibility of contradiction, the most comfortable and probably the most costly ever placed in a theatre for a general audience. They are gothic chairs, with high carved backs, of California laurel wood, polished, with hair and spring seats—five springs and five pounds of curled hair to each, covered with solferino leather and ornamented with white boss nails. These chairs have no legs, but are secured to a raised bench by hinges and India-rubber springs, and, without the front rising, can, at the will of the sitter, be tipped back 25 degrees or more and will return to their natural place on the pressure being removed. This chair is a California design and is vastly superior to the fixed and rigid cast iron chairs used in Pike's Opera House and Booth's new theatre. New York, one of which was taken up by Mr. Barrett and sent out here as a specimen and to show the contrast. It cost but one-third the money of the California laurel chair. Each chair has 22½ inches allotted it, while other methods of seating give only 17 inches, and there is no possibility of crowding more persons in than there are chairs. Underneath each chair is a square hat-box, in which the chapeau is safe from injury by the boots of those behind or on the side. The space between the rows of chairs is 3 feet 10 inches wide, and visitors can pass those seated without compelling them to stand. The aisles in the dress circle are 6 feet wide. All the aisles in the parquette and dress circle will be handsomely carpeted. This and the carpet and matting in the corridors will be the only upholstery in the house, and there will be nothing to encourage or harbor fleas. The total number of exits and entrances to the dress circle and parquette are eight, and their aggregate width, measuring each at its narrowest point, is 58 feet. By these exits, the house, however crowded, could be cleared in less than three minutes, without danger, no matter how alarmed and panic-stricken the audience might be.

The upper circle has five rows of plain oak chairs on iron pedestals and secured to the floor, and there is room for another row of seats when required. The large space on each side, behind the aisles, affords an excellent promenading place from which almost the whole house can be seen, and can be filled with spectators when there is an unusual demand for admission. There are many people who go to the theater less often than they would because they are unwilling to give $1 for admission, and do not like to be seen in second priced seats. The back row of the upper circle for seeing and hearing is equal to any place in the house, and yet those who occupy it are out of sight of all in the higher priced part of the house, except, probably, those who occupy the first balcony boxes.

The gallery has a very easy incline, and is less elevated than in most theatres of the same capacity. It has ten full rows of benches, all provided with comfortable backs; besides these, there are a number of broken circles fitted with seats. In this part of the house the same care has been given as in others, that every one who pays to see the show shall see all that goes on on the stage, and the gods of California will have no reason to nightly pray the master of ceremonies to "hoist the rag," as they irreverently term the painted drapery called the border.

The ordinary seating capacity of the theatre is 1,478, but with extra seats and utilizing standing space, etc., about 2,150 persons can be accommodated without any inconvenience to those having regular seats.

VENTILATION, EXTINCTION OF FIRE, ETC.

Besides the large fan-shaped ventilator in the centre of the auditorium ceiling and its nine satellites, communicating with a ventilator on the ridge of the roof of the building, 18 feet by 30, there are, in the walls behind the gallery and the upper circle, 8 large windows, all of which open to their fullest dimensions for the admission of air. At the back of the stage, also, are six window spaces. These should give nearly air enough, but, in addition, there are 30 or 40 openings in the outer walls, and in the partitions between the circles and corridors for the free passage of air. There are, besides the windows spoken of, thirteen skylights in the roof of the building, giving light to the large property room over the auditorium and through the rigging floor above the flies, to the stage. The saving of gas by having full daylight rehearsals, etc., will be $100 a month, and go largely to make up for the amount of gas burnt in lighting up the promenade halls, etc. For the extinction of fire there are two 3-inch hydrants, 50 feet of hose attached, one in each fly-gallery with which the stage can be flooded in one minute. In the main corridor of the house are two other hydrants of the same size to which hose will be attached, and which will deluge any part of the front if necessary, or can be used to keep a fire on the stage from passing the proscenium arch.

ENTRANCE TO UPPER CIRCLE AND GALLERY.

We have yet to describe the entrance to the upper circle and gallery, to have omitted which might have led the reader to suppose that the proprietors of the Theatre had by mistake done what it is said a London architect once did for a purpose —erected a theatre without a gallery staircase. It was said he had an interest in some adjoining property, which it became necessary for his employer to buy as the easiest remedy for the defect. The entrance to the gallery and upper circle is at the Kearny street end of the building. The exterior opening, as we have said, is 9 feet wide. In the level hall between the door and the foot of the staircase is the ticket-office, and also a wide door communicating with the theatre door. A flight of stairs some 10 or 11 feet wide, by an easy ascent, leads to the first landing, from which there is an opening to the smaller music hall. A second flight of stairs leads to the corridor or promenade hall of the upper circle. This is the same in form as the one below, but of course, though its length is the full breadth of the theater, it is narrower in the other direction. It will be suitably furnished in comfortable but plainer style than the corridors below. The entrance to the upper circle seats is from each side, and where there are below the wings of the corridor, on this floor, on each side, is that standing and promenading space behind the tier of seven arches, which we have already described in the view of the house from the footlights. To facilitate the access of visitors to this circle to the middle seats, an aisle about five feet wide runs between the back row of chairs and the bulkhead which supports the gallery front. Out of the promenade hall, behind the upper circle are two good stairways leading right and left to the gallery above. So spacious are these exits, and there are so many wide spaces where a crowd could move rapidly, that more than 1,500 people might get into the street in case of an alarm in two minutes without injury to any one, unless they wilfully precipitated themselves down the stairs.

GENERAL REMARKS—COST, OWNERS, LESSEES, ETC.

The whole building, that is, the theatre and the two music halls, are built so that by removing a temporary brick wall in an archway already fitted with doors, it can be thrown into one for festive occasions. It was intended to celebrate the event of the completion of this magnificent Temple of Thespis with such a ball, but it was found impossible to complete the theatre at the time originally determined on except by taking the workmen off the other part of the building. There will be an occasion even more worthy of such a ball, and that will be the entertainment of those visitors who shall arrive by the first through train from the Atlantic to the Pacific. The Pacific railroad ball on the night of the day on which the welcome train from the East arrives in this city will be a notable event in the annals of California life.

The enterprise of building this theater, as first suggested, was to be undertaken by an association of capitalists. This scheme fell through, and Charles R. Peters, H. P. Wakelee and three other gentlemen assumed the labor and cost themselves. Every brick and every timber that has gone into this edifice has been laid under the personal supervision of Mr. Peters, who has spent his whole time on the work since the excavation commenced on August 6th last.

The total cost of the building and land, with auditorium and stage furniture, will reach, by the time the music halls are finished, $350,000. The expenditure of this vast sum, in a neighborhood which had until then been only covered by wooden buildings, has doubled the value of the land in the vicinity, and given an impetus to business in that locality which will cause the demand for good buildings, and therefore for available lots, to continue for some time.

The fortunate lessees of this noble building are Messrs. Barrett and McCullough, two young gentlemen who firmly established themselves in the favor of the people of this city, while fulfilling professional engagements at Maquire's Opera House. Superior to all petty feelings of rivalry, they became fast friends long before they entertained the thought of associating themselves in business. As lessees and part proprietors of the California Theatre, they have before them a career which might excite the envy of the most prosperous and most eminent of their profession.

DESIGNERS, CONSTRUCTORS, ETC.

The general design of the building, and the arrangement of the auditorium, with one or two trivial modifications, and all the plans, are the work of Charles L. Bugbee, of this city, architect. W. M. Hussey has had charge of the masonry; Hall & Bond of the carpenter work; Middleton & Hobson of the gas fitting and plumbing; Bryant & Strahan of the carving; P. Hibbard of the stair building; Jas. Green of the plastering; John Kehoe of the tin roofing; J. Kiltredge of making and hanging the iron doors, etc.; Whittier, Fuller & Co. furnished the mirrors, plate glass, etc.; J. Comb had charge of the painting; J. Duff did the fresco work; J. Brewster had charge of the glazing; George P. Kimball & Co. of the iron work;

P. Healy of the stone cutting; Otto Shrader painted the proscenium; Kennedy & Bell furnished the carpets; N. P. Cole & Co. the furniture; Piper & Rice the bricks; Adams & Co. and Holmes & Co., the lime and cement; M. Dolet & Co., the gas lamps; Rockwell, Coye & Co. the hardware; Hanscom & Co., the iron front; the pictures came from the houses of J. C. Duncan & Co. and Currier & Winter; the dress circle and parquette chairs from Warren Holt; other furniture from E. S. Spear & Co.; plaster ornaments from J. Patterson; W. Denny (marine painter.) is artist. Mr. Grobb is draughtsman. P. E. R. Whitney, Chief Engineer of the Fire Department, directed the water works. All these gentlemen are citizens of San Francisco.

Messrs. Haughwout & Co. of New York, and Bliss & Co. of New York, furnished the gas fittings. With the exception of the latter—the carpets, the statuary and a few other trifling articles—everything in the theater is the material of California growth or manufacture and worked by California artificers.

THE STAGE

The depth of the stage, measured from the foot lights to the rear walls, is 77 feet and the width from side wall to side wall, is 80 feet. The height to the underside of the rigging floor, is 50 feet. There are seven pairs of grooves. Each main scene, or pair of flats, will be 28 feet wide by 20 feet high. The chamber under the stage is 15 feet high, and the full size of the stage. The fittings of the stage embrace all modern novelties, and the whole has been built under the immediate superintendence of John Torrence; much of the machinery and mode of working being his own design.

Every convenience for artists has been thought of, and there are besides green-room, orchestra-room, supernumeraries' property-room, wardrobe, painter's room, etc., two sets of excellent dressing-rooms, each opening out of their own corridor one for ladies and the other for gentlemen.

It is expected that everything will be in readiness for the first reception of the public on Monday week, January 18th, the same day as that fixed for the opening of Booth's new theatre, a kindred enterprise.

The story of the opening night was recounted by the *Alta California*:

106:2   OPENING NIGHT OF THE CALIFORNIA THEATRE

Brilliant Assemblage—Theatre Crowded to Its Utmost Capacity—2,479 People in the House—Poem by Frank Bret Harte, Esq.—Compliment to Denny's Painting—Barret & McCullough Called Before the Curtain—Etc.

The opening of the California Theatre, on Bush street, was the sensation of yesterday. Those who had seats were preparing to go, those who had not were trying to figure out how they could get standing room, and still others wanted to see the assemblage as it filed into the building. Anticipating that the crowd would come all together, a barricade was placed across the entrance so that only one couple at a time could pass, and the delay at the door enabled the ushers to seat the visitors as fast as they presented themselves in the vestibule. Mr. Barrett and Mr. Rogers were inside the railing to tell the ticket-holders which entrance would take them most directly to their seats.

By a few minutes after eight o'clock all were in their places, the orchestra, under the direction of Prof. Geo. Evans, played an overture, the curtain was rung up, displaying a room scene, and Mr. Barrett stepped out to pronounce the opening address, written by Frank Bret Harte, Esq. The elocutionist complimented the poet

106:2. *Alta California,* Jan. 19, 1869.

by committing to memory the words of the poem, and spoke them with feeling, good taste and appropriate action. . . . Mr. Barrett was complimented with hearty applause on his entrance, and received for his elocution a share of the applause bestowed upon the poet.

THE PLAY

After a brief pause the curtain was rung up again, and Bulwer's elegant comedy, "Money," was commenced. The first to appear on the stage was Mr. W. H. Sedley Smith, as Sir John Vesey, who received a courteous welcome and a bouquet from some old-time admirer. The other members of the company were applauded as they came on, but Mrs. Judah was recognized as an old favorite, and treated accordingly. When Mr. McCullough, as Alfred Evelyn, made his appearance, the reception was prolonged into an ovation. Mr. Raymond, who appeared as Graves, established himself as a favorite at once; the gallery took up his stereotyped expression of "Sainted Maria," and repeated it for his own amusement. The play was very satisfactorily rendered; there was a little nervousness on the part of Miss Gordon, the Clara Douglass of the evening, but her graceful actions and exquisite taste in dressing made amends for any lack of power. Mr. W. F. Burroughs, as Sir Frederick Blout, made a very good impression; he is an actor of ability. Mr. Holmes made a fair representative of Sir Benjamin Stout. The other characters were represented by Mr. John Wilson (as Dudley Smooth,) Mr. E. J. Buckley (as Lord Glossmore,) Mr. Franks (as Mr. Sharp,) and Mrs. E. J. Buckley (as Georgina Vesey:) these characters were all well personated. Mr. W. H. Sedley Smith is a fine old man actor, as was seen last night, yet he undertook the character of Sir John Vesey at short notice, as Mr. Edwards was unable to appear because of illness. To say anything of the playing of Mr. McCullough or Mrs. Judah is needless; it is enough to know that they were in the piece to ensure the success of at least two of the characters.

THE ACT DROP

Between the first and second acts the green curtain was let down for the purpose of preparing the spectators for the treat in store—the view of the magnificent painting by G. J. Denny. Impatient cries came from the gallery, and then the curtain was drawn up revealing the view of the Golden Gate, with the *Western Continent*, the *Golden City*, the *Challenge*, etc. At first there was a prolonged round of applause, and then the gallery gave three cheers, and repeated them again, and again—a well deserved tribute to the artist.

THE SCENERY

The scenic effects came in for a share of the compliments of the evening—every new set received a round of applause. The apartments of Sir John Vesey were handsome and in good taste, but the elegant salons of the wealthy Alfred Evelyn made the others look dingy by comparison; here was displayed the roofing in of the room with a handsome ceiling. The furniture also was in admirable taste. . . .

CAPACITY OF THE HOUSE

There were 2,479 spectators in the theatre last night, realizing $2,135 for the management. . . .

107. SECOND McVICKER'S THEATRE
Chicago, Illinois
Opened August 15, 1872

James McVicker continued in his role as one of the most active theater builders and theatrical managers in the West. His first theater, which was built in Chicago in 1857, was destroyed in the great Chicago fire of 1871. It had been completely renovated only nine weeks before its destruction in that fire. Immediately after the holocaust McVicker began to build another playhouse, the first one to open following the terrible conflagration, and called by Noah Ludlow "the best in the West." It was on the site of McVicker's first theater.

The opening of the second McVicker's Theatre was an important event in the rebuilding of the city of Chicago and received much publicity in the newspapers. The Chicago *Tribune* reviewed the opening.

107:1 The opening of McVicker's Theatre, last evening, was an event in the rebuilding of the city to be marked with a white stone. It was the dedication to its appropriate uses of the first public building erected within the limits devastated by the great conflagration. As our readers have already been informed, all the seats sold several days ago, therefore an immense crowd was to be expected. But the size of the assemblage and the enthusiasm manifested even surpassed expectation. The doors were opened at half-past 7 o'clock, but long before that hour the vestibule and sidewalk were filled with an excited multitude. People gathered faster than they could be admitted, and, by 8 o'clock, the press was fearful. The vestibule was full, the adjacent walks were full, and a long line of persons, anxious for admission, extended as far as State street. There was nothing to do but to exercise the most exemplary patience, and wait until the way should be gradually cleared to the auditorium. At 8 o'clock punctually the play commenced, but at least 1,000 people were still without. As they slowly forced their way along the passage, or were forced by the pressure of those about them, they had time to study the architecture of the entrance, the gilded pillars that support the massive portico, the bronzed figures that guard the doorway, and the elaborate frescoing of the vestibule. Ladies and gentlemen, old and young, rich and poor, were indiscriminately mixed in the confused and intricate mass of humanity. It was nearly 9 o'clock, and about the ending of the first act, when the last spectator filed in and settled per-

107:1. Chicago *Tribune*, Aug. 16, 1872.

256

spiringly into his elegantly-upholstered chair.

It was not the play that the majority of the people had come to see. That was evident in the long and patient attention of every spectator to the various details of the handsomest theatre auditorium in the West. Lorgnettes were levelled at the ceiling, and many a long, admiring look was given to the proscenium, whose elaborate ornamentation and chaste coloring in white and gold were a pleasure and delight to the beholder. . . .

A reporter for the Chicago *Tribune* gave greater detail about the theater:

107:2 McVicker's Theatre is completed, and on the eve of being opened to the public. We have on several occasions given partial descriptions of this edifice, but the prospect of being speedily devoted to its intended uses, renders a new description with fuller details not inappropriate. Less time is consumed in building theatres than formerly. The principal work upon the present structure has been done within the last five months. Since it has been under cover, the progress has been so rapid as to be almost marvellous. The size of the lot on which the theatre stands is about 85 x 200 feet; of the extra depth, the stage occupies about 55 feet, the auditorium 91 feet.

THE FRONT
The theatre is built after plans drawn by Messrs. Wheelock & Thomas, who rank among the most skillful architects in the city. It may be confessed, however, that the front, in grandeur of executions and beauty of detail, does not even compare favorably with other specimens of their skill, seen here and there about the rising city. Its appearance is anomalous and does not suggest to the mind the use for which the building is intended. The openings are too numerous, and the two octagons designed to relieve the monotony of

107:2. Chicago *Tribune*, Aug. 11, 1872.

the *facade* give simply a look of oddity without a hint either at utility or beauty. The builder has been even more unfortunate in the material than in the design. Either from mistaken economy, or from some reason that does not appear upon the surface, brick has been chosen for the facing material instead of stone, at a very trivial diminution of cost. The brick, however, has been painted white, which is an improvement, and partially gives the impression of stone, although in a rather ghastly manner. The defects that we have pointed out are almost the only objections that even the most captious critic can make to what is undoubtedly now the finest theatre in the West.

EXTERIOR ORNAMENTATION
The details of the ornamentation of both of the exterior and interior, when figures are involved, have been executed by Signor Giovanni Meli, whose skill in molding has supplemented in an excellent manner the finished taste of the architects. The window caps of the entire front are ornamented with grotesque human heads, human and animal, giving the building an exceedingly unique appearance. The entrance to the main vestibule is by a sort of *porte cochere,* the floor of which will be nearly on a level with the sidewalk. Above this are placed four female figures, representing the four seasons—Spring on the right hand and winter on the left. Each of these figures carries a torch, the two right-hand figures bearing the symbol of intellectual enlightenment in the right hand and the others in the left. The drapery of all is in the Greek style, variously and gracefully arranged. The hair is also arranged in antique Greek fashion, the fillets with which it is bound being tastefully varied. The countenances are expressive. Spring bears in one hand a cluster of flowers; Summer is represented by Ceres holding in one hand a sheaf of wheat; Autumn bears a vessel containing an assortment of fruit, and Winter bears in one hand a lighted fire in an antique

vase. These figures are all modelled with elegance, and are gracefully varied in posture. The ornaments surmounting the *facade* are in tolerable taste, and, in conjunction with the portico, will give an appearance of unity of design which will somewhat modify the objections we have made.

THE VESTIBULE

Under the portico, on each side of the entrances, are placed on truncated columns, two large female figures, over seven feet in height, representing Tragedy and Comedy. The face of the first is heroic in expression, and the attitude is admirable. In the left hand it bears a serpent coiled, which tries in vain to strike, and in the right, which is clasped upon the breast, a naked dagger. The head is ornamented with a coronet. The style of dress is Egyptian, and the robes are full and flowing, revealing only a small portion of the figure. The figure of Comedy, which stands immediately opposite, is also spirited in design, and finely executed. The face is intellectual and very expressive. The style of dress and the coiffure is Grecian. All of the ornamentation and figures mentioned above, are of terra cotta, bronzed, which has all the effect of real bronze. Several of them are finished and ready for the place they are intended to occupy. The outside is 24 x 50 feet. The ticket office stands in the old place in the centre. The walls and ceiling are handsomely frescoed. The lobby connecting with the auditorium is reached through masive doors of black walnut, at the further end by a flight of a few broad steps. On each side of these doors is a niche which will contain busts as soon as they can be got ready. One of these will be a bust of Shakespeare from a head in possession of ex-Mayor Rice, said to be the most correct extant.

THE AUDITORIUM

The auditorium of the theatre is about 91 feet in depth by 82 feet in width, and 52 feet in height from the centre of the parquet to the dome. Its seating capacity is 1,800, which can be increased if desired to 2,600. A black walnut railing separates the parquet from the dress circle. There are two galleries, so gracefully sloped and modelled that the stage can be seen from every seat which they contain. The gallery railing is neatly executed by the younger Meli, from designs by Messrs. Wheelock and Thomas, and is of scroll work, with figures and shields at intervals. The upper tiers are reached by stairs rising from the lobby on either side of the main entrance. The frescoing is by Heath and Milligan, and although very well done is not sufficiently elaborate in detail. The handsomest portion is the dome and its immediate surroundings. The inner section is designed in panels ornamented with bunches of flowers, and a blue and white border surrounding it is really the most attractive work of the artist in colors. The prevailing tints of the walls are negative and lack the warmth and brightness essential to the light and cheerful effect essential to a place of amusement. The parquet, dress-circle and second tier are seated with patent chairs of the newest adjustable pattern, handsomely upholstered in crimson velvet. The coloring of the wood, iron-work, &c., of the proscenium is all white and gold.

LIGHT AND VENTILATION

The light and air of heaven find free admission through twenty windows opening from the auditorium into the alleys on either side. Ventilation is, therefore, ample for all occasions. The means of egress are sufficient for any emergency. There is a side door opening from the auditorium into the alley on the north side of the theatre, and also a door at each end of the lobby opening outwards. Not counting the exit from the stage, the theatre has, therefore, four convenient openings for escape in case of serious accident.

106. California Theatre, San Francisco. Published in John P. Young's *History of San Francisco* (San Francisco, 1912). Courtesy of the California State Library.

109. Interior, Wade's Opera House, San Francisco. Engraving, published in B. E. Lloyd, *Lights and Shades in San Francisco* (San Francisco, 1876). Courtesy of the California State Library.

INTERIOR VIEW OF WADE'S OPERA HOUSE.

107. Second McVicker's Theatre, Chicago, 1878–79 (?). Photograph by Copelin. Courtesy Chicago Historical Society.

The arrangements for lighting at night are complete and perfect. The chandeliers, candelabra and gas jets are carefully disposed, and the effect when all are lighted will be brilliant in the extreme. The principal chandelier, which depends from the dome, is of immense size, and will shed upon the array of beauty and fashion beneath it the light of noonday from its two hundred burners. Chandeliers, smaller, but equally elegant, placed at intervals about the dress circle and galleries, will assist in the general splendor and enhance the effect.

The gas will be lighted from a new process invented by Professor Samuel Gardiner, Government electrician. It will be done by passing a current of electricity over a tiny coil of platinum wire placed by each burner just as the gas is turned on. The machinery is so nicely arranged and adjusted that the burners in any circle, or in different parts of the stage, can be separately lighted or extinguished, and again relighted, without interfering with any others.

THE PROSCENIUM

Although the general appearance of the auditorium is handsome, it is the proscenium which has given it its chief beauty. It is this tasteful piece of work that entitles the theatre to the proud position of the finest theatre in the country outside of New York. It is in two *étages*, and extends from the footlights on each side of the stage to the circles, a distance of about 30 feet. Each stage is divided into three openings, two of which are false. The true stage box occupies the compartment or panel next to the stage. The false openings will be filled by immense plates of silvered glass, that will add to the brilliancy of the general illumination of the theatre. The whole proscenium is highly decorated in the renaissance style, with pillars, pilasters, and a handsome entablature. The openings are all elliptical and the prevailing style of architecture, as shown by the capitals of the columns and pilasters, is Ionic. The arch of the lower *étage* is ornamented by figures in *bas relief* representing cherubs supporting vases. The space between the upper and lower *étage* is adorned by a balustrade enriched with diamond work. The arch of the upper stage box is supported by two large and elegantly designed caryatides, shading their faces with their hands, terminating in scroll work and foliage, and bearing handsome gasoliers. The unity of effort is preserved by a beautiful entablature, surmounting continuously both the opening of the stage and the entire space covered with ornamentation on either side.

The frieze is adorned with nine *bas reliefs* representing heads of Roman matrons and soldiers upon shields supported by cherubs, terminating in arabesques, which are placed alternately. The figures are in terra cotta and the *bas reliefs* in *carton pierre*. All of these are from the studio of G. Meli & Son, and show knowledge of the human form, and skill in execution worthy of the consummate artist. It is something for Chicago to be able to boast of having within her borders a sculptor who was a pupil of Terani, who was himself the pupil of the divine Canova. The beauty of the interior is principally due to Messrs. Wheelock and Thomas, after whose designs it was built, and to whom a very large portion of the credit for the ornamental beauty of rebuilt Chicago will be due. We are pleased to learn that Signor Meli is already beginning to meet with that encouragement which his remarkable skill and talent deserve. He has commissions for moulding figures for Giles' elegant new jewelry store, and will assist in ornamenting Aiken's beautiful new theatre, Potter Palmer's new hotel, and various other new buildings in course of erection. Our capitalists and builders should certainly not think of going elsewhere for decorative talent, when what they desire can be obtained at home more cheaply, and of even finer quality than abroad.

STAGE AND SCENERY

The stage is of the same size of Booth's Theatre, New York, and has a height, breadth, and depth, equal to all exigencies. The scenery is under the skillful management of Mr. Howard Rogers, scenic artist, and Mr. J. C. Alexander, machinist. Twenty four full sets of scenery have already been painted, and others will be added as needed. The furniture of the stage is in readiness, and is ample for all purposes, and exceedingly elegant. The painting galleries have been placed at such a height that the full size of the stage can be commanded for all essential effects. No drapery will be used in front of a wood scene, so that the spectator will seem to see nothing but the forest, and the illimitable depths of the sky beyond. The stage will be furnished with the usual number of traps, and will be perfect in every detail.

The general view of the auditorium will be very handsome. The delicately beautiful colors of the proscenium, the graceful outlines of the galleries supported by the slender Corinthian shafts of iron, in the light of the crystal chandeliers will show to excellent advantage. The floors are covered with rich carpets which deaden unpleasant sounds, and make listening easier and more agreeable. . . .

108. SECOND BOSTON MUSEUM
Boston, Massachusetts
Opened September 2, 1872

In 1872 the venerable Boston Museum was thirty years old and much in need of extensive repairs. The complete renovation of the playhouse took place under the direction of the acting manager, R. M. Field. The theater opened on September 2 with an excellent cast in Sheridan's *School for Scandal*. A special program issued for the opening performance explained the renovation in detail.

108:1 OPENING OF THE THIRTIETH DRAMATIC SEASON! BOSTON'S FAVORITE COMEDY THEATRE

Entirely Re-Constructed and Re-fitted at an Enormous Expense!

Description of the Alterations and Improvements

THE EXTERIOR

The stone-work of the front building has been newly worked, cleansed and pointed, presenting now a remarkably light and fresh appearance. The balconies, and the thirty-six gas brackets holding the large globes, have been re-painted, the former a light brown color, and re-tipped with gilt, and the lettering which extends along each of the three balconies entirely re-gilded. New iron gates, of an ornamental design, are substituted for the heavy doors formerly used at the Tremont Street entrance, and a new staircase of very easy ascent, each "tread" ornamented with brass-work especially made therefore, takes the place of the old one leading from the street to the box-office landing. Passing elegant new ticket-gates, designed by Mr. F. W. Mozart, the Grand Hall of Curiosities is found to be entirely re-fitted and re-embellished, Mr. Anthony Hanson, under whose direction the building was constructed in 1845, having charge here of the carpenter work, and Mr. Cyrus T. Clark of the painting and decorating. The ceiling and columns have been made as beautiful as a skillful use of the brush could make them, light colors, gilding and panel work taking the place of the former severe simplicity of this part of the Museum, while the statuary, busts, and paintings have all passed through the renovators' hands. Thirty-six brilliant drop lights, furnished by the Tucker Manufacturing Company, and ranging along the first and second floors, give,

108:1. Program for reopening of the Boston Museum, 1872; Univ. of Georgia Library.

with the gorgeous new pedestal lights at the foot of the new grand staircase at the further end, a novel and splendid effect that no description could well exaggerate. Passing up the large stairway toward the auditorium, the narrow and low-studded passageway is found to have been converted into a high-domed and beautiful paneled vestibule, with an elegant chandelier dependent from the centre, the roof having been raised several feet, and the vestibule constructed from designs by Messrs. Cummings and Sears, architects.

THE THEATRE

The interior of the auditorium and its connecting lobbies and staircases has been entirely remodeled, scarcely a line of the house remaining as before. The old level gallery has been entirely removed, and a balcony of horseshoe form, sloping towards the stage and with one more row of seats in front, has been substituted. The front railing is of light iron work. The parquet floor is raised next to the stage eight inches, and then sloped up gradually to the old level at the back; this leaves the orchestra floor down, and makes the front seats more desirable, without injury to the others. The parquet circle has been lowered and sloped towards the stage, to conform to new lines of balcony. Steps have been put from ends of circle to parquet, making one of easier access to the other. The lines of seating in parquet have been curved to correspond with the new lines of stage front, and a new iron and upholstered railing has been placed around the orchestra. A new staircase has been made to balcony with easy steps and a broad landing, the heavy rails, balusters and posts being of black walnut, and the large post at foot terminating with a bronze figure carrying a cluster of gas lights. The arrangement of staircase is such that more room is given for the entrance lobby, and the substitution of light iron columns for the heavy square wooden ones between parquet and lobby gives the whole a more

open and roomy effect, while facilitating ingress and egress and allowing more standing room. Great attention has been paid to the strength and safety of construction. The old work that has stood the test of twenty-six years of hard service has been replaced by other even stronger.

The broad exit to Court Square has likewise been considerably improved, a neat fence taking the place of the heavy door formerly in use, and this passage will be both lighted and open during every performance.

HEATING AND VENTILATION

The heating arrangements having proved ample on all occasions, have only been modified sufficiently to conform to new work; but the great care has been taken to provide a system of *thorough ventilation*, ample for all emergencies.

In a Theatre the problem of how to remove the foul air is simplified by the fact that a powerful motive agent (the heat of the burning gas), is always available so long as an audience occupies the building. This power has been taken advantage of in this instance by constructing a shaft over the dome sunburner, connecting with a large ventilator on the roof, causing a large draught of hot air through the roof. A monitor ventilator, four feet by thirty, has been built from this shaft to the one which takes the air from the rear balcony ceiling, and the entire attic floor over the auditorium has been raised up and re-floored, leaving an open space of two feet between new floor and new ceiling; this space is connected with the hot air shaft and with thirty-eight perforated ornamental ventilators in ceiling. In addition to this and for use in warm weather, ten new dormer windows have been placed in roof, and open blinds substituted for sashed in windows over dome in lobby. Fresh air is introduced under the parquet circle and through entrance halls, and forty-three perforated ventilators under balcony ceiling connect the lower part of the house with ventilators above, the air being filtered through wire net work in the risers of balcony steps. The entire opening to the outer air from the auditorium amounts to *three hundred and sixty square feet*. It is believed that no building of its class has so effective a system of ventilation in active and efficient operation.

ILLUMINATION

The lobby is lighted by a cluster of gas-burners, suported by the bronze figure on stair-post; the sides and back of parquet circle and balcony by brackets on walls; but the principal illumination of the body of the house is from the central sun-burner in the eye of the dome, and thirteen large double brackets on the frieze over balcony and near cove of ceiling. These were all made expressly for this house from special designs by the architect. The sunburner has ninety lights, and is similar to the English pattern, the reflectors being of cast-iron, enameled in white, and the light being exceedingly soft and brilliant. The large brackets near ceiling are intended to assist in throwing an even light on the dome and below, to aid in the ventilation by creating upward currents of air through the perforated openings over, and to do away with much discomfort to occupants of balcony seats, by removing the light and heat of the gas from their immediate neighborhood.

THE ACOUSTIC PROPERTIES

Of the auditorium were always good, and have been somewhat improved by the use of wood sheathing for the new balcony, ceiling, dome, etc.

THE DECORATION

The raised decorative work is mostly done in "carton-pierre," backed and relieved by sawed and turned wood-work. All new ceilings and panels are covered with fine canvas before being painted on.

THE DOME, ETC.

The rim around sunburner is richly ornamented, and from it radiate the thir-teen panels of the dome centre. The central surfaces of these are covered with a raised diaper pattern, surrounded by gilt mouldings, the ribs separating the panels having laurel and ribbon moudings and gilt beads, and terminating in brackets and pendants.

Two small dome panels for the centre of spandrils next to the proscenium and a flat band of perforated panels for ventilation connects the dome with the cove, which is treated with darker color on a light ground in a stenciled pattern. Next under the cove and immediately over the gallery columns is a highly ornamental frieze, in perforated and sunk and raised work, divided at intervals by panels from which spring the large gas brackets; the lines being carried down from ceiling to gallery by brackets and ornamental columns.

THE GALLERY

The gallery front railing is of light and strong wire work of a rich ornamental pattern, closely studded with cast iron rosettes, and finished above and below with a border or fringe of cast iron work, and divided into sections corresponding with columns by carved wood brackets, and the whole being capped by a rail, upholstered in crimson plush and finished with a gilt moulding. The under and front surface of the balcony are decorated with "carton-pierre" and wood mouldings.

THE PARQUET

Is separated from the circle by a low paneled and upholstered railing, and the orchestra is enclosed by a rail of the same material as the balcony, but of a different pattern. Three flat arches have been thrown over the entrance to the parquet, supported on fluted iron columns, with turned and carved capitals. All the walls of the auditorium are sheathed for three feet and a half high with alternate strips of ash and black walnut cap, and this same finish extends around lobbies and stairways.

THE PROSCENIUM

Being the central and foremost feature, the frame within which the mirror is held up to nature, is more lavishly decorated than other parts of the house. The construction of the stage and the uses of the Theatre being such as to render proscenium boxes undesirable, no attempt has been made to introduce them; but the surface of arch and sides of opening have received an architectural treatment suited both to the rest of the auditorium and to showing the setting of stage and scenery and costumes to the best advantage. On either side the design commences with a base heavily moulded and ornamental and with three buttresses. On this base are two paneled and fluted pilasters with carved capitals, the whole supporting a heavy bracketed cornice with cresting or crown ornament above. In the large panels between the pilasters, on either side, are placed symbolical wood carvings, showing musical instruments, shields, armor, books, banners, and other paraphernalia of the stage; the whole being entwined with branches and wreaths of laurel, oak, and palm. Above the cornices and rising from behind the crests on each side are supplementary panels, with pilasters and cornices surmounted by scroll work and enclosing a small arch in relief, supported by small terminal figures in "carton-pierre" and overhanging circular frames which enclose medallion heads. Around the proscenium and extending to the floor on the outer edges are heavy "ball and billet" and other turned mouldings. The main surface of the arch is filled with the same embossed work which forms the centre of the dome panels, and in the middle is placed the principal carving, a group of musical instruments, laurel and oak branches, etc.

COLORING AND GILDING

It has been the endeavor of both architect and decorative painter to make the whole appearance of the house light and cheerful, and at the same time to avoid the cold and ineffective treatment commonly known as "white and gold." To do this the panels and other prominent surfaces have been tinted a delicate straw color, with borders of warm grays; a few of the smaller ribs and mouldings being brought out by the use of pure white. For cutting in the recessed ornaments, delicate and rich shades of crimson have been sparingly employed; and to bring out prominent points, gilding has been liberally used. The walls and ceilings are treated with delicate shades of warm grays and paneled with bands of color. Around the walls, under the balcony and across stage front, are bands of stenciling in color.

SEATING

The parquet has been entirely reseated with "Jackson's cabinet pattern seats," of liberal size; the iron work, as well as that of all the other seats, are being gold bronzed; and the upholstery being in heavy crimson enameled cloth. The parquet circle and balcony and part of balcony circle have the "Cooper Institute chair," upholstered in crimson plush. All the chairs have the "tilting seat." The balcony circle has on either side the patent "Jackson chairs," and also light, roomy seats of iron and wood, upholstered in crimson enameled cloth.

CARPETINGS, ETC.

The entrance and other lobbies and stairways have been carpeted with heavy cocoa matting, and the parquet and circle aisles with handsome and costly carpeting of colors suited to the decoration.

THE STAGE

Improvements have been very extensive, an entirely new stage, with all the modern appliances, and extending from wall to wall, having been built under the direction of Mr. Warren Marden, for many years the Master Machinist of the establishment.

A new Drapery Act Drop, and tormentor wings and front borders have been painted by Mr. Edward Cotter, the new Scenic Artist of the theatre, whose works promise great popularity for this department of the Museum.

The reconstruction of the theatre has been from the designs and under the superintendence of Mr. John A. Fox, Architect.

All the constructional work has been done under the immediate personal supervision of Mr. F. W. Mozart, Theatrical Machinist and Builder, assisted by Mr. A. Hanson and others.

The stairs, by Mr. Geo. Edgerton.

The decorative painting, gilding and "carton-pierre" work is by Mr. William A. McPherson.

Painting of the front building, exterior and interior, by Mr. Cyrus T. Clark.

The three carvings for proscenium and brackets for gallery front, by Mr. Victor Charmois, of Messrs. Lawrence, Wilde & Hull.

The gas piping, wall brackets, etc., by Mr. N. W. Turner.

Gas fixtures of front Hall by N. W. Turner and the Tucker Manufacturing Company.

The wire balcony and orchestra railing by Messrs. Morss & Whyte.

The central "sunburner" and dome gas brackets were made by John Shirley Jr. of Providence, R.I.

The iron columns are from Messrs. Thatcher's "Fulton Iron Foundry."

Iron work by Mr. Wm. H. Low.

Mill-work by Messrs. Manson & Peterson, East Boston.

Plumbing by Mr. T. H. Capper.

Plastering by Mr. John Mack.

Upholstering by Mr. F. S. Somers.

Carpets by Messrs. J. H. Pray & Sons.

Cocoa mattings by Messrs. Peasley & Bond.

New stage and machinery by Mr. Warren Marden.

New act drop curtain, borders and scenery by Mr. Edward Cotter.

Lithographing plans by Messrs. H. W. Longfellow & Co.

109. WADE'S OPERA HOUSE
San Francisco, California
Opened January 17, 1876

The year 1876 was one of great economic instability, and yet two of the largest theaters the West coast had seen opened their doors during this time—Wade's Opera House and Baldwin's Academy of Music.

Wade's Opera House was the dream of a local dentist, Dr. Thomas Wade, whose great ambition was to build the most magnificent opera house ever seen in San Francisco. The idea was a grand one, but the time was not right. The newspaper *Figaro* carried the following notice:

109:1   The Real Estate circular says: "Ground has been secured, either by lease purchase, for the erection of a large theatre on the north side of Mission Street, one hundred and twenty-five feet west of Third, just opposite Dr. Scudder's Church. The land has a frontage of one hundred or one hundred and five feet on Mission, by a depth of two hundred and seventy-five feet. The lot has a side entrance on Jessie and a ten-foot alley on the east; the latter is owned by Michael Reese. The lessees have received notice to quit before July next. The buildings are common brick and frame ones. One of the lots purchased has a frontage of fifty-five feet, by a depth of one hundred and sixty feet to Jessie Street in the rear; the sum paid for it was $25,000 ($454 per front foot), which is a reasonable price. We have purposely avoided mentioning this matter for several reasons, though we have been cognizant of the project for a long time. The statement, as is usual in projected theatre items, is overdrawn. In the first place the land has not been purchased; and the whole scheme hangs fire and will probably be abandoned. Capitalists think even more than twice in these money-tight times before investing $200,000 in a theatre on Mission Street."

109:1. *Figaro,* Mar. 8, 1873.

Unfortunately, Dr. Wade did not heed this advice, but found financial backers and built his mammoth opera house, which, of course, received a vast amount of publicity from the newspapers. This was particularly true as the project neared completion. Every week saw some new item about the great opera house and its wonders. On the eve of the opening *The Evening Post* wrote of the coming event and briefly described the new house:

109:2   This magnificent temple of the drama, which has been described at length in our local columns, will open on Monday, when the grand spectacle of "Snowflake" will be produced on a scale of splendor unequaled on this continent. Already nearly 2,000 seats have been sold, the larger portion at a high premium, for the opening night. A general rehearsal was held last night, in which the whole ballet appeared, and everything worked like a charm. The corps de ballet, which has been in active rehearsal at Union Hall for some weeks past, numbers 400, and it is only the vast capacity of the stage which enables it to be seen to advantage. Before the programme the "Star Spangled Banner" will be sung by the entire Fabbri Opera Troupe, and cannot fail to produce a splendid effect. The scenic effects are very fine, and are greatly aided by the new foot lights known as "float lights," which are enclosed in tri-colored glasses, red, green and white, so arranged that the stage can be illuminated with three different colors. The orchestra, consisting of twenty instruments—is the largest in the United States. That at Booth's Theatre, New York, only contains sixteen. During the progress of the piece a novelty will be introduced—

A CARRIAGE DRAWN BY FOUR LIVE PONIES.
"Snowflake" has cost in its production $30,000, an amount not so surprising as it would appear at first view when among other things it may be mentioned "en

109:2. *The Evening Post*, Jan. 15, 1876.

passant" that no less than five hundred dresses are required for changes of character alone. The theater itself is on the European model. There are three galleries and a pit, the front part of which is styled the parquette. The back part and the gallery immediately above the dress circle, the next gallery is the family circle, and the top gallery, after the time honored custom, is devoted to the gods. The seating capacity of the theater is for 2,234 persons, divided as follows: Parquette, 458; orchestra circle, 208; dress circle, 322; 22 Mezzonine boxes, 100; 12 stage boxes, 100; family circle, 402; gallery, 500; extra sliding seats in aisles, say 150. So great is the public anxiety to be present for the opening night that for Monday at least we might multiply these figures by two. Mr. Bert deserves every credit for his exertions in giving to our citizens such a splendid place of amusement and to our city such a beautiful public building, and we hope its success will bear a just proportion to his untiring energy.

The playhouse, which had been designed by S. A. Bugbee and Son, was described by the New York *Dramatic News* (March 18, 1876) as "a magnificent structure, perfect in all its details, the acoustic qualities unequalled, and the stage the largest in America, excepting the old Bowery." The cost of Wade's Opera House, however, was not $200,000 as predicted by *Figaro*, but $750,000!

110. BALDWIN'S ACADEMY OF MUSIC
San Francisco, California
Opened March 6, 1876

Soon after the opening of Wade's Opera House, a second huge theater opened its doors —Baldwin's Academy of Music. The playhouse was part of a hotel-theater complex built by Edward J. Baldwin, who was to manage the hotel, while the theater was managed by Thomas Maguire, the veteran theater-builder and owner on the west coast. Like Wade's Opera House this was a large, opulent playhouse with all the red plush, gilt, and crystal so popular in the theatrical house of the day.

A special press viewing of the theater three days before the official opening was described in the *Alta California*.

110:1 BALDWIN'S ACADEMY OF MUSIC.— This theatre was lighted up last evening and thrown open to the members of the Press. It was the universal opinion that a more handsome theatre does not exist to-day in the United States. The prevailing color of the house is a rich deep crimson, bordered with gold; plate-glass mirrors at the sides reflect again and again the beauties of the auditorium. The impression on first entering is that one is standing in some magnificent parlor. The crown of the whole, however, lies in the dome of the auditorium. The concave ceiling, directly over the stage, and which breaks away from a gorgeous lambrequin, is in blue and white tints, representing the clouds and sky, in which are seated two symbolical figures, representing Music and Drama, with cherubim playing around them. They are as correctly drawn and vigorously colored as a well-wrought oil painting. In a second section of the vault, more directly over the gallery, is a second emblematic group, consisting of a fewer number of figures, but as highly artistic as the first one. The proscenium boxes are eight in number. They are upholstered in crimson rep and satin, the paper being of a crimson ground figured with various golden forms. By a novel arrangement of the partitions, any two of the boxes may be thrown into one. The carpeting and furnishing of these boxes are rich and tasteful. At the back of the dress circle are ten mezzanine boxes, richly carpeted and decorated. Above the stage is a copy of one of the authentic portraits of Shakespeare. The drop curtain consists of two rich, crimson silk draperies, which part in the middle and are drawn up to the sides,

110:1. *Alta California,* Mar. 4, 1876.

revealing a well arrayed stage 50 feet in breadth, 35 feet deep and 36 feet high.

The theatre, which in all justice may be called a *bijou*, will seat 2100 persons comfortably. The opening will take place next Monday evening, when Mr. Barry Sullivan will appear as the Duke of Gloucester in the tradgedy "Richard III."

111. CENTRAL CITY OPERA HOUSE
Central City, Colorado
Opened March 4, 1878

The discovery of gold in Colorado in 1859 caused a population explosion similar to that in California ten years earlier. The original strike was in the foothills of the Rockies near Pike's Peak, and some fifty thousand men had rushed to that area. Towns were established overnight, and within a short time Central City became the most important town in the West.

In 1860 an actor, J. S. Langrishe, moved to Central City and opened a log theater. He was so successful that the season lasted three months, a longer theatrical season than could be claimed by many larger cities at this time. Langrishe continued to visit Central City three months a year for fourteen years.

A disastrous fire in 1874 destroyed the town within a few hours, but the rebuilding began immediately, and, after the essential homes, banks, and stores were rebuilt, the people of the city decided to erect an opera house for musical and dramatic performances. Among the miners who settled in Central City were a number of Welshmen, who, with their love of singing, felt that the opera house was a necessity, while other citizens of the town longed for a return of the drama.

Because of the division between those who wanted an opera house and those who preferred a return of dramatic performances, this is one of the few theaters in America that had a double opening night—the first night devoted to music and the second to drama.

The pride of the people of Central City is seen in the glowing review of the new opera house in the town's newspaper, *The Evening Call*, "Published every afternoon (Sundays ex-

108. Interior, Second Boston Museum, Boston. Courtesy of the Harvard Theatre Collection.

110. Baldwin's Hotel and Academy of Music, San Francisco. Engraving, published in B. E. Lloyd, *Lights and Shades in San Francisco* (San Francisco, 1876). Courtesy of the California State Library.

111. Central City Opera House (restored), Central City, Colo., 1937. Photograph by Newbury. Courtesy of the Denver Public Library Western Collection.

111. Interior, Central City Opera House (restored), Central City, Colo., ca. 1937. Courtesy of the Denver Public Library Western Collection.

cepted,) in the Miller block, over Goldman's Fruit Store."

111:1   DEDICATED

OPENING OF THE MOST MAGNIFICENT OPERA HOUSE WEST OF THE MISSOURI RIVER

A History of the Enterprise and the Men Who Engaged in it.

The Concert Last Night by Our Home Talent an Overwhelming Success

The Wealth and Beauty of Central and Surrounding Towns Fill the House from Pit to Dome.

The Dramatic Performance To-Night

If ever the people of Central had reason to feel proud of the first city of the mountains, it was last night upon the opening of her magnificent opera house, which to-day stands the finest temple of the Muses west of the Missouri, and far ahead of any thing of the kind ever projected in the Rocky Mountains. As the vast audience filed into the beautiful theatre, an audience representing the wealth, beauty and intelligence of the mountain towns, many were the expressions of delight and astonishment which fell from the lips of those who for the first time viewed what may be looked upon as Central's pride, and which is a credit to Colorado. The beautiful fresco work, brought out in bold relief by the scintillations of one hundred gas jets, the handsome drop curtain, and the house filled to its utmost capacity, with fair women in rich and costly dresses, and brave men, was a sight seldom seen, and certainly not soon to be forgotten in these regions.

A LITTLE HISTORY

A slight history of the beautiful building which now graces Eureka street, may not

111:1. *Evening Call,* Mar. 5, 1878.

be uninteresting to the majority of readers of the CALL. Ever since Central has been known as a city, she has been famed throughout the State for her musical talent. It has got to be a conceeded fact, which all will admit without argument, that the amateur musical talent of Central, not only surpasses that of any western town, but even compares most favorably with that of some of the larger and metropolitan cities of the east.

Something over a year ago, the amateur society of Central produced for their own as well as their friends' amusement, Balfe's complete opera, "The Bohemian Girl," the different characters being taken by some of our most respectful citizens. And such was the complete success of the representation that its fame soon spread over the state, and it was stamped by all, and especially the press, as the most successful amateur musical performance ever given in Colorado. This success stimulated our amateurs to still nobler efforts, and at the same time showed the necessity of having some first class hall or theatre for such productions, and opened the eyes of some of our capitalists to the want of an opera house. The impulse once given, it was immediately resolved to erect a temple which would be a lasting monument to the honor of the city and the state.

ONE YEAR AGO

Just one year ago last night, a party of enterprising gentlemen of capital organized the company, with a capital stock of $50,000; plans and specifications were drawn, sufficient money subscribed to purchase the present site, and work immediately commenced under the immediate supervision of the architect chosen—Mr. R. S. Roeschlaub, of Denver, The walls, which are built of solid granite, taken from our grand old hills, arose as if by magic under the direction of Messrs. Mullen and Sartori, who had the contract for the masonry work, and in a short space of time the building has assumed shape and was closed in. How well these gentlemen performed their portion of the contract, the building itself, the most substantial in the state, bears ample testimony, and it is with pleasure the CALL records the fact as an act of justice to two of the most competent mechanics in our midst.

The masonry work being completed, the building was immediately turned over to Messrs. McFarlane & Co., who had the contracts for the carpenter work. The rapid and workmanlike manner in which these gentlemen performed their portion of the work, is well known to every man of the community, and will remain a record of their worth as builders as long as the opera house stands. The CALL takes a special delight in recording these facts, as the Messrs. McFarlane & Co., as well as Messrs. Mullen & Sartori, are among our most respected and responsible citizens.

The fresco and scenic work, which commands the universal admiration of all who behold it, was done by Mr. Massman, of San Francisco, a gentleman whose reputation as a scenic artist is now firmly established in Colorado, in connection with the Presbyterian church in Denver, as well as our own opera house.

The furnaces, hot air pipes and heating apparatus, were furnished by Bacon & Sons, of Denver, work like a charm, and make the building very comfortable. The size of the building is 55 x 115 feet, with a stage 43 x 52. The dress circle and parquette are furnished with patent opera chairs, and will seat about 500 persons. The gallery will seat about 250 persons, and is furnished very comfortably.

THE COST

It was at first supposed that $12,000 would be sufficient to complete the building ready for occupancy, but, this being expanded, a further draught of $6,000 was made and immediately paid by the stockholders. It may be safe to say that the entire building as it now stands cost between $20,000 and $25,000. . . .

The reviewer proceeds to extol the concert in elaborate detail, mentioning people from out of town and describing the dresses of the women. Just one fault was mentioned: "The only drawback of the evening was the poor working of the gas."

A more objective and detailed description was given by the Denver *Rocky Mountain News.*

111:2 . . . A NEWS reporter was shown over the completed edifice yesterday by Mr. A. Von Schulz, manager of the opening ceremonies and entertainments. Mr. Roeschlaub, who was present, also furnished every facility for gathering information of the work done and money expended, which now amounts to about $23,000. The exterior is massive masonry, plain but imposing. Four outer doors, opening direct upon the sidewalks, and level with the street, lead to a vestibule the entire width of the building. From the vestibule two stairways lead to the large and very comfortable gallery, which is swung across the rear of the auditorium, but not carried down the sides—a good arrangement, for several reasons. The gallery seats are the best in the house both for seeing and hearing, though there is not a bad seat anywhere. To the right and left of the gallery stairs in the vestibule are two large entrances to the parquette and dress circle. The box office is below the gallery stairs. A short flight of easy steps lead to these entrances, from which the floor slopes gently to the stage, giving every spectator a clear view of the performers. The orchestra is placed a little below the level of the front seats, so that the "big fiddle" and its engineer do not loom up above everything else in the building, as in our (alleged) Denver opera house. The interior is well heated and lighted, the central chandelier being a counterpart of the one in the Central Presbyterian church in this city. There is not much "gingerbread"

111:2. Denver *Rocky Mountain News,* Mar. 5, 1878.

about the wood work of the interior, which is "neat, not gaudy," but the frescoing is fine, very fine, as elegant in its line as anything in the country. The artist appears to have been more "at home" in the theatre than in the church, and there is little comparison between his work in the opera house and that in the Central church, though both are well done. The centre piece is an "open dome" and one can almost imagine he is looking through the roof at the sky overhead with angry clouds hurrying by *en route* to Georgetown and Pike's Peak direct without change, as the railroad guides say. The side and corner pieces represent symbols of the various arts—music, drama, etc. The drop curtain is also very fine, representing a Rhine scene, shown through parted drapery. The great stage is fully equipped with handsome new scenry—everything is new about the building, from roof to basement—and there are four elegant dressing rooms, besides all the space necessary for the multitudinous "properties" of the profession. Indeed, the most striking feature of the opera house is its generous proportions as compared with most western or suburban theatres. There are no "candle-box" arrangements anywhere. Its exits are so ample that the whole audience can walk out almost at once. Taken all in all it is a theatre of which any city might be proud, and is as far superior to anything Denver has or ever had that no comparison need be instituted. . . .

Central City's position of prominence was not to last long. It is estimated that over $85,000,000 in gold was mined in the Central City area from 1860 to 1890; then prosperity of the region ended as quickly as it had started. The population of the town dwindled from 10,000 to only 400, and the Opera House was used only occasionally, then not at all.

In 1932 a group of people felt that the Central City Opera House should be revived, and with the aid of famous designer Robert Ed-

mond Jones, it was opened once again, this time as a major tourist attraction for the summer crowds that go to Colorado. The playhouse is still in operation today as and important summer theater.

112. TABOR OPERA HOUSE
Leadville, Colorado
Opened November 20, 1879

It was 1878 that Horace Tabor made his famous silver strike in Leadville, Colorado, and a new town came into being some ten thousand feet up in the Rockies. Tabor's strike led to the discovery of huge beds of silver carbonate, and Leadville became the silver Capital of Colorado. Overnight the population of the area grew to 30,000, and Horace Tabor became an exceedingly rich man.

A year after the strike, Tabor opened his Opera House to provide entertainment for the miners, and here some of the most famous actors and actresses of the period came to perform. Two days before the opening of the Opera House the Leadville *Daily Chronicle* told of the new theater.

112:1   THE TABOR GRAND
It Is the Finest Edifice in the Land
And Will Be Thrown Open
Thursday Night
Jack Langrishe and
His Star Troupe on Deck
That large fine-fronted massively-built brick building on Harrison Avenue fifteen feet beyond the Clarendon Hotel is Tabor's Opera House. Ground was broke for its foundation just one hundred days ago tomorrow morning, and at four o'Clock Thursday afternoon this week the workmen therewith chest their tools and receive their reward of "well done good and faithful servants." At that time Messrs. Tabor and Bush will have expended on this building over thirty thousand dollars, and nowhere in the West

112:1. Leadville *Daily Chronicle,* Nov. 18, 1879.

has that amount of money created so creditable a building. Of course the Opera House portion is that part of the structure in which the local public are immediately interested. There are thousands of citizens in this city who have been impatiently waiting for the completion of this, the first class place of amusement in Leadville. That is, it is to be the only legitimate theater or the only place where respectable people need not be afraid to go. This has been the one great need in Leadville for months. There has been solemn preaching and hard work in overwhelming quantities, but of respectable amusements there has been little. For the full supply of this great want this community is wholly indebted to the public spirit and generous enterprise of Hon. H. A. W. Tabor and Mr. William H. Bush.

Now let's go up and see what they have done for us. No, you don't go in there. The ground floor, all excepting a large store room and a private office for the Clarendon Hotel, has been let out for mercantile purposes. We will pass through those heavy, though easily swinging doors and a flight of stairs broad enough to admit a regiment of soldiers leads us to the second floor of the house. Here is the Opera House. It has a parquet and dress circle. The entrance to the latter is up a second flight of stairs. The parquet is seated with Andrew's patent orchestra chairs. You don't know what they are? Never in Booth's, Wallack's, or the Union Square Theater in New York, or the Walnut Street Theater in Philadelphia? Well, these chairs in Tabor's are the same. They are elegantly upholstered in plush. The aisles are beautifully carpeted; the ceilings to the hall are handsomely frescoed; the ventilation is perfect; the blending beauty of the whole being fully brought out by brightly burning lights from seventy-two jets. The entire house is furnace warmed; the fire extinguishing arrangements are perfect; in fact, to tell the whole story in one chapter, Tabor's Opera House in Leadville is the most perfect place of amusement between Chicago or St. Louis and San Francisco.

The stage is a whole hall within itself, but this belongs to the amusement matters and not to us, the dear public. However, that drop curtain is nice. It is really a tastefully-painted landscape scene, and isn't that life-sized portrait of Lieutenant Governor Tabor at the top perfectly natural? When that expression was caught the governor had just been interrupted in a recital of his recent million-dollar purchase at Chicago. The next sends us wandering through the beautifully foliaged forest. It is an admirably executed scene. Following this unrolls a curtain which takes you and I back to the garden of our childhood days. The next the painter calls a palace arch. The fifth is a plain chamber scene. Here it is that Juliet steps from her bed chamber in the silent hours of the night, and leaning from the vine wreathed balcony peers out on the moonlight lawn and in the soft plaintive tone begot by an ardent love cries out, "Romeo, Romeo, where art thou, Romeo?" The sixth scene reveals the interior of a well appointed New England kitchen. From this we are transported to a cold, dismal prison, which is artistically delineated in the seventh scene. The eighth and last representation now ready for the stage is a street scene, intended for Harrison Avenue, on the night of July 4th, 1881. These paintings would certainly do credit to the best scenic artist in the land.

It may be that Mr. J. B. Lamphere is the best. It was he who painted them. On either side of the stage are two boxes, one above the other. They are richly carpeted, mirrored and upholstered. The orchestra which is to be composed of fifteen pieces will be seated in a circular box on a level with the parquet.

Now but one thing remains to be told. This really elegant place of amusement is to be opened day after tomorrow (Thursday) night. The play is to be the "Serious

Family." The company which has been engaged for thirteen weeks, arrived at the Clarendon this afternoon. They are in charge of J. S. Langrishe.

The Leadville *Daily Chronicle* gave more details of the stage.

112:2 . . . The building is built of stone, brick, and iron, and is one of the most substantial and costly architectural structures in the stage. It has a frontage on Harrison Avenue of sixty feet, and is three stories high. The height of the building in the clear, is sixty feet, the lower or ground floor being furnished into two elegant and spacious stores, and the entrance to the theater, twelve feet in width, occupying the center of the block. The total cost of the building was something more than $40,000. The auditorium has a seating capacity of eight-hundred and eighty. There are two large handsomely finished proscenium boxes on either side of the stage, and a model horseshoe gallery comfortably seated and affording a fine view of the stage from every angle. The parquette and dress circle are supplied with the latest style of patent opera chairs, with adjustable seats, and upholstered in crimson velvet. The stage, 35 x 58 feet, is perfect in all its various arrangements, and is one of the largest west of New York. There is a suite of five luxuriously furnished rooms on the second floor occupied by Governor Tabor, the owner, and W. H. Bush, lessee, as office and private apartment. The upper or third story is furnished off into rooms occupied in connection with the Clarendon Hotel. In the rear is the store-room of the Claredon, 40 x 60 ft. . . .

It was not easy for actors performing in Leadville to become adjusted to the altitude. The famous actor, Otis Skinner, in his autobiography recalls Leadville in 1882.

112:3 My first essay in the part [Anthony] at Leadville, Colorado, ten thousand feet above sea level, at which elevation the least physical effort is trying to the unacclimated, was nearly disastrous. My nervousness had sent me pell-mell into the stirring scenes with no thought of husbanding my physical resources. By the time I had reached the middle of the big speech, I was all in. The blood was pounding in my ears and in my temples, and my chest was heaving in asthmatic convulsions. I just did get through, and when the calls came I had only strength enough to fall out in front of the curtain and to fall back again. I soon learned that in *Anthony* the race is not always to the swift. A few more performances served to set the pace right and leave me breath enough to finish, and shortly I found *Anthony* a "property of easiness."

Leadville in 'eighty-two was a wide-open town, saloons, gambling houses, dance-halls and variety shows, all ablaze after night-fall. Roulette, keno and faro were to be found every few blocks on the main street in shabby establishments open as the day to the passer-by. In one of them, whose door was never closed night or day, there was an outer anteroom where prominent citizens of Leadville could meet and talk politics. On the table in the center of this room was a well-worn copy of the Bible which some one, generally a lean and grizzled miner, was invariably reading, while from the hall at the back came the click of the marble in the little stalls of the roulette wheel; or the drone of the keno caller as he read the numbers: "Seventy-two—eight—eleven—twenty-four!" "Keno!" "Hell!"

The chief variety theatre was a tawdry affair, afflicted with much cheap gilt and bright paint, where sorry-looking "serio-comics" in lurid dress sang to an audience that threw silver dollars at their feet. These

112:2. Leadville *Daily Chronicle*, Jan. 1, 1880.

112:3. Otis Skinner, *Footlights and Spotlights* (Indianapolis: Bobbs-Merrill, 1924), pp. 118–20.

daughters of Danaë would ogle and nod as they sang and work very hard to start the silver shower, which, when begun, resembled a hail-storm. The ability of these nymphs to sing, dance and pick up a coin in simutaneous action was much admired. I saw one poor black-face banjo player bob and pantomime at the occupants of the bench rows without result until, either in pity or disgust, a drunken miner threw him a dime. . . .

The Tabor Opera House in Leadville still stands today, although it no longer houses performances.

113. TABOR GRAND OPERA HOUSE
Denver, Colorado
Opened September 3, 1881

With the opening of Tabor's Grand Opera in 1881, Denver proudly took its place with those regional centers in the United States that could boast important theaters. H. A. W. Tabor in 1879 had built the Tabor Opera House in Leadville, a playhouse that had been called "the finest in the land," but the new Denver playhouse was to be on an even grander scale. A reporter from the *Tribune* visited the theater before its opening and wrote the following description:

113:1   AN INTERIOR VIEW.
A Glance at the Auditorium of the Tabor Opera House.

How it looks to One Standing at the Entrance to the Parquet.

The Gorgeousness of the Ancients Revived.

A Rare Combination of Architectural Beauty, Rich Coloring and Solid Wealth.

The Most Beautiful Theater in America.

There are few persons in Denver who have not seen the exterior of the Tabor

113:1. Denver *Tribune*, Sept. 4, 1881.

Grand Opera house; there are still fewer who have seen the interior. Those who have been so fortunate as to secure little slips of paper bearing the signature of either Manager Bush or architect W. J. Edbrook, and thus been enabled to view the gorgeousness of the building, have given their less fortunate friends descriptions so glowing that for weeks past all Denver has been on the tiptoe of excitement to see what the new temple of the dramatic and musical muses looks like. This curiosity has not been to know how wide the grand entrance is, or the thickness of the carpet on the aisles: and nobody has been particularly anxious to know whether the floor of the stage is of spruce or of pine. The desire has been to know how the Tabor Grand Opera house differed from other theaters—much having been said about the originality of the architecture and decorations—and just how it will look on the opening night. There will be fifteen hundred persons at the dedication of this masterpiece of the architectural and decorative arts to the drama to-morrow evening. There will be thousands who would be there if they could. Both those who will be present and those who will not are curious to know something about the appearance of the new theater.

A GLIMPSE AT THE INTERIOR
will heighten the pleasure of the former in preparing them for the treat in store for them and it will serve as "the next best thing" for the latter.

In entering into a description of this fairy-like place—or in attempting to describe its beauties—one must lose sight of lengths, widths, heights and depths; for, to say that the handsome railings around the balconies were four inches and a half wide and that the massive cornice were so many feet in thickness, would be much like attempting to describe a poetic creation by giving the dimensions of the objects represented. The interior is so complete, in such perfect harmony that one

112. Tabor Opera House,
Leadville, Colo., ca. 1883.
Courtesy of the Denver
Public Library Western
Collection.

112. Interior, Tabor Opera House, Leadville, Colo., ca. 1883. Courtesy of the Denver Public Library Western
Collection.

113. Interior, Tabor Grand Opera House, Denver, 1881. Courtesy of the Denver Public Library Western Collection.

almost forgets to be critical. The writer has, therefore, discarded the dry measurements as uninteresting and really unimportant in comparison with the grandeur and poetic beauty of the theater. Let the gentle reader imagine that he has passed through the marble entrance into the dazzlingly bright rotunda and on into the foyer of the parquet. Although the heavy curtain, hanging across the main entrance to the auditorium between two massive mirrors, shuts out the view of the stage and the theater itself, yet there is so much beauty all around one that he lingers before going further.

THE RAYS FROM THE
GLISTENING CHANDELIER,

hanging immediately in the center of the foyer, cast a bright light on the ceiling, rich in its dark colorings and warm the scene into poetic life. On either side, broad handsomely-carpeted stairways lead to the balcony above, and on the massive richly-carved newel posts at the foot of the stairways are gas fixtures of unique design. The artistic and decorative carving on these posts, which are of highly polished cherry, is worthy of a careful study, and is in itself a work of art of the highest type. But what attracts most attention in the foyer of the parquet are the two large panel paintings. They are on either side of the entrance to the parquet, large mirrors separating them from the entrance.

The ground of the panels is of gold, with maroon velvet reliefs; narrow, delicate strips of gold surrounding the panel and forming the frame. On this gold ground is the painting. One of the panels represents the *Fleur de Lis* rearing its head above the marsh grass; the other is a cluster of sunflowers. Both panels are painted in a strong, clear style, and their decided colors are in perfect harmony with the rich walls and ceilings. Pushing aside the soft curtain, one enters the parquet. He can not view all of the theater, for the balcony above him prevents him from seeing the ceiling or the walls. But

he can see all the lower part of the house; the base of the polished pillars that run to the ceiling on either side of the proscenium. He can see the boxes that are on the parquet floor, with their soft, strangely colored draperies.

INTOXICATED WITH A GLIMPSE

of the beautiful scene, he hurries on until he stands at the entrance to the parquet, or auditorium. From this point his eye can drink in the beauties of the entire scene. The first impression one has is that he has been suddenly transported to some enchanted scene. What he sees is so unlike anything he has ever seen before that he can not at first realize that he is in a theatre. The glistening mirrors, the gaudy gilt and the painfully bright white gloss paint that form the make-up of the conventional theater are nowhere to be seen. In fact, there is nothing in the Tabor Opera house that resembles the theaters of to-day except the general idea of arranging the seats so that spectators may see what is going on on the stage. He looks in vain for the square window-like stage boxes that he finds in the Eastern theaters. He misses the prominently gay dome with its stars and pictures of angels, and fairies and mermaids and all sorts of improbable things which the artists have painted on the ceilings of many of the older theaters. The Tabor Grand Opera house is radically unlike most play houses, and yet one has to examine its arrangements so in harmony and the effect is so pleasing that nothing more is to be desired, although one can not at first tell what makes this beautiful effect. There is a peculiar and fascinating combination of the ancient with the modern in the architecture, and it strikes one that while every convenience that modern art could suggest has been attained, the massiveness and strange beauty of the

ARCHITECTURE OF THE ANCIENTS

has been revived. It is old, yet new. It is like a realized dream of the grandeur of the great works of a thousand years ago. Architect Edbrook followed what is known as the "Modified Egyptian Moresque" style, and the decorations are in keeping with the construction. As one looks at the high ceiling with its massive girders forming a graceful square around the dome in the center, from which swings a brilliant chandelier; then at the pagoda-like arrangement of the boxes, and at the proscenium arch, beautiful in its simplicity and richness, he finds one thing present in all—reality. There is no tinsel used. There is a solidity, a richness about everything that one must examine and realize before he can appreciate. Governor Tabor might have saved $30,000 by using cheap woods in the interior construction of the Opera house, in the place of the highly polished and carved cherry which is to be found in all parts of the building, even where it will never be seen, unless one takes the trouble to peer into nooks to look for it. What attracts attention at once are

THE NOVEL BOXES.

Although the theater would be beautiful without them, yet it would lose it chief charm were they constructed in any way other than as they are. History tells of boxes in the olden time theaters of Southern European countries, for people of note, that were much like them; and yet these are so novel, so original as to not be the counterpart of anything. Not only is originality shown in the construction of the boxes separately, but in the manner in which they are arranged. In most theaters private boxes are partly on the stage; that is, in the proscenium. They are not at all satisfactory places from which to view the play. Indeed, one cannot see the center of the stage unless he sits in the extreme front of the box. In constructing the boxes as he did in the new Opera house, Architect Edbrook not only avoided the stereotyped styles, but gained two decided advantages, viz: the boxes are handsomer, more unique, and a better view of the stage can be had from them than from the old-style proscenium boxes and, as they are located in the auditorium, they naturally shorten the sides of the galleries, which, in most theaters, extend to the proscenium, making it impossible for persons occupying back seats on the sides to see the stage. It was a happy thought that suggested a shortening of the galleries and the construction of the boxes in this novel style. The boxes are so peculiar in appearance that it is difficult to give one a correct idea of them. There are three on either side of the theatre, rising one above the other. They seem to be entirely distant from the walls of the building and

LOOM UP, PAGODA-LIKE,

to within about twenty feet of the ceiling. They are surmounted by a roof that is like the covering of a Turkish Mosque. This roof is of a delicate blue, and on its slender and graceful peak is a ball of gold. Each box has rich curtains, and when they are drawn one can readily imagine that the effect is beautiful. Perhaps a better idea of these boxes may be given by describing one of them. Take, say, the box on the right side of the theater in the parquet. It is on a level with the stage; and its occupants can glance down upon those occupying seats in the orchestra. The formation of the floor of the box is an half circle—not quite so large, perhaps. There is a delicate railing surrounding the outer side of the box. This railing is not more than twenty inches in height, so low that in the upper box, way up near the ceiling one at first feels a little timid about venturing near the edge. There are curtains to each box, which can be so arranged as to partially or completely hide the occupants from those in the audience or on the stage. The entrance to the box is through a curtained doorway, the framework of which is of slender posts of cherry, richly carved. What impresses one most is the airiness, and delicacy of construction of these boxes; they appear to be formed of skeleton like frames and rich curtains. There is very little solid work about them. The floors are covered with heavy carpets the designs and colours of which are in keeping with the colorings through the building, and especially with the rich Bourbon tapestry hangings. The figures in the tapestry on the walls represent a poetic combination of lovers and flowers. The curtains which may be drawn around the boxes if desired are especially handsome. They are of silk plush of a soft sage green, maroon and old gold in colors. The ceilings are hung with tapestry gathered into a pleted half circle. One may reach these boxes from a stairway which runs from the lower to the upper one in the rear and completely hidden from view from the parquet, balcony or amphi-theater. This arrangement will make it convenient and pleasant for those who like to "visit" between the acts. One can run from one box to another without being seen from the auditorium.

Besides those six closed boxes there are six open boxes, if they may be so called. They are not really boxes but little places separated from the rows of seats. These boxes immediately adjoin the closed boxes, and while making pleasant places for small parties, they also add to the beauty of the theater. It is these boxes that cause the abrupt ending of the galleries. Abrupt is hardly the word, for the railing that runs around the balconies is not broken at any point, but curves and winds around the boxes in one continuous and graceful line.

What are quite as beautiful, if they are not quite so novel, are

THE PROSCENIUM
AND THE DROP CURTAIN.

And yet the designers have shown much originality in both of these. The artist conceived the idea of making the proscenium the frame for the picture that is, for the scenes that shall be presented on the stage. The execution has not fallen short

of the conception of the painter, Mr. Robert Hopkins. The groundwork is of gold paper of a celebrated French manufacture, and imported especially for this purpose. The bright gilt is relieved by narrower slips of copper-gold, and by an odd figure painted in maroon and ultra-marine green and gold. In the center of the top of the arch is painted a collection of musical instruments, the fool's cap and bells, and the dagger. On either side of the bottom of the arch arc exquisitely painted representations of large Japanese pots, in a decided blue. From these pots a delicate laurel vine climbs up the sides of the arch. What gives beauty to the proscenium arch, and what really makes it complete, is the large painting in the semi-circle panel, 19–32 feet. immediately above it. The painting is in oil, and as a work of art is entitled to great praise. The subject is "Hector's Adieu to Andromaque." The subject was evidently selected with a view to harmony, for the colorings are not only in keeping with the intent of the picture, but also with the surrounding decorations. The proscenium arch and the beautiful painting which surmounts it and makes the symmetry perfect, are not complete without the drop curtain.

While, as before stated, the proscenium arch forms a figurative frame for the stage pictures, it forms a literal frame for the drop curtain.

THE DROP CURTAIN.

This is also the work of Mr. Robert Hopkins. It will rank as one of the most artistic pieces of scene painting of the day. Before describing the curtain it may add to the interest in it to say that there is a connection between the painting over the arch and the scene on the curtain. The former represents history and the latter poetry—the two things from which the drama springs. Mr. Hopkins has shown a true poetic fancy in his conception of this scene and much artistic ability in its execution. He got his idea from Kingsley's lines, which read thus:

"So fleet the works of men
Back to the earth again—
Ancient and holy things fade like a
dream."

He has painted these lines at the bottom of the curtain. The picture is in spirit with the lines. In the foreground is seen a massive structure of the most magnificent architecture imaginable. In the perspective are other handsome buildings. But the mark of decay is on all. They are moss-grown, rotting away and tumbling down. All seems to be dying, but nature. The sky is radiantly beautiful and is the very incarnation of life. These three—the arch, the painting surmounting it and the drop curtain—form a picture that one does not soon tire of looking at.

THE CEILING

The ceiling does not at first glance show all its beauties. Looking up to it from the parquet, a height of 65 feet, it strikes the beholder as being modest and harmonious, and that's all. But upon a closer examination its massiveness and richness are discovered. It is divided into a square by heavy girders, with smaller panels in front and in the rear. In the center of the square is the dome, 30 feet in diameter. The beauty of this is in its simplicity. There are no stars, no figures, nothing whatever but the sky. An artist is risking a great deal when he paints a marine picture without a vessel or some object to relieve the stretch of water; or a sky scene with nothing but clouds to relieve the plain coloring. The artist has not failed in this. He has represented an early evening sky of a greenish blue, with fleecy clouds seeming to float lazily by.

The colorings in the ceiling are decided and rich without being flashy. There is considerable gilding on the large girders, the ground of which is of deep buff. The cornice is painted in strong colors, brightened with a dash of blue, gold and red here and there. The work on the ceiling is seen to good advantage in the foyer of the amphitheater where a heavy arch, corresponding with the proscenium arch, separates the foyer from the main auditorium. The walls of the theater are covered with rich paper of seven different designs, all in keeping with the general architecture and decorations. A bright gold is the reigning color, relieved by dark and decided columns. The effect is warm and rich without being gaudy.

One of the most important results that Architect Edbrook labored to attain was fine acoustic properties. His success is flattering to his ability, for one cannot sit in any part of the house where he cannot hear all that is said on the stage. The arrangement of the balconies, the quality of the wood used in constructing the floors, the formation of the dome and the arrangement of the stage have all aided in bringing about this happy effect. There is a more abrupt pitch in the balconies than in most theaters and from the fact that they do not extend all the way to the stage, and thus make the auditorium choked, the acoustics are probably better than they otherwise would be. As it is the sound upon leaving the stage rushes straight up, seemingly gathering volume as it goes. Were the dome in the ceiling large and deep much of the sound would be lost. But the dome is small, of very slight curve, and the sound rolls over it without losing much if any of its strength. The Tabor Grand has an advantage over nearly every theater in the country in that it is not necessary to illuminate it in the daytime, if so desired. Light is admitted through two large windows of cathedral stained glass, one on the north side of the building and the other on the east side, up in the amphitheater. It might be stated here that there was an object in so constructing the Opera house that it would not need to be made light by artificial means in the day time. Conventions and meetings may not only be held there, but it is said that Governor Tabor has a plan for uniting the stage more closely with the church, which may bring the Opera house into use in the daytime. The Governor's idea is to throw the house

OPEN ON SUNDAY

and invite the different devines of the city to preach there in the afternoon. The religious services in McVicker's theater in Chicago have proven a popular Sunday afternoon feature in that city for some time past, and there is no doubt that like services would be hailed with real pleasure in Denver.

A general description of the house having been given, the minor, though not less interesting points, must follow in a less consecutive order. Theater-goers will find the chairs in the new Opera house not the least agreeable feature. They are not only very handsome and very comfortable, but each one is supplied with a hat rack. It is made of wire and is tacked on under the seat, and all gentlemen will have to do will be to stick their silk hats between the wires and enjoy the play in the happy consciousness that nobody is kicking dents in them. These seats are from A. H. Andrews & Co., of Chicago.

The seating capacity of the house is 1,500, including the boxes. There are 600 seats in the parquet, 300 in the balcony and 350 in the amphitheater. There is sufficient room in each of the balconies to add a hundred or more seats without discomfort, if it is found necessary.

THE GALLERY OF THE GODS.

It is worthy of note that this amphitheatre is far superior to the balcony of many theaters. In many, if not in the majority of the New York theaters, the gallery "where the gods do congregate" is a dark, cramped and decidedly unpleasant place to be in; where there is a musty, unsavory smell of peanut shells and dried quids of tobacco, and where the floor is often dangerously slippery with tobacco juice, which the "gods" take delight in dexterously squirting at each other. It is not so in this case. The amphitheater is

almost as desirable a place to sit in as one of the chairs in the parquet. The ceiling rises high above the topmost seat, and light and air in abundance enter through the large window in the rear. There is a retiring room attached, even to the gallery.

The one point that should not be overlooked by any means is that there is

NOTHING CHEAP IN THE BUILDING.

Indeed, expensive woods have been used where cheaper material would have answered the same purpose. This fact is the more wonderful and the more commendable when the disposition of this Western country to make a false show is considered. Even in the remote corners of the ceiling, where stencil work could not have been detected from frescoing the latter was done with as much care, as it had been in the most conspicuous places in the theater.

There is, perhaps, no better criterion for one to base his judgement of the character of the work in the interior of the new Opera house upon, both as to

SOLIDITY, RICHNESS AND BEAUTY,

than the double columns of cherry that run from the floor of orchestra to the cornice in the cove, forming a support, apparently, for the heavy girders that cross the ceiling. These pillars, it might have been stated in connection with the description of the proscenium, add greatly to the beauty of the arch. To look at them, one would think these massive yet powerful pillars were carved from solid pieces of wood, so cleverly has the mechanic put them together. They are of cherry, highly polished, and almost without ornament, except near the top where they join the cornice.

About half way up the pillars are gas fixtures of the most elegant and graceful designs—rich, yet not gaudy, being of delicately formed and highly polished brass work. At the top of the pillars there is a gilded carving, which is a pleasant relief to the long, unbroken column of dead color.

THE GAS FIXTURES.

The gas machinery of the theater is perfect, every appliance known to gas engineering that could be used to advantage having been procured. The engineer can control every jet in the house by simply touching a valve. All the machinery governing the gas pipes is grouped together in a very short space on the right side of the stage, just at the first entrance and immediately back of the proscenium aisle. In the arrangement of the pipes for lighting the stage the attempt has not been to merely secure light, but to get at the same time the best effects. There is a set of lights for every row of scenes and they are so well protected that a fire in the "flies" will be a thing unheard of in this theater.

THE GRAND CHANDELIER.

Those who sit in the galleries will not be blinded by the dazzling light of the centre chandelier, as is frequently the case in Eastern theaters, where economy in making the ceilings low has been thought of more importance than the eyesight of persons occupying seats in the upper gallery. The ceiling of the Opera house is high, so high that at first glance one who has been used to seeing the top gallery literally hanging from the ceiling, thinks the height of the theater is too great for the size of the auditorium. But where he comes to define his criticisms he finds that while the ceiling looks high, yet the architecture of the building is such that the proportions and contour are perfect. The grand chandelier hangs twenty-eight feet from the ceiling. It does not interfere with the lines of sight to all parts of the stage from any part of the house. It is the handsomest and most original in its design of any chandelier in any of the theaters of this country. While not so large as those in the largest of the Eastern theatres, it is far more elegant. There are hundreds of crystal pendants on it, but not so many as to hide the beauty of the brass work, the frame itself. There will be two circles of light, one about twice as large as the other, and the combined gas jets of the two number one hundred and forty-four. The design of the small gas fixtures about the building are in keeping with this grand chandelier, the prevailing style being light, graceful and elegant. The gas fixtures were made by H. M. Wilmarth, of Chicago.

There are an hundred points of beauty that have not been noticed—beauties that are of minor importance when compared with the more prominent feature of the house. One can find an art study in a bit of carving or in a scrap of coloring or frescoing. This can be appreciated when it is remembered that nearly every pillar of wood is elaborately carved. The carving is genuine, too, not done by machinery and then glued on. One can look in every direction and find new beauties in the architecture, in fact, the entire interior, look at it as one may, is one grand picture, made up of innumerable studies. The aim of the architect and the artist was to secure imposing yet soft lines and warm coloring without the introduction of anything flashy.

THE FOYERS.

Although one finds the interior of the auditorium far richer and more attractive than the foyers, yet the latter have not been slighted. The foyer of the parquet, which one enters after leaving the rotunda, is gorgeous with mirrors, glistening chandeliers, richly colored ceiling and the bold, decided panel paintings of the sunflowers and *Fleur de Lis* before described. The foyer of the balcony is large and richly decorated in colors that harmonize with those of the other parts of the house. The foyer of the amphitheatre, or upper gallery, is handsomer than that of the first circle, although it may not find the "gods" so appreciative as it deserves. The ceiling is high, the foyer wide and the colorings and massive supports form a combination of lines and shades that can be found in no other part of the house. All these foyers are handsomely carpeted and the stairs are covered with axeminster, into which the feet sink softly as one goes up and down. In the balcony the seats are separated from the foyer by handsome curtains. This carries out the general idea of the architecture, that of making the lines soft and moving, and this the curtains accomplish much better than walls. This idea alone is an evidence of a desire to break away from old rules and create something new. A passing thought of the writer may give many an idea of how the interior impresses one by the recollections or suggestions it inspires. It seems that no more appropriate surroundings could have been designed for the play of "Othello." Everything is dark, yet tender; undulating, yet rigid.

THE ENTRANCE AND THE ROTUNDA.

Unfortunately the grand entrance and the rotunda of the Opera house will not be completed for the opening night. Bare walls will stare blankly at the gay crowd as it passes through into the foyer, where polished marble and richly stained glass and gorgeous colors should have beamed a welcome. But it will not be that way for long. The entrance will be the handsomest to any theater in America. It will be a fit introduction to the solid beauty that one will find upon entering the auditorium. It is twenty-four feet wide and fifty feet deep. It will be entirely of marble, and the aim will be to make it the most beautiful combination of colored marbles, polished and carved, of any work of its character ever before attempted. The walls will be artistically wainscoated and pilastered, supporting a richly carved cornice. At the end of the entrance a short flight of massive iron steps lead one to the rotunda, which will be one of the most pleasing parts of the building. It was perhaps because the box office is here that

the desire was to make the rotunda so attractive. A soft, intoxicating light will fill the place, subdued and given color by the cathedral glass dome which surmounts the rotunda. It is of the same width as the grand entrance and thirty-two feet in depth. The walls, to the cornice, are sixteen feet high and from that point the dome gradually swells to a height of twenty-five feet in the center. The cornice will be of cherry, carved fantastically, but without other decoration, and the framework of the dome light will be made of the same wood. The glass lights in the dome are so constructed that any of them can be opened. At intervals of space there will be small pieces of crystal-like glass cut into a convex shape, which will reflect hundreds of prismatic rays upon the rotunda beneath. From the center of the dome hangs a chandelier so unique and novel in design that the writer confesses his inability to comprehensively describe it. It is not large, and the style is more airy and delicate than massive and grand. Even the representative of the firm that manufactured it confessed his inability to define the design. It looks like a number of things. One might take it for a temple, or a grotto, with delicate pillars surmounted by a Turkish dome. Then it might serve as a bird cage. Whatever its design, it is ornamental, and will attract much attention. The Manager's office will be on the left side of the rotunda. It will be furnished with elegance, the chairs, desk, etc., all being finished in cherry. Retiring rooms will also open from the rotunda, where the toilet may be re-arranged before entering the foyer if desired.

FOR ONE'S COMFORT.

What will perhaps be more appreciated in the new Opera house than any other feature, are the arrangements that have been made to secure the entire comfort of theater-goers. There are but few theaters in the East that have retiring rooms for ladies even, and when the Academy of

Music in Philadelphia was built, the fact that it had rooms in which ladies might arrange their toilets, was hailed as the greatest boon that had ever been given to the theater-goers of the city. The new Opera house not only has spacious rooms, elegantly upholstered, for ladies, but there are also smoking rooms for gentlemen. These rooms open from each of the three foyers. They will make delightful places to spend an half hour in for a smoke or chat.

THE STAGE.

Unless a full description of the stage, with interpretations of stage technicalities, were given, one could not get a better idea of the new Opera house stage than from the simple statement that there is nothing lacking in it that is known to the art. The arrangement of the stage is perfect. It is large and yet not so big as to be barn-like, and it is most admirably designed. Back of the proscenium it is fifty feet in depth and seventy-two feet wide. As the stage scene, that is, taking the lines from the sides of the proscenium arch, to be fifty by thirty-four feet in width. There will be eighteen feet on either side the stage for the sliding of the scenes, etc. The arrangement for lowering and hoisting the drop scenes are complete, and while they appear complicated to one not posted in scene shifting and dropping and stage carpentry in general, yet he can also see that there is perfect order and no trouble to be feared of the scenes getting mixed. The scenery has been prepared with much more care than is usually given to such work. In most theaters, scenery is gotten up by men who haven't the slightest idea that any one will pronounce their work artistic. All they desire is to have their daubs answer a purpose— represent a house, a street, or a lake, relying much upon the poetic fancy of the play-goers who sit in front to supply what they have failed to impart to their scenes. But it has not been so in the Tabor Grand Opera house. Mr. Hopkins, the artist, has

painted twenty-four sets of scenes, all of them of merit and many of them deserving the name of works of art. There is nothing crude about the work. The manner of joining the scenes together is as novel as the scenes are beautiful. They can be put together in any fashion and yet form a complete scene. For instance, the two pieces forming a street scene can be transposed in position and still form a street scene, although different from the other. The dressing rooms are all on the Curtis street side of the stage. One can not take a dozen steps through the dark entries without finding one of these little rooms opening either on one side or the other. Some of them are larger and better furnished than the others, but all are comfortable, and the actors will not be cramped for room in changing their costumes.

THE MEN WHO BUILT IT.

About all that remains to be said is to tell by whom this beautiful temple of the muses was designed and decorated. The architects were W. J. Edbrooke and F. P. Burnham, who also designed the Tabor block. Mr. Edbrooke has been on the scene of construction of the building almost daily since the first stone was laid. The Opera house building and the handsome theater in it form one of the broadest pieces of architecture in the West, and almost the perfection of art has been obtained at every point. It is said that one hundred thousand dollars have been spent in the fitting up of the interior of the theater after the walls were plastered, and nearly half of this fortune was expended on the hard woods in which the interior in finished.

The decorations were made by J. B. Sullivan & Brother, of Chicago, Mr. J. B. Sullivan himself having been in Denver superintending the work since May last. Although this firm have done many artistic pieces of work in the theaters of Chicago and in churches and in lodge rooms all over the country, and right here in Colorado, for that matter, having just completed the decoration of the handsome Opera house at Colorado Springs, yet never before, so Mr. Sullivan says, have they attained the perfection that is to be found in the work just finished.

The stage and its arrangements were built under the direction of Mr. John C. Alexander, one of the best stage carpenters in the country. He has been in Denver and at the theater superintending the work since February last. To him the credit is largely due that the stage of the Tabor Opera house is the most perfect in its appointment of any in the country.

114. COLUMBIA THEATRE
Chicago, Illinois
Opened September 12, 1881

James H. McVicker's great rival as a theater builder and owner in Chicago was J. H. Haverly, who had owned the New Adelphi Theatre, billed as the "largest theatre in Chicago," and seating some 2,000 persons. The playhouse was not a good one, the construction being shoddy, and was in reality nothing more than a firetrap. Haverly reconstructed and redecorated the theater in 1878 and succeeded in making the old house presentable. His lease on the land expired in 1882, however, and Haverly turned to constructing a new theater, the Haverly, which in 1885 was renamed the Columbia Theatre.

114:1   In 1882, when J. H. Haverly's lease to the ground on which the old Adelphi stood, expired, he secured the financial cooperation of John B. Carson, then of Quincy, Ill., but now of Chicago, to construct a new theater building. The site selected for the new structure was on a lot just west of Dearborn Street on Monroe Street, facing north. The design of the new theater was made and carried out

114:1. A. T. Andreas, *History of Chicago*. 3 vols. (Chicago: A. T. Andreas Co., 1884–86), 2:666–67.

on a most elaborate plan, and it is notable that the building was constructed and opened to the public within eighty-eight days after the ground was broken, James D. Carson having control of the building operations. The building is seventy feet wide and has a depth of one hundred and ninety feet. It is six stories in height and is surmounted by a pyramidal tower. The first-story front is constructed of iron, and the upper portion is built of finely polished white Lemont stone in a composition of the French Renaissance and Queen Anne style, and the whole presents an ornamental, yet substantial and imposing, appearance. The total seating capacity of the entire house is two thousand. The stage is seventy by fifty-four feet and is provided with every appliance to make it complete, having large and well appointed dressing-rooms on the main floor for the use of the "stars," while others equally convenient and well arranged are provided for the support of the companies playing.

The theater was opened by Mr. Haverly on September 12, 1881, Robson and Crane appearing in Shakespeare's *Twelfth Night*. He continued as proprietor until June, 1883, when financial reversals caused him to re-lease the property to Charles H. McConnell, who became the proprietor at that time. During the summer following he made such alterations and additions as gave that theater a world-wide reputation. The changes were made in the front of the building and in the lighting and ventilating facilities. But the chief attraction now is the art galleries, which were added to the theater in the summer of 1884. The two stores, which formerly occupied the space on each side of the grand entrance, were entirely transformed, and the foyer was re-arranged. The ceilings and walls of these apartments are a mass of golden Lincrusta-Walton, and the whole is made resplendent by blazing incandescent lights. The foyer is separated from the auditorium only by portières, and the apartment is decorated in a royal manner. Two marble statues, "Ino and Bacchus" and "Jeptha's Daughter," from the chisel of C. B. Ives, of Rome, occupy a conspicuous position, and the walls are hung with high-class paintings of the modern school. The art galleries were Mr. McConnell's pet project, and they have proved to be a most receptive feature. For a considerable time afternoon receptions and concerts were given by the management semi-monthly, and these were always attended by the fashionable people of the city. The collection embraces some notable paintings, which are classified under the chapter devoted to the consideration of Art in this volume. A terra-cotta bas-relief of Sarah Bernhardt is shown, and Venetian carved ebony figures of male and female Egyptians, and "The Seasons" inlaid in copper on panel, with ebonized frame, are conspicuous art objects exhibited. The art apartments are further embellished with cabinets, mantels, bronzes, bric-a-brac, Bohemian-glass vases, settees, screens, ebony, gilt and marble pedestals, bronze busts, Egyptian lamps, etc.

On February 2, 1885, a stock company was organized, and Mr. McConnell sold out a large interest in the theater. On February 2, 1885, Mr. McConnell transferred the theater to the Columbia Theater Company, incorporated with a capital stock of $200,000, of which, J. M. Hill is president and manager; J. S. McConnell, treasurer and acting manager; and C. H. McConnell, secretary. The change of name from Haverly's to the Columbia Theater occurred at the close of the Irving engagement, Miss Ellen Terry, the actress, having had the honor of re-christening it.

115. BROADWAY THEATRE
Denver, Colorado
Opened August 18, 1890

The opening of Denver's Broadway Theatre attracted much attention, and the play-

house was heralded as "one of the most luxurious playhouses in the world." Again there was the neo-Oriental motif that was found in Tabor's Grand Opera House in Denver, which had opened some nine years previously. Of particular note was the emphasis on the "fireproofing" of the structure. The Denver *Republican* carried an extensive description of this new theater.

115:1   IN THE NEW BROADWAY

DESCRIPTION OF THE INTERIOR OF THIS
BEAUTIFUL DENVER THEATER

One of the Most Luxurious Playhouses
in the World—
Indian Designs of Architecture
and Drapery——
A Fireproof Stage of Most Generous
Dimensions——
Twenty-five Boxes and Seating
Accommodations for 1,630 Persons—
The Artistic Drop Curtain and
Beautiful Lights

The ring of hammers and a chorus of echoing grunts from hundreds of saws in the hands of an active army of carpenters has, at last, made the interior of the beautiful Thespian gem, known as the Broadway theater ready for occupancy. This evening, Miss Emma Juch, the distinguished American prima donna, will formally open the elaborate theater which the energy of Bush & Morse has built for Denverites to enjoy. The theater has previously been reviewed in THE REPUBLICAN, but as over $90,000 worth of additional improvements have recently been made in the construction of its magnificent interior, a representative of this paper yesterday made a personal inspection of the paragon of architecture for a more full description.

The cost of the theater portion of the building alone will now equal $175,000.

115:1. Denver *Republican*, Aug. 18, 1890.

HAVERLY'S THEATRE, CORNER DEARBORN AND MONROE STS.

115. Broadway Theatre, Denver, ca. 1885. Courtesy of the Denver Public Library Western Collection.

114. Haverly's Theatre (later renamed Columbia Theatre), Chicago, 1882. Engraving, published in *Chicago, Illustrated and Descriptive* (Chicago: N. F. Hodson & Co., Nov., 1882). Courtesy Chicago Historical Society.

115. Interior, Broadway Theatre, Denver, ca. 1900. Photograph by McClure. Courtesy of the Denver Public Library.

In its construction Colonel Wood of Chicago has made the greatest effort of his life. He has succeeded, and can fold his arms proudly to-night when an admiring audience of 1,600 people will mingle with the universal praise for Bush and Morse that will burst from the appreciative lips of their fellow-citizens.

In augurating their new enterprise Messrs. Bush & Morse have adopted the right policy to clothe the impression of the opening with cause for pleasant and lasting remembrances in the hearts of their patrons. They will open to the public a theater in itself a gilded gem of splendor and convenience, first-class in all its appointments, with a practical manager and executive staff, and a standard operatic attraction. First impressions are always lasting in theater dedications. The Broadway's success is assured.

The managerial post will be held by M. B. Leavitt, a gentleman whose name alone is a sesame for theatrical success. The resident manager will be H. B. Lonsdale, a thoroughly practical theatrical man, whose brief sojourn in Denver thus far has surrounded him with a circle of admiring friends. A. Benton will be the custodian of the cash. Sam Leavitt, a nephew of the manager, will officiate at the box office as assistant treasurer. The balance of the staff consists of T. M. Harrington, stage carpenter; T. Lathrop, property man; S. American, electrician; Professor Koenigsburg, leader of orchestra; John Lyons, door-keeper; J. Hall, advertising agent, and W. H. Jones, chief usher.

READY FOR BUSINESS

The theater's exterior, even in its uncompleted form of construction, is already familiar to Denverites. While the theater portion proper, in the rear of the magnificent hotel apartment and theater building is finished, the front portion of the exterior has not received its finishing touches. As regards the entrance, however, the arch is complete. After passing over an elegant stretch of imported encaustic tiles for 130 feet, the visitors this evening will form a good impression of the theater before they reach the luxurious interior. On each side of the wall of the entrance is a row of marble slabs that reaches the entire length to the doors of the theater. Over the arch the words "Broadway Theatre" are carved and surrounded by a handsome bed of terra cotta. All the terra cotta used in the construction of the house is of fire-proof porous. The box-office is on the right, near the entrance. Manager Lonsdale will also have a private office in this portion of the building. On the left, and directly opposite the box-office, will be established a cafe, where it will be an impossibility for young men to escape regaling their sweethearts with an oyster supper, when the season opens. The entrance to the gallery and balcony is on Lincoln avenue, while the entrance to the parquette is on Broadway.

THE STAGE

The stage is a stage of steel. On its surface is a flooring of polished boards, the only wooden-work in its construction. Hydraulic cylinders operate the curtain, while all the scenery is operated by the counterweight system, which makes it the acme of simplicity in its mechanical workings. There are four trap-doors in the stage. The dimensions of these traps vary. When the reader realizes that the stage is forty feet deep and seventy-five feet in height, a conception of the magnitude of its size can be obtained.

There is an array of iron girder arches beneath the stage. What brick is used is composed of the fire-proof quality. The scenery has all been subjected to a coat of asbestos paint, that precludes the possibility of making it susceptible to fire.

DRESSING ROOMS IN PLENTY

The iron staircases lead from the stage to a series of dressing-rooms on each side of its spacious dimensions. The dressing-rooms are all that comfort could suggest. They are the embodiment of cleanliness, and larger, in fact, than many "furnished rooms for rent" that hang their placards on the outer wall.

The "star" dressing-rooms are two in number. No doubt the luminaries who occupy the luxurious apartments will be evening stars exclusively. A large porcelain bath-tub, one that enjoys the sole distinction of being the only one in usage in a theatrical dressing-room, adorns one of the rooms. There are twenty dressing-rooms all told. After climbing the iron stairway to an altitude of about sixty feet, one can see the beauties of the paint loft and artists' room.

The carpenter's shop is located separately from the main building, in the rear. A thick partition prevents the possibility of a conflagration. Two long iron fire-escape stairways have been erected on the side of the building facing Eighteenth avenue. In fact, the entire construction of the beautiful Thespian temple has been planned with an intention to have it beat a salamander's record, if occasion ever presents itself for the test.

THE CURTAIN

Twilight, according to tradition, let her curtain down and pinned it with a star. Perhaps, in point of liberality of dimension, that curtain holds a perpetual supremacy, and not being operated by hydraulic cylinders nothing but a twinkler would successfully hold it in place.

However, in point of artistic design, rich harmony of colors and tasteful execution of good workmanship, the Broadway theater curtain is unexcelled. The scene is a glimpse of India, to harmonize with the architecture of the interior of the theater. It represents a street scene with citizens in native garb. In lieu of cable or electric cars, a towering mode of street transit is portrayed by the colossal form of an elephant, upon whose monstrous spinal column the regulation canopy is seen. Groups of natives are pictured standing near a great wall, behind which tropical trees wave greeting to the audience. A *palanquin* is also within the range of observation. The border of the curtain is richly tinted in colors that blend with pleasing effect with the complexion of the interior of the auditorium. The curtain was painted by Thomas G. Moses of Chicago, an artist whose skillful brush has executed similar good work in the metropolitan centers of the East. The inside main curtain has been introduced to a thick coat of asbestos and shaded in pretty, delicate color of blue. The drop curtain is thirty-four feet high and forty feet in width, being one of the largest in the country. The foot-lights number forty and are incandescent electric lights, protected by a layer of tin, which forms a strong reflector.

THE BOXES

On each side of the stage are canopy boxes of rich design. Then come a number of mezzanines, all beautifully furnished. The curtains to the boxes are of the Indian pattern. The backs of these paradisiacal patterns are richly paneled with *jute velour*. A row of incandescent lights peep askance to the audience behind a thin layer of small curtains that are interwoven in the fret-work around the front of the boxes. The railing of each box is handsomely upholstered with plush of olive green. Counting thirteen foyer stalls in the rear of the parquette, there are twenty-five boxes all told. These have all been taken for this evening, Mr. Leavitt having surrendered his box to accommodate the unprecedented craze for seats. Mr. Bush and a party of five friends will occupy one of the boxes this evening. Doubtless his heart will swell with pride more than once when he witnesses the magnificent triumph of the enterprise which he and Mr. Morse have given to Denver.

THE SEATING CAPACITY

In the parquette the chairs will be of the regular pattern, upholstered in plush of olive green, which a man that is addicted to color blindness might call old gold. The chairs are placed in variations of attitude calculated to bid defiance to Leghorn hats of generous brims, which ladies ofttimes wear to the horror of the unfortunate who sits behind them.

There are 461 chairs in the parquette, all numbered with neat silver plates. In the dress circle are 165 chairs, in the balcony 347, and family circle 257. In the gallery just "400" can crowd themselves. While this may not be strictly the 400 of McAllister renown, the complement of gods are indifferent so long as they get a good view of the stage. The total seating capacity of the house is 1,630. The foyer extends around the entire rear portion of the auditorium. Entrances to all the boxes are made from the foyer.

BEAUTIFUL FRESCOING

The fixtures constituting the electrollers of five lights each are of Roman gold, made expressly for Bush and Morse. They are worked in Indian design. The frescoing of the walls and ceiling on the interior of the building is in itself a study of artistic merit. It is fully in keeping with the general standard of excellence that characterizes this great triumph of architectural skill. The colors consist of old blues and sienna, the designs harmonizing with the general construction of the house. Far above the heads of the audience the ceiling is decorated with a series of frescoing that seems to wave greeting from the departed spirit of the Bard of Avon as his portrait looks down upon the handhome interior. A delicate shade of blue, interspersed with rich gilt, makes a pleasing effect. The proscenium border is also decorated in mild, but tasteful form. The dimensions of the proscenium arch are thirty-eight feet six inches in width and thirty-two in height.

FIVE CAR-LOADS OF SCENERY

The scenic effects have not all reached here as yet owing to a delay in transit, but in this respect the present company will not suffer, as Miss Juch's special train carries five car-loads of scenery.

THE ORCHESTRA

The orchestra pit is surrounded by a brightly polished railing, behind which the orchestra can safely play "Annette Rooni," or any other operatic aria they may desire. The orchestra will consist of twelve musicians, under the leadership of Professor Koenigsburg. A piano will also be a musical adjunct, when needed. Every seat for the performance this evening has been sold, which is sufficient evidence of the public's appreciation of the enterprise displayed by the new candidates for favor in the theatrical circles of Denver. There is but little doubt that the Broadway will always be a standard attraction in Denver.

116. THE AUDITORIUM
Chicago, Illinois
Opened December 9, 1889

The Chicago Auditorium opened formally on December 8, 1889, with the President of the United States, Benjamin Harrison, and his Vice-President, in attendance. It was then the largest playhouse in the United States and was to maintain that position for a number of years to come. Not only was the seating capacity of the theater tremendous, but the acoustics of the house was absolutely a marvel. A person in a natural voice on the huge stage could easily be heard in the rear seats of the second gallery.

The Chicago *Tribune* devoted to the opening of the Auditorium three pages which are reproduced here.

116:1   DEDICATED TO MUSIC AND THE PEOPLE

The Celebrated Auditorium Formally Opened with Ceremonies of Unprecedented Impressiveness

---

PRESIDENT AND VICE-PRESIDENT
OF THE NATION PRESENT

116:1. Chicago *Tribune*, Dec. 10, 1889.

Governors of Several States and Prominent Officials Add Directly to the Occasion

---

WEALTH AND FASHION FROM ALL PARTS OF THE COUNTRY ATTEND

Universal Praise for the Chicago Enterprise that Carried to Success an Undertaking of Such Vast Magnitude

---

IMPOSING SCENE WITHIN THE BUILDING— THOUSANDS THRONG THE ADJACENT STREETS

The scene was a great one, yet behind the magnificence there arose in memory another different from it in many respects that occurred in the same building.

Then the flag of the nation was entwined everywhere among the rafters of an incomplete structure. Then the banners of the States floated over delegations from every part of the Union. Then the representatives of the Republican party presented two names to the people for President and Vice-President—the names of Harrison and Morton. The cheers, the music, the waving of flags—who that were present can forget the occasion when a chapter in our national history was written?

Last night instead of rafters the hall was roofed with ivory and gold and starred with electricity. Long lines of white boxes on either side, and rising tier on tier overflowed with beauty and fashion. Instead of the excitement of a political struggle was the calm of a people assembled to dedicate to freedom and the arts a temple worthy of both. And there in one corner of the stage—a stage where more than a thousand were seated, though they looked like a handful—were two men whose names on the former occasion were on the lips of the multitude. Two promises had been kept. The Auditorium was completed; Harrison and Morton were present as President and Vice-President, respectively, in the place that witnessed their nomination.

It was not the time for a gratification of a party spirit, but for a feeling of patriotism far wider—a feeling of gratefulness for belonging to the peaceful and progressive Republic and for living in a city to whose enterprise and enlightenment this hall was a monument.

Here history had been made; here harmony now reigned.

SCENE OF GRANDEUR

Imagine that stage, only a little spot of it being taken up by a thousand or more persons, and its burden looking like a mite in comparison with the assemblage before it. You could not feel the sense of immensity till you turned from the footlights and looked back under the white and gold-ribbed vault of the body of the Auditorium to the balconies, which flattered the eye and then bewildered it; for, first, there sloped back from the parquet a stretch like a flower garden; then came the curving balcony, black with thousands, as if more people were there than anywhere else; above it the straight line of the second balcony, with banks of sightseers; and last and highest of all the gallery, where occupants looked like dots. Now came the triumph of architecture— for, while you felt the largeness, you also felt the compactness of the whole. Despite the distance, you know that these dots in the gallery were near you, and could hear every note and word uttered on the stage. And you were not satiated or overpowered by the decorations. In light there is no satiety; and richness was kept from being overpowering because it was expressed in white and gold. It was sumptuous and chaste.

THE EXERCISES

The Mayor speaks. He is collected, and looks dignified. He is no doubt saying what is proper, but he does not enchain attention, and his intonation sadly recalls a preacher in a country church.

113. Tabor Grand Opera House, Denver, ca. 1881. Courtesy of the Denver Public Library Western Collection.

THE AUDITORIUM—Congress Street, Michigan and Wabash Avenues.

116. The Auditorium, Chicago. Albertype, published in *Select Chicago, Illustrated in Albertype* (New York: A. Wittemann, 1889). Courtesy Chicago Historical Society.

116. Interior on opening night, Auditorium, Chicago, Dec. 9, 1889. Engraving, from a drawing by H. F. Farny; published in *Harper's Weekly* (Dec. 28, 1889). Courtesy Chicago Historical Society

THE INTERIOR OF THE CHICAGO AUDITORIUM.—Drawn by H. F. Farny.—[See Page 1035.]

Then comes the cantata by Mr. Frederick Grant Gleason, with its fine swing and rhythm. He is a Chicagoan, and so is the author of the poem, Miss Harriet Monroe. They are both young; but who save the young should sing the achievements of our young city! Theirs is now her hope, and to them belongs her future.

Mr. Tomlin, who has trained generations of Chicago singers, swings his baton over that great chorus. As a new ship feels the first wind of ocean, the great building tastes the music and thrills with delight. Here is a place for song life's fullest utterance. The noblest hymns are surely yet unsung, and this shall be their birthplace. In imagination you may hear their strains, and in imagination see the masses who will hear them. It makes one reverent to think that the Auditorium has received its baptism of sound.

And now comes the petted plaything of two continents, the warbling Patti. How soft she is; how caressingly inviting; how essentially feminine! No wonder she bewitches the people, for has she not bewitched old Father Time, and made him drop his scythe and pause in his relentless way to listen! Would he touch her raven locks with gray! Behold! They have stolen sunset gold and made it sunrise. And those tresses are in harmony with the Auditorium's scheme of color—a subtle compliment to Chicago. Patti is a Vivian, and the sad old world is her Merlin. Let her play her tricks even here and warble in the ear of dignity. She gives comedy to the seriousness of the occasion by lending to it the coquetry of her sex.

PEOPLE ON THE STAGE

If you were near enough to the stage you much have studied faces. In the temporary right-hand box near the mass of singers on the stage was President Harrison, looking complacent and pleased. Beside him and almost invisible is the dark modest face of the man who planned and carried out the Auditorium—Ford Peck. Perhaps you would not have believed it if told who he was—he looked so young. Behind him was the good-natured, kindly face of Vice-President Morton, with whose simple benignity the spectators fell in love. There is his stately wife—a woman to grace such a scene. And then, through dignitaries of Church and State, you looked upward beyond them all—behind the bright coats of the military and the brilliant costumes of the ladies—and saw the last and most hidden of all in that honored section—you caught a glimpse of one to whom Illinois and the whole country delight to honor. It is well that the bulk of the spectators cannot see him, for their plaudits would not let him remain in that obscurity. But you recognize him, for you know the dark eyes, and the iron gray beard and hair. It was Walter Q. Gresham.

The Governor and his suite are on the opposite side of the stage; but the exercises are beginning. The great organ peals forth; but let the critics tell of the music. We are too excited to listen to it.

Once more in the night air, with memories that will last the longest lifetime and with some thoughts that are not selfish to sweeten life, we may look back at the Auditorium, from which its thousands are swarming like bees from a hive. How solemnly and sternly rises this strong tower, "four square to all the winds of heaven!" It is a reminder of duty and of a people's destiny. It looks toward the West —toward the future. It is almost prophetic. Friend, have we seen the curtain rise tonight on the last act of that drama of humanity of which Bishop Berkeley wrote? You remember the last line, do you not?

Time's noblest offering is the last.

EXERCISES IN THE AUDITORIUM

Impressive Music and Elegant Speeches— Cheers for the President

It was soothing to step into the concert hall before the lights blazed up, even after the benediction of the soft evening. The golden walls were figured with big graceful shadows thrown by the semi-circles of quiet light; the chorus of the many waving fans in the boxes and on the stage where the singers sat was as gentle as the zephyrs moved by those same fans; the singers themselves looked in the distance like the creatures of a mirage; there was no defining of individual figures, only a faint pretty blending of quietly-waving colors that looked as though they might have been a skillfully painted foreground of the southern sky behind them. There was no harsh noise; so seats were banged down by the ushers; no ribald servitor yelled: "Op'ry glasses; books of the op'ry"; the heaviest footfall was hushed in the yielding carpets. The early-comers breathed the spirit of their surroundings, settled back in their easy-chairs, and lolled.

The balconies softly filled up; dim figures began to steal down the parquet aisles and settle in the seats; occasionally a box which had stared with proper aristocratic vacancy at the gathering in the vulgar $50 seats would blossom out in the rich colors of handsome costumes. But there was nothing rude in the change that came of the face of the house. It was gradual and lazy.

The stage boxes were a little slow in filling up. Now and then a figure would glide into the star-spangled bannered recesses and there would be a sudden awakening from the delicious indolence and a whispered chorus of: "Is that not him?" or "Is that he?" A longer look would bring the assurance that the newcomer was only somebody or another who had nothing but money, and the release to dreaming would ensue.

THE PRESIDENT AND VICE-PRESIDENT

A little after 8 o'clock, there was a very pronounced awakening. The Hon. Levi P. Morton, Vice-President of the United States, came in and quietly took his seat.

A hearty burst of handclapping greeted him. Another moment and the outlines of a short chunky man were visible at the right stage entrance. There was absolutely no way of mistaking him. Before the electric light had run a fiery course across the ceiling and the hall was glittering and blazing in every corner, "His Excellency Benjamin Harrison," as the program called him, was bowing to a cheer that started musically up on the stage with the singers and ran up to the roof, where the galleries got it and fired it back again.

Then the lights flashed, the band roared out the familiar welcome, "Hail to the Chief," and the crowd only waited for the coming of another idol to be assured that the Auditorium was open at last.

They had Benjamin Harrison. They were to have Adelina Patti later on.

They waited. They didn't exactly wait patiently, but they were gentlemanly and ladylike in their impatience, of course. They applauded Theodore Dubois' Triumphal Fantasie and they whispered:

"Four more numbers to Patti."

They cheered Mayor Cregler's basso profundissimo periods, but they nodded across the hall:

"Patti will be here shortly."

Ford Peck was cheered to the echo, and boundless enthusiasm greeted President Harrison, but neither expression of feeling entirely concealed the murmur:

"So much longer to Patti."

Every pause in Mr. Gleason's cantata was filled in with applause and every pause found a comment:

"Beautiful, but it isn't Patti."

At last Mr. Runnells in eloquent language, which was heartily cheered, sized up the Parthenon, the Pyramids, and the Acropolis with the Auditorium, and found them shy.

And then—but that must come in the proper place.

EVERY BIT OF SPACE TAKEN

When Mr. Eddy and the orchestra began to play Mr. Dubois' piece written for the Auditorium's big organ and band, the house looked somewhat disappointed. Not that it wasn't brilliant, for it would have been that if all the seats had been vacant. But although all the balconies were jammed, many of the boxes were unoccupied, and in the body of house at least a thousand seats were bare. They had been paid for, and the owners were ripping their fine raiment out on Congress street in a life-and-death struggle with a coarse and vulgar mob; but naturally everybody who noticed the ragged state of the house blamed it on the speculators.

"Hope they will lose every ticket they bought," said all the people who had expected to see bank Presidents and reigning belles squatted in camp stools in the aisles. And the poor speculators, who were getting kicked by the mob and punched by the "coppers" outside were not to blame at all, as a few minutes showed. As soon as the blockade was cleared away the seat-owners began to swarm in, and before the last notes of the triumphal fantasia had boomed out there was not room enough in the house to afford a sitting place for a living skeleton. It was at this moment that Prof. Swing, who is strong on music, said to Mr. Milward Adams: "Beautiful, that fantasia, is it not?"

"Wonderful," replied Mr. Adams. "Out of sight. Fifteen thousand dollars in the house."

It was Mayor Cregler's turn after Mr. Eddy, M. Dubois, and the organ, and the Mayor stepped forward with easy dignity, and made a short, sensible speech in that voice which almost scared some of the bass singers into a reformation. Many times during the address the audience applauded, but when he referred to Mr. Peck in pleasant terms a roar of applause, the heartiest of the evening, made him feel that he had said a happy thing. The audience was impatient in a good-humored way through the rest of the Mayor's speech.

MR. PECK CALLED ON

They were in ambush for Mr. Peck and when his Honor concluded the opportunity came to spring on their victim. Mr. Peck was sitting modestly in his box fanning himself with a souvenir program when the mention of his name in loud tones by several thousand persons startled his composure. He blushed, climbed out of the box and bowed low. Then he made a quiet, simple little response of thanks, winding it up with what might be called the hit of the evening. He invited the audience to call on Mr. Benjamin Harrison for a speech. Now Mr. Harrison was not down for a speech. He figured in the program as "in attendance," and it was considered rich enough honor that he should figure in the night's festivities as a silent onlooker. But the people, as soon as they had recovered their breath from the shock of the bold suggestion, took kindly to it. Gen. Crook, Mr. Morton, and two other gentlemen around the President, began to pound their hands together, the boxes took up the refrain, and then the populace, which had by this time lost some of its awe of the Executive, let out all the expressions of its enthusiasm in a cannonade of applause.

THE PRESIDENT RESPONDS

Mr. Harrison faced it bravely. He stepped slowly to the front of the stage and bowed. He looked stronger and heartier than he had looked earlier in the day, and in the crowd of famous men around him he was, for the moment at least, the most distinguished-looking figure. His speech was earnest, manly, and just about the thing for such an occasion. He delivered in a good voice, which could be heard in any quarter, and nearly every sentence gained a recognition from the audience. What the shorthand writer heard him say is printed in another part of this paper.

The President had sunk blushing into his seat, when the orchestra struck up "America" and the full chorus joined in the fine, roaring, swinging old hymn. They played and sang it so well that they had to sing it over, and they sang it better the second time than the first. Mr. Morton's face fairly glowed with patriotism, and Mr. Harrison beat time instinctively.

All this, of course, was interpolated, and when the patriotism of the crowd was satisfied the regular order of things had to be resumed. Mr. Gleason's curtain, of which the musical sharp tells you elsewhere, met a cheering reception from the audience. Mr. John S. Runnells' address was the next thing to be heard and Mr. Runnells was applauded noisily before he had said a word. His oration proved that the preliminary outburst of applause had not been wasted. He made every man there feel proud that he had come to such a fine place, and he prophesied some great things for the future of the Auditorium.

And then—

MME. PATTI APPEARS

The audience had been stringing up to a high pitch. A general appearance of nervousness was noticeable. The ladies fidgeted and the men rolled and unrolled their programs. The chorus cast expectant glances towards the north entrance to the stage. The fiddlers grated their bows. The house shuddered in a brief spasm of applause.

And then—

Well, Patti. The choristers near the north entrance pressed back. The orchestra men began to move their hoarse fiddles. The figure of Mr. Milward Adams appeared and the radiant face of Mr. Milward Adams beamed gloriously down on the house. For an instant Mr. Adams held every eye, and then in a moment all his radiance was extinguished.

Patti had come.

She sang "Home, Sweet Home." She didn't sing it the way your mother used to. She sang it better. She sang it so well that President Benjamin Harrison rose from his seat and smote his right hand with his left as everybody else was doing. In response to the honor the madame

sang a Swiss echo song, but although the audience cheered and cheered she declined to sing again.

Then Governor Fifer delivered an eloquent address in a manly style, receiving hearty applause, his glowing tribute to Mr. Peck calling forth a rousing expression of approval.

This ended the night. . . .

HISTORICAL AND STATISTICAL
Interesting Information About the Greatest Building in the World

The genesis of the great Auditorium Building dates back almost four years, and the development from the primitive idea which contemplated simply a handsome and commodious theater to the massive pile which now adorns the Lake-Front is worth a brief review. In 1885 a number of Chicago capitalists decided to take measures to supply one of the greatest needs of the city, and to make the provisions on a scale commensurate with the present and future requirements of America's destined metropolis. It was soon realized that the initial idea, although a bold and promising one, was far behind the actual wants, not to speak of the aspirations of Chicago. The prospect grew. It was decided to build not only a grand hall, fitted to hold national conventions, and of the largest possible mass-meetings, but to combine in the one building also a magnificent hotel and an office block rivaling any existence. The plans were not changed; they simply grew. For a year or more ways and means were discussed and the elaboration of plans for the noblest structure of the nineteenth century went slowly but irresistibly on.

Finally the ground was selected and acquired. The site occupies magnificent frontages on Congress street, Michigan avenue and Wabash avenue. There were three residences, a hotel and a skating-rink on the ground, and all these had to be demolished. It was not until January, 1887, that the work of excavation was begun. This was of itself a stupendous undertaking. The excavations for the foundations were carried to a uniform depth of twelve feet below the sidewalk, and the trenches were dug out to a depth of seventeen to twenty-five feet. Over 80,000 cubic yards of loam, clay and sand were removed, and upon the solid clay the foundations were laid.

THE FOUNDATIONS AND WALLS

The building was begun June 1, 1887. For the foundations of the main building two traverse layers of twelve-inch timber were first laid. Above these came a five-foot layer of concrete, and in this three layers of railroad bars and T-beams were imbedded. The enormous tower required special treatment. Its foundations were made double secure by laying them on the same plan as that used in the main building, but using double thicknesses of timber and concrete and five layers of iron. To guard against inequalities of settlement, the tower was loaded with a weight equal, foot by foot, with that borne by the completed portion. More than 800 tons of pig-iron, in addition to vast loads of brick, were used to weight foundations of the tower. As the superincumbent masonry was put in place, the temporary load was removed, and when the building was completed tower and main structure stood as one, without crack, flaw or join. There was absolutely no settlement in any part of the building.

The work progressed steadily without a break from its initiation to its successful completion. The building has a total street frontage of 710 feet, of which 382 are on Congress street, 187 on Michigan avenue, and 141 on Wabash avenue. The tower weighs 15,000 tons, there are 15,000,000 brick in the building, and the amount of masonry and iron involved is almost incalculable.

THE REPUBLICAN CONVENTION

Before the building was half finished an occasion for the use of the main hall presented itself and justified the promoters of this grand undertaking in their daring project. This was the meeting of the Republican National Convention of 1888. The unfinished Auditorium was turned over to the Executive Committee, fitted with seats for the purpose designed, and prepared for the historic event. All who had the fortune to be present at the meetings of the Convention, united in testifying that for convenience of delegates and visitors, acoustic properties and all other requirements of a great meeting, the hall was perfect.

Meanwhile the work of decoration went on uninterruptedly. The hotel was rented to a New York firm and will be opened January 15, 1890. The office buildings on the Wabash avenue front were rented as fast as completed, and are occupied mainly by artists, students, and the Chicago Conservatory of Music. As soon as the echoes of convention oratory had died out work was resumed on the grand hall and theater. This has been continued until the present time, hundreds of skilled workers being employed in every department. The result is seen in the magnificent proportions, the gorgeous and elaborate decorations, and the perfect seating capacity of the grandest hall on the American continent. Seats, every one with a clear view of the stage, are provided for 4,500 persons, and the view is as perfect as the acoustic properties of the great Auditorium. The stage, in both breadth and depth, rivals the most famous of the ancient or modern structures, and taken for all in all the building stands unsurpassed. For convention purposes the hall outranks anything ever constructed, and over 11,000 people can be accommodated within its walls.

FINANCIAL AND OTHER POINTS

Compared with the solidity of this wonderful development of Chicago enterprise the useless pyramids spring into insignificance and the Eiffel Tower is but a toy. The cost of the great structure has been over $2,700,000 and the ground on which it stands is worth $1,000,000. It has been built in three years, while the Grand Opera-House in Paris, with half its seating capacity, cost over $9,000,000 and occupied thirteen years in construction. The Auditorium is purely a Chicago enterprise, built by Chicago men on the designs of Chicago architects, and stands today a fitting monument to Western vim and pluck. Everything connected with it is on the grandest scale. It possesses the finest organ in the world, the most magnificent hall for concerts, stage-plays, or public gatherings, and its adaptability to the needs of the Western metropolis is unlimited. Chicago by common consent has been settled upon as the one and only city in which to hold National Conventions. Its hotel accommodations and perfect summer climate are now supplemented by the long-needed desideratum of an audience-hall, superior to any on the face of the globe, and fitted for all public gatherings incident to the World's Exposition of 1893.

A precise description of the Auditorium is found in the *Architectural Record*:

116:2   The Auditorium Building illustrates how the versatile Western American can combine sentiment with thrift, and demonstrates how he can endeavor to cultivate the service of Mammon simultaneously with an effort to attain his highest artistic ideals. The wish of Chicago to possess an Opera House larger and finer than the Metropolitan, a hall for great choral and orchestral concerts, a mammoth ballroom, a convention hall, an auditorium for mass meeetings, etc., etc., all under the same roof and within the same walls, gave birth to the Auditorium proper. The desire that the Auditorium be made self-sustaining, and not like the Metropolitan Opera House, a perpetual financial burden to its owners, rendered necessary the external subordination of the Auditorium itself to the business building and hotel, which, together with it, form the Auditorium Building.

When the design of the Auditorium Building was first intrusted to its architects only two-thirds of the ground and less than one-half of the money finally absorbed by the work were placed at their disposal. But, little by little, the enthusiasm of Mr. Ford W. Peck, the chief promoter of the enterprise, met with such response from the business men of Chicago as to warrant the acquisition of greater area for the building site and expansions of scope and scale far beyond the limits contemplated in the conception and development of the original design.

The form in which we find this building is, therefore, the resultant of many conflicting causes and influences. At first glance it may seem a most delightful state of things for the architects of a great building to be compelled by force of circumstances to erect a larger and more costly structure than that called for by the first instructions of their client. But the situation appears far from delightful when viewed more subjectively. After months of arduous toil the many conflicting conditions of the various problems have been harmonized and adjusted to each other, and the many thoughts brought forth by their study have been crystallized into a complete and well-rounded design and expressed in nearly two hundred plans and diagrams. Presto! the conditions change!! All that has been so laboriously thought out and so carefully adjusted must be re-traversed and readjusted; not once, but a score of times; in fact, for each successive widening of the financial horizon of the enterprise. While there is an obvious gratification and pleasure in the consciousness of the widening of one's opportunities, yet this pleasure may be bought at too high a price. Such was the case with some of the developments in the growth of the design of the Auditorium, particularly af-

116:2. "Chicago's Auditorium," *Architectural Record* 1:415–34 (July 1891).

ter building operations had been fairly inaugurated and many conditions had thereby become fixed and inflexible.

But we are dealing with the Auditorium as it is; not with the Auditorium as it might have been had the original project been carried out, nor as it would have been had the final intentions and resources of its owners been known to its architects at the outset.

Considering first the exterior of the building: it is found dignified, impressive, simple and straightforward. Every square foot of street exposure serves commercial purposes, and serves them well. Utilitarian interests have nowhere been sacrificed, not even in the great tower, which, primarily conceived, without thought of its commercial utilization, as a means of indicating the main entrance of the Auditorium and giving it accent and emphasis in an expanse of utilitarian frontage, is now filled from cellar to roof with hotel rooms, and with offices which extend even into the machicolated cornice. Still one sees that the Auditorium is not an ordinary business building, but that its exterior is the embodiment of something nobler and higher than the desire to erect an inclosure for a rent-trap.

As the Auditorium, as such, nowhere penetrates to the street fronts, but is surrounded and surmounted by office building, hotel, etc., the wants and peculiarities of these became dominant in determining the fenestration, and with it the general expression of the exterior. It is to be regretted that the severe simplicity of treatment rendered necessary by the financial policy of the earlier days of the enterprise, the deep impression made by Richardson's "Marshall Field Building" upon the Directory of the Auditorium Association and a reaction from a course of indulgence in the creation of highly decorative effects on the part of its architects should have happened to coincide as to time and object, and thereby deprived the exterior of the building of those graces of plastic surface decoration which are so characteristic of its internal treatment.

In taking up the consideration of the interior, the office building presents no features worthy of especial remark, except perhaps regret that it should have been pressed to completion so long in advance of other parts of the structure as to deny it a share of the richer material of finish and the more elaborate detail accorded to the hotel and auditorium.

The hotel is in one sense a marvel of planning. It is only a fringe, showing a street frontage of 587 feet with an average depth of but 45 feet skirting two sides of the auditorium, the predominant claims of which for space absorb the area usually devoted to the "working department" of hotels. The difficulties arising therefrom appear to have been overcome, for space has been found for kitchen, laundry, bakery, store-rooms and the other adjuncts of the hotel. All appear to be conveniently located and to communication with each other and with the parts of the hotel which they are intended to serve. Despite the limitations of space incident to the peculiar formation of the site, the hotel contains a number of public rooms of decided architectural pretensions and character. The main dining-room in the tenth story is architecturally noteworthy. Its ceiling is a barrel vault, divided into panels by the arched top chords of the supporting roof trusses, in which are set incandescent electric lights as an important part of the decoration. The vault is intersected in each panel by two lunettes which, however, are rather bald in treatment. They should have had sculptured or painted decorations in keeping with the mural paintings in the large segmental tympani at the ends of the barrel vault.

The banquet hall is an unusually interesting room, not only because of its construction and location, which is over the auditorium, between trusses of 118 feet span, but also because if its peculiar artistic conception and treatment, at once aggressively unconventional and original and still extremely delicate and refined. In fact, the banquet hall is the culmination of the boldness, originality and refinement which are characteristic of the decoration of this building.

The hotel office, the restaurant, the café and the main parlor are all rooms worthy of notice and study. The latter, 45 x 95 feet in size, is remarkable because of its connection with a loggia extending along its entire frontage, giving a most interesting outlook upon Michigan avenue, the lake front and over Lake Michigan.

In its construction the hotel presents many interesting features. As a multiplicity of pillars would have been objectionable in the public rooms which occupy the first story of the Congress street front, and which were intended in the original design to take up all of the second floor of the same, the floors from the first story upward are carried on 140 riveted girders 2 feet high and of 36 feet clear span each. The front on which these girders occur is 360 feet long and being but 40 feet deep, is given lateral stiffness by four heavy brick walls extending from bottom to top of building. The absence of interior columns resulting from the use of the girder construction permitted a degree of freedom in the handling of partitions and the division into rooms was found quite useful.

The most daring and conspicuously successful structural features of the hotel are the truss constructions of 118 feet span carrying the banquet hall, weighing 660 tons, over the auditorium, and those carrying over the stage, with a span of 110 feet, a load of 2,500 tons composed of stage machinery, rigging-loft, fly-galleries and four stories of hotel rooms and working departments, all of fire-proof construction. None of these were contemplated in the original plans of the building or prepared for in its foundations. The modest eight-story European hotel first contemplated would have been amply

served by the present restaurant and by auxiliary eating halls intended to have been located above the same in the second story. With the increase in area and height of the building came the necessity for a large table d'hôte dining-room and for the banquet hall, as well as for the enlarged kitchen, store-room, servants' quarters, etc., etc. The dining-room itself was placed in the tenth story, with a frontage of 187 feet toward Lake Michigan, while the space required for all of the others could only be secured over the ceilings of the auditorium and stage. An effort was made, by the introduction of long beams and rails in the walls, to distribute this unexpected additional load, as far as possible, over walls and foundations. Eleven auxiliary trusses of from 75 to 118 feet span were constructed, and connected with the original roof trusses with the utmost care as regards general design and detail, and then protected against injury from fire by incombustible non-conducting inclosures of porous terra cotta and plastering upon wire cloth.

Another remarkable piece of construction is a trussed girder of 40 feet span carrying a centre load of 230 tons in the second story over the main staircase of the hotel. This, however, seems to have been uncalled for. Equally good results as to plan and artistic design could have been attained without the structural complications resulting from the omission of the pillars whose work this girder is intended to do.

The Auditorium proper, with its accessories, occupies an area of 35,800 square feet, out of a total area of 63,500 feet for the site of the building. Its cubic contents are 2,800,000 cubic feet out of a total of 8,300,000 feet for the entire building. Its general dimensions are 118 by 246 feet. To this must be added the spaces occupied for entrances and exits, for parlors and smoking-room, organ chamber and stage dressing-rooms, which encroach upon and penetrate the surrounding business and hotel buildings, some in one story only, others through from two to six stories. Again stair and elevator shafts of the business buildings and hotel make encroachments upon the auditorium. These overlappings and interpenetrations form a Chinese puzzle, which cannot be understood unless illustrated by a complete set of plans and sections. On the main floor the stage occupies a depth of 70 feet, the orchestra 12 feet, the parquette 104 feet and the main foyer 60 feet. The main floor contains about 1,400 seats, arranged in generous sweeping curves and stepped up upon the lines of Scott Russell's isacoustic curve, with a total rise of 17 feet. Advantage is taken of this rise to obtain under the higher parts of the parquette an entrance foyer 80 x 118 feet, and a series of wardrobe and cloak rooms of quite generous capacity. These are at the end of the auditorium, partly under the main foyer and partly under the parquette, opening from the entrance foyer and extending along both sides of the parquette. On the outside of the same are corridors 14 feet wide.

This unusually great rise of the main floor has also made practicable the arrangement of six entrances, similar to the "vomitoria" of the Roman amphitheatre, by which the lower half of the parquette seats are reached without rendering it necessary to climb to the upper level of the main floor. Excessive crowding upon the main stairs is also avoided. The boxes, forty in number, are arranged in two tiers upon each side of the parquette. The lower tier forms an arcade of semicircular arches with rather light treatment and but little effect of inclosure, while the upper boxes are entirely open. In fact, there is nothing at all of the box-like and stuffy effect produced by the conventional treatment of the open box. When these boxes are filled with richly-dressed women, the mass effect of the

rich colors and stuffs is exceedingly fine and blends quite harmoniously with the forms of the architectural detail and the colors of the decorations.

The main balcony, elliptical in plan, is 80 feet deep at the end, but quite narrow at the sides. It covers the main foyer and overhangs the parquette 20 feet at the end, but is not wide enough at the sides to completely cover the boxes. The seats are also arranged on the lines of the Scott Russell isacoustic curve, which here develops into a rise of about 40 feet from the lowest to the highest seat. Advantage has been taken of this to form two foyers, of which the lower one is 40 and the upper one 20 feet wide. Both have ample retiring and cloak rooms for the exclusive use of the occupants of the balcony. This balcony contains about 1,600 seats, the lower two-thirds of which are reached through twelve "vomitoria" opening out of the balcony foyers. The upper part of the balcony has no foyer, but free communication is established by a broad cross aisle.

Above the balcony are two galleries, each with about 500 seats. The second gallery is not over but in front of the first gallery, advantage having been taken of the favorable sight lines, due to the great depth of the house, to interpose the second gallery between the first gallery and the stage. Approach to the second gallery is had by way of horizontal bridges from the first gallery.

It will be seen from the foregoing that the Auditorium contains (including the boxes) 4,200 seats. Among the various uses to which the house is applied are many which do not require so great a seating capacity. Arrangements for reducing the size of the house have therefore been made by providing over each of the two galleries a section of movable ceiling, hung on hinges at one side and on chains passing over winches at the other. When the entire house is open, these sections of the gallery ceilings are turned upward on their hinges until raised so as to fold into panels provided for the purpose in the ceiling decoration. When it is desired to shut out either gallery from the house, these sections of their respective ceilings are lowered and turned downward on their hinges until the lower edges come down to the gallery railings, which are especially prepared for their reception. The lowered portions of the ceiling then form part of the general ceiling treatment of the hall, and the galleries are entirely shut off without impairment of the general architecture or decorative effect. If still further reduction of seating capacity is required, it is effected by a system of vertical curtains between the pillars on the line of the middle of the main balcony, by which means a further reduction in seating capacity of about 700 seats can be effected, so that when reduced to its smallest dimensions the house will contain but 2,500 seats. On the other hand, increased seating capacity for conventions, etc., is obtained by continuing the stepping of the parquette seats into the main foyer, by forming two floors of seating upon the stage, by reseating the boxes and the box corridors, etc., until a total capacity of 7,000 seats is reached. Throughout this article capacity refers to numbered seats, and is independent of standing room, etc.

The dimensions of the stage are 70 x 110 feet. The height from the floor to the rigging loft is 95 feet. The stage floor is divided into sections, all of which are separately or jointly movable in the vertical plane. This movement is effected by twenty hydraulic jacks, the plungers of which range from 6 to 24 inches in diameter and which are operated under a pressure of 100 pounds per square inch. The valves controling these jacks are concentrated in such a manner that the person operating them is always in communication with and under the control of the stage manager. The possible downward movement from the stage floor varies for

different parts of the stage from 8 feet 6 inches to 18 feet 6 inches, and the range of movement above stage level is for parts of the stage as much as 18 feet. It is possible with this apparatus to create variations and graduations of level of stage floor almost instantaneously in any direction, up or down or oblique, for any part of the stage floor. Simulations of steps, terraces, rocks, hills, caves, pits, can be produced by the mere movement of a few levers. So also can wavelike or rocking motions of greater or smaller portions of the stage floor be effected in open scene. This hydraulic apparatus is modeled upon that patented by the "Asphalia," of Vienna, and applied by it in the opera houses of Buda-Pesth, Prague and Halle. The ingenuity of American builders of hydraulic elevators and the special conditions prevailing in this building have, however, caused the introduction of many improvements and modifications of the European apparatus.

It has been stated that parts of the stage have a downward movement of 18 feet 6 inches. This brings the floor of the cellar under the stage to a general depth of 6 feet below high water of Lake Michigan, or to 4 feet below the average level of the surface of the lake. Four pits, of an area of about 150 square feet each, extend still 30 inches deeper for the purpose of receiving the framework of the lowered platforms. As the stage is only about one thousand feet distant from Lake Michigan and the intervening soil is a mixture of clay, sand and water, the influx of this water had to be guarded against. This was accomplished by excavating under the entire area of the stage to a depth of averaging 3 feet below that of the finished floor. A sump had first been dug to a somewhat greater depth and the excavation kept free from water by the action of a steam pump. A thin bed of concrete was first spread over the entire surface. This was covered with a layer of Trinidad asphalt one inch thick. Over this were

116. Interior, Auditorium, Chicago, 1889. Courtesy of the Auditorium Theatre Council.

116. Interior (partially restored), Auditorium, Chicago, 1965. Courtesy of the Auditorium Council.

laid four sheets of heavy felt paper, each well saturated with asphaltum. These were again covered with an inch of asphalt. Then another five layers of felt and another inch of asphalt. At all the edges abutting against the inclosing walls the asphalt and the felt are carried up to high-water level. To resist the upward pressure due to a possible head of over 8 feet of water the asphalt was covered with Portland cement concrete and steel rails of aggregate weight somewhat in excess of that represented by the aggregate water pressure over the entire area of the excavated space and of sufficient transverse strength to take care of the irregularities of strain caused by the varying depths of the different parts of the cellar. Where the asphalt and felt are turned up at the inclosing walls they are held in place by special retaining walls calculated with reference to the hydraulic head to be resisted. The area so treated is nearly 8,000 square feet. The treatment has been entirely successful. There have been two leaks, one caused by the breaking of a pipe, brought about by the settlement of a wall, the other caused by the melting of asphalt next an inclosing wall, due to the proximity of the furnace of one of the steam boilers. Both leaks were stopped without difficulty and before any damage had been done by the inflowing water.

The hydraulic jacks which furnish the motive power for the movement of the stage floor extend from 12 to 24 feet below the cellar floor, and from 7 to 18 feet below the foundations of the surrounding walls. The shafts containing these hydraulic jacks were cut through a soft and treacherous soil, some almost adjacent to foundations loaded full up to the extreme bearing capacity of the soil. The shafts were polygonal in plan, lined with 8 x 8 inch timbers cut to fit accurately at the angles and inserted from below, around the excavation as rapidly as the same progressed, and carefully wedges in, layer after layer. Whenever necessary a steam-

pump was used to free them from water. After the shafts were completed the foot of each was filled with concrete, the cast-iron cylinders were set, and after being fixed in proper position in both the vertical and horizontal planes, the spaces between the cylinders and the shaft walls were filled with sand. With the exception of a movement sympathetic with that of the foundation of adjacent walls, the shafts and cylinders are in the position and condition in which they were originally set. The movement due to the compression of soil under wall foundations was to a great extent anticipated, and arrangements for compensation for the same, by wedges and screws, were part of the design. Of the two floors below the stage, so much as is not required for the movable parts of the stage floor and the mechanism connected therewith, is utilized for dressing-rooms, store-rooms, workshops, etc., the entire construction being of incombustible material, except only the floor of the stage proper, and of the intermediate stage and traps, all of which is made of 3-inch plank. On this stage there are no "sky borders," and in fact no "borders" or "flies" of any kind. The entire stage is surrounded by the "horizon," which is a panoramic representation of the sky in every graduation from clear to extreme cloudiness. These graduations are painted on an endless canvas, so mounted and attached to a special mechanism, that changes of sky effects can be made in open scene, either gradually or quickly as the action of the play demands. All scenic effects are produced by drops extending across the entire stage, perforated where necessary, and so treated as regards perspective effect as to produce all the illusions of closed stage setting.

All of these drops as well as the border lights are counterbalanced so that they can be raised or lowered from the stage floor, and not from the fly galleries. The fly galleries are utilized as stations for light effects and for storage of scenery. Fly galleries, as well as rigging loft, are built entirely of iron, the floors being made of iron strips, 3-16 x 2 inches, placed one inch apart and riveted to the floor-beams. All suspension ropes for drops, etc., are of steel, and all sheaves are of cast-iron. Even the battens to which the drops are fastened are made of iron, the only combustible used in connection with stage construction and mechanism being the cables, by means of which the counter-weights of the drops and the drops themselves are raised and lowered.

As the curtain-opening which is required for scenic representation upon the stage is but 47 feet, while for choral concerts, conventions, balls, etc., a much greater opening is desirable, there has been provided to meet this exigency, what has been called "the reducing curtain." This is an iron framework 75 feet wide and 40 feet high, covered with plastering on wire cloth richly ornamented on the side facing the audience. Within this reducing curtain there is an opening 47 feet wide and 35 feet high. The smaller opening within the reducing curtain is closed by an iron curtain of ordinary make, and within this is the regular drop curtain of silk embroidered with gold thread. The reducing curtain weighs 10 ½ tons and the small iron curtain weighs 5 tons. For raising and lowering each of the three curtains there is a separate hydraulic apparatus, also for the horizon and for the paint bridge. The valves regulating all of these are on the stage within easy control of the stage manager. On both sides of the stage, to a height of four stories above and two stories below the same, are dressing-rooms, and the space between the ceiling of the auditorium and its roof is utilized for storage of scenery, properties, etc., the iron trusses being protected from fire by coverings of porous terra cotta.

Turning now to the consideration of the artistic development of the interior of the Auditorium proper we find that the color scheme of the decoration is extremely simple. The prevailing tone is ivory—gold leaf has been liberally used in connection with the same. The plastic decoration is either shaded as old ivory or incrusted with gold.

Over the proscenium arch is a painting in the nature of a processional, the figures being life size upon a background of gold. Upon the walls inclosed by a framework of architectural forms are two large paintings. All three of these paintings are illustrations of passages in Mr. Sullivan's essay on "Inspiration," read before the Western Association of Architects some years ago. The entire color effect is at once rich, quiet and delicate. It is carried through lobbies, foyers, retiring-rooms, etc., and is repeated in the Recital Hall— a small concert hall seating 500 people, placed above the auditorium.

The architectural and decorative forms found in the auditorium are unconventional in the extreme and are determined to a great extent by the acoustic effects to be attained. Hence the house is low— lowest at the stage end, thence flaring outward and upward to the extreme width and height of the room. The surfaces of the walls and ceilings are well broken. A series of concentric elliptic arches effect the lateral and vertical expansion from the proscenium opening to the body of the house. The soffits and faces of these elliptic surfaces are ornamented in relief, the incandescent electric lamps and the air inlet openings of the ventilating system forming an essential and effective part of the decoration.

The elliptic curves of the balcony are complementary to those of the ceiling. As the ceiling finally resolves itself into rectilinear forms these are taken up, and, when the galleries are shut off, continued by the fronts of the two galleries. The fronts of galleries and balcony have a plastic treatment accentuated by groups of incandescent lamps which continue the effect of the ceiling illumination and decoration. The organ occupies on one side of the house the space ordinary given up to proscenium boxes. The organ pipes are concealed by two grilles and a colonnade. The arrangement and treatment seem quite spontaneous and do not betray the fact that up to the time when the walls had been carried 30 feet high and the architecture and decoration of the interior drawn, it had only been intended to have a small stage organ concealed somewhere in the "flies." Still, not only has the organ been made to play an important part in the architecture of the house, but room has been found for its 7,000 pipes, and its bellows, also for its complicated electric mechanisms, for the carillons, drums, echo organ, etc., the chimes in one of the fly galleries, the echo organ between ceiling and roof at the farthest end of the house.

Much attention has been paid to the heating, cooling and ventilation apparatus. Fresh air, taken from the top of the building, is forced into the house by a fan having a wheel 10 feet in diameter and 4 feet 6 inches in face. The fresh air comes down through a shaft in which it is subjected to the action of a heavy spray. This, at all seasons of the year, washes from the air much of the dust and soot with which it is charged. In winter, warm brine is used to prevent the shower from freezing. In summer from twelve to twenty tons of ice are used for cooling the shower and with it the air. Salt is mixed with the melting ice to still further lower the temperature. For warming the air in winter it is carried through steam coils so subdivided and provided with valves that very minute graduations of temperature can be affected [effected]. A system of ducts carries the air into the different parts of the auditorium, to the stage and to the various corridors, foyers and dressing-rooms. The general movement of air is from the stage outward and from the ceiling downward. The air is removed from the house by the operation of three

disk fans, two of 8 feet diameter and one 6 feet in diameter. Ducts are carried to these exhaust fans from openings in the risers of all the steppings for the seats throughout the house, and from registers in every foyer, corrider, cloak-room, dressing-room, toilet-room, etc.

Besides this main ventilating apparatus there are ten smaller fans used for the ventilation of the engine rooms, stores, kitchens, laundries, banquet hall, bathrooms, water-closets, etc. Especially noteworthy is an exhaust fan, connected by means of suitable ducts with every one of the four hundred rooms containing plumbing fixtures in the hotel.

But a description of the machinery plant in ever so sketchy a manner would far exceed the possible limits of any magazine article. A mere enumeration of the parts of the same will convey an idea of the difficulties encountered by its designers. There are in use eleven boilers, capable of evaporating 54,000 pounds of water per hour, the equivalent of 1,800-horse power. There are fourteen steam engines, aggregating 1,200-horse power capacity. Of these, three serve for driving fans and laundry machinery while eleven are used for generating electric current, there being the same number of dynamos, which furnish current for over one thousand lamps and for fifteen electric motors of which eleven are used for driving fans, two for the organ, the other in connection with kitchen mechanisms. There are in the building ten passenger and four freight elevators; all hydraulic power for the same being generated by four compound duplex pumps. For pumping drinking water there are six pumps; for boiler-feed and for raising water of condensation, seven pumps; and for the air-washing apparatus, one pump, a total of eighteen pumps of various sizes. There are also seven hydraulic motors for driving such mechanisms as ice-crushers, knife-cleaners, etc. The entire apparatus is divided into two separate and distinct plants, one for the hotel only and the other for the auditorium and the business building combined. The heating apparatus of both plants is so arranged and connected that the exhaust steam is fully utilized. This is so effectively done that in cold weather steam is rarely seen escaping from the exhaust pipes, all being utilized and condensed in the heating coils and radiators. Circulation through the miles of pipes is maintained with a back pressure upon the cylinders, never yet exceeding three pounds per square inch, and in the early days of the apparatus, before the gradients of the pipes had been disturbed by settlements of the building, with a back pressure of less than one pound per square inch. An object of interest is the switch-board on the stage of the auditorium, which controls and regulates 4,000 lamps. This is set behind the reducing curtain and is hung on hinges in such manner that when the reducing curtain is down and the house is used as an opera house or theatre, the switch-board is to the right of the curtain opening, as in all theatres. When the stage is to be widened, the switch-board is turned out 90 degrees so as to leave clear the entire opening of 75 feet, produced by raising the reducing curtain.

But there has been enough discursive statement of details of arrangement, construction and appointment, and it remains only to attempt to summarize briefly the results achieved.

Regarding business building, hotel and external treatment enough has already been said. There remains the Auditorium proper in its relations to its various purposes and the structural and the financial problems and their solutions.

Before disposing of the Auditorium proper, attention must again be called to the reducing curtain and its functions. For operatic and dramatic performances, for lectures and for concerts not involving the use of a mass chorus the reducing curtain is down and the house is simply a

mammoth theatre or opera house with a proscenium or curtain opening of 47 feet. When, however, the house is used for a concert by a great chorus, for a political convention, a ball or a fair, the reducing curtain is raised and the entire stage becomes part of the auditorium. The chorus seats rise tier upon tier 75 feet wide, 70 feet deep, closed in on the sides with suitable decorations and covered with a series of sounding boards suspended from the rigging loft. If used for a ball the entire parquette, orchestra and stage are floored over and the stage inclosed by a continuous set scene in panoramic form, apparently a continuation of the arcade formed by the lower boxes, the arches filled with tropical foliage and flowers, in the centre of which is the orchestra. The arrangement for conventions has already been referred to.

The success of the room is greatest when used as a hall for mass concerts. The chorus seems thus to blend with the audience, and the house is so open that one can see at a glance almost the entire audience and the whole chorus. The sight of thousands of men and women in festive array is always pleasing, and when every one of these has ample space for sitting in comfort, has fresh air and can see and be seen and hear every modulation of sound in its full effect the result is inspiring. But little less effective and successful is the Auditorium as an opera house.

The stage settings are generally complete and sumptuous, the effect of the music as perfectly transmitted to the farthest corners of the house as the most critical can wish. It should here also be stated that the value of the stage appointments and mechanisms asserts itself at every performance. With stage hands one-third in number of those required for similar work in the Metropolitan Opera House all changes and transformations are made quickly and smoothly and there has never yet been a case where the actors have waited for the stage. On the contrary, the stage is always set before the actors or singers have made their changes of costume, etc.

All of this is, of course, also of value for dramatic performances, of which there has been a number of successful ones in the house, the two galleries being shut off. While the actors were easily heard and understood in every part of the house, objection was made by many to the fact that distance from the stage made observation of play features too difficult for full enjoyment of the performance. As a hall for orchestral concerts or for virtuosi on individual instruments the hall has proved all that would be wished for, as also for use as a lecture hall. Its effect as a ball-room is almost that of fairy land, and as a convention hall it permits every spectator to see and hear all that is being said and done upon the platform, and would in this particular also seem to have fulfilled its purpose were it not for the demand in the case of National Nominating Conventions for a greater seating capacity.

The many peculiarities of the hall in acoustic properties, brilliancy and illumination, purity of atmosphere, conveniences of ingress and egress, comfort of seats, number, size and elegance of foyer, promenades, etc., and the many coat-rooms, retiring and toilet-rooms, etc., distributed throughout all parts of the house, all these assert themselves in each of the many uses for which the Auditorium has been built, and leave no doubt of its unqualified success and show that it fulfills the expectations of its founders.

As to the success of the building considered as a piece of architectural engineering, the verdict while in the main favorable, must be qualified by the regret that the preparations for resisting the strains caused by the growth of the building into larger proportions and heavier weights than at first contemplated had not been confined to the superstructure, but had been begun with the foundations. But as

this could not have been expected under the conditions prevailing, the visible effects of certain irregularities of settlement of foundations must be considered as the price paid for many admirable features in the completed building, which had been deemed financially unattainable when the foundations were designed and built.

The problems in steam, mechanical and hydraulic, engineering have been successfully solved. The only difficulties encountered in the practical operation of the plant were remedied without great labor or expense. It may interest many to know that the source of complaint was the noise produced by the rush of large columns of water under great head through the supply pipes of the Tower Elevator. This was remedied by substituting a compression tank for the gravity tank as a source of water supply for these elevators. Another was the difficulty of maintaining the water column in the long suction pipes of the elevator, the service of which was from the nature of the case very irregular. In the case of one set of pumps a special contrivance for "priming" was provided, in the case of the other the tank was raised above the level of the pump valves. Minor difficulties in regulating air supply from and to fans were remedied by readjustment of dampers, valves, etc.

In quite a number of instances the folly of a municipal regulation prescribing vent pipes for traps was demonstrated. Owing to the great height of the building the friction of the air in these vent pipes became so great that they failed to do their intended duty. "Sanitas" and other antisiphoning traps were substituted for the S traps, and the inoperative trap vents were disconnected, since which there has been no further trouble.

The two electric light and power plants, each at the time of its construction the largest in the world, were really an evolution brought about by a series of experimental efforts which after many vexatious failures finally produced an efficient and easily controlled apparatus.

Whether or not the enterprise is an unqualified financial success can hardly be definitely stated. So much, however, is certain: Chicago has an Auditorium far better as an opera house or a concert hall or a ballmoor than either the Metropolitan Opera House or the Music Hall of New York, and the certainty that its owners will not be assessed to assure its maintenance is already established beyond the possibility of doubt. That a dividend will be realized upon the investment is more than probable. Time is, however, required for a southward movement of the business centre of Chicago sufficient to fill all the stores and offices with tenants at rentals approximating those paid in similar premises a few blocks north of the Auditorium. Even now there is a small surplus revenue, which, however, is being applied to the payment of a floating debt incurred by reason of the failure of the management to dispose of a part of its capital stock which is still held in the treasury.

The Auditorium remained the outstanding theater in Chicago until 1929, when the Civic Opera Company moved to the Civic Opera Building. There was much discussion at that time about demolishing the Auditorium building, but it survived to celebrate its fiftieth anniversary in 1939. It was opened sporadically until 1941, then closed. It was used by the U.S.O. during World War II as a recreation center and for a time housed a bowling alley. In 1947 the building was purchased by Roosevelt University and the office building and hotel used for educational purposes. The Auditorium, however, stood vacant, too costly for renovation by the young university. In 1960 the Auditorium Theater Council was formed to "restore, operate and manage the Auditorium Theater as a civic enterprise." The Council, under the leadership of Mrs. John V. Spachner, raised the needed money to begin the restoration under the guidance of the important Chicago architect, Harry M. Weese.

The Auditorium is once again in use as a theater and concert hall and is beguiling its audiences today as it did when first opened in 1889.

117. STEELE MacKAYE'S SPECTATORIUM
Chicago, Illinois

The Chicago Exposition of 1893 presented Steele MacKaye with his greatest challenge, a challenge that was never realized because of the financial panic of 1893. The project is worth mentioning, however, since it was one of the most fantastic theater projects ever conceived.

The Chicago Exposition celebrated the four hundredth anniversary of the discovery of America in 1492, and so the name "Columbian Celebration" was applied to the event. MacKaye envisioned the building of a gigantic theater that would be able to contain the story of the epic voyage of Columbus and his men. Anton Dvořák was commissioned to write the music for the extravaganza, and he produced the New World Symphony to tell the story in music. The Spectatorium, on the lake shore at 56th Street just north of the fairgrounds, was under construction when the financial panic hit, and there was no money to complete it. MacKaye, however, built a smaller model to exhibit the effects he had planned for the Spectatorium. This scaled-down Spectatorium was set up in a building on South Michigan Boulevard between Madison and Monroe streets that had previously housed the Chicago Fire Cyclorama. MacKaye had it reconstructed and called it the Scenitorium. It was opened to the public on February 5, 1894.

A reporter from the (Lincoln) Nebraska *State Journal* interviewed MacKaye:

117:1   AN ADJUNCT TO THE FAIR
———————————
Mr. MacKaye's Representation of the
Voyage of Columbus
———————————
A REVOLUTION IN SCENIC EFFECTS
———————————

117:1. Nebraska *State Journal*, Apr. 4, 1893.

302

A Building Which Is Destined to Play an
Important Part in the Columbus
Celebration—Mr. MacKaye Talks

Chicago, April 21—(Special)—There
has been a great deal of curiosity excited
concerning "The MacKaye Spectatorium,"
an immense building which is being
erected in Jackson park on the Lake
shore, Chicago, by the Columbian Celebration company for the production of a
spectatorial entitled "The World Finder."
While the enterprise has been under way
for a long time very little of definite
knowledge is known concerning it, but
THE JOURNAL is now able to present a
complete description of many of the novel
appliances to be seen there this summer.
The word "Spectatorium" alludes to the
building. This building, according to plans
shown, is of wood covered with white
staff and has an area of 500 feet by 350
feet not including the semi-circle which
forms the real wall of the building and
encloses the scenic area. In style the building is an entirely new combination of the
Romanesque and Renaissance style of
architecture which is not only picturesque
but also very pleasing to the eye. The
theatre portion of the building proper,
which includes the stage and audience
chamber, is arranged on a much different
plan than the ordinary theatre the audience chamber occupying one-sixth of the
space. The audience chamber is situated
in the center of the semi-circle, which
forms the stage area, and has a
seating capacity of 8,000 persons. The
stage proper, so to speak, is represented
by an opening in the center of this circular arc, this opening being 150 feet long
by seventy feet high. From the wall of the
scenitorium or stage department which
is nearest the audience to the outer wall
of the same is a distance of 180 feet, making the stage portion of the building a
space included within two concentric arcs
180 feet apart. The measurement on the
inside perimeter or arc from the back wall

on the other is 600 feet. It will thus be
seen that while the stage has a perimeter
of 600 feet only 170 feet of this is open to
the view of the audience. Herein lies a
great part of the novelty of "The Mac-
Kaye Spectatorium" stage. The stage portion, or, as it is called, the scenitorium, has
a concrete or cement bottom, and the
sides are also cement to a height of eight
feet, making a perfectly water tight box
of semi-circular shape. On the bed of
cement is laid concentric lines of railroad
track, enough rails being used to make a
single line over twelve miles long, or a
complete track, on which an engine could
pass, of six miles. These tracks are used
to transport the scenes from a point of
concealment to the section within lines of
sight. The machinery by which these cars
or, as they are called, stages are moved
consists of steel cables travelling over
sheaves alongside and between the tracks
and immense drums at one end. When a
scene is wanted these drums which work
on a friction clutch system, are brought
into play, the cables wind around on them
and the scene comes from behind the wall
into observation. These drums have a
two-fold purpose, inasmuch as they not
only bring the scene into view, but also
take it back to its place of concealment.
In comprehending the working of this
novel machinery it is necessary to understand that when the stage is clear, the
space at each end of the scenitorium is
filled with the telescoping stages bearing
the scenery, and going into place directly
behind the other, as trains do on parallel
tracks. Now, as to the scenery itself. Unlike the ordinary scenery, which is made
either of painted canvas, or of papier
mache, the scenes in "The MacKaye
Spectatorium" are constructed of practical
building material and to use an ordinary
theatrical word there is no setting of
scenery or anything of that kind, each
scene being built independently of all
others on the track or stage which bears
it from the point of concealment into the

range of sight. In presenting a stage view, however, it is very frequently necessary to use more than one of these stages or tracks as for instance, in the view of San Salvador seven independent stages are used, each one of which comes into place over a set of rails on which it travels alone, the whole filling the stage from the back wall to the very edge of the proscenium.

A feature of the stage department is that the scenitorium is always filled with water at a depth of six feet, and all the land used, for instance the street of Granada or the island of San Salvador, is drawn into sight over the water. As most of the views are marine in character the presence of this water is absolutely necessary in all save two scenes—that of the monastery of La Rabida and the scene at Granada. This water forms the miniature ocean on which Columbus' fleet makes its voyage. The three caravels which represent those of the fleet in which the great discoverer sailed are exact facsimilies of the Santa Marie [Maria], the Pinta and the Nina, even to the last detail of mast, spar and rope. They are not in any sense property ships, but are practical and in the production will be manned by bona fide sailors. These ships, like the scenes, are mounted on stages which travel on the rails, but are so constructed that they are susceptible to both wind and waves. The modis operandi of getting a scene from its concealment within the boundaries formed by the lines of sight, is very simple. The cables for any one scene all run to drums on the same shafting, and to start this scene it is only necessary to shift the friction clutch by which the drum revolves with the shaft; when a portion of the scene has travelled sufficiently far to require another to follow it, another friction clutch is thrown into position and so on until all the drums are working. If it was necessary all can be started at once.

Some idea of the immense power necessary to handle these scenes can be gained from the fact that twenty-eight stages, or trucks, combinedly weigh 1,200 tons and in one single scene power is required to mobilize 600 tons at once. This is not by any means all the power required, as there is a cyclone machine which is said to take 400 horse power, a wave-maker which takes as much more to say nothing of the cyclone machinery for putting air in motion. Outside of this, it is necessary at moments in the production to utilize 300,000 candle power of light and as the electric light plant is to be a portion of the equipment of the spectatorium, power will also be required to run these dynamos.

There are so many novelties in the way of lighting and atmospheric effects. In "the MacKaye Spectatorium" none of the foot lights, so called, or border lights are used, their places being taken by two great lights representing the sun and moon and by numerous smaller lights which are necessary, but which do not appear to the audience at all. One of these lights, the sun, will have the lighting capacity of fifty arc lights, representing 100,000 candle power. The light is so governed and managed that it can represent with exact fidelity, any phase of day, for instance, it can be made to give the gray light of morning, to gradually rise to the full glistening light of meridian splendor and to gradually decrease in effulgence until attended with all the hues of the tropical twilight, it settles to its bed of repose in the west. This is accomplished by the arc of a circle at the top of the scenitorium. This arc has a radius of 220 feet and extends from the line of vision to the east side of the line of vision on the west, the sun at mid-day being very near the center of the proscenium opening and directly over the top of the scene. The arc on which this luminary travels is parallel to the plane formed by the base of the scenitorium, or stage floor, and 150 feet distant from it. It carries this luminary from one end of the arc to the other and also carries an electric motor, by which the luminary can be raised or lowered at will and if necessary, in fact, can be dropped clear to the bottom of the seventy feet of water in the reservoir already aluded to. The other light, representing the moon, travels a similar but smaller arc and can be handled and managed as easily as is the greater light. This light has an illuminating power represented by 20,000 candle power. The rear wall of the scenitorium, or as much of it as can be seen by the audience, is not, properly speaking, a scene, nothing but the sky being represented. By a peculiar arrangement, which is not as yet explained, there is made to appear on this background of sky the constellations of the southern hemisphere, each star being given its correct magnitude by the light which attends it, and each being set at the proper place in the firmament from a chart furnished by the ablest astronomers of the day. By a combination of these light effects, it is possible to obtain any condition desired and every phase that attends the natural course of nature, even to the most subtle modulations of a tropical day. Not only can be presented the effulgent light of the meridian sun at noontide and the mellow, silvery light of the moon in a clear light, but also the hazy, murky atmosphere of the approaching hurricane with its thick bank of clouds obscuring the heavens and the atmospheric conditions which attend the breaking of the storm. By an entirely new device it is possible to obtain a curtain of mist, with real falling, pattering raindrops. Another novelty is the lighting in the presence of the real rainbow, which appears upon this curtain of mist, gradually growing out of the darkness until it attains its full glory, and as gradually disappearing from sight.

Another novel mechanical effect which will be used is the wave-maker, by which the mimic ocean can be made to present any phase desired. On the morning of the departure from Palos it is clear, calm, un-ruffled; later in the same day, when the beacon light is passed, it is stirred into faint ripples which makes music as the boats move through them and again it can be churned with the great, white-capped storm waves upon which the vessels pitch and toss. In conjunction with the wave-maker is the wind machinery by which every condition of air in motion can be shown from the gentle murmur of the western zephyr to the devastating cyclone.

One of the more novel of the many lighting features has been named the "luxaueator." This name is original with Mr. MacKaye and is derived from two Latin words which liberally translated mean a curtain of light. A portion of the appliances used for this light is in plain sight of the audience. This portion consists of a row of electric lights all around the proscenium opening. These lights are placed at the apex of a conical shaped reflector, the base of which is turned outward. These reflectors are made of brightly polished nickel and the first impression one gets of them is that they are a row of bells, the electric lamp itself not being visible. The proscenium opening is on a curve instead of straight and all around the opening is a sombre coat of black paint. When the luxaueator is used, a switch is turned and the lamps at the apex of these reflectors glow with an immense voltage of electricity. The effect of this is to present an optical illusion by which the blackness all around the proscenium opening is carried into the rectangle itself and there appears to be a vanishing line just at the mouth of these bell-shaped reflectors. The same switch which turns on the luxaueator also cuts off the stage lights. When the luxaueator is being used the audience sit in a mellow, soft light while the stage is apparently in dense darkness, but in reality the stage is light enough for all practical purposes of those employed thereon.

There have been many new words coined in connection with this enterprise and Mr. MacKaye, the author and inventor, was asked to give an explanation to THE JOURNAL as to the exact definition of the word "spectatorio," which he applies to the presentment to be given within the walls of the spectatorium. He responded as follows: "The spectatorio is a form of scenic production which may be defined as a combination of grand spectacle and grand oratorio and from this combination it takes its name. The story of a spectacle may be told either in spoken words or by pantomime, but from the colossal scale of the production, it is best fitted for pantomimic work, although it may be most artistically divided between pantomimic, for the more distant and extensive scenes, and speech for those which more nearly approach the public.

"There are there species of music employed in the spectatorio. First, the symphonic, which follows all the cosmic changes of the scene and all the dramatic action of the story, interpreting the sentimental mood and meaning of each change. Second, the incidental music. This occurs in the scenes themselves and forms a part of the incident of the story, illustrating, with the instruments of the time, the music of the age, and forming merely an archeological exhibit in music art. Third, choral music. In a spectatorio this form is an adaptation of the old idea of the Greek chorus very much enlarged in its scope and character by its association with the modern scene.

"For the purpose of the spectatorio the chorus is divided into two grand sections. One of these sections, composed entirely of male voices and located in the spectatorium proper, or the audience chamber of the building, in plain sight of the public, represents the visible or material world, and gives expression to the sentiment of that world toward the historic events which transpire during the progress of the story. The other section, located in the scenitorium, behind the scenes, is invisible and represents the mystic or ideal

world. It is composed of male and female voices, and reveals the ideal view of the human story. When any great historic event has reached its climatic expression in the scene, these choruses celebrate that event—the chorus of the spectatorium from the material and the chorus of the scenitorium from the ideal point of view. During the progess of the story the invisible chorus performs also another function. At the climax of a scene it interprets the ideal value of the human act presented by the scenic picture, but during the progress of the story the spiritual contentions which are supposed to be going on among the dramatis personae are suggested to the public by the voices of the invisible chorus. To accomplish this the mystic chorus is again divided into two sections, one composed entirely of male voices giving expression to the demoniac idea, while the other, composed entirely of female voices, expresses the divine idea. As, for instance, during the voyage of Columbus, when the great navigator encounters, with his crew, the meteors, the storms, the mirage, the alterations of hope and fear, which ultimately bred despair in the sailors, the voices of the invisible chorus celebrate the different emotions which pervade the breast of Columbus and those of his crew. During the storm the demoniac chorus sings the song of superstitious terror to the sailors, and they, hearing it, seek Columbus and beseech him to listen, but his ears are deaf to the songs of fear. As the diabolic song dies away into the darkness of the storm the divine chorus is heard singing the inspiring song of hope and faith to Columbus. This song he hears, and seeking his crew, beseeches them to listen; but they, in their turn, are inaccessible to the song of hope, illustrating a great spiritual truth, namely, that every heart hears only that song which is akin to its own character—the coward that of fear upon the slightest pretext, the brave man that of hope, even in the presence of the most discouraging circumstances. This is only one of the many instances illustrating the spiritual use of the chorus and suggesting the spiritual value of this order of entertainment, which may be properly named a spectatorio."

The dismantling of the Spectatorium elicited a major article in the Chicago *Journal*.

117:2   RAZING AN ELEPHANT

MACKAYE'S SPECTATORIUM
BEING DEMOLISHED

It Absorbed Over Half-a-Millon Dollars,
It Sold for $2,250, and Now a
Wrecking Company
Is Turning It Into Old Junk—
The Most Colossal
Fiasco of the Age

Steele MacKaye's Spectatorium is being demolished. An army of workmen has taken possession of the unfinished pile and within a few weeks all visible traces of the most colossal theatrical fiasco of the age will be obliterated.

All Summer long the towering, incomplete structure has glowered down upon the dainty State and foreign pavilions at the north end of Jackson Park. Although the structure is outside of the park enclosure, it appears to be within the limits of the Exposition and thousands of strangers, approaching Jackson Park from the lake, have wondered why, among all the massive and beautiful buildings of the Dream City, this unsightly colossus should have been left incomplete. On that fair picture of classic architecture, which the most inventive architects and artists of America have made memorable for all time, the Spectatorium has appeared as an indelible blemish.

Probably never in the history of the world was so vast an amount of money expended on a structure which brought so little at forced sale. Up to the day that

117:2. Chicago *Journal,* Oct. 12, 1893.

work was abandoned upon the building $550,000 had been sunk in this enterprise. It was projected as the largest and grandest auditorium that the Western world had ever seen. It was sold for old junk for the sum of $2,250.

Steele MacKaye, the projector of the enterprise, was an actor, a dramatist, and theatrical manager of long experience. In recent years he had been known to the Western public principally by his drama of the French Revolution, launched under the title of "Anarchy," and subsequently rechristened "Paul Kauvar." In New York City he had extensive vogue as a teacher of dramatic art and a successful director of stage performances. He was regarded as brilliant but erratic. Some people called him a genius—others a visionist.

Several months before the opening of the Exposition MacKaye came to Chicago with the scheme of a vast theatre only second in dimension to the Roman Coliseum, shaping itself in his mind. He proposed to present in the vast structure an allegorical representation of the discovery of America by Columbus on a scale never before attempted by a theatrical organization. Most actors and a greater chorus than had ever before participated in a dramatic or lyric stage performance were to be employed. The glories of the old Greek and Roman days were to be revived. Marvellous effects in electric stage lighting, invented by the projector, were to be introduced. The modern stage was to be revolutionized.

JUMPED AT THE SCHEME

MacKaye was glib and enthusiastic. He evidently believed in his project, and he made other people believe in it also. Some of Chicago's best-known and most conservative financiers listened to MacKaye and succumed to his eloquence. The Spectatorium Company became a fact.

Steele MacKaye, Ben Butterworth, Powell Crosley, Sidney C. White, Jr., and Howard O. Edmunds were the incorporators of the company. It was capitalized at $2,000,000, and first mortgage bonds to the extent of $800,000 were issued. Of these $553,000 were subscribed for. Stock was sold at $1,000 per share and among the prominent people who invested in the enterprise were: George M. Pullman, Murry Nelson, E. L. Brewster, Edson Keith, John Cudahy, I. J. Gage, C. J. and F. W. Peck, H. E. Bucklen, ten shares each. Others interested from two to five shares each were: F. H. Head, C. H. Deere, Arthur Dixon, J. J. Mitchell, E. H. Phelps, F. G. Logan, N. B. Ream, David Henderson, A. C. McClure, Andrew Mc-Nally, Ben Butterworth and P. E. Studebaker.

Work was begun upon the building under the most favorable auspices. Plenty of money for the prosecution of the scheme seemed to be assured. With the structure under way the projector began to prepare for the performances which were to make the enterprise memorable. Dramatic papers teemed with advertisements of the scheme and the local newspapers were resorted to in order to gather together the nucleus of the proposed chorus. Hundreds of young men and women, with musical inclinations and histrionic ambitions responded. The best were selected. They were to attend rehearsals without pay. The instruction was to be recompense for the outlay of time. Salaries were not to begin until the Spectatorium was opened to the public. Young Chicago became enthusiastic over the prospect. Even chorus girls of experience were inoculated with the Spectatorium fever. The operatic and extravaganza companies found it difficult to fill the places vacated by those who were attracted by the glowing prospects offered by the MacKaye manifestos.

The building grew apace. Newspaper columns were filled with glowing accounts of the progress of the work. Projector MacKaye frequently submitted to being interviewed in order to let the public know how the colossal structure was progressing. A model of the great stage, with the newly invented lighting devices worked out in miniature detail, was constructed at and outlay of many thousands of dollars, and a favored few invited to inspect it. Among the few are the principal stockholders; everybody looked and admired and said, "Wonderful." Prospects for the completion of the colossus were bright.

Then came a change. Rumors of trouble —financial trouble—in the affairs of the Spectatorium began to float about. Contractors claimed they were not getting their money and refused to labor on promises. A receivership followed. That was on June 1st, when over half-a-million had been expended, and the building was still a little more than a skeleton. Twelve days later Contractor William Mayor still further intricated the legal aspect of the case by going into the Circuit Court and charging against the incorporators.

WRECK OF A GREAT ENTERPRISE

The condition in which the building was left rendered it unsafe in itself and a menace to the Exposition. On July 18 the Building Commissioner ordered it to be removed. No action was taken on this order, but on September 21 the Chicago Title and Trust Company, which had been made receiver for the company, after submitting a statement to the court showing that the liabilities of the concern were $400,000 with only $4,000 as assets in unpaid subscriptions, asked leave to sell the building and dispose of the option on the real estate. This was granted and the building was knocked down to the highest bidder at public sale for $2,250.

The work of removing the immense structure is being done by the Chicago Wrecking Company, of which Moses Harris is president. This unique company makes a business of removing buildings for the salvage in them. Its yards on South Halsted street are filled with the skeletons of great iron structures, the vertebra of

117. Steele MacKaye's proposed Spectatorium, Chicago. From a watercolor by Childe Hassam, 1893 (based on an architect's drawing). Reproduced from Percy MacKaye, *Epoch* (New York, 1927) by permission of the estate of Percy MacKaye. Photograph courtesy of The Hoblitzelle Theatre Arts Library, The Humanities Research Center, The University of Texas at Austin.

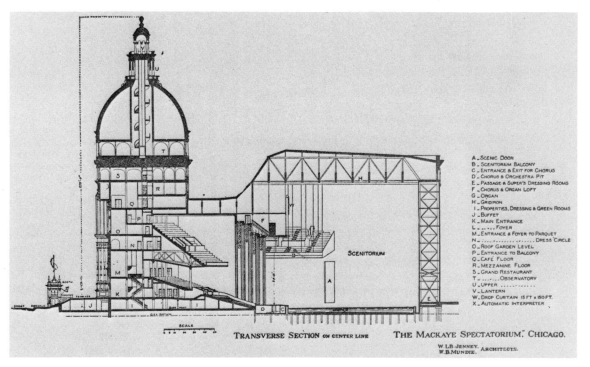

A _ SCENIC DOOR
B _ SCENTORIUM BALCONY
C _ ENTRANCE & EXIT FOR CHORUS
D _ CHORUS & ORCHESTRA PIT
E _ PASSAGE & SUPER'S DRESSING ROOMS
F _ CHORUS & ORGAN LOFT
G _ ORGAN
H _ GRIDIRON
I _ PROPERTIES, DRESSING & GREEN ROOMS
J _ BUFFET
K _ MAIN ENTRANCE
L _ .... FOYER
M _ ENTRANCE & FOYER TO PARQUET
N _ .... DRESS CIRCLE
O _ ROOF GARDEN LEVEL
P _ ENTRANCE TO BALCONY
Q _ CAFÉ FLOOR
R _ MEZZANINE FLOOR
S _ GRAND RESTAURANT
T _ .... OBSERVATORY
U _ UPPER ....
V _ LANTERN
W _ DROP CURTAIN 15 FT x 150 FT.
X _ AUTOMATIC INTERPRETER

TRANSVERSE SECTION ON CENTER LINE   THE MACKAYE SPECTATORIUM, CHICAGO.

W. LB. JENNEY, ARCHITECTS.
W. B. MUNDIE,

117. Transverse section, Spectatorium, Chicago. Reproduced from Percy MacKaye, *Epoch* (New York, 1927) by permission of the estate of Percy MacKaye. Photograph courtesy of The Hoblitzelle Theatre Arts Library, The Humanities Center, The University of Texas at Austin.

118. Castle Square Theatre, Boston. Courtesy of the Harvard Theatre Collection.

defunct building enterprises and the odds and ends of architectural decadence. A builder can buy anything there from a pound of nails or a quart of second-hand bolts to a bushel of door knobs. If he wants a few tons of structural iron he can also be accommodated. Out of that historic junk yard railroads could build depots with steel girders galore, and California's mid-winter exposition could find the material to build half the structures necessary to house the exhibits.

This is the company that is removing the Spectatorium and 200 men are being employed doing it.

"There are 400 tons of steel beams in the building," said Mr. Harris this morning, "but the amount of building material in the pile is very hard to estimate. If it requires good engineering skill to erect such a building as the Spectatorium, I am quite sure it is an equal feat of engineering to take it all down again. No man not entirely acquainted with his business could do this at all, and few would be able to do it without sustaining a heavy loss. Where does the point come in? Oh! that's my business. Special machinery is requisite to get the big girders down from their present position. The work is of a very dangerous character. Some of the men we employ are experts in their line. A good house wrecker, as we call him, earns from $5 to $6 a day. We have a man on every job of importance constantly patroling the building and repairing every spot which shows signs of weakness. If there is any place which he can not repair, he instantly reports to headquarters. Work is then at once stopped and the building made safe before our men are allowed to again work on it."

REMOVING THE BUILDING

Mr. Harris was asked what time it would take his company to remove the Spectatorium, and replied:

"It will take at least three months, but these things are as uncertain as the sale of the salvages. I shall try and dispose of the steel on the ground, and I have offered it all for $30 a ton, which is cheap considering the character of the material put into the building. If I can't get this sold that way, it will have to be broken up for scrap. So you see I may stand to lose considerable there which I shall have to make up in other ways. . . ."

In failing health for months and desperately worried over finances, MacKaye died on February 25, 1894. The Scenitorium performances continued sporadically without him for a time, and then they, too, succumbed.

118. CASTLE SQUARE THEATRE
Boston, Massachusetts
Opened November 19, 1894

Just one hundred years after the opening of the rather crude Federal Street Theatre in Boston, a new playhouse was dedicated that was called one of the "finest, safest and best equipped" theaters in the country. William H. Birkmire, in his work *The Planning and Construction of American Theatres*, described the new playhouse in detail.

118:1   Thespis has not a more beautiful temple in the country than Boston's new and most magnificent home of the drama, the Castle Square Theatre, one of the finest, safest, best equipped, most comfortable and most elaborately furnished buildings devoted to dramatic purposes. The entire press of New England, as well as the representative journals in the States, have united in the fullest measure of praise of its grandeur.

The situation of the theatre, as every Bostonian is aware, is on the spacious square formed by the junction of Tremont, Chandler, and Ferdinand streets. As far as the public convenience is concerned the site is a happy selection. The Providence

118:1. William H. Birkmire, *The Planning and Construction of American Theatres* (New York: Wiley, 1901), pp. 9–15.

309

depot, and the Columbus Avenue station of the Boston and Albany Railroad, are not five minutes' walk distant; the prominent street-car lines of the city and the West End, the South Boston, and Cambridge lines are but a few steps removed; the elevated railway has a station at Castle Square; and altogether the location is as easy of access as that of any other theatre in the city.

What but a few months before the opening night, November 19, 1894, was an unsightly building has been transformed into a gorgeously appointed theatre.

Before passing through the principal entrance on Tremont Street, we are confronted by an arcade with a height of thirty feet from the ground, classic in style, and built of brick and terra cotta.

Two engaged columns of the Corinthian order stand on either side, on pedestals eleven feet high, and support an elaborately moulded terra-cotta frieze and cornice. Great garlands in terra-cotta relief intertwine theatrical insignia, and on each side of the arch a group of six immense wrought-iron lanterns of colonial style cast a brilliant light over the whole scheme of decoration. From the roof of the arch rows of electric globes send their brilliancy down and emphasize the artistic finish of the large 16' x 16' vestibule. On the right and left sides of the vestibule are great terra-cotta panels each bearing the figure of a Greek dancing girl. In front and above are immense stained-glass windows, bearing in many-colored glass the outlines of a mediaeval castle and the name of the theatre.

Passing through the main doors from the vestibule we enter the "grand foyer." Turning to the right or left we reach the mezzanine balcony by the grand staircases with their handsome electro-bronze newels and balusters, the top of the newels being set off by large electric-light globes.

The grand foyer, or lobby as it is sometimes called, is circular in form, 19 feet wide, including staircases, and 60 feet in length. The staircases are each 8 feet wide, built of iron and marble.

By glancing at the ceiling of the foyer we are shown the Gustavian domes blazing with light, which shed their brilliance over the most beautiful paintings that have ever decorated the ceilings of a theatre.

Scarcely are the beauties of the domes considered when we discover succession after succession of similar domes, with myraid circles of cherubs reaching away into a seemingly endless distance. The effect is so real and so astonishing, the purity and transparency of the glass is so wonderful, that we had not noticed great mirrors set over the entrance-doors at such angles as to reflect in their clear depths almost every part of the entire theatre.

From the foyer on the right is situated the ladies' parlor, 12 feet wide by 20 feet long, a dainty resting-place furnished as in the days of Louis XVI. Its pretty onyx marble fireplace, combined with the silken finish of the walls, its soft carpet in delicate design and colors, and the gilded furniture, lend to it an indescribable charm which is heightened by large mirrors covering two of its walls.

The beauty of the foyer is difficult to surpass. Exits from the auditorium, hung with draperies in softest red, are numerous. Cloak-rooms, dressing-rooms, and toilet-rooms are situated with generous regard to comfort and convenience. The floors are of neat designs in mosaic tiling. Great arches, panelled, and beautified with exquisite paintings, are seen on every side. Directly opposite the vestibule doors are dainty Sienna marble fountains, with gold faucets. The walls are finished in satin effect, and the harmony of coloring in this part of the theatre defies description.

As we enter the auditorium through the doors shown upon the view from the stage, we see a series of domes supported upon steel construction of the balcony, and a scheme of decoration after the Italian Renaissance style, the relief work being in cream and gold. Directly over the auditorium an immense circular electrolier, 40 feet in diameter, spreads its twenty arms out from the centre of the dome, and its three hundred and eighty incandescent lamps of frosted glass send their rays to every part of the auditorium are no wooden beams, bracings, or floors; with a grand illuminating effect.

Encircling this electrolier is another division of the dome, suspended from the electrolier a short distance, resplendent with floating cherubim trailing a bewildering mass of ribbons and garlands of flowers in their merry race around the wide-spreading branch of three hundred and eighty electric lights. No less attractive are the proscenium arch, and the boxes, twenty in number, furnished with superb designs in stereo-relief. Beautiful beyond all is the sounding-board, a portion of which is shown in the plate view of the boxes, with a depth of fifteen feet over the proscenium arch, bearing the most exquisite work in painting about the theatre. Twelve dancing girls, life size in figure, present themselves in artistic abandon. The work was so elaborate that it was first executed on canvas in New York and then brought to the theatre to grace the sounding-board. The magnificence of the auditorium is entrancing. Wherever art has laid her finger she has left an impress of beauty. The grand sweep of the balconies, the soft harmony of the colorings, the beauty of the relief decorations, and the masterfulness of the paintings have impressed us with the fact that we have found an aesthetically perfect theatre.

While art has left its impressions, mechanical science appeals to us for a hearing. Every hygienic law has been considered in the construction. Pure air is forced into the building by a system of ventilation perfect in its conception. Each floor has a hollow space to admit the air from the immense air-ducts, supplied by a mammoth blower. The air is carried to every seat and forced into the house through the hollow-legged chairs.

We are attracted by the general roominess about the auditorium, and at once discover another distinctive feature in the seating arrangements. Every chair is of more than ordinary width as to admit of free passage even when the audience is seated; even to the back set of the second balcony, the chosen throne of the "gallery gods." This majestic critic, the terror of all "thespians," is seated in comfort. He sits in a chair covered with finest plush.

If we now turn to a view of the stage, we find that the proscenium arch is 40 feet wide and 34 feet high to the overhead girders, and its soft velvet curtain hides an ideal stage, 68 feet wide and 45 feet in depth.

Almost every appliance known to the theatrical world has entered into the construction of this theatre. Its electrical equipment of one thousand 32-candle-power lamps is as nearly perfect as modern science can make it.

Broad entrances on each side lead to the streets adjoining, and a cavalcade of horses can enter at one side, making a circuit of the stage and return.

The switchboard which controls the light effects is a marvelous piece of mechanism. It is similar to that used at the Metropolitan Opera House, N.Y.

The theatre is fully equipped with the most approved fire-apparatus. Instead of single standpipes, a complete duplicate set is used. Adequate standpipes on each side of the stage are augmented by axes, hooks, brackets, and fire-extinguishers on each fly-gallery, paint-bridge, gridiron, and roof. In the construction, only iron, marble, and brick have been used. There in fact, no wood-work of any kind, even composition mouldings taking the place of wood in the door-trimmings.

The seating capacity is from 1600 to 1800.

The general outlay of the Castle Square Theatre is shown by the plan, which fully describes the main floor or parquette circle, with all the necessary entrances and stairways leading to the various portions of the house.

The main entrance to the grand foyer is from Castle Square, the entrance to the right from Chandler Street, and that from the left an alley leading to Tremont Street. The main entrance, from Castle Square, is 16 feet wide, the Chandler Street entrance 10 feet wide, and that from Tremont Street also 10 feet.

The balcony is reached from the grand foyer; the gallery from stairways to the right and left adjoining the Chandler Street and alley entrances. These latter stairways are each 6 feet wide and built of iron and slate.

From the foyer and lobbies the auditorium is reached by ten wide doorways. The auditorium is 79 feet 6 inches wide, 85 feet 6 inches deep, and 70 feet in height to the top of the dome ceiling. All calculations are taken from the curtain-line. The outer line of the footlights from the curtain-line is 6 feet, the orchestra rail 11 feet, and the latter is drawn from a point upon the centre-line of the opening extending backward 58 feet, and from the same point the seat-rows of the parquette, 2 feet 8 inches apart, are drawn.

The parquette circle is arranged in steps which are described from a point upon the centre-line extending into the auditorium 9 feet 6 inches.

The first stepping of the circle is 2 inches, and each successive step is increased by ½ inch for 13 steps.

The various aisles of this main floor are divided as shown, 3 feet wide at the orchestra-rail and 5 feet nearest the outer circle.

The boxes, six in number, are reached through small reception-rooms connected by a passage leading to the lobby on the right and the left of the entrance from Tremont Street.

There are also upon this floor, connected to the lobbies, check-rooms, writing-room, telephone-room, and toilets attached to the ladies' parlor and the smoking-room.

The check-room to the right under the balcony staircase is 7 feet 6 inches wide by 14 feet long, and the left check-room under the corresponding staircase, is the same size. Adjoining this left check-room are the telephone and writing rooms, 7 feet 6 inches wide by 16 feet long. The toilet adjoining the ladies' parlor is 7 feet 6 inches by 16 feet, and that of the smoking-room 10 feet 6 inches by 12 feet.

The boxes are each 8 feet deep, with a portion of the circle deducted, by 8 feet in width, with the passages leading to the reception-rooms of the boxes are 3 feet 9 inches wide.

The stage is commodious and easy of access to the street, at the right through a passage 10 feet wide, and at the left through the alley or court. The dressing-rooms, in addition to those shown upon this plan adjoining the office, are placed upon the floor above.

Selected Bibliography of the American Theater, 1716-1899

Students interested in knowing the location of primary source materials concerning the American playhouses of the period before 1900 will find that the following major libraries have collections worth consulting: Boston Public Library, Brown University Library, Columbia University Library, Free Library of Philadelphia, Folger Shakespeare Library, Harvard University Theatre Collection, Library of Congress, Museum of the City of New York, New York Public Library Theatre Collection, Princeton University Theatre Collection, University of North Carolina Library, University of Pennsylvania Library, Yale University Library, and Hoblitzelle Theatre Arts Library of the University of Texas. These repositories are rich in primary materials of the eighteenth- and nineteenth-century American theater, particularly of the eastern part of the United States.

The theater in the Midwest is well represented in the libraries of the Chicago Historical Society, Chicago Public Library, Filson Club Library, St. Louis Public Library, and Tulane University Library. The theater in the Far West is represented by materials in the Western Collection of the Denver Public Library, Bancroft Library of the University of California at Berkeley, and Theatre Library of the University of California at Los Angeles.

Various state and local historical societies also have large collections of materials relating to the theater in their respective areas: California State Library, California Historical Society, Connecticut Historical Society, Maryland Historical Society, Massachusetts Historical Society, New-York Historical Society, Pennsylvania Historical Society, Missouri Historical Society (Columbia and St. Louis), and Rhode Island Historical Society.

There are several general histories of the theater that can be helpful to the investigator:

Coad, Oral Sumner, and Mims, Edwin, Jr. *The American Stage*. The Pageant of America, vol. 14. New Haven: Yale Univ. Pr., 1929.

Dunlap, William. *A History of the American Theatre*. 2 vols. in 1. New York: J. & J. Harper, 1832.

Hewitt, Bernard. *Theatre U.S.A. 1665 to 1957*. New York: McGraw-Hill, 1959.

Hornblow, Arthur. *A History of the Theatre in America*. 2 vols. Philadelphia: Lippincott, 1919.

Hughes, Glenn. *A History of the American Theatre, 1700–1950*. New York: French, 1951.

Sayler, Oliver. *Our American Theatre*. New York: Brentano, 1923.

Seilhamer, George O. *History of the American Theatre.* 3 vols. Philadelphia: Globe Printing House, 1888–91.

Taubman, Howard. *The Making of the American Theatre.* New York: Coward, 1965.

Newspapers are one of the most important sources for American theater history during the eighteenth and nineteenth centuries, and the author has consulted the following newspapers in the course of his work: Boston: *Advertiser, Gazette, Traveller, Transcript*; Central City, Colorado: *Evening Call*; Charleston: *Courier, Morning Post and Daily Advertiser, South Carolina Gazette*; Chicago: *Journal, Tribune*; Cincinnati: *Daily Commercial*; Columbia, S.C.: *Herald*; Denver: *Republican, Rocky Mountain News*; Leadville, Colo.: *Daily Chronicle*; Lincoln, Neb.: *State Journal*; New Orleans: *Times-Picayune*; New York: *Brooklyn Eagle, Commercial Advertiser, Daily Advertiser, Dramatic Mirror, Dramatic News, Evening Post, Gaine's Mercury, Herald, Independent, Morning Chronicle, New York Gazette and Weekly Postboy, New York Mirror and Ladies Literary Gazette, Rivington's Gazette, Spectator, Spirit of the Times, Times, Tribune*; Philadelphia: *Claypool's American Daily Advertiser, Evening Bulletin, National Gazette, Poulson's American Daily Advertiser, United States Gazette*; St. Louis: *Missouri Republican*; San Francisco: *Alta California, Daily Evening Bulletin, Evening Post, Figaro*; Virginia City: *Territorial Enterprise*; Washington, D.C.: *Daily Chronicle, National Intelligencer*; Williamsburg, Va.: *Virginia Gazette.*

Among the dozens of magazines and journals consulted, the following proved most helpful: *Aurora, Architectural Forum, Architectural Record, Dramatic Mirror and Literary Censor, Galaxy, Lippincott's Magazine, Minerva, Mirror of Taste and Dramatic Censor, Rambler's Magazine and New York Theatrical Register, New York Magazine, Theatrical Censor, Theatrical Censor and Critical Miscellany, Scientific American.*

Numerous local histories of the theater published in recent years would be helpful for the student interested in American playhouses.

There are also hundreds of memoirs and autobiographies of major theatrical figures that reveal many details concerning the playhouses in which they worked. As a detailed listing of these works is included in the bibliography of *Famous Actors and Actresses on the American Stage* (Documents of American Theater History), only a few of them have been listed here.

It should be emphasized that this is merely a selective bibliography of works concerning American playhouses before 1900 and should not be considered in any way exhaustive.

Andreas, A. T. *A History of Chicago.* 3 vols. Chicago: A. T. Andreas Co., 1885.

Ashe, Thomas. *Travels in America, Performed in 1806.* 3 vols. London: Phillips, 1808.

Bernard, John. *Retrospections of America, 1797–1881.* Ed. by Laurence Hutton and Brander Matthews. New York: Harper & Bros., 1887.

Birkmire, William H. *The Planning and Construction of American Theatres.* New York: Wiley, 1901.

Blake, Charles. *An Historical Account of the Providence Stage.* Providence: G. H. Whitney, 1868.

Brown, Thomas Allston. *A History of the New York Stage from the First Performance in 1732 to 1901.* 3 vols. New York: Dodd, 1903.

———. *The Showman's Guide.* New York: n.p., 1874.

Bryan, W. B. *History of the National Capital.* New York: Macmillan, 1916.

Bunn, Alfred. *The Stage: Both Before and Behind the Curtain.* 2 vols. Philadelphia: Lea & Blanchard, 1840.

Clapp, Henry Austin. *A Record of the Boston Stage.* Boston and Cambridge: James Munroe & Co., 1853.

Cooke, John Esten. *The Virginia Comedians.* 2 vols. New York: D. Appleton & Co., 1854.

Cowell, Joe. *Thirty Years Passed among the Players in England and America.* 2 vols. New York: Harper & Bros., 1884.

Crawford, Mary Caroline. *The Romance of the American Theatre*. Boston: Little, 1913.

Daly, Charles P. *The First Theatre in America*. New York: Dunlap Society Publications, 1899.

Dixon, William Hepworth. *New America*. 2 vols. London: Hunst & Blackett, Pub., 1867.

Dunlap, William. *Diary of William Dunlap*. 3 vols. New York: New York Historical Soc., 1930.

Durang, Charles. "The Philadelphia Stage. From the Year 1749 to the Year 1855. Partly compiled from the papers of his father, the late John Durang; with notes by the editors [of the Philadelphia Sunday *Dispatch*]." Never published in book form. Complete files pasted in six volumes with 300 engravings and autograph letters, in library of Univ. of Pennsylvania, Philadelphia.

Durang, John. *The Memoir of John Durang, American Actor*. Ed. by Alan S. Downer. Pittsburgh: Univ. of Pittsburgh Pr., 1966.

Fennell, James. *An Apology for the Life of James Fennell*. Philadelphia: Moses Thomas, 1814.

Gagey, Edward M. *The San Francisco Stage*. New York: Columbia Univ. Pr., 1950.

Gibson's Guide and Directory on the State of Louisiana. New Orleans: J. Gibson, 1838.

Graydon, Alexander. *Memoirs of a Life, Chiefly Passed in Pennsylvania*. Harrisburg: John Wyeth, 1811.

Hall, Basil. *Travels in North America*. 3 vols. Edinburgh: Cadell & Co., 1829.

Hapgood, Norman. *The Stage in America, 1897–1900*. New York: Macmillan, 1901.

Henderson, Myrtle E. *History of the Theatre in Salt Lake City*. Salt Lake City: Deseret Book Co., 1941.

Hill, George Handel. *Life and Recollections of Yankee Hill*. Ed. by William K. Northall. New York: W. F. Burgess, 1850.

———. *Scenes from the Life of an Actor*. New York: Garrett & Co., 1853.

Hillyer, Katherine, and Best, Katherine. *The Amazing Story of Piper's Opera House in Virginia City, Nevada*. Virginia City: Enterprise Pr., 1953.

Hunter, Alexander, and Polkinhorn, J. H. *The New National Theatre, Washington, D.C. A Record of Fifty Years*. Washington, D.C.: R. O. Polkinson & Sons, 1885.

Ireland, Joseph N. *Records of the New York Stage*. 2 vols. New York: T. H. Morrell, 1866–67.

Jefferson, Joseph. *The Autobiography of Joseph Jefferson*. New York: Century Co., 1889.

Jeffery, Jno. B. *Jno. B. Jeffery's Guide and Directory to the Opera Houses, Theatres, Public Halls, Bill Posters, etc., of the Cities and Towns of the Western, Southern and Middle States of America*. Ed. and pub. by the author, 1878.

Leavitt, M. B. *Fifty Years in Theatrical Management, 1859–1909*. New York: Broadway Publishing Co., 1912.

Leman, Walter M. *Memories of an Old Actor*. San Francisco: A. Roman Co., 1886.

Lossing, Benjamin J. *Life and Times of Philip Schuyler*. 2 vols. New York: Mason Bros., 1860, 1873.

Ludlow, Noah Miller. *Dramatic Life As I Found It*. St. Louis: G. I. Jones & Co., 1880.

MacKaye, Percy. *Epoch*. 2 vols. New York: Liveright, 1927.

McVicker, James. *The Theatre: Its Early Days in Chicago*. Chicago: Knight & Leonard, 1884.

Managers in Distress: The St. Louis Stage, 1840–1844. St. Louis: St. Louis Historical Documents Foundation, 1949.

May, Alonzo B. "May's Dramatic Encyclopedia of Baltimore. Histories of Baltimore Theatres from 1750 to 1901." Ms in archives of Maryland Historical Society.

Mudd, A. J. "Early Theatre in Washington City." *Columbia Historical Society Records* 5:64–86 (1902).

———. "The Theatre of Washington from 1835 to 1850." *Columbia Historical Society Records* 6:222–66 (1903).

Murdoch, James E. *The Stage*. Philadelphia: J. M. Stoddart & Co., 1880.

Murray, Charles Augustus. *Travels in North America*. London: R. Bentley, 1839.

Northall, William Knight. *Before and Behind the Curtain*. New York: W. F. Burgess, 1851.

Odell, George C. D. *Annals of the New York Stage*. 15 vols. New York: Columbia Univ. Pr., 1927–49.

Power, Tyrone. *Impressions of America in 1833–1835*. 2 vols. London: Carey, Lea, & Blanchard, 1836.

Pyper, George D. *The Romance of an Old Playhouse*. Salt Lake City: Seagull Pr., 1928.

Russailh, Albert Bernard de. *Last Adventure, San Francisco in 1851*. Tr. by Clarkson Crane. San Francisco: Westgate Pr., 1931.

Ryan, Kate. *Old Boston Museum Days*. Boston: Little, 1915.

Scharf, J. Thomas. *A History of St. Louis City and County*. 2 vols. Philadelphia: Louis H. Everts & Co. 1883.

———, and Westcott, Thompson. *A History of Philadelphia, 1609–1884*. 3 vols. Philadelphia: Everts & Co., 1884.

Skinner, Otis. *Footlights and Spotlights*. Indianapolis: Bobbs-Merrill, 1924.

Smith, Sol. *The Theatrical Apprenticeship of Sol Smith*. Philadelphia: Casey & Hart, 1846.

———. *Theatrical Management in the West and South for Thirty Years*. New York: Harper & Bros., 1868.

Soulé, Frank; Gihon, John H.; and Nisbett, John. *The Annals of San Francisco*. New York and San Francisco: D. Appleton & Co., 1855.

Stone, Henry Dickinson. *Personal Recollections of the Drama, or Theatrical Reminiscences*. Albany, N.Y.: C. Van Bentuysen & Sons, 1873.

Taylor, Bayard. *Eldorado, or, Adventures in the Path of Empire*. 2 vols. New York: G. P. Putnam & Sons, 1850.

"Theatre Buildings." San Francisco Research, vols. 15–17. Sponsored by the City and County of San Francisco. Works Project Administration Project 10677, O.P. 665–08–3–167, 1938–42. Mimeographed.

Thompson, Thomas Hinckley, and West, Augustus Albert. *Illustrated History of Sacramento City and County*. Sacramento: Thompson & West, 1880.

Tompkins, Eugene, and Kilby, Quincy. *The History of the Boston Theatre, 1854–1901*. Boston: Houghton, 1908.

Towse, John R. *Sixty Years in the Theatre*. New York: Funk & Wagnall's, 1916.

Tyler, Lyon Gardiner. *Williamsburg, the Old Virginia Capital*. Richmond: Whittet & Shepperson, 1907.

Vandenhoff, George. *Dramatic Reminiscences*. New York: T. H. Cooper & Co., 1860.

———. *Leaves from an Actor's Notebook*. New York: D. Appleton & Co., 1860.

Wemyss, Francis Courtney. *Chronology of the American Stage from 1752–1852*. New York: W. Taylor & Co., 1852.

———. *Twenty-six Years in the Life of an Actor and Manager*. New York: Burgess, Stringer & Co., 1847.

Willard, George O. *A History of the Providence Stage, 1762–1891*. Providence: News Co., 1891.

Willis, Eola. *The Charleston Stage in the Eighteenth Century*. Columbia, S.C.: State Co., 1924.

Wood, William B. *Personal Recollections of the Stage*. Philadelphia: H. C. Baird, 1855.

Index of Theaters
Arranged Alphabetically

References are to entry, not page, numbers.

Index of Theaters
Arranged Geographically

References are to entry, not page, numbers.

CALIFORNIA. *Sacramento:* Eagle Theatre, 70; *San Francisco:* American Theatre, 75; Baldwin's Academy of Music, 110; California Theatre, 106; Jenny Lind Theatre, 1850, 71, June 1851, 73, Oct. 1851, 74; Maguire's Opera House, 78; Metropolitan Theatre, 77; Wade's Opera House, 109.

COLORADO. *Central City:* Central City Opera House, 111; *Denver:* Broadway Theatre, 115; Tabor Grand Opera House, 113; *Leadville:* Tabor Opera House, 112.

DISTRICT OF COLUMBIA. *Washington:* Ford's Theatre, 61; National Theatre, 38; United States Theatre, 24; Washington Theatre, 1804, 25, 1821, 28.

ILLINOIS. *Chicago:* Auditorium, 116; Columbia Theatre, 114; Crosby's Opera House, 83; McVicker's Theatre, 1857, 79, 1872, 107; Rialto Theatre, 66; Rice's Theatre, 69; Steele MacKaye's Spectatorium, 117.

LOUISIANA. *New Orleans:* American Theatre, 1824, 62, 1840, 67; St. Charles Theatre, 1835, 64, 1843, 68.

MARYLAND. *Baltimore:* Holliday Street Theatre, 20.

MASSACHUSETTS. *Boston:* Boston Museum, 1841, 46, 1872, 108; Boston Theatre, 55; Castle Square Theatre, 118; Federal Street Theatre, 17; Haymarket Theatre, 22; New Exhibition Hall, 14; Tremont Street Theatre, 35.

MISSOURI. *St. Louis:* Bates Theatre, 72; St. Louis Theatre, 65; St. Louis Varieties Theatre, 76.

NEVADA. *Virginia City:* Piper Opera House, 82.

NEW YORK. *New York City:* Abbey Theatre, 102; American Theatre, 101; Astor Place Opera House, 50; Barnum's New Museum, 85; Bijou Opera House, 93; Booth's Theatre, 86; Bowery Theatre, 1826, 33, 1828, 36, 1837, 39, 1839, 43, 1845, 48; Broadway Theatre, 49; Brougham's Lyceum, 53; Burton's Theatre, 51; Casino Theatre, 95; Chapman's Temple of the Muses, 47; Chatham Garden Theatre, 31; Chatham Theatre, 44; Cruger's Wharf Theatre, 8; Daly's Theatre, 91; Empire Theatre, 100; Fifth Avenue Theatre, 1869, 87, 1873, 89, 1892, 98; Garden Theatre, 97; Garrick Theatre, 104; Hammerstein's Olympia, 105; Herald Square Theatre, 103; John Street Theatre, 11; Knickerbocker Theatre, 102; Lafayette Theatre, 32; Laura Keene's Theatre, 57; Lyceum Theatre, 96; Madison Square Theatre, 92; Manhattan Opera House, 99; Metropolitan Theatre, 56; Mitchell's Olympic Theatre, 45; Nassau Street Theatre, 1750, 4, 1753, 7; National Theatre, 41;

Index of Personal Names and Theatrical Specialties

References are to entry, not page, numbers.

Abbey, Henry E. (theatrical manager), 90, 102

Abbott, Mr. (theatrical manager), 40:1

Alba, Signor (artist), 39:2

Alexander, J. C. (stage machinist), 107:2, 113:1

Allegri, Signor (scene designer, artist), 52:1, 53:2

Anderson, James (stage manager), 44:2, 44:3

ARCHITECTS. Barnett, George I., 76:2; Billings, H. and J. E., 46:1; Brunel, Marc Isambard, 23:3; Buckling, Mr., 42:1; Bugbee, Charles L., 106:1; Bugbee, S. A., and Son, 109:2; Bulfinch, Charles, 17:2, 17:3; Burnham, F. P., 113:1; Cabot, E. C., 55:1; Clarke, M. L., 65:1; Cummings and Sears, 108:1; Edbrooke, W. J., 113:1; Folsom, William H., 81:1, 81:2; Fox, John A., 108:1; Gifford, James J., 61; Grain, Peter, 32:1; Haight, Charles C., 101:1; Harrison, E. L. T., 81:1; Hausmann, William M., 61:3; Haviland, John, 27:1, 27:3; Kimball and Wisedell, 92:2; Lessig, Charles W., 61:3; Macomber and Peter, 61:3; McElfatricks and Co., 104:1, 105; Mangin, Mr., 23:4; Peck, Ford, 116:1, 116:2; Pollard, Calvin, 39:2; Preston, Jonathan, 55:1; Purdy, Samuel, 44:2; Reichardt, Mr., 40:1; Reinagle, Hugh, 29:2, 31:2, 35:2; Roeschlaub, R.

S., 111:2; Rogers, Isaiah, 35:1; Sera, Joseph, 33:2, 36:2, 36:3, 40:1; Strickland, William, 27:2, 30:3, 37:2; Syrjala, Sointu, 61:3; Trimble, J. M., 48:1, 49, 49:1, 53:2, 56:1, 57:1, 80:2; Weese, Harry M., 116:2; Wood, Col., 115:1

ARTISTS. Alba, Signor, 39:2; Allegri, Signor, 52:1, 53:2; Chizzola, Signor, 39:2, 40:1, 40:2; Ciceri, Charles, 23:2, 23:4; Clark, Cyrus T., 108:1; Comb, J., 106:1; Cotter, Edward, 108:1; Coyle, Mr., 33:2; Denny, G. J., 106:1, 106:2; Duff, J., 106:1; Edgar, Mr., 35:2; Evers, John, 29:2; Gariboldi, Signor, 89:1; Goatscher, Philip, 94:1; Guidicini, Signor, 39:2; Guidocci, Signor, 80:2; Hardy, Mr., 35:2; Harvest and Youngling, 54:1; Hayes and Hawthorne, 59:2; Heath and Milligan, 107:2; Heister, G., 42:1, 49:1, 53:2; Hillyard, Mr., 58:1; Hoban, Mr., 15:1; Hodges, Mr., 30:1; Hopkins, Robert, 113:1; Hoyt, Henry, 97:1; Hubbard, Mr., 35:2; Isherwood, H., 35:2; Lamphere, J. B., 112:1; McPherson, William A., 108:1; Maiben, Henry, 81:1; Meli, G., and Son, 107:2; Milbourne, Mr., 18:2; Moline, Signor, 52:1; Morris, William, 81:1; Moses, Thomas G., 115:1; Ottinger, George Martin, 81:1; Patterson, J., 106:1; Reid, H. Logan, 98:1; Reinagle,

Mitchell, William E. (actor, theatrical manager), 45, 45:1, 45:2, 45:3
Molini, Signor (artist), 52:1
Morris, William (artist), 81:1
Morse, Mr. (theater owner), 115:1
Moses, Thomas G. (artist), 115:1
Mosher, James (theatrical manager), 20:2
Mozart, F. W. (builder, stage manager), 108:1
Mullen and Sartori (builders), 111:1
Murray, Walter (actor, theatrical manager), 3, 4, 4:4, 5, 7, 8

Niblo, William (theatrical manager), 34:1, 50, 52, 52:1

Ottinger, George Martin (artist), 81:1

Palmer, Albert Marshman (theatrical manager), 88, 88:1
Palmo, Ferdinand (theatrical manager), 51, 51:1, 51:2
Pastor, Tony (entertainer, theatrical manager), 84, 84:2
Patterson, J. (ornamental plasterer), 106:1
Peck, Ford (architect), 116:1, 116:2
Pelby, William (actor, theatrical manager), 35, 35:1
Pepin, M. (theatrical manager), 27:1
Peters, Charles R. (builder, theater owner), 106:1
Phillips, Aaron (actor, theatrical manager), 62:1
Phillips, James (builder), 39:2
Pike, Samuel (theater owner), 80, 80:2
Piper, John (theatrical manager and owner), 82:2
Placide, Alexander (theatrical manager), 16, 16:1, 19, 19:2
Platt, Mr. (theater owner), 38:2
Plumsted, William (merchant, theater owner), 3, 3:1
Pollard, Calvin (architect), 39:2
Powell, Charles Stuart (theatrical manager), 17:1, 17:3, 22, 22:1, 22:2
Preston, Jonathan (architect), 55:1
Price, Stephen (theatrical manager), 29:2
Prince, Charles P. (theatrical manager), 70:2
Purdy, Samuel (architect), 44:2

Ralston, William (theater owner), 106
Raymond, Mr. (builder), 49:1
Reichardt, Mr. (architect), 40:1
Reid, H. Logan (artist), 98:1
Reinagle, Alexander (theatrical manager), 18:1, 20:1, 20:2, 24:2, 25
Reinagle, Hugh (architect, artist), 29:2, 31:2, 35:2
Rice, John B. (actor, theatrical manager), 69, 69:1, 69:2
Richards, Mr. (artist), 18:1, 18:2, 30:1
Robinson and Evard (theatrical managers), 73:1, 75:4
Roeschlaub, R. S. (architect), 111:2
Rogers, Howard (artist), 107:2
Rogers, Isaiah (architect), 35:1
Rooker, Mr. (artist), 30:1
Rowbotham, Mr. (theater owner), 38:2
Rowe, James S. (theatrical manager), 62:4, 64:2
Rush, William (artist, sculptor), 18:1
Russell, Richard (stage manager), 62:4, 64:2

Saint-Méry, Moreau de (author), 18:3
Sanford, C. W. (builder), 32:1
Sanger, Frank (theatrical manager), 100
Sargent, Franklin (theatrical manager), 96:1
SCULPTORS. Ives, C. B., 114:1; Rush, William, 18:1
Sefton, Mr. (stage manager), 52:1
Sera, Joseph (architect, artist), 33:2, 36:2, 36:3, 40:1
Sharpley, Sam (theatrical manager), 84
Shirley, John (gas fixtures), 108:1
Simpson, Edmund (theatrical manager), 29:2, 41:1
Sinclair, Catharine (actress, theatrical manager), 77, 77:1
Smith, J. R. (artist), 49:1, 65:1
Smith, Sol (actor, theatrical manager), 62, 63:2, 65, 65:1, 65:2, 67, 67:1, 67:2, 68, 68:1, 68:2, 76:1, 76:2
Smith, W. H. (stage manager), 46:1, 47:1
Smith, W. Russell (artist), 27:4, 59:2
Spofford, Teleston and Co. (theater owners), 45:3
STAGE MACHINISTS. Alexander, J. C., 107:2, 113:1; Ciceri, Charles, 23:2; Conklin, George, 29:2, 31:2; Galbraith,

325